renewals

D1496319

08752656

A. Wilson Greene

BREAKING THE BACKBONE OF THE REBELLION

The Final Battles of the Petersburg Campaign

Savas Publishing Company

Manufactured in the United States of America

Breaking the Backbone of the Rebellion:
The Final Battles of the Petersburg Campaign
A. Wilson Greene

© 2000 A. Wilson Greene

Includes bibliographic references and index

Printing Number
10 9 8 7 6 5 4 3 2
First Edition

ISBN 1-882810-48-1
Library of Congress Card Number 99-63648

Savas Publishing Company
202 First Street SE, Suite 103A
Mason City, IA 50401

(515) 421-7135 (editorial offices)
(800) 732-3669 (distribution)

This book is printed on 50-lb. acid-free paper. It meets or exceeds the guidelines for permanence and durability of the Committee on Production Guidelines for Book Longevity of the Council on Library Resources

Dedicated with love and respect to Allen S. Greene,
who took his young son to countless Civil War battlefields
and other old places many years ago and thus provided
him with a lifelong passion for history.

Thanks, Chief

"One good battle &
the back of the rebellion is broken."

Montgomery C. Meigs
Quartermaster General of the United States Army
July 18, 1861

TABLE OF CONTENTS

List of Maps

List of Photos and Illustrations

Foreword

The Siege of Petersburg proved the longest campaign of the Civil War. It pitted the greatest general of each side, Ulysses S. Grant for the North and Robert E. Lee for the South, directly against each other. Lee's masterful defense of Petersburg and Richmond prolonged the life of his army, of his capital, and of his country for nine-and-a-half months. Yet Grant's characteristic ability to learn from experience and his successful application of the Federals' many potential advantages eventually doomed those two cities and, along with them, the Army of Northern Virginia and the Confederacy itself.

A campaign between two such great commanders, involving such significant stakes and causing such crucial consequences, invites extensive study. Surprisingly, however, few authors have concentrated on Petersburg. Usually, it has been touched upon simply as a part of a broader history of the Civil War or as part of a biography of the entire military career of one of the participating generals. Only within the past twenty years have authors focused upon the overall campaign and upon its component battles. During those two decades, important books have been written on the entire siege; on Ben Butler's preliminary foray against Petersburg (June 9); on Grant's First, Third, Fourth, and Fifth Offensives (from mid-June to early October); and on the penultimate battle at Five Forks on April 1.

Yet the Siege of Petersburg did not end at or because of Five Forks. Neither the arrogant boastfulness of Phil Sheridan, never hesitant to exalt himself at the expense of the truth, nor the exhaustion of some authors, weary after writing about the entire war and anxious to hurry on to Appomattox and be done with the book, can discredit the fundamental reality that the siege raged on for one final, bloody, decisive day.

April 2,1865, rather than April 1, proved the day of decision, as blue brigades broke through Petersburg's outer defenses, severed the last supply lines into the city, reached the Appomattox River above town, and rendered Lee's entire position astride James River untenable. This breakthrough battle at last receives rightful recognition in A. Wilson Greene's breakthrough book, *Breaking the Backbone of the Rebellion: The Final Battles of the Petersburg* Campaign.

This book places the battle in the overall context of the siege. It gives increasing attention to operations in 1865, especially to the fateful fighting at Watkin's Farm and Jones's Farm on March 25. The pace picks up as Grant unleashes his Final Offensive, March 29. The heart of the book is the decisive fighting on April 2, especially the VI Corps' breakthrough at Boisseau's house, its drive southward to Hatcher's Run, and the XXIV Corps' subsequent strike for Petersburg, barred only by the heroic garrisons of Fort Gregg and Fort Alexander.

Throughout, the book combines stirring narrative with keen analysis. Personal vignettes of individual soldiers and junior officers punctuate perceptive passages on the generalship of senior commanders. Thorough research undergirds this work; wise and mature understanding of the Civil War pervades it.

Such significant scholarship is no surprise to anyone who knows Will Greene. Initially a National Park Service historian and still a much-sought-after battlefield tour guide, he is renowned for his ability to communicate the connection between tactics and terrain. Then as the first President of the Association for the Preservation of Civil War Sites and now as the Executive Director of Pamplin Historical Park he has rendered tremendous contributions in saving historic battlefields. Most recently, as founding Director of the National Museum of the Civil War Soldier, he is reaching out to make the American public as well as Civil War specialists aware of the experiences of Federal and Confederate fighting men.

To these triple talents as guide, preservationist, and museum director, he has now established his reputation as an author of a major book of history. *Breaking the Backbone of the Rebellion* at last provides the needed coverage of the Day of Decision at Petersburg. Wilson Greene's book will endure as the definitive history of the decisive breakthrough at Boisseau's house, which doomed Petersburg—and, along with it, doomed Richmond, the Army of Northern Virginia, and the Southern Confederacy as well.

Richard J. Sommers
Carlisle, Pennsylvania

Preface
and Acknowledgments

"One good battle & the back of the rebellion is broken."

Brigadier General Montgomery C. Meigs, Quartermaster General of the United States Army, expressed this optimistic opinion about the future of the Civil War in a letter to his father on July 18, 1861. Three days later, Meigs had his "good battle" near Manassas Junction, Virginia along the banks of Bull Run, but the outcome of that engagement far from fractured the effort of eleven Southern states to create a new nation. Instead, the armed uprising would consume nearly four more years and 600,000 American lives, until events on an early April day in Dinwiddie County, Virginia would, at last, break the backbone of the rebellion.

* * *

The Civil War has garnered more attention than any other chapter of American history. Participants in the conflict understood the enormous significance of their war, and began to write about its conduct and consequences even before they determined its outcome. Scores of unit histories and memoirs appeared in the four decades after 1865 buttressed by a number of periodicals seemingly devoted to describing every conceivable aspect of the war. The Civil War Centennial provided the catalyst for a new round of scholarship producing a small library of books that remain classics in their field. But no period since the war's veterans laid down their pens has added more to our knowledge of the United States's most seminal event than the one that began in the mid 1980s and continues into the new century.

The lives of many important wartime figures have received attention for the first time even while fresh and insightful studies revise the standard impressions of more familiar names. Topics unrelated to the military conduct of the war are finding long-deserved voices. Thoughtful histories of the regiments, brigades, and armies that tramped from Texas to Pennsylvania between 1861 and 1865 appear every month, improved by statistical analysis unthinkable in the era before cliometrics.

It is the campaign studies, however, that continue to produce some of the best new work in Civil War military history. Since 1985, readers have benefited from dozens of new treatments of the war's battles and the contexts in which they occurred. Most of the significant Civil War engagements have either been reexamined or studied for the first time during the last fifteen years. In several cases, pivotal clashes have commanded the attention of multiple authors whose books on the same topic have emerged almost simultaneously.

The Petersburg Campaign (often misidentified as the Siege of Petersburg) offers something of an exception to this uninterrupted parade. In the Preface to his 1991 book, *The Last Citadel: Petersburg, Virginia, June 1864-April 1865*, Noah Andre Trudeau observed that "In spite of its length and the amount of combat activity surrounding it, the Petersburg siege has received remarkably little attention from historians." That is still true almost a decade later. Trudeau's book, in fact, represented the first attempt to treat the entire Petersburg Campaign between two covers. To be sure, a small number of monographs published during the last twenty years have focused upon individual aspects of the Petersburg Campaign (some of them quite good), but a number of gaps in the Petersburg story remain. This book is an attempt to fill one of those voids.

In 1992, while serving as the president of a land trust called the Association for the Preservation of Civil War Sites, I became involved in the acquisition of several tracts on which the decisive combat of the Petersburg Campaign occurred on April 2, 1865. The Pamplin Foundation, created by the philanthropic descendants of the land's wartime owners, provided the funding for the purchase and development of a historical park on this property, now named Pamplin Historical Park & The National Museum of the Civil War Soldier. My move to Dinwiddie County in 1995 to serve as Pamplin Historical Park's executive director motivated me to learn more about the events that unfolded in the park on April 2 than was attainable from the paucity of available secondary sources.

The focus of this study is the attack by the Union Sixth Corps that, on the morning of April 2, 1865, broke through a portion of the Confederate line in what is now Pamplin Historical Park. The story's primary protagonists are the 14,000 Federal soldiers commanded by Major General Horatio G. Wright who made that attack and the roughly 2,800 Confederates and their comrades in Lieutenant General Ambrose Powell Hill's Third Corps who attempted to stop it.

However, the Breakthrough (a shorthand title I have coined for this particular military action, to distinguish it from other, less critical "breakthroughs" at Petersburg) did not occur in a vacuum. The men who fought this battle had been in constant contact with the enemy for nearly eleven months and had emerged from a winter encampment uniquely influential on the strategic thinking of the army commanders and the morale of the soldiers they led. Its conduct was the result of a series of engagements that began on March 25,1865 at Fort Stedman, spread to the entrenched Confederate picket lines southwest of Petersburg, and concluded a week later at Five Forks. Similarly, the Breakthrough triggered a full day of combat across the Petersburg front and caused the battlefield death of General Hill, one of the highest-ranking Confederate officers to be killed in combat. The ultimate consequence of the Breakthrough was the capture of Petersburg on the morning of April 3. All of these topics come under scrutiny within these pages. The surrender of Richmond and, six days later, the Army of Northern Virginia, found their antecedents in the decisive action of April 2.

This is the shared story of all the officers and men, Union and Confederate, who participated in the climactic days at Petersburg. It has been my intention, as it is with most historians, to avoid slanting the tale toward one side or the other, and to render judgments only as the evidence warrants. As anyone who has attempted to write about the last weeks of the war will testify, however, the volume of that evidence is skewed in favor of Federal sources. For every one surviving Confederate battle report, their are twenty written by their blueclad opponents. Manuscript sources abound in Northern repositories—but are scarce in the South. This disparity almost inevitably results in a narrative dominated by the words and perspectives of the Union participants. In no way should this imbalance imply an author's bias in the approach to this study, for there was glory and tragedy enough during the final battles at Petersburg to equally satisfy partisans of the blue or the gray.

*   *   *

I am indebted to a number of individuals and institutions for making available the source material that did surface, and for helping me arrange those documents into a coherent account. Dr. Arthur W. Bergeron, historian at Pamplin Historical Park, knows at least as much about the Breakthrough as I do and has contributed immeasurably to whatever merit this book may possess. Dr. Richard J. Sommers of Carlisle, Pennsylvania not only shared with me his mastery of the collections at the United States Army Military History Institute, but challenged my understanding of the Petersburg Campaign on numerous occasions, much to the benefit of this book's tactical accuracy. David Ward of Lakeville, Connecticut generously sent me many manila envelopes filled with material from his private collection of Sixth Corps accounts. John Metz of Richmond and George Skoch of Shaker Heights, Ohio contributed the outstanding maps that enhance the narrative.

The staffs of several libraries and archives deserve special mention, although each institution cited in the Bibliography provided courteous and efficient assistance. Perhaps it is the stereotype of apathetic government functionaries that makes the staff of the Manuscript Division of the Library of Congress seem so exceptional. No researcher in the Southern Historical Collection at the University of North Carolina or the Perkins Library at Duke University fails to emerge impressed with the helpful, thoroughly professional archivists who manage those unique collections. I received cordial attention worthy of particular thanks at the Virginia Historical Society and the North Carolina State Archives in Raleigh. Ms. Kelly Nolin of the Connecticut Historical Society went out of her way to help a wayward Virginian navigate around her relevant papers. The interlibrary loan staff of the Appomattox Regional Library lent invaluable assistance in tracking down obscure tomes.

Several individuals came forward to provide sources I would never have otherwise found. My gratitude in that regard is expressed to Dr. David F. Cross of Rutland, Vermont; Charles E. Heller of Olathe, Kansas; Robert K. Krick of Fredericksburg, Virginia; Jack Mandaville of Maple Grove, Minnesota; Fred Robinson of Chesterfield, Virginia; Ed Root of Coopersburg, Pennsylvania; John Sargent of Morrisville, Vermont; and Vermonter Don Wickman for passing along information on the boys from the Green Mountain State.

Several friends and colleagues deserve particular thanks. Dr. Earl J. Hess of Knoxville, Tennessee provided information on William MacRae. William Marvel of South Conway, New Hampshire waded through the entire manuscript and did more for my punctuation and grammar than the entire English Department of several schools. Between social obligations, he also reminded me that each quotable story from a veteran's pen will not pass the test of corroboration. Every manuscript needs a harsh and unrelenting critic, and Dr. George C. Rable of Tuscaloosa, Alabama by way of the Dawg Pound and Riverfront Stadium, filled that role for this one. He challenged every conclusion and almost every prepositional phrase and I am very grateful to him for it.

Theodore P. "Ted" Savas, my publisher and a friend to everyone interested in reading good Civil War military history, demonstrated infinite patience as the deadline for this project slipped into the new millennium. His endurance was matched only by that of my wife, Margaret, who tolerated 5:00 a.m. alarms, unwashed dishes, and countless weekends alone to support the completion of the story of a battle that took place, partly, in the flower gardens of her backyard.

A. Wilson Greene

Dinwiddie County, Virginia

December 1999

CHAPTER ONE

Battles and Leaders
in 1864 Virginia

A weary figure in blue stepped into the midnight darkness at Parke Station on the United States Military Railroad, a few miles south of Petersburg, Virginia. His journey had commenced nearly five days earlier near Kernstown in the Shenandoah Valley. As the sharp crack of a picket's rifle reminded the young officer, the long war that in recent weeks had receded from his immediate presence had not yet run its course. He and his comrades in the Union army's Sixth Corps had more work to do.

Captain Elisha Hunt Rhodes, the 22-year-old son of a Rhode Island mariner, had enlisted in the 2nd Rhode Island in June 1861. Along with his unit, Rhodes had participated in all of the major Eastern Theater campaigns of the Civil War—rising, meanwhile, from private to the commanding officer of his regiment. The 2nd Rhode Island had shared the fate of the Army of the Potomac until July 1864, when a Confederate offensive down the Shenandoah Valley spilled into Maryland and threatened the nation's capital. The Northern high command responded to the crisis by dispatching the Rhode Islanders and the rest of the Sixth Corps to Washington from their positions south of Petersburg.

For several months, the Sixth Corps and other Federal troops dueled with a small but determined Confederate army led by the irascible Lieutenant General Jubal A. Early. The venue for their contest quickly shifted south of the Potomac River and into the vital Valley of Virginia drained by the twin forks of the Shenandoah. A series of battles commencing on September 19 east of Winchester culminated near the banks of Cedar Creek exactly one month later. There, Early's army met a crushing defeat that all but eliminated it as a strategic factor in the Shenandoah Valley.[1]

Following a relatively calm interlude, the Sixth Corps soldiers learned in late November that they would return to the Army of the Potomac, which remained locked in continual combat near Petersburg with General Robert E. Lee's indomitable Army of Northern Virginia. Rhodes and the 2nd Rhode Island left their camp at Kernstown on the morning of December 1 and marched to Stephenson's Depot, where they took the trains to Washington. The next day the New Englanders boarded the steamer *City of Albany* and proceeded down the Potomac to Alexandria. At daylight on December 3, an entire fleet of transports bearing the First Division of the Sixth Corps set course for Union army headquarters at City Point, at the confluence of the Appomattox and James rivers eight miles northeast of Petersburg. Arriving on the afternoon of December 4, the troops transferred from ships' decks to the jolting cars of the United States Military Railroad and embarked upon a twelve-mile journey to Parke Station, a supply depot named after Major General John G. Parke, the commander of the army's Ninth Corps. "Here we are again in the trenches before Petersburg after our five months' absence in Maryland and the Valley of the Shenandoah," Rhodes confided to his diary. "I was sorry to leave the Shenandoah, for we have had a fine campaign, but duty is duty, and I do not complain. If it will end the war I am satisfied to go to any point they choose to send me." Events would justify Rhodes's faith in the wisdom of his reassignment. In less than four months, he and his comrades would participate in a dramatic operation that would lead to the capture of Petersburg and Richmond and induce the very result Rhodes sought.[2]

> "I was sorry to leave the Shenandoah, for we have had a fine campaign, but duty is duty, and I do not complain."

* * *

On December 5, the 2nd Rhode Island moved into a portion of the Union line between two strong points, Battery 26 and Fort Wadsworth, neither of which had existed when the Sixth Corps left to confront Jubal Early in the summer. In fact, much had changed during those five months,

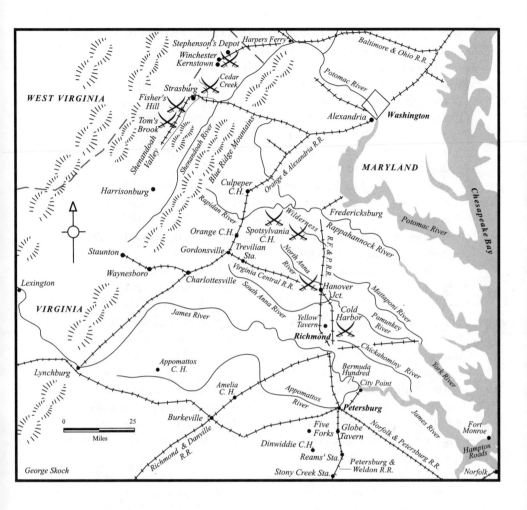

George Skoch

although the overarching Union goal of isolating Petersburg from the rest of the Confederacy remained unaltered, if elusive.[3]

Petersburg's military importance rested on its relationship to Richmond. Located 23 miles south of the Confederate capital at the head of navigation on the Appomattox River, Petersburg was the seventh-largest city in the Confederacy, and second only to Richmond in population and prestige in the Commonwealth of Virginia. A score of tobacco factories, four cotton mills, and numerous elegant public buildings and private homes distinguished the "Cockade City" in 1861. Five railroads and several major wagon roads guided commerce through Petersburg in addition to the shipping trade provided by the Appomattox. Much of that commerce found its way north into Richmond. By the last winter of the war, Richmond's material and military survival depended upon the transportation nexus at Petersburg.[4]

Despite its significance, Petersburg had seen little of the war prior to 1864. Major General George B. McClellan's Peninsula Campaign in the spring of 1862 alerted Confederate authorities to the need to defend Petersburg, for the city offered Northern invaders an unlocked back door to Richmond. Beginning in the summer of 1862 and continuing through the spring of the following year, Captain Charles H. Dimmock supervised the construction of a series of fifty-five artillery batteries and connecting works ringing Petersburg in a ten-mile arc resting on the river both above and below the town. But after McClellan's failure, Union efforts to capture Richmond always emanated from the north—that is, when the Yankees were not contending with Confederate offensives orchestrated by Lee and the Army of Northern Virginia.[5]

The strategic initiative in Virginia shifted for good in March 1864. Ulysses S. Grant, the 42-year-old architect of the Union's most impressive victories in the Western Theater, arrived in Washington to receive the well-earned rank of lieutenant general and title of general-in-chief of all United States armies. Grant made his headquarters in the field and traveled with the principal combat force in the East, Major General George G. Meade's Army of the Potomac. Although Meade would remain in command of this army for the duration of the war, Grant's presence diminished Meade's role, and the lieutenant general assumed de facto control.

Grant prepared a massive offensive for the spring of 1864, components of which would commence along the Gulf of Mexico, in north Georgia, and on three fronts in the Old Dominion. A small army under Major General Franz Sigel would move up the Shenandoah Valley in the western part of the state, presenting a threat to Confederate communications and

Lieutenant General Ulysses S. Grant

Library of Congress

supplies in this bountiful agricultural precinct. Sigel's failure and that of his successor had opened the path for Jubal Early's adventures in the summer and fall.

A larger force under Major General Benjamin F. Butler was slated to approach Richmond from the east and south, cut the railroad leading to Petersburg, and prevent the Confederates from detaching troops from their capital or points south to reinforce the Army of Northern Virginia.

Butler stumbled almost as miserably as Sigel, his Army of the James giving Petersburg its proudest hour of the Civil War in the process. On June 9, a motley collection of townsmen, mostly old men and young boys, successfully defended the city against a bumbling gaggle of Butler's cavalry until veteran Confederate troops appeared on the scene.

Grant's main effort depended, logically enough, on the Army of the Potomac. Grant told Meade to focus on Lee and to pursue the legendary commander wherever the road might lead. That path turned out to be one of the longest and bloodiest of a long and bloody war. Grant and Lee clashed first in the Wilderness, a tangled and trackless landscape west of Fredericksburg. On May 5 and 6, nearly 30,000 soldiers fell in featureless thickets set ablaze by the discharge of weapons, charring corpses and roasting the wounded. Lee inflicted the most losses and turned both of Grant's flanks on the last day of the battle, but unlike his predecessors, Grant did not retreat across nearby river barriers to lick his wounds.

Grant focused instead on the next strategic point, the village of Spotsylvania Court House. Whoever controlled Spotsylvania held the shortest road to Richmond and, predictably, Lee's strategic options were firmly tethered to the protection of his capital. For nearly two weeks, May 8-21, the armies collided again, contending for key points along the Confederate trenches and killing one another with alarming efficiency. Brought to a stalemate at Spotsylvania, Grant disengaged and once again moved to his left, southeast, keeping in contact with his waterborne supply lines. Lee stopped Grant's progress at the North Anna River, and between May 23 and May 27 fought a series of small actions defending the rail junction connecting the Shenandoah Valley with Richmond.

Stymied, Grant plunged deeper into central Virginia through the well-watered lands northeast of Richmond. The armies remained in constant contact, Grant looking for a way around or through Lee, and the Confederate commander brilliantly juggling his outnumbered forces to meet every threat. On June 3, the Federals launched a massive attack along nearly seven miles of Confederate fortifications centered on a roadside inn called Cold Harbor. Lee repulsed these assaults with relative ease, leaving some 7,000 dead and wounded Federals on the killing fields of Hanover County. These losses merely added to a butcher's bill that in 30 days claimed nearly 82,000 casualties along a 60-mile corridor reeking of gore.[6]

Grant had effectively run out of maneuvering room. Lee blocked his path into Richmond and the broad James River flowed between the Federals and another attempt to march around Lee's right flank. The Federal commander enjoyed few options on the fourth day of June, the least attractive of which was to settle in for a McClellanesque siege east of

Richmond. The Army of Northern Virginia, weakened in numbers but still formidable behind its elaborate fortifications, defied Grant to hazard another frontal assault like the one that had failed the day before. A movement to the west would necessitate establishment of a new Union supply line, land-based and prohibitively vulnerable to Confederate cavalry. This left only the logistically daunting alternative of a secret crossing of the James and a movement against Petersburg. Grant immediately laid his plans.

The rewards for success were potentially great. All but two of the railroads feeding Richmond from the unconquered Confederacy funneled through Petersburg, making control of the town a key to the strangulation of the Southern capital. Moreover, General Pierre Gustave Toutant Beauregard's diminutive army provided scant protection for the Cockade City. Charged with defending the region south of Richmond, including Petersburg, most of the Creole general's troops were positioned to contain Butler's hapless legions on the peninsula called Bermuda Hundred, between the James and Appomattox rivers.[7]

Petersburg offered a tempting prize ripe for the picking, but reaching the town was the problem. Grant proposed to disengage an army of 100,000 men from direct contact with the enemy, cross a river at least 2,100 feet wide and 100 feet deep, and reassemble 40 miles away for an attack, all of which had to be achieved without Lee's knowledge. Should the Confederate commander discover the plan, he could at the very least rush to Petersburg via the shorter axis and man the imposing Dimmock Line before Grant could deploy. A more frightening scenario would bring the Army of Northern Virginia howling down upon the Federals while they were crossing the James, presenting the prospect of the destruction of the Union army in detail.

On June 12 the operation began. One Federal corps boarded transports and followed Virginia's inland waterways to Hampton Roads then up the James River to reunite with Butler. Most of the army marched overland, crossed the Chickahominy River, and either ferried across the James or tramped over an enormous pontoon bridge erected by Union engineers in just eight hours. In the meantime, one Union corps noisily demonstrated in front of Lee's lines south of the Chickahominy, prompting the Confederate commander to discount warnings sent by Beauregard with increasing frequency and urgency that a move was afoot to attack Petersburg.[8]

That action commenced on June 15 when, at 7:00 p.m., after cautiously approaching the eastern perimeter of the Dimmock Line, nearly 14,000 Federals unleashed an assault against some 2,200 men of

Beauregard's skeleton force. Such odds dictated that the Confederates give way, and blueclad soldiers rushed into the abandoned works. With reinforcements at hand and a bright moon to light their way, the Northerners had an unobstructed path into Petersburg—but they balked. Timid subordinate generalship coupled with a lack of offensive spirit among some of the rank and file, lost Grant the chance to capture Petersburg with minimal cost. That forsaken opportunity would lead to nearly ten more months of combat at a combined price of 70,000 casualties.

During the next three days, more and more of the Union army arrived on Petersburg's doorstep, knocking loudly and achieving limited admittance. A desperate Beauregard gradually persuaded the incredulous Lee that the Federal hordes were now in his front and not east of Richmond. Lee gradually permitted a trickle and then a flood of reinforcements to bolster the beleaguered Petersburg defenders, now manning a new line hastily erected closer to the city. On June 18, both armies assembled almost in their entireties, and once again the Federals attacked. Exhaustion, poor coordination between corps, and an understandable lack of enthusiasm for assaulting earthworks combined with Lee's fresh troops to spell failure for this day's offensive. Between June 15 and 18, Grant lost an additional 10,000 men in return for the capture of a few miles of now-meaningless trenches.[9]

Resignedly, Grant altered his strategy to minimize dependence on further frontal assaults. Once again he would adopt the maneuvering that had brought him from the Wilderness to Richmond—moves to his left, seeking the right flank of Lee's attenuated lines. Grant's targets would be, one by one, the highways and railroads leading into Petersburg.

The first of these transportation arteries were the Jerusalem Plank Road and the Petersburg Railroad, both leading south into the Carolinas. Between June 22 and 24, the Federals pushed westward, reaching the tracks of the Petersburg Railroad before two Confederate divisions drove them back. At a cost of 2,300 men, Grant succeeded in gaining permanent control of the Jerusalem Plank Road, giving notice in the process that the Petersburg Railroad would be next in his sights.[10]

The Sixth Corps had played a major role in the fighting along the Jerusalem Plank Road, as it had during most of the trauma of the previous six weeks. Portions of the corps had reached a critical road junction in the Wilderness on May 5, preventing its capture by the leading elements of the Confederate army. Throughout that battle troops displaying the Greek Cross (the corps insignia) found themselves in the thickest of the fighting on both flanks of the Union line. At Spotsylvania, beloved corps commander, Major General John Sedgwick, met an instant and much-lamented death at the hands of a Confederate sharpshooter. Three days later his men attempted to avenge their leader's loss by capturing a short section of the Confederate line known to history as The Bloody Angle. The corps played a supporting role at the North Anna River but found itself in the vortex of the maelstrom of Cold Harbor. Its combat record, reliable discipline, and location on the flank of the army's Petersburg deployment made it a likely choice to rescue Washington from Jubal Early in July. Success in the Valley bonded the corps to Major General Philip Sheridan, sent by Grant in August to orchestrate Early's demise.[11]

While Sheridan and the Sixth Corps engineered victory in the Valley, the effort to capture Petersburg continued. Both armies embraced the spade as warmly as the sword, the Confederates improving their already impressive works ringing Petersburg as the Federals constructed a parallel system of trenches at distances ranging from more than one-half mile to just a few-score yards. At one point southeast of the city, the terrain offered an unusual opportunity to break the impasse. A regiment of Pennsylvania coal miners began digging a shaft aimed directly below a Confederate fort. Their concept included exploding a huge charge of black powder under the Rebel bastion, followed with an attack designed to seize commanding high ground overlooking Petersburg. Grant approved the scheme more as "a means of keeping the men occupied" than as a blueprint for ending the campaign. But as the days passed and the Pennsylvanians readied their mine for detonation, Grant determined to use this unorthodox tactic to take the city.[12]

On July 30 at 4:40 a.m., some 8,000 pounds of powder jarred the ground like an earthquake, lifting the Confederate fort into the sky and killing or wounding at least 278 Southern soldiers in the spectacular process. A huge crater measuring 170 feet long, 60 to 80 feet wide, and 30 feet deep greeted the Union troops who approached the gigantic scar, filling them with awe and trepidation. A corridor lay open to the hill at Blandford Church, which, if occupied with Union artillery, would have rendered Petersburg indefensible.

But once again, as on the evening of June 15, poor leadership cost the Federals an opportunity to capture the Cockade City. Eleventh-hour changes to the battle plan removed specially trained black troops from the front ranks of the attackers. Officers responsible for directing the replacement soldiers demonstrated a lack of understanding about how to proceed—or worse, spent the morning safely ensconced in bombproof shelters imbibing liquid courage. Instead of skirting the Crater and dashing for the high ground, the leaderless Federals plunged into the gaping hole, where they milled helplessly amid increasingly crowded and chaotic conditions.

The shaken Confederates took advantage of these Federal lapses to seal the ends of the breach in their line and coordinate a series of counterattacks against the Crater. Southern cannoneers lobbed rounds into the huddled Unionists, and from 8:30 a.m. until early in the afternoon, grayclad infantry assaulted the ever-more desperate enemy clinging to the slopes and perimeter of the enormous death trap. By 2:00 p.m. the battle was over. Grant's men either ran the gantlet back to the original Union lines, surrendered to their Confederate opponents, or died on the red clay of the Crater, made slippery with the blood of corpses stacked eight deep. Union losses totaled nearly 4,000 in what Grant called "the saddest affair I have witnessed in the war."[13]

The experience at the Crater convinced the Union commander that his conception of targeting the transportation routes into Petersburg promised the surest, if not the swiftest path to ultimate victory. His strategy would include initiating simultaneous offensives north of the James River and on the Petersburg front to keep Lee from shifting his outnumbered forces to meet successive threats.

The Petersburg Railroad offered Grant his next objective. Between August 18 and 21, portions of two Union corps pushed west and seized the vital tracks south of Petersburg. Beauregard and Lee called on elements of Lieutenant General Ambrose Powell Hill's Third Corps, aided by Beauregard's troops, to drive the Yankees back. Three days of spirited fighting along the railroad and the parallel Halifax Road left the Federals bloodied but victorious. Lee's rail line to the Carolinas now contained an apparently irreparable gap, presenting the Confederate chieftain with a logistics problem of significant proportions.[14]

Although Lee had warned the Confederate government in June that he would be hard-pressed to maintain the Petersburg Railroad, Union cavalry raids had damaged the only two alternate routes, the Richmond & Danville Railroad and the South Side Railroad. Until they could be repaired, Lee had no choice but to devise a makeshift supply line from the south. Employing the Petersburg Railroad as far north as Stony Creek, some eighteen miles below Petersburg, Lee transferred materiel to wagons for transport cross-country to Dinwiddie Court House. At Dinwiddie, the all-weather Boydton Plank Road provided a reasonably reliable route into Petersburg. Nevertheless, soldiers in the trenches and civilians in both Petersburg and Richmond felt the pinch of short supplies—a condition that would only worsen as the campaign continued.[15]

After a few weeks respite, Grant prepared another twin offensive on both sides of the James. On September 29 and 30, Union forces captured and then held a key Confederate position east of Richmond named Fort Harrison. This combat attracted most of Lee's attention and troops, opening an opportunity on the Petersburg front to exploit the weakened and divided Army of Northern Virginia.

Grant's goals were the two primary transportation routes still running unfettered into Petersburg from the south and west: the Boydton Plank Road and the South Side Railroad. With the Petersburg Railroad effectively blocked and the Jerusalem Plank Road firmly in his grasp, the Union commander needed only to sever these remaining links to isolate Petersburg from the rest of the Confederacy. This accomplished, Grant knew that Richmond must certainly wither as well.

While Union troops made progress at Fort Harrison, other Federals probed west and then north toward the Boydton Plank Road. From September 29 through October 2, fighting erupted in the woods and farm fields southwest of Petersburg, centered along byways like Squirrel Level, Church, and Duncan roads, and on lots owned by families named Peebles, Pegram, Jones, and Boisseau. Once again, Lee entrusted A. P. Hill with direction of the Confederate defense, and Hill in turn relied on two of his division commanders, major generals Henry Heth and Cadmus M. Wilcox, to carry the brunt of the fighting. When the guns fell silent after four days of sporadically intense combat, both the Boydton Plank Road and South Side Railroad remained in Southern hands. Grant's so-called Fifth Offensive at Petersburg (sometimes styled the Battle of Peebles's Farm) had not achieved its goals. Grant's nearly 3,000 casualties merely earned him a westward extension of his siege lines. Likewise, the Confederates were forced to improve the hasty entrenchments they had constructed in advance of the Plank Road, to guard against future Federal initiatives that seemed to recur on a monthly basis.[16]

Heth's Division and two brigades of Wilcox's, those of brigadier generals James H. Lane and Samuel McGowan, received orders from Hill to entrench a permanent defense line from Battery 45 at the southwest corner of the Dimmock Line, southwest to Hatcher's Run, a distance of about six miles. The new works ran southeast of and parallel to the Boydton Plank Road and thus protected the makeshift supply route Lee had concocted in August. These entrenchments would be the responsibility of Heth's and Wilcox's troops for the duration of the campaign.[17]

Just like clockwork, Grant launched another offensive on October 27, once again focusing on the Boydton Plank Road and the South Side Railroad. The Federals committed 43,000 troops to this effort in addition to the usual diversionary attacks north of the James. This time the Yankees reached the Boydton Plank Road before A. P. Hill slashed them with devastating counterattacks. The fighting centered on Burgess's Mill, near where the Plank Road crossed Hatcher's Run at the far southwestern end of the Confederate line. The armies suffered more than 3,000 total casualties, most of them wearing blue, before darkness ended the battle. The Federals withdrew from their temporary foothold on the Plank Road and receded into their ever-lengthening lines. For a sixth time since mid-June, Lee managed to maintain his tenuous grip on Petersburg.[18]

Now, the elements and advancing season combined to assist the exhausted Confederates. Cold autumn rains poured down on the Petersburg front, turning the dirt roads upon which the armies depended into ribbons of mud, the weakening November sun taking longer to dry them between storms. Grant recognized that the time for active campaigning had come to an end, but took comfort in the triumphs of Phil Sheridan in the Shenandoah Valley. Thanks in part to Sheridan's achievements—and despite Grant's evident failure around Petersburg—the November elections returned Abraham Lincoln to the White House and promised another Congress devoted to prosecuting the war to a successful conclusion. With political imperatives for action no longer a factor, Grant contented himself with consolidating his territorial gains, extending his entrenchments, and preparing winter camps. Lee and his battle-worn soldiers welcomed the break.

*   *   *

The 1864 campaign season wrought catastrophic changes upon the Army of Northern Virginia and its command structure. Between May 4 and June 3 alone, confrontations with Grant's army claimed 37% of Lee's general officers while more than 31,000 of the rank and file left their blood in the woods and fields of Orange, Spotsylvania, and Hanover counties. The fighting around Petersburg and Richmond from June through October only exacerbated these grim statistics. Some 13,000 Southerners fell north of the James and south of the Appomattox during the summer and fall. Including the nearly 10,000 losses suffered by Jubal Early in the Shenandoah Valley, the Army of Northern Virginia had bled away the equivalent of more than 80% of the manpower with which it started the year.[19]

In October, General Lee acknowledged to the secretary of war the peril inherent in such attrition:

> I beg leave to inquire whether there is any prospect of my obtaining any increase to this army. If not, it will be very difficult for us to maintain ourselves. The enemy's numerical superiority enables him to hold his lines with an adequate force, and extend on each flank with numbers so much greater than ours that we can only meet his corps, increased by recent recruits, with a division reduced by long and arduous service. We cannot fight to advantage with such odds, and there is the gravest reason to apprehend the result of every encounter.[20]

Lee hoped that conscription and the substitution of disabled soldiers and blacks for able-bodied white troops assigned to non-combat details would bridge his manpower gap, but neither of these expedients yielded significant results. The Army of Northern Virginia would have to rely on its surviving veterans to achieve a victory that by late autumn looked increasingly unlikely.[21]

The most important survivor was Lee himself. During a six-month period when the army lost each of its infantry corps commanders and its chief of cavalry to illness, wounds, or death, "Marse Robert" remained an inspiration to his troops and their infant nation. His record of achieving victories against great odds since his accession to army command in June 1862, and his dignified determination, prompted everyone vested in the Confederate cause to cast faith-filled eyes in his direction.[22]

At the conclusion of the fighting in October, Lee conducted a tour of inspection from north of the James down to Petersburg. Upon arriving in the Cockade City, he decided to move his headquarters from Violet Bank on the north side of the Appomattox into Petersburg itself. The fallen leaves had exposed Violet Bank to Union batteries south of the river, rendering it unsuitable for further use. Lieutenant Colonel Walter H. Taylor of Lee's staff selected the Beasley House on High Street in the city's west end and made it a comfortable domicile for his general, noting that this was the first time that Lee agreed to locate his quarters in a private home. The 57-year-old commander showed signs of weakening health in the autumn of 1864, but his energy level remained high. In fact, after just a single night's rest, the general continued the examination of his lines, allowing him an opportunity to complete a full assessment of his army's commanders, deployment, and strength.[23]

That army retained the basic organizational structure established in 1863 and counted many familiar faces among its senior leadership. Lee had been recently cheered by the return of Lieutenant General James Longstreet, his most experienced corps commander, to active duty. Longstreet had been accidentally wounded by his own men on May 6 in the Wilderness amid circumstances eerily similar to those under which

Thomas "Stonewall" Jackson had been shot the previous year. After a long convalescence, and despite the inability to use his crippled right arm, "Old Pete" resumed command of the army's First Corps on October 20.[24]

Longstreet's command bore responsibility for operations north of the Appomattox River. This would prove to be a relatively static sector during the remainder of the campaign, an assignment that suited the recovering Georgian's limited stamina and renowned mastery of the defensive. Longstreet's subordinates included two of the division commanders assigned to the First Corps at the outset of the spring campaign, major generals Charles W. Field and George E. Pickett.

A 36 year-old Kentuckian and member of the United States Military Academy's class of 1849, Charles Field had little direct experience with his commander. Severely wounded at Second Manassas in August 1862 while serving in Jackson's wing, Field endured a lengthy recuperation until assigned divisional command in the First Corps in February 1864. Longstreet protested Field's assignment so stridently, preferring the appointment of someone from his own inner circle, that he drew a strong rebuke from President Jefferson Davis. Davis's admonition ended the controversy, but did little to establish a strong basis of trust between the two generals. Subsequent events, however, proved that the corps commander's reluctance to accept Field was unwarranted. Field and his division became mainstays throughout 1864 and had fought well as recently as September during the contest for Fort Harrison. Field's Division remained the primary force north of the James.[25]

George Pickett and his division developed a unique record in the First Corps and in the army as a whole. Shielded by circumstance from an intense volume of combat and consequent attrition early in the war, Pickett and his Virginia brigades earned their notoriety on July 3, 1863 at Gettysburg by lending their name to one of history's most famous charges. Pickett's Gettysburg experience tarnished his military reputation and depleted his division. At the outset of the spring campaign, Pickett's command remained near Richmond, struggling to regain its combat readiness rather than joining the Army of Northern Virginia in the field. Reuniting with the army in late May, Pickett's troops manned the fortifications between the James and Appomattox rivers, containing Butler's Federals in Bermuda Hundred. Of the nine infantry divisions that composed the Army of Northern Virginia in the spring of 1864, Pickett's was and would remain the least esteemed in the eyes of the army's commander.[26]

The third division of the First Corps was in the Shenandoah Valley when Longstreet returned to the field. Major General Joseph B. Kershaw's

Georgia, Mississippi, and South Carolina brigades enjoyed a long and honored association with the Army of Northern Virginia. Unlike Field and Pickett, Kershaw lacked a professional military background. The 42-year-old South Carolinian had been a politician and a secessionist firebrand. Blessed with unusual intelligence and a natural bearing for command, Kershaw had distinguished himself in every engagement in which he had participated. Early's defeat in mid-October and the relative quiet that descended on that theater of the war during the following weeks prompted Lee to recall Kershaw on November 15. Less than a week later, Kershaw's Division took its place beside its old First Corps comrades north of the James.[27]

Kershaw's arrival was soon balanced by the departure of Major General Robert F. Hoke's Division, which had been temporarily attached to Lee's command during most of the Petersburg Campaign. Hoke's brigades arrived in Virginia from the Carolinas in early May in response to the threat posed by Ben Butler's approaching army. The young Tarheel (Hoke was just 26 years old) played a pivotal role in Butler's defeat as a part of Beauregard's small command south of the James. Lee borrowed Hoke in early June and plugged his division into a key portion of the lines at Cold Harbor. After Beauregard's departure in September to take command of the Confederacy's Military Division of the West, Hoke's four brigades served north of the James beside the First Corps.

On December 19, Beauregard wired Richmond of the imminent threats to South Carolina posed by Major General William T. Sherman's relentless advance, and a Union armada presumably targeting Wilmington, North Carolina, the principal Confederate port on the Atlantic coast. Beauregard requested reinforcements to defend the Carolinas, and Lee asked Longstreet to detach a division for the job. Naturally enough, Longstreet selected the only outsiders in his command. Three days before Christmas the last of Hoke's men left the Petersburg-Richmond front en route to Wilmington.[28]

Hoke's departure offset some 70% of the increased strength occasioned by the return of the army's Second Corps. That organization had been absent from the Army of Northern Virginia since June, when Lee made the audacious decision to detach one-third of his entire force to repulse the Union army under Major General David Hunter (Sigel's successor), which had ravaged the Valley towns of Staunton and Lexington. At the head of the corps rode Jubal A. Early. Called "my bad old man" by the army commander, Early offered a combination of profane speech, surly disposition, and unusual military acumen to earn a unique reputation among Lee's subordinates. Early rose to corps command during the late spring relieving the ailing Lieutenant General Richard S. Ewell.[29]

Lee would not have entrusted his newest corps commander with such a daunting responsibility had he not felt "Old Jube" was up to the task. Yet, Lee's selection of the Second Corps for independent duty probably had as much to do with the composition of its troops as with the competence of its commander. Its ranks included Stonewall Jackson's old Army of the Valley, those legendary warriors of 1862 who earned international fame for themselves and the quirky genius who led them. Effecting Hunter's demise accounted for only the first of Early's assignments. Once this notorious Yankee had been dispatched, Early was to reclaim the Valley and use it once again as a corridor to the Potomac—perhaps even threatening Washington. That is exactly what the 47-year-old Virginian accomplished. Early struck terror into the heart of the Federal capital, Maryland, and Pennsylvania until Grant mustered the right combination of troops and leadership that ultimately resulted in Early's defeat. As autumn's brisk winds gave hint of the fast-approaching Valley winter, and Grant began to dismantle Sheridan's command, General Lee decided that his second great experiment in the Shenandoah Valley had ended. The time had come to bring the Second Corps home.[30]

None of Lee's units experienced more attrition at the highest levels of command than the Second Corps. Neither Ewell nor the three division commanders who fought under him at the Wilderness occupied their posts in the fall. Early's own division was now led by Brigadier General John Pegram, a native of Petersburg but with a wartime career centered in the West. Assuming command of Early's old brigade in the spring of 1864, his service in the Virginia Theater proved short-lived as he fell painfully wounded at the Wilderness. Pegram recovered in time to inherit Early's old division in the Shenandoah Valley in September. A solid officer, Pegram exuded the youthful dash so appealing to Victorian sensibilities, and his courtship of the Baltimore belle, Hetty Cary, provided an interesting social diversion for the careworn gentry.[31]

Major General Robert E. Rodes's Division traveled south under the leadership of Brigadier General Bryan Grimes, a North Carolinian and accomplished amateur soldier. Grimes assumed division command by virtue of being senior brigadier in a unit deprived first of Rodes at Third Winchester in September, and the next month of Rodes's successor, Major General Stephen Dodson Ramseur, mortally wounded at Cedar Creek. Like Pegram, Grimes had no experience at the divisional level although his performance as a brigadier left room for optimism.[32]

General Robert E. Lee

Library of Congress

The third of the Second Corps divisions entered the 1864 campaign under Major General Edward "Alleghany" Johnson, who departed the scene on May 12 as a prisoner of war. The general-officer corps in the Army of Northern Virginia suffered catastrophic casualties during the first three weeks of May, necessitating a profusion of command changes at the army's highest levels. Within fourteen days a young Georgia brigadier, John B. Gordon, moved from command of his six regiments to lead first Early's and then Johnson's divisions, the final appointment being one that endured until the corps returned to Petersburg in December.[33]

The 32-year-old Gordon had risen from captain to major general on sheer ability, having joined the army with a background in business and law in north Georgia. His heroics at Sharpsburg and other early battles attracted Lee's attention, and the army commander personally commended Gordon's performance in the Wilderness, leading to his elevation to divisional command.[34]

The need to match the December transfer of the Union Sixth Corps from the Valley to Petersburg precipitated Lee's decision to strip Early of his army, if not his title and grade. On the 8th, Gordon's and Pegram's divisions departed from Waynesboro, taking the trains to Richmond and then traveling south across the Appomattox.

Grimes's Division followed six days later, the newly arriving troops taking position on the army's right. Lee left Early in the Valley with a token force, but with the rank and therefore potential to return to command of the Second Corps. This meant that an acting corps commander would be needed for the troops en route to the Petersburg front, and Lee bestowed that honor upon Gordon. Lee would increasingly turn to the spirited Georgian for counsel and companionship during the remaining months of the war. Brigadier General Clement A. Evans, a 31-year-old Georgia jurist and politician, assumed control of Gordon's Division.[35]

Gordon's returning veterans found the men of Hill's Third Corps waiting for them in the trenches south and west of Petersburg. Hill's order of battle had remained relatively stable throughout the year, and was the only one virtually unaffected by the giant sideshow conducted in the Shenandoah Valley. That is not to say, however, that the Third Corps completely avoided command disruptions in 1864.

Corps commander Powell Hill had risen from service as a field officer to the leadership of the Light Division in 1862. During the first eighteen months of the war, the 37-year-old Virginian distinguished himself as perhaps the best combat officer at that level in the army, although his relationship with Stonewall Jackson had been stormy. Upon Jackson's death in May 1863, Hill received promotion to lieutenant general and command of the newly-organized Third Corps. Hill's performance as a corps commander rarely lived up to expectations. Perhaps Hill had been promoted beyond his level of competency, or maybe the ill-defined health problems that plagued him throughout the last years of his life began to take their toll. Hill periodically required medical leave, placing more responsibility on his capable cast of subordinates.[36]

Hill's division commanders included major generals William Mahone, Henry Heth, and Cadmus M. Wilcox. Of this trio, only Mahone entered the spring campaign without a divisional command. This diminutive graduate of the Virginia Military Institute led a brigade for more than two years with average distinction at best. Longstreet's wounding at the Wilderness precipitated a command shuffle that lifted Mahone to the head of Major General Richard H. Anderson's Division of Hill's corps. These increased responsibilities so animated Mahone's potential that by the end of the campaign season he was recognized as one of the army's finest division commanders. Mahone spearheaded the counterattack at the Crater, and earned his major-generalcy as a reward.[37]

Henry Heth was the senior division commander in the corps. Like his cousin George Pickett, Heth had graduated last in his West Point class. He spent the first two years of the war in western Virginia and Kentucky and then came east in early 1863 in time to command a brigade of Hill's Division at Chancellorsville. The same reorganization that resulted in Hill's promotion to corps command elevated Heth to divisional leadership, and it was his troops who precipitated the Battle of Gettysburg. Heth was allegedly the only officer Lee called by his given name, but the 38-year-old Virginian hardly merited such special consideration. Mentally capable and socially captivating, Heth too often acted impetuously to achieve greatness. The collapse of his division on the morning of May 6 compromised the safety of the entire army, and Heth believed that Lee never forgave him for this blunder.[38]

Heth's Division consisted of four brigades. Brigadier General Joseph R. Davis led a predominantly Mississippi unit, an appropriate assignment for the nephew of the Confederate chief executive. Brigadier General William MacRae commanded the five North Carolina regiments previously directed by Brigadier General William W. Kirkland, who fell wounded in June. Despite a small stature and wholly unimpressive physical presence, MacRae proved to be a tonic for his Tarheel charges. "General MacRae soon won the confidence and admiration of the brigade, both officers and men," remembered Brigadier General James H. Lane. "His voice was like that of a woman; he was small in person, and quick in action. . . . He could place his command in position quicker and infuse more of his fighting qualities into his men, than any officer I ever saw." Colonel William McComb of the 14th Tennessee replaced the veteran brigadier James J. Archer who was captured at Gettysburg and died shortly after his release from a Federal military prison. McComb's Brigade contained the army's only Tennessee regiments. Brigadier General John R. Cooke led the last of Heth's brigades. Cooke's four splendid North Carolina regiments remained intact from the Wilderness to the end of the war. Cooke's father led the Union cavalry during the Peninsula Campaign in 1862, while his brother-in-law, Major General J. E. B. Stuart, commanded the Confederate cavalry until his death in May 1864. Cooke's record as a brigadier was unsurpassed in the Army of Northern Virginia, and when Heth acted as corps commander during Hill's occasional absences, Cooke replaced Heth at the head of the division.[39]

The last of Hill's divisions benefited from the leadership of one of Lee's most dependable lieutenants. Cadmus M. Wilcox, a native of North Carolina raised in Tennessee, had graduated near the bottom of his West Point class but pursued an army career that yielded distinction in Mexico and a text on rifle practice in the 1850s. His service as a brigade commander in Longstreet's corps reached its zenith during the Chancellorsville Campaign. Wilcox transferred to the Third Corps during the army's post-Jackson reorganization. Following the death of Major General William Dorsey Pender after Gettysburg, Lee elevated Wilcox to command Pender's former division. Outgoing and likable, the 40-year-old Wilcox earned a reputation in the army for his insistence on discipline and top performance in the line of duty. Wilcox's star had not ascended as rapidly as Mahone's or Gordon's, but Lee and Hill knew that they could rely on his four brigades to hold a line, plug a gap, or execute a charge with skill and determination.[40]

Wilcox's four brigades hailed from the Carolinas and Georgia. Brigadier General Alfred M. Scales, Pender's protege, led five North Carolina regiments from the Wilderness all the way to Petersburg. Periodic illness-induced absences failed to tarnish the reputation of this Tarheel politician-turned-general. Brigadier General Edward L. Thomas, like Scales innocent of formal military training, also distinguished himself during three years as the commander of his four Georgia regiments. Lee briefly considered Thomas as the replacement for Pender, testifying to the capabilities of this 39-year-old planter.[41]

The other North Carolina brigade in Wilcox's Division belonged to James Lane, a Virginian who migrated south before the war to teach at North Carolina's military institute. Lane served as major of the 1st North Carolina Volunteers in the war's initial land battle at Big Bethel, earning the loyalty and affection of his troops who called him the "Little General." He transferred to the command of the 28th North Carolina and fought in the campaigns of 1862, being wounded twice during the Seven Days Battles. When Lane's brigade commander died at Sharpsburg in September, the men of the brigade petitioned for Lane's promotion, which was approved in November. Lane's five regiments, his old 28th plus the 7th, 18th, 33rd, and 37th North Carolina, participated in all of the army's engagements prior to Petersburg. No brigade fought with more pluck at Gettysburg, perhaps an outgrowth of the responsibility it felt for the accidental volley that had felled Stonewall Jackson two months earlier. Lane received a third battle wound at Cold Harbor, disabling him until the early autumn. His stalwart Carolinians, however, participated with distinction in all of the Third Corps actions on the Petersburg front.[42]

The last of Wilcox's brigades represented South Carolina, the only Palmetto-State infantry unit in Hill's corps. Its commander, Sam McGowan, shared a lack of professional military training with the other brigadiers in the division. At 45, McGowan was older than any general officer in the division and had spent his antebellum years building a successful law practice and political career in Abbeville, South Carolina. McGowan gained some martial experience as a volunteer during the Mexican War and continued to serve as an officer in the state militia. Participating in the bombardment of Fort Sumter and as a staff officer at First Manassas, McGowan initially exercised line authority in the field as lieutenant colonel of the 14th South Carolina. Quickly rising to the command of his regiment, McGowan suffered two wounds in 1862. When Brigadier General Maxcy Gregg died near Fredericksburg in December of that year, McGowan inherited Gregg's Brigade despite being junior to two other regimental commanders in the unit.

McGowan's Brigade contained five regiments: his old 14th, the 1st (Provisional Army), 12th, 13th, and Orr's Rifles. The 1864 campaign had been particularly grueling for these South Carolinians. McGowan's Brigade was one of two Confederate units responsible for defending the horrific Bloody Angle at Spotsylvania, a battle that severely depleted the brigade and resulted in the wounding of its commander. A few days later, McGowan's regiments suffered more than 200 casualties in a sharp fight at the North Anna River. Engaged under interim commanders at Cold Harbor, along the Jerusalem Plank Road, and north of the James River in the summer, the brigade welcomed General McGowan back to the field in August. Immediately, McGowan led his troops into combat at Reams Station and the next month at Peebles's Farm. No Confederate brigade surpassed McGowan's in the volume and intensity of its 1864 combat experience.

The general himself earned a reputation as an earnest, straightforward man, quick in perception and extraordinarily capable as a communicator. "As a military man he was very successful," wrote one observer. "Although not so rigid and minute in his discipline and management as many others, he excelled most officers of equal rank in efficiency. He was an excellent drillmaster, a constant maintainer of good order and regularity, and (which is his great merit) has always succeeded in inspiring confidence in himself and in imparting to others the magnetism of his own enthusiasm."[43]

In the autumn of 1864, the Army of Northern Virginia included a Fourth Corps commanded by Lieutenant General Richard H. Anderson. Anderson's two divisions had once comprised Beauregard's army, but upon the departure of that officer for Wilmington and coastal South Carolina, the troops remained in Virginia and were officially melded into Lee's command.[44]

Their leader, known to some as "Fighting Dick," had been a corps commander since May 7, when Lee tapped him to replace the wounded Longstreet. When Old Pete returned to the field in October, Anderson received his new assignment in order to preserve the separate identity of his troops and to give Anderson a post commensurate with his rank. Anderson turned 43 in the fall of 1864 and had fought under Lee since the Seven Days, first in command of a brigade and then a division under Longstreet. The post-Chancellorsville reorganization sent the South Carolinian and his division to Hill's corps, but Anderson's previous association with the First Corps explained in large part why he inherited Longstreet's position—despite his lackluster record at the divisional level. "His courage was of the highest order, but he was indolent," wrote a member of Longstreet's staff. "His capacity and intelligence [were] excellent, but it was hard to get him to use them." Anderson had enjoyed outstanding moments acting for Longstreet, most notably on the march to Spotsylvania from the Wilderness. Of all the corps leaders in Lee's army, "Fighting Dick" Anderson was the least talented and held the least important command.[45]

Robert Hoke's Division belonged to Anderson's corps but served north of the James with Longstreet. This left only Major General Bushrod R. Johnson's Division reporting directly to Anderson, further diminishing the South Carolinian's status as an equal among the army's lieutenant generals. Johnson graduated from West Point in 1840 and served in the Mexican War, but resigned from the army to become a teacher, a profession that brought him to Nashville before the war. Despite his Ohio origins and his Quaker upbringing, Johnson enjoyed an eventful and varied career as a Confederate officer. He served in the Western Theater and fought with Longstreet at Chickamauga and Knoxville in 1863. In early May, he and his Tennessee brigade transferred to Virginia and participated in Beauregard's actions against Butler south of the James. Later that month, he received promotion to major general and spent the rest of the war engaged in Lee's defense of the Cockade City. Johnson's new division occupied an important part of the line east and southeast of Petersburg with four brigades composed of Virginians, Carolinians, and Alabamians.[46]

Lee's Artillery Reserve still employed Brigadier General William Nelson Pendleton at its head, although the 54-year-old Virginian's duties were administrative in nature. Field command of the guns rested with the corps artillery chiefs, Brigadier General Edward Porter Alexander, under Longstreet, Colonel Reuben Lindsay Walker, under Hill, and Colonel Hilary P. Jones, under Anderson.[47]

Lee's cavalry belonged to Major General Wade Hampton of South Carolina, successor to the legendary "Jeb" Stuart. Several months passed after Stuart's death before Lee decided to advance the 46-year-old Hampton to Stuart's position, but during that time Hampton reinforced the excellent combat record he had earned as a division commander. Brigadier General Matthew C. Butler inherited Hampton's former division, and General Lee's second son, Major General William H. F. "Rooney" Lee, led the army's other division. The wounded Major General Fitzhugh Lee's troopers remained in the Shenandoah Valley during the fall, leaving Hampton with just two divisions around Petersburg.[48]

The Army of Northern Virginia possessed one additional body of troops in the fall of 1864 under the direction of a familiar lieutenant. Richard S. Ewell had been a stalwart with the Army of Northern Virginia since its earliest days. A West Pointer and career soldier, Ewell rose quickly through the ranks to become the heir-apparent to Stonewall Jackson when that incomparable officer perished in 1863. Possessed of a wooden leg and a new wife, Ewell as a corps commander suffered from comparisons to his famous predecessor. The strain of his duties rendered him unfit for vigorous service by the end of May, and Lee placed him on sick leave. Shortly thereafter, Ewell assumed command of the Department of Richmond. This diminished assignment entrusted Ewell with the remnants of Bushrod Johnson's Tennessee troops, Brigadier General Martin W. Gary's cavalry, mixed artillery batteries, reserves, militia, and local defense forces composed of government clerks and workers in the war industries.[49]

*   *   *

Lee returned to his Petersburg headquarters after completing his inspection, but by month's end he had shifted his command post yet again. Responding to General Grant's strategic preference for moving around the Confederate right, Lee accepted the invitation of the William Turnbull family to establish army headquarters at their home on Cox Road, two miles west of Petersburg. Walter Taylor once more saw to the comfortable accommodations of his chief, happily accepting the invitation of Mr. Turnbull to use the spacious parlor of "Edge Hill" for his own habitation. By the end of November, Lee had moved into the finest quarters he would occupy during the war, and what would remain his home until the fateful day that awaited him in April.[50]

His army defended a front stretching from the piney woods east of Richmond south across the James River, through Chesterfield County, over the Appomattox River, and encircling Petersburg from the east, to the south, and finally to the southwest, beyond Burgess's Mill at Hatcher's Run. This contorted front represented a perimeter of more than 37 miles, bolstered to be sure by powerful fortifications but defended with an outnumbered and inadequate force.

The official army returns for November 30 listed 75,630 officers and men present for duty in the Army of Northern Virginia and the Department of Richmond. But that figure included Early's corps, detached in the Valley, which reduced Lee's actual numbers on the Petersburg-Richmond front to 62,674. One month later, the Second Corps had arrived but Hoke's Division had departed. Deducting also the many soldiers too ill to man their posts, Lee could count on only 57,438 men, including Ewell's department, to defend his lines. Despite the addition of Pickett's, Bushrod Johnson's, and Ewell's Richmond troops, Lee's army was smaller than it had been in early May. More ominously, it represented less than half of the Federal strength arrayed against it.[51]

Coping with this large and growing disparity had concerned General Lee for months. "Without some increase in strength, I cannot see how we can escape the natural military consequences of the enemy's numerical superiority," he had written in August. His early November inspection revealed that he could post, on average, only one man for every four-and-one-half feet of line. Such weakness limited Lee's strategic options to those of the defensive, although the gray gambler continued to look for opportunities to assume the tactical offensive. In late November, reports of a possible Union movement westward toward the rail junction at Burkeville prompted Lee to examine the possibilities of concentrating blows on both sides of the James against whatever Federal forces remained, but Grant's failure to execute the rumored advance caused Lee to shelve these plans.[52]

Grant did send a strong force south along the Petersburg Railroad toward an important bridge near Hicksford in early December. Lee responded by detaching Hampton and Hill to intercept the Yankees. Miserable weather and the threat of Confederate opposition turned back the Federals without a significant engagement. Lee's primary task during the winter remained the defense of the Confederate capital, to be accomplished in large part by holding firm at Petersburg. If the long-term military prospects of such a strategy seemed barren, evacuating Richmond and Petersburg presented serious perils as well, as inventoried by one Confederate officer. "Apart from the military value of the morale which would have been lost by such a step," wrote artillerist E. P. Alexander, "was the strategic value of the position as a railroad centre & head of navigation, & the enormous value of the Tredegar Iron Works & the Richmond Arsenal & all the stores & factories & machinery & skilled labor concentrated there, which could never be moved. Civilized armies cannot fight like savages without bases of supply. Should they try it their fighting would at once degenerate even below the value of the fighting of savages."[53]

Unfortunately for Lee, events in other sections of the Confederacy continued to affect his local military situation. Sherman's capture of Savannah in December provided the launching pad for a new campaign into the Carolinas in January. Lee quickly detached an infantry brigade to assist the resistance to Sherman, and then ordered M. C. Butler's cavalry division, accompanied by Wade Hampton, to South Carolina as well. The loss of so much of his mounted force, not to mention the stalwart Cavalry Corps commander, seriously diminished Lee's army. His only hope of replacing these troopers rested with the return of the horsemen still operating with Early in the Shenandoah Valley, a transfer that would not occur until early spring.[54]

In late January the Confederate Congress took a step intended to redress an organizational shortcoming and recognize the service and talents of the Confederacy's greatest commander. The legislators created the position of general-in-chief of the armies, a post clearly designed to place Lee on an equal footing with Grant. On February 6, President Davis appointed Lee to the job. This action, merely a gesture so late in the war, bestowed an honor upon a deserving man and offered a little comfort and cheer to the soldiers and citizens of a failing cause, but little else. Lee unmistakably maintained direct command of the Army of Northern Virginia, but also inherited the burdens of a deteriorating Confederate military situation. The Army of Tennessee had been ruined outside of Nashville in December. Sherman had isolated Georgia from Virginia and was driving through South Carolina. Within a month of Lee's appointment, Sheridan dealt Early's remnant army its death blow, freeing "Little Phil's" veteran cavalry for potential service elsewhere in Virginia. Above all loomed Ulysses S. Grant and his legions, visible above

Petersburg's parapets and doubtless waiting for the first break in the weather to resume the relentless combination of maneuver and hammer blows which had so severely constricted Lee's military options.[55]

*   *   *

The forces that Grant used to pin Lee to his Petersburg entrenchments had experienced an attrition and command reorganization in 1864 every bit as dramatic as those that had transformed and diminished the Army of Northern Virginia. The Army of the Potomac, however, remained at the heart of the lieutenant general's plans to vanquish Lee and terminate the Confederate experiment.

The most successful of that army's leaders, George Meade, retained the post that he had held since June 1863. In his late forties, Meade had reached the pinnacle of a military career that began with his appointment to the United States Military Academy in 1831. He saw service in Mexico and plodded diligently along in the old army, discharging various engineering functions. His rapid rise through the Army of the Potomac derived principally from outstanding performances on the Peninsula, in the 1862 Maryland Campaign, and at Fredericksburg. Following the disaster at Chancellorsville in the spring of 1863, Meade was thrust into overall command while the army marched northward to counter Lee's second large-scale incursion across the Potomac. A few days later, the armies clashed at Gettysburg, and Meade emerged as the first Northern general to whip Lee in a major campaign. The victorious Meade found himself an overnight hero.

One military man during the winter of 1863-1864, however, clearly superseded Meade in the esteem of his countrymen, and that man was Ulysses S. Grant. Grant's decision to reject a Washington-based headquarters in favor of a command post in the field condemned Meade to a secondary role in the spring campaign. Meade unselfishly volunteered to step aside as army commander to make room for someone of Grant's own selection, but the new lieutenant general quickly elected to keep Meade. That confidence proved well-placed. "General Meade has more than met my most sanguine expectations," Grant told the secretary of war in mid-May, while recommending Meade for promotion to major general in the regular army. "He and Sherman are the fittest officers for large commands I have come in contact with."[56]

With a few exceptions, Meade and Grant functioned well together in what must have been an uncomfortable and periodically demoralizing role for the victor of Gettysburg. "In point of reality the whole [responsibility for army command] is Grant's," wrote one of Meade's staff officers in August. "He directs all, and his subordinates are only responsible as executive officers. . . ." Meade's relationship with his corps commanders was not so harmonious or effective. "He was totally lacking in cordiality toward those with whom he had business, and in consequence was generally disliked by his subordinates," thought a War Department official. "With General Grant Meade got along always perfectly, because he had the first virtue of a soldier—that is, obedience to orders . . . but the almost universal dislike of Meade which prevailed among officers of every rank who came in contact with him, and the difficulty of doing business with him, felt by every one except Grant himself, so greatly impaired his capacities for usefulness . . . that Grant seemed to be coming to the conviction that he must be relieved." The general-in-chief did consider sending Meade to command the forces in the Shenandoah Valley during the summer of 1864, but at year's end Meade's position at the head of the Army of the Potomac remained secure.[57]

Only one of the five corps commanders who entered the Wilderness with Meade camped with the Army of the Potomac at Petersburg in December. Major General Gouverneur K. Warren maintained command of the Fifth Corps despite a checkered performance at the head of Meade's old organization. A distinguished West Point graduate, the 34-year-old New York native led a pedigreed Zouave regiment from his home state and later a brigade in the Army of the Potomac. His fame derived from service as the army's chief engineer at the Battle of Gettysburg, where he alertly recognized danger on Little Round Top and summoned reinforcements at a critical moment. Promotion and restoration to line command followed.

Warren's generalship in the Overland Campaign mixed tactical and administrative competence with a stubbornness and overcaution that would ultimately lead to his undoing. His refusal to execute an ordered attack on May 12 during the Battle of Spotsylvania almost resulted in his dismissal, and Warren's standing and reputation in the army suffered accordingly. He continued to quarrel with Meade and others throughout the year, although the Fifth Corps played a prominent role in important actions like that at the Petersburg Railroad in August. "He was a man of fine intelligence, great earnestness, quick perception, and could make his dispositions as quickly as any officer, under difficulties where he was forced to act," explained Grant. "But I had . . . discovered a defect which was . . . very prejudicial to his usefulness. . . . He could see danger at a glance before he had encountered it. He would not only make preparations to meet the danger which might occur, but he would inform his commanding officer what others should do while he was executing his move." Divisions under brigadier generals Charles Griffin, Romeyn B. Ayres, and Samuel W. Crawford, all experienced at their level of command, lay encamped at year's end between the Jerusalem Plank Road and Halifax Road south of Petersburg.[58]

Positioned on Warren's right, the Second Corps had earned a reputation as the finest in the Army of the Potomac, largely due to the leadership of Major General Winfield S. Hancock. That worthy officer assumed corps command prior to the Gettysburg Campaign, during which he received a serious wound that would plague him the rest of his life. In late November his lingering injuries, combined with a desire for a more independent assignment, prompted him to accept responsibility for recruiting and organizing a new Veteran Volunteer Corps with headquarters in Washington. Hancock was replaced by Major General Andrew Atkinson Humphreys, who received the temporary command (later to be made permanent) of the Second Corps.[59]

> "When he does get wrathy, he sets his teeth and lets go a torrent of adjectives that must rather astonish those not used to little outbursts."

At age 54, Humphreys owned more than three decades of military experience, most of it as an engineer in the old army or as a staff officer under McClellan early in the war. For less than a year in 1862 and 1863, Humphreys led a division of infantry, but immediately after the Battle of Gettysburg he accepted a promotion to become chief of staff to General Meade and the Army of the Potomac. The fiery Humphreys preferred line authority, however, and Hancock's departure created an opening for which he was eminently qualified. His appointment met with wide approval throughout the army. Though Humphreys was highly esteemed for his intelligence and easy-going nature, his use of language elicited much notice in army circles. "He was one of the loudest swearers that I ever knew," observed Charles A. Dana of the War Department. Theodore Lyman, a veteran of Meade's staff, agreed: "When he does get wrathy, he sets his teeth and lets go a torrent of adjectives that must rather astonish those not used to little outbursts."[60]

Humphreys's division commanders included Major General John Gibbon and brigadier generals Nelson A. Miles and Gershom Mott. Gibbon protested Humphreys's appointment as temporary Second Corps commander, feeling that his seniority in the corps entitled him to any promotion of a less-than-permanent nature. Grant would soon mollify Gibbon with a corps command of his own outside the Army of the Potomac. In order to relieve the Second Corps from its dangerous and fatiguing position on the army's right, east of Petersburg, on November 28 Meade directed Humphreys to move to the far left, south and west of the city, to a place where the opposing lines lay much farther apart.[61]

The troops who relieved them on the eastern sector belonged to the Ninth Corps. This organization entered the 1864 campaign independent from the Army of the Potomac under the familiar guiding hand of Major General Ambrose E. Burnside, but in late May Meade's army absorbed it in the interest of command efficiency. Burnside remained in charge of his troops until the administrative fallout from the Crater fiasco claimed him as its highest-ranking casualty. On August 14 Burnside's chief of staff, John G. Parke, assumed control of the corps, and Burnside faded forever from active command.[62]

Parke graduated second in his West Point class and spent his entire pre-war military career as an engineer, thus sharing that professional background with Meade, Humphreys, and Warren. Parke's earliest wartime service came as a subordinate to Burnside during that officer's successful 1862 campaign in North Carolina. The 37-year-old Pennsylvanian served as army chief of staff while Burnside commanded the Army of the Potomac during the Fredericksburg Campaign, and Parke later led troops under Burnside in the Department of the Ohio. Once again in the role of chief of staff in 1864, the likeable and popular Parke was a logical choice to succeed his unfortunate superior by virtue of his rank, long association with the corps, and previous experience in line authority.[63]

Parke's three divisions swapped places with the Second Corps in December, thus assuming the disagreeable assignment of guarding the Army's right flank, extending from the Appomattox River east of Petersburg to near the Jerusalem Plank Road south of the city. Brigadier generals Orlando B. Willcox and Robert B. Potter had been division commanders since well before the beginning of the spring campaign, while Brigadier General John F. Hartranft earned his divisional command by meritorious service while in charge of his brigade.[64]

Brigadier General Henry J. Hunt headed the army's artillery branch as he had since 1862. Hunt was considered one of the foremost authorities on artillery in the old army, and his service with the long arm during the war did nothing to tarnish that reputation. In addition to a large reserve, Hunt exercised administrative oversight if not command authority over artillery brigades attached to each corps. Major John G. Hazard led the Second

Corps guns, Colonel Charles S. Wainwright fulfilled that function for the Fifth Corps, and Colonel John C. Tidball served as the Ninth Corps artillery chief.[65]

Meade's Cavalry Corps had been eviscerated by the same order that transferred Phil Sheridan to the Shenandoah Valley. Sheridan took with him two of the three mounted divisions with which he had campaigned since the spring, leaving only Brigadier General David M. Gregg's troopers with the Army of the Potomac. The 31-year-old Gregg was a much-esteemed officer, universally liked, whose abrupt and unexplained resignation in February 1865 would surprise everyone.[66]

An officer whose permanent departure elicited less shock and regret commanded the other Federal army on the Petersburg-Richmond front. Ben Butler's achievements at the head of the Army of the James improved but little following his singular failures in the spring of 1864. When in late December he returned from North Carolina after another aborted offensive, Grant finally lost patience with his politically-minded subordinate. The general-in-chief banished Butler to his home and named Major General Edward O. C. Ord as Butler's successor. Ord, a West Pointer and favorite of Grant's since their service together in 1862, had been wounded in September while commanding a corps under Butler. His return to health coincided with the completion of the 1864 election cycle, rendering the well-connected but militarily under-endowed Butler mercifully expendable.[67]

The Army of the James had completed a major reorganization just prior to Ord's accession. The army's two infantry corps, the Tenth and Eighteenth, each contained a division of United States Colored Troops, but this mix of white and black units within the corps created problems. Moreover, Butler sought to enhance the racial pride and cohesiveness of his black units. Therefore, he eliminated the two corps in favor of an all-white Twenty-fourth Corps and an all black Twenty-fifth Corps. John Gibbon received command of the Twenty-fourth Corps, thus resolving his dissatisfaction with being bypassed to succeed Hancock. "It was difficult to conceal my pleasure and satisfaction at the receipt of this news," wrote Gibbon. "It relieved me from the embarrassments of a position which I regarded as a false one, enlarged my sphere of duty under a commander (Ord) for whom I had great respect and regard, made me more independent and second in command in the Army of the James instead of seventh as I was in the Army of the Potomac." Despite his raw ambition and petulance, Gibbon had compiled a sterling record as a brigade and division commander and made a good choice to lead the three divisions of his corps, directed by brigadier generals Robert S. Foster and Charles Devens, and Colonel Thomas M. Harris.[68]

The Twenty-fifth Corps included Butler's black regiments and the United States Colored Troops who had served with Burnside and Parke in the Ninth Corps. Their leader was Major General Godfrey Weitzel, a Cincinnati German not yet 30 years old who had graduated second in his class at the United States Military Academy. Like so many of Grant's corps commanders, Weitzel possessed a strong engineering background. His association with the influential Butler as chief engineer and his subsequent service in the Trans-Mississippi Theater advanced the career of this competent soldier. Ironically, Weitzel had firmly opposed arming blacks while in Louisiana in 1862, but now found himself at the head of the only all-black army corps in American history. His division commanders at year's end included brigadier generals Charles J. Paine, Edward A. Wild, and William Birney.[69]

The Army of the James bore responsibility for the Union trenches north of the James River, running from Signal Hill (Fort Brady) northward to New Market Road. The army's cavalry, a division under Brigadier General August V. Kautz, guarded the right flank of this line. Brigadier General Edward Ferrero, the Brooklyn dancing master who had commanded Burnside's black troops at the Battle of the Crater, connected with Ord's left on the south bank of the James in command of three brigades designated as the Defenses of Bermuda Hundred. Thus Grant's huge siege line mirrored Lee's from the sandy pineland of eastern Henrico County, across the James and Appomattox rivers, and into the old tobacco fields of Dinwiddie County.[70]

The return of the Sixth Corps in December reunited Meade's army, except for the two cavalry divisions that remained in the Valley with Sheridan. The Sixth Corps, like the Second and Ninth, operated under different leadership at year's end. Major General Horatio G. Wright inherited command on May 9, 1864, following the death of popular long-time corps commander, John Sedgwick.[71]

The 44-year-old Wright hailed from Connecticut and graduated second in the West Point class of 1841. His distinguished standing at the Military Academy marked him for a career with the engineers, a craft he practiced throughout his tenure in the pre-war army and a speciality that he shared with Meade and the army's other corps commanders. Wright's early wartime service included stints as an engineering officer in Virginia, commanding troops on the south Atlantic coast, and as the head of the Department of the Ohio in Cincinnati. Not until 1863 was Wright assigned to the Army of the Potomac. As a division commander under Sedgwick,

Wright displayed a steadiness that impressed his superiors more than it garnered public attention. Admired in army circles for his pleasant personality and predilection for prompt and precise action, Wright handled the Sixth Corps in the Overland Campaign with "heroic gallantry and marked ability." Grant expressed no hesitation in sending Wright and his corps to protect Washington during Early's summer offensive. The inspirational role played by Sheridan at the Battle of Cedar Creek, however, did overshadow Wright's solid performance in the Valley. Early had overwhelmed the Federals while Wright acted as army commander, until Sheridan's dramatic arrival rallied the bluecoats and helped earn a Union victory. Nevertheless, Wright won the reputation as a man of high intellect with a marked capacity for command—if rarely brilliant or flashy in combat. His relatively low profile stemmed from his late association with the Army of the Potomac, a secondary role at Gettysburg, and his understudy status with both the enormously popular Sedgwick and the highly publicized Sheridan.[72]

Wright struck an imposing physical figure as well. One observer noted that the general "wore a rounded face of florid hue with puffy cheeks and bulging forehead, had brown locks which if licensed to grow, would vie with Hyperion's, for the tendency to curl was there; as it was, they were more luxuriant [sic] than his poverty of mustache and goatee, both of which were, oddly, of a lighter shade. Wright verged on six feet and though bulky of form, his figure was symmetrical. Erect in the saddle . . . he presented a martial appearance." The men of the Sixth Corps accepted Wright, but usually compared him unfavorably with Sedgwick. "The soldiers of the 6th Corps do not like [Wright] very well," confessed a member of the 37th Massachusetts. "We used to like General Sedgwick (or Uncle John as we used to call him.)"[73]

Only one of Wright's Petersburg subordinates had much experience handling a division. Brigadier General George Washington Getty, although an artillerist by training, assumed command of an infantry division in 1862 and served in that capacity for most of the war. A graduate of West Point and classmate of future Confederate opponents like Richard Ewell and Bushrod Johnson, the 45-year-old Getty transferred to the Sixth Corps just prior to the Wilderness Campaign, where he was severely wounded while playing a key role in that bloody engagement. He returned to command in time to help save Sheridan's army with a heroic stand at Cedar Creek.

Getty's battlefield behavior testified to his courage, a trait admired by the men in his division. His personal modesty and reticence contributed to a public obscurity unwarranted by his fine record. Getty married a woman from Staunton, Virginia, whose family staunchly supported the Confederacy, but Getty's devotion to the Union never faltered. "True in all soldierly instincts . . . intent on his duty . . . always to be found at the head of his men, who trusted in him implicitly," he was, thought one of his officers, "the model of an educated American soldier gentleman."[74]

Colonel James M. Warner led Getty's First Brigade. A 28-year-old Vermont native, Warner had graduated next to last in the West Point class of 1860. He spent the first year of the war at an isolated post in Colorado, but came east in 1862 to command a heavy artillery regiment in the Washington defenses. Grant called these Vermonters to the field during the fighting at Spotsylvania, where Warner promptly fell wounded. He returned to duty in time to lead a brigade during Sheridan's victories in the Valley. The men of his Pennsylvania and New York regiments respected Warner, one thinking him "the best officer now present. He is a clever, gentlemanly fellow, and I like him very much."[75]

Getty's Second Brigade commander enjoyed a much longer association with his troops than did Warner. Brigadier General Lewis A. Grant also hailed from Vermont, but pursued a career in law, not the military. The 34-year-old attorney had risen within the 5th Vermont from major to colonel, then took charge of the renowned Vermont Brigade, of which his old regiment was a part. Wounded at Fredericksburg, sufficiently successful to earn a Medal of Honor for his service at Salem Church, and brilliant at Cedar Creek, Grant earned the grudging respect, if not the affection, of his men. They called him "Aunt Liddie" and considered him possessed of a "fussy old womanish disposition." Major Aldace F. Walker, Warner's successor as commander of the 1st Vermont Heavy Artillery in Grant's brigade, noted that his general "had by diligent study, made himself so thoroughly acquainted with the red tape of the Regulations, that he became a martinet in his disposition to require the performance of many of its absurdities." Despite his bureaucratic tendencies, Walker credited Grant with unquestioned bravery and energy.[76]

Getty's Third Brigade was composed primarily of New York units leavened by one regiment each from Maine and Pennsylvania. The Pine Tree State outfit had been formed from the reenlisting veterans of three disbanded regiments, including the old 7th Maine. Colonel Thomas W. Hyde had been in command of that regiment and, upon his return to the army from a short leave, found himself the ranking officer of his brigade. Just 23 years old, Hyde had attended Bowdoin College and as the major of the 7th Maine earned a Medal of Honor for his accomplishments at Antietam. "It was a proud thing for a boy to command a brigade," admitted the youthful Hyde, who would learn the responsibilities of his elevated authority during the relatively quiet winter months.[77]

Wright's First Division had been his own, and upon his promotion to corps command, Brigadier General David A. Russell moved up to take his place. However, Russell was killed at Third Winchester (Battle of the Opequon) in September 1864, and Brigadier General Frank Wheaton succeeded him. Wheaton was the unusual Union soldier with prewar experience as an officer but no formal military education. The 31-year-old Rhode Islander entered the Civil War as lieutenant colonel of the 2nd Rhode Island, but rose to brigade command in December 1862. Wheaton's father-in-law, General Samuel Cooper, was the ranking officer in the Confederate Army, and his mother-in-law was the sister of the Confederate commissioner to England, James Mason. Wheaton's loyalty was never an issue, although compared to Getty, he was not particularly beloved in the ranks.[78]

Wheaton's First Brigade was the second of the two Sixth Corps brigades associated with a single state. The 1st New Jersey Brigade contained six regiments from the Garden State and suffered the fourth highest number of killed and mortally wounded of any brigade in the war. Colonel William H. Penrose had commanded the New Jerseyians since May 9, 1864, having previous experience as colonel of the 15th New Jersey. Penrose received a commission in the regular army at the outset of the war by virtue of his father's standing as an officer, and transferred to the volunteer service in 1863. He conducted himself like a professional soldier and demanded much of his citizen-soldiers, a characteristic that prevented him from being warmly embraced by his men.[79]

Wheaton's Second Brigade returned to Petersburg under the command of Brigadier General Ranald S. Mackenzie. The 24-year-old Mackenzie had graduated first in the West Point class of 1862 and immediately entered the engineers, in which capacity he served with distinction from Second Manassas through the Overland Campaign. In July 1864, Mackenzie received a line command as colonel of the 2nd Connecticut Heavy Artillery and went to the Valley where, like his brigade commander, Colonel Joseph E. Hamblin, he was wounded at Cedar Creek. Mackenzie temporarily succeeded Hamblin in command of the brigade and continued in that capacity until late in the winter, when he was transferred to replace Kautz at the head of the cavalry division of the Army of the James. Hamblin, a 36-year-old New York insurance broker, recovered from his Cedar Creek wound and resumed his place at the front of the brigade.

Major General Horatio G. Wright

Hamblin's return was greeted with almost universal celebration in the Second Brigade. "A brave officer of magnificent figure and bearing, and a gentleman by instinct," Hamblin had worked his way up through the ranks of the brigade's 65th New York. "All glad to see Gen. Ham[b]lin," testified a Connecticut captain. The brash young Mackenzie enjoyed a much briefer connection with the unit, and although Grant called him "the most promising young officer in the army," his troops felt differently. "Our best intelligence . . . which has caused as much joy as all of Sherman's victories is the departure of Brig. Gen. Mackenzie for the Army of the James," wrote an officer in the 2nd Connecticut Heavy Artillery. "He left us yesterday amid the shouts of his entire command. . . . I think he goes singularly unregretted—as there are not 2 persons in the entire brigade but what are more than glad that he had left us, and sincerely pray that they may never see his face again."[80]

Colonel Oliver Edwards led the Third Brigade of the First Division. Not quite 30 years old, Edwards had returned from Illinois to his native Massachusetts in 1861 to volunteer for service. In 1862 he received command of the 37th Massachusetts and led it competently through Spotsylvania, where he succeeded to brigade command in the Second Division. When the Sixth Corps went to the Valley, Edwards switched to the First Division and took command of the mixed brigade of Massachusetts, Rhode Island, Pennsylvania, and Wisconsin troops that he led at Petersburg. Edwards was highly regarded and battlewise.[81]

The Third Division of the Sixth Corps contained just two brigades. Its commander since April 1864, Brigadier General James B. Ricketts, was numbered among the many Sixth Corps casualties at Cedar Creek, and Brigadier General Truman Seymour filled his place. Seymour had joined the Sixth Corps as a brigade commander at the outset of the Overland Campaign, but his tenure with the corps had been brief. Captured at the Wilderness, he spent the next three months as a prisoner of war. His exchange allowed him to return to the corps. His seniority and experience as a brigade, division, and even independent commander, made Seymour the logical choice to replace the incapacitated Ricketts.

Like so many of the officers in Wright's command, Seymour hailed from New England. The 40-year-old Vermonter had graduated from the United States Military Academy, fought with valor in Mexico, and defended Fort Sumter in April 1861. One observer called Seymour, "a fiery and irrepressible sort of party." His disastrous leadership at the Battle of Olustee and his brigade's collapse at the Wilderness marked him as the potentially weak link in Wright's triumvirate of division commanders.[82]

Seymour's First Brigade marched under the direction of Colonel William S. Truex, who had moved up on May 14 at Spotsylvania from his position as commander of the 14th New Jersey. Less than three weeks later, Truex fell wounded at Cold Harbor and could not return to duty until after the Valley Campaign had run its course. The 45-year-old Truex attended West Point and saw action in the Mexican War. He held field commands in the 5th and 10th New Jersey regiments before accepting the top position in the 14th New Jersey. His brigade also included units from New York, Pennsylvania, and Vermont.[83]

Seymour's Second Brigade had been his own in the Wilderness and had retained its organizational integrity throughout the year. It contained the only Ohio and Maryland troops in the corps, while two veteran Pennsylvania regiments and one of the heavy artillery outfits from New York completed this polyglot command. Colonel J. Warren Keifer rode at its head. This 28-year-old Buckeye had been the colonel of the 110th Ohio, but acceded to brigade command during the 1864 Valley Campaign, where he won a brevet for gallantry. An intelligent and articulate man who would within a generation become Speaker of the United States House of Representatives, Keifer, like Seymour and Truex, shared the handicap of limited experience at his level of authority.[84]

Colonel Charles H. Tompkins commanded the Sixth Corps artillery brigade since the spring of 1863. Tompkins went on leave in January, however, and Captain William A. Harn of the 3rd New York Battery, and then Captain Andrew Cowan of the 1st New York Battery, took command of Wright's guns. Most of Cowan's cannoneers had been with the Army of the Potomac since the earliest days of the Peninsula Campaign, and, like the other gunners in blue, were thoroughly competent and well-equipped.[85]

* * *

Elisha Hunt Rhodes and his comrades in the First Division led the way from the Valley back to Petersburg. Seymour's troops followed Wheaton's on December 3. Once Gordon's and Pegram's Confederates left northwestern Virginia, Getty's division decamped, and by December 16 the entire Sixth Corps had assembled along the Petersburg lines. Wheaton relieved Crawford's Fifth Corps division; when Seymour arrived, his troops filed in on Wheaton's left, between Fort Wadsworth and a point midway between Vaughan and Squirrel Level roads, replacing Ayres's Fifth Corps troops. Getty continued the line to the west, relieving Gibbon's Second Corps units between Seymour's left and Fort Fisher, near Church Road. This placed the Sixth Corps squarely between Parke on its right and Humphreys on its left, several miles south and west of Petersburg. Wright arrived in person on December 12 to assume command of his corps.[86]

The Army of the Potomac, Burnside's Ninth Corps, and the Army of the James entered the 1864 campaign season with twenty-nine infantry officers at the army, corps, or divisional command level. At the end of the year, only nine of those men, fewer than one-third of them, still occupied

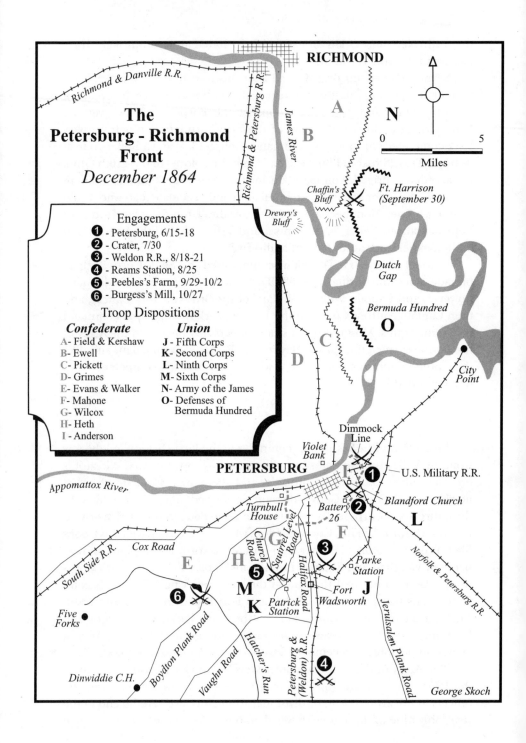

RICHMOND

A

B

N

0   5

Miles

Richmond & Danville R.R.

**The
Petersburg - Richmond
Front**
December 1864

Richmond & Petersburg R.R.

James River

Chaffin's
Bluff

Ft. Harrison
(September 30)

Drewry's
Bluff

Engagements

❶ - Petersburg, 6/15-18
❷ - Crater, 7/30
❸ - Weldon R.R., 8/18-21
❹ - Reams Station, 8/25
❺ - Peebles's Farm, 9/29-10/2
❻ - Burgess's Mill, 10/27

Troop Dispositions

Confederate
A- Field & Kershaw
B- Ewell
C- Pickett
D- Grimes
E- Evans & Walker
F- Mahone
G- Wilcox
H- Heth
I - Anderson

Union
J - Fifth Corps
K- Second Corps
L- Ninth Corps
M- Sixth Corps
N- Army of the James
O- Defenses of
    Bermuda Hundred

Dutch
Gap

Bermuda Hundred

O

C

D

City
Point

Dimmock
Line

Violet
Bank

I

❶

U.S. Military R.R.

PETERSBURG

Blandford Church

Appomattox River

Turnbull
House

Battery
26

❷

L

F

Cox Road

South Side R.R.

G

Church Road

Squirel Level Road

Halifax Road

❸

Parke
Station

Norfolk & Petersburg R.R.

E

H

❺

M

K

Patrick
Station

Fort
Wadsworth

J

Jerusalem Plank Road

Five
Forks

❻

Boydton Plank Road

Vaughn Road

Hatcher's Run

Petersburg &
(Weldon) R.R.

❹

Dinwiddie C.H.

George Skoch

their original positions. Attrition had afflicted brigade and regimental leaders with even greater severity.[87]

Grant's official returns at the end of the year showed 121,718 officers and men present for duty on the Petersburg-Richmond front. This compared unfavorably with the 155,221 composing the combat-ready forces of Meade, Burnside, and Butler at the campaign's inception, but the reduction of effectives by some 30,000 reveals only part of the story. The shattered landscape from the Rapidan River to the Boydton Plank Road was littered with the corpses of thousands of boys in blue. Thousands more filled hospitals and convalescent beds throughout the North, or languished in Confederate prisons. These soldiers represented some of the best fighting material available to Grant. Not only was the War Department unable to replenish the ranks with equal numbers, but the quality of the replacements that did report failed to measure up in all cases to the men whose shoes they filled. Grant's inability to capture Petersburg in 1864 stemmed from multiple reasons—not the least of which was the Army of Northern Virginia. The Union forces who made those repeated attempts, however, did not enjoy the same seasoned leadership with which they entered the campaign, nor was the caliber of the average man in the ranks equal in experience or motivation to the veterans who plunged into the Wilderness in early May.[88]

Grant still possessed a more than two-to-one numerical advantage over Lee, but eight months of experience demonstrated that those were not particularly favorable odds when Confederate fortifications were factored into the equation. Grant's strategy of targeting the supply routes into Petersburg remained sound, but the freezing and thawing of a central Virginia winter boded ill for the mobility required to pursue that scheme. The Union war effort, however, would not hibernate until spring. Sherman's capture of Savannah, Georgia, in late December and his subsequent request to march overland through the Carolinas caused Grant to alter his plans. The general-in-chief had anticipated transporting Sherman's army to Virginia by water to operate against Lee, but Sherman's audacious proposal seized Grant's imagination.

"If North and South Carolina were rendered helpless so far as capacity for feeding Lee's army was concerned, the Confederate garrison at Richmond would be reduced in territory, from which to draw supplies, to very narrow limits in the State of Virginia," wrote Grant. "I approved Sherman's suggestion therefore at once."

With "Uncle Billy's" bummers marching north, Union forces reducing Fort Fisher and aiming to close the Confederacy's principal Atlantic port at Wilmington, North Carolina, a waterborne Federal army poised to land in the Tarheel State, and additional blueclad forces targeting the industrial interior of Alabama, Grant reduced the role of Meade's and Ord's stationary divisions to that of a ready reserve. "From about Richmond I will watch Lee closely, and if he detaches much more, or attempts to evacuate, will pitch in," he told Sherman. "In the meantime, should you be brought to a halt anywhere, I can send two corps of thirty thousand effective men to your support, from the troops about Richmond."[89]

Thus as winter's mantle descended on the troops along the Petersburg lines, officers and men turned from thoughts of envelopments and bayonet charges to the more mundane skills of perfecting fortifications and preparing winter quarters. The men in blue hoped, and the warriors in gray feared, that this would be the last winter of the war. "As I looked across the plains to the rebel lines I could not but wonder where I and the rebel pickets would be next New Years," wrote Corporal Lewis Bissell of the 2nd Connecticut Heavy Artillery. "I hope to be at home and hope the rebel will be at his and the war ended."[90]

NOTES

The following abbreviations are utilized in these notes:

CHS: Connecticut Historical Society
CV: Confederate Veteran
Duke: William R. Perkins Library, Duke University
HEH: Henry E. Huntington Library
HSWP: Historical Society of Western Pennsylvania
LC: Manuscripts Division, Library of Congress
MOLLUS: Military Order of the Loyal Legion of the United States
NA: National Archives
NCDAH: North Carolina Department of Archives and History
NT: National Tribune
PMHSM: Papers of the Military Historical Society of Massachusetts
SHC: Southern Historical Collection, University of North Carolina
SHSP: Southern Historical Society Papers
SHSW: State Historical Society of Wisconsin
USAMHI: United States Army Military History Institute
USC: South Caroliniana Library, University of South Carolina
UVM: Bailey/Howe Library, University of Vermont
VHS: Virginia Historical Society

VTHS: Vermont Historical Society

YU: Bernhard Knollenberg Collection, Manuscripts and Archives, Yale University Library.

1. There are any number of excellent sources about the 1864 Shenandoah Valley Campaign. One of the best comprehensive treatments of this decisive chapter of Civil War history is Jeffry D. Wert, *From Winchester to Cedar Creek* (Carlisle, Pa., 1987). Battlefield parks at Fisher's Hill and Cedar Creek allow modern visitors an opportunity to study this campaign on the ground. Historic land is preserved at Third Winchester and Tom's Brook as well, although in 2000 there are few facilities to accommodate visitors at those sites.

2. Robert Hunt Rhodes, ed., *All for the Union: The Civil War Diary and Letters of Elisha Hunt Rhodes* (New York, 1985), 198-200; Elisha H. Rhodes, "The Second Rhode Island Volunteers at the Siege of Petersburg, Virginia," in *Personal Narratives of Events in the War of the Rebellion, Being Papers Read Before the Rhode Island Soldiers and Sailors Historical Society*, 100 vols. (Providence, 1878-1915, reprint, Wilmington, N.C.,1992), X, 434-436. Rhodes belonged to the 2nd Rhode Island Volunteer Infantry. All such volunteer infantry regiments will be identified simply by their numerical and state designations. Cavalry and artillery units will be specifically designated as such.

3. Rhodes, *All for the Union*, 200; Rhodes, "The Second Rhode Island Volunteers," 436. Nothing remains of Battery 26, but Fort Wadsworth is well preserved in 2000 and administered by Petersburg National Battlefield.

4. Noah Andre Trudeau, *The Last Citadel: Petersburg, Virginia, June 1864-April 1865* (Boston, 1991), 4-6; William C. Davis, *Death in the Trenches: Grant at Petersburg* (Alexandria, Va., 1986), 8; William D. Henderson, *Petersburg in the Civil War: War at the Door* (Lynchburg, Va., 1998), 1-10. Petersburg earned its nickname during the War of 1812 when President James Madison commented upon the headgear adornments of volunteer troops from Petersburg. In 1860, the city numbered 18,266 residents, including 3,164 free blacks and 5,680 slaves. In 2000, Petersburg is a city of some 35,000 with a richly preserved architectural and historical legacy.

5. Richard Wayne Lykes, *Campaign For Petersburg* (Washington, 1970), 9-10; Henderson, *Petersburg in the Civil War*, 55; Trudeau, *The Last Citadel*, 4,6. Some 4,000 soldiers and 1,000 slaves began work on the so-called Dimmock Line in August 1862. Much of those defenses remain in 2000 throughout Petersburg National Battlefield and in the City of Petersburg.

6. The Overland Campaign from the Wilderness to Cold Harbor is the subject of several outstanding monographs. Noah Andre Trudeau, *Bloody Roads South: The Wilderness to Cold Harbor, May-June 1864* (Boston, 1989) is among the best. Individual accounts of the major battles are also in ample supply. Gordon C. Rhea, *The Battle of the Wilderness, May 5-6, 1864* (Baton Rouge, 1994), and *The Battles*

for *Spotsylvania Court House and the Road to Yellow Tavern, May 7-12, 1864* (Baton Rouge, 1997), William D. Matter, *If It Takes All Summer: The Battle of Spotsylvania* (Chapel Hill, N.C., 1988), J. Michael Miller, *The North Anna Campaign: "Even to Hell Itself"* (Lynchburg, Va., 1989), and Louis J. Baltz III, *The Battle of Cold Harbor, May 27-June 13, 1864* (Lynchburg, Va., 1994) are all recommended. William Glenn Robertson writes about the action at Petersburg on June 9 in *The Battle of Old Men and Young Boys, June 9, 1864* (Lynchburg, Va., 1989). Important parts of the Wilderness, Spotsylvania, and Cold Harbor battlefields are preserved by the National Park Service. Hanover County maintains a critical portion of the North Anna Battlefield at Ox Ford.

7. The two railroads were the Richmond & Danville, and the Virginia Central. Grant did target the Virginia Central in his plans to isolate Richmond. The Union army in the Shenandoah Valley would move eastward along the railroad from Staunton while a cavalry force led by Major General Philip H. Sheridan would cut the line west of Richmond and link up with the Valley force. This portion of Grant's grand strategy would come to grief at Lynchburg and Trevilian Station, respectively, in mid-June. General Pierre Gustave Toutant Beauregard headed the Department of North Carolina and Southern Virginia. His small army was independent of the Army of Northern Virginia, so, unlike the Federals, the Confederates did not enjoy unity of command in the state.

8. For accounts of Grant's plans for and execution of the crossing of the James see Trudeau, *The Last Citadel*, 14-25 and Davis, *Death in the Trenches*, 34-39.

9. The fighting between June 15 and 18 is sometimes styled the Battle of Petersburg. Trudeau, *The Last Citadel*, 29-55, Davis, *Death in the Trenches*, 39-53, and Lykes, *Campaign for Petersburg*, 10-16 offer detailed, intermediate, and brief accounts, respectively, of these four days of combat. Thomas J. Howe, *The Petersburg Campaign: Wasted Valor, June 15-18, 1864* (Lynchburg, Va. 1988) is the only monograph devoted exclusively to this portion of the campaign. Much of the ground on which these battles occurred is preserved as a part of the main unit of Petersburg National Battlefield.

10. Lykes, *Campaign for Petersburg*, 17-19 and Trudeau, *The Last Citadel*, 56-87, discuss the Battle of Jerusalem Plank Road. That highway survives on much of its wartime route as U.S. 301, Crater Road, in Petersburg, and farther south as VA 35. Jerusalem is now Courtland, Virginia. The Petersburg Railroad is often called the Petersburg & Weldon Railroad or simply the Weldon Railroad in accounts of the campaign.

11. The Sixth Corps enjoyed a long if relatively unspectacular combat record in the Army of the Potomac prior to 1864. Organized on May 18, 1862, the corps participated in the Seven Days Battles east and north of Richmond, captured Crampton's Gap in South Mountain during the Maryland Campaign, and was present but not heavily engaged at the battles of Antietam and Fredericksburg. The Sixth Corps fought for two days at Second Fredericksburg and Salem Church during the Chancellorsville Campaign, but was only lightly engaged at Gettysburg. On November 7, 1863, the Sixth Corps won a brilliant little victory at

Rappahannock Station and then entered winter camp around Brandy Station and Culpeper Court House during the winter of 1863-1864. For a tidy summary of the organization's history, see Frank J. Welcher, *The Union Army 1861-1865: Organization and Operations*, 2 vols. (Bloomington, Ind., 1989), I, 394-420.

12. Ulysses S. Grant, *Personal Memoirs of Ulysses S. Grant*, 2 vols. (New York, 1885, reprint, New York, 1974), II, 307-310. Grant had experience with exploding mines under Confederate fortifications at Vicksburg in 1863.

13. Grant to Major General Henry W. Halleck, August 1, 1864 in *The War of the Rebellion: A Compilation of the Official Records of the Union and Confederate Armies*, 128 vols. (Washington, 1880-1901), Series 1, vol. 40, pt. 1, 17. Hereafter cited as *OR*. All references are to Series 1, vol. 46 unless otherwise noted. The best single source on the Battle of the Crater is Michael A. Cavanaugh and William Marvel, *The Petersburg Campaign: The Battle of the Crater, "The Horrid Pit," June 25-August 6, 1864* (Lynchburg, Va., 1989). See also Trudeau, *The Last Citadel*, 98-127, Davis, *Death in the Trenches*, 64-89, and Lykes, *Campaign for Petersburg*, 24-35. The Crater—the single-best-known feature of the Petersburg Campaign—is a major attraction at Petersburg National Battlefield and is in a remarkable state of preservation, although not retaining anything like its original dimensions.

14. The only single volume covering the engagement along the Petersburg-Weldon Railroad is John Horn, *The Petersburg Campaign: The Destruction of the Weldon Railroad, Deep Bottom, Globe Tavern, and Reams Station, August 14-25, 1864* (Lynchburg, Va., 1991). See also Trudeau, *The Last Citadel*, 142-174, Davis, *Death in the Trenches*, 99-104, and Lykes, *Campaign for Petersburg*, 36-38. Casualties during the four days of fighting numbered 4,279 Federals and about 1,600 Confederates. The Petersburg (Weldon) Railroad Battlefield is substantially intact in 2000 but threatened with imminent industrial development. The National Park Service uses Fort Wadsworth as a place to interpret the August fighting.

15. Horn, *The Destruction of the Weldon Railroad*, 112; Douglas S. Freeman, *R. E. Lee: A Biography*, 4 vols. (New York, 1934-1935), III, 452-453, 487. Most of the route from Stony Creek to Dinwiddie Court House carried the charming appellation of Flat Foot Road. In 2000, Flat Foot Road is VA 626 in Dinwiddie County.

16. One of the most impressive works of Civil War military history treats Grant's Fifth Offensive. Richard J. Sommers, *Richmond Redeemed: The Siege at Petersburg* (Garden City, N.Y., 1981) provides a micro-tactical narrative of the action both on the Petersburg front and north of the James. Trudeau, *The Last Citadel*, 202-217 discusses this aspect of the campaign in more modest depth. The battlefields of September 29-October 2 enjoy little protection or interpretation and have been severely compromised by the construction of a massive industrial facility. The National Park Service preserves the Union forts and connecting entrenchments between Squirrel Level Road and the "fishhook," including forts Welch, Gregg, and Wheaton, but these works were not, of course, present during

the fighting. Some of the October 2 fighting occurred at what is now Pamplin Historical Park.

17. Cadmus M. Wilcox, "Autobiography," in Cadmus Wilcox Papers, LC, 8-12; Cadmus M. Wilcox, "Defence of Batteries Gregg and Whitworth, and the Evacuation of Petersburg," in *SHSP*, 49 vols. (Richmond, 1876-1944), IV, 20; Joseph Mullen, Jr., Diary, September 30-October 2, 1864, Museum of the Confederacy; William A. Templeton to Sarah B. Templeton, October 3, 1864, in Templeton Family Papers, USC. Wilcox stated that the Confederates were occupying "a line of hastily constructed rifle pits" on September 30, and Sommers refers to the Confederate line prior to October 2 as "incomplete." There can be little doubt that the works that would be the target of the Sixth Corps attack on April 2, 1865, preserved in Pamplin Historical Park and on adjacent lands, originated prior to October 2. The elaborate fortifications that greeted the Sixth Corps on April 2, however, did not exist until after the fighting at Peebles's Farm. Major Harry Hammond of McGowan's staff wrote in early October, "we are completing heavy works on this front and have a line laid out running between the Weldon and Southside roads which the engineers say we will continue to the North Carolina line if that be necessary in order to prevent the enemy from gaining any ground west of where they are now." See Hammond to his wife, October 8, 1864, in Hammond, Bryan, and Cummings Family Papers, USC. The rest of Wilcox's Division, Scales's North Carolina Brigade and Thomas's Georgia Brigade, were on the west end of the Dimmock Line and north of the Appomattox, respectively.

18. The Battle of Burgess's Mill is treated in Trudeau, *The Last Citadel*, 218-250. There is no publicly accessible ground preserved on this battlefield.

19. Douglas S. Freeman, *Lee's Lieutenants*, 3 vols. (New York, 1942-44), III, 512-514; Trudeau, *Bloody Roads South*, 341; Trudeau, *The Last Citadel*, 55, 80, 127,189, 217, 248, 250; Gary W. Gallagher, "The Shenandoah Valley in 1864," in Gary W. Gallagher, ed., *Struggle for the Shenandoah: Essays on the 1864 Valley Campaign* (Kent, Ohio, 1991), 16. Determining casualty figures for Civil War battles is usually an exercise in approximation (despite seemingly precise numbers provided by some sources) and this is no more true than when assessing Confederate losses during the last year of the war. The figures listed in the text are estimates. The Army of Northern Virginia started the spring campaign in 1864 with between 62,000 and 65,000 men.

20. *OR* 42, pt. 3, 1134. The Confederate secretary of war was James A. Seddon.

21. Freeman, *R. E. Lee*, III, 517-518.

22. Emory M. Thomas, *Robert E. Lee: A Biography* (New York, 1995), 349-350; Freeman, *R. E. Lee*, III, 542.

23. Freeman, *R. E. Lee*, III, 515; Thomas, *Robert E. Lee*, 351-352; Walter H. Taylor, *Four Years with General Lee* (New York, 1877, reprint, New York, 1962), 141. Thomas documents Lee's "sour disposition" during this period, his failing eyesight, and his florid complexion to speculate that the effects of cardiovascular disease may have been exerting themselves upon the general. Violet Bank is operated as a public museum by the City of Colonial Heights and preserves the

remaining portions of Lee's headquarters. The Beasley House still stands in 2000 at 558 High Street and is interpreted with a nearby historical marker, but the building is privately owned and not accessible to the public. Lee maintained his office in an outbuilding on the property, still extant in 2000. See N. L. Oberseider and Suzanne Savery, *Four Self-Guided Walking Tours: Petersburg Virginia* (Petersburg, 1995), 34-35, for a description of the house and dependency.

24. Freeman, *Lee's Lieutenants*, III, 613; James Longstreet, *From Manassas to Appomattox* (Philadelphia, 1896, reprint, Secaucus, N.J., 1985), 572-575. For a good description of Longstreet's wounding, see Rhea, *The Battle of the Wilderness*, 366-374. A table of organization for the Army of Northern Virginia, Early's command in the Shenandoah Valley, and other troops on the Petersburg-Richmond front as of October 31, 1864 may be found in *OR* 42, pt. 3, 1187-1197.

25. Freeman, *Lee's Lieutenants*, III, 310-312. Field survived the war and enjoyed a varied career which included service in the Egyptian army, doorkeeper at the United States House of Representatives, and Superintendent of the Indian Reservation at Hot Springs, Arkansas.

26. Freeman, *Lee's Lieutenants*, III, 627. Pickett was not quite 40 years old in the autumn of 1864. He graduated last in the famous West Point class of 1846 that included George B. McClellan and Thomas J. Jackson. Pickett was the senior major general in the army, but his Gettysburg legacy deprived him of a more important or trusted role in the army's hierarchy. In late 1863, Pickett became the commander of the Department of North Carolina and Southern Virginia with headquarters in Petersburg. In fact, Pickett married LaSalle Corbell at St. Paul's Church in Petersburg in September 1863. The best treatment of Pickett's life is Lesley J. Gordon, *General George E. Pickett in Life & Legend* (Chapel Hill, N.C., 1999), in which the strained relations between Lee and Pickett are well documented.

27. Freeman, *Lee's Lieutenants*, III, 343, 627. Kershaw returned to South Carolina after the war and enjoyed a distinguished career as a jurist.

28. Daniel W. Barefoot, *General Robert F. Hoke: Lee's Modest Warrior* (Winston-Salem, N.C., 1996), 162-198; T. Harry Williams, *P. G. T. Beauregard: Napoleon in Gray* (Baton Rouge, 1955), 238-241; Freeman, *Lee's Lieutenants*, III, 617-618; Freeman, *R. E. Lee*, III, 522-523; *OR* 42, pt. 3, 1279-1280, 1287. Hoke earned a fine reputation as a regimental and brigade commander, but Freeman accused him of a lack of cooperation at the head of a division. *Lee's Lieutenants*, III, 593, 618. Beauregard grew discontented in his anomalous position as an independent commander subsumed by Lee and the Army of Northern Virginia. He was also unhappy about Lee's decision in June to send Early instead of him to the Shenandoah Valley, and by John Bell Hood's appointment in July to replace Joseph E. Johnston in command of the Army of Tennessee outside of Atlanta. Thus, when the opportunity arose to send Beauregard south, Lee, Davis, and Beauregard himself saw the chance to resolve a difficult situation.

29. Jubal Early lacks a modern, scholarly biography, a remarkable circumstance given his pivotal role in the Army of Northern Virginia. Millard K. Bushong, *Old Jube* (Boyce, Va., 1955) is the best available option.

30. Freeman, *Lee's Lieutenants*, III, 523-524. Early turned Hunter back at Lynchburg on June 17-18. There are several good monographs on Early's 1864 summer campaign, the best of which is Benjamin Franklin Cooling, *Jubal Early's Raid on Washington 1864* (Baltimore, 1989).

31. Pegram's Division had been commanded by Major General Stephen Dodson Ramseur until Early reorganized his Valley army in September by giving Ramseur Major General Robert E. Rodes's Division, thus creating the vacancy for Pegram. Freeman, *Lee's Lieutenants*, III, 582,629.

32. Freeman says of Grimes that he had a "quick and fiery temper, but in action showed judgment as well as skill and courage," *Lee's Lieutenants*, III, 630. Grimes's letters have been published in Gary W. Gallagher, ed., *Extracts of Letters of Major-General Bryan Grimes, to his Wife, Written While in the Service in the Army of Northern Virginia* (Wilmington, N.C., 1986). For a comprehensive biography of Grimes, see T. Harrell Allen, *Lee's Last Major General: Bryan Grimes of North Carolina* (Mason City, Ia., 1999).

33. Ralph Lowell Eckert, *John Brown Gordon: Soldier Southerner American* (Baton Rouge, 1989), 72,80; Freeman, *Lee's Lieutenants*, III, 391.

34. Eckert, *John Brown Gordon*, 72. Gordon is one of the most fascinating and impressive figures among the luminaries from Lee's army. After the war, Gordon served Georgia as a United States senator and as governor. He also led the United Confederate Veterans and wrote one of the most quotable, if not entirely factual, of the Confederate postwar memoirs entitled *Reminiscences of the Civil War* (New York, 1903, reprint, Baton Rouge, 1993). Gordon's account of his role in the May 6 Confederate attack north of the Orange Turnpike at the Wilderness serves as an example of his sometimes questionable version of events.

35. Eckert, *John Brown Gordon*, 102; Freeman, *Lee's Lieutenants*, III, 628; Freeman, *R. E. Lee*, III, 520-522. Gordon remained in de facto command of the Second Corps until the end of the war, but never officially received the promotion to lieutenant general that normally came with that level of responsibility.

36. There have been several biographies of Hill, the most recent being James I. Robertson, Jr., *General A. P. Hill: The Story of a Confederate Warrior* (New York, 1987). Robertson advances the theory that Hill suffered from prostatitis for nearly twenty years, contracted from a venereal disease. The symptoms included frequent, painful urination, nephritis, urethral strictures, fever, chills, and insomnia. These maladies made it difficult for Hill to ride and led to extreme fatigue and depression, according to Robertson.

37. Freeman, *Lee's Lieutenants*, III, 552-553. Mahone's life is treated in Nelson M. Blake, *William Mahone of Virginia: Soldier and Political Insurgent* (Richmond, 1935). Mahone represented Virginia in the United States Senate after the war as a virtual Republican and maintained a home in Petersburg at 137 South Sycamore Street, in 2000 the Petersburg Public Library.

38. Freeman, *Lee's Lieutenants*, II, 506-507, III, xxxiv, 443. Heth, with some justification but no malice, held Hill responsible for the problems on May 6 at the Wilderness. There is no biography of Heth, although his memoirs have been published. See James L. Morrison, ed., *The Memoirs of Henry Heth* (Westport, Conn., 1974).

39. The four brigades described in the text formed the basic composition of Heth's division, although there were variations throughout the fall of 1864. See *OR* 42, pt. 3, 1240, 1366, for examples. McComb commanded all of the Tennessee troops in the Petersburg-Richmond defenses as of January 1865 when the 17th & 23rd, 25th & 44th, and 63rd Tennessee regiments transferred to McComb's brigade from Ewell's Department of Richmond. See *OR* 42, pt.3, 1370 and *OR* pt. 2, 1112. McComb would be promoted as of January 20, 1865 to brigadier general. Robertson, *General A. P. Hill*, 302; George C. Underwood, *History of the Twenty-Sixth Regiment of North Carolina Troops in the Great War 1861-'65* (Goldsboro, N.C., 1901), 83; Freeman, *Lee's Lieutenants*, III, 633; Trudeau, *The Last Citadel*, 498. MacRae's brigade sharpshooters "afforded the strongest evidence of [MacRae's] extraordinary power in infusing into the minds of his soldiers morale of the highest order," according to Major Charles M. Stedman of the 44th North Carolina. For a description of this elite portion of MacRae's Brigade, see Charles M. Stedman, *Memorial Address Delivered May 10th, 1890, at Wilmington, N.C., by Hon. Charles M. Stedman. A Sketch of the Life and Character of General William MacRae, with an Account of the Battle of Reams Station* (Wilmington, N.C., 1890), 12.

40. Freeman, *Lee's Lieutenants*, III, 202-203. Of Wilcox's action on May 3, 1863 during the Chancellorsville Campaign, Freeman wrote, "Cadmus Wilcox that day gave military history an example far outliving his time, of the manner in which one Brigade, courageously led, can change the course of battle and retrieve a lost day." Freeman, *Lee's Lieutenants*, II, 626. Wilcox believed that he deserved promotion to division command in the fall of 1862 when both John Bell Hood and George E. Pickett received major generalships instead. He held Longstreet responsible for this perceived slight and requested to be transferred to the Western Theater until Lee smoothed his ruffled feathers. Wilcox's brother, a Confederate congressman from Texas, died in February 1864 and Wilcox felt a certain responsibility for the welfare of his widowed sister-in-law and her children. He again sought a transfer, this time to the Trans-Mississippi Theater, in order to be closer to this family, but once again, Lee could not spare him. This caused Wilcox significant anxiety throughout the Petersburg Campaign, but there is no direct evidence that it impaired his generalship. See Jeffry D. Wert, *General James Longstreet: The Confederacy's Most Controversial Soldier—A Biography* (New York, 1993), 210-211 and Freeman, *Lee's Lieutenants*, III, 630-631.

41. Lee's reluctance to appoint Thomas also stemmed from his Georgia origins in a division in which Carolinians predominated. Sensitivity to geographic considerations weighed almost as heavily in Confederate military politics as ethnic

and party affiliations influenced Federal personnel decisions. Freeman, *Lee's Lieutenants*, III, 201.

42. There is not yet a published biography of Lane, but his brigade and its second commander are amply profiled by William K. McDaid, " Four Years of Arduous Service: History of the Branch-Lane Brigade in the Civil War," unpublished Ph.D. dissertation, Michigan State University, 1987. Lane's predecessor in brigade command was Brigadier General Lawrence O'Bryan Branch.

43. James Fitz James Caldwell, *The History of a Brigade of South Carolinians First Known as Gregg's and Subsequently as McGowan's Brigade* (Philadelphia, 1866, reprint, Dayton, Oh., 1984), 103-104, 173-245. The Battle of Reams Station occurred on August 25, 1864. An attempt to drive the Federals away from their newly-won control of the Petersburg Railroad and to ensure that the Federals did not threaten Lee's new rail head at Stony Creek, the battle was a tactical victory for the Confederates. It failed, however, to dislodge the bluecoats from their blocking position along the railroad further north around Globe Tavern.

44. Freeman, *Lee's Lieutenants*, III, 631.

45. Joseph Cantey Elliott, *Lieutenant General Richard Heron Anderson: Lee's Noble Soldier* (Dayton, Oh., 1985), 83-84, 121; G. Moxley Sorrel, *Recollections of a Confederate Staff Officer* (Jackson, Tenn., 1958, reprint, Wilmington, N.C., 1987), 128.

46. Charles M. Cummings, *Yankee Quaker, Confederate General: The Curious Career of Bushrod Rust Johnson* (Columbus, Oh., 1993). Cummings writes that Johnson and his commander, Dick Anderson, were "somewhat kindred spirits—unassertive, gentlemanly, lacking inspirational color or showmanship." Anderson and Johnson also shared the same birthday, although at 47, Johnson was five years Anderson's senior. See Cummings, *Yankee Quaker, Confederate General*, 309. Johnson's Division consisted of Elliott's Brigade of South Carolinians commanded by Brigadier General William H. Wallace, Brigadier General Matthew W. Ransom's Brigade of North Carolinians, Wise's Brigade of Virginians commanded by Colonel John T. Goode until Brigadier General Henry A. Wise returned in December, and Brigadier General Archibald Gracie's Brigade of Alabamians.

47. Freeman, *Lee's Lieutenants*, III, 632; *OR* 42, pt. 3, 1244-1248. The Second Corps artillery remained in the Valley under the command of Colonel Thomas Hill Carter. Sometime in the winter of 1865, a portion of Early's artillery, including Colonel Carter, returned to the Petersburg front. Walker would receive promotion to brigadier general in February 1865.

48. Hampton assumed control of the cavalry on August 11, 1864. But unlike Stuart, Hampton did not revel in the deadly business of war. Manly Wade Wellman, *Giant in Gray: A Biography of Wade Hampton of South Carolina* (New York, 1949, reprint, Dayton, Oh., 1988), 152; Freeman, *Lee's Lieutenants*, III, 633.

49. Percy Gatling Hamlin, "*Old Bald Head*" (*General R. S. Ewell*): *The Portrait of a Soldier* (Strasburg, Va., 1940), 184; Donald C. Pfanz, *Richard S. Ewell: A*

Soldier's Life (Chapel Hill, N.C., 1998), 404-425; Freeman, *Lee's Lieutenants*, III, 510.

50. Taylor, *Four Years With General Lee*, 141; Freeman, *R. E. Lee*, III, 525-526. The Turnbull House is no longer extant, but in 2000 there is a small marker indicating its location in the yard of a postwar home along U.S. 1 near the intersection with VA 226 in Dinwiddie County. See Chapter Ten, note nineteen for a discussion of the fate of Edge Hill on April 2, 1865.

51. *OR* 42, pt. 3, 1236, 1237, 1248, 1358, 1362; Jennings Cropper Wise, *The Long Arm of Lee*, 2 vols. (Lynchburg, Va., 1915), II, 911-916; Freeman, *Lee's Lieutenants*, III, 618; Freeman, *R. E. Lee*, III, 518. The numbers given in the text differ slightly from those cited by Freeman and are based on the figures provided in the *OR.*

52. *OR* 42, pt. 2, 1200, pt. 3, 1222-1223; Freeman, *R. E. Lee*, III, 516. In some places, parallel lines of works required Lee to post extra troops along the same linear front.

53. Freeman, *Lee's Lieutenants*, III, 616; Trudeau, *The Last Citadel*, 262-285; Gary W. Gallagher, ed., *Fighting for the Confederacy: The Personal Recollections of General Edward Porter Alexander* (Chapel Hill, N.C., 1989), 512. Hicksford is now Emporia, Virginia.

54. Freeman, *Lee's Lieutenants*, III, 633, 638-639. Brigadier General James Conner's South Carolina Brigade was the infantry shifted south.

55. Freeman, *Lee's Lieutenants*, III, 634-635. The Battle of Waynesboro on March 2, 1865 caused the demise of Early's army. For more information on the significance of this engagement, see Chapter Four. For more information regarding Lee's strategic situation at this stage of the war, see Noah Andre Trudeau, "A Mere Question of Time: Robert E. Lee from the Wilderness to Appomattox Court House," in Gary W. Gallagher, ed., *Lee the Soldier* (Lincoln, Neb., 1996), 538-546; Thomas, *Robert E. Lee*, 353; Sommers, *Richmond Redeemed*, 207; and Freeman, *R. E. Lee*, III, 518-524. Alan T. Nolan in *Lee Considered: General Robert E. Lee and Civil War History* (Chapel Hill, N.C., 1991), 112-133 advances the provocative proposition that after Lincoln's reelection, and perhaps earlier, Lee knew that the war was lost, and therefore should have surrendered the army in the interest of saving lives and property.

56. Freeman Cleaves, *Meade of Gettysburg* (Norman, Okla., 1960), 229; *OR* 36, pt. 2, 695. Cleaves's is a comprehensive and reliable biography of Meade.

57. George R. Agassiz, ed., *Meade's Headquarters 1863-1865: Letters of Colonel Theodore Lyman from the Wilderness to Appomattox* (Boston, 1922), 224; Charles A. Dana, *Recollections of the Civil War With the Leaders at Washington and in the Field in the Sixties* (New York, 1898), 189, 226. On Meade's potential command in the Valley, see A. Wilson Greene, "Union Generalship in the 1864 Valley Campaign," in Gallagher, ed,. *Struggle for the Shenandoah*, 42.

58. For Warren's troubles during the Overland Campaign, see Rhea, *The Battle of the Wilderness*, 432-433, Matter, *If It Takes All Summer*, 232, and Stephen Sears, *Controversies and Commanders: Dispatches from the Army of the Potomac*

(Boston, 1999), 255-261. Grant's quote is found in Grant, *Personal Memoirs*, II, 445. For evidence of Warren's poor relations with Meade and others see, Horace Porter, *Campaigning With Grant* (New York, 1897, reprint, Alexandria, Va., 1981), 251-252, and Allan Nevins, ed., *A Diary of Battle: The Personal Journals of Colonel Charles S. Wainwright 1861-1865* (New York, 1962), 476. The Fifth Corps occupied the line between Battery 24 and Church Road until the arrival of the Sixth Corps in December when the Fifth Corps concentrated farther east. See Welcher, *The Union Army*, I, 389. Griffin and Crawford had commanded divisions throughout the year; Ayres rose from brigade command after Cold Harbor. Warren's letters and a sympathetic biographical treatment may be found in Emerson Gifford Taylor, *Gouverneur Kemble Warren: The Life and Letters of An American Soldier 1830-1882* (Boston, 1932, reprint, Gaithersburg, Md., 1988). Warren's tenure as commander of the 5th New York Zouaves is detailed in Alfred Davenport, *Camp and Field Life of the Fifth New York Volunteer Infantry* (Duryee Zouaves) (New York, 1879, reprint, Gaithersburg, Md., 1984).

59. David Jordan, *Winfield Scott Hancock: A Soldier's Life* (Bloomington, Ind., 1988), 169-173; Joseph T. Glatthaar, "Black Glory: The African-American Role in Union Victory," in Gabor S. Boritt, ed., *Why the Confederacy Lost* (New York, 1992), 157.

60. Porter, *Campaigning With Grant*, 329; Dana, *Recollections of the Civil War*, 192; Agassiz, ed., *Meade's Headquarters*, 73. Humphreys was also a fastidious man. Lyman said that he was "continually washing himself and putting on paper dickeys." Agassiz, ed., *Meade's Headquarters*, 6. Dana noted that he rode about with a black felt hat with the entire brim turned down, giving him the appearance of a Quaker. Dana, *Recollections of the Civil War*, 192. A good description of Humphreys's accession to command of the Second Corps may be found in Henry H. Humphreys, *Andrew Atkinson Humphreys: A Biography* (Philadelphia, 1924, reprint, Gaithersburg, Md., 1988), 258-262.

61. Humphreys, *Andrew Atkinson Humphreys*, 265. Both Miles and Mott had been brevetted as major generals of volunteers in the summer of 1864. The ranks provided in the text for them and for all officers are the full rank of the officer in question at the time, not the brevet rank. The Second Corps occupied the line between Fort Dushane and Fort Fisher, covering the army's far left and rear, with headquarters at the Peebles House. Welcher, *The Union Army*, I, 336.

62. William Marvel, *Burnside* (Chapel Hill, N.C., 1991), 372, 409-413. Marvel argues a convincing case that Burnside was made the scapegoat for the Crater, and that this much-maligned officer deserves a better reputation than that which history has generally accorded him.

63. Agassiz, ed., *Meade's Headquarters*, 213; Nevins, ed., *A Diary of Battle*, 467. Parke was promoted to major general effective July 18, 1862, making him the senior officer at that rank in the Army of the Potomac. There is no published biography of Parke.

64. Welcher, *The Union Army*, I, 437-438. Before the Petersburg Campaign ended, Willcox, Potter, and Hartranft would receive brevet promotions to major general.

65. *OR* 42, pt. 3, 1115-1122. Information on Hunt's rise to command of the Army's artillery and the way that branch was organized may be found in L. Van Loan Naisawald, *Grape and Canister: The Story of the Field Artillery of the Army of the Potomac, 1861-1865* (New York, 1960, reprint, Washington, 1983), passim, but especially 182, 329-330, 489-490. Hunt was brevetted major general of volunteers for his service at Gettysburg. Hazard, Wainwright, and Tidball were all brevet brigadier generals by the end of the war.

66. *OR* 42, pt. 3, 1122; Stephen Z. Starr, *The Union Cavalry in the Civil War*, 3 vols. (Baton Rouge, 1979-1985), II, 417-418. Gregg had received a brevet to major general of volunteers on August 1, 1864.

67. For Butler's removal, see Howard P. Nash, Jr., *Stormy Petrel: The Life and Times of General Benjamin F. Butler, 1818-1893* (Rutherford, N.J., 1969), 214-215. Ord assumed command on January 8, 1865.

68. Trudeau, *The Last Citadel*, 378; Edward G. Longacre, *Army of Amateurs: General Benjamin F. Butler and the Army of the James, 1863-1865* (Mechanicsburg, Pa., 1997), 243-244; John Gibbon, *Personal Recollections of the Civil War* (New York, 1928, reprint, Dayton, Oh., 1988), 277; *OR* 42, pt. 3, 1123-1125. Harris's division joined the Twenty-fourth Corps from the Shenandoah Valley on December 24. Gibbon's Second Division under Brigadier General Adelbert Ames was detached in early January for duty in North Carolina and did not rejoin the corps. See Welcher, *The Union Army*, I, 500-501. Devens received a brevet promotion to major general following the Battle of Chancellorsville and Harris had been brevetted brigadier general for his service at the Battle of Cedar Creek.

69. Dudley Taylor Cornish, *The Sable Arm: Black Troops in the Union Army, 1861-1865* (New York, 1956, reprint, Lawrence, Kans., 1987), xvi, 266, 281; Welcher, *The Union Army*, I, 504; *OR* 42, pt. 3, 1126-1127. Paine's division along with Ames's of the Twenty-fourth Corps transferred to North Carolina in early January and did not rejoin the corps. Weitzel, like all the ranking officers in the Twenty-fifth Corps, was white. Birney would receive a brevet major generalcy before the Petersburg Campaign concluded. The artillery brigade of the Twenty-fifth Corps was all white as well.

70. Welcher, *The Union Army*, I, 230; *OR* 42, pt. 3, 1127. Ferrero would receive a brevet promotion to major general in December 1864, despite his dubious conduct at the Battle of the Crater. Fort Brady is preserved as a part of Richmond National Battlefield Park, as are much of the Union and Confederate lines north of the James.

71. Sedgwick's standing with his troops may be judged by the remarks of Dr. George T. Stevens, a surgeon in the 77th New York of the Sixth Corps: "Never had such a gloom rested upon the whole army on account of the death of one man as came over it when the heavy tidings passed along the lines that General Sedgwick

was killed. . . . No soldier was more beloved by the army or honored by the country than this noble general. His corps regarded him as a father, and his great military abilities made his judgment, in all critical emergencies, sought after by his superior as well as his fellows." George T. Stevens, *Three Years in the Sixth Corps. A Concise Narrative of Events in the Army of the Potomac, From 1861 to the close of the Rebellion, April 1865* (Albany, N.Y., 1866, reprint, Alexandria, Va., 1984), 327-328. Sedgwick, in turn, thought highly of Wright and had indicated that he wished for Wright to succeed him in corps command if he became incapacitated, even though another Sixth Corps division commander was senior to Wright. See Matter, *If It Takes All Summer*, 103.

72. Porter, *Campaigning With Grant*, 166; Dana, *Recollections of the Civil War*, 191; Agassiz, ed., *Meade's Headquarters*, 300. A recent student of the Overland Campaign is very critical of Wright's inaugural performance as a corps commander: "[Wright's] behavior revealed a general paralyzed at the prospect of taking risks." Staff officer Charles A. Whittier, considered Wright a "well-mannered, temperate man—not at all deficient in physical courage, but when responsibilities came on him he took to drink." There is no other hint in the literature that Wright abused alcohol under stress. See Rhea, *The Battles for Spotsylvania Court House and the Road to Yellow Tavern*, 315-316. Wright's profile remains low with modern students of the Civil War for all the reasons provided in the text and because he lacks a published biography.

73. James E. Taylor, *The James E. Taylor Sketchbook With Sheridan Up the Shenandoah Valley in 1864: Leaves from a Special Artist's Sketchbook and Diary* (Dayton, Oh., 1989), 122; Aldace F. Walker, *The Vermont Brigade in the Shenandoah Valley 1864* (Burlington, Vt., 1869), 16-17. Corporal Edward A. to "Dear Sister," January 24, 1865, ts. in the collection of Pamplin Historical Park. Taylor erroneously gave Gates as Wright's middle name. It was Gouverneur.

74. Walker, *The Vermont Brigade in the Shenandoah Valley*, 17-18. Getty was a native of the District of Columbia and received a brevet promotion to major general in August 1864.

75. James Harper to "Dear Al," March 2, 1865, in John Harper Papers, HSWP. Warner had been brevetted a brigadier general in August 1864.

76. Hazard Stevens to "Dear Mother," January 21, 1865, in Hazard Stevens Papers, LC; Walker, *The Vermont Brigade in the Shenandoah Valley*, 18-20. Grant had received a brevet major generalcy as a result of his performance at the Battle of Cedar Creek. The Battle of Salem Church was a part of the Chancellorsville Campaign and was fought on May 3 and 4, 1863. In addition to the biographical sketches on Grant in the usual compendiums, see the Collection Files, Minnesota Historical Society, for a full description of Grant's life. Grant had a son he christened Ulysses Sherman Grant.

77. Thomas W. Hyde, *Following the Greek Cross or, Memories of the Sixth Army Corps* (Boston, 1894, reprint, Gaithersburg, Md., 1988), 235. Hyde's brigade had been commanded by Brigadier General Daniel D. Bidwell, who was killed at Cedar Creek. Hyde received his Medal of Honor in 1863 while serving as assistant

secretary of war. An excellent description of his exploits at Antietam is found in John M. Priest, *Antietam: The Soldiers' Battle* (Shippensburg, Pa., 1989), 295-299.

78. James Harper to "Dear Al," March 2, 1865, in John Harper Papers, HSWP. Wheaton was promoted to brevet major general during the Petersburg Campaign.

79. Mark Mayo Boatner III, *The Civil War Dictionary* (New York, 1959), 436; Joseph G. Bilby, *Three Rousing Cheers: A History of the Fifteenth New Jersey from Flemington to Appomattox* (Hightstown, N.J., 1993), 49-50. At Petersburg, the 32-year-old Penrose was a brevet brigadier general.

80. James Deane, "Following the Flag: The Three Years Story of a Veteran", ts. in CHS, 29; Grant, *Personal Memoirs*, II, 541; Homer Curtis to "Dear Friends," March 20, 1865, in Homer Curtis Letters, YU; Michael Kelly, Diary, March 19, 1865, CHS. One New Yorker described Hamblin in particularly glowing terms:

> a tall, well proportioned, genteel looking man with a bold, fearless face which seemed to me, a perfect model of manly beauty. There was an honest frankness, a rosy freshness, a genial cheerfulness that went direct to the heart and gave the impression that there was nothing narrow, mean, or small in the composition of its owner. There was an easy air of graceful dignity blended with good nature and sociability. In bodily formation this man, chiseled in marble, would have rivaled the Apollo Belvedere. He was one of nature's masterpieces and the finest I ever saw. By his many engaging qualities he won the affection of the men; they loved, honored, almost idolized him.

See Thomas P. Southwick, *A Duryee Zouave* (Brookneal, Va., 1995). Hamblin was promoted to brevet brigadier general for his actions at Cedar Creek. Ironically, Mackenzie was the nephew of Confederate commissioner John Slidell of Louisiana, like Wheaton's in-law, James Mason, the subject of the controversial Trent Affair. Kautz assumed command of a division in the Twenty-fifth Corps.

81. Wert, *From Winchester to Cedar Creek*, 19. Edwards had been promoted to brevet brigadier general for gallantry at Spotsylvania. He was absent from the Petersburg front for much of the winter, but returned in late February.

82. *OR* 42, pt. 2, 440, 460, 465; Agassiz, ed., *Meade's Headquarters*, 299. Ricketts received a brevet promotion to major general on August 1, 1864. The Battle of Olustee was fought near Lake City, Florida on February 20, 1864 and resulted in Seymour losing more than one-third of his force.

83. Matter, *If It Takes All Summer*, 416, n. 24; Baltz, *The Battle of Cold Harbor*, 92; *OR* 42, pt. 3, 880. Truex would receive a brevet promotion to brigadier general for his gallantry on April 2, 1865.

84. Keifer's brevet promotion was dated October 19, 1864. His perspectives were published as *Slavery and Four Years of War: A Political History of Slavery in the United States*, 2 vols. (New York, 1900). He served in the Spanish-American War and lived until 1932.

85. Tompkins is listed as being on leave in January but no explanation is provided for his absence. Apparently he returned to duty sometime after the

Appomattox Campaign. See *OR* pt. 2, 331,744; pt. 3, 1068; Naisawald, *Grape and Canister*, 533. Tompkins held the brevet rank of brigadier general and both Harn and Cowan had been brevetted majors.

86. Welcher, *The Union Army*, I, 413, 899; Hyde, *Following the Greek Cross*, 239; Hazard Stevens to "Dear Mother," December 13, 1864, in Hazard Stevens Papers, LC; Bernard A. Olsen, ed., *Upon the Tented Field* (Red Bank, N.J., 1993), 292. Fort Fisher exists in 2000 in excellent condition as a part of Petersburg National Battlefield. Vaughan, Squirrel Level, and Church roads survive on approximately their original beds as secondary roads through Dinwiddie County.

87. The nine officers who remained in command at the same levels with essentially the same units (reorganizations not withstanding) included Meade as army commander; Gibbon (although in January, as noted in the text, he would leave for the Army of the James) and Mott in the Second Corps; Warren, Griffin, and Crawford in the Fifth Corps; Getty in the Sixth Corps; and Potter and Willcox in the Ninth Corps. I have not included Butler, who was on his way out the door as commander of the Army of the James, although technically not relieved until January, or Adelbert Ames, whose division left for North Carolina in January. For Tables of Organization see *OR* 36, pt. 1, 106-119, 42, pt. 3, 1114-1127.

88. Meade reported 83,826 present for duty on December 31, 1864. I included the General Headquarters officers, Twenty-fourth Corps, Twenty-fifth Corps, Kautz's cavalry division, and the Defenses of Bermuda Hundred to arrive at 37,892 present for duty on the Petersburg-Richmond front from Butler's command. See *OR* 42, pt. 3, 1114, 1123. For the figures prior to the Wilderness, I used Present for Duty Equipped for the Army of the Potomac April 30, 1864 in *OR* 36, pt. 1, 198 (97,273), returns for the Ninth Corps for April 1864 in Andrew A. Humphreys, *The Virginia Campaign of '64 and '65* (New York, 1883, reprint, Wilmington, N.C., 1989), 14 (19,331), and the figures in Humphreys, *The Virginia Campaign*, 137, for the Army of the James (38,617). It bears repeating that readers should consider these and practically all Civil War-era strength and casualty figures as estimates. Such precise numbers always carry the risk of conveying misplaced concreteness in what must necessarily be an imprecise historical exercise. Replacement troops for Grant's forces in 1864 included volunteers motivated by the same patriotic instincts that impelled the war's earliest soldiers. However, the new levies also arrived through conscription or were recruited with the aid of huge bounties, making the decision to join the army more of an economic than an altruistic one. More than half of all conscripted Union soldiers entered the army as a result of the fall 1864 draft. Localities paid nearly $300,000,000 in bounties. In some districts, a man could earn nearly $1,000 by enlisting, at a time when a soldier's pay was less than $200 a year. See Eugene Converse Murdock, *Patriotism Limited 1862-1865. The Civil War Draft and the Bounty System* (Kent, Oh., 1967), 13, 205-206.

89. Grant, *Personal Memoirs*, II, 401-405.

90. Mark Olcott with David Lear, *The Civil War Letters of Lewis Bissell. A Curriculum* (Washington, 1981), 333.

CHAPTER TWO

The Sixth Corps
Prepares for the Spring Campaign

U pon its arrival in the Petersburg area, the Sixth Corps returned to a region of the Old Dominion markedly different from its recent haunts in the Shenandoah Valley. Instead of rolling fields picturesquely framed by the peaks of the Blue Ridge, Massanutten, and Little North mountains, Wright's troops found themselves in relatively flat, undistinguished terrain cut by numerous marshy streamlets and swamps. "This part of Virginia is of the region which has been cultivated without being renewed since Colonial days," snarled one Union officer, "and has grown up in pines which cover the exhausted soil and is properly called, in other parts of Virginia, the Wilderness."[1]

The Sixth Corps occupied a front of approximately four miles running east and west at a distance of some three to four miles south and southwest of Petersburg. Four country roads—Johnson, Halifax, Vaughan, and Squirrel Level—penetrated Wright's lines running north and south. A fifth thoroughfare, Church Road, initially defined the left flank of the corps. The Petersburg Railroad also sliced through Sixth Corps territory, its tracks there dismantled thanks to Warren's victory in August. A number of tiny creeks and intermittent streams fed a sluggish waterway called Second Swamp that drained the eastern half of Wright's front. West of the Petersburg Railroad, the drainages combined south of the Union line to form Arthur's Swamp, both systems flowing south toward North Carolina's Albemarle Sound rather than emptying into the nearby Appomattox River. This region was tired farmland mixed with timbered tracts before the arrival of the armies, but now the landscape assumed a barren appearance, reflective of the military need for fields of fire and building materials.[2]

"We have got a first rate shanty, and when we ar in it we ar warm anuf."

Once assured of their immediate security, the troops focused on establishing camps. The imperfect occupation of the area by the Fifth Corps left Wright's men with an ugly environmental legacy. "The troops preceding had erected ungainly and squalid shanties of every shape and size, and left the ground covered with filth and pitted with holes," reported a Sixth Corps inspector. The men responded by constructing drainage ditches, which "reduced the once wide-spread and noisome swamp to a harmless rivulet." Thomas Hyde's brigade sarcastically nicknamed their sanitation engineering "the Dutch Gap Canal," after Ben Butler's enormous effort to cut a new channel in the James River, and in short order the ground became much more habitable.[3]

Possessed of terra firma, the soldiers began erecting quarters designed to serve as home for the duration of the winter. The army practiced little standardization when it came to temporary lodgings, so the quality and appearance of each shelter varied with the skill, energy, and building materials employed by any particular group of bunkmates. Some regiments simply pitched their tents. Others augmented their canvas with a base of logs, while many men built wooden huts that provided the best protection against a Southside Virginia January. "We have got a first rate shanty," boasted one Wisconsin soldier, " and when we ar in it we ar warm anuf."

Private William L. Phillips of the 5th Wisconsin described in some detail the design of his winter quarters built shortly after the return of the Sixth Corps to the Petersburg lines:

> We have just finished a house 7 by 10 we packed the timber 1/2 mile on our shoulders it was heavy green pich pine a small piece of it is a load for any man. . . . it is made of haves of pine logs about 8 inches through it is layed 5 feet high then covered with tent cloth the gable ends are closed up with

boards the fire place and the door occupyse one end and the bunk acrost the
other the bunk is made by driving 4 croches into the ground about 2 feet
high then a cross peaces and little poles layed on these we covered with pine
bows about 6 inches thick then covered with dry leaves this makes a captol
bed rite before the bed there is a low bench we can sit by the fire and lean
our backs against the bed when we eat we spread a rubber cloth on the bed
and turn right around on our seat and stick our feat under the bed and eat our
hard tack and sow belly or beaf and drink our coffee as contented as kittens.

Officers generally enjoyed a higher standard of living than enlisted
men. Major Mason W. Tyler of the 37th Massachusetts bragged that "I have
now got quite a grand house, a real palace, so to speak." Tyler's residence
measured fifteen feet by six and a half feet, with a seven-foot ceiling in the
center. He shared his quarters with just one other officer. On the other
side of the company street, it was not unusual for four or more privates to
crowd into one hut. Sergeant Albert C. Harrison of the 14th New Jersey
reported in January that some noncommissioned officers in his regiment
were completing a gabled dwelling that included flooring and built-in
bunks. The surgeon of the 77th New York believed that the quarters in his
outfit were more comfortable than any they had built previously.
Occasionally, the troops exploited unusual circumstances to improve their
housing. Some men in the 10th Vermont commandeered an abandoned
freight car, removed its axles and wheels, and converted the conveyance
into a domicile.[4]

Colonel Hyde noted that by this stage of the war the army had not only
developed a certain genius for adapting to life on the front lines, "but had
learned the value of hygiene" in preserving the health of the men. The 5th
Wisconsin, for example, published orders on December 28 prescribing the
depth and width of the drainage ditches surrounding quarters, forbidding
the disposal of garbage within the company streets, and recommending
the airing of bedclothes and structures for at least two hours per day,
weather permitting. Noncommissioned officers would be held responsible
for ensuring that the men in their squads washed frequently and changed
their underclothing at least once per week! Failure to enforce these
regulations would result in demotions for those charged with the
responsibility. Apparently, these personal grooming guidelines did not
include barbering standards. Private Franklin Jones of the 10th New Jersey
wrote home that he submitted to a haircut, but his orderly sergeant
forbade him to trim his beard, because it "was admired buy the rigament i

will let you know how long it is i can turn it up and it comes half way up my nose and thay tell me that it is a grate help to wone hear in the summer time on a count of the dust. . . ."[5]

Despite these hygenic precautions, men still fell ill. The Sixth Corps erected field hospitals near the camps which elicited praise for their appearance and efficiency. "Our hospital is in the form of a cross," wrote Hospital Steward John N. Henry of the 49th New York in Getty's division. "The central tent [is] raised higher than the rest with arms composed of two tents on either side, one at the head & three at the lower Side forming on the ground plot a regular Catholic cross composed of nine hospital tents. It will hold 50 patients without crowding." A First Division officer thought his unit's hospital "the most tastefully arranged camp that I have seen since I have been in the army." An elaborate wooden fence surrounded the hospital and beautiful arches formed from fresh evergreens adorned each entrance. One of Meade's staff called the Sixth Corps establishments "model hospitals," and a surgeon believed that every care and comfort that could be offered patients was available at the Sixth Corps facilities.[6]

Once a soldier is secure, warm, and dry, his thoughts turn toward his stomach. The men of the Sixth Corps ate as well as most Union troops around Petersburg in the winter of 1865. There are few references to hunger in the Federal ranks. Much of the credit for this accomplishment belonged to the modern and efficient logistics that kept supplies moving to the front lines. The Union base at City Point teemed with activity as ships docked along the wharves on the James, unloading every possible necessity and not a few luxuries for soldier consumption. Warehouses stored roughly 9,000,000 meals at any given time, and the bakeries at City Point produced some 100,000 loaves of bread each day.[7]

These provisions reached the field via the United States Military Railroad, a network that combined the tracks of the old City Point Railroad with new rails that led behind the Union siege lines. "No other such railroad was ever seen before, or ever will be again," observed one New Englander. The railroad's most distinguishing feature was its construction along the natural terrain contours. "It looks queer to see the cars run up and down hill as they do here," observed Private John J. Ingraham of the 121st New York. "I don't think there is a place on the road that is graded." Private George W. Buffum of the 5th Wisconsin agreed. "We have got a great curiousity here; that is our railroad," he wrote his niece. "It runs the whole length of our line within 80 rods of our breastworks. It is made on top of the ground without any digging at all. It is up hill and down." Yet, as many as fifteen daily trains made the journey from City Point to the front with such efficiency that at times bread was unloaded still warm from the ovens.[8]

Most army rations were prepared in messes, small groups of soldiers who shared accommodations and split the chores of cooking and clean-up. "We are drawing rations," wrote a Wisconsin private. "We draw hard tack, pork, beans, dried ap[p]le, beef, sugar, coffee, soap, candles, oh, and mackeral and 3 loaves of soft bread. We have plenty to eat now." In mid-winter, however, the military hierarchy began to assign company cooks to prepare food in central kitchens. "We are having Company Cook houses built so to have the rations cooked the same as at the Forts," testified a Connecticut soldier. Men would report to the cookhouse door at the appropriate bugle call and receive their rations, including a tin cupful of hot coffee. The meals, always adequate in quantity, often lacked variety and nutrition. The 37th Massachusetts was selected in late December to revive a remedy for this starchy monotony, a usually repulsive concoction called dessicated vegetables. The commissary intended to serve the unpopular product cooked instead of in its usual form as a hard, dry cake. "It is earnestly desired that a fair trial of its merits be made," read a circular from the brigade commissary. "As the Department is particularly anxious to ascertain whether the article meets the approbation of the soldiers, you are requested to make at as early a day as possible a report of the trial in your Regiment." The record does not reveal the Bay Staters' verdict.[9]

The men sought other alternatives to supplement their army diet. Civilian sutlers established shops near the camps and sold the troops all manner of delicacies sure to please a dulled palate. Private Lothrup L. Lewis of the 1st Maine Veteran Volunteers procured an impressive list of edibles including pies, bologna, mackerel, tripe, peaches, and apples that he bought practically every day during the winter. Officers fared even better. "We have a mess of four persons, and we manage to live very comfortably," boasted one New England major. "This morning we had corned beef hash, and to-morrow morning we expect to have fried pudding. Last night we had scalloped oysters. Our sutler has not come up yet, so that we have had to run hither and yon to buy what we wanted." Occasionally, the men received permission to buy items of their choosing directly from the army commissary department at prices considerably less onerous than those charged by sutlers. One Wisconsin soldier crowed that, armed with some cash from home and an order from an officer to shop at the commissary, "we bought 7 pounds of indian meal and 1 pound of rasins and 1/2 pound of butter and 3 eggs and 1 nutmeg . . . we mixed up our pudding with the eggs and rasins and boild it in a bag . . . we had a captol dinner of soft bread and butter plumb pudding and apple sauce." Colonel Hyde appropriated a Frenchman named Francois from one of the regiments in his brigade after discovering that the immigrant had been a cook at the Cafe Riche in Paris before the war. The menu at Hyde's headquarters substantially improved thereafter.[10]

The same transportation system that so efficiently delivered food to the front also ensured that the troops received adequate clothing. Although the well-fed Private Lewis mentioned seeing barefoot men in the Sixth Corps camps in early February, few other witnesses remarked upon a shortage of shoes or any other type of apparel. One critical commodity did elude the logisticians at City Point, however. The army relied on wood to prepare fortifications, construct housing, cook food, and provide warmth. Finding firewood became a significant challenge as the winter dragged on. "Wood is very scarce with us & it is next to impossible for me to get enough for to cook my food with," complained a New Yorker. The artillery batteries used their wagons to carry timber from the fast-disappearing forests, but the infantry had to tote their own logs to their camps from increasingly distant woodlots. By late January, this often meant a hike of two miles just to gather enough fuel for the day's requirements.[11]

During the second week of February, Keifer's brigade of Seymour's division moved from its camps just west of the Petersburg Railroad to the fortifications between Fort Fisher and Fort Gregg, known as "the fishhook," at the western end of the army's refused left flank. Miles's division of the Second Corps had been in that area but received orders to move southwest and extend the Union front toward Hatcher's Run. Miles instructed his men to dismantle their huts and bring the materials with them to rebuild quarters behind their new lines. This left Keifer's men homeless for more than a week, scrambling to find lumber in a treeless neighborhood and cursing their Second Corps comrades. Meanwhile, Hamblin's brigade occupied Keifer's old camps and found them "muddy but rather pleasant."[12]

The weather caused more universal discomfort than the occasional shifting of camps. A cold snap in February prompted numerous complaints. "The weather has been very cold for a long time, much more so than I ever knew it to be before [or] since I've been a soldier," grumbled Private George A. Cary of the 1st Maine Veterans. Major Tyler of the 37th Massachusetts agreed: "I think yesterday [February 12] and to-day have been the coldest days of the season, and last night the wind blew so that it tore our tents pretty much all to pieces, and came near leaving us looking through bare poles into the face of heaven which, in the existing state of the temperature, was not so nice." Private Buffum was on guard duty on the 12th and wrote his family that "I had on for clothing 2 pairs of stockings, 2 pairs of drawers, 1 pair pants, 1 blouse, 1 dress coat, 1 overcoat, 2 pair mittens, 1 shirt. I was cold then."[13]

In March temperatures moderated, but the wind proved particularly bothersome. "The weather is very peculiar here," wrote Colonel Keifer. "When it does not rain, it is windy, and then the sand flies through the air in such quantities, as to almost blind a person. Our quarters became so full of sand as to make it very uncomfortable." Chaplain Frank C. Morse of the 37th Massachusetts told his wife that his eyes hurt from having so much windblown dust circulating through his tent.[14]

Lieutenant Homer Curtis of the 2nd Connecticut Heavy Artillery penned a colorful and obviously heartfelt description of these trying conditions to his friends in New England:

> It is the dustiest of all my days. The dust nearly as white as snow is flying in clouds every where that the wind flies and penetrating with it every nook and crevice of every habitation in this whole line. Dust in the bed where we sleep—dust in the bread that we eat—dust on our clothes, our papers & our books—dust in our ears, eyes, nose and mouth—gritty dust in our teeth and under our finger nails Dust in clouds—dust in piles—dust above—dust below. Dust, dust, dust, dust—dust everywhere—everything dust—no dust returning to dust here, where every body and everything is already dust. The flying dust beats against and through my canvas roof rattling and falling like snow. It falls and rests on everything so that you can write your name legibly in dust anywhere.[15]

The soldiers may have had to contend with occasional cold fronts and blustery winds, but very little snow fell in the Petersburg area that winter. "I have sean snow but three times hear and that did not lay a day," testified the well-whiskered Franklin Jones. Sergeant George J. Howard of the 5th Vermont concurred: "We have at no time this winter here had more than one half inch in depth of snow. The frost has not penetrated the ground but a few inches at any time." Moreover, warm spells, like the one in early February, reminded Yankees of spring at home. "The winter just suits me," crowed Private Phillips of the 5th Wisconsin. "It isent never very cold nor there is no snow." Images and descriptions of soldiers wading through waist-deep drifts around Petersburg are more products of fancy than meteorological verity.[16]

Because the Sixth Corps assumed responsibility for a previously fortified portion of the Union perimeter, the men of the Greek Cross at first merely occupied the defenses that had been prepared by their predecessors. Quickly, however, Wright's officers organized fatigue parties to strengthen the engineering network protecting the Sixth Corps from attack. "The breastworks in front of the 3d Division have been repaired during the past week and abbattis built in front of them," reported Lieutenant Colonel J. Ford Kent of the corps staff on January 9.[17]

These improvements occurred along the entire corps front, with special attention placed on augmenting the advanced line of obstructions. "Where we do Picket it would be almost impossible now for the Rebles to get through to our Picket line," bragged Andrew Burwell of the 5th Wisconsin. "For in the open fields we have set what we call Johnny catchers and those are long poles set into the ground with the uper end about as high as a man's head and they are so thick a rabbitt could not crawl through and in the woods the small timber and brush is cut down and left lying on the ground in all shapes so that a cat could not get through without being heard. . . ."[18]

Assistant Surgeon Joseph Case Rutherford of the 10th Vermont explained to his son how the barriers worked:

> An abbittie is made of tree tops with the limbs cut off about 4 feet long and their limbs are sharpened. These are stuck into the ground with their points toward the enemy and are placed so thick that a man cannot get through them. This is in a row parallel with the breast work. The trip wires are placed in front of the abbittis. They are woven in among the stumps & brush so thickly that a man cannot possibly get through them. The guns of our batteries are so placed that they can sweep every inch of the ground in front. If the enemy should attempt to take our works we could completely destroy him while he was trying to get through these obstructions.[19]

The most substantial winter engineering project undertaken by the Sixth Corps involved the expansion of Fort Fisher, situated just east of Church Road, into the biggest of the Union forts on the Petersburg front.

This enlargement began shortly before the Sixth Corps occupied that sector and continued through late February. As many as 1,000 troops at a time worked on Fort Fisher, although not every soldier-laborer pitched in with full dedication. "Detailed to work on fort Fisher all day didn't work very hard though," Private Cary confessed to his diary on February 21. Major Tyler of the 37th Massachusetts estimated that when completed the fort could hold as many as 3,000 men. Fort Fisher's location just 2,000 yards from the main Confederate line distinguished it as the closest Union point to the South Side Railroad, and lent the bastion a significance that would be underscored during the spring campaign.[20]

Few Sixth Corps troops failed to notice the observation and signal tower rising behind Fort Fisher. This unusual structure eventually reached 145 feet in height and offered a stunning panorama of the surrounding country. "I had a fine prospect one day last week which was worth more than a view of Niagara Falls," wrote Chaplain Morse, who, equipped with field glasses, had gained permission to ascend the tower. "We could see the rebels very distinctly, their defences, camps, etc. We also had a fine view of Petersburg. . . ." It is easy to imagine the advantages such a post offered to those officers responsible for obtaining information regarding enemy dispositions, a fact not lost upon one Confederate. "The observatory erected by [the Federals] in front of [Brigadier General William] M[a]cRae's Brigade is completed, and is some 200 feet high," testified this Maryland officer. "From its top the curious Federals have the satisfaction of seeing all that is going on in our lines. They will next mount a telescope to ascertain what we eat and the color of our hair. Go ahead, Mr. Yankee! But use it for religious purposes, as the top of your observatory is the nearest you will ever get to heaven."[21]

Labor on the fortifications comprised one of a number of daily activities that quickly assumed a deadly-dull routine. A typical day in the Sixth Corps camps began with reveille at 6:30 a.m., followed 30 minutes later by breakfast. Surgeons' call sounded at 7:45 a.m., prompting a response from those troops feeling in need of medical attention. Guard mounting occurred at 8:00 a.m., and company drill for those not assigned to fatigue duties took place between 9:00 a.m. and 10:00 a.m. A signal summoned the men to dinner at noon, allowing the troops a two-hour break until battalion drill at 2:00 p.m. Another rest period ensued between 3:00 p.m. and 4:30 p.m., after which the officers held a dress parade. Return to the camps took place at sundown, tattoo at 8:30 p.m., and taps

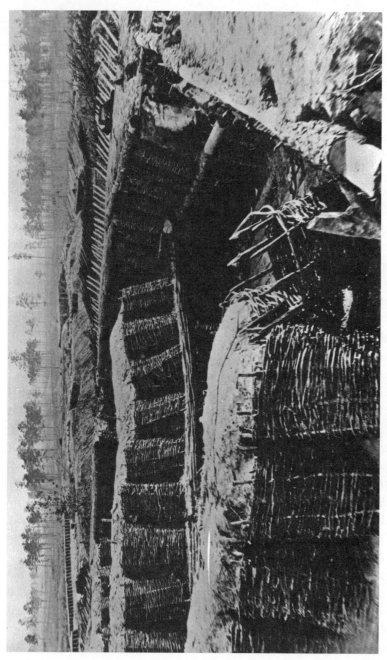

Elaborate Union fortifications at Petersburg. *National Archives*

ended the day at 9:00 p.m., when "the lights must be extinguished and noise cease." "This winter had very few excitements and a great deal of hard work," confirmed Colonel Hyde. "We had a brigade dress parade every afternoon . . . and went through the whole of the bayonet exercise to the sound of the bugle."[22]

Company and regimental officers also devoted considerable energy to maintaining discipline among their troops. Time-honored traditions of cleaning, polishing, and scrubbing filled the time and reminded the independently-minded volunteer that he was still subject to army orders. "They are prety strict with us here," reported Private Phillips. "We have to keep our buttons and brass scoured and our Cow hides blacked and if we come out with a spot of rust on our gun or bayonet or without our hair as slick as a Niggers heel the old lieut colonel wil put us on extra duty or in the guard house or make us shoulder a rail and walk in front of the sentinal two or three hours and if you are not there just at the minute at roll cal or drill it is the same. . . ." On the other hand, the men who presented the best appearance often received rewards such as reduced guard duty, easier assignments, or extra furlough. "There is 7 men excused from camp guard every morning," explained Phillips. "We are taken over to head qrs and inspected. The cleanest and best apearing man is taken for colonels orderly[.] 7 of the cleanest men that is left is excused from guard that day and night. 6 of the next cleanest and best apearing stands at head qrs."[23]

Amid the stultifying regimen of winter camp life, the Sixth Corps maintained its guard against potential Confederate attacks. Each front-line regiment divided the entrenchments it defended into segments marked with a company letter. Should an alarm be sounded, every soldier would rush to his company's designated sector, ready to repel an assault. Those units serving at the front line slept in their clothes with guns and accoutrements by their sides. At first light, all the troops would be awakened, arms stacked, and the men poised to move at a moment's notice. Sunrise so diminished the threat of a surprise that the troops were dismissed to pursue the usual round of camp duties. "Eternal vigilance is the rule; for the Johnnies are feeling for weak places to break through the lines," reported a Connecticut soldier in February.[24]

The army's first defensive perimeter consisted of the well-prepared picket line located between the main works of the opposing forces. Most Sixth Corps privates served as pickets twice a week, noncommissioned officers less frequently. "When a man is on picket at night he is monarch of all he surveys," wrote Corporal Lewis Bissell of the 2nd Connecticut Heavy Artillery. "No one living has more absolute power than he. His word is law. It is death to the man who dares to disobey his commands at night or in fact at any time. A nation's welfare and destiny are resting on him. It is a business that cannot be trifled with. If anything can test a man's bravery and patience it is picket duty in front of a treacherous foe for there is no knowing when or from where he will come."[25]

A division officer occupying a bullet-proof hut on the picket line held command of his unit's details for three days. The pickets themselves drew 24 hours of uninterrupted duty during which time they were prohibited from sleeping under penalty of death. The picket line was a series of entrenched positions spaced about 50 feet apart, depending upon the local terrain, with a vidette line consisting of "gopher holes" established about 50 yards in advance of the fortified posts and manned during the night. Each picket post contained four to seven men. The videttes in front rotated hourly.[26]

A quiet and irregular war-within-a-war characterized affairs on the Sixth Corps picket line. Instead of a steady and predictable exchange of musketry whenever a head appeared above the dirt, danger arrived sporadically, usually just before dawn, and by several stratagems. "When a few prisoners were wanted," wrote Lieutenant J. F. J. Caldwell of Samuel McGowan's South Carolina Brigade, "(and they were sometimes our only chance for information of the enemy's movements,) Gen. [Cadmus M.] Wilcox would order one or more of his battalions of sharpshooters to capture some. . . . They would move out of our picket line a little before day, creep close to the enemy, form, rush in (generally by the flank) and sweep up and down the works. They always captured some prisoners and a good deal of plunder, and sometimes killed a few of the enemy. . . . At dawn they would return to our lines."[27]

Major Thomas J. Wooten of the 18th North Carolina led the sharpshooters of James Lane's Brigade. Wooten often worked in conjunction with McGowan's troops to effect such raids on the Federal picket line, popularly termed, "Wooten's seine-haulings." The major would carefully reconnoiter his targets during the day, then lead a body of picked men in pairs to the Union outposts, where in a flash they would surround individual Federal videttes and whisk them into Confederate lines. These attacks netted so many prisoners that they elicited written commendations from Lee and Hill. Thomas Hyde reported that one such foray resulted in

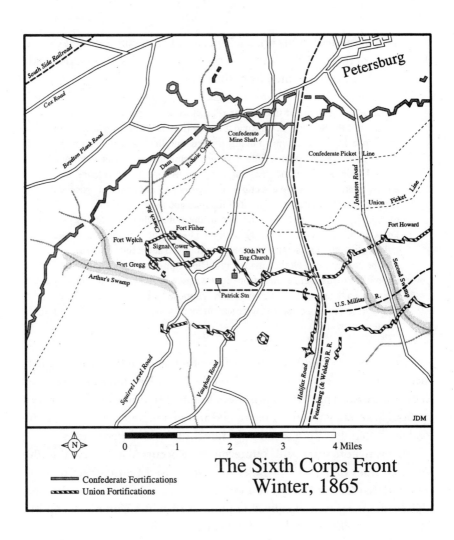

The Sixth Corps Front
Winter, 1865

the loss of about half of his brigade's pickets. Lieutenant Colonel Charles A. Milliken of the 43rd New York described another episode that plucked a lesser number of Hyde's men from the ranks:

> Between the hours of five and six o'clock A.M. . . . the vidette posts on the right of the Squirrel Level Road, hearing (but not seeing, on account of the dense fog,) the enemy moving toward our line, fired to alarm the supports, when the enemy fired a volley simultaneously with them and dashed upon the main line, reaching the posts as soon as the videttes. The enemy approached in two directions one party of 50 or 60 men approached the line near the abatis on the right of the road and the other 40 or 50 strong on the right of the Division picquets at the point where the 2nd & 3rd Division line connects. One party obliquing to the right and the other to the left. The videttes and sentinels were being relieved at the time of the attack, and the enemy being clothed in the Light Blue Uniform of our troops it was impossible to distinguish them from our own men, which prevented most of the men on the posts from firing as they supposed them to be the videttes and sentinels falling back, and were surrounded by the enemy who captured fourteen men and wounded one.[28]

Not every Confederate picket-line incursion met with complete success. On New Year's eve an attack on the Third Division's front resulted in the capture of a number of prisoners and the wounding or killing of four others. However, Seymour's men rallied and snared four of the raiders who explained that they were seeking "hardtack and some overcoats."[29]

An even more successful countermeasure occurred in front of the 10th Vermont lines of Truex's brigade. A newly-arrived Confederate deserter reported that some 200 of his comrades intended to launch a raid that very night with an eye toward collecting plunder from the Union picket posts. The officer in charge of the Federal videttes ordered the man held, and threatened to stretch his neck if his story proved false, to which the deserter allowed that "he had it in for that bunch of blockheads and wanted to see them annihilated." The Federal officer arranged a trap by assigning each of his pickets a specific place around the vidette-post fires, creating a formation by which any attackers could be surrounded and captured. "Our instructions were to keep a good fire, and if attacked, at the first alarm, that each man should go to his place selected, allow the rebels to rush into the enclosure around the fire, give them our regulation yell, and charge with fixed bayonets." The plan worked as designed and nearly 200 astonished Confederates dropped their guns and surrendered.

The 10th Vermont also put an end to one of the more ingenious ways by which Confederate marauders captured Union pickets. One of the Federal vidette posts rested just beyond a brick chimney, the sole remnant of a burned home. From time to time, relief parties for this station discovered their predecessors missing with no apparent explanation. Declining to question the loyalty of these men, the Yankees puzzled over the bewildering disappearance of their comrades. At last, a Confederate deserter provided the key to this mystery. The Southerners had constructed a tunnel leading from a secure position behind their own picket line to the ruined house, and covered the exit with the old chimney's hearthstone. This subterranean passageway provided the Confederates with the means to pop out just behind the unlucky Union picket post. The raiders, dressed in stolen Federal overcoats, would masquerade as a relief detail, thus catching the unsuspecting Union pickets completely off guard and easily capturing them.

The Federals verified the existence of the tunnel and prepared a surprise for its clandestine patrons. They rigged a 12-pound artillery shell in the pit under the fireplace so arranged that the least movement of the stone would detonate the projectile. After restoring the ground to obscure their handiwork, the vengeful Yankees retreated to await the next nocturnal Confederate appearance. About nine o'clock that night, they heard an explosion from the direction of the old house. Rushing to the scene, they discovered the hearthstone blown away and the remains of some badly shattered rebels buried by debris. The blast had caved-in the tunnel, closing one small chapter of the vicious little war that raged along the picket lines.[30]

These dramatic incidents shared the stage with more mundane episodes. Occasionally, the Federals would set ablaze what woods remained between the lines to discomfit their opponents. Sergeant Berry Benson of McGowan's Brigade recalled the time that the resulting fire raced toward the Confederate posts so quickly that guns and haversacks were burned, and even the vigilant General Lane's whiskers and eyebrows were singed in the process. Some unlucky Southerners felt their cartridge boxes explode against their bodies while escaping the flames.[31]

The no-man's land between the picket lines sometimes became a killing ground in a different way. One day, a North Carolina sharpshooter brought down a wild turkey with a well-aimed shot, but the coveted game fell in a patch of woods half-way to the Union picket posts. Reluctant to venture out where he might become a victim himself, the hungry Southern hunter waited until a Sixth Corps soldier, witness to the shooting, crawled forward into the woodlot to claim the bird for his own stew pot. The Tarheel leveled his rifle and dispatched the Federal, and, thus emboldened, dashed out and retrieved the turkey.[32]

Despite such contretemps, Sixth Corps sentries often established amicable relationships with their Confederate counterparts. "Our picket line and the Johnnies is snug together," wrote George Buffum. "We leave our guns on the post and go out and talk to one another." Spirited trading occurred, although officers on both sides discouraged overt fraternization. Newspapers were a favorite commodity along with tobacco, coffee, and specialty items like jack knives or uniform insignias. "It was a very simple process," according to South Carolinian William Miller. "A Yankee out on the picket line would shake a paper or bundle of coffee and hollow at us as to what he had to exchange with us and he would place it on a stump or some elevated place and go off; then we would go and get it and leave our package for the party to come for. I never knew or heard of either party cheating." The men also exchanged animated conversation, especially pertaining to the course of the war in other theaters. "There is generally some fun in tantalizing [the Confederate pickets] and hearing the sharp sayings which are yelled back and forth," mused Captain Dayton E. Flint of the 15th New Jersey. "Some of the 'Rebs' are pretty witty, and occasionally get the best of it, so far as talking goes."[33]

Sometimes the congenial feelings between the picket lines reached remarkable extremes. Private Henry Houghton of the 3rd Vermont crossed between the lines to harvest firewood and encountered a Confederate on a similar mission. The two enemies agreed to cut down the same tree together, the Rebel and Houghton hacking on opposite portions of the trunk. "After it fell I chopped down one side of the log and he the other, then we split it and he had one half and I the other, then we swapped hats and went back to camp and I am quite sure I wore that hat until just before the last review in Washington," remembered Houghton.[34]

Sixth Corps troops usually acquired new equipment in more orthodox ways. A number of units received new firearms and accoutrements including the Mann's patented cartridge box. "These are carried on the front of the body," wrote Lewis Bissell, and "are made to carry sixty rounds . . . There is a knapsack to go with the new cartridge box."[35]

Preparing camps, building quarters, perfecting fortifications, drilling, and going on picket duty demanded much of the troops' time during the winter, but the men still occupied themselves with the pursuit of pure fun. Captain Flint of the 15th New Jersey enjoyed the occasional horseback ride to visit other Jerseymen along the lines. The men wrote letters home, played chess and checkers, and pitched quoits. Musical performances by army bandsmen garnered rave reviews. Major Richard F. Halstead of Wright's staff assembled an all-star band of 40 musicians from the Sixth Corps and presented concerts that delighted large crowds. Miss Mary L. Masters of Boston even composed an original tune entitled, "The Old Sixth Corps," one verse of which went:

> Our truest, bravest heart is gone
> And we remember well
> The bitter anguish of that day
> When noble Sedgwick fell;
> But there is still another left
> To lead us to the fight,
> And with a hearty three times three
> We'll cheer our gallant Wright![36]

Such wholesome pastimes competed with the usual camp vices for the soldiers' leisure hours. A member of the 121st New York reported to his wife that, "In this regt. i know of many young men that left home determined to resist all temptations of a demoralizing influence but they have one by one like the autumn leaf fallen & into habits . . . not likely to honor them or help them in their future." Profanity, drunkenness, and gambling headed the list. "Thousands of young men have learned to love ardent spirits & to get beastly intoxicated on the same here whenever they could procure it let the cost be as extravagant as it may," wrote this offended New Yorker. "Some think they cannot be a soldier without using profanity at the beginning & end of each sentence they utter. . . . Gambling like swearing is carried on to a great extent by a large majority of the men, first they commence . . . playing for pies, apples, cigars or any other small innocent stakes, by & by they are captivated by the play & venture large sums of money, the result is conclusive, many lose ther[e]by all or nearly all their hard earning[s] which are generally pocketed by some more artful & successful player."[37]

The soldiers gladly received visitors in camp, few quite so welcome as the gentleman from Maine so full of patriotic fervor that he determined to give each man in the Army of the Potomac a dollar. "He kept on for quite a time too," reported Colonel Hyde, "till he realized how many of them there were." Even more popular were the female guests, although by March new regulations prohibited ladies from spending the night in camp. Wives, sisters, and other distaff callers returned to City Point in the evenings after rounds of cheering their loved ones.[38]

City Point also housed women of more questionable virtue. An entire village of prostitutes, lining three parallel streets about four blocks long, flourished near the wharves. In some 120 log or clapboard houses, these "soiled doves" charged three dollars per visit and cleared as much as $300 per day. After pay days, long lines developed in the neighborhood, although between payroll musters the whores were known to "take their time and do many special things." In addition to dispensing sexual favors, these women would write letters home for illiterate soldiers, adding a commendable capitalist versatility to their astonishing stamina as businesswomen. The soldiers' fondness for what Sergeant John F.L. Hartwell of the 121st New York called "licentiousness" did not come without additional price, however. Many men seemed to "cast aside all honor & like a beast go about seeking whom they may discover but generally get devoured themselves, disease of the most loathsome kind fastens upon them & they die with rottenness," wrote Hartwell.[39]

Reproductive activities in the Sixth Corps were not limited to the houses of ill repute at City Point or the conjugal visits of wives. "The boys are having considerable fun over a circumstance which has just happened in a New Jersey regt.," reported Warren Williams of the 5th Wisconsin. "It appears a woman soldier has been in that regt. whether she is married or not I cannot say . . . she has done a soldiers duty. . . . she was out on picket and now she has a nine pound soldier. . . . I think she ought to have a pension dont you. Who will say we cannot whip the south when the north [can] raise soldiers right in the field."[40]

The Irish Brigade's celebration of St. Patrick's Day marked the highlight of the winter social season. Officers from throughout the army attended horse racing between the Fifth and Second corps, foot races, and musical entertainment, while plates of sandwiches washed down with the usual libations added to the festive atmosphere. The Peebles House behind the left end of the Sixth Corps line provided the venue for this extravaganza. "Nearly every Brigadier, Brigade commander & Major General have entered their horses," wrote one observer. "The fair sex of our northern states was represented by quite a number of officers wives," reported a soldier in the 6th Vermont. "Very pretty women too unless I have the idea that all women are, not having seen one for so long before." Not only did various riders injure themselves in falls from their mounts, but construction of Fort Fisher suffered as well. "Perhaps some of the surviving members of the regiment remember what happened when they were sent on St. Patrick's day with the teams to get pine poles to be used for strengthening Fort Fisher, and failed to get past the Irish Brigade that was celebrating the day with races and games of all sorts," suggested the historian of the 121st New York. "They had an enjoyable day, but the toting of a log [or] cord of wood all night, and extra picket duty somewhat canceled the pleasant remembrance of it." It may be imagined that on March 18 other celebrants struggled with the after-effects of overindulgence as well.[41]

Yet, according to Chaplain Lemuel T. Foote of the 151st New York, drunkenness did not pose the ubiquitous problem in the Petersburg camps that it had during previous campaigns. "I have not seen during the month a single case of intoxication, nor do I think [there] has been such a case," Foote reported on January 31 with, perhaps, a little exaggeration. "This is in fact owing to the wholesome effect of orders issued from the commanding officer of the Div. restricting the sale and use of whiskey to officers in the limits of the Div."[42]

Some of this good behavior might have been attributable to the sustained interest in religion that permeated the Union army as it had since the second winter of the war. "Yesterday evening I preached in the chapel tent belonging to the Christian Commission," wrote Chaplain Morse. "It is a very large chapel and it was filled to overflowing. There is a good interest there and quite a number are seeking religion every evening." Chaplain Foote conducted two services every Sunday and two evening prayer meetings during the week. "These services have been well attended and we are looking for a gracious outpouring of the Spirit that shall result in the conversion of many souls," he wrote. The Christian Commission also sponsored religious gatherings every night in the Sixth Corps camps. This is not to say that every soldier embraced godliness with unbounded fervor. Chaplain Foote confessed that "the greatest obstacle that I meet with is the same that the Christian minister meets everywhere[:]

the natural disinclination of the heart to accept the experimental truths of the gospel of Jesus Christ as revealed in his word." Lieutenant Colonel Hazard Stevens of Getty's staff numbered himself among such skeptics: "In this division there are only six chaplains although there are seventeen regiments each of which is entitled to one. They are usually considered rather worthless."[43]

A number of the chaplains provided spacious and attractive buildings to stimulate attendance. By far the most famous of these military churches belonged to the 50th New York Engineers. With professional construction techniques honed by years of service in the field, the New Yorkers departed from their usual menu of bridges and roads to raise a Gothic-style structure that could accommodate, by one optimistic count, some fifteen hundred persons. Lewis Bissell described the church as built of "pine logs set upright. The floor is of hewn logs. . . . The spire is well worth seeing. It is framed of small sticks, about the size of a broom stick, fastened and matched together. The doorway represents an arch of marble and is made of pine poles bent to the required shape and form." The building assumed the appearance of a short cross, and on the inside, the left-most aisle was reserved for officers, while a gallery over the entrance served blacks. A rustic chandelier provided light. The 50th New York church hosted secular entertainments during the week in addition to Sabbath services. "It is used for all kinds of purposes . . . evening plays . . . a regular gymnasium, great singers, regular clowns," reported a New Englander.[44]

If the word of God brought contentment to Sixth Corps soldiers, so did the appearance of the army payroll in late February and early March. "A paymaster's arrival will produce more joy in camp than is said to have been produced in heaven over the one sinner that repenth," observed one Union soldier. Both Union and Confederate troops experienced irregular and often long-deferred pay musters. "Our brigade has just been paid, and I assure many men were made happy," confirmed James Harper of the 139th Pennsylvania on March 2. "Pay was received for four months to Dec. 31st. although there were many in our regiment who had ten months coming."[45]

Many soldiers wishing to visit loved ones at home sought a furlough during the winter, although the army sparingly doled out such leave. "The order is at present that not more than five per cent of the officers of any regiment can be absent at one time," stated Chaplain Morse. "Those going to Massachusetts and other states north of it can have twenty days' leave."

50th New York Church (Poplar Grove)

National Archives

Even if one received permission to journey north, other obstacles intervened. Warren Williams believed that he might have succeeded in gaining a furlough, but the financial and emotional stress of going home posed too steep a price. "If it did not cost so much I should have applied for a furlough," he wrote his family. "It would cost me about fifty dollars to go and come and I think the money would do you more good than six or eight days visit from me would and then the idea of a second parting I do not like so I have concluded to keep a stiff upper lip and stay the year out unless something turns up to call me home." Permission to leave camp for a shorter period, to pay a social visit to City Point for example, required an army pass, stimulating an illicit business in these documents. "We have made a large number of arrests today, of soldiers engaged in selling passes—They are stolen from [Colonel Theodore S.] Bowers," reported Provost Marshal General Marsena Patrick on January 12.[46]

The men of the Sixth Corps worried about promotions, contributed funds for the erection of a monument to their beloved former commander, John Sedgwick, and followed the progress of Sherman's campaign through the Carolinas. Sergeant James Denton of the 1st New Jersey grumbled that advancement in the army depended upon one's political affiliation. While asking his brother to advise him on the progress of a pending promotion, Denton expressed pessimism: "I think somtimes that I will give up all hoaps for it seams that no man can git Nothing without he is A dam black Rebublican. I swear that I will sea them fouther in hell then wat tha ar at Present befor I will com to that." Pennsylvanian James Harper noted that Warner's brigade was assessed $1,000 for its portion of the Sedgwick monument fund, each of the five regiments in the brigade paying $200. "It seems a little strange that our share is always out of all proportions," complained Harper. "However, we have paid over $200 to Co[l]. Warner, and have done our duty in this praise-worthy matter." Commenting on a 100-gun salute fired along the corps front to celebrate Sherman's capture of Columbia, South Carolina, Lieutenant Homer Curtis observed with mixed emotions that, "We play second fiddle[,] rather it seems to me Sherman does the fighting and gets the glory. We lie here and hurrah and occasionally fire a salute. Easy for us but not very glorious." But others like Captain Charles G. Gould of the 5th Vermont viewed Sherman's success with less ambivalence: "Genl. Sherman will soon make connexion on our left and then with Sheridan on our right we are 'going in'—'Goodbye Richmond' when they connect with our line."[47]

> "Genl. Sherman will soon make connexion on our left and then with Sheridan on our right we are 'going in'—'Goodbye Richmond' when they connect with our line."

Sherman's progress to the south, misunderstood machinations at army headquarters, and the improving weather all increased combat preparations in the Sixth Corps camps as February gave way to March. Orders arrived on the night of February 25 for the corps to "pack up everything and sleep with our straps on" in response to a report that the Confederates were about to evacuate Petersburg. Although this precaution proved to be a false alarm, rumors circulated that the corps would be returned to the Valley. Such a transfer sat well with Sergeant Altus H. Jewell of the 77th New York when he learned of Jubal Early's defeat at Waynesboro. "I had rather be there than down here for a change," Jewell told his sister. "If we go to the Valley we won't have [Early] to fight."[48]

Within another week, however, many in the Sixth Corps realized that their recent orders portended a more local effort to win the war. "We're all jacked up ready to move at a moments notice," said John J. Ingraham. "I think there will be another advance soon. . . . If this is true, which I hope it might be, I think Gen Lee's time is short." Ingraham's comrade in the 121st New York, Sergeant John F. L. Hartwell, recognized as only a veteran soldier could, that the resumption of campaigning would entail hardships and risks, despite the general optimism prevailing in the camps. "I . . . expect nothing else than to be tumbling over stumps and into bug holes during our nights march," admitted Hartwell. "I confess I dread it very much as any sensible man should. Only think of my gettin my new pants besmeared with filth to say nothing of fatigue and running against lead & chuncks of iron which are very apt to make a series of vent holes in ones body." In spite of these potential hazards, Hartwell and the rest of the Sixth Corps prepared in various ways for the inevitable action everyone knew was a mere matter of time.[49]

Beginning on March 7, Generals Meade and Wright conducted formal reviews of each Sixth Corps division, starting with Seymour's. Colonel Keifer fairly beamed when describing his brigade's fine display, an affair attended by numerous civilian dignitaries as well as the army commander:

> I had the honor of turning out my Brig. this afternoon & having it received by Maj. Genl. Meade. Mrs. Lt. Genl. Grant, Secy [of War Edwin M.] Stanton's daughter and niece, Judge [George] Woodruff & wife of N.Y. City, and a large number of ladies and gentlemen attended the review with Genl Meade. . . . I may say [no] Brigade in the field ever looked better or marched better than did mine. Gens. Meade & Wright were highly delighted, as were the other distinguished ladies & gentlemen, at their appearance.[50]

On the 15th it was the Second Division's turn when Meade and Wright were joined by Senator Henry Wilson of Massachusetts and Congressman

Justin S. Morill of Vermont. "The dust flew like snow so we were all white with dust when we got back," observed one Maine participant. On March 20, General Wheaton's men put on the show. The surprise guest reviewer was Rear Admiral David Dixon Porter, who accompanied Wright, Meade, artillery commander Henry J. Hunt, and other luminaries. New Englander Homer Curtis left a vivid description of the event:

> Our Divn formed out on the parade and after an hours waiting in the sun Gen. Wheaton came out with his staff and took of his position in front and presented arms to the reviewing officers. Gen. Meade & Wright & Rear Admiral David D. Porter—they rode down the lines and then we marched in review. The 2nd C.A. [Connecticut Heavy Artillery] distinguishing itself as usual. I never saw either Meade or Adl. Porter before. . . . Gen. Meade is a grizzly old graybeard looking savage as a meataxe. A very different looking man is the Admiral. His smooth face nearly eclipsed by a black cap and blacker . . . mustache.[51]

The Federal high command continued to wrestle with one particularly troubling issue as the campaign season approached: desertion. Soldiers had been slipping into the Confederate lines throughout the winter. General Lane observed in early December that "desertions from the enemy are of nightly occurrence." Sergeant-Major Robert R. Hemphill of McGowan's Brigade wrote about the same time that, "night before last five deserters from the 5th New Hampshire Regiment came to our tent. They were mostly foreigners and recruits, tired of the service and glad of an opportunity to escape." Sergeant Berry Benson affirmed in February that the trickle of Federal fugitives continued: "Last night 20 Yanks came over to our picket line; they were mostly foreigners, unable to speak English, and being dressed, some of them, in citizens' clothes, it is supposed they were immigrants pressed into the service immediately on their arrival."[52]

The notion that the Northern army consisted of foreign hirelings tricked or forced into the military played well in the South, implying that only the ignorant, gullible, or unwilling would participate in the Union war effort. There was some basis in truth to this stereotype. Corporal William E. H. Morse of the 1st Maine Veterans noted in January that 46 new recruits reported to his regiment: "One of them is Portuguese, and can understand very little English. The most of them are foreigners." In reality, though, many of the Billy Yanks who chose to desert were native-born Americans who did so with premeditation, motivated by greed or cowardice. A soldier in the 121st New York testified that "a few bounty jumpers & Subs desert

Brigadier General Frank Wheaton

Massachusetts MOLLUS Collection, Carlisle Barracks, Pennsylvania

occasionaly from our side but they are of no account <u>any where</u> & we are just as strong without such men as they are generally <u>cowards</u> of the lowest grade and dare not face a veteran soldier of the good old stock." The 40th New Jersey, for example, earned an especially noxious reputation in this regard. Lured into the service with large bounties between December 1864 and February 1865, dozens of these men skedaddled in Trenton, cash in hand, while many others deserted at Petersburg, apparently trusting their chances for survival behind Southern lines more than as a combatants. Such behavior infuriated the veterans of the Sixth Corps, who treasured their organization's good reputation. "I should like to see one of them sneaking of[f] he would get a hole in his hide if I could shoot strate enough and if I failed to hit him I would take after him with fixed bayonets," fumed a member of Wheaton's division. "That is the general feelings of all the boys." According to one student of the regiment, "the vast majority of these scoundrels [were] native born Americans."[53]

Executions remained the primary deterrent to desertion, as they had been since the return of the Sixth Corps in December. "I have just been witness to another of those horrible sights which is a regular thing in our army every Friday, the Shooting or Hanging of some Deserter," wrote Private James R. Holmes of the 61st Pennsylvania. The army conducted these punishments as a public spectacle to be viewed by the condemned man's comrades as an object lesson. "Jane, I seen the worst sight yesterday that I ever saw in my life," wrote a Wisconsin private to his wife. "Our whole division was marched out to see a man shot for deserting." Lewis Bissell of Connecticut described one such grim scene in graphic detail:

> The division formed three sides of a square, the fourth side being left open. Here the grave was dug. . . . The doomed man rode in an ambulance with a chaplain. His coffin was carried in front of him. First came an officer on horse back riding with drawn sabre. He was followed by a band of music, then twelve men with arms reversed, next the coffin[,] then the criminal[,] following him twelve more men with arms reversed. In this formation they marched around the line to the open grave. Here they halted. The coffin was placed a few feet in front of the grave. The criminal was helped out of the ambulance and the chaplain prayed with him. Then two men took him, placed him on his coffin, fastened a handkerchief over his eyes and tied his feet and hands. At a signal twelve muskets were discharged and the criminal fell dead across his coffin, his heart pierced with eight or ten bullets. He was buried and his grave leveled.[54]

Although Colonel Charles Wainwright wrote in February that "desertion to the enemy was about stopped among our men by the hanging process," in reality both the act and the consequence continued even as the army drilled and reviewed in preparation for impending combat—perhaps because of that prospect. "There is a man to be shot in our Division to day for desertion and jumping bounties," penned Assistant Surgeon Joseph C.

Rutherford on March 8. "It is a solom[n] thing to think of and I most wish there was some way that he might live though he richly deserves his punishment. . . . I shall not go to see the execution as I dislike such scenes very much." A few days later, Colonel Keifer attended the imposition of the death penalty on Private James Kelley of the 67th Pennsylvania, a soldier in his brigade. Keifer shared Doctor Rutherford's feelings about executions: "I abhor such scenes. I doubt also their propriety. I also doubt whether the discipline of the army or the preservation of its organization demands such a punishment." Captain Michael Kelly of the 2nd Connecticut Heavy Artillery had no such doubts. He described in great detail the January execution of a New Jersey soldier, concluding his account by observing that "it was an awful day and a very effective one." Effective or not, the

> "There is a man to be shot in our Division for desertion. . . It is a solom[n] thing to think of and I most wish there was some way that he might live though he richly deserves his punishment."

executions continued throughout the month, even as well-dressed Washington officials and their ladies gazed with admiration upon the spit and polish of nearby parading troops.[55]

The numbers of those troops increased during the winter from a variety of sources. Not all of the new soldiers were the "bounty jumpers & Scallowags" complained of by Provost Marshal Marsena Patrick. The 15th New Jersey received 200 replacements in March while the New Jersey Brigade expanded to absorb the mixed blessing of the 40th New Jersey as a completely new unit. Chaplain Winthrop Henry Phelps of the 2nd Connecticut Heavy Artillery noted that 28 recruits joined his regiment on January 18, described as "good looking able men" by Lewis Bissell of the regiment. Corporal George H. Mellish of the 6th Vermont told his mother that his company had received six new recruits. "Since I wrote last we have had a new arrival—a lot of 'Fresh-Fish'. . . . They were all pretty good looking and good appearing fellows. . . ." Still, the poor performance at the Battle of Hatcher's Run by some of the new men, derided as "damb slinks or coffee coolers," fueled the disrespect toward the army's recent arrivals felt by many old soldiers.[56]

Despite the advantages of increased manpower, most veterans preferred the presence of one tested comrade to the addition of ten inexperienced recruits. "We dont want any new men," admitted James Harper of the 139th Pennsylvania. "The strength of our regiment increases slowly . . . and we prefer to serve what remains of our term by ourselves." Veterans returning from sick leave swelled the ranks of their regiments. "All during the winter, soldiers and officers had been coming back to our regiment so that we probably numbered more men and officers than at any time since the battle of Winchester," remembered Lieutenant David Soule of the 2nd Connecticut Heavy Artillery. "Some had been in hospitals from wounds and disease, but the war department had hustled all back that had not been discharged." The 5th Vermont posted 148 men on the sick list in February, a number that dropped steadily with the approach of spring. Their brigade mates in the 4th Vermont welcomed back 40 men exchanged in March who had been captured at the Petersburg Railroad in June. Staff officer Hazard Stevens quantified the results of these accretions as early as January 25: "Our old division [Getty's] is constantly increasing. We now have nearly 5,000 men effective. During the campaign we were reduced to 3500 at one time."[57]

Increases in troop strength, mild and improving weather, military successes in other theaters, and, most of all, the perception that the wind had turned against the Confederate ship of war, all led to a cautious optimism among Sixth Corps troops on the eve of the 1865 spring campaign. "Our military affairs look encouraging, and it is not probable that the coming campaign will be anything like so bloody as the last. We may even have no more hard fighting," predicted staff officer Stevens. "Our superiority, especially in numbers is constantly on the increase and I rather anticipate a campaign of more marches than battles." Sergeant Harrison of the 14th New Jersey also saw the end in sight. "The boys are all in good health and lively as crickets as the spring opens," he wrote his parents. "Slowly the Angel of Peace is descending to visit the American People once again. Slowly but surely is old Lee being entrapped and he will one of these days find the trap sprung." Colonel Keifer agreed: "I feel very confident of our ability to crush Lee's army, if we are properly handled." Hazard Stevens shared this outlook as well: "I think the Con theif eracy as A. Waud calls it, is beginning to crumble, the back bone is bent a little at least."[58]

Buoyancy in the Federal camps derived more from an evaluation of diminishing Confederate morale than from all the new troops and the battlefield triumphs of Sherman and Sheridan combined. Reports circulated through the Union army of disturbances between paroled Confederate soldiers and Southern civilians, indicating serious trouble on the Rebel homefront. The Confederate effort to enlist blacks struck Yankee observers as hard evidence of the South's desperate fortunes. Most dramatically, the presence of Confederate deserters along the Petersburg lines demonstrated indisputably that Jefferson Davis and Robert E. Lee were losing their hold on the men upon whom they depended to achieve Southern independence.[59]

"Me-thinks the Rebel Cross does not float so defiantly now as it did in the more palmy days of the Confederacy," wrote Vermonter George Mellish. "They begin to think the North [has] too many guns for them and they knowing that makes all the difference in the world. . . . The mass of them won't fight with desperate fury—they will adopt a more reasonable course altogether—Desert." Colonel Keifer was not quite so sure that the Confederates would go down without resistance, but he shared Mellish's analysis of Southern morale: "The last struggle, it is possible, may be desperate upon the part of the rebels, to succeed in their nefarious designs, but it is at hand. Evidence of discontent and weakness are everywhere visible in the rebel strongholds. The spirit of the Rebel Army is broken. . . ." A Connecticut captain, writing in early March, recorded that "a good many thinks, officers & men, this is the month that will wipe out Lee."[60]

The Sixth Corps may have detected serious cracks in the psychological armor of the Confederate war effort, but the physical evidence of Rebel defiance that confronted them across the lines continued to impress all observers. The Southern defenses included an elaborate picket line, multiple rows of intimidating obstructions, and a powerful rampart of earth and logs swept by artillery for its entire length across an open field of fire. The presence of these imposing fortifications provided a grim and unsettling backdrop to every activity in the Union winter camps.

The Confederates' picket line ran parallel to and about one-half mile in advance of their main works. The wood-cutting parties from both armies continually reduced the forest cover between the forward lines so that by March, barely a pine tree stood to shield the opposing armies from one another. "It may be well to say that this intrenched picket line was a continuous trench and parapet, affording a good cover for its defenders, and in fact, a line of field fortifications in all except relief and the accessories, such as abattis, fraise, & c., generally found in advance of a line of field entrenchments," testified Brigadier General John G. Barnard, Grant's chief engineer. "Such obstructions had originally existed in a rude but effective way, in the shape of slashings of timber, but these had been mainly cleared away by our own troops and those of the enemy for fuel, under the tacit understanding between the advanced forces of the combatants so often witnessed in war."[61]

Behind the picket line, Confederate engineers laid out as many as four rows of abatis, "so intertwined and fastened down that it was difficult to overcome or remove," plus fraise and chevaux-de-frise. These obstructions presented as daunting an obstacle as the ones Federal correspondents boasted about in their letters home. One soldier described the barriers as representing gigantic rakes with four rows of teeth. The sharpened logs pointed outward "with an unyielding and aggressive air," thought a Northern officer, "as if to say, Come and impale yourselves on us." The Southerners had even located their latrines amid the obstructions, presenting an additional and disgusting impediment to any potential attacker.[62]

The main Confederate line, plainly visible from the observation tower and other vantage points along the Sixth Corps front, represented the apex of mid-nineteenth century military engineering. The parapet, constructed of earth and logs six feet high, twelve feet thick at the base, and four feet wide at the top, occasionally included headlogs which completely protected the defenders when firing, except for the slender aperture through which they aimed their rifles. A moat, sometimes filled with standing water, measured six feet deep and eight feet wide. Narrow openings in the line protected by traverses provided passage for the Confederate pickets and wood gatherers, and access to the sinks. Various artillery positions thoroughly blanketed the cleared field of fire, virtually eliminating all defilade for approaching troops.[63]

The Confederates also strengthened their defenses with the aid of impounded water, called inundations. The largest and most effective of these liquid barriers confronted the Sixth Corps along Old Town or Rohoic Creek opposite Fort Fisher and to the left of Lane's North Carolina Brigade. Colonel Thomas Mann Randolph Talcott of Lee's staff superintended the construction of this military dam, which rendered an assault across its expanse utterly impractical. The Southerners also built at least one mine shaft filled with explosives in front of their lines.[64]

This advanced military engineering, a powerful deterrent to attack, received continual attention from the allegedly demoralized Confederates. "The men all along the lines are kept constantly at work, making alterations in some parts, and reviewing others, so as to make them stand the effects of the winter better," testified General Lane. Their labor did not go unnoticed in the Sixth Corps camps. "There is unusual activity within the rebel lines just now," reported Lewis Bissell. "They keep building strong works and mounting heavy guns."[65]

Private Oscar Waite of the 10th Vermont was numbered among the Sixth Corps troops who spent the winter of 1865 admiring the energy and tenacity of his enemies: "All winter the rebels have been working like beavers, strengthening and perfecting their works, until there don't seem to be any chance for further improvement. . . . Opinions seem to differ as to Gen. Lee as a tactician or an invader, but all agree that when it comes to defensive operations, 'Old Bob' understands his business."[66]

Thus, as nature's icy grip loosened on the men of the Sixth Corps and their comrades in Grant's two armies, the expectation of renewed hostilities carried an ambiguous message. Lincoln's soldiers had fared reasonably well during the fourth winter of the war. The necessities of life had appeared in adequate quantity, occasional diversions mitigated the monotony, and the ranks had increased to levels not seen since the previous spring. Moreover, evidence mounted that the Confederate war effort had reached the last ditch. Yet, the omnipresent and still dangerous Army of Northern Virginia, ensconced securely behind fortifications that all agreed were "not calculated to encourage assaults," qualified this cautious optimism. How had Lee's men survived the winter? Had the Confederacy's sails really gone slack, or did the coming of spring mean another deadly and futile encounter with the perpetually indominatible followers of Lee?[67]

NOTES

1. Maj.-Gen. Wesley Merritt, "The Appomattox Campaign," in *War Papers and Personal Reminiscences 1861-1865: Read Before the Commandery of the State of Missouri, Military Order of the Loyal Legion of the United States* (St. Louis, 1892, reprint, Wilmington, N.C., 1992), 110. Merritt's comments referred to Dinwiddie County in general.

2. Welcher, *The Union Army*, I, 413; George B. Davis, Leslie J. Perry, Joseph W. Kirkley, *Atlas to Accompany the Official Records of the Union and Confederate Armies* (Washington, 1891-1895, reprint, New York, 1978), Plate LXXVII; Petersburg Quadrangle, United States Department of the Interior, Geological Survey, 1969, Photo revised, 1987. Most of the Sixth Corps line lay in Dinwiddie County, although that portion of the line east of Johnson Road was in Prince George County. Johnson, Vaughan, Squirrel Level, and Church roads all exist in 2000 on or close to their wartime routes. Halifax Road and the Petersburg Railroad have swapped alignments where they intersect the Union lines. The railroad is now west of the highway, a relationship that was reversed at the time of the campaign. Arthur's Swamp is a tributary of the Nottoway River, which joins the Blackwater River near the North Carolina state line to form the Chowan River, which in turn feeds into Albemarle Sound near Edenton, North Carolina. See Freeman, *Lee's Lieutenants*, I, 695-696.

3. Inspection Report of Maj.[Lt. Col.] Hazard Stevens, 2d Div, 6th Corps, Feb.7, 1865, 3rd Brigade, Record Group 94, NA; Hyde, *Following the Greek Cross*, 239. The narrative focuses on the Sixth Corps camps during the winter of 1865, but the experience of Wright's troops generally mirrored that of the rest of the army.

4. George W. Buffum to wife, December 22, 1864 and January 1, 1865, in George W. Buffum Letters, 1864-1865, SHSW; William L. Phillips to "Father and Mother," December 26, 1864, in William L. Phillips Letters, SHSW; Mason Whiting Tyler, *Recollections of the Civil War With Many Original Diary Entries and Letters Written from the Seat of War, and with Annotated References* (New York, 1912), 319; Olsen, ed., *Upon the Tented Field*, 294; Stevens, *Three Years in the Sixth Corps*, 429; Oscar E. Waite, "Three Years With the Tenth Vermont," (2 vols.; VTHS), II, 239. For a delightful essay on life in winter camp, see John D. Billings, *Hardtack and Coffee, or The Unwritten Story of Army Life* (Boston, 1889, reprint, Gettysburg, Pa., 1974), 73-89.

5. Hyde, *Following the Greek Cross*, 240; Descriptive List and Order Book, 5th Wisconsin Infantry, Record Group 94, NA; Franklin Jones to "Dear Wife and Children," February 18, 1865, in Franklin Jones Papers, New Jersey Historical Society. Jones died of chronic diarrhea on May 19, 1865, so he never tested his theory about the summertime utility of long whiskers.

6. John Michael Priest, ed., *Turn Them Out to Die Like a Mule: The Civil War Letters of Hospital Steward John N. Henry, 49th New York, 1861-1865* (Leesburg,

Va., 1995), 413; Tyler, *Recollections of the Civil War*, 332-333; Agassiz, ed., *Meade's Headquarters*, 316; Stevens, *Three Years in the Sixth Corps*, 429. The Sixth Corps maintained both field hospital facilities and a permanent hospital at City Point. The Second Division field hospital was near Patrick Station on the United States Military Railroad, close to the left end of the corps line.

7. Site Bulletin, City Point Unit, Petersburg National Battlefield. A good portion of the Union supply base at City Point is preserved by the National Park Service as the City Point Unit of Petersburg National Battlefield. One soldier in the 37th Massachusetts did describe a shortage of rations in the Sixth Corps: "The rations we draw this winter are very good what there is of them, but that is not half enough to eat. It is a general complaint throughout the corps." Edward A. to "Dear Mother," January 1, 1865, ts. in the collection of Pamplin Historical Park.

8. Trudeau, *The Last Citadel*, 298; John J. Ingraham to "Dear Sister," February 23, 1865, in John J. Ingraham Papers, Cornell University; George W. Buffum to "Sarah," January 18, 1865, in George W. Buffum Letters, 1864-1865, SHSW; wayside exhibit panel, Main Unit, Petersburg National Battlefield.

9. George W. Buffum to "Sarah," January 18, 1865, in George W. Buffum Letters, 1864-1865, SHSW; Inspection Report of Maj.[Lt. Col.] Hazard Stevens, Feb. 7, 1865, Record Group 94, NA; George Henry Bates to "Parents," February 4, 1865, in George Henry Bates Letters, Schoff Civil War Collection, University of Michigan; Billings, *Hardtack and Coffee*, 125-126; Order Book, 37th Massachusetts Infantry, Circular, Office Brigade Commissary, December 26, 1864, Record Group 94, NA. Dessicated vegetables were not new to the army. They had justly earned the disdain of soldiers for their unappetizing appearance and unappealing flavor. The troops nicknamed them "desecrated vegetables." Bell Irvin Wiley, *The Life of Billy Yank: The Common Soldier of the Union* (Indianapolis, 1942), 242. For more irreverent analysis of dessicated vegetables, see James I. Robertson, Jr., *Soldiers Blue and Gray* (Columbia, S.C., 1988), 70, and Billings, *Hardtack and Coffee*, 138-139.

10. Lothrup Lincoln Lewis, Diary, February 27, 1865, in Lothrup Lincoln Lewis Collection, LC; Tyler, *Recollections of the Civil War*, 319; William L. Phillips to "Father and Mother," December 26, 1864, in William L. Phillips Letters, SHSW; Hyde, *Following the Greek Cross*, 241. The 1st Maine Veteran Volunteer Infantry was organized on August 21, 1864 by consolidating the 5th, 6th, and 7th Maine regiments. All future references to the 1st Maine Veterans are to this unit, not the original 1st Maine Infantry which was mustered out of service on August 5, 1861.

11. Lothrup Lincoln Lewis, Diary, February 5, 1865, in Lothrup Lincoln Lewis Collection, LC; Nevins, ed., *A Diary of Battle*, 496; Ann Hartwell Britton and Thomas J. Reed, eds., *To My Beloved Wife and Boy at Home: The Letters and Diaries of Orderly Sergeant John F. L. Hartwell* (Madison, N.J., 1997), 333; Tyler, *Recollections of the Civil War*, 324.

12. Letters Sent Book, Sixth Army Corps, 1864-1865, Record Group 393, NA; Homer Curtis to "Dear Friends," February 10, 1865, in Homer Curtis Letters, YU. Miles's division shifted position as a result of the Battle of Hatcher's Run on

February 5-7, 1865. See Chapter Four for a discussion of this engagement. The 121st New York occupied the former camp of the 126th Ohio of Keifer's brigade. Lieutenant Philip R. Woodcock wrote that the regiment "fixed up our shanties good shape. 4 of us in a tent. . . . We are now near the Yellow House or Warren's Station. The R.R. runs only a few feet from our camp." See Philip R. Woodcock, Diary, February 9, 1865, in David Ward Collection, Lakeville, Connecticut.

13. George A. Cary to "My Dear Mother," February 15, 1865, in Cary Family Papers, University of Maine; Tyler, *Recollections of the Civil War*, 329; George W. Buffum to "wife and family," February 16, 1865, in George W. Buffum Letters, 1864-1865, SHSW. One wonders what had happened to Tyler's "palace."

14. J. Warren Keifer to "My Dear Wife," March 22, 1865, in Joseph Warren Keifer Papers, LC; Philip R. Woodcock, Diary, March 23, 1865, in David Ward Collection, Lakeville, Connecticut; Frank C. Morse to "My dear Nellie," March 24, 1865, in Frank C. Morse Papers, Massachusetts Historical Society. Sergeant John F. L. Hartwell of the 121st New York confided to his diary on March 23 that, "the air was full of sand most of the day so as to make it impossible to see but a very short distance at any time. Tents and any quantity of chimneys were blown down." See Britton and Reed, eds., *To My Beloved Wife and Boy at Home*, 340.

15. Homer Curtis to "Dear Friends," March 23, 1865, in Homer Curtis Letters, YU. Lieutenant Woodcock of the 121st New York identified March 16 as "the most windy day we have had . . . dust flew awful." Philip R. Woodcock, Diary, March 16, 1865, in David Ward Collection, Lakeville, Connecticut.

16. Franklin Jones to "My dear wife and children," February 26, 1865, in Franklin Jones Papers, New Jersey Historical Society; George J. Howard to "My Dear," February 26, 1865, in George J. Howard Letters, VTHS; John J. Ingraham to "My Dear Friend," February 3, 1865, in John J. Ingraham Papers, Cornell University; Olcott and Lear, *The Civil War Letters of Lewis Bissell*, 350; William L. Phillips to "Father and Mother," January 26, 1865, in William L. Phillips Letters, SHSW. Many soldiers maintained a close record of the weather, and their notations confirm that the winter of 1865 at Petersburg was relatively mild and snowless. See for example Ethel Lowerre Phelps, ed., "A Chaplain's Life in the Civil War: The Diary of Winthrop Henry Phelps," St. Paul, Minn., 1945, in Winthrop Henry Phelps Papers, LC. Sergeant John F. L. Hartwell of the 121st New York wrote his wife on February 25 that "We have no snow here nor have we had since I came back [on January 25] but [what] we have is Virginia mud knee deep everywhere." See Britton and Reed, eds., *To My Beloved Wife and Boy at Home*, 333. Lieutenant Michael Kelly of the 2nd Connecticut Heavy Artillery recorded in his diary on January 4, 1865 that "snow deep, 5 inches," but the next day he wrote that it was "awful muddy & slushy," indicating a quick thaw. See Michael Kelly, Diary, January 4-5, 1865, CHS. Private James L. Bowen of the 37th Massachusetts remembered that "The winter was very unpleasant. Little snow fell, but there was an abundance of rain and the armies literally lived in mud." See Bowen, "Lee in the Toils," in *Philadelphia Weekly Times*, May 2, 1885.

17. Letters Sent Book, Sixth Army Corps, 1864-1865, Part II, Entry 4407, Record Group 393, NA.

18. Olcott and Lear, *The Civil War Letters of Lewis Bissell*, 366; Andrew Burwell to "Dear Mary," February 3, 1865, in Burwell Letters, University of Southern Mississippi.

19. Joseph Case Rutherford to "My dear Son," March 8, 1865, in Joseph Case Rutherford Papers, UVM.

20. Trudeau, *The Last Citadel*, 289; Waite, "Three Years with the Tenth Vermont," II, 239; Tyler, *Recollections of the Civil War*, 336-337; Olcott and Lear, *The Civil War Letters of Lewis Bissell*, 344; George A. Cary, Diary, February 21, 1865, in Cary Family Papers, University of Maine; Lothrup Lincoln Lewis, Diary, February 13, 1865, in Lothrup Lincoln Lewis Collection, LC; William L. Phillips to "Father and Mother," February 12, 1865, in William L. Phillips Letters, SHSW. Sergeant Hartwell of the 121st New York referred to Fort Fisher as "a new Fort" in his diary entry of January 3, 1865, and William Phillips of the 5th Wisconsin mistakenly reported that the fort was an expansion of an existing Confederate installation. See Britton and Reed, eds., *To My Beloved Wife and Boy at Home*, 326. Construction actually began in mid-October by the Union Ninth Corps and the fort was named by October 23. The small, original redoubt had its gorge stockaded by December 28. Shortly thereafter, work began on its expansion. Fort Fisher was named in honor of Lieutenant Otis Fisher of the 8th U.S. Infantry who was mortally wounded on September 30, 1864 near the fort's future site. "He was ever brave and ready in action, hightoned and chivalrous, and his loss is sincerely mourned," wrote Brigadier General Orlando B. Willcox. See *OR* 42, pt. 1, 554. Fort Fisher is very well preserved in 2000 at the intersection of Flank and Church roads within the boundaries of Petersburg National Battlefield.

21. J. Williard Brown, *The Signal Corps, U.S.A., in the War of the Rebellion* (Boston, 1896, reprint, Baltimore, 1996), 394; Frank C. Morse to "My dear bosom companion," March 4, 1865, in Frank C. Morse Papers, Massachusetts Historical Society; Homer Curtis to "Dear Mother," February 21, 1865, in Homer Curtis Letters, YU; Olcott and Lear, *The Civil War Letters of Lewis Bissell*, 343; Samuel Z. Ammen, "Maryland Troops in the Confederate Army," 2 vols., I, 170, in Thomas Clemens Collection, USAMHI. Work on the signal tower began on December 20, but inclement weather delayed its completion until late February. Sergeant Berry Benson of McGowan's South Carolina Brigade wrote on February 2, 1865 about the last stages of its construction. See Berry G. Benson, "Reminiscences," 595, in Berry G. Benson Papers, SHC. Also, Corporal Lewis Bissell of the 2nd Connecticut Heavy Artillery wrote on February 19 about the tower still being under construction. Sergeant Hartwell of the 121st New York told his wife that a "100 foot pine tree used as a look out post for pickets" provided another opportunity for scanning the Confederate lines. "Very few soldiers dare climb to the dizzy top but I have been up 3 times & the last time had a field glass," Hartwell wrote. "I enjoyed the sight greatly & remained up there for nearly an hour getting a plan of a portion of their works in our immediate front." See Britton and Reed, eds., *To My Beloved Wife and Boy at*

Home, 335. The site of the famous signal tower lies along the east side of Church Road north of its intersection with Squirrel Level Road. Nothing remains on the ground to identify its precise location.

22. Circular, HQ 3rd Bde., 1st Div., 6th A.C., January 9, 1865, Part II, Entry 4418, Record Group 393, NA; Hyde, *Following the Greek Cross*, 240.

23. William L. Phillips to Henry L. Phillips, January 25, 1865, and William L. Phillips to "Father and Mother," February 19, 1865, both in William L. Phillips Letters, SHSW; Michael Kelly, Diary, January 8-9, 1865, CHS.

24. Rhodes, "The Second Rhode Island Volunteers," in *Rhode Island Soldiers and Sailors Historical Society*, X, 443-445; Edward S. Roberts, "War Reminiscences," in *Connecticut Western News* (Canaan, Conn.) January 4, 1912.

25. Warren Williams to "My Dear Companion & Children," March 9, 1865, in Warren Williams Papers, University of Wisconsin, Milwaukee; Andrew Burwell [Salutation missing], March 24, 1865, in Burwell Letters, University of Southern Mississippi; Olcott and Lear, *The Civil War Letters of Lewis Bissell*, 333. William L. Phillips of the 5th Wisconsin wrote that as a private he had "to go on picket 48 hours out of every 8 days and 24 hours camp guard. . . ." See Phillips to "Grandfather and Grandmother," January 4, 1865, in William L. Phillips Letters, SHSW.

26. Olcott and Lear, *The Civil War Letters of Lewis Bissell*, 332; Rhodes, "The Second Rhode Island Volunteers," X, 447; Roberts, "War Reminiscences," in *Connecticut Western News*, January 11, 1912; Lothrup Lincoln Lewis, Diary, January 6, 1865, in Lothrup Lincoln Lewis Collection, LC.

27. Caldwell, *The History of a Brigade of South Carolinians*, 253-254.

28. James Lane, "History of Lane's North Carolina Brigade," in *SHSP*, IX, 354; William H. McLaurin, "Eighteenth Regiment," in Walter Clark, ed., *Histories of the Several Regiments and Battalions from North Carolina in the Great War 1861-'65* (5 vols.; Goldsboro, N.C., 1901, reprint, Wendell, N.C., 1982), II, 59; Hyde, *Following the Greek Cross*, 241-242; Charles A. Milliken to Major Charles Mundee, January 9, 1865, Letters Received Book, Sixth Army Corps, 1862-1865, Part II, Entry 4414, Record Group 393, NA. William L. Phillips of the 5th Wisconsin described in vivid detail one of the Confederate raids in which the Southerners employed owl hoots and quail whistles as signals for their attacks. Phillips barely escaped both capture and wounding during this December 30, 1864 episode. See William L. Phillips to "Father and Mother," January 1, 1865, in William L. Phillips Letters, SHSW.

29. Olsen, ed., *Upon the Tented Field*, 294-295.

30. Both of these episodes, perhaps more colorful than literally true in all regards, are related in Waite, "Three Years With the Tenth Vermont," II, 240-242.

31. Benson, "Reminiscences," 599, 610-611, in Berry G. Benson Papers, SHC.

32. Samuel Dorrah [salutation missing], n.d., in Samuel Lewers Dorrah Papers, 1861-1868, USC.

33. Olcott and Lear, *The Civil War Letters of Lewis Bissell*, 338; Bilby, *Three Rousing Cheers*, 232; George W. Buffum to wife, December 11, 1864, in George W. Buffum Letters, 1864-1865, SHSW; William J. Miller, Memoir, 12, in William J.

Miller Papers, Winthrop University; Benson, "Reminiscences," 594, in Berry G. Benson Papers, SHC; Dayton E. Flint to "My dear Sister," February 21, 1865, in Dayton E. Flint Papers, Civil War Miscellaneous Collection, USAMHI.

34. Henry Houghton, "The Ordeal of Civil War: A Recollection," in *Vermont History*, XLI, 45. Major Mason Tyler of the 37th Massachusetts confirmed that such wood-cutting experiences were not unique to Houghton: "Just below Fort Fisher the opposing lines are so near together that the men from both sides chop wood from the same trees and are on perfectly good terms." Tyler, *Recollections of the Civil War*, 337. See also James Armstrong, *Carolina Light Infantry's Record in the Great War: The Story of a Gallant Company* (Charleston, S.C., 1912), 9.

35. Olcott and Lear, *The Civil War Letters of Lewis Bissell*, 335; Bilby, *Three Rousing Cheers*, 231; *The Winsted* (Conn.) *Herald*, February 24, 1865. William E. H. Morse of the 1st Maine Veterans wrote on February 14, 1865 that "today I am given a new musket and equipments. . . ," "The 'Rebellion Record' of an Enlisted Man," in *National Tribune Scrapbook* (Washington, 1909), 97-98.

36. Dayton E. Flint to "My dear Sister," February 21, 1865, in Dayton E. Flint Papers, Civil War Miscellaneous Collection, USAMHI; Hazard Stevens to "Dear Mother," March 10, 1865, in Hazard Stevens Papers, LC. A copy of "The Old Sixth Corps" is in the George W. Getty Papers, Gibson-Getty-McClure Family Papers, LC. "The Old Sixth Corps" contains eight stanzas of dubious literary quality. The absence of sheet music prevents a judgment of its musical value, although the lyrics' rhythm suggests that it could be sung to the tune of "The Bonnie Blue Flag." One copy of the lyrics advises that "Soldiers can receive 14 songs for 50 cents, 30 for $1, sent by mail, postage free, to all parts of the army, by addressing G.P. Hardwick, Washington, D.C."

37. John F.L. Hartwell to "My Beloved Wife & Boy," March 16,1865, in Britton and Reed, eds., *To My Beloved Wife and Boy at Home*, 336-337. Hartwell made it clear that he managed to avoid descending into any of these bad habits.

38. Hyde, *Following the Greek Cross*, 241; J. Warren Keifer to "My Dear Wife," March 9, 1865, in Joseph Warren Keifer Papers, LC; James Harper to "Dear Al," March 2, 1865, in John Harper Papers, HSWP.

39. Thomas P. Lowry, *The Story The Soldiers Wouldn't Tell: Sex in the Civil War* (Mechanicsburg, Pa., 1994), 29; Britton and Reed, eds., *To My Beloved Wife and Boy at Home*, 337. It is assumed that the daily income cited in the text included gratuities.

40. Warren Williams to "My Dear Family," February 20, 1865, in Warren Williams Papers, University of Wisconsin, Milwaukee. Williams's regiment was in Wheaton's division, which also contained the New Jersey Brigade, but Williams did not identify the regiment to which the pregnant soldier belonged. The *Portsmouth* (N.H.) *Daily Morning Chronicle* of March 30, 1865, reported under "Infantry Item" that a corporal of the 18th New Hampshire fell ill on duty at Petersburg, was taken to the hospital, and there delivered a baby boy. The paper suggested that the corporal deserved a promotion. The 18th New Hampshire belonged to the Ninth Corps, but the incident may have been the same one mentioned by Williams and

simply corrupted in the retelling. I am indebted to William Marvel, a historian uniquely qualified in such matters, for acquainting me with this source.

41. Charles W. Wall to "Dear Mother," March 16, 1865, in Wall Family Papers, Cornell University; J. Warren Keifer to "My Dear Wife," March 17, 1865, in Joseph Warren Keifer Papers, LC; Agassiz, ed., *Meade's Headquarters*, 321-322; George H. Mellish to "Dear Mother," March 17, 1865, in George H. Mellish Papers, HEH; Isaac O. Best, *History of the 121st New York State Infantry* (Chicago, 1921, reprint, Baltimore, 1996), 205.

42. Report of Chaplain Lemuel Thomas Foote to Brig. Gen. S[eth] Thomas, January 31, 1865, in Lemuel Thomas Foote Papers, LC.

43. Frank C. Morse to "My own dear Nellie," February 1, 1865, in Frank C. Morse Papers, Massachusetts Historical Society; Lemuel T. Foote, Report to Brig. Gen. S[eth] Thomas, January 31, 1865, in Lemuel Thomas Foote Papers, LC; Andrew Burwell to "My Darling Wife," March 22, 1865, in Burwell Letters, University of Southern Mississippi; Hazard Stevens to "Dear Mother," March 4, 1865, in Hazard Stevens Papers, LC.

44. Bilby, *Three Rousing Cheers*, 231; Frank C. Morse to "My dear Nellie," February 2, 1865, in Frank C. Morse Papers, Massachusetts Historical Society; Olcott and Lear, *The Civil War Letters of Lewis Bissell*, 350; Agassiz, ed., *Meade's Headquarters*, 311-312; Michael Kelly, Diary, March 9, 1865, CHS. The church was a part of a little village of tidy Gothic-style cottages that composed the regiment's winter camp. See Trudeau, *The Last Citadel*, 297. Construction on the church was in progress by January 22, but as late as March 13, the engineers continued to improve their structure. Lieutenant Philip R. Woodcock of the 121st New York wrote in his diary that day, "Went over to see the chapel which is being built by the 50th N Y Engineers. A splendid piece of architecture. [It is] the prettiest thing I have seen." See Thomas James Owen to "Dear Father, Mother, and Sister," January 22, 1864 [sic], in Dale E. Floyd, ed., *"Dear Friends at Home. . .": The Letters and Diary of Thomas James Owen, Fiftieth New York Volunteer Engineer Regiment, During the Civil War* (Washington, 1985), 71, and Philip R. Woodcock, Diary, March 13, 1865, in David Ward Collection, Lakeville, Connecticut. Of course, this was not the only army church constructed and patronized by the Sixth Corps during the winter. Sergeant Hartwell of the 121st New York mentioned that he "worked on the Brigade Chapel" in his diary entry of January 28, 1865. See Britton and Reed, eds., *To My Beloved Wife and Boy at Home*, 330. The 50th New York Engineers' church was located along the Union lines between Squirrel Level and Vaughan roads.

45. Quoted in Robertson, *Soldiers Blue and Gray*, 78; James Harper to "Dear Al," March 2, 1865, in John Harper Papers, HSWP; Roberts, "War Reminiscences," in *Connecticut Western News*, January 4, 1912; William McVey, Diary, February 28, 1865, in William McVey Papers, Ohio Historical Society. One must imagine that payday brought a certain joy to at least one neighborhood at City Point as well.

46. Olcott and Lear, *The Civil War Letters of Lewis Bissell*, 337; Frank C. Morse to "My own dear Nellie," February 10, 1865, in Frank C. Morse Papers,

Massachusetts Historical Society; Warren Williams to "My Dear Companion & Children," February 26, 1865, in Warren Williams Papers, University of Wisconsin, Milwaukee; David S. Sparks, ed., *Inside Lincoln's Army: The Diary of Marsena Rudolph Patrick, Provost Marshal General, Army of the Potomac* (New York, 1964), 458.

47. James Denton to "Dear Brother," January 20, 1865, in James Denton Letters, Rutgers University; James Harper to "Dear Al," March 2, 1865, in John Harper Papers, HSWP; Philip R. Woodcock, Diary, February 28 and March 1, 1865, in David Ward Collection, Lakeville, Connecticut; Homer Curtis to "Dear Mother," February 20, 1865, in Homer Curtis Letters, YU; Charles G. Gould to "Dear Mother," March 19, 1865, in Captain Charles Gilbert Gould Collection, UVM. Efforts to raise funds for a Sedgwick monument began in November 1864, while the corps was still in the Shenandoah Valley. On October 21, 1868, a statue of the general was dedicated at the United States Military Academy at West Point, cast in bronze from three Confederate cannons captured by the Sixth Corps in battle. See Richard Elliott Winslow III, *General John Sedgwick* (Novato, Cal., 1982), 177.

48. Olcott and Lear, *The Civil War Letters of Lewis Bissell*, 345; William B. Adams to "Sister Dora," February 26, 1865, in William Bryant Adams Papers, Maine Historical Society; Altus H. Jewell to "Dear Sister," March 8, 1865, in Sgt. Altus H. Jewell Papers, USAMHI.

49. John J. Ingraham to "My dear Friend," March 14, 1865, in John J. Ingraham Papers, Cornell University; John F.L. Hartwell to "My Beloved Wife," March 19, 1865, in Britton and Reed, eds., *To My Beloved Wife and Boy at Home*, 339-340.

50. J. Warren Keifer to "My Dear Wife," March 7, 1865, in Joseph Warren Keifer Papers, LC.

51. Charles C. Morey to "Dear Mother," March 17, 1865, in Charles Carroll Morey Papers, Stuart Goldman Collection, USAMHI; George A. Cary to "Dear Friends," March 15, 1865, in Cary Family Papers, University of Maine; Homer Curtis to "Dear Friends," March 21,1865, in Homer Curtis Letters, YU. Captain Michael Kelly of the 2nd Connecticut Heavy Artillery did not appreciate the high-level review. "Very warm, almost as the 4 of July," he wrote. "Many of the men fell out, some had to go in the ambulances & be carried to camp, some to hospital. We were all pretty well played out, so many hours on foot, waiting in line under a hot sun & marching. Its no fun to us, we don't like it, we want to fight & wind up this war, that's what we came for." See Michael Kelly, Diary, March 20, 1865, CHS. Lewis Bissell placed the First Division review on March 22, but this is in error because he dated the letter in which he described the review as *Monday* March 22. March 22, 1865, was a Wednesday. Olcott and Lear, *The Civil War Letters of Lewis Bissell*, 352. Philip R. Woodcock indicated that on March 19, General Meade participated in his [Hamblin's] brigade's monthly inspection and "complimented us highly on our appearance." Philip R. Woodcock, Diary, March 19, 1865, in David Ward Collection, Lakeville, Connecticut.

52. James Lane, "Glimpses of Army Life in 1864," in *SHSP*, XVIII, 415-416; Robert R. Hemphill to "My dear Calvin," December 3, 1864, in *The Medium,*

(Abbeville S.C.), October 11, 1900; Berry Benson to his father, February 27, 1865, in Berry G. Benson Papers, SHC.

53. Morse, "The 'Rebellion Record' of an Enlisted Man," in *National Tribune Scrapbook*, 96; John F.L. Hartwell to 'My Dear Wife," March 9, 1865, in Britton and Reed, eds., *To My Beloved Wife and Boy at Home*, 334; William L. Phillips to "Father and Mother," February 19, 1865, in William L. Phillips Letters, SHSW; Bilby, *Three Rousing Cheers*, 235. The Confederates did not treat deserters as prisoners of war. Instead, the government offered them the option of seeking sanctuary in the South or being smuggled back into the North at an unguarded point. Such a policy encouraged selfish or demoralized Federals to abandon their comrades.

54. Ida Bright Adams, ed., "The Civil War Letters of James Rush Holmes," in *The Western Pennsylvania Historical Magazine*, XLIV, no.2, 124-125; George W. Buffum to "wife and family," January 7, 1865, in George W. Buffum Letters, 1864-1865, SHSW; Olcott and Lear, *The Civil War Letters of Lewis Bissell*, 334; Bilby, *Three Rousing Cheers*, 231. The victim of this sentence was Corporal Peter Cox of the 4th New Jersey, a deserter. George Henry Bates and Michael Kelly of the 2nd Connecticut Heavy Artillery also described this execution, but misidentified the condemned man as Peter McCox. See Bates to "Parents," January 8, 1865, in George Henry Bates Letters, Schoff Civil War Collection, University of Michigan, and Michael Kelly, Diary, January 6, 1865, CHS. Fridays seemed to be the designated day for executions. See Sergeant Londus W. Haskell to "Dear Mother," January 1, 1865, in Jeffrey D. Marshall, ed., *A War of the People: Vermont Civil War Letters* (Hanover, N.H., 1999), 285.

55. Nevins, ed., *A Diary of Battle*, 498; Joseph C. Rutherford to "My dear Son," March 8, 1865, in Joseph Case Rutherford Papers, UVM; J. Warren Keifer to "My Dear Wife," March 11, 1865, in Joseph Warren Keifer Papers, LC; Michael Kelly, Diary, January 6, 1865, CHS. Edward Roberts of the 2nd Connecticut Heavy Artillery described Kelley's execution in some detail: "I . . . saw a deserter shot he followed his coffin around between two lines of soldiers the coffin was carried by four men he following with a platoon of soldiers front and rear the Band played it was a sad scene he bore it manfully not a muscle moved. . . ." Edward S. Roberts, Diary, March 11, 1865, CHS. Not every Union soldier opposed capital punishment, of course. Provost Marshal General Marsena Patrick expressed no regret regarding a March 18 execution except that the firing squad jumped the gun and unleashed its volley at the command "aim." See Sparks, ed., *Inside Lincoln's Army*, 481. There are many other examples of March executions in the Sixth Corps. See for instance Wilbur Fisk to "Editor Freeman," March 24, 1865, in Wilbur Fisk Papers, LC, published as Emil and Ruth Rosenblatt, eds., *Hard Marching Every Day: The Civil War Letters of Private Wilbur Fisk, 1861-1865* (Lawrence, Kans., 1992), 318; Morse, "The 'Rebellion Record' of an Enlisted Man," in *National Tribune Scrapbook*, 97-98; and John Preston Campbell to "Dear Father," March 14, 1865, in Corporal John Preston Campbell Papers, Civil War Miscellaneous Collection, USAMHI.

56. Sparks, ed., *Inside Lincoln's Army*, 471; Bilby, *Three Rousing Cheers*, 233-235; Phelps, ed.,"A Chaplain's Life in the Civil War," in Winthrop Henry Phelps Papers, LC; Olcott and Lear, *The Civil War Letters of Lewis Bissell*, 338; George Mellish to "Dear Mother," March 18, 1865, in George H. Mellish Papers, HEH; William L. Phillips to "Father and Mother," n.d., in William L. Phillips Letters, SHSW.

57. James Harper to "Dear Al," March 2, 1865, in John Harper Papers, HSWP; David E. Soule, "Recollections of the Civil War," in *New Milford* (Conn.) *Gazette*, June 28, 1912; George G. Benedict, *Vermont in the Civil War: A History of the Part Taken by the Vermont Soldiers and Sailors in the War for the Union 1861-65* (2 vols.; Burlington, Vt., 1886-1888), I, 202,175; Hazard Stevens to "Dear Mother," January 25, 1865, in Hazard Stevens Papers, LC.

58. Hazard Stevens to "Dear Mother," February 27, and January 25, 1865, in Hazard Stevens Papers, LC; Olsen, ed., *Upon the Tented Field*, 298; J. Warren Keifer to "My Dear Wife," March 18, 1865, in Joseph Warren Keifer Papers, LC. Sergeant John F. L. Hartwell wrote his wife on March 24 that "everything looks favorable for a speedy close of this War by unconditional submission to the laws of the 'Govt' by those now in rebellion." He carefully outlined Lee's strategic options of surrender—desperate attack, or evacuation to the mountains—and concluded that the Confederate commander was "in a bad fix and will soon be in a worse one if he dont look out." See Hartwell to "My Dear Wife," March 24, 1865, in Britton and Reed, eds., *To My Beloved Wife and Boy at Home*, 342. Not every Sixth Corps veteran felt so optimistic. Homer Curtis told his family on February 6 that he did not "anticipate any great results from the movements afoot—as I have a firm belief in the proverbial 'bad luck' of the Army of the Potomac—but I hope there will be nothing very disastrous at least. Our army seems fated to achieve nothing substantial in the way of victory. Will it be to the end?" Homer Curtis to "Dear Ma & Sisters," February 6, 1865, in Homer Curtis Letters, YU.

59. Nevins, ed., *A Diary of Battle*, 498-99.

60. George Mellish to "Dear Mother," March 13, 1865, in George H. Mellish Papers, HEH; J. Warren Keifer to "My Dear Eliza," March 5, 1865, in Joseph Warren Keifer Papers, LC; Michael Kelly, Diary, March 1, 1865, CHS.

61. Brevet Major General J. G. Barnard, *A Report on the Defenses of Washington to the Chief Engineers, U.S. Army* (Washington, 1871), 150. Two published Confederate reports provide a somewhat different description of the Confederate picket line's location and configuration. Lieutenant James Fitz James Caldwell of McGowan's staff placed the Confederate picket line an average of five hundred yards from the primary works, but given the verifiable location of the Confederate rifle pits established after March 25, this seems too close to the main line. See Caldwell, *The History of a Brigade of South Carolinians*, 252. Sergeant Berry Benson, another member of McGowan's Brigade, specified that the picket posts were "a succession of small earthworks at about twenty-yard intervals called rifle pits." See Susan Williams Benson, ed., *Berry Benson's Civil War Book* (Athens, Ga., 1992), 174. Only isolated fragments of the original Confederate picket line

remain, so it is impossible to reconcile the discrepancies in these descriptions. Given the length of time the Confederates defended their lines and the inherently dangerous position occupied by the pickets, it is easy to imagine constant improvements to what were originally rifle pits, lending them the appearance if not the absolute reality of an uninterrupted line of works.

62. Agassiz, ed., *Meade's Headquarters*, 334; Lewis A. Grant, "The Old Vermont Brigade at Petersburg," in *Glimpses of the Nation's Struggle. A Series of Papers Read Before the Minnesota Commandery of the Military Order of the Loyal Legion of the United States* (St. Paul, Minn.,1887, reprint, Wilmington, N.C., 1992), 395; James P. Matthews, "How General A. P. Hill Met His Fate," in *SHSP*, XXVII, 28; Hazard Stevens, "The Storming of the Lines of Petersburg by the Sixth Corps, April 2, 1865," in *PMHSM* (14 vols.;Boston, 1907, reprint, Wilmington, N.C., 1989), VI, 418.

63. Stevens, "The Storming of the Lines of Petersburg," in *PMHSM*, VI, 418; Caldwell, *The History of a Brigade of South Carolinians*, 254; Major Lemuel A. Abbott, *Personal Recollections and Civil War Diary, 1864* (Burlington, Vt., 1908), 262; Keifer, *Slavery and Four Years of War*, II, 193; Benson, "Reminiscences," 557-558, in Berry G. Benson Papers, SHC. The Confederates revetted their works by placing logs on all the interior exposed surfaces and around the shoulders of the narrow openings and artillery embrasures. They also constructed a banquette or firing step to allow the riflemen access to the slits below the headlogs or so that they could fire over the parapet. Pamplin Historical Park preserves an outstanding section of these original works in which all the engineering features described (save the wooden elements long ago rotted away) may be observed. Much of the rest of the line survives elsewhere on private property, including the author's. Pamplin Historical Park has reconstructed at full scale a portion of the Confederate line as an outdoor exhibit.

64. Westwood A. Todd, "Reminiscences of the War Between the States April 1861-July 1865," 283, in the Westwood A. Todd Papers, SHC; Lane, "Glimpses of Army Life in 1864," in *SHSP*, XVIII, 416; Julius A. Lineback, Diary, January 21, 1865, in Julius A. Lineback Papers, SHC; Giles B. Cooke, "When With General Lee," in *CV* (40 vols.; Nashville, 1893-1932), XXXVII, 183; Caldwell, *The History of a Brigade of South Carolinians*, 251, n.1; George H. Mills, *History of the 16th North Carolina Regiment in the Civil War* (Rutherfordton, N.C., 1897, reprint, Hamilton, N.Y., 1992), 59, 63. There are no visible remains of the dam along Rohoic Creek, which broke with spectacular results in January but was quickly repaired. Two military dams may be seen in Pamplin Historical Park, although neither played a role in the April 2, 1865 attack. Remains of what may be the mine shaft described by Mills extending from the Confederate works near the modern intersection of Squirrel Level and Defense roads were found in 1997 during the construction of the New Millennium Studios in Petersburg.

65. Lane, "Glimpses of Army Life in 1864," in *SHSP*, XVIII, 416; Olcott and Lear, *The Civil War Letters of Lewis Bissell*, 352. Work on the Confederate fortifications continued throughout the winter and early spring. On March 26, an

officer in the 2nd Maryland Battalion of William McComb's Brigade reported that, "Our works still demand additions, and at 9 o'clock I am detailed to take charge of a fatigue detail from the brigade to strengthen the fortifications." See Ammen, "Maryland Troops in the Confederate Army," I, 177, in Thomas Clemens Collection, USAMHI.

66. Waite, "Three Years With the Tenth Vermont," II, 243.

67. Benedict, *Vermont in the Civil War*, I, 579.

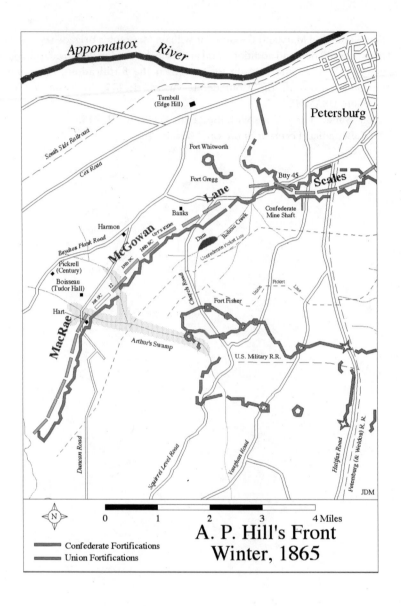

Appomattox River

Petersburg

Turnbull (Edge Hill)

South Side Railroad

Cox Road

Fort Whitworth

Fort Gregg

Btty 45

Scales

Lane

Banks

Confederate Mine Shaft

Harmon

McGowan

Orr's Rifles

14th SC

14th SC

Dam

Bobove Creek

Confederate Picket Line

Pickrell (Century)

Boisseau (Tudor Hall)

Boydton Plank Road

1st SC

12

Union

Picket

Line

Picket

Church Road

Fort Fisher

Hart

MacRae

Arthur's Swamp

U.S. Military R.R.

Duncan Road

Squirrel Level Road

Vaughan Road

Hatfax Road

Petersburg (& Weldon) R. R.

JDM

N

0   1   2   3   4 Miles

A. P. Hill's Front
Winter, 1865

Confederate Fortifications
Union Fortifications

Chapter Three

A. P. Hill's Corps

Survives the Winter

L aughter echoed throughout the parlor of the large frame house on Duncan Road. Three young officers, and a fourth man obviously their senior, exchanged playing cards along with good-natured banter while heat from a wood stove supplemented the warm fellowship of the occasion. The building they occupied, just behind Confederate lines some six miles southwest of Petersburg, served as the workplace and residence for more than half a dozen South Carolinians and their general, who bore responsibility for some 1,400 troops camped outside their door.

Brigadier General Samuel McGowan, the leader at the whist table and of all the soldiers in the immediate vicinity, had established his headquarters in the home of Joseph and Ann Boisseau in early October 1864. The Boisseaus were respected residents of Dinwiddie County and proprietors of a large farm situated a few hundred yards south of the Boydton Plank Road. McGowan and his staff had reconfigured the commodious two-and-a-half-story dwelling into a combination office and dormitory. The South Carolinians spent the winter of 1864-1865 tending to the needs of their men while passing their leisure time in various elevated pursuits. "We frequently entertained one another with recitals from the poets and dramatists," reported one of the general's aides. "General McGowan led in this, having committed to memory many passages of Milton, Shakespeare and others. I learned [Richard Henry] Wilde's 'My Life is Like the Summer Rose' from his recital."[1]

Brigadier General Samuel McGowan

National Archives

Both in the discharge of his official duties and during social occasions, McGowan hosted many visiting officers that winter, including his military neighbors, William MacRae and Henry Heth, whose own headquarters were located a few hundred yards southeast on Duncan Road and one-half mile northwest along the Boydton Plank Road, respectively. Division commander Heth passed the winter with the help of a friend named Ficklin, who operated blockade runners out of Wilmington, North Carolina. In exchange for cotton traded at Liverpool, Ficklin returned to the Cape Fear River laden with consumer goods. At his enterprising friend's invitation, Heth sent a wagon to Wilmington that Ficklin stuffed with "canned goods, coffee, tea, sugar, hams, twenty gallons of brandy, and the same amount of whiskey, a dozen boxes of fine cigars, etc." Heth's headquarters may have rung even more joyously than McGowan's when the contents of Ficklin's wagon reached their destination.[2]

Of course, the Confederate rank and file never shared the exalted lifestyles of brigade and division commanders. The powerful works that so impressed Wright's soldiers protected the makeshift encampments of portions of Heth's and Cadmus M. Wilcox's divisions of A.P. Hill's corps, the units assigned to the lines opposite the Federal Sixth Corps. McGowan's Palmetto-Staters and James Lane's North Carolina Brigade occupied the ground closest to Wright's Yankees. McGowan's five regiments held the earthworks between MacRae's troops on their right and Lane's on their left. The 1st South Carolina anchored McGowan's right, adjoined in order to the left by the 12th, 13th, 14th, and Orr's Rifles, which linked with Lane's Brigade on its left. Lane's units, in turn, covered the fortifications from just southwest of the Banks House, across Church Road, and a little beyond the impounded waters of Rohoic Creek below Battery 45, where they connected with Brigadier General Alfred M. Scales's Tarheel regiments. McGowan's and Lane's camps stretched along nearly two and one-half miles of the Confederate front.[3]

A scarcity of building materials in the early winter and a desire for protection from potential artillery bombardment compelled many of these men to burrow into the ground for their initial shelter. One of Wilcox's soldiers described his dugout as containing 100 square feet sunk six feet into the earth and covered with a matrix of logs. He then installed a layer of boughs and leaves on which he stacked a pile of dirt "till it is shaped like a potato hill." Equipped with a chimney, this subterranean abode performed creditable service. By mid-winter, however, most of the underground quarters had been replaced by conventional huts similar in design to those built by the Federals. "The camps are as well selected as circumstances will permit, and are well drained," reported McGowan's brigade inspector. "The police of camps and quarters is fair and improvement is noted."[4]

Some Confederates chose to utilize canvas for their winter shelters. Sergeant-Major Robert R. Hemphill of Orr's Rifles helped his colonel, George M. Miller, transform a large officer's wall tent and fly into a rustically elegant domicile:

> The entrance is to the south and the chimney is just beside the door. We
> have a small fire place which is lined with rock, the chimney being made of
> wood and mud. At the back of the tent we have a bedstead, made of rough

plank, about 4 feet wide and 6 ½ feet long and to make it downy we have some pine leaves under our blankets and for a pillow we have a pair of saddle bags. At the left hand corner as we enter and in the rear of the tent we have a forked stick driven into the ground on which we hang our haversacks and Col. Miller's sword. Col. Miller has a pine stool with a back to it and I have a buggy cushion which I picked up on one of our movements and which I put on a stick of wood and make a seat. In a crack in the chimney Col. Miller lays his pipe and I carry mine in my pocket and at the head of our bed we have two or three bags of smoking tobacco drawn from the Government.[5]

Just like their Unionist counterparts, Lee's soldiers erected a hodgepodge of temporary quarters, expedients that gave the camps a ramshackle appearance. Hill's troops transformed the level ground behind their sector of the works into a collection of small military villages in which various pleasant diversions tempered the austerity of martial routine.[6]

The winter of 1864-1865 witnessed a renewal of religious interest in the Army of Northern Virginia. Some 60 temporary chapels served various regiments, although the level of pious fervor during the previous two winters equaled and perhaps exceeded the righteous enthusiasm displayed in the Petersburg camps. In December, a group of the most highly-respected chaplains formed an association to systematically address the veterans' spiritual needs. One soldier testified that the preachers conducted prayer meetings twice per week, with two additional services on the Sabbath. "Their are several preachers with our Brigade now among them Mr. Wingate & Mr. Pritchard from Raleigh—and they are trying to start a revival," wrote Captain James A. Graham of the 27th North Carolina of John R. Cooke's Brigade, "but it seems to work rather slowly." Perhaps the men of Graham's regiment preferred to attend the popular school over which the captain presided. "There will be about one hundred and fifty scholars in all—some of whom do not know the letters," wrote Lieutenant Colonel Joseph C. Webb. "The men seem to enter into it with a determination to learn."[7]

Although the basic tenets of military drill held fewer mysteries for most Confederate soldiers than the complexities of the English language, Southern officers did not neglect routine training during the winter. Competitions between regiments in rival divisions provided an additional stimulus to maintain mastery over the soldiers' art. Sam McGowan took particular pride in the precision of his unit and frequently challenged Harry Heth's brigades to compare proficiencies.

On one occasion in March, McGowan invited General Cooke to a match testing both facility in drill and scrutiny under inspection. Cooke replied that he would bring two of his regiments, either one of which would prevail over the best McGowan could muster. Cooke's confidence may have unnerved the South Carolinian, who attempted to change the rules by selecting the finest regiment from Wilcox's entire command to defend the division's honor. Cooke understandably objected to such an arrangement, but stood by his boast that either one of his top two regiments was the superior to the pride of McGowan's own brigade—and he would be willing to let McGowan choose which of the two Tarheel outfits would compete.

The day for this grudge match arrived and an eager audience gathered at Heth's headquarters (Cooke thus had the home-field advantage), including numerous brigade commanders, John B. Gordon, Wilcox, Heth, and Robert E. Lee himself. Cooke brought along the 15th and 27th North Carolina regiments and McGowan selected the former as his opponent. "To the delight" of the North Carolinians and, no doubt, General Heth, Cooke's unit prevailed in both drill and inspection. Lieutenant Colonel Webb observed General Lee during the review and noted the commander's approbation. Heth then asked the 27th North Carolina to go through the manual of arms, an exercise from which the division commander derived "especial gratification."[8]

The soldiers spent their evenings in camp writing letters, mending clothing, smoking or chewing tobacco, and making or listening to music. Scarcely a tent, dugout, or hut lacked at least one occupant who possessed an instrument and some degree of philharmonic skill. Of course, a number of the units in Hill's command maintained regimental bands which performed for the officers and men. Orr's Rifles mustered a musical aggregation of ten which routinely entertained its camp mates around a roaring fire. One source identified the 1st South Carolina band, also in McGowan's Brigade, as being composed predominantly of "free persons of color." Julius A. Lineback, who served with the 26th North Carolina band in MacRae's Brigade, made note of a January serenade performed for General Heth at the request of General Lane. The Tennessee Glee Club, a vocal group in William McComb's Brigade, sang hymns and performed other selections both for the benefit of their comrades and for their brigade and division commanders.[9]

Although Confederate soldiers largely entertained themselves, the occasional visitor offered welcome diversion. One particularly memorable personality made the rounds in Wilcox's Division in December. Introduced with much fanfare as Professor R. O. Davidson, this flamboyantly scientific gentleman unveiled a plan for subduing the Northern army and ending the war.

Professor Davidson had supposedly invented a flying machine styled the "Artis Avis," or " Bird of Art" to the classically educated. The airship, as Davidson described it, was manufactured of hoop iron and wire covered with white oak and powered by a one-horse-power steam engine. One aeronaut would command each Artis Avis, equipped with various navigational devices and carrying a payload of artillery shells. A foot-activated spring allowed the aviator to rain projectiles onto the enemy scaring away the Yankees he did not kill. The professor assured his listeners that a successful prototype had been tested, but that the Confederate government had declined to fund production of a fleet. Thus, he now appealed directly to the men who would benefit the most from his innovation.

While some men in Edward L. Thomas's Brigade ridiculed the idea, enough endorsed the scheme to contribute $116.00 toward the project. Many in McGowan's Brigade responded similarly to the sharper's appeal for a dollar from each soldier. "Quite an idea if he can only succeed and who knows but what he will," wrote a soldier in the 45th Georgia. "He says he will be ready for active operations by the middle of February next." Predictably, no Artis Avis ever appeared, and the learned con-artist disappeared along with the wages of the gullible soldiers.[10]

The troops received more tangible commodities than Professor Davidson's hollow promises, some of which brought great joy to the ranks. In early February, the women of Hillsborough presented the 27th North Carolina with new flags, occasioning a ceremony attended by Mrs. General Cooke and other ladies. A different kind of delight resulted from the occasional whiskey ration distributed throughout the camps. One February night, the entire Confederate picket line in front of Wright's Sixth Corps erupted in cheers. The Federals, at a loss to understand the cause of such Rebel jubilation, learned from a deserter that liquor had been provided to their chilly opponents.[11]

Naturally, nearby Petersburg offered a more dependable source of alcohol. Easy access to intoxicants created such problems that by late fall, William Nelson Pendleton, Lee's artillery chief and an Episcopal cleric, appealed to Petersburg's elected officials to abolish this traffic:

> I have been requested by Gen'l Lee to endeavor to secure your cooperation with the military authorities in repressing the great evil of intemperance prevailing among a class of our Soldiers in consequence of the facility with which quantities of spirits are obtained & dispensed in your city. Fruitful of mischief as is this vice, it must, by all proper means, be restrained in our

army otherwise in vain will be all the sacrifices & sufferings of our virtuous population in this war of defence against a powerful enemy pressing for our destruction. Drunkenness, you need not be told, is ruinous to military discipline, and destructive to efficiency. Soldiers thus demoralized cannot be relied upon in a great & protracted struggle while they become nuisances to the inhabitants near whom they are quartered. For the sake, therefore, of your own city & its people, as well as for the cause of our common country, in the name of our honoured commander-in-chief, I ask of you such action as may be in your power toward represing this evil within your limits. It is hoped you can prevent in great measure, the present enormous traffic in spirits and aid in breaking up those places of resort for evil indulgence which soldiers frequent, especially at night. . . .[12]

The men of Hill's corps enjoyed visits to the Cockade City for more than just the allures of the bottle. Romance perfumed the air, and soldiers on the front lines followed its scent armed with passes and passion. "I cannot but feel very lonely while seeing so many of our boys walking along the streets with a fairy pinned to their arm and leaning on with every manifestation of affection," lamented a Virginia artillerist. "A great many of the soldiers are marrying around and in Petersburg," wrote another observer, "some for life, some for the war and some for one winter only." There may have been a man or two whose feelings for his partner ebbed in an even shorter time.[13]

The desire to visit home rarely waned. Shortly after the first of the year, a new system of granting furloughs to seven men out of every hundred brought cheer to the camps. "This measure is both wise and kind in that it is a relaxation in which men stand of so much need," one Virginian commented. A week later, this same soldier found himself the beneficiary of an even more liberal policy: "An order was received today granting four extra furloughs to our company, and to be given to meritorious men, in which category our captain was pleased to class me. I anticipate a very fine time in Richmond for eight or ten days. . . ."[14]

Not everyone enjoyed a winter vacation, but for some of Lee's soldiers life in camp proved far from intolerable. "I am in as good health as I ever was in my life and am having a pretty good time," wrote one North Carolinian. Such an assessment is at odds with the popular image of life in Lee's army during the last winter of the war, an image crafted in part by the architects of the Lost Cause mythology. Typical of this perspective was the North Carolina captain who, writing after the war, described his version of the Southern patriot in the Petersburg trenches: "Half-clad and half-rationed these brave, devoted men held the lines for nine long months, including one of the most terrible winters that ever spread its

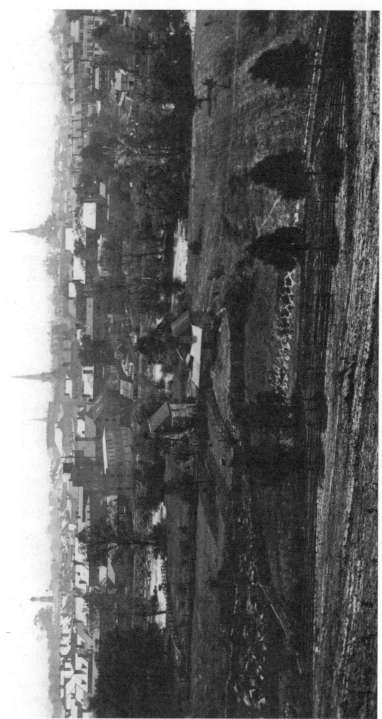

View of Petersburg from north of the Appomattox River. *National Archives*

white mantle over the earth. Barefooted in the snow, the men stood to their posts on picket, or at the port holes." This portrait certainly exaggerates weather conditions that winter and suggests a pervasive suffering that the historical record does not support. Yet, the army's hardships at Petersburg were real.[15]

R. L. Proffit of the 18th North Carolina wrote home on November 27, 1864, crowing about the quality of his newly-completed quarters and assuring his family that he was in good health and high spirits: "If no disturbance[,] we can enjoy our selves for the winter . . . but I fear rations are going to be short." It did not take a prophet, however, to realize that this Tarheel's prediction would come true. Since the early autumn, officials in the Bureau of Subsistence had warned of impending food deficiencies facing the Army of Northern Virginia.[16]

The Commissary Department confronted many difficult challenges during this last winter of the war. Union armies ranged across much of the South, controlling or laying waste to areas where agricultural production formerly fed Confederate soldiers. The Trans-Mississippi, much of Georgia, and now the Shenandoah Valley no longer provided crops and livestock needed at the Petersburg-Richmond front. Deteriorating railroads undermined the remaining transportation routes linking Petersburg to the unoccupied Confederacy. Although blockade runners—like Heth's friend Ficklin—devoted space to luxuries or consumer goods that could have been better used to import subsistence for the army, the foodstuffs they did carry were vital. The fall of the port of Wilmington and General Sherman's destruction of the rail connections from Charleston in early 1865 eliminated another important supply source for Lee's men.

That is not to say that ample food did not exist. Mountains of government provisions lay stockpiled in depots awaiting transportation to the front. Even more frustrating, Southern farmers sometimes refused to sell their produce to Confederate agents because of the government's inadequate compensation. "My officers are without funds, and their efforts to secure subsistence stores are paralyzed in consequence of same," wrote Major James Sloan, Commissary of Subsistence in North Carolina, on February 2. "Producers are refusing to sell, even at market prices, because they say the Government will not pay."[17]

General Lee warned Jefferson Davis that unless the administration effected some change in the supply system, "dire results" would ensue. The president acted quickly and in February replaced Colonel Lucius B. Northrup as Commissary General of Subsistence with Brigadier General Isaac M. St. John. St. John's "prompt and vigorous measures to procure supplies for the army" elicited praise from Lee. In early March, the Bureau of Subsistence reported that "the subsistence necessary for the troops operating in Virginia and North Carolina is only limited by the amount of specie and Confederate money available for its purchase." Some 12,500,000 rations of bread and 11,500,000 rations of meat could be acquired for military use in those two states alone.[18]

The soldier on the firing line knew little about the intricacies of Confederate procurement policies other than how they affected his own digestive system. Before Christmas, the official daily ration in the Army of Northern Virginia consisted of one pound of beef or one-third pound of bacon, one pound of flour or meal, sixteen ounces of rice, and small quantities of vinegar, salt, and soap. Those troops on front line duty in the trenches received a bonus allotment of coffee and sugar. "'Tis true," observed an officer in the 27th North Carolina, "the rations we get are sometimes not such as a man with a good appetite could wish for, still we make out with them, and never really suffer for food." Another Tarheel agreed. "While rations are short, there is enough to subsist on," wrote John Shaffner. Chaplain Eugene W. Thompson of the 43rd North Carolina admitted that some of the men in his unit complained about the quantity of their food, but reported home that, in his opinion, the rations were "tolerable." General Lane believed that, thanks to the special solicitation of Governor Zebulon Vance, North Carolina soldiers fared better than any other troops in Lee's army, "as much as some ignorant people are disposed to laugh at the 'Old North State.'"[19]

The veterans of Samuel McGowan's Brigade painted a much less rosy portrait of their daily fare. "We experienced a greater suffering for food . . . than we had ever known before," remembered Lieutenant Caldwell. "The ration of food professed to be a pound of cornmeal and a third of a pound of bacon. But we received scarcely the full weight of the former, and the latter we had frequently to do without entirely." The absence of the meat ration, caused in part by a flood that disrupted rail connections between Petersburg, Danville, and Greensboro, North Carolina, elicited particular complaints. "We have been without meat for three or four days at a time," wrote Captain Samuel L. Dorroh of the 14th South Carolina. "Get sugar & coffee in place of meat. You know cornbread & coffee is dry liveing." Private Joseph W. Templeton of the 12th South Carolina noted that he had been without meat for two weeks, and tried to remedy the problem by accompanying a foraging expedition to North Carolina in search of bacon. "We are rather short [of food], but I don't think it likely they will catch us without enough to make a fight on," wrote Major Harry Hammond of

McGowan's staff. "I only hope that the want of full rations will not affect the spirits of our troops, and I do not believe it will their health or strength."[20]

The soldiers attempted to supplement their official diet in various ways. Sometimes the food was brought to them. The women of Richmond and Petersburg, flushed with patriotism and holiday spirit, promised to supply a "Great National Dinner" to their heroes in gray, but the well-intentioned ladies raised expectations they could not redeem. By the time they parceled out the available food, the quantity barely made a dent in the soldiers' appetites. "We each received a few mouthfuls—a tea spoonful of apple butter to a man," grumbled Julius Lineback. "I got a little piece of turkey and two small pieces of meat and about four good mouthfuls of lightbread," reported a Georgian a few miles up the line. Private John Walters, a Virginia artillerist, noted that his battery's portion amounted to a third of a loaf of bread per man. "If this is, as it pretended, the nation's acknowledgment to the army and an evidence of the people's appreciation of our toils and suffering, let no one in the future say 'republics are grateful.'" Musician Lineback dismissed the "Great Bake" as a "great humbug. . . . Instead of cheering the men and putting new enthusiasm into them, this pitiful effort only made more plain the desperate condition of affairs in the Southern Confederacy & had rather a depressing effect." But Sergeant–Major Marion Hill Fitzpatrick of the 45th Georgia recognized that "it was too large an undertaking to try to give the whole army such a dinner." Georgian John Coxe, the beneficiary of a disappointingly thin ham sandwich, shouted, "God Bless our noble women! It was all they could do; it was all they had." Then every man in Coxe's tent broke down and cried.[21]

A better diet required ingenuity, cash, or both. John Walters reported that he gained nine pounds between the fall and early January because he could purchase extra food around Petersburg. Few Confederates, however, enjoyed such means. Another Virginia cannoneer explained that fishing expeditions frequently yielded a succulent catfish "which would occasion great joy among [the angler's] messmates." Troops also scrounged for food on land. Some scavengers favored "the Dinwiddie persimmon," described as "a very delightful fruit" and plentiful behind Confederate lines. One camp story related how General Lee had spotted a soldier of the 14th South Carolina in a persimmon tree. "What are you doing up that tree, sir," asked the general. "Don't you know those persimmons are green?" The quick-thinking private claimed to be "merely trying to draw my stomach down to the size of my rations."

Men lucky enough to go on sanctioned foraging trips, like Private William C. Templeton of the 14th South Carolina, benefited firsthand from the collected bounty. "I was in five countys," testified Templeton, "dynwidee brunswick lunburg notaway and meckalinburg. . . . I got Plenty to eat." Officers could buy an additional ration per day, which went far toward alleviating their hunger, but raised questions about the equity of a system that compelled enlisted men to subsist on less.[22]

Thus, it is difficult to generalize about the food supply in Hill's corps during the last winter of the war beyond recognizing that it was never plentiful and occasionally inadequate. Soldiers like Virgil Cavin of the 38th North Carolina stated his viewpoint plainly: "we dont get a nuff to eat out here. We only draw one pint of corn meal a day and a quarter pound of meat." Confederate prisoners reported to their Sixth Corps captors that two days' rations might consist of one pint of meal and some rice. On the other hand, a Georgian in Edward Thomas's Brigade wrote both in January and in March that "we get plenty of meat, but little plenty of bread." In March, a North Carolinian told his wife that "Rations are bountiful just now. To-day I drew good bacon, meal, peas, sugar & coffee." This mixed testimony tempers historian Douglas Southall Freeman's conclusion that Lee's army, "in a word, was starving on its feet," in the winter of 1864-1865. Still, compared to Wright's Sixth Corps Federals, Hill's men fared poorly.[23]

Food shortages accounted for just one of several privations that characterized life on the Confederate lines southwest of Petersburg. South Carolina Sergeant Berry Benson noted that his unit, a part of McGowan's command, sank a well near its camps "but sometimes it is dry then we have to go farther. None of it is very good water." The scarcity of firewood proved even more troublesome. Soldiers consumed the surrounding forests to build their fortifications and their quarters, drastically reducing the fuel supply in a much-cultivated land. The remaining wood lots became precious commodities as the troops relied on firewood to prepare meals and to provide heat. J. F. J. Caldwell testified eloquently about the consequences of this mid-nineteenth century energy crisis:

> We suffered for firewood. The growth about the camp, never heavy, was soon consumed by the troops; and for the last two months of our stay here we were obliged to carry logs on our shoulders for the distance of a mile or more, in order to have any fire at all. What we did get was most generally green pine or swamp wood. Gen. McGowan set the wagons of the brigade to hauling wood for us during the latter part of the winter, but the distance of the wood from camp, the roughness of the roads, the small number of wagons we had, and the wretched condition of the teams, prevented us from receiving anything beyond the merest apology for fuel.

It was not unusual to see returning pickets balancing quantities of firewood across their shoulders for use in warming their cabins and cooking their rations.[24]

With results as uneven as those involving the distribution of food, Hill's men hoped the government would supply their clothing needs. The occasional package from home containing a pair of socks or a warm scarf helped dent the chronic shortage of uniforms that had plagued the Confederacy since the outset of the war. The classic "butternut," dressed in a variety of jackets, trousers, and headgear cadged from untold sources, is a mainstay of Civil War literature.

"Shoes were scarce. More than once a soldier left a bloody track on the frozen picket line."

That is not to say that Lee's men achieved total self-reliance in regard to their apparel. North Carolinian R. L. Proffit reported in late November that, "we have just drawn a full suit of clothing . . . all I lack is an overcoat." Captain James Riddick of McGowan's staff inspected the brigade in late February and pronounced its condition as "tolerably well supplied with clothing." Yet Lieutenant Caldwell recalled that the uniforms received by the troops that winter were "coarse and flimsy. I do not remember the issue of a single overcoat, and but few blankets. Shoes were scarce. More than once a soldier left a bloody track on the frozen picket line."[25]

The smartly dressed Federals made frequent mention of their opponents' tattered appearance—particularly when Rebel prisoners or deserters paraded past them. Andrew Burwell of Wisconsin marveled at the Confederates captured in February along Hatcher's Run: "Some had on old straw hats some old slouch hats and all descriptions of clothes some had long coats some short jackets and pants of all kinds and description and no overcoats of any kind they use their old Blankets to put on their shoulders." Watching the Confederate pickets across the lines reminded Connecticut Corporal Lewis Bissell of observing a group of women "with cloaks, shawls, double bustles and hoops, and they had thrown over their shoulders blankets and tents which flapped in the wind." An officer on Meade's staff admired the Rebels' wiry physiques, but decried their "matted hair, tangled beards, and slouched hats, and the most astounding carpets, horse-sheets and transmogrified shelter-tents for blankets." Although the Confederates indisputably lacked the spit-and-polish appearance of their well-clothed enemies, they did a remarkable job with the practical application of available materials to ward off winter's chill.[26]

Other camp conditions, less troublesome than deficiencies in food, firewood, and clothing, contributed to the discomfort that defined the Petersburg winter. A lack of soap drew a pointed comment from the inspector of MacRae's Brigade, who noted that efforts to manufacture the article from "offal & spoilt Beef" had partly corrected the problem. Unwanted camp guests of the four-legged variety irritated some Confederates. "These rodents were very numerous and almost as large as squirrels," noted an Alabamian. "At night they were a great annoyance to us by running over our faces as we slept."[27]

These cumulative hardships reduced the ranks of Lee's army. As of December 31, 1864, illness and a lack of shoes or clothing diminished the number of effective soldiers in the Army of Northern Virginia by more than 10,000. Two months later, the sick rolls contained more than 5,300 names, about the same as in the Federal armies that numbered twice Lee's in aggregate strength. Thus, in addition to the morale-numbing impact of enduring varying degrees of privation, the poor diet, worn-out clothing, and unsanitary conditions rife in the Army of Northern Virginia consigned loyal soldiers to the hospital.[28]

The daily routine for those still fit for duty differed little from activities in the Union camps. The soldiers emerged early from their huts, coughing, stretching, and yawning as they prepared to face another dull and laborious day. Those not assigned to fatigue duty on the fortifications or rotating to the picket line engaged in company drill in the morning, battalion or brigade drill in the afternoon, and dress parade before supper. "General Lee has issued orders . . . to drill 8 hours a day," explained Berry Benson. "That is a little too much I think, but he knows best." Lieutenant Colonel Webb of the 27th North Carolina required his officers to recite lessons on tactics each evening until 10:00 p.m., and justified the practice to his family by explaining, "I am sure that if drill and discipline will avail anything, our Brigade will not lose next spring, & summer, any of the laurels which it has won."[29]

Not every Confederate kept quite so busy. John F. Shaffner, a North Carolina surgeon, informed an unknown correspondent about how he spent his day:

> It is generally past nine o'clock when I breakfast. At 10 A.M. the Div. Ex. Board assembles. Of this I am now a member. We generally adjourn by 1 P.M. Then I read or write until 4—at which hour I dine. By 6 P.M. a crowd usually assembles at my tent, for a game of Whist or Euchre, by which

means we spend the evening. About 10 the game is dismissed, and then I occupy myself about an hour in smoking and gazing steadily into the fire.[30]

General Lane made special mention of the exemplary animal husbandry practiced by his brigade. The unit's horses and mules were quartered in "comfortable log stables" near the Tarheel camps, well cared for in all regards. Likewise, Lane's troops maintained the brigade's wagons and tack throughout the winter by using oil produced from the hooves of the Commissary Department's slaughtered beeves. The Carolinians even recycled. Following an artillery bombardment, the Southern cannoneers would collect large quantities of Yankee shell fragments for the foundries, "getting eight cents a pound for the iron and ten for the lead."[31]

Despite the absence of combat or the likely threat of an immediate attack, Hill's officers maintained vigilant discipline in their camps. Volunteer soldiers, even the veterans of the Third Corps, demonstrated an independent spirit that sometimes required corporal punishment. The men respected this system as long as it met their unofficial standard of fairness. On March 2, an officer in the Purcell Battery apparently crossed the line when he bucked a man for insubordination, creating "signs of mutiny" in the battery and among some Tennesseans in McComb's Brigade. The 2nd Maryland Battalion arrived "to quell the disturbance," without further incident, but the Confederate soldier showed once again that limits existed to what he would tolerate in the service of his country.[32]

Perhaps the tension evident from this incident arose in part because every Confederate soldier knew that winter's end meant the beginning of a potentially decisive spring campaign. Hill's corps prepared for the coming conflict in a variety of ways, including responding to General Lee's frequent inspections of their front. General Heth recalled that, "There was hardly a week that [Lee] did not come to my headquarters . . . and request me to accompany him to the lines." Confederate scouts disguised as Federals conducted bold forays up to and sometimes through the Union picket lines to gather information. Shifts in Union deployment garnered immediate attention in the Confederate camps. Lieutenant Colonel Webb noticed in early March that the Yankees had massed troops opposite the right of Heth's line and in front of Cooke's Brigade, "prepared to make another attempt to turn our right flank, which they will try as soon as the ground is sufficiently dry for moving artillery, the wind is drying the ground very rapidly, and in all probability before this reaches you a bloody battle will have been fought near this place." Anticipation of imminent attack ended furloughs and spurred improvements in the fortifications.[33]

Confederate desperation during the last winter of the war may be gauged by the government's willingness to arm slaves. Since the summer of 1863, voices in the South had called for the enlisting of blacks, a proposition that challenged one of the basic tenets of Southern nationhood. Throughout 1864, every suggestion that slaves officially serve as soldiers in the Confederate army met implacable resistance. By January 1865, however, the deteriorating military situation at Petersburg and elsewhere prompted General Lee to adopt a pragmatic approach to the issue. Lee wrote Virginian Andrew Hunter that the question boiled down to whether the Negro was going to be employed as a soldier against the South or for it: "I think, therefore, we must decide whether slavery shall be extinguished by our enemies and the slaves be used against us, or use them ourselves at the risk of the effects which may be produced upon our social institutions. My own opinion is that we should employ them without delay."[34]

Lee reiterated his support for converting slaves into Confederate soldiers on several occasions during the winter. In February, he corresponded with the Confederate sponsor of a slave soldier bill. "With reference to the employment of negroes as soldiers . . . I think the measure not only expedient but necessary. . . . Under good officers and instructions, I do not see why they should not become good soldiers," wrote Lee. Henry Heth remembered speaking with the general-in-chief during one of Lee's inspection visits. When Lee asked Heth how the Confederacy might carry on the war without additional men, the division commander replied, "The only solution of that problem that I know is to put the negroes in the army." Lee agreed. "I recommended that some time since," he lamented, "but to do so was not considered advisable."[35]

By late February, the Confederate chief executive completed his own philosophical transformation on the question. Jefferson Davis wrote an Alabama correspondent that, "It is now becoming daily more evident to all reflecting persons that we are reduced to choosing whether the negroes shall fight for or against us, and that all arguments as to the positive advantages or disadvantages of employing them are beside the question, which is simply one of relative advantage between having their fighting element in our ranks or in those of our enemy." Expressions of support for arming the blacks poured in from Confederate units on the front lines, providing lawmakers with a clear rationale for enacting the necessary legislation.[36]

On March 4 and 5, 1865, the Virginia General Assembly passed its own law authorizing the enlistment of slave soldiers, but the measure withheld the guarantee of emancipation for those who served. A week later, the

Confederate Congress also approved a provision (by only one vote in the Senate) permitting the president to requisition a quota of black troops from each state. Reaction within the army varied. Twelve officers of the 49th Georgia of Thomas's Brigade, including the regimental commander, immediately forwarded a plan to General Lee outlining means for expediting the addition of slaves to their unit, including a clear expression of support for fighting beside black men: "When in former years, for pecuniary purposes, we did not consider it disgraceful to labor with negroes in the same field, or at the same work bench, we certainly will not look upon it in any other light at this time, when an end so glorious as our independence is to be achieved." The plan received endorsements from division commander Wilcox and acting corps commander Heth. Not every Confederate soldier shared this enthusiasm for black comrades-in-arms. Tarheel artillerist James W. Albright confided to his diary on March 15-16, "the first order to raise negro troops appears in to-day's papers—from to-day, I date the history of our downfall as a nation."[37]

There is some intriguing evidence that practical application on the front lines may have anticipated the legislation in Richmond. Adjutant Jacob Siebert of the 93rd Pennsylvania reported that in late February Confederate prisoners claimed that blacks were already drilling in the streets of Petersburg. Private Franklin Jones of the 10th New Jersey quoted a Confederate deserter on February 26 who complained about the presence of black troops in the ranks: "Wone from South Carolina came in and he sed that when the war broke out he had 50 big nigars beside the little wons and now he had to in struck the nigar in the manuel of arms and that was more than he could bair." Three weeks later, Joseph Rutherford, the assistant surgeon of the 10th Vermont, told his wife that, "the rebs have at last got the nigger on the brain—and in front of our corps (6th) they have the colored gentry on picket. But they cannot trust them. When a picket is relieved the relief does not bring a gun but takes the one the man he relieves has. So much for the rebel nigger soldier."[38]

The prospect of impending battle, with or without slave comrades, forced every man in Lee's army to reevaluate both the probable fortunes of the Confederate war effort and his own proper relation to that cause. An experience in the 11th North Carolina of MacRae's Brigade provided some insight into the doubts that haunted the devoted veterans of the Army of Northern Virginia. About the first of March, the unit's three-year term of enlistment expired. Although Confederate conscription laws bound most of the troops to continuing military service, the regiment's officers invited the soldiers to ceremonially reenlist. The unit dutifully mustered on its camp parade ground as the officers called each company to step forward to the colors and renew its commitment. When Company K's turn arrived, only Sergeant Jacob S. Bartlett answered the call. His reluctant comrades remained in the army, of course, but their actions spoke volumes about their attitudes.

Federal officer Hazard Stevens predicted that large numbers of Confederates would be captured without resistance at the first opportunity, thus removing themselves from the war while maintaining their honor. North Carolinian Julius Lineback prayed that a negotiated settlement would soon bring peace: "Oh, that something would be done to stop this hopeless struggle, and let us go home." But some Southern soldiers were not content with symbolic protests of their continued service, or reliance on the Yankees or the politicians to relieve them of their military responsibilities. In the winter of 1865, many Johnny Rebs decided to terminate the war, or at least their role in it, on their own terms.[39]

The rate of desertion in the Army of Northern Virginia had waxed and waned during the final months of 1864. But with the onset of winter, and particularly in February, the army hemorrhaged its manpower in torrents. General Lee alarmingly informed Adjutant General Samuel Cooper that, "Hundreds of men are deserting nightly, and I cannot keep the army together unless examples are made of such cases." Lee reported 1,094 desertions between February 15 and 25, 779 during the next ten days, and 1,061 between March 9 and 18. In barely more than four weeks, nearly 3,000 Confederate soldiers left the ranks, or about one in every nineteen men. The actual numbers may have been higher and will never be known.[40]

Defections from Wilcox's and Heth's commands proved especially heavy. From February 15 through 25, those two divisions reported 503 desertions—almost as many as the rest of the army combined. Similarly, during the next ten days, more soldiers were absent without leave from both Wilcox's and Heth's units than from any of the army's other divisions. Only later in the month did they surrender this dubious distinction to George Pickett's brigades.[41]

This flow of men into the Sixth Corps lines elicited numerous comments and reams of informal (and often exaggerated) tallies from the Federals. "You never saw anything like the desertions that are occurring among the Rebs these days," wrote Major Mason Tyler of the 37th Massachusetts. "We average about twenty a night on our division line, and on the Ninth Corps I understand they have about one hundred a night." "The rebs are deserting fast," reported Warren Williams of the 5th Wisconsin. "34 came into our brigade last night[,] 25 in one place[.] during the week past about 75 have come in. This brigade line extends only about 3/4 of a mile so you can judge for yourselves how fast they come in as the whole line of this army is over 20 miles in length." Private William B. Adams of the 1st Maine Veterans estimated on February 26 that about 100 deserters per night entered his brigade's lines. Vermonter Joseph Rutherford described an entire company of 55 men, including their officers, skedaddling en masse. Colonel Keifer merely told his wife that "desertions still continue to be numerous from the enemy," while Corporal Lewis Bissell of the 2nd Connecticut Heavy Artillery wrote that "the boys talk about the Johnnies as at home we talk about suckers and eels. The boys will look around in the evening and guess that there will be a good run of Johnnies."[42]

Confederate sources confirmed this phenomenon, but usually with less precision than that provided by Lieutenant Caldwell, who numbered the AWOL soldiers in McGowan's Brigade at exactly 104. An officer in the 27th North Carolina merely admitted, "There have been a good many desertions from our army lately," and the regiment's commander referred to the desertion rate as "alarming." Another Tarheel confessed that unauthorized absences had become "very frequent," and in his unit the rate averaged about three per day.[43]

Many Confederate deserters acted during the night while serving on picket duty. This could be a deadly business, however, because a deserter always risked being mistaken for a participant in one of the occasional Confederate picket-line forays. In such instances, the side-swapper might come under fire instead of being peaceably welcomed into Union lines. Of course, Southern officers issued orders to shoot deserters, so a nocturnal dash toward the Federals could result in drawing fire from either direction.

On the night of February 19, 24 men of Company I, 33rd North Carolina, hatched a clever plan. They gathered a large number of blankets and made of them a comfortable bed for the unsuspecting captain who presided over that portion of the picket line. Tucking-in the grateful officer, who apparently determined that this act of kindness represented his troops' expression of their esteem, the soldiers waited until their cozy superior had fallen asleep. Then they made their move, "bringing arms and equipments—everything they had but those lucky blankets—upon which the Capt. may be sleeping now," gleefully reported Lieutenant Homer Curtis of the 2nd Connecticut Heavy Artillery. "If so I hope it is very sweetly indeed."[44]

Wood cutting and gathering between the lines, a daylight enterprise, also offered bold Confederates the chance to desert. Taking advantage of a morning fog on March 5, four Southern fuel collectors wandered forward of their comrades to a point where they were difficult to see in the mist. A corporal suggested they throw down their axes and make for the Union lines. Approaching the Federal videttes, they signaled with a paper their intention to surrender. The Yankees waved their caps and in the Rebels came. At other times, the Union wood choppers played a more active role in assisting deserters. During one of the frequent occasions when soldiers from both sides were cutting trees in the same area between the lines, some Confederates made known their desire to come over. At opportune moments, the Federals would shed their overcoats and place them over the shoulders of the Southern deserters. Then, the figures in blue garments would drift casually toward the Union line, secure in the safety of the informal truce that existed among the wood collectors. "Our boys worked in that way and got quite a number in all," boasted Private John J. Ingraham of the 121st New York.[45]

Other Confederate wood cutters were not nearly so subtle. A daring sergeant and four of his men drove their six-mule team and wagon, used to collect the timber, straight through the Union picket line to safety. When the non-commissioned officer called out disingenuously to the Confederate videttes to stop his "runaway" team, the grayclad pickets gave unsuccessful chase and, finding themselves close to the Union lines, "concluded to desert in company" as well.[46]

Sentries and wood collectors had a sanctioned reason to be near or between the picket lines. Another class of Southern visitor to the neutral ground between the armies also succumbed to the temptations of the Union. The enterprising traders who went in search of coffee, newspapers, or other consumer items sometimes swapped their allegiance as well. The 10th Vermont's Joseph Rutherford described an incident that occurred one morning when a Johnny Reb found a willing Federal to trade a good Southern knife for some Yankee soap: "After the bargain was made the Union Soldier got the soap to hand to the reb when the reb looked round behind him to see if any of his companions was looking—and said 'never mind the soap Yank. I am going where there is plenty of it' and started to run into our lines as fast as he could leg it." He reached the Union fortifications safely where, presumably, he indulged in a good scrubbing.[47]

What motivated so many of Lee's men to forsake cause and comrades? Lewis Bissell quizzed deserters on this very question. Some claimed simply to be sick of fighting, while others, according to the Connecticut corporal, had never been devoted soldiers. "Many of the deserters are men who kept out of the army just as long as possible," wrote Bissell. "Then when conscripted they deserted at the first opportunity."[48]

The Federals had ample first-hand experience with this brand of reluctant patriot in their own ranks. Sergeant George J. Howard of the 5th

Vermont wrote his wife explaining how the Federal soldiers themselves encouraged their enemies to desert:

> The boys are having a gay time here in our Division since the 'Peace Conference' coaxing 'Johnnies' to desert and we are quite successful too; on the night of the 21st we got forty-eight . . . and turned them over to the corps headquarters and got a recpt for them. It began first by the pickets chopping wood for fires from the same tree between the picket lines, next by changing in carrying wood to the fires; and then to trading tobacco knives, sugar, coffee, and soap etc. and finally our boys told the 'Johnnies' they had better come over and go north and take the big wages now offered for laborers to which some three hundred . . . has consented within the last ten days, and been sent north from our Division alone. This is sport for the boys but it makes rebel officers threaten us with shooting and hanging if they can catch us for [luring] their men away. 'We recon' they will not be troubled with men in the army in a few more months.[49]

Howard's reference to job openings addressed a common concern among discouraged Confederates who considered leaving the ranks. Practically all such men loathed the possibility of being compelled to take up arms against their former companions once accepted into the Union lines. General Grant realized this and on August 31, 1864, promulgated orders exempting Confederate deserters from service as Union soldiers. In early January 1865, however, Grant sweetened the pot. Special Orders No. 3 provided a further incentive to Confederates to surrender to the Federal authorities:

> Hereafter deserters from the Confederate Army who deliver themselves up to the U.S. forces will, on taking an oath that they will not again take up arms during the present rebellion, be furnished subsistence and free transportation to their homes, if the same are within the lines of Federal occupation. If their homes are not within such lines they will be furnished subsistence and free transportation to any point in the Northern States.
>
> All deserters who take the oath of allegiance will, if they desire it, be given employment in the Quartermaster's and other departments of the Army, and the same remuneration paid them as is given to civilian employees for similar services. Military duty, or service endangering them to capture by the Confederate forces, will not be exacted from such as give themselves up to the U.S. military authorities.
>
> Deserters who bring arms, horses, mules, or other property into our lines with them will, on delivering the same to the Quartermaster's department, receive in money the highest price such arms, horses, mules, and other property are worth. . . .[50]

This policy may explain why the bold sergeant brought in his wood-cutting team and wagon and why most of the deserters carried their guns. "The inducement for desertion held out by the enemy is not to be despised," wrote a North Carolina surgeon, whose garbled grasp of the program's details does not diminish his judicious assessment of its temptations: "Genl Grant offers a bounty of $30.00, and a new suit of clothes, with free transportation to any portion of the Northern States." Major Tyler of Massachusetts confirmed that the Federals sent over "on every opportunity General Grant's orders in regard to deserters," sometimes at great risk to the messengers who entered Confederate lines bearing copies of Grant's program.[51]

Some left the ranks to line their pockets; others deserted to line their stomachs. "I have seen veterans of three full years who have faced death incessantly who believe in the southern cause as sincerely as I do, finally be conquered by gnawing hunger and desert to the enemy in the hopes of a full meal," wrote Sergeant James E. Whitehorne of the 12th Virginia on March 31. "I hate the idea, but I won't criticize."[52]

Sometimes homesickness and fear of the future combined with the lack of food to create a crisis of loyalty for Confederate soldiers. Virgil Cavin of the 38th North Carolina made it clear in a letter to his family on March 21 that his willingness to remain with the army had just about expired:

> We dont gite but a pint of meal a day and I can eat that at one meal. . . . I cant stay here and live on the rashings we gite. . . . I want to see you all the worst ever I did. I dont no What to do. . . . I want to come home if I can gite there and could stay there. . . . I hate to stay here and starve which I think we will do if the yanks gits the roads cut of which I think they will do. . . . I dont think there is three days rashings in Petersburg at this time. hilary I want to see you the worst ever I did in my life if i could jest gite home to see you all and gite something good to eate which I dont gite here.

Many Federals cited hunger as the chief complaint of the deserters who entered their lines.[53]

If poverty of the haversack led to poverty of the spirit, so too did the supplications of the soldiers' correspondents who, with increasing urgency, implored their own Johnny Rebs to give up the fight. Where once civilians had buoyed the resolve of the men on the front lines, many now encouraged the troops to reflect their own crisis of confidence and leave the army. Captain Graham of the 27th North Carolina understood the problem: "If the people at home would only write cheering letters to their friends in the army instead of counselling them to commit this base crime everything would go on so much better with us." Many soldiers and civilians reinforced each other's sense of hopelessness. "The men have an idea that all is lost, and that further carnage is useless," wrote Surgeon Shaffner. "The teachings of our home people have forced this idea upon the army." Even General Lee cited disheartened civilians as a chief cause of desertion: "It seems that the men are influenced very much by the representations of their friends at home, who appear to have become very despondent as to our success. They think the cause desperate and write to the soldiers, advising them to take care of themselves, assuring them that if they will return home the bands of deserters so far outnumber the home guards that they will be in no danger of arrest."[54]

The men of MacRae's Brigade responded to this problem by addressing a circular to one of their North Carolina representatives in Richmond, appealing to the state's Congressional delegation to go among the citizens of North Carolina and "endeavor to unite them again in an honest and hearty support of our cause, thus renewing in our soldiers that enthusiasm and pride which has caused them in the past to win for their State and themselves an undying name." MacRae and 46 of his officers laid the blame for desertion at the feet of "those of our citizens at home who by evil counsels and by fear have been made to despair of the success of our cause, and are constantly, while the soldiers are home on furlough and through the mails, instilling into them opinions which too often culminate in desertions."[55]

Another kind of letter from home also induced desertion. Men from the Carolinas in particular received correspondence that winter from loved ones who stood in the path of the malevolent Sherman's approaching hordes. Frightened, defenseless, and impoverished, the authors of these missives forced devoted followers of Lee to choose between their duties as soldiers and their responsibilities as husbands and fathers. One Tarheel trooper expressed this dilemma poignantly in a letter to his pregnant wife in mid March:

> "The men have an idea that all is lost, and that further carnage is useless. The teachings of our home people have forced this idea upon the army."

I have lived [as a] soldier long enough now not to dread its vicisitudes personally, but the thought of my family being cut off from me, and in the enemy's lines makes my heart heavy indeed. Your condition just now, my wife, rendering you so helpless to yourself whilst I have no command of my time is enough to destroy not only the wits, but composure of a husband . . . It gri[e]ves me so much to think I cant be by you in your time of suffering.[56]

Virginian Robert Stiles remembered letters that "would have seared your very eyeballs to read, but that . . . could not be read without tears—letters in which a wife and mother, crazed by her starving children's cries for bread, required a husband and father to choose between his God-imposed obligations to her and to them and his allegiance to his country, his duty as a soldier." Walter Taylor, an officer on Lee's staff, referred to "hundreds of letters" in which mothers, wives, and sisters told of their inability to support themselves or their families and appealed to their men to come home and rescue them from their fates.[57]

Governors who formed home guard units, aided by zealous recruiting officers, only induced more soldiers to leave the front lines. Citing a blatant example in Georgia, Lee beseeched the secretary of war for an end to this insidious system and the arrest of officers who solicited such recruits for their own purposes. "It has been one of the greatest evils of the service since the beginning of the war, and has caused the loss of a much greater number of men than have ever been brought into service by means of such special organizations," Lee growled.[58]

Private Noah Collins of the 37th North Carolina in Lane's Brigade deserted on the night of March 30. Collins's rationale embodied a general war weariness. Angry with his officers and Confederate leadership, and despairing of ultimate Confederate success, Collins saw the opportunity to end his personal role in the South's quest for independence and took it:

Being sorely pressed down in mind, with regard to my savage treatment [by] my officers; who for no possible offense that I ever committed had been base principle enough to deny me a single furlough of indulgence during the whole war; which was robbing me of my legal, or lawful right and fellow soldiers customary privileges[,] and the failure on the part of our head Rebel officials, to enter into any conciliatory, or peace making measures, with the Northern head officials, on the Hampton Roads Review; when nearly every person possessed of sound reason, both North and South well knew that this great Southern Rebellion was virtually crushed at that time; and that it was no better than wilful murder on the part of our head Rebel officials, to continue the flagitious or grossly wicked and bloody war any longer; consequently I resolved to hazzard my life and health no longer for the support of a completely fallen cause, which could no longer be contended for. . . .

North Carolinian Virgil Cavin expressed the same sentiment more succinctly: "I would give the confederacy to get home." Berry Benson of McGowan's Brigade concluded that "the desertions were prompted mostly by pure weariness of the war, and very rarely, (almost never) by sympathy with the Union cause."[59]

Desertion afflicted every brigade in the Army of Northern Virginia, but Tarheels seemed to be the most frequent offenders. "The desertions are chiefly from North Carolina regiments, and especially those from the western part of that State," wrote Lee to the secretary of war. New Englander Mason Tyler told his mother that, "Almost all the deserters that we get now seem to be from the Old North State. They say that their State and their soldiers want to come back into the Union and they individually believe it their duty to encourage it by setting the example." Berry Benson observed that "It was generally accounted that N.C. and Florida troops were the worst about this. . . . It was [Brigadier General Joseph] Finegan's Florida brigade that deserted so numerously that, one night, the enemy's pickets called over to us on picket: 'Tell Gen. Finnegan to come over and take command of his brigade.'" Private John B. Southard, of the 49th New York in Thomas Hyde's brigade, wrote home that "They have been deserting to us very heavily from especially North & South Carolina & Georgia until within the last few days they have put troops from Va & Miss in our front and they don't come in so fast."[60]

While the origin of the Floridians' particular malaise may rest with conditions unique to that unique brigade, the preponderance of North Carolina deserters is easier to explain. Tarheel soldiers faced the worst possible combination of factors conspiring to induce a loyal soldier to leave the ranks. General Lee's specific mention of western North Carolina evoked the ambivalent sentiments regarding secession and Confederate nationhood which that part of the state experienced from the very outset of the war. The highland regions of both Carolinas shared a latent and sometimes blatant Unionism with places like western Virginia, eastern Tennessee, and the northern tier of counties in Georgia and Alabama. Moreover, in mid-February, General Sherman appeared poised to enter the state after leaving a trail of smoldering destruction in South Carolina. Any rational Tarheel would harbor deep concerns about the fate of his home and family when the blue scourge reached his county. North Carolina was also convenient. While many Confederate deserters sought refuge in the Union lines, some men from North Carolina simply slipped away and made the 50-mile trip to the state border and from there to their homes or other safe refuges. Finally, because fully half the troops in Heth's and Wilcox's divisions hailed from the Old North State, it was statistically more likely that Tarheels would find their way into the Sixth Corps lines more frequently than troops from any other jurisdiction.[61]

The Confederates employed several measures to deter desertion. The army's standing policy of shooting troops who attempted to defect, while daunting in the abstract, lost most of its bite in the application. In many instances, Southern soldiers could not bring themselves to shoot discouraged comrades in the back. Instead, grayclad pickets fired their rifles high, thus technically obeying orders but avoiding the grim consequences of an aimed discharge.[62]

As the stream of desertions continued from the picket line, officers took additional steps to make crossing into Yankee territory more difficult. They cracked down on the unauthorized exchange of newspapers between the lines, because the Northern press widely disseminated Grant's terms to deserters. More officers on the picket line and the assignment of only reliable men to vidette duty also helped. Colonel Keifer testified that as desertions mounted in mid-February, Southerners strengthened picket lines to accommodate sharpshooters whose increased rate of fire made it more difficult for deserters to run the gantlet. Rumors circulated through the Union ranks that Lee was shifting new and more reliable divisions to the front lines to replace those in which desertion flourished, as if the Army of Northern Virginia had such reserve units available for these assignments.[63]

The Confederates also launched their own propaganda campaign. "The rebel officers tell their men that Grant has agreed to exchange deserters with Lee so if they desert they will have to come back and suffer the penalty," wrote New Englander Lewis Bissell. Of course, that penalty might be death. In March, Lee ordered that the troops be reapprised of this Article of War at their daily drills and dress parades. Furthermore (in a measure that evokes comparison to the humorless airport security regulations of contemporary America), General Orders Number 8 deplored the "evil habit [that] prevails with some in this army of proposing to their comrades in jest to desert and go home." Lee specified that "the penalty for advising or persuading a soldier to desert is death; and those indulging in such jests will find it difficult on a trial to rebut the presumption of guilt arising from their words."[64]

Attempting to prevent desertion presented one challenge; dealing with those who had already left the ranks offered another. As the wave of winter desertions began to crest in mid-February, General Lee issued one of the more powerful of his wartime policy statements. Released to the troops as General Orders Number 2, Lee's message reached both those who had deserted and those who might consider the act in the future:

In entering upon the campaign about to open, the general-in-chief feels assured that the soldiers who have so long and so nobly borne the hardships and dangers of the war require no exhortation to respond to the calls of honor and duty. . . .

The choice between war and abject submission is before them. . . . They cannot barter manhood for peace nor the right of self-government for life and property.

But justice to them requires a sterner admonition to those who have abandoned their comrades in the hour of peril.

A last opportunity is afforded them to wipe out the disgrace and escape the punishment of their crimes.

By authority of the President of the Confederate States, a pardon is announced to such deserters and men improperly absent as shall return to the commands to which they belong within the shortest possible time, not exceeding twenty days from the publication of this order, at the headquarters of the department in which they may be. . . .

By the same authority it is also declared that no general amnesty will again be granted, and those who refuse to accept the pardon now offered, or who shall hereafter desert or absent themselves without leave, shall suffer such punishment as the courts may impose, and no application for clemency will be entertained.[65]

It is not known how many deserters responded to this amnesty offer, but enough failed to do so that Lee sent detachments of North Carolina troops south to hunt deserters or prevent runaways from reaching their homes. Brigadier General Robert D. Johnston's entire four-regiment brigade spent either all or part of the winter of 1864-1865 in northern North Carolina for the sole purpose of catching deserters. The 5th, 20th, and 23rd North Carolina left the Shenandoah Valley and adopted positions along the Staunton and Roanoke rivers to guard "every road and ferry" against the escape of fellow Tarheels and others from their military obligations. In February, the 12th North Carolina joined their comrades. "There were so many men, mostly conscripts, deserting from Lee's army and passing through North Carolina, that the Confederate authorities sought to check it by drawing a cordon of troops across their route," wrote a veteran of the 23rd North Carolina. "Some of the companies were sent back to their neighborhoods to catch deserters. . . . The battalion of sharpshooters went to cope with the recalcitrant mountaineers. . . ." The 23rd caught about as many deserters as they had men in their unit, "which was not many," admitted the regimental historian.[66]

When deserters were captured, one of two fates awaited them. Virgil Cavin described an incident in which the army meted out severe corporal punishment to two would-be deserters: "They caught Mitt Fioeddler & Alx

Spaugh and brought them back & gave them one lick from 8 hundred fifty men each." As staggering as such a sentence may have been, Cavin's comrades avoided the maximum penalty for desertion—execution.[67]

J. F. J. Caldwell stated that only five of the 104 deserters from McGowan's Brigade were captured, but each of those five was tried, convicted, and condemned to death within twenty-four hours. A young boy among them had his sentence commuted, but the other four, all members of the 1st South Carolina, faced a firing squad composed of their regimental comrades and in the presence of the entire brigade. The guilty parties requested a full baptism before meeting their fates, which proved to be a difficult matter, according to Caldwell:

> Our couriers could not find a Baptist chaplain, and the Presbyterian ministers about us prayed to be excused. I could not blame them, for the rite could not be administered except by wading thirty yards or more into a pond of ice-cold water with a muddy, mirey bottom. But we secured, at last, the services of a Methodist chaplain: whereupon General McGowan exclaimed, 'Hurrah for the Methodists!' Then the men were shot.[68]

Berry Benson provided some details regarding how the South Carolinians administered the death penalty:

> Twelve men are detailed as executioners, drawn from the command by lot . . . six of these are provided with guns containing only powder, six with powder and ball. The prisoner is tied to a stake, his hands tied behind his back, his coffin by his side. A handkerchief is then bound over his eyes, and directly the command 'Fire!' is given, and the terrible scene is ended.

It is unclear how often this ghastly spectacle played out during the winter, but there can be no doubt that Lee approved of such justice as one means to stem the manpower drain that threatened to sap the viability of his army.[69]

Yet it is easy to exaggerate the problem. For every man who ran away, for whatever reason, a dozen or more endured the hardships, resisted the temptations, and stood by their comrades in arms. Even the briefest glance at the army's correspondence in early 1865 reveals the presence of undaunted optimism about the conflict's outcome, continued devotion to the Confederate cause, and a determination to see the war through to a successful conclusion rather than accept the unthinkable consequences of defeat.

Chaplain Thompson of the 43rd North Carolina admitted shortly after Christmas that "our prospects at present are very gloomy." But when considering the option of abandoning the fight, Thompson knew the choice he would make:

> I sometimes look at subjugation and I tell you it is appalling. It is to have our fair fields confiscated; it is to have our beloved church desecrated, our innocent women to be the prey to brutal lust, our cherished institutions ruined, our whole country wasted and forever spoiled, and our entire population reduced to a state of poverty, degradation and vassalage unknown before in the history of the world. Are we ready for such a fate as this. Will we submit to it? If it is Heaven's decree I submit, if not I think I am honest when I say I am ready to risk my life to prevent it. . . .[70]

Others drew Thompson's sharp picture of the alternative to victory, evoking the fate of a defeated South as ample motivation for sustaining the war. "If croakers would but consider a moment the consequences of subjugation they would certainly talk different," wrote a Georgian in Thomas's Brigade. "Pen cannot describe nor tongue tell the degradation and suffering of our people if we ever submit. . . . After passing the present crisis there is on us, I have no doubt things will brighten soon and we will prove ourselves worthy of freedom by learning the true value of it in these dark times." Sergeant James Whitehorne of the 12th Virginia felt that he had come too far with the Army of Northern Virginia to forsake it now: "I have been in this Holy Cause for four long years and it is truly a Holy Cause to me. I have fought and suffered and bled for the Confederacy and I would rather my bones bleach on some red hill of the Old Dominion than be subjugated."[71]

Surgeon Shaffner expressed his optimism on New Year's day, despite acknowledging that the army was "now enveloped in more gloom than at any previous crisis. . . . I have never doubted the purity and justness of our cause, and though I have felt very despondent during portions of the late campaign, I do not now despair of the Republic. . . . We will certainly, sooner or later, emerge victors from this contest." Lieutenant Colonel Webb of the 27th North Carolina concurred with Shaffner a few weeks later: "I feel as ever, confident of our success. Gen'l Lee's Army is numerically stronger now than when he opened the Campaign of 64, while in experience it is two fold stronger. That Grant has an inferior Army, to the one we fought last year, no one doubts." With the advent of spring, men like staff officer Harry Hammond actually looked forward to the next campaign. "I feel more cheerful than usual," he told his wife, "and am not without good hope that fortune will be on our side this summer. . . . This army is still a bulwark that holds the invasion at bay, and may turn the tide with good fortune."[72]

These expressions of determination and confidence found free vent at a number of mid winter gatherings held by units in Wilcox's Division. On the night of February 1, the regiments in McGowan's Brigade conducted a torchlight march from their camps to the Boisseau House, accompanied by a band, and called upon General McGowan to validate their enthusiasm for continuing the good fight. "[McGowan] was completely taken by surprise; but commenced & warming up as he progressed, made a capital effort, abounding in fun & anecdotes—spoke about an hour," remembered a South Carolinian. The general concluded his speech amidst enthusiastic cheers and then enjoyed a serenade by the musicians.[73]

This festive occasion at McGowan's headquarters arose from the adoption of resolutions drafted by the general and endorsed almost unanimously in his brigade. Their language compensates in clarity of purpose for what it lacks in brevity:

> Resolve, 1st. That the war in which we are engaged is a war of self-defence; that in the beginning, nearly four years ago, we took up arms in defence of the right to govern ourselves, and to protect our country from invasion, our homes from desolation, and our wives and children from insult and outrage.
>
> 2d. That the reasons which induced us to take up arms at the beginning have not been impaired, but, on the contrary, infinitely strengthened by the progress of the war. Outrage and cruelty have not made us love the perpetrators. If we then judged that the enemy intended to impoverish and oppress us, we now know that they propose to subjugate, enslave, disgrace and destroy us.
>
> 3d. As we were actuated by principle when we entered the service of the Confederate States, we are of the same opinion still. We have had our share of victories, and we must expect some defeats. Our cause is righteous and must prevail. . . .
>
> 4th. To submit to our enemies now, would be more infamous than it would have been in the beginning. It would be cowardly yielding to power what was denied upon principle. It would be to yield the cherished right of self-government, and to acknowledge ourselves wrong in the assertion of it; to brand the names of our slaughtered companions as traitors; to forfeit the glory already won; to lose the fruits of all the sacrifices made and the privations endured; to give up independence now nearly gained, and bring certain ruin, disgrace and eternal slavery upon our country. Therefore, unsubdued by past reverses, and unawed by future dangers, we declare our determination to battle to the end, and not to lay down our arms until independence is secured. Is life so dear, or peace so sweet, as to be purchased at the price of chains and slavery? Forbid it Heaven![74]

The sentiments expressed by the South Carolinians found similar voice in Lane's Brigade. The 18th, 28th, and 37th North Carolina regiments passed like-worded resolutions between February 5 and 10, and directed that they be forwarded to the Confederate Congress, the secretary of war, Governor Vance, and newspapers in the state. They pledged reenlistment for the duration of the war, a rejection of "the absurd proclamations of Abraham Lincoln," and a commitment to devote "our property, our lives, and our honor and our all, never to submit to Abolition tyranny nor Yankee rule." Just as in McGowan's Brigade, a few of Lane's soldiers refused to endorse these documents, but there can be no doubt that an overwhelming majority of the North Carolinians supported continued prosecution of the war.[75]

One Confederate soldier used music to express his fidelity to the Confederate cause. Cannoneer James W. Albright composed a song to the tune of "Annie Laurie" which he called, "We'll fight until we die!" whose lyrics mirrored the rhetoric used in the McGowan and Lane resolutions:

> The clash of arms is ringing
> All o'er our Southern land,
> But, 'round brave Lee is clinging
> A fine, devoted band-
> A fine, devoted band-
> Whose cry is <u>Liberty!</u>
> And for Southern Independence
> We'll fight until we die!
>
> The Yankee thieves have pillaged
> Many a Southern home,
> And our sweethearts, wives & children
> Now penniless do roam-
> Now penniless do roam-
> Let vengeance be our cry,
> While for Southern Independence
> We'll fight until we die!
>
> Then, boys, let's do our duty,
> In this the hour of need-
> Ne'er forsake this glorious cause
> Until our land is freed-
> Until our land is freed-
> 'Twere better for to die,
> Than give up Independence,
> When the goal is so nigh![76]

It is tempting to dismiss this eleventh-hour bravado as just so much whistling past the graveyard. Most students of the war see little real possibility that the Confederacy could have prevailed on the battlefield after Abraham Lincoln's reelection. Yet, there is abundant evidence that demonstrates optimism and increased morale in Lee's army as winter waned and the spring campaign season approached. Surgeon Shaffner returned to the army on March 10 after a brief absence and found "the troops in excellent health, and in much better spirits than I had anticipated. . . . Rations are quite abundant—more so than when I left." Lieutenant Colonel Tazewell L. Hargrove of the 44th North Carolina observed about the same time that "the army is in better spirits than it has been for a month or two past and is much more hopeful." Lieutenant Colonel Webb assured his family that "there are plenty of men, who will remain true and who are determined, that will make this country a warm climate, till the Yankees are willing to cede to us the right of self-government." One immediate result of this increased morale was a reduction in the desertion rate along Hill's front beginning in mid-March. "Desertions are not quite so heavy just now," wrote a Federal on March 16. Berry Benson agreed: "Our soldiers are in much better spirits than they were: desertions are rare in this part of the army."[77]

If resolve led to increased morale, then higher spirits nurtured a sanguine outlook toward the coming campaign. "Our resources, wisely and vigorously employed, are ample, and with a brave army, sustained by a determined and united people, success with God's assistance cannot be doubtful," thought Lee. Brigadier General William H. Forney, in command of Wilcox's old brigade in William Mahone's Division, wrote that "all that is required of us is to stand firm—the Yanks are not anxious to meet us." A North Carolinian summarized the renewed buoyancy that lifted the Army of Northern Virginia in March while recognizing the one indispensable factor in any formula for Confederate victory: "with a blind confidence in the wisdom and skill of our noble Commander, [the troops] are ready to do anything at his bidding."[78]

*   *   *

The men of Wright's Sixth Corps sensed that one crisis had passed in the Army of Northern Virginia and that the spring promised the advent of another—one quite possibly drenched with blood. Hazard Stevens grudgingly admired his opponents across the barren landscape of Dinwiddie County, while maintaining confidence in the eventual outcome of the campaign. "Their tenacity and stubbornness are wonderful," Stevens wrote. "The rebels are determined and will make a strong resistance in the spring."[79]

The nature of that resistance would determine the outcome of the Petersburg Campaign and, ultimately, of the Civil War itself.

NOTES

1. J. F. J. Caldwell, "Reminiscences of the War of Secession," in Yates Snowden, ed., *History of South Carolina*, 5 vols. (Chicago, 1920), II, 830; John Milner Associates, Inc., *Historic Structure Report for Tudor Hall Dinwiddie County, Virginia* (2 vols.; West Chester, Pa., 1995), I, passim. The exact date of McGowan's arrival at the Boisseau House and the circumstances under which he took possession of the home are unknown. However, Lieutenant Caldwell wrote that the brigade arrived in the neighborhood on October 2 and began building fortifications the next morning, so it is probable that McGowan assumed residence at the Boisseau House at about the same time. See Caldwell, *The History of a Brigade of South Carolinians*, 243.

The Boisseau House, Tudor Hall, is preserved as a part of Pamplin Historical Park. A portion of the home is furnished to represent McGowan's headquarters based on limited direct evidence of the appearance of the rooms and conjecture derived from descriptions of similar accommodations. Lieutenant Caldwell thought that McGowan "could get more fun into a game of whist than I had imagined it possible to inject into that serious recreation." Duncan Road, VA 670, exists in 2000 on a track similar to its wartime course. This byway was also known as Harmon Road, after a homeowner of that name whose house stood near the road's intersection with the Boydton Plank Road. For a brief, reliable history of Tudor Hall, see Arthur W. Bergeron, Jr., *Tudor Hall: The Boisseau Family Farm* (Richmond, 1998).

2. Caldwell, "Reminiscences of the War of Secession," II, 830; Henry Heth, Memoir, 164, in Heth-Seldon Papers, University of Virginia. MacRae's headquarters were located either in the Hart House itself or on the adjacent grounds. The dwelling still stands in 2000 near Duncan Road and is a part of Pamplin Historical Park. Heth occupied the Century House, the Pickrell home, which also survives in 2000 as a private residence on the southeast side of Boydton Plank Road, U.S. 1. Heth documented visits by Lee to his headquarters, but no specific mention of "Marse Robert" at the Boisseau House has surfaced. Heth, Memoir, 165-166.

3. Caldwell, *The History of a Brigade of South Carolinians*, 259; Lane, "History of Lane's North Carolina Brigade," in *SHSP*, IX, 357. The regimental alignment of Lane's Brigade is not known. Scales's Brigade extended Wilcox's line to the east as

far as Lieutenant Run. See Inspection Reports and Related Records Received by the Inspection Branch in the Confederate Adjutant and Inspector General's Office, Wilcox's Division, November 30, 1864, filed as Inspection Report P, No. 37, Inclosure 46, Microcopy No. 935, Roll 12, Record Group 109, NA. The Banks House is preserved as a detached portion of Pamplin Historical Park south of U.S. 1 near Hofheimer Way. Battery 45 retains excellent integrity in 2000 near the intersection of Boydton Plank Road and Defense Road in the City of Petersburg and is identified by a small monument.

4. Inspection Reports and Related Records Received by the Inspection Branch in the Confederate Adjutant and Inspector General's Office, Wilcox's Division, December 31, 1864, filed as Inspection Report P, no. 46, Microcopy No. 935, Roll 14, Record Group 109, NA; Marion Hill Fiztpatrick to "Dear Amanda," November 3, 1864, in Henry Vaughan McCrea, *Red Dirt and Isinglass: A Wartime Biography of a Confederate Soldier* (Marianna, Fla., 1992), 524; Jeffrey C. Lowe and Sam Hodges, eds., *Letters to Amanda: The Civil War Letters of Marion Hill Fitzpatrick, Army of Northern Virginia* (Macon, Ga., 1998), 181-182; Inspection Report for McGowan's Brigade, January 27, 1865, filed as Inspection Report P, No. 53, Inclosure 4, Microcopy No. 935, Roll 15; Inspection Report for McGowan's Brigade, December 27, 1864, filed as Inspection Report P, No. 46, Inclosure 8, Microcopy No. 935, Roll 14, both in Inspection Reports and Related Records Received by the Inspection Branch in the Confederate Adjutant and Inspector General's Office, Record Group 109, NA. The troops along Hill's front occupied a portion of the defense line that stood a mile or more from the main Sixth Corps entrenchments. Thus, Hill's men discovered that they had little need of bombproof quarters, because incidents of artillery or mortar fire at that range were rare.

5. Robert R. Hemphill to "My dear Calvin," December 3, 1864, in *The Medium* (Abbeville S.C.), October 11, 1900.

6. The windstorm on March 23 that hurled dust with such abandon in the Union camps also spread fires in the Confederate camps. A Marylander in McComb's Brigade wrote in his diary, "About 1 o'clock p.m., there was a most terrific storm and from the carelessness of some one, the woods about three miles from us caught on fire, and the flames spread with great rapidity. In a short time some of the houses in our camp caught fire. We had hard work to keep the whole camp from being destroyed. Fortunately there were but three houses burned and several injured. To night the whole country seems to be on fire. The conflagration has reached the Federal camps, and as they have more woods than we, and the wind setting upon them, I expect they are having a lively time." Ammen, "Maryland Troops in the Confederate Army", I, 167, in Thomas Clemens Collection, USAMHI. The remains of two soldier huts have been excavated, marked, and backfilled behind the Battlefield Center at Pamplin Historical Park. The Park has reconstructed several soldier dwellings based on the dimensions of the originals and contemporary descriptions as a part of a demonstration camp.

7. Bell Irvin Wiley, *The Life of Johnny Reb*, 182; Robertson, *Soldiers Blue and Gray*, 186-188; William W. Bennett, *A Narrative of The Great Revival which prevailed In The Southern Armies* (Philadelphia, 1877, reprint, Harrisonburg, Va., 1989), 413-414; James A. Graham to "My dear Mother," February 24, 1865, in James A. Graham Papers, SHC; Joseph Caldwell Webb to "My dear Aunty," January 24, 1865, in the Lenoir Family Papers, SHC. One Confederate described the sanctuary used by Joseph R. Davis's Brigade as "a rude log house with four fireplaces in it, large enough to hold about 200 men." See Ammen, "Maryland Troops in the Confederate Army," I, 172, in Thomas Clemens Collection, USAMHI. The soldiers also participated in outdoor recreation. South Carolinian William J. Miller remembered that, "We younger soldiers played ball often and in the winter time we had snow. I have often seen whole regiments and brigades snowballing each other." Given the sparse snowfall that winter, these battles must have been brief and infrequent, or perhaps Miller confused the winter. See William J. Miller, Memoir, 12-13, in William J. Miller Papers, Winthrop University.

8. Benson, "Reminiscences," 606, in Berry G. Benson Papers, SHC; Joseph C. Webb to "My dear Aunty," March 15, 1865, in Lenoir Family Papers, SHC. The sources do not indicate which regiment defended McGowan's honor, but Sergeant Benson did identify the 1st South Carolina as the unit which competed against a regiment from MacRae's Brigade a few weeks earlier.

9. Wiley, *The Life of Johnny Reb,* 156-158; Robertson, *Soldiers Blue and Gray*, 83-84; Robert R. Hemphill to" My dear Calvin," December 3, 1864, in *The Medium* (Abbeville S.C.), October 11, 1900; Richard Rollins, "Black Southerners in Gray," in Richard Rollins, ed., *Black Southerners in Gray: Essays on Afro-Americans in the Confederate Armies* (Murfreesboro, Tenn., 1994), 21-22; Julius A. Lineback, Diary, January 4, 1865, in Julius A. Lineback Papers, SHC. The Marylanders had their own glee club as well. See Ammen, "Maryland Troops in the Confederate Army," I, 167, in Thomas Clemens Collection, USAMHI.

10. "A Confederate Airship. The Artis Avis Which was to Destroy Grant's Army," in *SHSP*, XXVIII, 303-305; Marion Hill Fitzpatrick to "Dear Amanda," December 8, 1864, in McCrea, *Red Dirt and Isinglass,* 531; Lowe and Hodges, eds., *Letters to Amanda*, 187-188. A discussion of the Artis Avis may also be found in J. Tracy Power, *Lee's Miserables: Life in the Army of Northern Virginia From the Wilderness to Appomattox* (Chapel Hill, N.C.,1998), 264-265. Davidson served in the 11th Mississippi Infantry and then as a clerk in the Treasury Department in Richmond.

11. James A. Graham to " My dear Mother," February 4, 1865, in James A. Graham Papers, SHC; Morse, "The 'Rebellion Record' of an Enlisted Man," in *National Tribune Scrapbook*, 97-98.

12. Pendleton to "Mayor & Council of the City of Petersburg," October 31, 1864, in William Nelson Pendleton Order Book, June 5, 1862-April 1, 1865, Museum of the Confederacy.

13. Kenneth Wiley, ed., *Norfolk Blues: The Civil War Diary of the Norfolk Light Artillery Blues* (Shippensburg, Pa., 1997), 207; R. P. Scarbrough quoted in

Trudeau, *The Last Citadel*, 260. Private John Walters, the lonely cannoneer quoted in the text, stated that, "As far as permits are concerned, they are almost unnecessary as we go down town as often as we wish, but having a permit relieves me from answering roll call." Walters's unit, the Norfolk Blues, was quartered in Petersburg, so access to town was easier than it would have been for the front line infantry outfits. See Wiley, ed., *Norfolk Blues*, 207. A soldier in the 2nd Maryland Battalion in McComb's Brigade received an invitation to visit Petersburg on February 10. "Dined with Mr. A. Took a walk with some young ladies this evening. Spent a most pleasant day," he recorded in his diary. See Ammen, "Maryland Troops in the Confederate Army," I, 166, in Thomas Clemens Collection, USAMHI.

14. Wiley, ed., *Norfolk Blues*, 185-187.

15. James A. Graham to "My dear Mother," February 4, 1865, in James A. Graham Papers, SHC; Benjamin F. Dixon, "Additional Sketch of the Forty-Ninth Regiment," in Clark, ed., *North Carolina in the Great War*, III, 154.

16. R. L. Proffit to "Dear F.M. & Sisters," November 27, 1864, in Proffit Family Papers, SHC; *OR* Series IV, 3, 653.

17. Freeman, *Lee's Lieutenants*, III, 619; Stephen R. Wise, *Lifeline of the Confederacy: Blockade Running During the Civil War* (Columbia, S.C., 1988), 192-213; *OR* pt. 2, 1221. For an excellent summary of the subsistence situation in the South during the last year of the war, see, Frank Vandiver, "The Food Supply of the Confederate Armies, 1865," in *Tyler's Quarterly Historical and Genealogical Magazine*, XXVI, 209-210.

18. *OR* pt. 2, 1210, 1246, 1297. Isaac Munroe St. John received his promotion on February 16, 1865.

19. *OR* Series IV, 3, 930-931; Joseph C. Webb to "My dear Aunty," March 15, 1865, in Lenoir Family Papers, SHC; John F. Shaffner [Salutation missing], January 1, 1865, in Fries and Shaffner Papers, SHC; Eugene W. Thompson to "Dear Friend," December 26, 1864, in Leonidas L. Polk Papers, SHC; James Lane, "Glimpses of Army Life," in *SHSP*, XVIII, 420.

20. Caldwell, *The History of a Brigade of South Carolinians*, 254-255; Samuel L. Dorroh to "Mother," February 9, 1865, in Samuel Lewers Dorroh Papers, 1861-1868, USC; Joseph W. Templeton to Sarah B. Templeton, February 8, 1865, in Templeton Family Papers, USC; Harry Hammond to his wife, February 7, 1865, in Hammond, Bryan, and Cummings Family Papers, USC.

21. Wiley, ed., *Norfolk Blues*, 184-185; Julius A. Lineback, Diary, January 3, 1865, in the Julius A. Lineback Papers, SHC; McCrea, *Red Dirt and Isinglass*, 535; Lowe and Hodges, eds., *Letters to Amanda*, 197; Coxe quoted in Ernest B. Furgurson, *Ashes of Glory: Richmond at War* (New York, 1996), 286. For an overview of the "Great National Dinner" of January 2-4, 1865, see Power, *Lee's Miserables*, 229-233.

22. Wiley, ed., *Norfolk Blues*, 185; Private John Cunningham Goolsby, "The Crenshaw Battery," in *SHSP*, XXVIII, 367; Daniel Augustus Tompkins, *Company K Fourteenth South Carolina Volunteers* (Charlotte, N.C., 1897), 25; William A.

Templeton to "Sister," March 15, 1865, in Templeton Family Papers, USC; Eugene W. Thompson to "Dear Friend," December 26, 1864, in Leonidas L. Polk Papers, SHC. The counties visited by Templeton included Dinwiddie, Brunswick, Lunenburg, Nottoway, and Mecklenburg, essentially the two tiers of counties between the Petersburg fortifications and the North Carolina border.

23. Virgil Cavin to "Dear Cosin," March 11, 1865, in Patterson-Cavin Family Papers, Duke; Olcott and Lear, *The Civil War Letters of Lewis Bissell*, 351; McCrea, *Red Dirt and Isinglass*, 533-534, 540; Lowe and Hodges, eds., *Letters to Amanda*, 195, 201; John F. Shaffner to "My darling Wife," March 14, 1865, in Fries and Shaffner Papers, SHC; Freeman, *Lee's Lieutenants*, III, 621. See also Harry Hammond to his wife, February 18, 1865, in Hammond, Bryan, Cummings Family Papers, USC, for testimony about improving rations in McGowan's Brigade.

24. Berry Benson to "Dear Sister," March 5, 1865, in Berry G. Benson Papers, SHC; Caldwell, *The History of a Brigade of South Carolinians*, 255.

25. R. L. Proffit to "Esteemed Sister," November 20, 1864, in Proffit Family Papers, SHC; Inspection Reports and Related Records Received by the Inspection Branch in the Confederate Adjutant and Inspector General's Office, Inspection Report for McGowan's Brigade, February 28, 1865, filed as Inspection Report P, No. 64, Inclosure 9, Microcopy No. 935, Roll 16, Record Group 109, NA; Caldwell, *The History of a Brigade of South Carolinians*, 255. The standard discussion of Confederate clothing during the war may be found in Wiley, *The Life of Johnny Reb*, 108-122.

26. Andrew Burwell to "Dear Mary," February 11, 1865, in Burwell Letters, University of Southern Mississippi; Olcott and Lear, *The Civil War Letters of Lewis Bissell*, 339; Agassiz, ed., *Meade's Headquarters*, 324.

27. Inspection Reports and Related Records Received by the Inspection Branch in the Confederate Adjutant and Inspector General's Office, Inspection Report for MacRae's Brigade, February 27, 1865, filed as Inspection Report P, No. 64, Inclosure 3, Microcopy No. 935, Roll 16, Record Group 109, NA; Isaac Gordon Bradwell, "Holding the Lines at Petersburg," in *SHSP*, XXVIII, 457.

28. Freeman, *Lee's Lieutenants*, III, 618; Thomas G. Jones, "Last Days of the Army of Northern Virginia," in *SHSP*, XXI, 65-66.

29. Joseph Caldwell Webb to "My dear Aunty," January 24, 1865, in Lenoir Family Papers, SHC; Benson, "Reminiscences," 610, and Benson to his father, March 25, 1865, both in Berry G. Benson Papers, SHC. Caldwell notes an increase in the amount of drill in February and March. See Caldwell, *The History of a Brigade of South Carolinians*, 255, 262. Reports regarding the frequency with which Confederates performed picket duty varied from every other day to once a week. See William S. Long, Memoir, in Breckinridge Long Papers, SHC; Caldwell, *The History of a Brigade of South Carolinians*, 253-254; William A. Templeton to "Sister," December 22, 1864, in Templeton Family Papers, USC; Ammen, "Maryland Troops in the Confederate Army," I, 166, in Thomas Clemens Collection, USAMHI.

30. John F. Shaffner [Salutation missing], January 15, 1865, in Fries and Shaffner Papers, SHC.

31. James Lane, "History of Lane's North Carolina Brigade," in *SHSP*, X, 207; Lane, "Glimpses of Army Life in 1864," in *SHSP*, XVIII, 414.

32. Ammen, "Maryland Troops in the Confederate Army," I, 167, 170, in Thomas Clemens Collection, USAMHI. This incident demonstrated not only the resistance to perceived abuses of discipline, but also the breakdown of morale within the Confederate army. The episode revealed "a mutinous spirit among officers and men, and a sad want of discipline among the Tennesseans," thought a Marylander. The Purcell Battery was a Virginia organization. "Bucking" was a form of physical punishment that required a soldier to sit with his hands and feet tied, his knees drawn up, his arms passed around them, and have a rod inserted horizontal to the ground, between his arms and the backs of his knees. Thus immobilized, the victim would soon experience significant discomfort.

33. Heth, Memoir, 165. Heth also noted that Lee would frequently stop to chat with Mrs. Heth and their daughter before conducting his inspections, "filling his pockets with apples and claiming a kiss for each apple he gave" the little girl. Headquarters Letter Book, 1863-1865, in Joseph Warren Keifer Papers, LC; Joseph C. Webb to "My dear Aunty," March 5, 1865, in Lenoir Family Papers, SHC; James A. Graham to "My dear Mother," February 24, 1865, in James A. Graham Papers, SHC; Jacob S. Bartlett, "The War Record of J.S. Bartlett A Private in Company E-First Regiment of North Carolina Volunteers From Yorktown to the Appomatox [sic]," 15, in J. S. Bartlett Papers, SHC.

34. *OR* Series IV, 3, 1012-1013. For excellent summaries of the debate over arming slaves in the Confederacy, see James M. McPherson, *Battle Cry of Freedom* (New York, 1988), 831-837, and Power, *Lee's Miserables*, 250-255.

35. Robert E. Lee to Hon. Ethelbert Barksdale, February 18, 1865, in St. Paul's Church Vestry Book, 69-70, VHS; Heth, Memoir, 167. Barksdale's bill and its companion in the Senate are discussed in Wilfred Buck Yearns, *The Confederate Congress* (Athens, Ga., 1960), 97-98.

36. *OR* Series 4, 3, 1110; McPherson, *Battle Cry of Freedom*, 836; Emory M. Thomas, *The Confederate Nation: 1861-1865* (New York, 1979), 296. For a summary of Davis's gradual acceptance of transforming slaves into Confederate soldiers, see William C. Davis, *Jefferson Davis: The Man and His Hour* (New York, 1991), 597-599. George C. Rable, *The Confederate Republic: A Revolution Against Politics* (Chapel Hill, N.C., 1994), 287-296, provides an outstanding account of the entire question of the Confederacy's struggle with the question of authorizing black combat troops.

37. McPherson, *Battle Cry of Freedom*, 837; Thomas, *The Confederate Nation*, 296-297; Mark Newman, compiler, "The Old Forty-Ninth Georgia," in *Confederate Veteran*, XXXI, 181; *OR* pt. 2, 1316; James W. Albright, Diary, March 15-16, 1865, in James W. Albright Papers, SHC. On February 22, General Horatio Wright reported that seven deserters from Lane's 18th North Carolina claimed that Tarheel soldiers voted against employing blacks as soldiers while Georgians favored

the measure and South Carolinians were divided on the question. See *OR* pt. 2, 639-640.

38. Jacob M. Siebert to "My Dear Father," February 24, 1865, in Siebert Family Papers, Harrisburg Civil War Round Table Collection, USAMHI; Franklin Jones to "My dear wife and children," February 26, 1865, in Franklin Jones Papers, The New Jersey Historical Society; Joseph C. Rutherford to "My dear wife," March 18, 1865, in Joseph Case Rutherford Papers, UVM.

39. Jacob S. Bartlett, "The War Record of J. S. Bartlett," 15, in J. S. Bartlett Papers, SHC; Hazard Stevens to "Dear Mother," January 29, 1865, in Hazard Stevens Papers, LC; Julius A. Lineback, Diary, January 25, 1865, in Julius A. Lineback Papers, SHC. Bartlett claimed that he was offered a commission as reward for his unique act of volunteering but turned it down. "A commissioned officer was not allowed to carry a gun in battle and I did not want the Yankees shooting at me and me with nothing to shoot back at them," he explained.

40. *OR* pt.2, 1258, 1265, 1292-1293, pt.3, 1353; Freeman, *Lee's Lieutenants*, III, 623-624. Freeman wrote that deserters equaled about 1/12 of all able-bodied Confederates. Theodore Lyman of Meade's staff believed that many more Confederates deserted to the rear than came into the Union lines, and estimated that Lee's losses from desertion in February alone must have equaled "a large brigade or a small division." Agassiz, ed., *Meade's Headquarters*, 305.

41. *OR* pt. 2, 1265, 1292-1293, pt. 3, 1353. 591 soldiers deserted from the rest of the army during that February period.

42. Tyler, *Recollections of the Civil War*, 333; Warren Williams to "My Dear Family," February 20, 1865, in Warren Williams Papers, University of Wisconsin, Milwaukee; William Bryant Adams to "Sister Dora," February 26, 1865, in William Bryant Adams Papers, Maine Historical Society; Joseph C. Rutherford to "My dear Wife," February 28, 1865, in Joseph Case Rutherford Papers, UVM; J. Warren Keifer to "My Dear Wife," March 1, 1865, in Joseph Warren Keifer Papers, LC; Olcott and Lear, *The Civil War Letters of Lewis Bissell*, 347.

43. Caldwell, *The History of a Brigade of South Carolinians*, 256; James A. Graham to "My Dear Mother," February 24, 1865, in James A. Graham Papers, SHC; Joseph C. Webb to "My dear Aunty," February 23, 1865, in Lenoir Family Papers, SHC; John W. Graham to "My Dear Father," February 22, 1865, in William A. Graham Papers, SHC. John Graham served in Matthew W. Ransom's Brigade of Bushrod R. Johnson's Division, not in Hill's corps.

44. Dayton E. Flint to "Dear Sister," February 21, 1865, reprinted in the *Washington* (N.J.) *Star*, April 20, 1911, in Dayton E. Flint Papers, Civil War Miscellaneous Collection, USAMHI; Homer Curtis to "Dear Mother," February 20, 1865, in Homer Curtis Letters, YU. The 33rd North Carolina served in Lane's Brigade.

45. Olcott and Lear, *The Civil War Letters of Lewis Bissell*, 347; John J. Ingraham to "Dear Sister," February 23, 1865, in John J. Ingraham Papers, Cornell University. Grayson M. Eichelberger of the 6th Maryland told almost precisely the

same story. See Grayson M. Eichelberger, Memoir, in Civil War Miscellaneous Collection, USAMHI.

46. A number of Union sources described such an episode with varying degrees of detail. It is probable that they all referred to the same event. See John Rumsey Brinckle to "My Dear Sister," February 26, 1865, in John Rumsey Brinckle Papers, LC; John H. Macomber, Diary, February 23, 1865, in John H. Macomber Papers, Minnesota Historical Society; Jacob Siebert to "My Dear Father," February 24, 1865, in Siebert Family Papers, Harrisburg Civil War Round Table Collection, USAMHI; William L. Phillips to "Father and Mother," February 25, 1865, in William L. Phillips Letters, SHSW; Houghton, "The Ordeal of Civil War," in *Vermont History*, XLI, 45.

47. Joseph Rutherford to "My Dear Wife," February 19, 1865, in Joseph Case Rutherford Papers, UVM.

48. Olcott and Lear, *The Civil War Letters of Lewis Bissell*, 344, 345. See Chapter Two for a discussion of desertions from the Union Sixth Corps.

49. George J. Howard to "My Dear," February 26, 1865, in George J. Howard Letters, VTHS.

50. *OR* pt.2, 587, 828-829. For Grant's assessment of Confederate desertion in the winter of 1865, see Grant, *Personal Memoirs*, II, 425-427.

51. Warren Williams to "My Dear Companion & Children," February 2, 1865, in Warren Williams Papers, University of Wisconsin, Milwaukee; Phelps, ed., "A Chaplain's Life in the Civil War," in Winthrop Henry Phelps Papers, LC; John F. Shaffner to "My darling Wife," March 19, 1865, in Fries and Shaffner Papers, SHC; Tyler, *Recollections of the Civil War*, 320-322; Peter Cullen to "The Honorable Mr. [Newton D.] Baker, Secretary of War, October 24, 1916, courtesy of Ed Root, Coopersburg, Pa. The scuttlebutt in the Sixth Corps was that the six-mule team and wagon earned the deserters $1,000. See Olcott and Lear, *The Civil War Letters of Lewis Bissell*, 345.

52. James E. Whitehorne, Diary, March 31, 1865, in J. E. Whitehorne Papers, SHC.

53. Virgil Cavin to "Dear Father & Mother & Brother," March 21, 1865, in Patterson-Cavin Family Papers, Duke; Franklin Jones to "Dear wife and children," February 18, 1865, in Franklin Jones Papers, The New Jersey Historical Society, for example.

54. James A. Graham to "My dear Mother," March 8, 1865, in James A. Graham Papers, SHC; John F. Shaffner to "My darling Wife," March 19, 1865, in Fries and Shaffner Papers, SHC; *OR* pt.2, 1254.

55. Petition from MacRae's Brigade, Army of Northern Virginia, February 24, 1865, in William A. Graham Papers, SHC. Five other such memorials were addressed to other representatives, each of them worded almost identically.

56. Meeta Armistead Capehart to "My own dear wife," March 16, 1865, in Meeta Armistead Capehart Papers, SHC.

57. Robert Stiles, *Four Years Under Marse Robert* (New York, 1903, reprint, Dayton, Oh., 1988), 350. More often than any other American soldiers,

Confederates faced the choice of defending their families from the enemy at their fence lines or protecting their country and comrades from the enemy across the battle lines.

58. *OR* pt. 3, 1353-1354.

59. Noah Collins, Memoir, 74-77, in Isaac Spencer London Collection, North Carolina Department of Archives and History; Virgil Cavin to "Dear father & mother," February 18, 1865, in Patterson-Cavin Family Papers, Duke; Benson, "Reminiscences," 581, in Berry G. Benson Papers, SHC.

60. *OR* pt. 2, 1254; Tyler, *Recollections of the Civil War*, 332; Benson, "Reminiscences," 580, in Berry G. Benson Papers, SHC; John B. Southard to "Dear Sister," February 28, 1865, in Southard Family Correspondence, New-York Historical Society. Of course, only troops from the Carolinas and Georgia were opposite Southard's regiment. Mason Tyler of the 37th Massachusetts wrote on February 26 that a whole company of South Carolinians deserted the previous night. "It is not often that we get them from that state." It does no dishonor to the Palmetto State to recognize that only McGowan's Brigade represented South Carolina on the Sixth Corps front, which partially explains Tyler's observation that South Carolina deserters were relatively scarce. Tyler, *Recollections of the Civil War*, 335.

61. A number of sources examine the attitudes of North Carolinians about secession and the prosecution of the war. See Daniel W. Crofts, *Reluctant Confederates: Upper South Unionists in the Secession Crisis* (Chapel Hill, N.C., 1989); John G. Barrett, *The Civil War in North Carolina* (Chapel Hill, N.C., 1963); and W. Buck Yearns and John G. Barrett, eds., *North Carolina Civil War Documentary* (Chapel Hill, N.C., 1980).

62. Olcott and Lear, *The Civil War Letters of Lewis Bissell*, 336; John J. Ingraham to "My Dear Friend," February 3, 1865, in John J. Ingraham Papers, Cornell University. Ingraham described an incident in which four of five members of a Confederate picket post deserted, "the fifth one could not pluck up courage enough to come with them but agreed not to fire at them when they started. To screen himself [from charges of disobedience of orders], he would fire three shots high so he would not hit them." One Union report indicated that a Confederate sharpshooter was promised a 30-day furlough if he brought in an aspiring deserter—dead or alive. See Anonymous Union Spy Intelligence Journal, February 18, 1865, in Schoff Civil War Collection, University of Michigan.

63. Olcott and Lear, *The Civil War Letters of Lewis Bissell*, 343; Hazard Stevens to "Dear Mother," March 1, 1865, in Hazard Stevens Papers, LC; J. Warren Keifer to Captain Charles H. Whit[t]elsey, February 15, 1865, in Letters Received, Sixth Army Corps, 1862-1865, Part II, Entry 4414, Record Group 393, NA; Charles G. Gould to "Dear Parents," February 23, 1865, in Captain Charles Gilbert Gould Collection, UVM.

64. Olcott and Lear, *The Civil War Letters of Lewis Bissell*, 351; *OR* pt. 3, 1357.

65. *OR* pt. 2, 1229-1230. General Orders Number 4 of the Army of Northern Virginia, issued a few days later, repeated the offer of amnesty and ordered those

enlisted men in the army who were under arrest, awaiting trial, or serving sentences for being absent without leave or desertion to be released immediately and restored to active duty. See Power, *Lee's Miserables*, 255.

66. John Franklin Heitman, Diary, February 27, 1865, in John Franklin Heitman Papers, Duke; Maj. James C. MacRae and Sergt.-Maj. C.M. Busbee, "Fifth Regiment,"; Walter A. Montgomery, "Twelfth Regiment,"; Brigadier-General Thomas F. Toon, "Twentieth Regiment"; Captain Vines E. Turner, A. Q. M. [&] Henry C. Wall, "Twenty-Third Regiment," all in Clark, ed., *North Carolina in the Great War*, I, 290, 650, II, 124, 262-263. The 7th North Carolina of Lane's Brigade left Petersburg on February 26 for High Point, North Carolina to arrest deserters and return absentees to the army. See Captain James S. Harris, "Seventh Regiment," in Clark, ed., *North Carolina in the Great War*, I, 386. Elements of Cooke's Brigade of Heth's Division also returned to the Old North State to hunt deserters. One recent student of Lee's army wrote, "For the most part . . . the order [allowing amnesty to returning deserters] was ineffective both as an incentive for absentees or deserters to return without punishment and as a deterrent for those inclined to desert in the future. See Power, *Lee's Miserables*, 256.

67. Virgil Cavin, undated letter fragment, in Patterson-Cavin Family Papers, Duke.

68. Caldwell, "Reminiscences of the War of Secession," in Snowden, ed., *History of South Carolina*, II, 830. Harry Hammond dated these executions to March 9, 1865. See Hammond to his wife, March 10, 1865, in Hammond, Bryan, and Cummings Family Papers, USC.

69. Benson, "Reminiscences," 609, in Berry G. Benson Papers, SHC; Freeman, *Lee's Lieutenants*, III, 624. Executions occurred throughout the winter, not just in response to the increased frequency of the crime in February and March. See Ammen, "Maryland Troops in the Confederate Army," I, 166,172, in Thomas Clemens Collection, USAMHI, for a description of the execution of a soldier in the 14th Tennessee on January 3, 1865 attended by McComb's Brigade, in which the victim lived nearly ten minutes after being shot. "It was a trying sight indeed," wrote one witness. "The man himself seemed to take it very easy. A minister prayed with him for a few minutes after he had been blindfolded."

70. Eugene W. Thompson to "Dear Friend," December 26, 1864, in Leonidas L. Polk Papers, SHC. As a non-combatant, Thompson faced less personal risk on the battlefield than the soldiers in his regiment, but his commitment to the army's cause mirrored that of his comrades.

71. McCrea, *Red Dirt and Isinglass*, 534; *Lowe and Hodges*, eds., *Letters to Amanda*, 196; J. E. Whitehorne, Diary, March 31, 1865, in J. E. Whitehorne Papers, SHC.

72. John F. Shaffner [Salutation missing], January 1, 1865, in Fries and Shaffner Papers, SHC; Joseph C. Webb to "My dear Aunty," January 24, 1865, in Lenoir Family Papers, SHC; Hammond to his wife, March 10 and March 25, 1865, in Hammond, Bryan, and Cummings Family Papers, USC.

73. Andrew B. Wardlaw to "Dear Wife," February 5, 1865, in Andrew Bowie Wardlaw Papers, USC; Benson, "Reminiscences," 595, in Berry G. Benson Papers, SHC.

74. Photocopy of Resolutions on Display at Tudor Hall, Pamplin Historical Park. Staff officer Major Andrew B. Wardlaw wrote this about these Resolutions: "Our Brig. adopted a capital set of resolutions, drawn up by Gen. McG., almost unanimously, except in the shabby Rifle Regt. The Pickens & Anderson companies are composed of narrow minded, prejudiced men & a good many of these refused at first to come up to the scratch, but the next day they were addressed by their Col. & made a rather lame redemption of their character. The Abbeville companies did what was expected of them." Andrew B. Wardlaw to "Dear Wife," February 5, 1865, in Andrew Bowie Wardlaw Papers, USC.

· 75. Lane, "History of Lane's North Carolina Brigade," in *SHSP*, IX, 357-61. The 7th and 33rd North Carolina did not pass similar resolutions because they were recruited for the duration of the war, so the question of voluntary reenlistment was moot with them. Wilcox's Division certainly enjoyed no monopoly on this brand of late-war patriotism. Many units throughout the Army of Northern Virginia adopted similar resolutions to those cited in McGowan's and Lane's brigades. For a thorough discussion of these documents see Power, *Lee's Miserables*, 245-249.

76. James W. Albright, Diary, March 1, 1865, in James W. Albright Papers, SHC.

77. John F. Shaffner to "My darling wife," March 10, 1865, in Fries and Shaffner Papers, SHC; Tazewell L. Hargrove to "My dear Father," March 8, 1865, in Willis G. Briggs Papers, SHC; Joseph C. Webb to " My dear Aunty," February 23, 1865, in Lenoir Family Papers, SHC; Theodore Vaill to "Dear Brother Chas.," March 16, 1865, in Theodore F. Vaill Papers, Northwest Corner Civil War Round Table Collection, USAMHI; Benson, "Reminiscences," 610 and Benson to his father, March 25, 1865, both in Berry G. Benson Papers, SHC.

78. *OR* pt. 2, 1230; William H. Forney to "My Dear Wife," February 9, 1865, in William H. Forney Papers, SHC; John F. Shaffner to his wife, March 16, 1865, in Fries and Shaffner Papers, SHC. Lee's private correspondence struck a more fatalistic note than his public proclamation: "Sherman & Schofield are both advancing & seem to have every thing their own way, but trusting in a merciful God, who does not always give the battle to the strong, I pray we may not be overwhelmed. I shall however do my duty & fight to the last." Lee to "My dear Mary," February 21, 1865, in Robert Edward Lee Papers, VHS.

79. Hazard Stevens to "Dear Mother," February 8, 1865, and February 12, 1865, in Hazard Stevens Papers, LC.

CHAPTER FOUR

Strategy and Combat
in February and March, 1865

oratio Wright believed in leadership by example. The Sixth Corps commander often forsook the desk at his headquarters and ventured into the field to see and be seen by his troops. Exercising that philosophy on the morning of January 4, 1865, Wright rode forward to examine the corps picket line with an engineer's eye toward ensuring its proper location and design. In the course of his inspection, the general suffered a severe fall from his mount, occasioning concern among his staff that he had sustained a serious injury. The surgeons suspected only broken ribs, but by the next morning the bedridden commander could barely move. Wright's condition gradually improved during the next two weeks, but not nearly enough to allow him to resume his duties. On January 17, Wright received permission to take a leave of absence to fully regain his strength. Brigadier General George W. Getty inherited temporary command of the corps until Wright returned, which would not be for more than a fortnight. During that interval, the Army of the Potomac experienced its first real combat of the new year, including a supporting role for a portion of the Sixth Corps.[1]

General Grant precipitated that fighting on February 4 when he ordered George Meade to initiate an offensive designed to interdict the route used by Robert E. Lee to bring supplies into Petersburg from the

Brigadier General George W. Getty

Massachusetts MOLLUS Collection, Carlisle Barracks, Pennsylvania

south. The Boydton Plank Road near Dinwiddie Court House offered the best target for such a mission. This was a job for cavalry, and Meade turned to the only mounted troops with the Army of the Potomac: the Second Division, under Brigadier General David M. Gregg. Meade designated Gouverneur K. Warren's Fifth Corps to provide close support for the horsemen along Stage Road east of Dinwiddie. Two of Andrew A. Humphreys's Second Corps divisions would, in turn, protect Warren by

keeping north of the Fifth Corps, between Warren and the permanent
Confederate lines. This large expedition, dedicated to a relatively small
purpose, left its camps between 3:00 a.m. and 7:00 a.m. on February 5.[2]

The Union cavalry easily reached Dinwiddie Court House but found
few wagons. By day's end, they had bagged just eighteen vehicles along with
50 prisoners. Warren dutifully brushed aside a small force at Monk's Neck
Bridge over Rowanty Creek, repaired the span, and proceeded west,
stretched out along Stage Road for several miles but in position to
concentrate should Gregg encounter significant enemy resistance.[3]

Humphreys executed the most dangerous assignment of the
operation, because his men deployed closest to the expanded Confederate
fortifications. Following the October fighting at Burgess's Mill on the
Boydton Plank Road, Powell Hill had improved his lines to and across
Hatcher's Run, and then northward to Burgess's Mill. The Federals knew
that these earthworks bristled with the bayonets of Heth's Division and
that, should Gregg and Warren find trouble, it would likely be from Heth.
Accompanied by two divisions led by brigadier generals Thomas A. Smyth
and Gershom Mott (Brigadier General Nelson A. Miles's division remained
in the Second Corps defensive lines three miles away), Humphreys
marched toward Hatcher's Run at Armstrong's Mill and Vaughan Road to
serve as a shield between Heth and Warren.[4]

Humphreys established communications with Warren, some four
miles to the southwest, and deployed Smyth's division northward along
Duncan Road, facing west toward the Confederate works, which were in
full view about 1,000 yards distant. He refused Smyth's right flank and,
recognizing its vulnerability, summoned Colonel Robert McAllister's
brigade of Mott's division to extend the line to the east. However, a
dangerous gap remained between McAllister and Smyth, and the
Confederates wasted little time exploiting it.

Lee discovered the Federal offensive before noon and reacted
instantly. He alerted both Heth's and Brigadier General John Pegram's
divisions, situated, respectively, in the earthworks north of Hatcher's Run
and near Burgess's Mill, to the possibility of an attack against them like the
one in October. He also summoned Brigadier General Clement A. Evans's
Division of Gordon's corps to reinforce Pegram and counter such a threat.
When he discovered the Federals along Hatcher's Run had halted their
advance, Lee planned a strike of his own. Scouts discovered the weakness
in Humphreys's dispositions, and Lee ordered Heth to strike the
pregnable portion of the Second Corps line with Cooke's, McComb's, and
MacRae's brigades.

In the meantime, a worried Humphreys had ordered one brigade from Miles's division to reinforce his tenuous position north of Armstrong's Mill. That unit began to arrive shortly after 4:00 p.m., allowing McAllister to shift toward the gap. While this movement was under way, Heth charged. The battle lasted more than an hour and involved multiple assaults. "The enemy, as usual, massed and fell on us—nearly the whole force against my brigade," wrote Colonel McAllister. "Thank God we three times rolled back the tide of battle." Cooke's Tarheels suffered the most during these unsuccessful attacks, observed by Lee himself from behind Heth's earthworks. "In the afternoon parts of Hill's and Gordon's troops demonstrated against the enemy on the left of Hatcher's Run, near Armstrong's Mill," Lee laconically reported the next day. "Finding him entrenched they were withdrawn after dark."[5]

Heth's attack may have failed, but its boldness, combined with the minimal gain achieved by the cavalry at Dinwiddie Court House, prompted Meade to terminate his operation and order the concentration of the entire expedition at the Vaughan Road crossing of Hatcher's Run. Before dawn on February 6, Gregg rejoined Humphreys and Warren in this neighborhood. Meade also called on a division of the Ninth Corps and Brigadier General Frank Wheaton's division of the Sixth Corps to move toward the scene of action near Hatcher's Run. Thus, Meade committed seven full infantry divisions, a part of an eighth, and virtually all of the army's available cavalry to the security of an offensive that had netted fewer than twenty wagons. Wheaton received orders to move about 8:00 p.m., February 5, and he followed Squirrel Level Road south several miles before establishing a fortified camp shortly after midnight.[6]

The next morning, February 6, both armies launched probes to determine the whereabouts of their enemies. On the north side of Hatcher's Run, Humphreys ascertained that Heth's Division had returned to its fortifications. South of the stream, Warren delayed his advance until 1:00 p.m., when Meade prodded him to move westward both on Vaughan Road and a parallel track two miles north that led toward Dabney's Saw Mill. This put the Fifth Corps on a collision course with Pegram's Division, which Lee had ordered to explore both of these byways on a west-to-east axis.

Opposing elements clashed shortly after 2:00 p.m. On Vaughan Road the Union infantry, buttressed by Gregg's cavalry, held its own and turned back the Rebels. The fighting along Dabney's Mill Road, however, assumed a life of its own, the meeting engagement acting like a magnet for every available unit, blue and gray, in the vicinity. Warren sent brigades from each of his three divisions first against Pegram, and later against Evans's

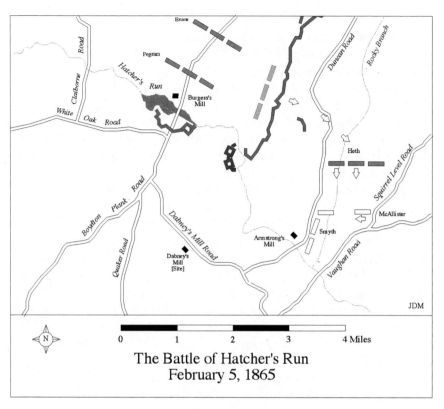

The Battle of Hatcher's Run
February 5, 1865

The Battle of Hatcher's Run
February 6, 1865

and William Mahone's divisions, the latter commanded that day by Brigadier General Joseph Finegan. The battle lines swayed to and fro, first one side and then the other gaining the advantage. Once the firing began, Wheaton received word to move forward and assist Warren if necessary. With the sound of battle echoing plainly across the frigid Dinwiddie landscape, Wheaton pushed west on Vaughan Road and met Meade, who directed him toward the front. A Fifth Corps staff officer urgently beseeched Wheaton's leading brigade, the Second, under the temporary command of Colonel James Hubbard of the 2nd Connecticut Heavy Artillery, to march west on Dabney's Mill Road and reinforce Warren's hard-pressed divisions.

Hubbard's men rushed forward, crossed Hatcher's Run, and hurried toward Dabney's Mill, loading their guns as they went. About three-quarters of a mile beyond the stream, Wheaton ordered the brigade into line of battle just as a mass of blue-uniformed fugitives, mostly from Brigadier General Samuel W. Crawford's Fifth Corps division, burst through the dense woods in their front. "Just here we met many running for their lifes to the rear," remembered one of Hubbard's officers. "We stopped all we could. A Lt. was one. I ordered him to halt, he would not, so I drew my sword on his backside." The stampede, however, proved too large to arrest despite Wheaton's efforts to form the panicked soldiers on Hubbard's flanks. The torrent became so powerful "that we were completely broken up and obliged to fall back to re-form," remembered one of Hubbard's subordinates. Gathering darkness and scattered but disconcerting friendly fire made even this retrograde movement dangerous for the Sixth Corps veterans. "Charged them and then ordered back . . . everything in confusion and a perfect whirlpool and panic," claimed a soldier in the 121st New York. At last, Wheaton established a new line about 300 yards to the east, assisted by one of Brigadier General Charles Griffin's Fifth Corps brigades. The skirmish firing gradually abated and by 10:00 p.m. Hubbard's weary troops fell back to the northeast side of Hatcher's Run and rejoined the rest of the division in Humphreys's unthreatened entrenchments. "We . . . lay down on our arms for the night in a rough cornfield," recalled a member of the 121st New York, "which was non[e] too dry for comfort."[7]

Amidst a "severe storm of sleet and snow" that night, officers on both sides assessed the day's action. Officially, Warren cast a positive light on the battle, but he admitted privately that "we are getting to have an array of such poor soldiers that we have to lead them everywhere, and even then they run away from us." A Confederate staff officer evaluated the performance of Lee's troops with similar disappointment: "Our men fight

badly, many of them . . . a sacrifice to the failure in duty of company &
regimental commanders, when their men gave ground."

The next day, Warren pressed forward again and slowly pushed back
the Confederate picket line in combat limited by exhaustion, minor
objectives, and execrable weather. Two of Wheaton's brigades supported
this effort but did not become embroiled in the day's incidental fighting.
During the night, the Federals withdrew without incident, offering an
anti-climactic ending to the Battle of Hatcher's Run.[8]

Meade reported 1,539 casualties between February 5 and 7, including
one killed, 21 wounded, and five missing in Wheaton's division. Lee's
losses are estimated at about 1,000, the most lamented being division
commander Pegram, felled by a sharpshooter's bullet on the afternoon of
February 6. The engagement allowed Meade to expand his permanent
fortifications southwest to the Vaughan Road crossing of Hatcher's Run, a
distance of about three miles. The Second Corps manned these works,
compelling part of the Sixth Corps to shift westward into the lines around
forts Fisher, Welch, and Gregg that had previously been occupied by
Humphreys's men.

Beyond the loss of the competent (and newly wed) Pegram, Hatcher's
Run meant little to Lee. He had realized long before the first week of
February that offensives around his right flank aimed at cutting the
Boydton Plank Road and South Side Railroad would likely continue until
his lines became too stretched or his ability to counterpunch too feeble to
protect his remaining supply routes. What to do about that eventuality
continued to dominate Lee's thinking.[9]

*   *   *

The gun smoke had barely dissipated along Hatcher's Run when Lee
assumed his new responsibilities as general-in-chief of all Confederate
armies, while maintaining direct command of the Army of Northern
Virginia. For weeks, Lee had recognized that the progress of Union armies
in the Carolinas exacerbated his army's precarious strategic situation
around Petersburg and Richmond. Sherman's legions were moving like a
swarm of amphibious locusts through South Carolina. Within a week the
blue tide would engulf the capital at Columbia and isolate Charleston,
forcing the evacuation of the cradle of secession. Another Federal force led
by Major General John M. Schofield targeted Wilmington, North Carolina,
and on February 22 Schofield would conquer that important city. Lee, of
course, wished to protect the states to his south from the Yankee invaders,
but the presence of these troops in the Carolinas portended disaster for the

defenders of Petersburg and Richmond as well. As early as January 29, Lee informed President Davis that should Grant receive any sizable reinforcements, "I do not see how in our present position he can be prevented from enveloping Richmond." Three weeks later, the general-in-chief wrote James Longstreet that, "If Sherman marches his army to Richmond . . . and General Schofield is able to unite with him, we shall have to abandon our position. . . ."[10]

"I do not see how in our present position [Grant] can be prevented from enveloping Richmond."

This critical relationship between Federal progress in the Carolinas and the viability of the Petersburg-Richmond defensive perimeter prompted Lee to execute a major command change the day Wilmington fell. He plucked the much-traveled and controversial General Joseph E. Johnston off the military shelf assigning the Virginian overall command in the Carolinas. Johnston's nearly impossible mission was to turn back Sherman before he could combine with Schofield. Should Sherman's juggernaut prove unstoppable, Lee would evacuate Petersburg and Richmond and rendezvous with Johnston's army along the railroad between Burkeville and Danville. Ironically, the legendary commander of the Army of Northern Virginia found the performance of his primary mission, the defense of Richmond, largely dependent upon the man whom he had replaced in that role almost three years earlier.[11]

Although Lee had confidence in Johnston, he fully realized the steep odds faced by Confederate forces to the south. To forestall the determination of the war on a doubtful contest of arms, Lee tried a diplomatic ploy. On March 2, he contacted Grant seeking an interview to explore "the possibility of arriving at a satisfactory adjustment of the present unhappy difficulties by means of a military convention." Grant quickly disavowed any authority to participate in such a meeting and assured the Lincoln administration that he would press "all advantages gained to the utmost of my ability."[12]

An ominous demonstration of that advantage occurred the very day Lee corresponded with Grant. Major General Philip H. Sheridan administered the coup de grace to what remained of the Confederates' Shenandoah Valley army at the Battle of Waynesboro. The complete rout of Lieutenant General Jubal A. Early opened the way for Sheridan and his blue cavalry to reinforce Grant at Petersburg. First Sherman and Schofield and now Sheridan promised to increase the numerical superiority enjoyed by Grant's forces beyond Lee's ability to resist. Lee counted some 56,000 men in the Petersburg-Richmond lines, while he estimated that the Federals could bring 160,000 to the James and Appomattox front. Johnston would do what he could in North Carolina, but under these circumstances, what course should the Army of Northern Virginia follow?[13]

To help answer that question, Lee sought the advice of his youngest corps commander. At 2:00 a.m. on March 4, John Gordon received Lee's messenger requesting an immediate meeting at army headquarters. The anxious Gordon rode through a bitter night and arrived at Edge Hill to find the general-in-chief wearing "a look of painful depression on his face." Lee invited Gordon to examine various reports revealing the desperate condition of Confederate military fortunes across the map. He then asked the respected Georgian "to state frankly what I thought under those conditions it was best to do."

Gordon listed three plausible courses of action. First, "make terms with the enemy, the best we can get." Of course, Gordon did not know that Lee had attempted to do just that by approaching Grant. Second, "retreat—abandon Richmond and Petersburg, unite by rapid marches with General Johnston in North Carolina, and strike Sherman before Grant can join him." This possibility had been discussed for more than a month. Should retreat be deemed undesirable, however, Gordon advocated one final option: "we must fight, and without delay."[14]

Armed with this counsel, with which he professed to agree, Lee journeyed to Richmond for a meeting with Jefferson Davis. There, word of Grant's refusal to parley preempted any discussion of a negotiated peace. The president's views on compromising Confederate independence were too well known to allow room for debate. Lee then expressed his conviction that it would be necessary to abandon Petersburg and Richmond, a grim prospect that Davis accepted without apparent protest. The general could not authorize the movement, however, until the muddy roads of Southside Virginia dried sufficiently in the spring sun to permit Lee's emaciated draft animals to haul loaded wagons long distances. Once in the open, Lee would strike southwest and unite with Johnston to face first Sherman, and then turn on Grant. In the meantime, Lee would have to attack Grant before Sheridan arrived from the Valley and threatened to cut Lee's communications with Johnston, thus preserving the one practical avenue for continued Confederate field operations. To stand still meant death for his army, thought Lee, whereas by fighting, the end would come only with defeat.[15]

Lee's vague notion of launching a spoiling attack to buy evacuation time for his army never found the chance to mature. On March 9, Lee wrote the new secretary of war, John C. Breckinridge, that he saw "no strong prospect" that Johnston could stop Sherman. A communication from Johnston two days later confirmed Lee's doubts. "Should Sherman and [Schofield's top subordinate, Major General Jacob D.] Cox unite," wrote Johnston, "their march into Virginia cannot be prevented by me." But then, Johnston added a new wrinkle to Confederate strategic thinking. "Would it be practicable," he asked Lee, "to hold one of the inner lines of Richmond with one part of your army, and meet Sherman with the other, returning to Richmond after fighting?"[16]

The idea intrigued Lee. If the Confederates could strike Grant in such a way as to compel the Federal commander to shorten his lines, Lee might reduce the number of his trench-bound defenders as well. The surplus could then combine with Johnston and assail Sherman as that officer approached the Virginia border. If successful, Lee and Johnston would countermarch to Petersburg and confront Grant on more equal terms. Even should Lee's initial offensive fail, he might still earn the breathing room needed to execute his original plan and completely evacuate the fortifications so as to combine with Johnston to the southwest. How and where to achieve the attack against Grant, Lee asked Gordon to decide. Johnston's failure to stop Sherman at Bentonville, North Carolina on March 19-21, and Schofield's rendezvous with "Uncle Billy" at Goldsboro, North Carolina on March 23 convinced Lee that the time to launch his "last grand offensive" had arrived.[17]

*   *   *

Grand strategic thinking occupied the general-in-chief at City Point as fully as it did the officers at Edge Hill in the late winter of 1865. Ulysses S. Grant formulated plans to pursue simultaneous offensives "which covered a theater of war greater than that of any campaigns in modern history," wrote one of the general's staff officers, including initiatives aimed at Mobile, Alabama and in east Tennessee. Of course, Grant watched Sherman's progress with abundant approbation as his trusted subordinate rolled through the Carolinas. He also kept an ear turned for reports from his other favorite lieutenant, Philip Sheridan. On March 5, news arrived of Sheridan's decisive victory over Early, but then a week passed with no definite information concerning the stumpy Irishman's whereabouts. During the evening meal at headquarters on March 12, two supremely disheveled figures appeared at Grant's cabin. The visitors brought a dispatch from Sheridan written on tissue paper and wrapped tightly in tinfoil to enable the couriers to ingest it should they have been intercepted en route.[18]

Sheridan's missive summarized his accomplishments since defeating Early at Waynesboro. "Little Phil's" cavalry had crossed the Blue Ridge Mountains and captured Charlottesville with the intention of moving south of the James to wreck the South Side Railroad from Appomattox to Farmville. High water and damaged bridges frustrated this plan, however, and Sheridan focused instead on the destruction of the James River and Kanawha Canal and the Virginia Central Railroad, prefatory to a rendezvous with Grant. The blue horsemen did their job with singular thoroughness, reported Sheridan, who now requested that forage and rations be sent to White House Landing on the Pamunkey River from where the column would make its way into Union lines.[19]

Sheridan's anticipated arrival helped Grant perfect his plan for the spring campaign around Petersburg and Richmond. Grant later called this period "one of the most anxious . . . of my experience during the rebellion," his apprehension arising from the fear that Lee, worn down by desertion and bereft of military options, would abandon the Petersburg-Richmond lines. "I knew that he could move much more lightly and more rapidly than I," wrote Grant, "and that, if he got the start, he would leave me behind so that we would have the same army to fight again farther south—and the war might be prolonged another year."[20]

To avert this unhappy circumstance, Grant longed to commence the spring offensive that he hoped would eliminate Lee's army and, combined with Sherman's progress in the Carolinas, end the war. But the Federals faced the same daunting logistical problems that delayed Lee's intention to execute the very plan Grant dreaded. The heavy rains that prevented Confederate vehicles from extricating themselves from the Petersburg lines also prohibited Grant from launching a campaign dependent on the mud-soaked roads. "It was necessary to wait until [the roads] had dried sufficiently to enable us to move the wagon trains and artillery necessary to the efficiency of an army operating in the enemy's country," observed the general-in-chief. Grant would also defer to Sheridan: "It was necessary that I should have his cavalry with me, and I was therefore obliged to wait until he could join me south of the James River."[21]

Sheridan would come, Sherman would press north, and sooner or later, nature would bake the sloppy byways of Dinwiddie County into a passable mix. Until then, Grant awoke every morning afraid that "Lee had gone, and that nothing was left but a picket line." Perhaps Lee would attempt to escape with that kind of stealth. Instead, he might hazard an

Sixth Corps winter quarters, February 1865. *Massachusetts MOLLUS Collection, Carlisle Barracks, Pennsylvania*

attack against some portion of the Union lines to create confusion sufficient to allow the Army of Northern Virginia to get away before the bluecoats could recover. As early as February 22, Grant sent instructions to the acting army commander, Major General John G. Parke, to be on the alert for such a tactic. "As there is a possibility of an attack from the enemy at any time . . . extra vigilance should be kept up both by the pickets and the troops on the line," wrote the general-in-chief. "Let commanders understand that no time is to be lost awaiting orders, if an attack is made, in bringing all their reserves to the point of danger. With proper alacrity in this respect I would have no objection to seeing the enemy get through."[22]

As February gave way to March, no Confederate attack occurred and travel conditions began to improve. Grant circulated explicit orders throughout the Army of the Potomac to prepare to pursue Lee should the Southerners quit their lines:

> From this time forward keep your command in condition to be moved on the very shortest possible notice in case the enemy should evacuate, or partially evacuate, Petersburg, taking with you the maximum amount of supplies your trains are capable of carrying. It will not be necessary to keep wagons loaded, as they can be loaded in a few hours at any time. If we do move[,] the line southwest of the Jones house will be abandoned.[23]

The line identified in Grant's orders included defenses maintained by the Sixth Corps. Naturally, these instructions and the news from North Carolina left Wright's troops alive to the probability that fighting would soon erupt again. "The effect of Sheridan's raid and Schofield's victory over Bragg has really made the rascals desperate and they have either got to get out of their present position or starve," explained a Vermont soldier to his wife.[24]

If Grant seemed to possess an uncanny prescience for understanding Lee's plans, he shared that intuition with others in his army. "We are hourly expecting some movement upon the part of the rebels, which will cause us to move," wrote Warren Keifer on March 23. "It seems certain that it is the intention of Genl. Lee to unite Johnson's [sic] army (now in North Carolina) with his, and then strike either this army or Sherman's and should he be successful in striking one, he would hope to be able to turn and defeat the other. This will be his grand Napoleonic tactics." Keifer could not have better described the Confederate strategy had he been present at the Turnbull House or in Davis's office on Clay Street in Richmond.[25]

Grant, Keifer, and others reached their conclusions not from information supplied by some well-placed spy or by the interception of secret Confederate correspondence, but from common-sensical analysis of their opponents' options. With the Northern commitment to prosecute the war an established fact, any competent military thinker realized that Lee could not remain stagnant at Petersburg and Richmond and hope to maintain his army indefinitely. He had to do something, and the alternatives boiled down to executing a surreptitious escape, with all or part of his forces, aided, perhaps, by an attack designed to render the evacuation more practical.

Grant's understanding of the military situation around Petersburg had the virtue of precision but the vice of reaction. His orders had been predicated upon response to a movement by Lee, while Sherman, Schofield, and Sheridan carried the offensive burden in distant theaters. This went against Grant's grain, and on March 24 he took steps to reclaim the strategic initiative he had monopolized since the Army of the Potomac passed the Rapidan River the previous spring. Learning of Sheridan's intention to cross the James, and expecting to enjoy the services of that esteemed officer and his veteran cavalry, Grant issued orders for a coordinated offensive to end the war. "On the 29th instant," Grant wrote to Meade, Sheridan, and Major General Edward O. C. Ord, commander of the Army of the James, "the armies operating against Richmond will be moved by our left, for the double purpose of turning the enemy out of his present position around Petersburg, and to insure the success of the cavalry under General Sheridan, which will start at the same time, in its efforts to reach and destroy the South Side and Danville railroads." In five days, Grant would bring the war to Lee before the Confederates could execute their own limited attack or disappear into the night down the railroads leading west and south out of Petersburg and Richmond.

But Grant's planning reckoned without John Gordon.[26]

*   *   *

Since receiving orders from Lee to perfect the details of the Confederate offensive, Gordon had "labored day and night at this exceedingly grave and discouraging problem, on the proper solution of which depended the commander's decision as to when and where he would deliver his last blow for the life of the Confederacy." Gordon canvassed the entire Union line and determined that, using a Confederate strongpoint east of Petersburg called Colquitt's Salient as his launching pad, he could attack Fort Stedman and its associated batteries.

Here, on a small plateau known as Hare's Hill, the lines stood merely 200 yards apart, with picket posts separated by one-quarter of that distance. The young Georgian believed that by capturing Fort Stedman and three forts thought to be to its rear, "the disintegration of the whole left wing of the Federal army" might be possible. Surely, success at Stedman would at least force Grant to constrict his lines, thus allowing Lee to detach troops to Johnston.[27]

Gordon met with Lee on March 22 and presented his plan. After due consideration, Lee approved it the next day. Gordon's tactical conception called for the clandestine removal of the Confederate obstructions in front of Colquitt's Salient, the capture of Union pickets by men posing as deserters, elimination of the barriers protecting Fort Stedman by 50 axemen, allowing Gordon's infantry to storm the fort, and finally the infiltration by 300 picked troops of the Union bastions supposed to be in Stedman's rear. These commandos, led by local guides selected personally by General Lee, would seize the artillery presumed to be mounted there, which, if used by their original garrisons against the Southerners in Stedman, would render the fort untenable. Once all of this had been accomplished, Gordon's troops would range north and south, widening the gap in the Union line, while cavalry dashed forward to wreak havoc on Federal communications in the rear.

Gordon would rely upon the bulk of his own Second Corps, three divisions strong, to achieve his success. Two brigades of Bushrod R. Johnson's Division were detailed to reinforce Gordon, along with four brigades of Hill's corps: Lane's, Thomas's, McComb's, and Cooke's. On March 24, Gordon requested even more manpower. Lee obliged by notifying Pickett's Division, north of the James, to board the cars and rush to Gordon's assistance, although the gray commander discounted Pickett's chances of arriving in time for the 4:00 a.m. assault. Major General William H. F. "Rooney" Lee's cavalry division would provide the horseflesh for the mounted portion of the attack. All told, Lee and Gordon committed about half of the infantry in the Army of Northern Virginia to this desperate offensive.

Completing all arrangements well before dawn on March 25, Gordon ordered a private to fire the gun that would trigger the operation. "As the solitary signal shot rang out in the stillness, my alert pickets, who had crept close to the Union sentinels, sprang like sinewy Ajaxes upon them and prevented the discharge of a single alarm shot," remembered Gordon. The Second Corps troops moved out on their dramatic mission, "the cool, frosty morning [making] every sound distinct and clear," recalled a division commander, Brigadier General James A. Walker, "and the only sound heard was the tramp! tramp! of the men as they kept step as regularly as if on drill."[28]

Gordon's offensive unfolded according to plan, his men removing the obstacles in front of Fort Stedman and seizing that installation along with three adjacent batteries. The assault caught the encamped Ninth Corps troops by surprise, and their first game attempt to regain their positions resulted in the capture of the bold Union brigade commander who led it. "Up to this point, the success had exceeded my most sanguine expectations," wrote Gordon, who now looked anxiously for word from his detachments supposed to be subduing the critical fortifications east of Fort Stedman.[29]

General Parke, Ninth Corps commander and senior Union officer on the field, reacted quickly to the emergency. He sent directives to Brigadier General John F. Hartranft, commander of Parke's reserve division, to dispatch his untested regiments to the danger point. Parke also ordered the unshaken troops already on the scene to initiate artillery fire against the captured forts and prepare to assist Hartranft in conducting a counterattack. These troops quickly sealed the ends of the breach, frustrating Gordon's efforts to expand the breakthrough. The failure of his parties to find, let alone capture, the forts upon which so much of his planning had been based also dismayed Gordon. In reality, these forts did not exist, but the search for them consumed valuable time, utilized by Hartranft to muster his Pennsylvanians for their baptism of fire.

By 7:45 a.m. the Ninth Corps had readied its counterattack, 4,000 strong, just as General Lee, who had ridden from the Turnbull House that morning to watch the battle, authorized the beleaguered Gordon to return to Colquitt's Salient. Many of Gordon's men would never regain their own lines. As Parke's troops closed in on the captors of Fort Stedman, some Confederates surrendered on the spot rather than run the cruel gantlet of fire sweeping the fallow cornfield between Stedman and the Southern earthworks. Scores who did make the attempt died trying.

The gunfire sputtered out before 9:00 a.m. Parke tallied some 1,000 Ninth Corps casualties, more than half of them taken prisoner in the initial Confederate attack. Gordon's losses numbered at least 2,700 (some estimates range as high as 4,000), every one literally irreplaceable at this stage of the war. Lee summarized the disaster in a letter to President Davis:

> I was induced to assume the offensive from the belief that the point assailed could be carried without much loss, and the hope that by the seizure of the redoubts in the rear of the enemy's main line. . . . Genl. Grant would . . . be obliged so to curtail his lines, that upon the approach of Genl Sherman, I might be able to hold our position with a portion of the troops, and with a

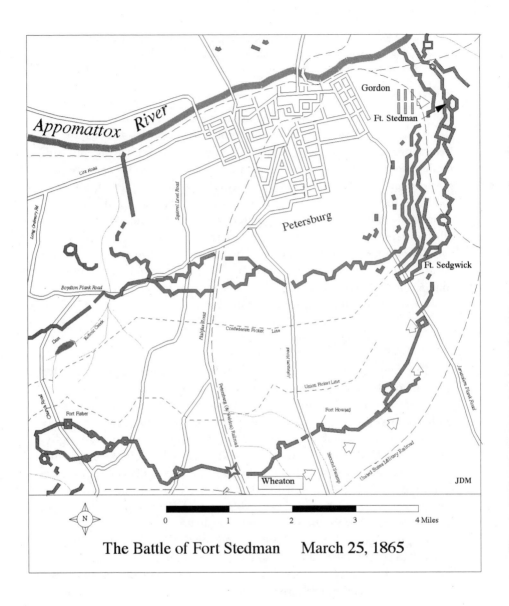

The Battle of Fort Stedman   March 25, 1865

select body unite with Genl Johnston and give him battle. . . . I fear now it will be impossible to prevent a junction between Grant and Sherman, nor do I deem it prudent that this army should maintain its position until the latter shall approach too near. . . .[30]

The same obstacles to retreat enumerated early in the month still stood between Lee and his only remaining option—evacuation of Petersburg and Richmond. Road conditions were improving but still inadequate. The administration required more time to prepare the government for departure, and the army needed to stockpile quantities of food and forage. Now, Lee found it necessary to rest and refit Gordon's exhausted command before it could undertake a major movement. On the afternoon of March 25, however, the Federals gave a clear signal that Lee's window of opportunity was closing. The tactical initiative retrieved by the Ninth Corps on the morning of March 25 would be exercised throughout that day by the Sixth and Second corps in a footnote to Fort Stedman that possessed enormous implications for the future.

*   *   *

The men of the 2nd Connecticut Heavy Artillery awoke on the morning of March 25 to the sound of distant firing, a disturbance they first interpreted as only a spirited clash of pickets. When the roar of artillery swelled across the brightening eastern horizon, the Nutmeggers realized that a full-blown engagement had exploded somewhere to their right. Horatio Wright also discerned trouble and wired General Parke, inquiring if the Ninth Corps required any help and offering to dispatch an entire division if necessary. Wright promptly received an answer that bespoke the seriousness of the yet undefined crisis east of Petersburg. "Send that division at once," came the reply from army headquarters.[31]

Wright selected Wheaton's command for the task, and by 7:00 a.m. orders had reached the First Division's brigade commanders to place their men under arms and commence their march to reinforce the Ninth Corps. "Just as we were eating our Breakfast we received orders to fall in," wrote Andrew Burwell of the 5th Wisconsin. Within an hour, Wheaton's troops swung into "the Sixth Corps quick step up the corduroy for the scene of action." The head of the column passed army headquarters by 8:15 a.m., and fifteen minutes later reached the Jones House, Parke's command post near the Jerusalem Plank Road. Along the way, the Sixth Corps troops experienced some long range shelling which inflicted negligible damage but impressed the soldiers that March 25 would be no ordinary day.[32]

Wheaton's three brigades covered roughly four miles before halting near Fort Sedgwick around 9:00 a.m., about the same time that General Hartranft completed his successful counterattack against Fort Stedman two miles to the northeast. Although the Sixth Corps supports had not been needed to repair the damage wrought by Gordon's assault, Parke was not yet ready to release them. "I think it would be well to let the division remain for some time until I can hear further from the line and from General Meade," Parke informed Wright. Wheaton's men would linger near Fort Sedgwick until about 11:00 a.m., when they were ordered back to their encampments.[33]

In the meantime, Gordon's repulse allowed the Union high command to pursue a suggestion made earlier by both Humphreys and Wright. Shortly after Wright had dispatched Wheaton to Parke's rescue, he sent an inquiry to the acting army commander regarding the advisability of a Union offensive along the Sixth Corps front: "As the enemy must have massed on right of our line, they must have left their own line weak. How would it do for us to attack along the whole length of our line?" At about the same time, General Humphreys wired Parke reporting that he had been reconnoitering in advance of the Second Corps entrenchments. "Shall I drive in the enemy's pickets all along my line," asked the eager Pennsylvanian, "and if I find his works slightly held, attack him?" Parke understandably declined to authorize such an offensive in the early morning hours of March 25, citing his provisional command over the other corps and the uncertain situation in the Ninth Corps front that required his full attention.[34]

Meade soon reestablished communications with his headquarters and started from City Point to assume direction of the army. By 8:30 a.m., Meade's staff had informed both Wright and Humphreys that Gordon's attack had failed, and granted permission to the Second Corps to "push the enemy . . . and determine whether or not there is any change on your front . . . . If you find that any advantage can be taken of this move of the enemy notify the general commanding." Humphreys's reconnaissances yielded very specific information about conditions in the Confederate lines. At 9:15 a.m., he reported that "the enemy have a strong picket line in pits, five or six men in each pit, pits about fifty feet apart; a thin line of battle in the works, single rank, men three feet apart, and artillery." Humphreys suggested that he drive back the Confederate picket line near the Watkins House along Duncan Road and follow up with a brigade-sized attack, exploited by a division and then by the entire corps if circumstances warranted.[35]

Wright, however, no longer shared his colleague's ardor to assume the offensive. Wheaton's departure had left his corps front dangerously weak, he thought, and his skirmishers told him that "the enemy's camps in front of Fort Fisher are vacated, but their picket line has been strengthened with intervals at five paces and strong reserves." Wright conveyed this information to army headquarters shortly after 8:00 a.m. An hour later, however, Meade sent clear directions that the Sixth Corps, like the Second Corps to its left, should press the Rebel picket line, drive it back, and ascertain whether an opportunity existed to assail the main Confederate works. Charles Griffin's division of the Fifth Corps had moved forward from its camps along Hatcher's Run to assist Wright if the Sixth Corps needed help until Wheaton returned.[36]

Dutifully, Wright reported moments later that his picket line stood poised to advance, but he reiterated that "on all parts of the enemy's line that can be seen there is no change, the lines and forts being fully manned. Shall the skirmish line advance under these circumstances?" Meade answered emphatically: "Yes. Drive in their pickets." Wright, however, apparently never received this order, because at 10:50 a.m. he wired army headquarters, "Not hearing from you and learning that the picket-line of the Second Army Corps is ready I shall push forward at once." Still, Wright balked. Thirty minutes later, he remained skeptical about testing the Rebel defenses: "Signal and other officers report the enemy line as strong as usual in my front." Having learned that Meade was expected at army headquarters at any moment, Wright held out some hope that his superior would reconsider the mandate that was now more than two hours old. "If I do not hear from [Meade] in ten minutes I shall advance my picket line, in pursuance of previous orders," Wright averred. Hearing nothing new, Wright promised at 11:30 a.m. to, "push forward immediately."[37]

During these exchanges between Meade and Wright, Humphreys not only launched his attack against the advanced Confederate positions but gained significant success. "We have taken the enemy's picket line in Watkins'-house field and are pushing forward to their main works," exulted Humphreys at 10:30 a.m. "We will hold all the ground we take." The only portion of the Second Corps front that had not advanced was that which connected with the Sixth Corps on Humphreys's far right flank. Griffin's division had been redirected to support Humphreys while the rest of Warren's troops waited to the south, ready to aid either Humphreys or Wright. With Wheaton's division rushing back to its original positions, three full Union corps were available to move forward and overwhelm what Meade and Grant hoped would be a severely depleted Confederate defense southwest of Petersburg.[38]

Wright's initial effort to capture the Confederate picket line reflected his continuing skepticism about the offensive's chances for success. Despite positive and repeated orders, Wright did not move until 1:00 p.m., and even then he committed but a skeleton force to what Meade intended to be a strong push against a wide portion of the Confederate front. Wright turned to Brigadier General Truman Seymour's Third Division, the troops on his left, closest to the Second Corps. Seymour assigned Lieutenant Colonel George B. Damon of the 10th Vermont responsibility for directing the division's pickets against their grayclad counterparts. Seymour also instructed Colonel Keifer to select two of his regiments to supplement Damon's men. The Buckeye commander designated the 110th Ohio and 122nd Ohio for the job.[39]

Wright and Seymour watched from Fort Fisher as the two Ohio units, under the overall command of Lieutenant Colonel Otho H. Binkley of the 110th, snaked out of the Union fortifications and took position in support of the Third Division pickets. That force consisted of about 160 men of the 14th New Jersey on the right and 230 men of the 10th Vermont on the left, stretched out for nearly a mile. All was quiet on the picket line and the off-duty men were enjoying a game of euchre when Damon appeared with startling news for the complacent videttes. "We are going to advance this picket line," announced Damon. "When you see the next post on your right advance you are to do the same. Fix bayonets, and deploy as you go, but do not cheer nor fire a shot until you reach the enemy's breastworks, which you are to capture and hold at all hazards." The Ohioans soon arrived with the 110th on the left and the 122nd to the right, one hundred yards to the rear of the now-stirring pickets, where they unslung knapsacks and fixed bayonets, prepared to support Damon's little force if its attack faltered. Damon took notice that the Confederate pits, some 300 yards distant, were strongly entrenched. The ground in front of this portion of the Union line was open except for a narrow belt of woods opposite Damon's left.[40]

With his arrangements perfected, Damon gave the signal to advance. The Vermonter reported that the whole line moved forward in unison, including Keifer's Ohioans. Keifer and Binkley told a different story. They stated that "only a portion" of the picket line advanced, and seeing this, the Buckeyes emitted "a triumphant shout" and started for the Confederate rifle pits under a severe musketry fire. Damon claimed that the attackers reached the picket posts in several places, but the leaden rain mingled with artillery blasts from the main Confederate fortifications forced the Federals to retire "in good order, to the original line." The bulk of the evidence suggests otherwise. Lieutenant Colonel Charles M. Cornyn of the

122nd Ohio testified that after reaching a point midway between the picket lines, "a check was given to the advance by the increased fire from the enemy, and the opening of their artillery, and an immediate fall-back took place." Binkley blamed the flanking fire that punished the ends of the short Union line for arresting his progress.

A Confederate account corroborates the Federal failure to reach their goal. "With a run and a cheer, the enemy closed up and seemed determined to take the works," wrote a South Carolinian. "But the fire of our pickets was too heavy, and after a moment's hesitation, the attackers broke and fled." Keifer committed some additional troops to protect the flanks of his exposed Buckeyes, but the advance had clearly foundered, "for want of proper direction, and in consequence of an improper selection of the place of attack," thought Keifer. Wright, who witnessed this mini-fiasco, promptly reported to Humphreys that his effort had miscarried but assured the Second Corps commander that "I shall try it again with troops enough for an assault, as soon as they can be got in position." He promised to renew the offensive in an hour, but Damon's little disaster had done nothing to decrease the timid pessimism that had characterized Wright's generalship since early morning. "The enemy is strong in my front," he reported, "and I think I may fail."[41]

Wright instructed Seymour to organize a second assault, but the division commander's orders drew a bitter protest from the distressed Keifer, who objected "to the useless slaughter of men under incompetent officers." Keifer then approached corps commander Wright with his concerns, and Wright responded with an order to Seymour to allow Keifer to choose the officer who would take command of the next offensive. The Ohioan first tapped Colonel Binkley, but then opted to lead the attack personally, a suggestion Seymour approved.[42]

Keifer responded instantly by deploying the bulk of his brigade in positions behind the Union picket line to reinforce Damon's bloodied veterans and the two Ohio regiments that had gone forward in the first attack. The 126th Ohio, less 100 men and two officers detached to garrison Fort Welch, advanced from the Union fortifications and took position on the left of Keifer's rapidly forming line of battle. Six companies of the 6th Maryland filed out of Fort Gregg and moved over to the right of the 126th Ohio. The 67th Pennsylvania established a second line about 25 yards to the rear of the first, in direct support of the 126th Ohio and 6th Maryland. One battalion of the 9th New York Heavy Artillery moved out of Fort Fisher and took position beyond the far left of Keifer's line, some distance to the rear. Including Damon's men, Keifer positioned approximately 2,500 troops for his assault.[43]

Keifer's would not be the only Federal troops involved in Wright's second attack. The corps commander ordered General Getty to commit the Second Division to reinforce Keifer. Accordingly, the Vermont Brigade marched out of its entrenchments to take position between the main Union fortifications and the picket line now occupied in such strength by Keifer's men. The 3rd Vermont and 4th Vermont comprised the front line of Brigadier General Lewis A. Grant's formation, with the 6th Vermont moving up close behind. The oversized 1st Vermont Heavy Artillery, in two battalions, occupied a supporting line in two ranks. Behind the heavies, the 5th Vermont took position on the left of a reserve line and the 2nd Vermont filed in to the right of the 5th Vermont. Grant's forces occupied the ground in front and a little to the left of Fort Fisher.[44]

Thomas Hyde's brigade massed to the right of Fort Fisher in support of the Vermonters, and Colonel James M. Warner's troops deployed to the left of the fort. The Vermont Brigade had orders to move forward to the picket line once Keifer had launched his attack. Hyde and Warner would then provide assistance as circumstances dictated. This arrangement demonstrates further that Wright maintained grave reservations about the wisdom of an attack against a position he deemed to be intimidatingly strong. Of the five brigades in Seymour's and Getty's divisions concentrated around the former "fishhook" section of the Union front, Wright designated only Keifer's (reinforced by the Third Division pickets) for strictly offensive purposes. Grant, Hyde, and Warner would play a supporting role, available to exploit an advantage, to be sure, but also in position to repulse a counterattack or cover a retreat by Keifer. Colonel William S. Truex's brigade remained in the fortifications along with a significiant minority of Keifer's troops in a purely defensive posture.[45]

The new deployment consumed an hour or more. During this interval, Keifer met with each of his regimental commanders to make certain they understood the task before them, described as "desperate work" by one Ohioan. By 3:00 p.m. all was ready. Keifer confidently directed that the brigade's flag be waved from the parapet of Fort Fisher as the cue that would trigger the assault.[46]

According to the Union plan, the signal would propel both Keifer's and Damon's troops against the Confederate picket line and indicate to Grant's Vermonters that they should move forward and occupy the advanced posts vacated by the Third Division attackers. Keifer wrote that "the men went forward & carried the entire line of the enemy's works and captured over three hundred prisoners. The men charged at a run and without firing a shot." Lieutenant Colonel Thomas W. McKinnie of the 126th Ohio stated that "the assault, upon the signal being given, was made with great promptness. The regiment leaped over our intrenched picket-line and rushed upon the rebel line under a heavy line of musketry, capturing almost all of the enemy's pickets in our front." Lieutenant Colonel Joseph C. Hill of the 6th Maryland confirmed that, "At the given signal the line moved forward, and with a shout of victory we entered and occupied the works."[47]

The two Ohio regiments that had attacked earlier in the day shared in the success of Keifer's front line. "At the given signal all started with a yell, fully determined this time to go through, and nothing but the natural obstructions could or did impede our advance," boasted Lieutenant Colonel Cornyn of the 122nd Ohio. "I take pleasure in saying that the colors of the 122nd Ohio . . . were the second planted on the enemy's works." The units in Keifer's second line, the 67th Pennsylvania and the 9th New York Heavy Artillery, encountered a little more difficulty during their attack. The New Yorkers had to cross "a deep marsh or swamp" and as a result "did not reach [the enemy's line] as soon as the other parts, but we were not far behind, capturing the rebel pickets in our front." The 67th Pennsylvania, mostly new recruits, experienced momentary confusion as they advanced under a storm of Confederate rifle fire. The regimental colors sustained 22 bullet holes, not counting the ball that shattered the flag staff, but the color bearer managed to lift his banner above the Confederate picket line "quite as soon as the color-sergeants of the regiments preceding him," according to the Pennsylvanians' commander, Major William G. Williams.[48]

Damon's Vermonters fully participated in this successful attack, earning plaudits from Keifer, who officially credited the officer he had privately maligned. Damon noted that at the signal, both the attacking force and the supporting column "advanced and carried the intrenched works of the enemy." Private Oscar E. Waite of the 10th Vermont remembered that "a few of the Rebels ran for their main line which only a part succeeded in reaching, but nearly all of this double line threw down their arms and surrendered as though glad of the opportunity." Lieutenant Colonel Horace W. Floyd, in command of both the 3rd and 4th Vermont, agreed that Grant's brigade also advanced at the signal flag, their goal being merely to occupy the Union picket line supposed to be vacated by Keifer's and Damon's attacking troops. "Upon reaching the works where I was to halt I found the troops had not left, and therefore, instead of halting I passed over them and reached the enemy's works in advance of any of the attacking party, capturing all the enemy's pickets in my front," wrote Floyd. It is not clear which hesitant troops Floyd's two regiments encountered during their advance. Possibly, the confusion in the 67th Pennsylvania

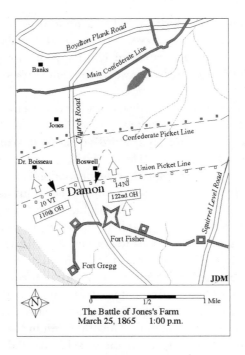

The Battle of Jones's Farm
March 25, 1865   1:00 p.m.

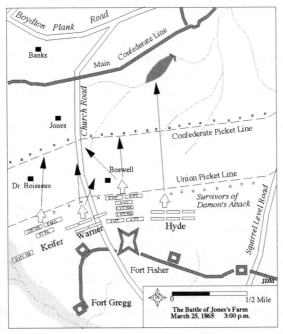

The Battle of Jones's Farm
March 25, 1865   3:00 p.m.

created an impression in Floyd's mind that none of the Third Division forces were advancing. In any event, the second battalion of the 1st Vermont Heavy Artillery accompanied Floyd's troops forward, and the Vermonter admitted that "the troops we passed came up soon after we had taken the line."[49]

Most of the rest of Grant's brigade also became engaged. The 6th Vermont moved forward on the left of the 3rd Vermont and 4th Vermont but did not arrive quite as quickly as Floyd's command. While the second battalion of the 1st Vermont Heavy Artillery helped capture the Confederate pickets in their front, their first battalion comrades obliqued to the right and linked with the 2nd Vermont. This unit moved from its support position in the third line to the right, along Church Road, and targeted the Confederate picket posts in front of the Jones House. "Seeing the enemy running in all directions to get out of our way, I ordered the Second Vermont Regiment to charge and take the Jones house, which was gallantly done," beamed the unit's commander, Lieutenant Colonel Amasa S. Tracy. The 2nd Vermont raised its colors to the left of the prominent two-story home, and the first battalion of the Heavies placed their flag to the right of the building. The other unit in the third line, the 5th Vermont, did not participate in the attack. "We did not have any fighting at all but were shelled pretty severely by their batteries," reported a regimental officer.[50]

At 3:10 p.m., Wright happily informed Humphreys that "I have just carried the enemy's picket-line in front of Fort Fisher, the enemy opening not heavily with artillery. I shall push forward to their main line with what troops I have, if further developments justify." The first of his troops to attempt to do this, however, advanced of their own volition, not in response to any explicit orders from the cautious Wright. Thomas Hyde watched as the Vermont Brigade charged to and beyond the Confederate picket line, but he envisioned more than just a support role in the capture of "a few miserable pickets." Hyde ordered his brigade forward, more than 2,000 strong, and aligned them to the right of Grant's troops between Church Road and Squirrel Level Road. He hoped to advance beyond the Confederate picket line and reach the main Rebel fortifications.[51]

Hyde received support from the 93rd Pennsylvania and the 62nd New York of Warner's brigade, and despite a severe artillery fire, the bluecoats plowed forward until they reached the inundation, or artificial pond, created by the damming of Rohoic Creek. This presented Hyde with an insurmountable obstacle. He also noticed that the Vermont Brigade had halted at the Confederate picket line to his left and rear. Stymied by the Rebel obstructions, isolated from his supports on the left, unprotected on the right, and subject to an increasingly accurate cannonade from the Southern works, Hyde sounded the recall and the brigade fell back to the same latitude as Lewis Grant's troops to their left.[52]

When Hyde halted his panting brigade, his right flank remained in the air, so it was with no small concern that he spied "a strong force" bearing down on it. "I at once refused the 1st Maine veterans and ordered the 122nd New York in with them," recalled Hyde. The momentum at the Second Battle of Jones Farm was about to shift.[53]

*   *   *

Despite their resounding victory at Fort Stedman, the Federals declined to conduct a counteroffensive against the Confederate lines at Colquitt's Salient. Reestablishing their broken positions and processing hundreds of prisoners, not to mention the always daunting prospect of challenging fixed fortifications, convinced the Ninth Corps that they had achieved enough for one morning. Thus, Gordon found no need to retain Henry Heth's and Cadmus Wilcox's troops in their reserve roles and ordered them to return to their camps southwest of Petersburg. Those elements of Cooke's, Lane's, McComb's and Thomas's brigades that had moved to their left on the evening of March 24 began to return to their bivouacs early in the afternoon—just in time to witness the Union assaults against their picket lines.

From the Confederate perspective, Keifer's, Grant's, and Hyde's attacks presented an awesome spectacle. "Saturday's fight along our front was a novel one," wrote General Lane, "and was confined almost entirely to the skirmish line, in full view of our main line of works." One of McGowan's men left a vivid account of the 3:00 p.m. attack:

> Soon they formed—not a line of skirmishers as before, but a solid line of battle. On they came, shoulder to shoulder, the stars and stripes flying over their heads. Again the fire broke from one of our rifle pits, extending to the right and left till the whole line, as far as rifles could reach, was crackling and sputtering. But forward still swept the line of blue, heeding neither their dead nor their wounded. Forward still, with a rush and a shout, the flag well to the front, and our hearts sink with the fear that they will go over the works at the first charge. . . . Our men, kneeling in the pits, take good aim and we can see how busy they are. It is but a minute before the enemy's line falters, appears about to break and flee. But look, the color bearer runs forward alone with his flag. With a shout that rings again, the blue line follows in a swift charge through our deadliest fire. They reach the works and turning rapidly to the right and left, they sweep the line in both directions for a long distance, taking possession of half a mile of rifle pits.[54]

The Southerners on the picket line resisted fiercely, at least until the overwhelming mass of blue engulfed them. The Confederate skirmishers "opened fire upon the enemy, many of them shooting into the very faces of the assailants. But it was of no avail," reported Lieutenant Caldwell of General McGowan's staff, who watched the battle from the main Confederate line. "The enemy swarmed up to the rifle pits, flapping their banners, and cheering and firing, and in scarcely more time than it has required to describe it, captured the picket line and swept up and down like a flame." According to Caldwell, some of the Confederate pickets fought to the last, others were shot while trying to escape, but the majority became prisoners. Sergeant Albert C. Harrison of the 14th New Jersey claimed that "the most part of the Rebel Pickets never fired a gun but stood in their works until they were taken by the shoulder and led back to our Provost Guards." Given the performance of the Southerners earlier in the afternoon, however, it is likely that the soldiers Harrison described surrendered subsequent to the capture of the picket posts.[55]

McGowan ordered his brigade to move out of its fortifications and advance about halfway to the captured positions, maintaining a "keen fire upon the Federals, which caused them to hug their works with tenacious fidelity," wrote Caldwell. Artillery fire supplemented the South Carolinians' musketry, coming primarily from two 12-pounder Napoleons and two 3-inch rifles manned by Captain Charles R. Grandy's Battery, the Norfolk Light Artillery Blues. These Virginia cannoneers had moved through Petersburg before dawn and reached the Boydton Plank Road near Battery 45, behind the inundation that would later prove so nettlesome for Hyde's brigade. The artillerists arrived at the Boisseau House near first light, where they remained throughout the morning and during the initial Union attack. When Keifer and Grant overran the picket line, orders arrived for Grandy's two sections to shift 300 yards to their left "at a hard gallop," where they "unlimbered, came into position, and fired upon the enemy, firing as rapidly as we could," according to one of the gunners. This cannonade failed to prevent the Federals from gaining and then holding the Confederate picket line, but additional Confederate fire from Fort Gregg and Battery 45 did add its metal to Grandy's blasts.[56]

This "galling fire of artillery" prompted Lieutenant Colonel Charles Hunsdon of the 1st Vermont Heavy Artillery to withdraw his battalion from the Jones House. "Shot and shell flew very promiscuously for some time," remembered a soldier from the 6th Vermont, while Keifer confided to his wife that "we were exposed to a terrible artillery fire until the close of the day," one projectile exploding so near the colonel that he was knocked to the ground from the concussion. In front of Hyde's position on the Union

Brigadier General Edward L. Thomas

Library of Congress

right, the gray cannoneers laid down a "heavy cross fire of artillery," but Hyde noted that although "the rebel cannon were worked for all they were worth . . . the balls were striking places that we had just left." It became clear that artillery alone might stop but would not dislodge the Yankees. That task would require infantry.[57]

Both McGowan's and Lane's men had formed a line of battle along and outside of the main Confederate fortifications. Together with the Southern cannoneers, they succeeded in keeping the Federals at bay, but their position confined them to a defensive role. Thomas's Georgians, however, observed the action from atop their winter huts after returning from their reserve duty in support of Gordon's attack. Moreover, their Peach State comrades had manned much of the now-captured picket line, so Thomas's troops became the likely candidates to muster a counterattack aimed at recovering the lost ground. Colonel Thomas Jefferson Simmons of the 45th Georgia met with Thomas and then dashed up to his veterans, ordering them and the 49th Georgia to fall in and march on the double-quick to engage the enemy.[58]

Colonel Simmons took command of the two Georgia units, which together numbered perhaps 400 men. They moved over the earthworks and reached a small rise north of the Jones House, where Confederate skirmishers had established a position about 250 yards from the captured rifle pits. "As we passed the crest of the hill, we saw the baleful foe on forbidden ground," remembered Captain John Hardeman of the 45th Georgia. Simmons maneuvered his small command into a surviving patch of woods east of Hyde's exposed right flank. "With a yell from one end of our line to the other that made the 'welkin ring,' we were up and at them like a 'thousand of bricks,'" wrote Hardeman. "Our line was good, our yell frightful, our fire murderous, and our victory complete."

Hyde saw (and presumably heard) the Georgians as they bore down on his vulnerable flank, defended by the 1st Maine Veterans and 122nd New York, which Hyde hastily deployed facing east. The Federal position became more tenuous as enfilading artillery fire screamed in from the main Confederate works. A shell decapitated Lieutenant Colonel Augustus W. Dwight of the 122nd New York before he could completely shift his unit in the proper direction. Hyde attempted to change the disposition of his men so that the Confederate guns could not perfect the range on his beleaguered brigade, but the loss—especially in the 1st Maine Veterans— was "frightful." One of the projectiles struck a picket post in which three Union officers lay huddled. Hyde watched as a severed foot, boot and all, flew over his head. The victim of this ghastly wound was a line officer to whom Hyde had refused a furlough a few days earlier.[59]

Hyde implied that despite the casualties absorbed by his brigade, he managed to blunt Simmons's attack, confining it to a ravine "from which no man attempted to emerge for hours without being a target for many balls." Other testimony suggests that Hyde's account understated the effect of Simmons's assault on his line. Colonel Warner, who had committed two regiments to Hyde's initial advance, reported that his units were "driven back in disorder." Confederate witnesses credited Simmons with recapturing the picket line "with a gallantry and coolness characteristic of the Georgia soldiers." At least one substantial body of Federals retreated to their original lines. About that time, Lieutenant Colonel Charles A. Conn of the 45th Georgia fell mortally wounded, his last words being "Forward boys, forward."[60]

Simmons led his counterattack between 3:30 p.m. and 4:00 p.m. Southern artillery fire continued to rain on Hyde's brigade even after the Confederate infantry assault had run its course. This combination of rifles and cannons compelled not only Warner's 62nd New York and 93rd Pennsylvania to retreat, but forced the 1st Maine Veterans and 122nd New York on the right end of Hyde's formation to withdraw as well. A member of the 45th Georgia claimed that the Confederates occupied their recaptured position for two hours. More likely, their conquest lasted only about half that time.[61]

The Federals immediately responded to Simmons's attack with long-range artillery salvos up and down the Confederate line. Several shells landed in MacRae's encampment near the Hart House east of Duncan Road, "striking amongst our cabins, knocking several of them out of all habitable condition," according to one displaced North Carolinian. Confederate counterbattery fire exploded a limber chest in Fort Fisher, killing twelve men instantly and wounding many others. The success of these random shots notwithstanding, victory or defeat along the Confederate picket line would be determined by infantry and not cannoneers.[62]

About 4:00 p.m., Wright and his lieutenants readied just such a large-scale effort. First, General Getty ordered Warner to retake the picket posts now occupied by the Georgians. Warner responded by forming a battle line consisting, from left to right, of the 102nd Pennsylvania, the 139th Pennsylvania, Hyde's 1st Maine Veterans, the 93rd Pennsylvania, and about 50 members of the 122nd New York. The 102nd Pennsylvania and the 139th Pennsylvania had not yet been engaged, their position being near the J. C. Boswell House, straddling Church Road in front of Fort Fisher, near the original Federal picket line. On Warner's right, Colonel Joseph E. Hamblin deployed the 65th New York and the 2nd Connecticut Heavy Artillery, supported by the other two regiments in his brigade, prepared to move forward along with their Second Division comrades. Finally, Colonel Oliver Edwards shook out a line of battle on Hamblin's right stretching almost as far as the picket line in front of Fort Wadsworth, the 2nd Rhode Island occupying the far right flank of what had become a

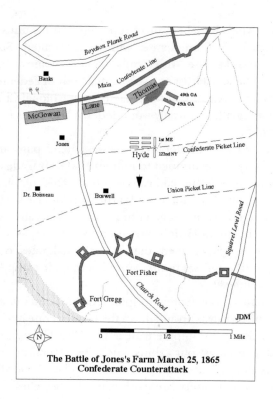

The Battle of Jones's Farm March 25, 1865
Confederate Counterattack

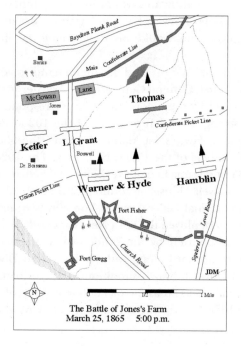

The Battle of Jones's Farm
March 25, 1865   5:00 p.m.

division-sized assault formation on a front nearly two miles wide. The New Jersey Brigade on the right, like Truex's brigade on the left, remained in reserve, but six of Wright's eight brigades had either been or were about to be committed to what Wright had tried to accomplish several hours earlier with just Damon's skirmishers and two Ohio regiments.[63]

A captain in the 45th Georgia looked across the open fields toward the Union fortifications and saw that "the hill was blue as far as we could see, both to the right and left." He estimated the force arrayed against Thomas's Brigade as "four brigades and two regiments of another." Even though the 14th Georgia and 35th Georgia had joined their comrades at the recaptured picket line, the massive host now deploying against them presented a sobering spectacle.[64]

The third Union offensive of the afternoon commenced with the firing of a section of guns from the 3rd Vermont Battery, summoned by Colonel Warner to help soften the Confederate artillery. This barrage, mingled with the longer-range fire from the main Federal line, consumed about 40 minutes. At 5:00 p.m., Warner gave the signal to charge. The brigade commander personally carried his unit's colors, and his regiments swiftly reached and then overwhelmed Thomas's Georgians. "The behavior of the troops was admirable," boasted Warner. "The pits and a crest about 300 yards beyond was carried, capturing many prisoners."

The 45th Georgia and 49th Georgia had expended practically all their ammunition in taking and holding their portion of the Confederate picket line, limiting their ability to respond to this new Yankee assault. The brigade's other two regiments did little to equalize the balance of power, so Thomas ordered his men to fall back. "We had a hill of two hundred and fifty yards to run up, the enemy firing into us both right and left," remembered Captain Hardeman. "We knew if we escaped it would be a miracle." Some of the Georgians did not hear the retreat orders and remained in the rifle pits, fighting briefly with the butts of their muskets before being subdued. An observer from McGowan's Brigade professed to be "highly incensed" at Thomas's expulsion, but without additional firepower there was nothing the overmatched Southerners could do. Of the four hundred men who made the charge with Simmons, about half came back. Casualties in the rest of Thomas's Brigade are not known.[65]

Hamblin's Federal brigade had orders to conform to the movement of Warner's men on their left; the troops were told not to fire until they could see the enemy. They, too, jumped off about 5:00 p.m. Hamblin rode up to Colonel Hubbard of the 2nd Connecticut Heavy Artillery and told him to "move directly forward," an order Hubbard repeated to his command, adding the modifier, "double quick." Sergeant Edward S. Roberts of the 2nd Connecticut Heavy Artillery recalled that:

> We advanced, the right of our regiment lapping into a piece of woods, but the rest charging over an open field. As soon as we appeared in sight the rebel pickets opened fire. This movement was made very steadily; the line of battle was perfect. The rebel pits were not continuous, but were made at intervals, small pits, crescent shape, with four men in each. As we advanced they continued the fire till we got within two rods of these pits, when the Johnnies threw up their hands and said: 'Don't shoot! don't shoot,' and they were let to pass us to the rear.[66]

Charging with "yells that would have shamed a tribe of Indians," Hubbard's New Englanders overran the Confederate picket line, where the remaining graycoats "threw down their arms and gave themselves up without any more fighting," heading for the Federal rear "like rats." The brief engagement cost the regiment 25 casualties. Hamblin could not stop the momentum of his attacking brigade, which rushed past the Confederate picket line, across the headwaters of Rohoic Creek, and up a slope where the Unionists received an iron salute from the Rebel artillery in the main line, a few hundred yards to their front. "Finding the brigade far in advance, without supports on either side and exposed to a sharp fire from the enemy on my right flank," Hamblin withdrew his regiments to a ridge about 300 yards beyond the captured picket line and dug in.[67]

The fire on Hamblin's right came from both enfilading artillery batteries and a small body of Southern infantry that emerged from the earthworks and threatened the Union flank. A portion of the 121st New York changed front to repel this weak attempt at a counterattack. "We reached the conclusion that the enemy's lines were thinly held," remembered an officer of the 121st New York, "else he would not permit us to peaceably hold the strong position we had taken and entrenched, within easy striking distance of his main line."[68]

The participation of Edwards's brigade on Hamblin's right also discouraged a Confederate counterattack. Wheaton's Third Brigade returned from its sojourn toward Fort Stedman early in the afternoon only to receive orders to mass between forts Wadsworth and Fisher in position to support Wright's offensive. Along with Warner and Hamblin, Edwards was told to engage the Confederate picket line, with the specific responsibility of guarding Hamblin's right flank. Moving around the marshy ground associated with the headwaters of Rohoic Creek, Edwards arrived on Hamblin's right and encountered the small force of Confederates mentioned by the 121st New York. "On the inner edge of the swamp we found the enemy on Hamblin's flank, and quickly drove them out, capturing about 100 prisoners," reported Edwards.

Lieutenant Colonel Elisha Hunt Rhodes and his 2nd Rhode Island turned back yet another flank attack, this time on Edwards's far right. "I quickly threw to the right and rear my right wing and opened fire which broke their line, and many surrendered, being unable to get back to their lines," remembered Rhodes. The 37th Massachusetts and the 5th Wisconsin refused Edwards's flank to the right and beat back yet another Confederate foray, this one attempted by a double skirmish line. But now, darkness had descended across the Jones Farm and its neighboring properties. The firing gradually diminished and then stopped altogether. Of all the Sixth Corps brigades involved in the March 25 offensives, Edwards's saw the least action, but a member of the 37th Massachusetts nevertheless thought the engagement, "a spicy and brilliant affair."[69]

This fighting on the Sixth Corps right entertained several prominent spectators. President and Mrs. Lincoln, General and Mrs. Grant, and General Meade all saw evidence of the hostilities from the parapet of Fort Wadsworth. "We gave three cheers for the President, and three for each of the generals," wrote the chaplain of the 37th Massachusetts, whose camp lay adjacent to Fort Wadsworth. At least two Federal soldiers were not so impressed by the appearance of the celebrities. "I had a good chance to see 'Uncle Abe,' wrote Private Edwin C. Hall of the 10th Vermont, "and I believe he is the homliest man I have seen for three years." Corporal George Bates of the 2nd Connecticut Heavy Artillery leveled a different brand of criticism at the president's entourage: "It seems we were highly honored the other day by having Mrs. Lincoln, Mrs. Grant, & other ladies at a safe distance from our engagement looking on. The *N.Y. Herald* calls this manly courage. I should like to be at such a safe distance every time there is an engagement. I am afraid it wouldnt call it courage though."[70]

*   *   *

While the Sixth Corps executed its three assaults between 1:00 p.m. and 5:00 p.m., the Second Corps concentrated on consolidating the gains it had achieved prior to Wright's first attack. Humphreys had reported the capture of the Confederate picket line in the Watkins House field along Duncan Road at 10:30 a.m. Miles's First Division, supported by elements of Mott's Third Division, had accomplished this feat while Wright spent the morning fretting about the strength of the Confederate skirmish line in his front.[71]

From his vantage point along the old Confederate picket line, Humphreys began to reevaluate his ability to capture the main Confederate line less than half a mile to his front. At 1:45 p.m., the Second Corps commander wired Meade that:

> Upon careful examination I find the works of the enemy as fully manned as ever, and considering the chances of success very doubtful I have not attacked. I understand that it was left to my discretion whether to make the attack or not. The troops still hold the picket-line taken from the enemy. I will order the dispositions for the attack to be made and await the decision of the commanding general of my judgment.

Immediately after transmitting this request for instructions, Humphreys ordered Miles and Mott to deploy their divisions in preparation to storm the main Confederate works, should Meade so desire. While arranging their units accordingly, both divisions received "a vigorous attack" from a substantial Confederate force. After 30 minutes, the Federals managed to repulse this assault, but Humphreys now understood that whatever weakness had existed in the Confederate line that morning clearly had been repaired. Shortly, word arrived from Meade reaffirming Humphreys's authority to make his own decision regarding the advisability of an attack. The Second Corps commander opted not to press his advantage any further.[72]

No lack of aggressiveness characterized Confederate leadership on the afternoon of March 25. While McGowan, Lane, and Thomas confronted Wright's corps to the northeast, the four brigades of Heth's Division and Brigadier General Young M. Moody's Alabamians of Bushrod Johnson's Division, spent the rest of the day attempting to recapture the picket line seized by Humphreys. Cooke's Tarheels and McComb's Tennesseans and Marylanders, like their comrades in Wilcox's Division, had returned from their supporting role in the Fort Stedman offensive to learn of the collapse of their brigade's sentries. "When we got within less than a mile of [our] old quarters the firing hurried us up," remembered Colonel Samuel H. Walkup of the 48th North Carolina. "We got [in]formed that the enemy had captured [our] picket line & most of our pickets. . . . We manned our works immediately & began firing upon the enemy in our old picket line. We then sent our Sharpshooters on their left flanks & drove the Yankees out of our pickets, without much loss[,] 2 killed and 4 wounded." MacRae's sharpshooters "moved directly to the front and broke through a strong line of battle, and, wheeling to the right, swept everything before them," wrote the commander of the 44th North Carolina, while the 2nd Mississippi of

Brigadier General Joseph R. Davis's Brigade "at the same time wheeled to the left and was equally successful."

At least two counterattacks struck the Second Corps line in addition to the 2:00 p.m. jab that claimed the tactical initiative from Humphreys. One assault began between 3:00 p.m. and 4:00 p.m. and another between 6:00 p.m. and 7:00 p.m., both of them targeting Mott's and Miles's divisions on either side of Duncan Road. In the latter attack, which ended after sunset, three regiments of Moody's Brigade lost 165 men captured as well as the battle flags of the 43rd Alabama and the 59th Alabama. A regiment from each of Heth's brigades, supported by the brigade sharpshooters and reserve regiments, charged the Federal line about dark. "The enemy were driven back to their reserve line," wrote a Marylander in McComb's Brigade. "We retired and the enemy advanced. We charged them again, and after a hotly contested fight of some two hours duration, were obliged to retire without retaking our rifle pits."[73]

The Confederate offensives in Humphreys's front, like those launched against Wright's brigades, achieved only limited results. Despite temporarily regaining some of their captured works, by and large, the Southerners failed to reestablish control over their old picket line and were compelled to fall back to their main entrenchments. A late afternoon advance by Brigadier General William Hays's division of Humphreys's corps succeeded in scattering the Confederate pickets along Hatcher's Run, completing a day's activity that witnessed the capture of some four miles of the forward Confederate line.[74]

*   *   *

Two particular hot spots continued to draw Federal attention after sunset. A group of grayclad sharpshooters occupied a house just southwest of the segment of the picket line captured by Seymour's division, near where the Sixth and Second corps battle lines intersected. Seymour assigned the ubiquitous Colonel Damon to dislodge these annoying marksmen. Damon tapped 150 men of the 5th Vermont and a section of the 3rd New York Battery commanded by Lieutenant George P. Fitzgerald to reduce the offending nest of Rebels. Fitzgerald unlimbered his guns at a range of 600 yards, aided in their deployment by staff officer Hazard Stevens. "I . . . soon knocked several holes in the house, causing the rebels to run out like rats," boasted Stevens, but the Confederates remained in a patch of woods undeterred by the shot and shell flying at them from Fitzgerald's artillery. A Second Corps brigade to Damon's left experienced no more success in capturing this house and its adjacent landscape, and the Federals eventually abandoned the effort.[75]

A little more than a mile to the northeast, a few Confederates had reoccupied the Jones House, captured then abandoned earlier by the 2nd Vermont and 1st Vermont Heavy Artillery. This commodious residence now occupied a location between the captured Confederate picket posts and the new line of skirmishers dispatched from McGowan's Brigade. In the fading light, Thomas Hyde "felt a bullet graze my arm through my overcoat, and saw the smoke of a musket from the roof of a large and comfortable-looking house between the lines." Incensed by the temerity of his would-be assassins, the young brigade commander ordered a stray company of Vermonters to drive away the Rebel sharpshooters. These troops did so, but soon "back the enemy came in greater numbers, and a dozen muskets flashed from the windows, now glistening in the setting sun." Colonel Tracy of the 2nd Vermont responded to Hyde's order to destroy the house, assigning a detachment from three of his companies under Captain Ward B. Hurlbut to do the job. "It was just getting dusk when we saw some figures moving stealthily about the house," reported a South Carolinian. "We opened fire, but were unable to drive them away. Presently a bright flame shot up, then another. In a few minutes the house was one huge flame of fire, lighting up the fields for a great distance around." The next morning, Cadmus Wilcox sent an official protest through the lines, eliciting an investigation by General Wright. When Hyde explained the circumstances surrounding this particular act of vandalism, Wright dropped the matter.[76]

With the exception of some light skirmish fire and the occasional artillery blast, the Jones House incineration ended hostilities for the Sixth Corps on March 25. That is not to say, however, that this long day's exertions were over. Although most of Grant's and Keifer's brigades returned to camp shortly after the fighting concluded, Hamblin's, Edwards's, Hyde's, and Warner's troops began entrenching a new picket line after sunset to secure the ground they had captured during the day. In some places, they merely refaced the Confederate rifle pits, but most of the new Union picket line was newly-built under trying conditions. Entrenching tools arrived after dark, and the labor consumed some four or five hours. Between 11:00 p.m. and 1:30 a.m., the bulk of the Sixth Corps troops began tramping wearily back to their shanties and tents, seeking the beds they had left so suddenly more than eighteen hours earlier.[77]

For hundreds of Wright's troops, however, the day's duties had still not concluded. Soldiers from Hyde's, Hamblin's, and perhaps other Sixth

Corps units stayed in the new earthworks as sentries. Lewis Bissell of the 2nd Connecticut Heavy Artillery remembered that night vividly:

> We were not allowed to build fires. It was very cold. During the day we had kept warm by fast marching but that night we suffered very much indeed. The boys' teeth chattered. We did not care to stand up anymore than was necessary besides we were tired out. Never in my life have I suffered so much from the cold as I did that night. I shook like a leaf for the next two days.[78]

The Confederates spent the evening in a similar fashion. After considering yet another attempt to recapture the works, McGowan's men received orders to establish a new picket line about halfway between their main entrenchments and the captured positions. "This was partially done by intrenching during the night," reported a South Carolina officer. Once the rifle pits had been dug and most of the Federal and Confederate forces had returned to their primary works, the only sounds that penetrated the frosty night air came from the wounded calling piteously from between the day's battle lines, seeking water or other forms of relief. Homer Curtis of the 2nd Connecticut Heavy Artillery ventured out into this no-man's land after midnight in search of fallen comrades:

> After looking around for some time vainly I was about to retire to our lines when I heard a groan, and saw the shadowy outline of a man moving along nearly parallel with our lines in a vague purposeless way and as though he might be wounded. I walked towards him and when near hailed him with 'Are you wounded, boy?' He glanced toward me or at least turned his head slowly and said, 'No I am lost.' I went close to him and seeing his gray jacket readily divined that he was not of us but I spoke pleasantly and said, 'I'll show you the way, here, you seem to be tired, I'll carry your musket.' He hesitated but gave me his Enfield and then started and said 'I guess I'm sold, captured aint I? What Regt. is yours?' I assured him he was all right, and told him my regt after he had informed me that he was from the 33d [sic] Georgia Vols, A. P. Hills Corps. I met Col. Hubbard just outside the videttes and introduced my new acquaintance to him. Col. pumped him as to force and position of the enemy but elicited little. He said there were only 3 brigades opposed to us but that was a plenty thank you for that was about our own force though Col. H. told him there were 2 Corps. We sent him to the rear and he seemed glad to get out of the reach of balls. I presume he intended to come over to us so I cannot take much credit to myself as to his capture, but it made quite a pleasant little incident and relieved for a moment the tedium of open air resting after a brush, which is worse than the brush itself.[79]

This unnamed Georgian became one of the last casualties in the most costly day of the campaign since the August engagement along the Petersburg Railroad. Although the fighting southwest of Petersburg did not prove as sanguinary as the contest for Fort Stedman, these little-known battles claimed a surprising number of victims. Union losses in the Second and Sixth corps that day were comparable to those suffered by the Federals at more famous engagements such as Wilson's Creek, Missouri; New Hope Church, Georgia; and New Market, in the Shenandoah Valley. Humphreys reported 51 killed, 462 wounded, and 177 missing, for a total of 690. More than half of this attrition occurred in Miles's division, the unit closest to the Sixth Corps, while Mott's division suffered heavily as well. Hays lost only 36 men while throwing his punches along Hatcher's Run.[80]

Wright's casualties were almost as severe as Humphreys's. Getty's division experienced the greatest losses, being involved not only in the 3:00 p.m. and 5:00 p.m. assaults, but absorbing the brunt of Thomas's counteroffensive as well. Getty lost 26 killed, 230 wounded, and 24 missing. Seymour's division (which is to say Keifer's brigade and the pickets from the 10th Vermont and 14th New Jersey of Truex's command) lost 11 killed, 101 wounded, and three missing. Wheaton's two brigades fought late in the day and, as would be expected, suffered less than their comrades in the Second and Third divisions. Hamblin and Edwards accounted for virtually all of the 10 men killed, 71 wounded, and three missing from Wheaton's command. Wright's total attrition on March 25 amounted to 479 men, roughly equivalent to the total strength of one of his 45 regiments.[81]

Confederate casualty figures are difficult to determine. Humphreys reported capturing 365 men in his front and estimated the number of killed and wounded Southerners "as fully three times his." A recent study determined that MacRae's Brigade suffered 123 losses on March 25, of whom 109 were captured and 14 wounded. Wright counted 547 Rebel prisoners and believed that Confederate losses in killed and wounded exceeded those for his corps. McGowan's Brigade lost 49 men on March 25, including 23 killed and wounded. An officer in the 45th Georgia stated that out of about 400 total men that went into the fight from his regiment and the 49th Georgia, 98 emerged from the 45th and about 100 returned from the 49th. It is reasonable to speculate that Lane's losses approximated those of McGowan, and that the 14th Georgia and 35th Georgia did not suffer as heavily as their comrades who made the initial counterattack. Perhaps 200 would be a plausible estimate of the number of killed and wounded to be added to the Confederate prisoners seized by the Sixth Corps, making the total casualties in front of Wright some 750. Bushrod Johnson estimated the losses in Moody's Brigade at 246, but those for

Cooke's and Davis's brigades are not known. Considering, however, that those Confederates executed three separate attacks, their killed and wounded probably exceeded the more than 500 such losses suffered by Humphreys's corps. All told, Lee may have lost as many as 1,600 troops in his unsuccessful defense of A. P. Hill's picket line on March 25.[82]

*   *   *

After receiving Meade's summary of the day's events, Grant broadly praised his lieutenant's performance: "It reflects great credit on the army for the promptness with which it became the attacking force after repelling an unexpected attack from the enemy." Meade reported near midnight that Wright held all the captured picket line and that Humphreys retained everything that he felt would be advantageous to him.[83]

March 25 certainly marked a day of triumph for the Army of the Potomac, but to what did the bluecoats owe their victory, and how would the combat that day influence the conduct of the upcoming campaign? There can be no doubt that John G. Parke performed with competence in his role as acting army commander. His actions in response to Gordon's attack at Fort Stedman were prudent, prompt, and thoroughly effective. To recognize that Gordon's was a hopeless mission does not detract from the professionalism displayed by his opponent that day. Parke's decision to defer authorizing an assault against the Confederate line southwest of Petersburg until the crisis east of the city could be resolved and communication with Meade reestablished, reflected cautious good sense. It must be recognized, however, that delaying the offensive suggested by Humphreys and Wright near dawn gave A. P. Hill's brigades a chance to return to their lines and eventually confront the Second and Sixth corps during their afternoon attacks.

Andrew A. Humphreys displayed commendable initiative and aggressiveness on March 25. His probes during the morning uncovered the weakness of the Confederate picket line in front of the Second Corps and, except for Hays's late afternoon thrust near Hatcher's Run, achieved everything the Second Corps would gain the entire day. With the assistance of Griffin's division of the Fifth Corps, Humphreys successfully defended what he had captured against three distinct Confederate counter blows. On March 25, the Second Corps restored some of the luster to a reputation that had suffered since their calamity at Reams Station the previous August.

Sixth Corps generalship on March 25 warrants less praise. Wright's instincts upon learning of the Confederate offensive east of Petersburg told him that opportunity beckoned in his own front. He correctly deduced that Lee had weakened his defenses opposite the Sixth Corps to support the attack against Fort Stedman. In fact, the bulk of Thomas's and Lane's brigades had gone to assist Gordon, leaving McGowan's South Carolinians and Scales's and MacRae's Tarheels to oppose five brigades of the Sixth Corps. Before mid-morning, however, Wright's confidence evaporated. Scouting reports contradicted what his intuition told him should be true. No discernible weaknesses could be detected in the Confederate front—or so Wright believed until almost noon, despite tangible evidence from Humphreys of Confederate vulnerability and positive orders from Meade to forge ahead.

Once Wright executed his attack, he committed only a tiny fraction of his available force and experienced a repulse. At this point, despite continued misgivings about his chances for success, Wright began to orchestrate the kind of offensive he should have conducted hours earlier. By 3:00 p.m., he had deployed Getty's division and Keifer's brigade in such a manner that their assault quickly overran the Confederate picket line. Thomas's counterattack enjoyed only temporary success because Wright and his subordinate commanders were prepared to respond with an overwhelming assault that permanently secured the captured rifle pits. The day ended with the Sixth Corps advanced as fully as Humphreys's troops.

The Union effort southwest of Petersburg lacked coordination and a clear articulation of objectives. To Meade's credit, he assigned Warren's corps as support to both Humphreys and Wright; in fact, one Fifth Corps division did play a minor role in the day's affairs. But at no time did the army commander move west of Fort Wadsworth to give personal direction to his subordinates. Nor did Meade ever specify a goal for Humphreys and Wright beyond exploring the situation in their front and taking advantage of any opportunities the corps commanders developed. To some extent, then, Meade preordained the piecemeal and spasmodic gains earned by Wright and Humphreys through his failure to adopt a clear and united course of action. Federal generalship on March 25 was reactive, if ultimately successful. Perhaps, under the circumstances, that is all that could have been expected.

Little more needs to be said about the conduct of Lee's "Last Grand Offensive" at Fort Stedman. Born of desperation but nurtured by careful planning and maximum commitment, Gordon's assault on the morning of March 25 could have succeeded only had the Federals demonstrated rank incompetence and demoralization. The Confederate commander had not been blind to the risk to his right flank entailed by this foredoomed endeavor. Lieutenant Caldwell remembered that, "On the night of the 24th of March, the brigade received orders to form and be ready to receive an attack," suggesting that Marse Robert had anticipated a Union thrust against his thinned ranks southwest of Petersburg. Once the drama at Fort Stedman had played out, Lee rushed Hill's troops back to their camps, and these weary brigades then hurled themselves at Humphreys and Wright in an effort to regain their captured picket lines. Unlike Meade, Lee thought enough of the situation there to give it his personal attention, but the Confederates had to content themselves with limiting the Federal gains to the advanced rifle pits. The Southern counterattacks found Union flanks and persisted with commendable determination, but they failed due to a lack of both coordination and the numbers necessary to evict an entrenched enemy.[84]

Not every Federal agreed that the triumph on March 25 southwest of Petersburg had been worth the cost. "This was an example of an attack in broad day against a simple infantry cover, which cost us, in killed and wounded, a number equal perhaps to that of the entire force of the enemy actually opposed to us," grumbled engineer officer John G. Barnard. Warren Keifer, whose brigade could claim as much credit for the day's outcome as any Sixth Corps unit, told his wife that "while I am delighted at our success, I question whether the position gained will in the end be of value to us. I most seriously question whether the loss to the enemy in killed, wounded and captured is worth to us even the small number of men lost by us."

Hazard Stevens, however, recognized that gaining a position just 700 yards from the enemy's primary defenses represented an important achievement. "The advanced positions thus gained were of incalculable advantage," he wrote. "From them all the intervening ground to the enemy's main line could be closely scanned, as well as his works themselves, and room was afforded to form an attacking column in front of our works and within striking distance of the enemy's." Writing with the perspective of hindsight, Andrew A. Humphreys summarized the significance of the battles southwest of Petersburg on March 25 in no uncertain terms: "It was this capture of the intrenched picket line of the enemy that made it practicable for General Wright to carry the enemy's main line of intrenchments by assault on the morning of the 2d of April."[85]

But on the morning of March 26, that decisive assault was still one week and thousands of intervening casualties in the future.

NOTES

1. *OR* pt. 2, 34, 42, 162, 536. Wright returned to the army on February 11. He spent a portion of his leave in Washington.

2. For the best outlines of the Battle of Hatcher's Run, see Trudeau, *The Last Citadel*, 312-322 and Humphreys, *The Virginia Campaign*, 312-315. Hatcher's Run would be David Gregg's last battle. On February 9, he resigned his commission, leaving the army the next day. "The whole division regretted his loss, as they had confidence in and esteem and affection for him," wrote the division's top medical officer. Colonel John Irvin Gregg, David Gregg's cousin and commander of the Second Brigade of Gregg's division, assumed divisional command on February 10. See *OR* pt. 1, 113, 622.

3. Monk's Neck Bridge over Rowanty Creek finds its 2000 incarnation along VA 669 about 1/2 mile east of VA 670 in Dinwiddie County. Rowanty Creek is formed by the confluence of Hatcher's Run and Gravelly Run, just a few hundred yards upstream from the bridge, which is sometimes spelled Monck's.

4. Heth's works survive in 2000 on private land in impressive condition. An attractive post-war mill occupies the site of the wartime Armstrong's Mill on the north side of Hatcher's Run just west of VA 670. The Vaughan Road crossing of Hatcher's Run in 2000 is along VA 613, one-quarter mile north of VA 670. None of the land off of the road network is publicly accessible.

5. James I. Robertson, Jr., ed., *The Civil War Letters of General Robert McAllister* (New Brunswick, N.J., 1965), 576-577; *OR* pt. 2, 1206. McAllister had received a brevet to brigadier general dating from October 27, 1864 for distinguished service at the Battle of Burgess's Mill (Boydton Plank Road). The brigade that relieved McAllister belonged to Colonel John Ramsey, who considered his arrival "very portentous and opportune." *OR* pt. 1, 207. William McComb had received his promotion to brigadier general effective January 20, 1865.

6. *OR* pt. 1, 297-298. Brigadier General John F. Hartranft's division represented the Ninth Corps in this operation.

7. "From the Old Nineteenth," in the *Winsted* (Conn.) *Herald*, February 24, 1865; Michael Kelly, Diary, February 6, 1865, CHS; *OR* pt. 1, 298-299; Philip R. Woodcock, Diary, February 6, 1865, in David Ward Collection, Lakeville, Connecticut; Britton and Reed, eds., *To My Beloved Wife and Boy at Home*, 331. The Fifth Corps brigade was Colonel Alfred L. Pearson's of Griffin's division. See *OR* pt. 1, 270-272.

8. "From the Old Nineteenth," in the *Winsted* (Conn.) *Herald*, February 24, 1865; *OR* pt. 1, 256, 299; Warren quoted in Trudeau, *The Last Citadel*, 320; Captain Charles H. Dimmock to Lissie, February 12, 1865, in Elizabeth Lewis Selden Dimmock Papers, VHS. Sergeant John F.L. Hartwell of the 121st New York recorded in his diary that, "Our blankets & clothes wer covrd with ice & frozen stiff." See Britton and Reed, eds., *To My Beloved Wife and Boy at Home*, 332. David

Thompson of the 27th North Carolina also criticized the performance of his comrades in this battle: "Our army is worst demoralized than it has ever been. . . . [T]he reason why we didnt whip those yanks . . . was that the men would not fight. The order was given to charge, but there was no charge in them . . . they would not go forward, if they had have charged as they have done before, we would have whipped the yanks." Quoted in James M. McPherson, *For Cause and Comrades* (New York, 1997), 161-162.

9. *OR* pt. 1, 67, 69; Trudeau, *The Last Citadel*, 322; Humphreys, *The Virginia Campaign*, 315. See Chapter 2 for the impact on the Sixth Corps of moving to the old Second Corps camps.

10. *OR* pt. 2, 1205. Lee officially assumed the duties of general-in-chief on February 9. See *OR* 51, pt. 2, 1082-1083. Lee quoted in Freeman, *R.E. Lee*, IV, 2 and *OR* pt. 2, 1250. The development of Confederate strategy between the Battle of Hatcher's Run and the Battle of Fort Stedman is admirably covered in Freeman, *R.E. Lee*, IV, 1-13. Schofield's capture of Wilmington is the subject of Chris E. Fonvielle, Jr., *The Wilmington Campaign: Last Days of Departing Hope* (Campbell, Cal., 1997).

11. *OR* 47, pt. 2, 1248, 1256-1257. Johnston had been removed as commander of the Army of Tennessee outside of Atlanta in July 1864. President Davis acquiesced in Johnston's appointment despite harboring a long-standing antipathy toward the prickly-but-talented Virginian, in part because of strong pressure from Congress. See *OR* 47, pt. 2, 1303 for Davis's rationale, and Rable, *Confederate Republic*, 286-287 for Johnston's support in the Senate.

12. *OR* pt. 2, 823-825. Lincoln tried diplomacy with Confederate commissioners at the Hampton Roads Peace Conference on February 3, seeking ways to end the war. This parley foundered, as Jefferson Davis knew it would, on the fundamental issue of Confederate independence. For a full discussion of this episode, see McPherson, *Battle Cry of Freedom*, 821-825. For Grant's correspondence with Lee and his proscription against negotiating peace terms from Secretary of War Stanton, see John Y. Simon, ed., *The Papers of Ulysses S. Grant*, 22 vols. to date (Carbondale, Ill., 1967-), XIV, 91, 98-99.

13. For accounts of the Battle of Waynesboro and Early's demise, see Philip H. Sheridan, *Personal Memoirs of P. H. Sheridan* (2 vols.; New York, 1888), II, 113-116, and Jubal Anderson Early, *Autobiographical Sketch and Narrative of the War Between the States* (Philadelphia, 1912, reprint, Wilmington, N.C., 1989), 461-464. Early's fate after Waynesboro is addressed in Freeman, *R.E. Lee*, IV, 507-509. Confederate strength returns may be found in *OR* pt. 1, 388-90, pt. 2, 1274. Thoughtful analysis of these figures is provided by Jones, "Last Days of the Army of Northern Virginia," in *SHSP*, XXI, 59-60 and Freeman, *R.E. Lee*, IV, 6.

14. Gordon, *Reminiscences of the Civil War*, 385-393, provides a colorful and dramatic account of this momentous conference. Gordon is the only source for the existence let alone the content of this meeting, however. The Georgian's habit of stretching the truth in his postwar writings raises questions about how much Lee actually relied on his young lieutenant to advise on grand strategy. Yet, Gordon's

careful biographer casts no doubt on the essential veracity of Gordon's narrative. See Eckert, *John Brown Gordon*, 107.

15. Freeman, *R.E. Lee*, IV, 9-10; Gordon, *Reminiscences of the Civil War*, 393-394. It is interesting that after Lee's return from Richmond, Gordon drew the conclusion from his conversation with the general-in-chief that the Davis administration opposed evacuation of Petersburg and Richmond.

16. *OR* pt. 2, 1295; 47, pt. 2, 1373. Johnston had suggested such a strategy as early as March 1, but Lee was not then ready to embrace it. See *OR* 47, pt. 2, 1298. John Cabell Breckinridge became Confederate secretary of war on February 6, 1865.

17. Col. Samuel M. Bowman and Lt. Col. Richard B. Irwin, *Sherman and His Campaigns; A Military Biography* (New York, 1865), 373-375. Mark L. Bradley, *Last Stand in the Carolinas: The Battle of Bentonville* (Campbell, Cal., 1996) is the best treatment of Johnston's last major engagement. It is singular that neither Johnston in his own stridently defensive memoirs nor a recent and sympathetic biographer emphasize the general's important role in influencing Confederate strategy at Petersburg, even if that strategy was unlikely to succeed. See Joseph E. Johnston, *Narrative of Military Operations During the Late War Between the States* (New York, 1874), and Craig L. Symonds, *Joseph E. Johnston: A Civil War Biography* (New York, 1992).

18. Porter, *Campaigning With Grant*, 386-387, 395-397.

19. Porter, *Campaigning With Grant*, 397; Sheridan, *Personal Memoirs*, II, 116-123; Grant, *Personal Memoirs*, II, 427-429.

20. Grant, *Personal Memoirs*, II, 424-425.

21. Grant, *Personal Memoirs*, II, 427.

22. Grant, *Personal Memoirs*, II, 424; Porter, *Campaigning With Grant*, 403; *OR* pt. 2, 631-632. Parke was acting commander of the Army of the Potomac because Meade had left that day to attend to the funeral of his son.

23. *OR* pt. 2, 962. The Jones House to which Grant referred was located near the Jerusalem Plank Road, several miles south of Petersburg. It is no longer extant.

24. Joseph C. Rutherford to "My dear Wife," March 18, 1865, in Joseph Case Rutherford Papers, UVM. Rutherford referred to the Battle of Kinston or Wyse Fork, March 8-10, in which Confederate troops under General Braxton Bragg unsuccessfully attacked Cox's army in North Carolina.

25. J. Warren Keifer to "My Dear Wife," March 23, 1865, in Joseph Warren Keifer Papers, LC.

26. *OR* pt. 1, 50.

27. Gordon, *Reminiscences of the Civil War*, 398-403. There are several good summaries of the Battle of Fort Stedman, providing differing perspectives, but similar analysis. See Trudeau, *The Last Citadel*, 330-354; Freeman, R.E. Lee, IV, 14-21; Freeman, Lee's Lieutenants, III, 646-654; Humphreys, *The Virginia Campaign*, 316-321; Gordon, *Reminiscences of the Civil War*, 395-413; Grant, *Personal Memoirs*, II, 431-433; Porter, *Campaigning With Grant*, 404-406, and John G. Parke's report in *OR* pt. 1, 316-319.

28. Gordon, *Reminiscences of the Civil War*, 410; Walker quoted in Trudeau, *The Last Citadel*, 338-339. Gordon told a much-repeated story about the rifleman who fired the signal shot, who, out of a sense of fair play, issued a verbal warning to the unseen Union pickets a few yards away. See Gordon, *Reminiscences of the Civil War*, 408-410. The two brigades from Johnson's division were Brigadier General Matthew Ransom's North Carolinians and Brigadier General William H. Wallace's South Carolinians.

29. Gordon, *Reminiscences of the Civil War*, 410. The Federal officer was Colonel Napoleon Bonaparte McLaughlen, who rushed into Fort Stedman in the dark and was captured while in the act of giving orders to men he supposed to be Federals.

30. Clifford Dowdey and Louis H. Manarin, eds., *The Wartime Papers of R. E. Lee* (New York, 1961), 917. Parke acted as army commander on the morning of March 25 because Meade was at City Point and the telegraph line between army headquarters and Grant's headquarters had been severed, leaving Parke the senior officer on the field.

31. "Capture of Richmond and Petersburgh," in The *Winsted* (Conn.) *Herald*, April 7, 1865; Homer Curtis to "Dear Friends," March 27, 1865, in Homer Curtis Letters, YU; *OR* pt. 3, 137.

32. *OR* pt. 1, 300-301, pt. 3, 138, 149; Andrew Burwell to "My darling Mary," March 26, 1865, in Burwell Letters, University of Southern Mississippi; Olcott and Lear, *The Civil War Letters of Lewis Bissell*, 353-359; William L. Phillips to "father and mother," March 26, 1865, in William L. Phillips Letters, SHSW.

33. Olcott and Lear, *The Civil War Letters of Lewis Bissell*, 357; *OR* pt. 1, 300-301, pt. 3, 137. Fort Sedgwick, popularly known as "Fort Hell," was destroyed in the 1960s to make way for a commercial building that, in 2000, stands vacant just east of Crater Road near its intersection with Morton Avenue in Petersburg.

34. *OR* pt. 1, 319, pt. 3, 121. Humphreys sent his message at 7:25 a.m. As previously mentioned, Meade was at City Point and out of telegraphic communication with the front. Therefore, Parke assumed temporary army command until Meade either returned to the army or reestablished direct communication with his field headquarters. It is important to note that although Parke's report explained that he deferred authorizing Humphreys and Wright to advance their lines early on the morning of March 25, he did tell Humphreys at 7:45 a.m. that, "If [the enemy's] lines are weakened in your front I think it well to take advantage of it." This was all the encouragement the aggressive Humphreys required. There is no record that Parke sent such a message to Wright. See *OR* pt. 3, 121.

35. *OR* pt. 3, 121-122. The Watkins House stood near the southeast corner of what in 2000 is the intersection of Duncan and Smith Grove roads, VA 670 and 673, in Dinwiddie County.

36. *OR* pt. 3, 139-140.

37. *OR* pt. 3, 140-143.

38. *OR* pt. 3, 124. Warren began the day at the Fifth Corps camps near Hatcher's Run behind the Second Corps on the army's far left flank and rear.

39. The reports covering Wright's first attack on March 25 may be found in *OR* pt. 1, 307-313. Lieutenant Colonel Damon timed the attack at 3:00 p.m., but all the other participants agreed that the advance occurred shortly after 1:00 p.m. For Humphreys's anticipation of Wright's advance on the right of the Second Corps, see *OR* pt. 3, 125, 142. Keifer had been colonel of the 110th Ohio before assuming brigade command, so it is not surprising that he would choose his old comrades for this honorable and important assignment.

40. Waite, "Three Years With the Tenth Vermont," II, 242. By the "breastworks," Damon clearly meant the entrenched picket line, not the main fortifications.

41. J. Warren Keifer to "My Dear Wife," March 25, 1865, in Joseph Warren Keifer Papers, LC; Benson, "Reminiscences," 613-615, in Berry G. Benson Papers, SHC; *OR* pt. 3, 143. Wright timed his dispatch to Humphreys at 1:15 p.m. This suggests that if the attack began at or shortly after 1:00 p.m., its duration was short indeed. Keifer expressed his disagreement with both the tactics and the selection of Damon as the leader of this offensive. Although the results seemingly sustained this judgment, one witness remarked on Damon's "coolness and bravery" during the engagement. See Joseph C. Rutherford to *Newport* (Vt.) *Express*, March 27, 1865, in Joseph Case Rutherford Papers, UVM.

42. J. Warren Keifer to "My Dear Wife," March 25, 1865, in Joseph Warren Keifer Papers, LC. Neither Wright nor Seymour comment on this sequence of events, leaving Keifer as the sole witness. It is clear that the incompetent officer to whom Keifer referred was Damon, whom Keifer misidentified as a member of Seymour's staff. Keifer believed that Seymour wished "to give [Damon] an opportunity to distinguish himself." Keifer had protested the selection of Damon prior to the first attack. It would have been highly irregular for Keifer to approach Wright without first gaining Seymour's permission to speak with the corps commander, but after the day's action, Keifer wrote his wife that, "What seemed likely to lead to a bad feeling between Genl. Seymour & myself was lost sight of after the battle." The discord which Keifer feared conceivably could have resulted from the brigade commander bypassing Seymour and going directly to Wright, but the evidence is inconclusive.

43. The reports of the regimental officers and Keifer himself may be found in *OR* pt. 1, 309-315. The 138th Pennsylvania did not, apparently, participate in the attack. Their whereabouts on the afternoon of March 25 are not recorded, but assumed to be in the main Union line. As mentioned in the text, Keifer retained a significant number of men in forts Fisher, Gregg, and Welch as a hedge against a Confederate counterattack should his own offensive fail. It is not possible to know precisely how many soldiers Keifer commanded on the front line. The estimate in the text is based upon the stated strength of Damon's pickets, an average strength of 400 men in each of Keifer's regiments, save the 67th Pennsylvania which reported 511 present for duty, and the 9th NY Heavy Artillery which numbered

more than 1,000 in its three battalions, minus the troops left behind to garrison the works. Private Lewis Rosenburger of the 6th Maryland reported that "the left wing of our Regt. was in Fort Gregg. The right was in action." See Rosenburger's diary, March 25, 1865, Carroll County Historical Society, Westminster, Maryland. The men of Truex's brigade who had not participated in the first attack, remained "all day behind the breastworks when the battle was raging on both sides of us." See Daniel Schaffner, Memorandum Book, March 25, 1865, in Schaffner Family Collection, Civil War Papers, Pennsylvania Historical and Museum Commission.

44. See *OR* pt.1, 304-307 for the reports from Grant's regimental commanders on the role played by the Vermont Brigade on March 25.

45. Hyde, *Following the Greek Cross*, 243-244; *OR* pt. 1, 302-304.

46. J. Warren Keifer to "My Dear Wife," March 25, 1865, in Joseph Warren Keifer Papers, LC; Solomon Rousculf, "Petersburg: The Part Taken in the Action of April 2, 1865 by the 126th Ohio," in *National Tribune*, June 18, 1891. All the accounts except one agree that the attack began at 3:00 p.m. Damon placed it at 4:00 p.m.

47. J. Warren Keifer to "My Dear Wife," March 25, 1865, in Joseph Warren Keifer Papers, LC; *OR* pt. 1, 314, 311.

48. *OR* pt. 1, 311-315. Major Williams belonged to the 126th Ohio but was in temporary command of the 67th Pennsylvania on March 25.

49. *OR* pt. 1, 305, 308-310; Oscar E. Waite to George Benedict, December 29, 1886, in George G. Benedict Papers, UVM. According to Waite, the surrendered Confederates eagerly ran toward the main Union line in order to escape the fire coming from their own fortifications. A knot of drunken Federal officers skulking in the rear saw "this horde of Rebels bearing down upon them," and "filled with consternation they started for our main line 'fleeing as from wrath to come.'" One cowardly Yankee tripped and fell, allowing the Confederates to overtake him, and begged for mercy until he realized his captors were, in fact, unarmed prisoners.

50. *OR* pt. 1, 304-307; Charles G. Gould to "Dear Parents," March 26, 1865, in Captain Charles Gilbert Gould Collection, UVM. This Jones House, not to be confused with the Jones House near the Jerusalem Plank Road, belonged to Robert H. Jones who married, in succession, two of the Boisseau girls from Tudor Hall. The site of the Jones House is privately owned on the west side of VA 672, Church Road, in Dinwiddie County.

51. *OR* pt. 3, 143; Hyde, *Following the Greek Cross*, 243-246; Stevens, "The Storming of the Lines of Petersburg," in *PMHSM*, VI, 431-432.

52. Hyde, *Following the Greek Cross*, 244-246. None of the sources from Hyde's brigade mention encountering resistance from a Confederate picket line in their initial charge. Perhaps Grant's attack created a ripple effect and uprooted the Confederate pickets to their right before Hyde arrived at the line. It is also possible that the portion of the picket line which Hyde attacked was undefended on the afternoon of March 25, the depleted Confederates relying on the flooded ground to protect their main works from surprise. The best military map of the area prepared by Nathaniel Michler does show the entrenched Confederate picket line

extending uninterrupted between Church and Squirrel Level roads. Michler's map labels Rohoic Creek as Indian Town Creek. See Davis, Perry, and Kirkley, *Atlas to Accompany the Official Records*, Plate LXXVII, 2.

53. Hyde, *Following the Greek Cross*, 245. The Federals did not give a name to the action on March 25 southwest of Petersburg. One Confederate source referred to the fighting described in the text as occurring at "the Jones Farm Battlefield," a reference to the combat that occurred there on September 30, 1864. See Noah Collins, Memoir, in Isaac Spencer London Collection, North Carolina Department of Archives and History, 72. Richard J. Sommers, a close student of the fighting southwest of Petersburg, refers to all the combat in this neighborhood on March 25 as the Battle of Watkins's Farm." Sommers to the author, June 5, 1999.

54. Captain John Hardeman to "Dear Captain," March 28, 1865, in Gregory A. Coco Collection, Harrisburg Civil War Round Table Collection, USAMHI; Lane, "Glimpses of Army Life," in *SHSP*, XVIII, 421; Caldwell, *The History of a Brigade of South Carolinians*, 264; Benson, ed., *Berry Benson's Civil War Book*, 177.

55. Caldwell, *The History of a Brigade of South Carolinians*, 264; Olsen, ed., *Upon the Tented Field*, 303.

56. Caldwell, *The History of a Brigade of South Carolinians*, 265; R. Thomas Crew, Jr. and Benjamin H. Trask, *Grimes's Battery, Grandy's Battery and Huger's Battery Virginia Artillery* (Lynchburg, Va., 1995), 48; Wiley, ed., *Norfolk Blues*, 210-211. The Crenshaw (Virginia) Battery, commanded by Captain Thomas Ellett, provided close support to Grandy's cannoneers. Private John Walters is the quoted artillerist.

57. *OR* pt. 1, 307; George H. Mellish to "Dear Mother," March 26, 1865, in George H. Mellish Papers, HEH; J. Warren Keifer to "My Dear Wife," March 25, 1865, in Joseph Warren Keifer Papers, LC; Morse, "The 'Rebellion Record' of an Enlisted Man," in *National Tribune Scrapbook*, 98; Hyde, *Following the Greek Cross*, 246.

58. Caldwell, *The History of a Brigade of South Carolinians*, 265; Noah Collins, Memoir, in Isaac Spencer London Collection, North Carolina Department of Archives and History, 72; Captain John Hardeman to "Dear Captain," March 28, 1865, in Gregory A. Coco Collection, Harrisburg Civil War Round Table Collection, USAMHI. Simmons was a 27-year-old native of Hickory Grove, Georgia who had been colonel of his regiment since October 13, 1862. After the war, Simmons would become the chief justice of the Georgia Supreme Court. See Robert K. Krick, *Lee's Colonels: A Biographical Register of the Field Officers of the Army of Northern Virginia* (Dayton, Oh., 1979), 318.

59. Captain John Hardeman to "Dear Captain," March 28, 1865, in Gregory A. Coco Collection, Harrisburg Civil War Round Table Collection, USAMHI; Caldwell, *The History of a Brigade of South Carolinians*, 265; Hyde, *Following the Greek Cross*, 246. Simmons did not identify the skirmishers he passed on the way to his attack. Perhaps they were survivors from the captured picket line, supplemented by men from Lane's and McGowan's brigades. No Confederate

source mentions the inundation in connection with the counterattack, suggesting that the Georgians' route lay west of the flooded ground.

60. Hyde, *Following the Greek Cross*, 246; *OR* pt. 1, 302; Papers Presented by Mark Newman "to The Committee of Ladies in Savannah Georgia for the Confederate Museum at Richmond, Va.," January 28, 1896, Museum of the Confederacy; Caldwell, *The History of a Brigade of South Carolinians*, 265; Captain John Hardeman to "Dear Captain," March 28, 1865, in Gregory A. Coco Collection, Harrisburg Civil War Round Table Collection, USAMHI. These seemingly irreconcilable accounts of the impact of Simmons's attack might be explained, in part, by a misapprehension of the cause of Hyde's initial withdrawal. Hyde described this movement as a voluntary action designed to rectify his isolation from supporting troops and his exposure to Confederate artillery fire, which had as yet done little material damage to his brigade. The Confederates may have assumed that this retreat came as a direct result of the Georgians' attack, which could not have been much later than the commencement of Hyde's withdrawal, if not virtually simultaneous to it. Existing evidence is not adequate to state with certainty the relationship between Hyde's shift and Simmons's assault, but there can be no doubt that the greater part of four Union regiments—the 62nd New York, 93rd Pennsylvania, 1st Maine Veterans, and 122nd New York—eventually withdrew in the face of the Georgians' fire. Which of those regiments were the Federals mentioned by Hardeman and Caldwell as retiring during Simmons's attack cannot be determined from the available sources.

61. Hazard Stevens to "Dear Mother," March 26, 1865, in Hazard Stevens Papers, LC; *OR* pt. 1, 302; Captain John Hardeman to "Dear Captain," March 28, 1865, in Gregory A. Coco Collection, Harrisburg Civil War Round Table Collection, USAMHI. The precise time when Simmons attacked is impossible to determine.

62. Julius A. Lineback, Diary, March 26, 1865, in Julius A. Lineback Papers, SHC; John Preston Campbell to "Dear Father," March 26, 1865, in Corporal John Preston Campbell Papers, Civil War Miscellaneous Collection, USAMHI. The long-range artillery duel could not have been very serious or effective. Colonel Hyde did not even notice that the Union artillery had opened. Lineback wrote that "I do not think that either side did much damage to the other. . . ." See Hyde, *Following the Greek Cross*, 247. Private John Walters of the Norfolk Blues, however, characterized the Federal artillery fire as "heavy" and claimed that one shell "passed within eight or ten feet of Gen.'l Lee's head, who was riding by at the time." No other source corroborates this near miss of the commanding general. See Wiley, ed., *Norfolk Blues*, 211.

63. *OR* pt. 1, 300-304; Rhodes, ed., *All for the Union*, 222; Alanson A. Haines, *History of the Fifteenth Regiment New Jersey Volunteers* (New York, 1883, reprint, Gaithersburg, Md., n.d.), 296. Hamblin placed the 65th New York on the left and the 2nd Connecticut Heavy Artillery on the right of his front line. His other two regiments were the 121st New York and 95th Pennsylvania. Prior to the actual

attack, Edwards's brigade shifted significantly to its left, reducing the field of combat to about a one-mile-wide front.

64. Captain John Hardeman to "Dear Captain," March 28, 1865, in Gregory A. Coco Collection, Harrisburg Civil War Round Table Collection, USAHMI; "Editor Constitutionalist," March 28, 1865, in Papers Presented by M. Newman "to The Committee of Ladies in Savannah Georgia for the Confederate Museum at Richmond Va." January 28, 1896, Museum of the Confederacy. Hardeman did not acknowledge the arrival of the other two regiments of Thomas's Brigade.

65. Benedict, *Vermont in the Civil War*, II, 726, 386; *OR* pt. 1, 302-304; "Editor Constitutionalist," March 28, 1865, in Papers Presented by M. Newman "to The Committee of Ladies in Savannah Georgia for the Confederate Museum at Richmond Va." January 28, 1896, Museum of the Confederacy; Captain John Hardeman to "Dear Captain," March 28, 1865, in Gregory A. Coco Collection, Harrisburg Civil War Round Table Collection, USAMHI. The adjutant of the 49th Georgia said that of the 238 men in his regiment that day, 11 were killed, 29 wounded, and 46 missing.

66. Roberts, "War Reminiscences," in *Connecticut Western News*, January 4, 1912; *OR* pt. 1, 300-301; Olcott and Lear, *The Civil War Letters of Lewis Bissell*, 353-359; "Capture of Richmond and Petersburgh," in The *Winsted* (Conn.) *Herald*, April 7, 1865.

67. "Capture of Richmond and Petersburgh," in the *Winsted* (Conn.) *Herald*, April 7, 1865; Soule, "Recollections of the Civil War," in *New Milford* (Conn.) *Gazette*, July 5, 1912; Theodore Vaill to "Dear Brother Charles," March 27, 1865, in Theodore F. Vaill Papers, Northwest Corner Civil War Round Table Collection, USAMHI; Homer Curtis to "Dear Friends," March 27, 1865, in Homer Curtis Letters, YU; Michael Kelly, Diary, March 25, 1865, CHS; *OR* pt. 1, 300. It is not possible to pinpoint the location of this fighting. Warner and Hamblin attacked across the ground between Church Road and Squirrel Level Road. The waterways mentioned in the Union reports are a series of small drainages that combine to become Rohoic Creek. The ground on either side of these drainages ascends slightly, and these land forms must be the ridges referred to by the participants. None of this ground is publicly accessible in 2000 and much of it has been obliterated by the construction of an outsized industrial facility.

68. Best, *History of the 121st New York*, 207. The sources do not identify the Confederates encountered by the 121st New York, but they were likely troops from Brigadier General Alfred M.Scales's North Carolina Brigade. Lieutenant Thomas D. Lattimore of the 34th North Carolina wrote that, "On 25 March the Thirty-fourth was thrown forward to support the picket line, which was about one mile in front of the main line of works. Superior numbers forced us to fall back to the works, losing considerably in killed, wounded and captured." See Clark, ed., *North Carolina in the Great War*, II, 589. The 22nd North Carolina of Scales's Brigade claimed credit for creating the inundation in front of Battery 45, placing that unit to the left of McGowan's, Lane's, and Thomas's in Wilcox's Division alignment. See Clark, ed., *North Carolina in the Great War*, II, 175.

69. *OR* pt. 1, 301-302; Rhodes, ed., *All for the Union*, 222; Charles Sterling Underhill, arranger, *"Your Soldier Boy Samuel": Civil War Letters of Lieut.Samuel Edmund Nichols, Amherst '65 of the 37th Regiment Massachusetts Volunteers* (Buffalo, N.Y., 1929), 126-127. William L. Phillips of the 5th Wisconsin reported that not all the members of his brigade behaved with honor during this portion of the battle: "Some of our brigade[,] the 2 rhode island [and] 37 mas was filled up with drafted men[.] some of the 2 rd tryed to run[.] their oficers took there revolvers and fired into them and told them that if they atempted to run that the rest of the reg should turn and fire on them[.] it is an ofal thing to see a lot of men in a panic they are dead to shame or any thing except trying to get away[.] they look and act like maniacs. . . ." Phillips to "Father and Mother," March 26, 1865, in William L. Phillips Letters, SHSW. The sources do not indicate which Confederate units Edwards encountered. Rhodes had received a promotion to lieutenant colonel in January. See Rhodes, ed., *All for the Union*, 208-209.

70. Frank C. Morse to "My dear Nellie," March 27, 1865, in Frank C. Morse Papers, Massachusetts Historical Society; Edwin C. Hall to "Dear Father," in Marshall, ed., *A War of the People*, 291; George Henry Bates to "Parents," March 31, 1865, in George Henry Bates Letters, Schoff Civil War Collection, University of Michigan; David Herbert Donald, *Lincoln* (New York, 1995), 572.

71. *OR* pt. 1, 196, 229, pt. 3, 125.

72. *OR* pt. 3, 125-126, pt. 1, 196, 237.

73. Samuel H. Walkup, Diary, March 25, 1865, in Samuel Hoey Walkup Papers, SHC; Stedman, *Memorial Address*, 12-13; John Franklin Heitman, Diary, March 25, 1865, in John Franklin Heitman Papers, Duke; Ammen, "Maryland Troops in the Confederate Army," I, 172, in Thomas Clemens Collection, USAMHI. Young Marshall Moody replaced Archibald Gracie in command of Johnson's Alabama brigade after Gracie was killed in December. For accounts of the attacks against the Second Corps on the afternoon of March 25, see *OR* pt. 1, 196-198, 200, 202-203, 206, 229, 233, 235, 241, 247, 249. See also DavidC. Love, *The Prairie Guards. A History of Their Organization, Their Heroism, Their Battles and Their Triumphs* (Columbus, Ga., 1890), 18, for an account from Davis's Brigade. Humphreys mistakenly reported the capture of the 69th Alabama battle flag when he meant the 59th Alabama, in *OR* pt. 3,127.

74. *OR* pt. 1, 213, pt. 3, 127. The captured picket line extended from Hatcher's Run on the Union left to beyond Squirrel Level Road on the Union right. Here and there, especially on Humphreys's front, the Southerners managed to retain a toehold on their original line, shielded from expulsion by darkness.

75. *OR* pt. 1, 308-309; Hazard Stevens to "Dear Mother," March 26, 1865, in Hazard Stevens Papers, LC; Benedict, *Vermont in the Civil War*, I, 202. The house may have been the Dabney residence, located near Duncan Road southwest of the Hart House. The Second Corps units involved to Damon's left were probably the First and Second brigades of Miles's division. The Second, or Irish Brigade, had run out of ammunition about the time of Damon's intended attack. Damon complained that the commander of an unnamed Second Corps brigade "declined

to move his troops to occupy the house" because of his concern about the security of his left flank, but the lack of cartridges probably played a role as well. See *OR* pt. 1, 196-201.

76. Hyde, *Following the Greek Cross*, 246-247; Benson, ed., *Berry Benson's Civil War Book*, 178; Benedict, *Vermont in the Civil War*, I, 577; *OR* pt. 1, 305; Caldwell, *The History of a Brigade of South Carolinians*, 265; Berry G. Benson, "Reminiscences," 612-613, in Berry G. Benson Papers, SHC.

77. For references to the construction of fortifications on the night of March 25 and the return to camp of the Sixth Corps, see Olcott and Lear, *The Civil War Letters of Lewis Bissell*, 358; Haines, *Fifteenth New Jersey*, 296; Homer Curtis to "Dear Friends," March 27, 1865, in Homer Curtis Letters, YU; *OR* pt. 1, 300, 303-304; Rhodes, ed., *All for the Union*, 222; "Capture of Richmond and Petersburgh," in The *Winsted* (Conn.) *Herald*, April 7, 1865; William B. Adams to "Sister Dora," March 26, 1865, in William Bryant Adams Papers, Maine Historical Society; Lothrup Lincoln Lewis, Diary, March 25, 1865, in Lothrup Lincoln Lewis Collection, LC; Regimental Order Book, 122nd New York Infantry, 1862-1865, Book Records of Volunteer Union Organizations, Record Group 94, NA.

78. Olcott and Lear, *The Civil War Letters of Lewis Bissell*, 355.

79. Caldwell, *The History of a Brigade of South Carolinians*, 266; Homer Curtis to "Dear Fannie," April 1, 1865, in Homer Curtis Letters, YU. The captured Georgian may have been from the 35th Georgia of Thomas's Brigade. The 33rd Georgia was not in Lee's army.

80. *OR* pt. 3, 172,177. Details of losses in the Second Corps are as follows: Miles's division: 27 men killed, 10 officers and 256 men wounded, 1 officer and 56 men missing; Hays's division: 4 men killed, 3 officers and 29 men wounded; Mott's division: 1 officer and 19 men killed, 14 officers and 150 men wounded, 1 officer and 119 men missing. The 69th New York of Miles's division lost 94 killed and wounded. The 120th New York of Mott's division lost 84 killed, wounded, or missing. These units reported the greatest regimental losses in the Second Corps on March 25. See *OR* pt. 1, 201, 249. The Battle of Wilson's Creek in southwest Missouri occurred on August 10, 1861 and most of its landscape is preserved as a national battlefield. The Battle of New Hope Church took place on May 25, 1864 northwest of Atlanta. The Battle of New Market, May 15, 1864, was a much-celebrated Confederate victory and is commemorated by a state-supported battlefield park.

81. *OR* pt. 3, 145; Letters Sent Book, Sixth Army Corps 1864-1865, pt. 2, Entry 4407, Record Group 393, NA. Various sources provide unofficial casualty figures for individual brigades and regiments in the Sixth Corps.

Keifer reported 4 killed and 17 wounded in the 110th Ohio; 1 killed, 23 wounded in the 122nd Ohio; 1 killed, 4 wounded in the 126th Ohio; 2 killed, 11 wounded, and 2 missing in the 67th Pennsylvania; no losses in the 138th Pennsylvania; 1 killed and 2 wounded in the 6th Maryland; and 35 wounded in the 9th New York Heavy Artillery, for a total of 103 in his brigade. See *OR* pt.1, 310.

Damon reported 2 killed and four wounded in the 10th Vermont. See *OR* pt. 1, 308.

Grant's brigade reported 2 killed and 8 wounded in the 2nd Vermont; 3 wounded in the 3rd Vermont; 2 wounded in the 4th Vermont; 1 killed and 7 wounded in the 5th Vermont; 1 wounded in the 6th Vermont; and 1 killed and 12 wounded in the 1st Vermont Heavy Artillery for a total of 37 in the brigade. See Benedict, *Vermont in the Civil War*, I, 579.

The 122nd New York reported 3 killed and 15 wounded. See Regimental Order Book, 122nd New York Infantry, 1862-1865, Book Records of Volunteer Union Organizations, Record Group 94, NA.

The 1st Maine Veteran Volunteers lost 73 killed and wounded according to William Bryant Adams as reported in a letter to "Sister Dora," March 26, 1865, in William Bryant Adams Papers, Maine Historical Society. William E. H. Morse in "The 'Rebellion Record' of an Enlisted Man," *National Tribune Scrapbook*, 98, listed the casualties in the 1st Maine Veterans as 5 killed and 56 wounded. George A. Cary estimated 75 killed and wounded in the 1st Maine Veterans. See Cary to "Dear Mother," March 24 [sic], 1865, in Cary Family Papers, University of Maine.

Altus Jewell of the 77th New York estimated that his unit lost 10 killed and wounded. See Altus Jewell to "Dear brother & sister," April 1, 1865, in Sgt. Altus Jewell Papers, USAMHI.

Hamblin reported 64 killed and wounded in his brigade. See *OR* pt. 1, 300. A listing of casualties for the 2nd Connecticut Heavy Artillery published in the *Winsted* (Conn.) *Herald* on April 7, 1865 listed 5 killed and 17 wounded. On March 27, Homer Curtis of that regiment reported 3 killed and 15 wounded. See Curtis to "Dear Friends," March 27, 1865, in Homer Curtis Letters, YU. Many of the accounts from the 2nd Connecticut Heavy Artillery mention the death of Sergeant-Major Goodwin Osborne, of whom Curtis said "a finer man never was called up to die for his friends by the hand of his & their foes."

John J. Ingraham reported 1 killed and 8 wounded in the 121st New York, but Philip R. Woodcock of that regiment thought his unit suffered 11 or 12 casualties including First Lieutenant Horatio N. Duroe killed and Lieutenant Langford Burton wounded. Duroe was described as "the largest man in the regiment, and a brave and impetuous officer." See John J. Ingraham to "Brother Oll," March 27, 1865, in John J. Ingraham Papers, Cornell University; Philip R. Woodcock, Diary, March 25, 1865, in David Ward Collection, Lakeville, Connecticut; Best, *History of the 121st New York State Infantry*, 207; Britton and Reed, eds., *To My Beloved Wife and Boy at Home*, 343-344.

Edwards reported 1 man wounded in the 2nd Rhode Island; 1 killed and 5 wounded in the 5th Wisconsin; 3 wounded in the 37th Massachusetts, no losses in the 49th Pennsylvania; 4 wounded and 3 missing in the 82nd Pennsylvania, and 5 wounded in the 119th Pennsylvania for a total in his brigade of 22. See *OR* pt. 1, 302.

82. *OR* pt. 3, 172-173, 182; Hess, "Lee's Tarheels," 712. Professor Hess has calculated that in MacRae's Brigade, the 11th North Carolina lost 27 men, the 26th

North Carolina 18, the 44th North Carolina 20, the 47th North Carolina 28, and the 52nd North Carolina 30. See also Letters Sent Book, Sixth Army Corps 1864-1865, pt. 2, Entry 4407, Record Group 393, NA; Caldwell, *The History of a Brigade of South Carolinians*, 266; Captain John Hardeman to "Dear Captain," March 28, 1865, in Gregory A. Coco Collection, Harrisburg Civil War Round Table Collection, USAMHI; Journal of Major-General Bushrod Rust Johnson, C.S. Army, March 15-April 16, 1865, in Bushrod Rust Johnson Papers, NA. A member of the 2nd Maryland Battalion of McComb's Brigade reported one killed, two wounded, and one missing during the day. See Ammen, "Maryland Troops in the Confederate Army," I, 168, in Thomas Clemens Collection, USAMHI. Scales's Brigade contributed to the butcher's bill during their counterattacks late in the day as well.

83. *OR* pt. 3, 113.

84. Caldwell, *The History of a Brigade of South Carolinians*, 265-266; Wiley, ed., *Norfolk Blues*, 211.

85. Barnard, *Report on the Defenses of Washington*, 150; J. Warren Keifer to "My Dear Wife," March 25, 1865, in Joseph Warren Keifer Papers, LC; Hazard Stevens to "Dear Mother," March 26, 1865, in Hazard Stevens Papers, LC; Stevens, "The Storming of the Lines of Petersburg," in *PMHSM*, VI, 417; Humphreys, *The Virginia Campaign*, 321. Stevens noted that "one salient point of the new fortified picket line in particular, considerably in advance of the captured rifle pits, embracing a slight knoll, just to the right of the Squirrel Level road, commanded an excellent view up and down their main line for a considerable distance."

CHAPTER FIVE

Prelude to Breakthrough
March 26-April 1

The morning of March 26 dawned quietly on the Sixth Corps front, revealing the portentous consequences of the previous afternoon's fighting. Exhausted Federals, who had spent a frigid night in the captured Confederate rifle pits or who had occupied new works erected on advantageous ground, gratefully returned to their camps, relieved by rested comrades. Across the way, the grayclad soldiers of Cadmus Wilcox's Division, whose gallant efforts had failed to prevent the loss of their advanced line, settled into hastily dug emplacements about halfway between their main entrenchments and their forsaken picket posts. Both armies declined to resume the bitter combat that had concluded at dark, concentrating instead on sorting out the opportunities and challenges wrought by the March 25 engagement.

General Wright began the day by addressing a gentle rebuke to his counterpart in the Second Corps, Andrew Humphreys, complaining about the location of Humphreys's new rifle pits. "The officers of the day, corps and division, report that the right of your picket-line has not advanced so far as our left, and that the latter has in consequence been compelled to incline to the rear," scolded Wright. "Can this be corrected by an advance of your right?" Humphreys promised to investigate the matter but took understandable offense at his peer's implication that the Second Corps had lagged behind. "I took the enemy's intrenched picket-line on my front . . . some time before the Sixth Corps took any part of the intrenched picket-line in their front," replied the miffed Pennsylvanian, "and the right of my rear picket-line had to be refused from the enemy's old picket-line because the picket-line of the Sixth Corps had not advanced, instead of the reverse." Early in the afternoon, Humphreys informed Wright that Nelson Miles, commanding his right-most division, insisted that no gap existed between him and the left of the Sixth Corps. Nevertheless, Humphreys agreed to order Miles to advance, if Wright would arrange to have his men keep pace. There the matter ended.[1]

The Federal triumph on March 25 brought under Union control the few trees that had survived the winter between the picket lines. Like a swarm of axe-wielding termites, the Yankees descended on these scattered copses, stripping the entire expanse between Wright's front and Wilcox's entrenchments. While the wood chopping progressed, a flag of truce arrived on the portion of the picket line manned by George Getty's division. The Confederates sought and received permission to recover the bodies of several officers killed on the previous day. The 5th Vermont's Captain Charles G. Gould accompanied Getty's officer-of-the-day to parley with his Confederate counterparts, "a fine looking set of fellows . . . very gentlemanly . . . well dressed and well mounted," thought Gould. In the Union rear, Joseph Hamblin conducted a brigade inspection and drill, but for the most part, March 26 proved a restful and peaceful Sabbath. Still, Wright suspected that the Rebels would not concede control of their former picket line without another fight. He issued orders that night for the entire corps to be under arms at 4:00 a.m. and to remain on the alert until an hour after daylight in order to respond should the Confederates assault. Wright also directed that two regiments from each division reinforce their picket posts at 4:00 a.m., the hour most likely to bring an attack.[2]

These precautions would prove prescient, but little that occurred in the Confederate ranks during that quiet Sunday presaged what was in store for the following morning. Although the Norfolk Light Artillery shifted nearly half a mile to its left to add firepower to the guns around Fort Gregg and Battery 45, no hostile Federal act provoked the Virginia cannoneers to discharge their pieces. Occasional picket fire did interrupt the stillness, particularly from the sentries in front of Samuel McGowan's Brigade, including the sharpshooter battalion of Captain William S. Dunlop. These South Carolinians enlivened their deadly pastime by outfitting a stick or ramrod with a Confederate uniform coat and slouch hat and hoisting it above a rifle pit. "Pop, went the rifles! Dummy was dropped, and a shout went up from the enemy," recalled one of the Palmetto State pickets. "After a little [while] Mr. Dummy looked up again, and again the rifles blazed away. The trick was played for some time before they found it out. And even then we could sometimes fool them by moving the dummy along as though it were a man walking."[3]

While the South Carolinians amused themselves at the expense of the Union marksmen, General Lee conducted a council of war at his Turnbull House headquarters west of Petersburg, attended by a number of high-ranking officers. The assemblage decided that the portion of the captured picket line crossing a gentle knoll called McIlwaine's Hill had to be recovered in order to prevent Union artillery from compromising key sections of the Confederate defenses. About 9:00 p.m., orders from Wilcox arrived at the Boisseau House. The major general instructed McGowan to commit his battalion of sharpshooters to join those of the rest of the division to achieve the task at hand. Captain Dunlop received a summons to appear at Tudor Hall, and the 30-year-old South Carolinian reported there at 10:00 p.m. McGowan told the captain of the importance placed by Lee on the impending operation and of the commanding general's promise to grant each survivor of the assault a 30-day furlough.[4]

The plan of battle called for the sharpshooters from McGowan's, Lane's, Scales's, and Thomas's brigades, about 400 rifles in all, to assail McIlwaine's Hill and recover the lost picket posts there and on the adjacent ground. Silence, secrecy, and the half-light of an early hour would be allies of the Confederate attackers. Once the sharpshooters had driven the Federals away, line infantry from Wilcox's command would move forward and secure the recaptured real estate. Dunlop assembled his men about 1:30 a.m. March 27, read them the orders for the assault "and the men and officers put upon their metal for the desperate adventure." They marched northeast on Boydton Plank Road where the sharpshooter battalions from the other three brigades joined them. Here, they formed line of battle, Major Thomas J. Wooten's command of Lane's Brigade taking position on the right of the front line with the South Carolinians to their left. Scales's and Thomas's contingents deployed in parallel lines immediately to the rear.

Each unit received specific instructions for the perilous operation. Wooten's men were to charge the knoll and then sweep to the right, scattering the Union sentries. Dunlop would perform similar service, clearing the rifle pits to the left of the crest. Scales's and Thomas's battalions would follow and occupy the summit, repulsing any Union counterattack until Wilcox's reinforcements arrived. The Southern officers exercised every precaution to ensure surprise, and no shots were to be fired until the bluecoats themselves opened hostilities. At 5:00 a.m., the column began to move. "The stillness of death settled down upon the dark valley which intervened between the lines, as this little band of devoted Confederates sallied forth with undaunted courage to encounter a foe five times their number, in a strong position well fortified," wrote the melodramatic Dunlop.[5]

The sharpshooters advanced slowly and steadily in the fog and gloom of an early dawn, their hearts pounding as the rustle of brush and the snapping of twigs underfoot threatened to unmask their stealthy approach.

"The crest of McIlwaine Hill blazed with the flashes of a thousand muzzles spurting death."

About 100 yards from the Union pickets, a dry tributary of Rohoic Creek fringed on either side by thickets slowed Wooten and Dunlop. The Carolinians eased themselves into the briars and crawled through the depression to the opposite bank, reforming into line of battle. Resuming their advance, the Confederates approached to within 30 to 50 yards of McIlwaine's Hill when a Federal vidette challenged them: "Halt! Halt!" demanded the blue-jacketed picket. His order evoked not obedience, but the piercing tones of the Rebel Yell. In a matter of moments, the Confederates dashed ahead amidst scattered volleys from the stunned Union defenders. The Northerners stood briefly and then skedaddled to the rear. "In the 'blackness of darkness' as at midnight we throttled them in their stronghold, and the crest of McIlwaine Hill blazed with the flashes of a thousand muzzles spurting death," according to a somewhat hyperbolic participant. "The right battalion changed direction to the right upon the center, and the left battalion to the left, and swept the hill of every solitary blue coat—tooth and toe nail—from center to circumference."[6]

The blow scattered the brigade pickets of Thomas Hyde and Lewis Grant, both of Getty's division. Hyde's men confronted the initial assault near the crest of McIlwaine's Hill, the battle quickly spreading to engulf Grant's Vermonters to their left. "We had a general row for a short time and I was in command of our Brigade Picket," wrote Captain Gould of the 5th Vermont. "I had my hands full for a while." Gould reported 38 wounded and missing among his sentries, most of them prisoners, and blamed his losses on the performance of Hyde's troops: "The Brig.[ade] on my right behaved very badly or we would not [have] lost hardly a man."[7]

About the time Wilcox's sharpshooters struck, the precautionary reinforcements, ordered by Wright to strengthen the picket lines before dawn, began to approach the scene of combat. "We saw what seemed to be a disposition of the enemy to mass a force on their line in front of my gun," remembered a Virginia artillerist positioned along the main Confederate

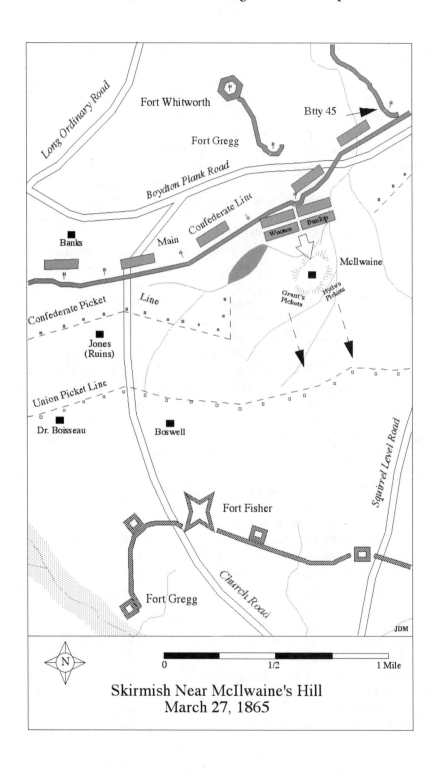

Skirmish Near McIlwaine's Hill
March 27, 1865

works. Southern observers could not determine the intentions of these fresh arrivals, but they did identify as many as three regiments. Fearing the formation of a Union counterattack, a 12-pounder opened fire from Wilcox's entrenchments. "We saw, one moment, the white smoke of the explosion, and the next, the whole force was scattered over the knolls in most undignified disorder," recalled an admiring secessionist.[8]

Once the sharpshooters secured McIlwaine's Hill and the Federal reinforcements made no attempt to regain the high ground, Lane, McGowan, and Colonel Joseph H. Hyman, in command of Scales's Brigade, sent elements of their units forward to hold the recaptured rifle pits. Some Confederate troops (probably McGowan's men) tested the picket line held by Warren Keifer's brigade to the southwest of McIlwaine's Hill, but achieved little. Dunlop claimed the Unionists launched three separate counterattacks aimed toward the knoll, all of which fell to grief before reaching McIlwaine's Hill—an assertion confirmed by no other witness. In fact, General Meade urged Wright at 11:55 a.m. to consider making just such an effort, but ultimately the army commander left the decision to the Sixth Corps commander, much as he had granted discretion to his subordinates two days earlier.[9]

By the time Wright received this communication, hostilities had ceased along the picket line. Both sides approved a flag of truce to recover the wounded and permit the Confederates to resume the retrieval of their slain from the March 25 fight who still littered the ground or reposed precariously in shallow graves. Officers freely mingled between the lines. The Confederates hardly impressed their Union counterparts with their optimism for the future. "I went down where they met [and] saw the Rebel Brig Genl Thomas," reported Lieutenant Robert Pratt of the 5th Vermont. "Quite smart looking . . . plenty of other commissioned officers. They pretended they felt confident of success but I know they lied." The truce lasted from 11:30 a.m. until 1:00 p.m., and only sporadic picket firing disturbed the rest of the day. After dark, the victorious Confederates retired a short distance to a new line of works that had been carefully designed to neutralize enemy occupation of McIlwaine's Hill.[10]

William Dunlop called the storming of McIlwaine's Hill "unquestionably one of the most daring and successful engagements of its dimensions ever witnessed upon any field during the great struggle." Northern commentators, such as Sergeant Abraham T. Brewer of the 61st Pennsylvania, judged the affair differently: "The advantage gained was slight and temporary. Little loss was inflicted upon our troops. Our bended picket line was soon straightened out, and the enemy brushed away, leaving his dead and wounded in our care." Corporal George H. Mellish of the 6th Vermont called the engagement "a little mush," while other Federals were equally dismissive. Yet, most of the day's casualties did belong to the Yankees. The Vermont Brigade officially reported 23 wounded and 26 captured. Losses in Hyde's brigade are unknown, but there must have been as many as suffered by the Vermonters. Keifer mentioned no casualties, and it is clear that Wheaton's division did not become engaged. A member of Dunlop's battalion reported one killed and three wounded, while the 37th North Carolina of Lane's Brigade suffered four wounded during its advance. It is safe to say that compared to the attrition experienced by the Confederates two days earlier, the impact of the fighting on March 27 was minimal.[11]

As it turned out, the outcome of this skirmish on McIlwaine's Hill had equally limited impact upon the strategic situation southwest of Petersburg. By March 27, Ulysses S. Grant had authorized a plan that had little to do with the tactical details along the Sixth Corps picket line.

* * *

The impending offensive outlined in Grant's March 24 orders relied on the imminent arrival of Philip Sheridan and his veteran cavalry. While generals Gordon and Parke struggled on the parapets of Fort Stedman, and Wright, Humphreys, Heth and Wilcox contended for the Confederate picket lines in Dinwiddie County, Sheridan began his trek from White House Landing on the Pamunkey River, northeast of Richmond, toward Meade's army south of Petersburg.

"Little Phil's" troopers were organized into two divisions led by brigadier generals Thomas C. Devin and George Armstrong Custer, and formed an unofficial corps commanded by Brigadier General Wesley Merritt. Although casualties sustained on the campaign from Winchester to White House, as well as the detachment of one brigade to guard prisoners captured in the Valley, reduced Sheridan's original strength of 10,000 sabres, a dearth of fresh horses to replace the mounts that had died or been disabled on the march created a much more serious problem. Merritt reported more than 1,300 dismounted men in his command and that an additional 2,161 horses were unserviceable, forcing the Federals to detach hundreds of horseless troopers to a camp near City Point. Sheridan estimated that due to this shortage, nearly 3,000 otherwise able men could not take the field.[12]

Sheridan encamped on the night of the 25th at Harrison's Landing on the north bank of the James River, and from there departed by boat for a meeting with Grant, leaving Merritt to direct the cavalry across the pontoon bridge at Deep Bottom. In short order, the diminutive Irishman met with the general-in-chief at his Appomattox Manor headquarters. Grant immediately set his admired lieutenant at ease by assuring him that Sheridan's decision to ignore his February directive either to join Sherman in North Carolina or return to Winchester would not be an issue. Furthermore, in deference to Sheridan's sacrifice of independent command by joining the Army of the Potomac, Grant would continue to recognize Sheridan's force as a distinct entity, reporting not to Meade but directly to the general-in-chief. Grant outlined the orders he had issued two days earlier, including the instructions for Sheridan's cavalry. The document stated that Sheridan would ride to the west of Petersburg and "then move independently under other instructions," language that led Sheridan, as well as members of Grant's staff, to infer that the general-in-chief intended for Sheridan's raid to conclude with a rendezvous with Sherman in the Tarheel State.

The prospect of cutting loose from the Army of the Potomac displeased Sheridan to no end. In his memoirs, he stated that he based his objection on the damage that would be done to public opinion should the Army of the Potomac require assistance from Sherman's army to defeat Lee. "My cavalry belonged to the Army of the Potomac," wrote Sheridan, "which army was able unaided to destroy Lee, and I could not but oppose any dispersion of its strength." It is more likely that Sheridan's disappointment stemmed from the prospect of missing out on the destruction of the Army of Northern Virginia, the capture of Richmond, and the virtual winning of the war.

In any event, Grant protested that such a prospect was not a part of his true strategy. He explained his fear that if the offensive should somehow fail to achieve entire success, the North would lose confidence in the likelihood of an early end to the war and precipitate a negotiated peace. Thus, the Illinoisan consciously wrote his orders to create the impression that a potential departure by Sheridan for North Carolina represented no deviation from the grand plan. The commanding general's actual scheme anticipated Sheridan's full participation in the culminating campaign of the war. Grant outlined his thinking in a private conversation with his agitated friend. "I told him that, as a matter of fact, I intended to close the war right here, with this movement, and that he should go no farther," wrote Grant. "His face at once brightened up, and slapping his hand on his leg he said: 'I am glad to hear of it, and we can do it.'"[13]

On the afternoon of the 26th, Sheridan accompanied Grant and President Lincoln on a voyage up the James. The party returned to City Point late that evening and Sheridan spent the night at the Eppes House, handsome headquarters of the armies' chief quartermaster, Brigadier General Rufus Ingalls. The next morning, Sheridan rode southwest to Hancock Station on the U.S. Military Railroad, where his troops had gathered after their previous day's crossing of the James. Little Phil busily oversaw the arrangements for the upcoming offensive until summoned by telegram to join Grant and the newly-arrived Sherman for an evening conference at City Point. Sheridan boarded the Military Railroad about 7:00 p.m., but the train promptly jumped the track, delaying Sheridan's arrival until near midnight. The tardy general found the lights still burning brightly in the little cabin that served as Grant's headquarters and residence, so Sheridan joined the conversation. The commanders were discussing Sherman's plans to move north into Virginia, and referenced Sheridan's role in the projected operations. Once again, the combative Irishman sensed an instinct to remove his command to North Carolina, and he expostulated vehemently against such a notion. Once again, Grant mollified him. Sherman lobbied Sheridan on behalf of a rendezvous in Tarheelia one more time on the morning of the 28th, "but when he saw that I was unalterably opposed to it the conversation turned into other channels," remembered Sheridan.[14]

The question of Sheridan's role in the looming offensive received one final clarification on the night of March 28, the eve of the impending movement. The cavalry remained on the cutting edge of Grant's planned offensive, of course, assigned to take the lead around the far right flank of Lee's army. Should the Confederates sally out to block this maneuver, Grant told Sheridan to "move in with your entire force in your own way, and with the full reliance that the army will engage or follow. . . ." If Lee declined to leave his entrenchments, Sheridan would cut loose from direct contact with the blue infantry and destroy the Richmond & Danville Railroad and the South Side Railroad. Once finished wrecking Lee's remaining supply lines, Sheridan might either return to the Army of the Potomac or join Sherman in North Carolina. Everything about this order suggested discretion for Sheridan, but Little Phil still worried that Grant preferred to dispatch him to Sherman's theater of operations. Sheridan's abiding concern indicated that he retained doubts about Grant's actual strategic intentions, despite the general-in-chief's verbal clarifications.[15]

In the meantime, Grant's instructions to the rest of his forces engendered less controversy. Gouveneur Warren's Fifth Corps and Humphreys's Second Corps received critical assignments to outflank Lee's westernmost fortifications and provide infantry support for Sheridan. Warren would move at 3:00 a.m., March 29, via Vaughan Road toward Dinwiddie Court House. Humphreys would follow, departing at 9:00 a.m., and forming a line facing northwest, extending from the Quaker-Vaughan roads intersection northeast to Hatcher's Run. Both corps were to drive Lee's troops back into their trenches should the Confederates attempt to interfere with their march. Once Warren and Humphreys had established communications, Warren would proceed to Boydton Plank Road and, in conjunction with Humphreys on his right, advance northeast along that important link in Lee's communications network.

Grant assigned the Army of the James a significant role in his grand strategy as well, thus coordinating all three of the Union commands around Petersburg and Richmond. Four divisions of Edward O. C. Ord's troops would move secretly from north of the James and occupy the lines evacuated by Humphreys. The divisions of brigadier generals John W. Turner and Robert S. Foster of Major General John Gibbon's Twenty-fourth Corps, Brigadier General William Birney's division of black troops from the Twenty-fifth Corps, and Brigadier General Ranald S. Mackenzie's division of cavalry, altogether some 18,000 men, began their 36-mile trek on the night of March 27-28. By the morning of the 29th, Ord's vanguard approached the banks of Hatcher's Run and began to take position in the trenches guarded since early February by Humphreys's veterans.[16]

Meade's other two corps, the Sixth and the Ninth, would not march in conjunction with Sheridan, Warren, Humphreys, and Ord. Wright's orders called for him to "be held in readiness to abandon the line of works now held . . . when its line of march would be indicated." Parke was to keep the Ninth Corps in its trenches confronting the eastern and southern approaches to Petersburg. The Ninth Corps commander would also act as Wright's superior whenever Meade's presence with the turning column removed him from direct communication with Wright.[17]

The men of the Sixth Corps welcomed Phil Sheridan back to the army and fully expected that wherever Sheridan went, so too would go Wright's command. "As soon as I heard that Sheridan was at White House I considered the 6th Corps as 'elected' for a trip somewhere with him," wrote a soldier in the 6th Vermont. On March 28, Oliver Edwards dined with the admired cavalryman and remembered that Sheridan promised that by the next day Edwards's brigade and the entire corps would be reunited with the man who had led them to victory in the Shenandoah Valley. Geography, however, overshadowed sentiment in Grant's selection of Warren's command to play the offensive's key infantry role. The Fifth Corps occupied an essentially reserve position in support of the Second and Sixth corps and would, therefore, require no front line replacements. Humphreys's men stood poised on the far left of the Federal

Colonel Oliver Edwards

Massachusetts MOLLUS Collection, Carlisle Barracks, Pennsylvania

entrenchments, closest to the objectives targeted by Grant and Sheridan. Thus, the Sixth Corps would have to be content merely to lash out at the Confederates opposite them if circumstances elsewhere created an opportunity for attack.[18]

With the exception of the actions on March 25 and 27, watchful waiting had characterized Wright's command for nearly two weeks. The rumors that circulated about March 15 of a Confederate withdrawal had stirred the Sixth Corps camps out of their winter routine. "At present the prospects for moving are good," wrote Sergeant Charles W. Wall of the 151st New York. "Sutlers are all ordered up to leave. The quartermasters are turning over all their old stuff. The agents for the Christian commission are getting up their Books & this while in winter quarters." Extra baggage had been packed away and sent to City Point and some officers substituted target practice for the usual drill. No wonder that the news of Sheridan's arrival kindled anticipation of active campaigning and the promise of victory among Little Phil's Valley veterans.[19]

The promise of active campaigning had a more chilling effect on Robert E. Lee. The Confederates knew as early as March 17 of Sheridan's approach toward Richmond, and ten days later learned that the Federal cavalry had crossed the James. Lee felt certain Sheridan would target the South Side Railroad beyond his right flank and therefore, until he could properly prepare to abandon the Petersburg-Richmond entrenchments, he would have to strengthen his right while maintaining a viable force elsewhere along his lines.

Lee possessed few options for redeploying troops to the west. His three small cavalry divisions, located either north of the James or eighteen miles south of Petersburg around Stony Creek Depot, promised the most obvious relief, but these units counted less than 6,000 saddles, little more than half of Sheridan's effective strength. The only infantry not assigned to the permanent defense lines belonged to George Pickett's all-Virginia division, a unit that had not seen significant combat since the previous June. One of Pickett's brigades, Brigadier General George H. "Maryland" Steuart's, had arrived at Petersburg on the 25th as support for Gordon's attack. Brigadier generals William R. Terry's and Montgomery D. Corse's brigades had halted north of Petersburg along Swift Creek when it became obvious that their services would not be needed at Fort Stedman. Brigadier General Eppa Hunton's Brigade was still north of the James, where Pickett had been sent in mid-March in response to Sheridan's potential threat to the Confederate capital. These twenty regiments numbered just 5,000 effectives and had suffered disproportionately from desertion, but they remained the only foot soldiers Lee could assign as an extension of his attenuated front. Anticipating the movement of Federal troops toward the Confederate right on March 28, Lee prepared to concentrate Pickett and the cavalry around an obscure Dinwiddie crossroads called Five Forks, an intersection along the shortest route to the South Side Railroad beyond the Confederate flank.[20]

The soldiers of the Sixth Corps, like General Lee, guessed on March 28 that a momentous operation was about to begin. Wright reiterated his orders to reinforce the picket lines at 4:00 a.m., but word of the conference at City Point between Grant, Sherman, and Sheridan, did more to convince the rank and file that something big loomed on the horizon. Rare orders for target practice and the issue of extra ammunition provided further clues. Wright erased any remaining doubts on the 28th by sharing the army's plans with his division commanders and encouraging them to keep a close watch on the enemy, reporting any movements they might discover. "Should [the Confederates] detach largely from our front, the corps will attack, moving probably to the left of the house burned on Saturday, in order to avoid the inundation to the right of that point," wrote Wright. "Such an attack must be made with vigor, as we must carry the enemy's line if we attempt it." The men of the Sixth Corps welcomed such a prospect. "No doubt a few days more will settle the fate of Petersburg," predicted Elisha Hunt Rhodes of the 2nd Rhode Island. "I shall be glad to welcome the dawn of peace, for I am tired of bloodshed. . . . Gen. Sheridan with the Cavalry Corps has rejoined the Army, and it looks as if work was to be done. Peach trees are in blossom. . . and the air is spring like."[21]

*   *   *

That spring like air helped transform the roads southwest of Petersburg into what Sheridan termed "a frightful state." His column of three mounted divisions, Devin's and Custer's under Merritt, and David Gregg's troopers now under Major General George Crook, used a variety of byways to make their way south to Reams Station and then west to Dinwiddie Court House. Sheridan assigned Custer to guard the wagon trains carrying subsistence and ammunition for the column, but Devin and Crook pushed ahead virtually without opposition and reached Dinwiddie Court House about 5:00 p.m. The county seat failed to impress General Sheridan: "Dinwiddie Court House, though a most important point in the campaign, was far from attractive in feature, being made up of a half-dozen unsightly houses, a ramshackle tavern propped up on two sides with pine poles, and the weather-beaten building that gave official name to the cross-roads." Sheridan established headquarters inside the tavern, and with the help of some coffee and a little wine provided by two young female residents, passed an enjoyable evening, listening to his staff sing to the accompaniment of a battered piano played by the girls.[22]

Warren moved out as directed at 3:00 a.m., following the Stage Road across Rowanty Creek at Monk's Neck Bridge, then west on Vaughan Road to its intersection with Quaker Road. Arriving shortly after 8:00 a.m., he advanced skirmishers northward on Quaker Road and sent word to Meade that Dinwiddie Court House was reportedly undefended. Meade responded at 8:45 a.m. with orders that Warren advance in strength up Quaker Road, cross Gravelly Run, and establish communications with the Second Corps on his right. Warren misunderstood, sending just one brigade up Quaker Road, although the army commander's intentions should have been clear based on the revised orders sent Warren the previous day. Impatiently, Meade hastened another courier westward on Vaughan Road to repeat his desire that Warren march north on Quaker Road and link up with Humphreys before extending his left to Boydton Plank Road. At noon, Warren replied that he had instructed Charles Griffin's division to advance along Quaker Road, followed by Samuel Crawford's brigades, with Brigadier General Romeyn B. Ayres's men left behind to guard the intersection of Quaker and Vaughan roads.[23]

The Second Corps began leaving its entrenchments near Hatcher's Run about 6:30 a.m., as Gibbon's troops from the Army of the James moved into position to relieve them. Methodically, and according to orders, Humphreys deployed each of his three divisions progressively southwestward from an anchor on the south bank of Hatcher's Run. First William Hays, then Gershom Mott, and finally Miles established a lightly entrenched line of battle facing northwest with a brigade from each division poised in reserve. The Union high command had grown very sensitive to the oft-repeated Confederate tactic of interposing a strong attack between the right of a flanking column and the left of the troops remaining behind in the trenches. Lee had done this in August at the Petersburg Railroad, in September at Peebles's Farm, in October at Burgess's Mill, and most recently at the Battle of Hatcher's Run. Humphreys aimed to ensure that he would leave no gap between his right and Ord's position. Meade's anxiety that Warren advance up Quaker Road stemmed from the army commander's concern that no opening between Warren and Humphreys be offered for Lee's exploitation.[24]

On the morning of March 29, Lee hardly contemplated a counteroffensive, but he had been informed that Federal infantry and cavalry had crossed Rowanty Creek and were headed west toward Dinwiddie Court House. Lacking certain knowledge of Union objectives, but suspecting that this budding offensive must be directed at the destruction of the railroads, Lee began implementing his defense. First, he ordered McGowan's Brigade to prepare to withdraw from its position at

Tudor Hall and march west to reinforce the troops around Burgess's Mill. Next, he sent word to Pickett to collect Terry's and Corse's brigades along Swift Creek, pick up Steuart's troops in Petersburg, and together take the South Side Railroad ten miles west of the city to Sutherland Station. Fitz Lee reported to his uncle from north of the James, and the gray chieftain told the cavalry commander to lead his division west to Sutherland Station, where Rooney Lee's and Major General Thomas L. Rosser's divisions would join him from the south. Marse Robert also delegated overall command of the cavalry to his nephew once it was united. Finally, Lee ordered Pickett's remaining brigade, Eppa Hunton's, to move across the James River and take position near Manchester from where it could either reinforce Pickett or move southwest by rail to protect the junction of the Richmond & Danville and South Side railroads at Burkeville.[25]

While Lee effected a concentration of his available reserves west of Petersburg, Lieutenant General Richard H. Anderson responded to the unfolding situation in his front. Anderson's nominal corps, in reality just the four-brigade division of Bushrod Johnson, guarded the far right of Lee's defense line. Johnson's entrenchments ran west from Burgess's Mill along White Oak Road to Claiborne Road and thence north, where they rested on the south bank of Hatcher's Run some four miles east of Five Forks and practically due south of Sutherland Station. Johnson's scouts had skirmished with the advance elements of both Humphreys's and Warren's corps and reported early in the afternoon that a strong Union force was pressing northward on Quaker Road. Anderson told Johnson to use his division to drive the Yankees back to Vaughan Road. The Buckeye Confederate directed three regiments of Brigadier General Henry A. Wise's Virginia brigade to move out from their trenches and follow Boydton Plank Road and Quaker Road south to meet the enemy. Brigadier General William H. Wallace's South Carolinians, Young Moody's Alabamians, and Brigadier General Matthew W. Ransom's North Carolinians followed Wise.[26]

Meanwhile, Brigadier General Joshua L. Chamberlain led the vanguard of Griffin's division northward along Quaker Road. After negotiating a crossing of bridgeless Gravelly Run, Chamberlain deployed his two outsize regiments among the buildings of the Lewis Farm. Ordering his men forward, Chamberlain encountered Wise's Brigade in a field north of the Lewis House. This clash escalated into a vicious meeting engagement that eventually embroiled most of Griffin's division with Wise's, Wallace's, and Moody's brigades. The battle lines swayed back and forth in the fields of the Lewis Farm as each side committed reinforcements to the fierce struggle. Chamberlain sustained a painful, if

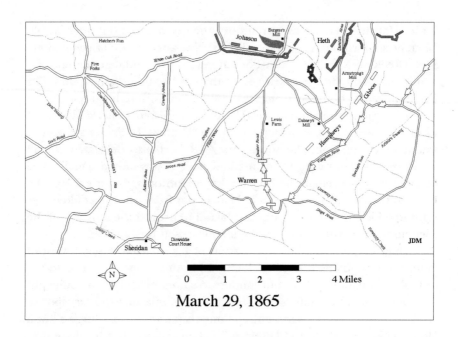

March 29, 1865

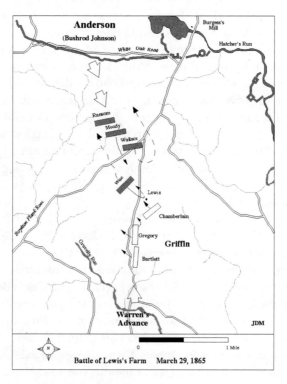

Battle of Lewis's Farm   March 29, 1865

not serious, wound but refused to leave the field, avoiding capture through a clever ruse. Eventually, Union numbers prevailed, and Johnson withdrew his battered brigades first to Boydton Plank Road, and then back to the entrenchments along White Oak Road. Crawford's division moved up to Boydton Plank Road near dusk, and Griffin's division occupied the intersection of Quaker and Boydton Plank roads.[27]

While the Fifth Corps fought the Battle of Lewis's Farm, Humphreys's men struggled more with the Dinwiddie landscape than with their Southern opponents. By day's end, the right flank of the Second Corps had skirmished lightly and occupied some advanced Confederate earthworks. On the left, Miles's division reestablished contact with Warren's right and entrenched a line running east toward the rest of Humphreys's corps, the far right flank of which rested on Hatcher's Run near Armstrong's Mill.[28]

As a steady rain began to fall after sunset, General Lee evaluated the significance of the eventful day's activities. Sheridan's occupation of Dinwiddie Court House might represent merely the opening gambit of a raid against the South Side and Danville railroads. Confederate cavalry would meet this threat and attempt to turn it back. However, the presence of so much infantry and, as Lee eventually learned, artillery as well, suggested a different purpose. Lee reasoned that Grant intended either to extend the Federal lines to the southwest or launch a major offensive against the Confederate right. Three of Pickett's brigades were already on their way to Sutherland Station, and now Lee instructed Hunton to join them. Marse Robert directed Colonel William J. Pegram's Third Corps artillery battalion to report with its twenty guns to the far right, and Lee also inquired of General Longstreet whether that officer could spare any First Corps infantry from north of the James. "Old Pete," who had failed to detect Ord's detachment of three infantry divisions, replied that sending Major General Charles W. Field's Division to Petersburg would necessitate summoning all the local defense troops and the Virginia Military Institute cadets to provide front-line defense against what he judged to be an undiminished Union presence.[29]

Lee also communicated with the Boisseau House, instructing McGowan to prepare his South Carolinians to march west by 10:00 p.m. The officers at Tudor Hall could not be sure what their mission might be, but they arranged to leave what had been their home for nearly six months. When no definite departure orders arrived by mid-evening, Lieutenant Caldwell wondered if the brigade might be needed at all, and some of McGowan's staff turned down their pallets and sought sleep. Just then a courier dashed up at full gallop bearing orders for the brigade to move out at once. The five South Carolina regiments plodded across the trampled

Sixth Corps Headquarters near Globe Tavern on the Petersburg (Weldon) Railroad, 1865.
Massachusetts MOLLUS Collection, Carlisle Barracks, Pennsylvania

fields of the Boisseau Farm for what would prove to be the last time, making their way through the rain to Boydton Plank Road and then southwest toward Burgess's Mill.

"It was an ugly night," reported one of McGowan's men. "The roads were soon trodden into slush, and we stumbled along, our feet heavy with the mud that clung to them. . . . Though there were fearful and doubting hearts among us to whom the power of the enemy was so plain that they feared we would soon be a conquered people, there was no prophet among us to tell that we were even then writing the last few pages of our war history."[30]

McGowan's men halted along the banks of Hatcher's Run, occupying an angle in the works where the entrenchments turned sharply to the right. The Carolinians had left about 150 of their brigade pickets at their posts on the Boisseau Farm. McGowan's former neighbors to the southwest, William MacRae's Brigade, also reported to Burgess's Mill having slogged through the mud with the South Carolinians. Lee had no reserves to replace these ten combat regiments that had evacuated his trenches astride Duncan Road, so Lane's Tarheels simply extended their thin ranks to the right, and William McComb's men spread out to their left to cover the vacant fortifications with a thin infantry veneer. Lane's movement affected the density of the rest of A. P. Hill's line between Lieutenant Run and Duncan Road, reducing the number of men in Wilcox's front from about 1,100 to just 888 per mile. Heth's soldiers fully recognized the peril faced by Hill's corps southwest of Petersburg. "We are expecting an advance here upon our works and fear the Yankees will also come in our right and rear," wrote Colonel Samuel H. Walkup of the 48th North Carolina of John R. Cooke's Brigade. "Our force is very weak." Private John Walters of the Norfolk Light Artillery Blues agreed that the events of March 29 portended ill: "I lay no claim to prophetic powers, but I would not be afraid to wager all that I have that . . . Grant will try our lines somewhere soon. . . ."[31]

The Sixth Corps also expected a decisive fight. "Great events are about transpiring here," wrote Colonel Keifer to his wife. "A great struggle is now impending. Tomorrow may be a day of carnage & blood between the contending armies around Richmond." Elisha Hunt Rhodes agreed that "something is about to happen. We are all ready to move. . . ." Chaplain Alanson Haines of the 15th New Jersey remembered that on March 29 "we were in a constant state of expectation, and lingered only from hour to hour in our old camp-ground. The wagons stood, loaded up; the mules were harnessed, and much of the time hitched, to start on the crack of the whip. Most of the mounted officers kept their horses saddled."[32]

Yet the afternoon of March 29 passed without incident along the Sixth Corps front. "We expected to move early this morning, but at this time (2 P.M.) we are still awaiting orders," wrote a Vermont captain. "Everything is now very quiet." A soldier from the 121st New York ventured out to the picket line and managed to trade some newspapers with the Confederates, as well as swap coffee for tobacco. General Wright reported that the Southerners displayed greater energy in preparing their defenses in his front than usual, but "otherwise there is no movement of any kind discoverable by the pickets or from the signal tower." Wright's last message of the day sent at 10:45 p.m. reaffirmed the static situation on his front: "It is believed that no troops have been withdrawn from the front of the corps." At that hour, McGowan was beginning his march to the west, but in the darkness and rain it is little wonder Wright did not realize it.[33]

*   *   *

General-in-Chief Grant left City Point on the morning of March 29, opting to shift his headquarters to the field while his armies executed their offensive. "I never knew the general to be more sanguine of victory than in starting out on this campaign," wrote a staff officer, and the results of the day did nothing to dampen Grant's optimism. His forces stood firmly astride Boydton Plank Road in two places—at Dinwiddie Court House and near the intersection with Quaker Road. Although Sherman's campaign through the Carolinas had reduced the importance of the Petersburg Railroad-Stony Creek-Dinwiddie Court House supply line, control of Boydton Plank Road marked a symbolic as well as substantive milestone in Grant's attempt to isolate the Army of Northern Virginia. Warren's temporary confusion and Humphreys's struggle with the tangled terrain of Dinwiddie County notwithstanding, this time Lee's predictable counter blows failed to reveal any Federal weakness. Sheridan's horsemen reached their goal with ease, and Ord effected his transfer to the Petersburg front virtually undetected.[34]

The day's events resolved whatever uncertainty remained in Grant's mind regarding the proper use of Sheridan's troopers. After reciting the outcome of the infantry actions, Grant wrote Sheridan that, "I now feel like ending the matter if it is possible to do so before going back. I do not want you, therefore, to cut loose and go after the enemy's [rail]roads at present. In the morning push round the enemy if you can and get onto his right rear. . . . We will act altogether as one army here until it is seen what can be done with the enemy."[35]

Lee had reacted to events on March 29 by committing his only reserves to bolster his right flank and protect his remaining rail supply lines, detaching troops from elsewhere along his attenuated front. The Army of Northern Virginia had been stretched as far as it could reach. On March 30, however, Lee received a meteorological reprieve from another problematical, if inevitable, test of arms.

The steady rain that commenced on the evening of March 29 continued unabated on the 30th. The abundant precipitation transformed the unsurfaced country roads upon which Grant's offensive depended into seemingly bottomless quagmires. "The roads had become sheets of water; and it looked as if saving of that army would require the services, not of a Grant, but of a Noah," wrote Colonel Horace Porter of Grant's staff. "Soldiers would call out to officers as they rode along: 'I say, when are the gun-boats coming up?'" Grant's concern both for the mobility of his troops and his ability to keep them provisioned so far from the Military Railroad prompted him to suggest to Sheridan that operations be suspended until conditions improved. Sheridan blanched at such advice and mounted a powerful pacer to pound his way to Grant's headquarters through the slop and make his case for no backward steps.[36]

Sheridan realized from overhearing a conversation between Grant and his staff that others shared his opposition to postponing the offensive. He reminded Grant that two years earlier Major General Ambrose E. Burnside had canceled his proposed crossing of the Rappahannock River above Fredericksburg and had become an object of ridicule for his "Mud March." Sheridan assured his commander that despite the weather, the cavalry could keep the field. Grant relented. "We will go on," he told Sheridan. Pressing his advantage, Little Phil requested the assistance of his old comrades of the Sixth Corps to undertake the destruction of Lee's right flank, but at this Grant demurred. The road conditions and Wright's location far to the east made Sixth Corps participation in an envelopment logistically impractical. With that news, Sheridan galloped away aboard his memorable mount to inspect his three divisions.[37]

At dawn on March 30, Sheridan ordered Devin's division and a brigade of Crook's command north to reconnoiter around Five Forks. Another of Crook's brigades trotted south from Dinwiddie Court House toward the Plank Road crossing of Stony Creek, with an eye toward forcing Rooney Lee and Rosser to detour far to the west in order to regain the main Confederate lines. The rest of Crook's troopers remained in reserve at the village while Custer struggled to extricate the supply wagons from the mud.[38]

Devin's brigades advanced north from Dinwiddie Court House to the angled intersection at the John Boisseau house. From there, blue columns rode ahead both on Courthouse Road leading northwest toward Five Forks and Crump Road which continued due north toward a junction with White Oak Road. About 3:00 p.m., the Union cavalry approached to within less than a mile of Five Forks when it came under spirited attack from a brigade of mounted Confederates. The skirmish ended when the bluecoats spotted Southern infantry and opted to retire and encamp a short distance to the rear.[39]

Major General Fitzhugh Lee's troopers provided the opposition for Devin's division during this small affray, and elements of George Pickett's Division contributed the infantry muscle. Fitz Lee's cavalry had been the first Confederates to reach the Five Forks area, but Pickett's foot soldiers were not far behind. During the night of March 29-30, Pickett had marched south from Sutherland's Station on Claiborne Road with his three brigades (Hunton had not yet caught up), crossed Hatcher's Run, and marched into position behind the entrenchments manned by Anderson's right flank. On the morning of the 30th, the Confederate general-in-chief rode to Sutherland Station and conducted a council of war attended by Pickett, Anderson, Harry Heth, and perhaps others. Lee decided that Pickett should proceed west on White Oak Road with his three brigades and two of Anderson's (Ransom's and Wallace's) and connect with Fitz Lee at Five Forks. Rosser and Rooney Lee were expected at the crossroads shortly as well, although Marse Robert could not know that Sheridan's blocking position across Stony Creek south of Dinwiddie Court House would extend their ride and delay their arrival. Pegram would accompany the column with six pieces of artillery. With Pickett in overall command, this mixed force of 10,600 men would assail the Federals at Dinwiddie Court House and blunt the Union offensive, protecting the rail lines in the process.

Pickett proceeded cautiously west on White Oak Road to cover the four miles to Five Forks. That element of Devin's command that had followed Crump Road to the right from the John Boisseau intersection approached the Confederate infantry column along White Oak Road, compelling Pickett to deploy his men in line of battle in order to repulse the pesky horsemen. These tactics delayed Pickett's appearance at Five Forks until 4:30 p.m. Even then, Rosser and Rooney Lee had not appeared and Pickett's men were tired. Fitz Lee and Pickett thus decided to establish an advanced line south of Five Forks and bivouac for the night, deferring their attack toward Dinwiddie Court House until the following day. The two missing cavalry divisions reported shortly thereafter, and the stage was set for the Confederates to assume the tactical initiative.[40]

*   *   *

The rain-soaked roads limited what Warren and Humphreys could accomplish on March 30, leaving Sheridan's cavalry with only tenuous connections to its infantry supports. Griffin's division of the Fifth Corps probed northward on Boydton Plank Road and provoked fire from the Confederate entrenchments near Burgess's Mill. Ayres's brigades conducted a more meaningful operation, slogging cross-country to a point south of the western end of Anderson's line below White Oak Road. Although these maneuvers elicited no important combat, the Fifth Corps had at least pinned its opponents inside their fortifications and threatened to overlap the Confederate right, interposing between Anderson's refused flank and the gathering Confederate host at Five Forks.[41]

The Second Corps experienced an equally uneventful day. "On the 30th [we] continued [our] advance, driving the enemy inside his entrenchments along Hatcher's Run from the Crow House to the Boydton road, pressing close up against them, but not assaulting," wrote General Humphreys. By evening, he had restored connections with the Twenty-fourth Corps on his right and Griffin's division of Warren's command on his left. General Lee juggled his units in response to these movements. Scales's Brigade evacuated its defenses on Wilcox's left and took position in the works near the intersection of Boydton Plank and White Oak roads. Two of these Tarheel regiments ventured a small attack at dusk resulting in the wounding of Colonel John Ashford of the 38th North Carolina. Thomas's Georgians filled in on Scales's portion of the line, much as Lane and McComb had covered the vacancy created by McGowan's and MacRae's departures. For their part, the South Carolinians shifted even farther to the right, providing the link between MacRae's and Scales's brigades to their east and Bushrod Johnson's brigades to the west.[42]

Southern deserters provided Meade with a reasonably clear snapshot of the tactical situation along the Confederate works. At 1:00 p.m., he wrote Parke that, "the enemy has undoubtedly weakened himself in your front," referring actually, to the diminution of troops opposite the Sixth Corps over which Parke exercised nominal command. "If this information should be confirmed during the day, you will be required to attack at early daylight tomorrow. You will, therefore, make all preliminary arrangements with that object in view." Wright received a copy of this message and promptly informed Meade that due to the foggy, misty conditions on that inclement afternoon, he could not confirm any movement in the Confederate works. Nevertheless, he affirmed that all arrangements for a dawn attack on March 31 would proceed as directed.[43]

Throughout the afternoon, as Grant and Meade sought to verify the Confederate troop deployments in front of Wright, Ord, and Humphreys, the Sixth Corps high command made plans for a frontal assault. George Getty suggested the specifics of the attack, and after dark, Wright's officers learned of their roles in the proposed action. Getty's division would take the lead, filing out of its works at Fort Fisher at 11:00 p.m. A single cannon shot at 4:00 a.m. would signal the Sixth Corps to commence its charge. A spirit of grim resolve settled over Wright's forces. "We are in for it again," wrote an officer in the 2nd Connecticut Heavy Artillery to his family. "I have just come in from Col's qrs where he called me to explain the move that is intended to be made. . . . I hope if we do go in that all of us will come out unscathed but that is scarcely to be expected and we may many of us fall. If I do among others please do not mourn very deeply for me for I trust we should all meet soon in a happier & more peaceful land than this." Elisha Hunt Rhodes shared this foreboding: "All the regimental commanders were ordered to report to Brigade Headquarters where we were told that the 6th Corps must attack Petersburg . . . at 4 o'clock and that we must not fail, but that we must take the enemy's work[s] no matter what it costs. We returned to our Regiments in a solemn frame of mind and made preparations."[44]

Colonel Keifer wrote to his wife on the evening of March 30 capturing the feelings of most members of Wright's corps:

> Tomorrow morning at daybreak our corps will charge the enemy's main works directly in my front. I of course always fear the result of an attack of that character, but think we will succeed, not withstanding the abattis, trenches and formidable works we shall encounter. We hope that we shall not encounter many of the enemy. . . . I have just had a conference with my Regt. Commanders, and made all possible arrangements for the assault. I trust in God that we will meet with success. I hope to get through the charge in safety, and trust that I may never be called upon to risk my life again, in the same way. . . .[45]

As it turned out, no one would compel him to do so—at least not on the morning of March 31. At 8:30 p.m., Meade relayed a message from Parke to Grant reporting that the Ninth Corps commander could discern no change in the Confederate lines in his front. Wright, added Meade, conveyed the same ominous intelligence. In light of this information, did

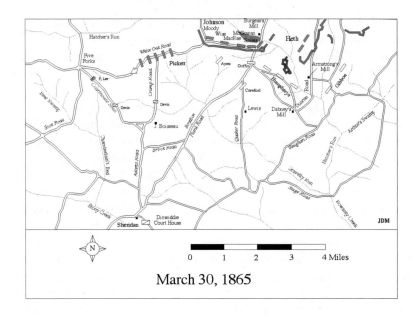

March 30, 1865

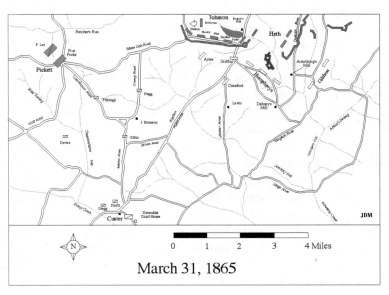

March 31, 1865

Grant still wish to hazard an attack? The general in-chief responded instantly: "You may notify Parke and Wright that they need not assault in the morning. They should, of course, watch their fronts and go in if the enemy strips to attack our left; but the idea of a general attack by them is suspended."[46]

Grant coyly told Meade that he had "pretty much made up my mind on the course to pursue," and promised to let the Pennsylvanian in on the secret in the morning. Grant appended a note to this dispatch, however, revealing at least part of his concept. The general-in-chief proposed to replace Griffin's Fifth Corps division on Boydton Plank Road with a division from the Second Corps, and shift all of Warren's command to the west to reinforce Ayres's troops resting south of the White Oak–Claiborne roads intersection. Grant did not tell Meade that he had previously corresponded with Sheridan, offering to detach Warren's entire Fifth Corps to cooperate with Little Phil in an assault against the far Confederate right, should circumstances allow. The confirmed presence of Pickett and the Confederate cavalry corps at Five Forks, however, made the prospect of a flank attack on the 31st prohibitively risky until Warren and Sheridan could establish better unity of command.[47]

Meade dutifully executed the orders Grant shared with him at 8:40 p.m. Humphreys would relieve Warren on Boydton Plank Road, and the Fifth Corps commander received notice to reinforce Ayres and stand ready to receive further instructions. To Parke and Wright went directives to abrogate the predawn offensive "but to be prepared to assume a threatening attitude and eventually attack if any opportunity presents itself. . . ." Wright acknowledged his new orders at 9:45 p.m. and affirmed that he had canceled the assault. He also volunteered that only one place on his front boded well for an offensive. Wright requested sufficient time, in the instance of future attack orders, to deploy his troops in the proper manner and at the right location. "At that point I believe I can go through the enemy's line," he told Meade.[48]

The telegraph lines continued to hum on that soggy night. Meade, revealing a touch of impatience with his cautious subordinate, replied that it simply was not possible to predict when attack orders would be sent and that, with what the high command had learned about Confederate detachments on the Sixth Corps front, Wright should not overworry about protecting himself from a Confederate assault. Instead, suggested Meade, Wright should hold his lines with two divisions and muster the third one opposite the vulnerable Confederate position, "where it will be ready promptly to attack and will also be on hand to meet any offensive movement of the enemy."[49]

Before that message could reach his headquarters, Wright composed a dispatch to Meade reacting to a note the army commander had forwarded from Warren earlier in the evening. This correspondence confirmed the departure of Scales's Brigade from the Sixth Corps front and implied that further detachments had occurred from Wilcox's Division. For some reason, Warren's information convinced the Sixth Corps commander of what he had failed to detect with his own forces all day. At 10:35 p.m., Wright asked Meade, "If so much of the force on my front has left, would it not be well for me to attack at daylight in the morning, according to the original programme?" Wright suggested wheeling to the left once his forces broke through while the enemy defended itself against a simultaneous assault by Ord, Parke, Humphreys, and Warren. "My division and brigade commanders fully understand what is to be done," the New Englander assured his commanding officer, "and, if your orders can reach me promptly, I can be ready to start the assaulting columns at early daylight."[50]

Meade passed Wright's bellicose proposal on to the general-in-chief shortly before midnight. Grant liked what he read. "You might notify [Wright] to arrange his preliminaries, and see if Parke can get ready also, and if so, give him definite orders as soon as it is known," he wrote Meade. Nevertheless, the lieutenant general doubted that enough time remained before daylight to reassemble the attack plans. While the Sixth Corps troops began filing out of their encampments, Grant contacted Ord and inquired if his divisions could muster promptly to support Wright in the morning. "Are your men so arranged as to enable you to assault at the same time?" asked the general-in-chief. Ord replied immediately that he could not prepare for an attack by daylight. Grant thus decided at 1:55 a.m., March 31, to cancel the on-again, off-again assault for the second time in five hours. A few minutes later, Meade informed Wright and Parke of this decision, news that greatly relieved the Sixth Corps rank and file. "How glad we were," recorded an officer in Hamblin's brigade. "At 2 AM all felt very sad expecting a terrible slaughter on our side," confirmed a soldier in the 121st New York. "I was glad it turned out as it did," agreed a member of the 5th Wisconsin, "for probabl[y] half of us would have been killed if we had went." The eventful if bloodless night ended with orders for the Sixth Corps to return to its fortifications.[51]

*   *   *

March 31 dawned gloomily as intermittent downpours continued to soak man and beast. The roads remained in execrable condition, prompting Grant to announce at 7:40 a.m. that no troop movements would be attempted that day. Efforts would be made to resupply the men, and the Confederate lines should be carefully observed to detect any changes, but that would be all, or so thought the general-in-chief. Grant reckoned, however, without the irrepressible initiative of Robert E. Lee.[52]

That morning, Lee rode along the Confederate works between Burgess's Mill and Anderson's far right flank. He had made several changes in his army's deployment during the previous 24 hours. MacRae's Brigade had shifted to the far side of Hatcher's Run. Hunton's Brigade of Pickett's Division had reported to Anderson along White Oak Road. Major General Bryan Grimes's Division of Gordon's Corps had shifted to the right, south of Petersburg, helping Thomas compensate for Scales's departure on the left end of Wilcox's front. Finally, A. P. Hill reported back from sick leave on the 31st, barely strong enough to ride but animated by the reports of Grant's incipient offensive and determined to do his duty in a time of crisis.[53]

Grant may have been content to wait for the sun and wind to solidify the roads, but on March 31, Lee exercised his preferred military philosophy and brought the war to the Federals on two fronts. Pickett and the cavalry already had orders to attack Sheridan at Dinwiddie Court House. During his journey along White Oak Road, Lee learned that the Union left flank opposite Anderson hung in the air, inviting a second offensive through the wide gap between Sheridan's cavalry and the Union infantry south of White Oak Road. Lee ordered McGowan's Brigade to march west and take position on the far right end of Anderson's line. Along with Hunton's Brigade, the South Carolinians would compensate Bushrod Johnson for the detachment of Ransom and Wallace to Pickett's sector. Johnson's two remaining brigades, Moody's Alabamians (commanded that day by Colonel Martin Luther Stansel of the 41st Alabama) and Wise's Virginians, would round out the strike force. McGowan's men followed White Oak Road westward, occasionally dipping into the woods to avoid detection by the Federals, and took position about 10:30 a.m. beyond the Claiborne Road–White Oak roads intersection.[54]

The command situation along White Oak Road invited trouble. Not only had Lee entrusted his offensive to just four brigades with no available reserves, but those units represented three different divisions from three separate corps unaccustomed to functioning together. General Johnson assumed tactical control of the operation while McGowan accepted responsibility for a demi-division consisting of his and Stansel's brigades. The ranking officer in the area, Richard Anderson, appears to have had little to do with superintending the attack.[55]

Johnson's battle plan called for McGowan's Brigade to move south and attack Warren's exposed left flank, flushing the Yankees across the front of Stansel's and Hunton's waiting infantry. Those two units would then charge the off-balance Federals, drive them from the field, and end their threat to the direct line of communications between Pickett and the rest of Lee's army. Before McGowan could deploy for his assault, however, Warren precipitated the combat by advancing two of Ayres's brigades, supported by a brigade from Crawford's division, toward White Oak Road. The New Yorker merely sought to secure his position by dispersing Confederate pickets south of the road and establishing his own advanced line well north of the main Fifth Corps deployment. He informed Meade of his decision to conduct this minor operation, despite the injunction against troop movements issued earlier in the morning. Ayres began his advance about the same time that McGowan began to deploy for his own assault.[56]

Stansel's Alabamians and Hunton's Virginians watched as the bluecoats approached their line. Reacting to this unexpected development, Johnson authorized them to attack immediately even though McGowan had not yet perfected his dispositions. Even before Johnson's directive reached them, however, the two Confederate brigades spontaneously lept to their feet and surged ahead. The South Carolinians soon joined in the attack, and the Federal line quickly reeled toward the rear. "We drove through the woods . . . and swinging round the right of the brigade so as to enfilade the Federal line, poured such volleys of musketry along their ranks as speedily set them flying along the whole line confronting Gracie's [Stansel's] brigade," wrote Lieutenant Caldwell. After some fierce fighting, McGowan, Stansel, and Hunton succeeded in routing all of Ayres's division and the brigade from Crawford's division sent to support it. Crawford committed his remaining two brigades to stem the gray tide, but they too were swept south across Gravelly Run. Although Wise's Brigade had moved out from its earthworks on the eastern end of Johnson's front, the Virginians had not joined the fight. Thus, three undersized and organizationally- unrelated brigades had combined to drive two veteran Union divisions from the field. It was a remarkable tactical achievement. "I have no idea that the brigade ever killed more men, even in the most sanguinary engagements, than it did this day," thought Caldwell.[57]

General Warren arrived on the scene during the chaos of the Federal retreat. Boldly seizing a regimental banner, he attempted to rally his demoralized troops, but to no avail. Not until the fugitives reached the south bank of swollen Gravelly Run and the protecting battle line of

Griffin's division did the panic subside. From the far bank of the stream, Griffin and his artillery supports held the winded Confederate juggernaut at bay. Meanwhile, Warren sent word to Humphreys requesting that the Second Corps provide help to his beleaguered divisions. Humphreys promptly committed two of Miles's brigades, which advanced early in the afternoon and collided with Wise's Brigade. The Virginians temporarily repulsed the Union advance, but the Confederate high water mark at the Battle of White Oak Road had passed. Meade's numbers, when boldly and competently employed, were bound to tilt the contest in the Union's favor. Just as the morning belonged to McGowan, Stansel, Hunton and Johnson, the afternoon would be dominated by Miles, Humphreys, Griffin and Joshua Chamberlain.[58]

Chamberlain's brigade, like the rest of Griffin's division, had moved to its left on the morning of March 31 and, by 1:00 p.m., had stabilized the situation in its front. Now, Warren turned his thoughts to a counteroffensive. He and Griffin approached Chamberlain, who still suffered from the wound he had received two days earlier at the Lewis Farm. "General Chamberlain, will you save the honor of the Fifth Corps?" Warren earnestly inquired. The Maine professor, with appropriate modesty (according to his own testimony), accepted the assignment. At 2:30 p.m., Warren gave the order to advance, and Chamberlain's brigade forded the swirling waters of the flooded creek.[59]

As the vanguard of Griffin's division, which was supported by the remainder of Warren's rallied corps, Chamberlain moved forward against only token opposition. Miles's attacks to the east had succeeded in driving Wise back into the earthworks along White Oak Road. This had compelled Johnson to withdraw his remaining three brigades to the line of temporary rifle pits erected earlier by Ayres's men south of the road. As Chamberlain emerged from the woods into a large clearing, a heavy fire greeted him from these works. Warren ordered Chamberlain to hold his ground, but already the embattled academic watched as his men dropped from deadly musketry. Chamberlain suggested that they secure their position not by entrenching, but by attacking. Griffin approved this idea and authorized Chamberlain to use Colonel Edgar M. Gregory's brigade in his offensive. "Riding forward I informed my officers of my purpose and had their warm support," wrote Chamberlain. "We sounded bugles 'Forward!' and that way we go."[60]

The Union attack first fell on Hunton's Brigade, overwhelming the Virginians and driving them back to the original Confederate line behind White Oak Road. Soon, the balance of the Southern forces also withdrew, and the victorious Federals pursued across the byway west of its intersection

with Claiborne Road. Warren considered a rush against the main
Confederate fortifications, but a reconnaissance late in the afternoon
convinced him that nothing could be gained by such a rash attack. Instead,
he consolidated his position and reestablished an unbroken connection
with Humphreys's troops on his right. The Second Corps had played a key
role in the dramatic Union victory. Thus, a day that had commenced with
fighting that prompted Griffin to conclude that "the Fifth Corps is
eternally damned," concluded with significant tactical achievements. The
most important of those gains centered on Warren's position astride White
Oak Road west of Anderson's right flank. Not only had this deployment
compelled Anderson and Johnson to retreat to their fortifications,
immobilizing them from any future adventures to the west, but it cut the
direct connection between the right flank of Lee's army and Pickett's Five
Forks detachment. The events of the day on Pickett's front would lend
additional consequence to Warren's victory.[61]

*   *   *

Figures stirred early on the morning of March 31 at Sheridan's
headquarters near Dinwiddie Court House. Little Phil reported to Grant
that the Confederates had constructed earthworks at Five Forks, but that all
the trains audible on the South Side Railroad had been heading west,
easing fears that General Joseph E. Johnston might be funneling troops
into Virginia from North Carolina. Sheridan saw opportunity, rather than
peril, in the strategic situation. "I believe I could, with the Sixth Corps, turn
the enemy's left or break through his lines, but I would not like the Fifth
Corps to make such an attempt," he wrote Grant. The general-in-chief
once again responded that despite Sheridan's persistent affinity for
Wright's command, it would not be possible to remove the Sixth Corps
from its position in the center of the Union army. "Besides, Wright thinks
he can go through the line where he is," Grant explained, "and it is
advisable to have troops and a commander there who feels so, to
co-operate with you when you get around." Grant offered Sheridan use of
the Second Corps in place of Warren, but before the cavalry chieftain
could consider that option, events north of Dinwiddie Court House forced
him to think not offensively, but about saving his command.[62]

While Lee, Anderson, and Johnson masterminded their offensive
plans at White Oak Road, Pickett set in motion the attack he had deferred
the previous evening. The curly-locked Virginian detached Fitzhugh Lee's
cavalry division, temporarily commanded by Colonel Thomas T. Munford,
to probe south from Five Forks and make contact with the Union troops in

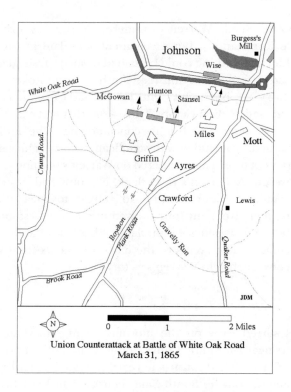

Union Counterattack at Battle of White Oak Road
March 31, 1865

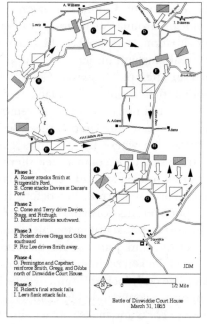

Phase 1:
A. Rosser attacks Smith at Fitzgerald's Ford.
B. Corse attacks Davies at Danse's Ford.

Phase 2:
C. Corse and Terry drive Davies, Stagg, and Fitzhugh.
D. Munford attacks southward.

Phase 3:
E. Pickett drives Gregg and Gibbs southward.
F. Fitz Lee drives Smith away.

Phase 4:
G. Pennington and Capehart reinforce Smith, Gregg, and Gibbs north of Dinwiddie Court House.

Phase 5:
H. Pickett's final attack fails.
I. Lee's flank attack fails.

Battle of Dinwiddie Court House
March 31, 1865

his front. Meanwhile, Fitz Lee, leading Rosser's and Rooney Lee's divisions, accompanied by Pickett's infantry, would head southwest from Five Forks on Scott Road with the goal of gaining a position west of Sheridan from which the Confederates could pile into the Union left flank. About 10:00 a.m., under clearing skies, Pickett's forces moved out.[63]

Sheridan was not insensible to a potential threat from the west, realizing that he had compelled Rosser and Rooney Lee to approach the Confederate battle lines from that direction by blocking the direct route from the south. Quite properly, then, the Union commander assigned elements of Brigadier General Henry E. Davies's brigade of Crook's division to patrol west of a swampy stream called Chamberlain's Bed, the course of which lay between Sheridan's position and a potential Confederate envelopment. Sheridan committed two of Devin's brigades to a strong reconnaissance north toward White Oak Road, one brigade approaching on Courthouse Road leading to Five Forks and the other using Crump Road to the northeast. Devin's Reserve Brigade, under Brigadier General Alfred Gibbs, remained behind at John Boisseau's along with the balance of Davies's troopers. Crook's remaining two brigades, Colonel J. Irvin Gregg's and Colonel Charles H. Smith's, bivouacked at Dinwiddie Court House while Custer's division still guarded the bogged-down wagon train far to the rear.

The Federal patrols found trouble. Devin's men encountered Confederates south of White Oak Road, confirming that the graycoats still controlled Five Forks. More worrisome was the news from west of Chamberlain's Bed that a force of Southern cavalry and infantry was heading toward Dinwiddie Court House. Sheridan reacted instantly. He ordered the remainder of Davies's brigade to move from Boisseau's to Danse's Ford on Chamberlain's Bed, to prevent a crossing there. Smith's brigade arrived from Dinwiddie Court House to assume a blocking position a mile downstream, at Fitzgerald's Ford. Gregg's regiments moved up in reserve near the intersection of Adams and Brook roads just south of Boisseau's. Sheridan thus deployed his six available cavalry brigades in a wide arc facing north, toward White Oak Road, and west, across the two established crossings of Chamberlain's Bed.[64]

It took Pickett until 2:00 p.m. to ready his assault across the marshy stream, swollen out of normal proportion by the recent rains. He assigned the cavalry, with Rosser's troopers in the lead, to force Fitzgerald's Ford. The infantry, with Corse's Virginians in the vanguard, would secure Danse's Ford. Once Munford heard the sound of Pickett's guns, he was to charge southward, adding to the Federal discomfiture from a third direction. But Pickett's plan did not proceed flawlessly. Rosser's attack at

Fitzgerald's Ford met stiff resistance—the swarthy Virginian sustaining a slight wound—and Smith's Federal cavalry holding its own. The infantry fared better. Corse's Brigade also encountered fierce fighting, but thanks in part to Davies's decision to detach part of his brigade to assist Smith, the Confederates eventually stormed across Danse's Ford and routed the remaining dismounted Union troopers.

The sound of combat alerted Devin's two brigades to trouble on their left and in their rear. The division commander accompanied part of Colonel Peter Stagg's Michigan Brigade to investigate the ruckus. The Wolverines quickly discovered Davies's men in a panic, and Devin summoned Colonel Charles Fitzhugh's brigade of his division to assist in stemming the developing disaster. Stagg and Fitzhugh achieved temporary success, but Pickett regained the momentum by committing Terry's Brigade to reinforce Corse. By then, Munford had launched his attack from the north, and Devin's horsemen found themselves assailed from front and flank. The hard-pressed Federals attempted to rally at the Boisseau House, but Pickett pushed forward to Adams Road south of the Union concentration point. In so doing, the Confederates cut off Stagg, Fitzhugh, and Davies from the rest of Sheridan's units to the south. Merritt told Devin to lead the three isolated brigades east to Boydton Plank Road and attempt to rejoin the rest of the command at Dinwiddie Court House. With Munford's Division in a threatening position to the north and Pickett to the west and south, an escape eastward offered Devin an attractive option to annihilation. The dismounted troopers would eventually make their way to the county seat near dark.

Characteristically, Sheridan acted with firm resolve during this crisis. Fearing that if Pickett continued to move east the Confederates would compromise Warren's left flank, Sheridan mustered the two remaining uncommitted brigades of his command, Gregg's and Gibbs's, and ordered them to attack Pickett from the south. Pickett wheeled into line of battle across Adams Road and faced his new opponents. In truth, of course, Pickett's intentions had always been to move toward Dinwiddie Court House, so Sheridan's claim that Gregg and Gibbs arrested Pickett's progress toward Warren's flank has no basis in fact. Nevertheless, a new phase of the Battle of Dinwiddie Court House now opened. Gibbs and Gregg fought for nearly two hours, between about 4:00 p.m. and 6:00 p.m., before Pickett's superior firepower decided the contest. Under renewed pressure from Fitz Lee, the Unionists fell back, taking Smith's stubborn brigade at Fitzgerald's Ford with them.[65]

Much like what had happened in the morning south of White Oak Road, the Confederate offensive north of Dinwiddie Court House had driven every Federal unit from the field. And, just as along Gravelly Run a few hours earlier, the bluecoats relied on a fresh division in reserve to salvage a critical situation. Sheridan had summoned George Armstrong Custer from his duty guarding wagons when affairs north of Dinwiddie Court House began to turn sour. Leaving one of his brigades with the train, Custer galloped ahead of Colonel Alexander C. M. Pennington's brigade and Colonel Henry Capehart's four regiments. Sheridan directed Custer to deploy his men about three-fourths of a mile north of Dinwiddie Court House. Quickly the troopers formed a line of battle, providing a rallying point for Gibbs, Gregg, and Smith. Union horse artillery unlimbered and added their bark to the formidable new position.

With Fitzgerald's Ford uncovered, Rooney Lee and Rosser splashed across Chamberlain's Bed and took position on Pickett's right flank. Daylight was fading, but Pickett determined to make one final attempt to destroy Sheridan's force and capture Dinwiddie Court House before darkness ended hostilities. His infantry charged across the open ground toward the Union line, denting Pennington's position but failing to effect a decisive breakthrough. Fitz Lee's cavalry tried to maneuver around Sheridan's left flank, but Charles Smith's weary troopers repulsed them, firing the last of their ammunition in the process. Nightfall silenced the gunfire, and the two sides settled into camps which, in places, lay only 100 yards apart.[66]

Confederate casualties at the Battle of Dinwiddie Court House are not positively known, but the best estimate is that some 360 cavalry and 400 infantry fell. Sheridan suffered 40 killed, 254 wounded, and 60 missing. The significance of the battle between Pickett and Sheridan transcended such numbers, however. As Sheridan told Colonel Porter that night, "This force is in more danger than I am—if I am cut off from the Army of the Potomac, it is cut off from Lee's army, and not a man in it should ever be allowed to get back to Lee. We at last have drawn the enemy's infantry out of its fortifications, and this is our chance to attack it." Sheridan reiterated his endless request that the Sixth Corps reinforce him, but Wright's men had their own problems to address on March 31.[67]

*   *   *

Grant's decision to cancel the dawn assault recommended by Wright on the night of March 30 sent the Sixth Corps soldiers back to their now-cheerless camps. The troops gamely cooked breakfast and attempted to re-erect their tents in the dripping predawn darkness of March 31. By mid-morning the rain relented, but not so the sounds of combat. At 9:30

a.m., General Ord reported that the Confederates had attacked his picket line. This elicited orders to Wright to prepare to assist the Army of the James should the Confederates become overly aggressive. "I will hold one division ready to move to your assistance and the others to follow, if necessary," Wright assured Ord. "Advise me if you wish them and designate their nearest route." As it turned out, Ord quelled the minor disturbance on his front without help, although he continued to explore the possibilities for a tactical strike into the afternoon.[68]

Affairs remained quiet along Wright's line, but the anxiety level in the ranks and among the officers was palpable. "We are under marching orders and expect to move in some direction soon," wrote Captain Charles C. Morey of the 2nd Vermont. "We are still in our old camp but all packed and ready to start. We hope and pray that we may be able to strike the death blow to rebelion [sic] before many days but perhaps we may fail[,] yet we hope for the best and will work hard for it and trust in God for the accomplishment. . . ." Colonel Keifer told his wife that "the whole army is kept upon the Qui viv[e]. We are under arms almost constantly to prevent surprises & if possible to detect and take advantage of any movement of the enemy." Sergeant John Hartwell of the 121st New York confided to his diary that when word came down to prepare to move to Ord's assistance, "we were all in a fever again to know what was before us to do."[69]

The Federals maintained an eagle eye on the Confederate line and reported that the Rebels had spent the entire day improving their fortifications. Headquarters issued the now-familiar orders to all division commanders to arouse the troops at 4:00 a.m. and reinforce the picket line from that hour until dawn to guard against surprise attacks. Had the Federals known the true state of affairs in Cadmus Wilcox's Confederate division that day, they would not have concerned themselves with defensive preparations. Wilcox reported that "at this time I was holding a line three or four miles long, with Cooke's, Davis's, and McComb's brigades of Heth's division, and Lane's and Thomas's of my division; on parts of my line the men were in one thin line ten feet apart, and no where was it held by men in double ranks." When Heth contacted Wilcox requesting a brigade to help blunt the menacing probes executed by Humphreys and Ord in the general vicinity of Burgess's Mill, Wilcox refused. "The withdrawing of a brigade would have been seen by the enemy and the lines so weakened that it could have offered but a feeble resistance," Wilcox explained. In order to strengthen this extremely weak position, Heth authorized General MacRae to return two of his regiments, the 11th North Carolina and the 52nd North Carolina, to positions on the east side of Hatcher's Run shortly after dark.[70]

The sun set on the Sixth Corps bivouacs this night in the absence of specific instructions to prepare for an attack. "At dark we were given to understand that nothing more would be required of us till morning," wrote a soldier in Hamblin's brigade, "so we went early to bed & wer[e] soon sound asleep." No such repose descended upon Union headquarters, now located at Dabney's Mill. General Grant had received reports from Sheridan about the eventful day near Dinwiddie Court House and acted upon the opportunity presented, ironically, by Pickett's tactical victory.[71]

Sheridan initially expressed concern for his security rather than promoting the offensive opportunity he championed with Colonel Porter later that evening. Accordingly, both Grant and Meade responded by directing a relief column, Griffin's division of Warren's corps, to move south along Boydton Plank Road to bolster Sheridan against the likely renewal of Pickett's attack in the morning. Grant also ordered Mackenzie's cavalry from the Army of the James to reinforce Little Phil. Within a short time, however, Meade, Grant, and Warren all recognized the enticing potential that Sheridan himself had observed once nightfall had ended the immediate threat to his exhausted troopers. At 8:40 p.m., the Fifth Corps commander wrote Meade suggesting an aggressive plan. Humphreys and the artillery would cover their own and Warren's positions near White Oak Road, allowing the Fifth Corps infantry to move southwest and attack the Confederates in their flank and rear, while Sheridan engaged the Rebels in front. "Unless Sheridan has been too badly handled," Warren said, "I think we have a chance for an open field fight that should be made use of."

Meade forwarded the proposal to Grant an hour later. "Would it not be well for Warren to go down with his whole corps and smash up the force in front of Sheridan?" he asked. "Warren could move at once. . . and take the force threatening Sheridan in rear, or he could send one division to support Sheridan at Dinwiddie and move on the enemy's rear with the other two." At the same moment, Grant dispatched a message to Meade at his headquarters along Vaughan Road near Gravelly Run that Griffin's relief division, combined with Sheridan's cavalry, provided "a chance for cutting up the infantry the enemy have entrusted so far from home." When the general-in-chief received Meade's proposition to commit Warren's entire corps to an offensive against Pickett, Grant replied, "Let Warren move in the way you propose and urge him not to stop for anything. Let Griffin go as he was first directed."[72]

The strategic vision Grant and Sheridan had cherished for nearly a week seemed to be unfolding: Union forces poised to smash an isolated Confederate contingent, opening the way to capturing the South Side Railroad, with Grant's favorite lieutenant in charge of the operation. The only flaw in this scenario, from Sheridan's perspective at least, was that Warren rather than Wright would be Little Phil's partner in victory. Grant told Sheridan to expect Warren at midnight and to assume overall command of the troops converging on his position.[73]

This expectation helped set the stage for the command controversy that would occur at the conclusion of the next day's combat. It was patently impossible for Warren to respond to orders received at 10:48 p.m. to report to Sheridan in little more than an hour. The Fifth Corps had fought a brutal battle on March 31. The road conditions had not greatly improved and the bridge across Gravelly Run on Boydton Plank Road had been destroyed, the stream itself running unfordably high. Most importantly, the distance from Warren's bivouac to Dinwiddie Court House was nearly six miles. Warren did the best he could. Because Ayres's troops were closest to the plank road, Warren sent his division instead of Griffin's down that highway to Dinwiddie Court House. Griffin and Crawford would march toward Pickett's rear to effect the pincers maneuver envisioned by Grant. Engineers busily reconstructed the bridge across Gravelly Run. But no one conveyed the true logistical situation to Sheridan, who knew nothing about when Warren received his orders and, therefore, had no reason to believe that the New Yorker would not join him at midnight as Grant had promised.[74]

Sheridan continued to labor in the dark, both literally and figuratively, when he sent a message to Warren at 3:00 a.m. April 1 attempting to coordinate the dawn attack strategy. He had heard nothing from the Fifth Corps commander and considered his reinforcing division three hours late. By the time his dispatch reached Warren, however, Sheridan's tactical plans had become moot: his quarry had fled.[75]

*   *   *

George Pickett's mixed command basked in the glow of the day's victory, made brighter by their cheering campfires, a comfort denied by Sheridan to his troopers the frosty night of March 31. "The rebels . . . had built up rousing great fires, around which they were moving, singing, yelling & shouting until near midnight," remembered one Federal. "We could hear the sounds of their voices plain." Those voices spoke of their performance in battle, an engagement, wrote one of the Southern participants, in which "the famous cavalry officer, General Phil Sheridan, with all his brag, was scared out of his boots."[76]

Sobering news received between 9:00 p.m. and 10:00 p.m. tempered whatever of this joy Pickett shared with his men. Some of Munford's outposts on Pickett's left had captured two infantrymen belonging to Brigadier General Joseph J. Bartlett's brigade of Griffin's Fifth Corps division. Warren had dispatched Bartlett to Sheridan's aid late in the afternoon, and his troops had reached the home of Dr. James Boisseau, north of Gravelly Run along Crump Road, when darkness arrested their progress. The presence of Bartlett's infantry on Pickett's left rear endangered the Confederate position and neutralized any advantage Pickett may have gained for a morning offensive. Before dawn, the Virginian issued orders for his forces to withdraw on both Courthouse and Scott roads, which merged at Five Forks. He could take comfort that he had blunted Sheridan's push for the railroad and that he could still protect that vital supply line from a position farther north.[77]

Pickett informed Lee on the morning of April 1 of his decision to pull back from the Dinwiddie Court House area. The gray chieftain's response was unusually sharp. "Hold Five Forks at all hazards," he scolded Pickett. "Prevent Union forces from striking the Southside Railroad. Regret exceedingly your forced withdrawal, and your inability to hold the advantage you gained." In this, Lee revealed his failure to understand the strategic framework in which Pickett rendered his decision. The division commander's instincts—that the presence of Bartlett's men near Dr. Boisseau's meant trouble—reflected precisely the Union plan of battle. Griffin and Crawford rejoined Bartlett about 7:00 a.m. Had Pickett remained in his evening encampments, his forces would have been trapped between these two powerful divisions and a reinforced Sheridan, with escape to the west his only option. By retreating northward, Pickett could still defend the railroad and seek to establish a direct connection with the rest of the army. As it turned out, Pickett's decision merely postponed disaster by some nine or ten hours, but that does not render the controversial Virginian's generalship any less correct.[78]

When the Confederates reached the Five Forks intersection, they began improving the shallow trenches they had constructed two days earlier. Pickett deployed his 10,000 troops on a line about one and three-fourths miles long. Ransom's and Wallace's brigades of Johnson's Division manned the left, protected to the east by a short "return," or refusal of the works running north. Steuart's, Terry's (now commanded by Colonel Joseph Mayo, Terry having been wounded on the 31st), and Corse's brigades extended the line west, to and beyond the road junction. Rooney Lee's horsemen guarded the far right flank, and a small mounted brigade led by Brigadier General William P. Roberts maintained tenuous communication with Richard Anderson's command to the east. Munford's cavalry and four guns bolstered Pickett's left flank while Willie Pegram unlimbered three guns near the crossroads and three more in support of Corse. Rosser's Division acted as a general reserve on the far side of Hatcher's Run, north of Five Forks.[79]

The ranking officers on the scene, Pickett and Fitz Lee, felt little anxiety for their new position, although Pickett would have preferred to establish his line on the far side of Hatcher's Run, had not the commanding general's orders been so explicit. After all, these were the same troops that had bested Sheridan the day before without the benefit of entrenchments, and moreover, Pickett had requested that Lee send him reinforcements and create a diversion to diminish his vulnerability. If the Federals had committed significant infantry to strengthen Sheridan's contingent, Pickett believed that Anderson would send him more troops to counterbalance the Federal shift. This thinking ignored the critical predicament faced by the Army of Northern Virginia on April 1. Longstreet's units north of the James offered the only possible source of reinforcement for Lee's right flank, and they would be available only if that officer could confirm that elements of Ord's army had moved south of the Appomattox. Even should some of Longstreet's men be released from duty in Henrico County, it would take many hours for Old Pete's brigades to transfer to the Petersburg front. In the meantime, Pickett would be on his own.[80]

While the Confederates completed their withdrawal and established their defenses near Five Forks, Sheridan spent the day reacting to the new Confederate deployment. The Union cavalry quickly detected Pickett's retreat and nipped at the Confederates' heels all morning. Ayres arrived about daylight, having moved west on Brook Road from Boydton Plank Road. Shortly thereafter, about 7:00 a.m., the head of Griffin's division, followed by Crawford's, appeared at the intersection of Courthouse and Crump roads near John Boisseau's, where they made contact with the cavalry. Mackenzie's weary troopers reached Dinwiddie Court House, but Sheridan allowed them to rest there.[81]

Shortly after noon, Sheridan decided on his battle plan. Custer's division would conduct a feint against the Confederate right while Warren would assail Pickett's left and turn the Confederate line in the gap between Pickett and Anderson. Once the Fifth Corps became engaged, Sheridan's cavalry would charge dismounted into the disrupted Confederate front. Such tactics might destroy the Confederate detachment or, at the very least, drive it westward, opening a clear path to the South Side Railroad which ran less than three miles north of Five Forks. Sheridan composed these plans with the knowledge that he had Grant's explicit authority to relieve Warren if Little Phil thought success depended upon removing that oft-times recalcitrant officer. "I did not wish to [relieve Warren], particularly on the eve of battle," remembered Sheridan, and at 1:00 p.m. he met with the New Yorker and explained the crucial role of the Fifth Corps in the impending offensive.[82]

Warren aligned his men along their axis of approach via Gravelly Run Church Road. It took until 4:00 p.m. for the Fifth Corps to deploy into attack formation. The intervening hours availed nothing to mollify Sheridan's seething impatience. The key to Warren's offensive belonged to Crawford's and Ayres's divisions, which were to strike the angle where the Confederate line bent back to the north. Griffin would follow Crawford from a reserve position to exploit the advantage gained, and Mackenzie's cavalry would skirt the ruined Confederate left and reach the road leading north in the Confederate rear, blocking escape in that direction.[83]

Warren believed that the target of his attack, the right angle in the Confederate line, was located near the confluence of Gravelly Run Church and White Oak roads. Reaching this junction between 4:15 p.m and 4:30 p.m. and encountering only light Confederate fire, Warren pushed north to where he then assumed the Confederate line must be. In fact, the return lay some 700 yards west of the intersection, so Crawford and Griffin marched northward, away from the enemy and into a tactical void. Ayres, on the left of Warren's formation, discovered the Confederates, and his attack easily routed the Rebels' left flank.[84]

A lack of command and control along the front line exacerbated the Confederate disaster. Tom Rosser had obtained some shad from the Nottoway River on his way to Five Forks and ordered them prepared at his encampment on the far side of Hatcher's Run. He invited Pickett and Fitz Lee to share in a delectable fish dinner, and both of these officers joined Rosser early in the afternoon. This left Rooney Lee the senior officer on the field. Lee's position on the far-right of the formation, however, isolated him from the rest of the troops. Even more ominous, he knew nothing about the temporary absence of his superiors. Thus, when Sheridan's attack struck, no Confederate commander was in position to direct a knowledgeable or comprehensive response.[85]

Once Ayres hit the Confederate left, the Union cavalry charged both the front and right of Pickett's line. Warren eventually regained his bearings and led Crawford's division south toward the Confederate rear. Pickett at last discerned the crisis and boldly galloped toward Five Forks to take charge of the deteriorating situation. He dispatched Mayo's Brigade to confront Crawford and realigned the remnants of Ransom's, Wallace's, and Steuart's brigades to face east, toward the approaching Union tidal wave. Rooney Lee and Corse continued to blunt Custer's assaults. The

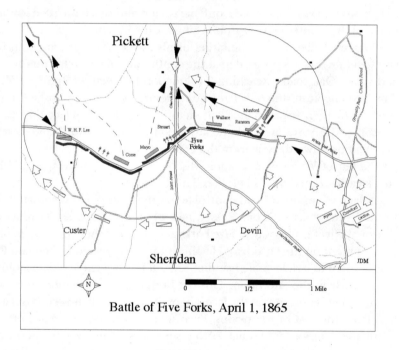

Battle of Five Forks, April 1, 1865

collapsing Confederate units thus fired in three directions simultaneously, but such a formation against a determined onslaught could not endure. As darkness descended, Pickett's resistance melted away. Some graycoats managed to escape to the northwest despite the best efforts of the Federals to capture them. As it was, Sheridan corralled roughly 2,400 prisoners while another 600 of Pickett's defenders fell killed or wounded. Union losses totaled 830.[86]

> "General, I trust you will reconsider your determinations.... Reconsider? Hell!"

The most prominent casualty of the day avoided bullet, shell, and capture—but not the wrath of his superior officer. About 7:00 p.m, at a time when total victory had been secured, someone from Sheridan's staff found Warren, who had participated with gallantry during the fighting, and delivered a devastating message: "Major-General Warren, commanding Fifth Army Corps, is relieved from duty, and will report at once for orders to Lieutenant-General Grant, commanding Armies of the United States." A stunned Warren sought out Sheridan on the bloody battlefield and found his commander shortly thereafter. "General, I trust you will reconsider your determination," Warren beseeched, in a tone one witness described as "very insubordinate." Sheridan roared back, "Reconsider? Hell! I don't reconsider my determination." Although junior in rank to the mediocre Samuel Crawford, Charles Griffin received command of the Fifth Corps and Warren rode away, his career in a shambles from which it would never recover—not even when an 1879 court of inquiry exonerated him from Sheridan's dismissal.[87]

While this drama unfolded at Five Forks, General Lee reacted to the first news of the disaster beyond his right flank. At 5:45 p.m., he ordered Anderson to withdraw Wise's, Moody's, and Hunton's brigades from the White Oak Road entrenchments and march them north to join the cavalry guarding the South Side Railroad near Church Crossing. This shift required that a skeleton force sidle westward to assist McGowan's Brigade in defending the earthworks evacuated by Anderson's three commands. Lee issued positive orders that Longstreet lead Field's Division to Petersburg from north of the James to compensate for Pickett's defeat. The Confederate situation had grown desperate indeed.[88]

A Union observer characterized the Battle of Five Forks as "one of the most interesting tactical battles of the war, admirable in conception, brilliant in execution, strikingly dramatic in its incidents, and productive of immensely important results." Sheridan himself immodestly considered his victory "unqualified." Pickett's losses were irreplaceable. The South Side Railroad loomed ahead in the darkness, apparently ripe for the taking, come sunrise. The integrity of Lee's defense along his entire Petersburg line fell under a shadow. Grant had to be apprised of Sheridan's triumph so that the general-in-chief could take measures to prevent a concentration against Sheridan, block Lee's ability to escape and, ultimately, eliminate the Army of Northern Virginia.[89]

Early in the day, Grant had dispatched Colonel Porter to act as headquarters liaison with Sheridan. Now, Porter passed through a memorable scene on his way to Dabney's Mill to report to Grant. Wagons, ambulances, stragglers, Confederate prisoners, and the walking wounded choked the roadways as the staff officer dashed southeast. "Everybody was riotous over the victory," Porter averred. When the messenger reached Boydton Plank Road far from the echoes of glory at Five Forks, one of his aides shouted the news of Sheridan's achievement. A passing figure in blue listened to this breathless report and promptly held his thumb to his nose in sarcastic salute. "No, you don't—April fool!" shouted the skeptic.

When Porter reached the roaring campfire at Dabney's Mill, his news elicited a more favorable response:

> I began shouting the good news as soon as I got in sight, and in a moment all but the imperturbable general-in-chief were on their feet giving vent to boisterous demonstrations of joy. For some minutes there was a bewildering state of excitement, and officers fell to grasping hands, shouting, and hugging each other like school-boys.

The normally reserved Porter found himself engulfed in the excitement and momentarily lost his own composure, leaping from his horse and slapping an astonished Grant soundly on the back in congratulations. Grant inquired about the numbers of prisoners Sheridan had taken and listened attentively to Porter's account of the battle. Then, with scarcely a word of comment, Grant retired to his tent where, by the light of a flickering candle, he could be seen writing in his order book. A few minutes later, he emerged and handed the papers to an orderly for dispatch over the field telegraph. Grant rejoined the knot of officers around the campfire and calmly stated, "I have ordered a general assault along the lines." Thought one observer, "These . . . words settled the fate of Petersburg and of Richmond."[90]

NOTES

1. Philip R. Woodcock, Diary, March 26, 1865, in David Ward Collection, Lakeville, Connecticut; *OR* pt. 3, 183-184.

2. Lewis A. Grant to George W. Getty, December 31, 1883, in Hazard Stevens Papers, LC; Charles Gilbert Gould to "Brother Aron," March 30, 1865, in Charles Gilbert Gould Collection, UVM; Britton and Reed, eds., *To My Beloved Wife and Boy at Home*, 343; *OR* pt. 3, 183. 4:00 a.m. was about the time that the first hint of the coming sunrise began to lighten the nighttime gloom, thus it was the earliest possible hour deemed feasible to undertake an offensive.

3. Wiley, ed., *Norfolk Blues*, 212; Benson, ed., *Berry Benson's Civil War Book*, 178-179.

4. Caldwell, *The History of a Brigade of South Carolinians*, 266; Major William Simpson Dunlop, *Lee's Sharpshooters; or, The Forefront of Battle* (Little Rock, 1899, reprint, Dayton, Oh., 1988), 250. McIlwaine's Hill straddles the Petersburg-Dinwiddie County line about one-half mile south of Confederate Fort Gregg. Union artillery placed on this rise would have allowed the Federals to target the Confederate works in the fort's vicinity. The land is privately owned in 2000 and unmarked for its historical significance.

It is unclear who attended the March 26 conference at army headquarters. Dunlop is the source for the existence of the meeting.

Sharpshooter battalions had been authorized by an act of the Confederate Congress in April 1862 and adopted by the army through General Orders Number 34 of May 3, 1862. Such units were actually formed in the Army of Northern Virginia during the fall and winter of 1863-1864, and at their height in May 1864 they numbered 34 battalions consisting of some 4,000 troops. The sharpshooters of MacRae's Brigade, for example, were selected on the basis of their performance under fire and wore a gold cross sewn on their left sleeves and the names of each battle in which they had participated sewn on their clothing. See George J. Winter, "A Battalion of Sharpshooters," in *Transactions of the Huguenot Society of South Carolina*, Number 79 (1974), 89, and Earl J. Hess, "Lee's Tarheels: Pettigrew's North Carolina Brigade in the Civil War," unpublished manuscript. The hand-picked men of these organizations possessed "intelligence, sound judgment... marksmanship [and] unfaltering courage," according to Dunlop. For information about Dunlop himself, see Robert K. Krick's introduction to the 1988 reprint edition of Dunlop's book.

5. Dunlop, *Lee's Sharpshooters*, 251-252; Benson, ed., *Berry Benson's Civil War Book*, 179. Lane described Major Wooten as "exceedingly modest, but a cool, cautious and fearless young officer, [who] was universally beloved by his men." See Lane, "History of Lane's North Carolina Brigade," in *SHSP*, X, 206. Captain John Young of the 22nd North Carolina commanded Scales's sharpshooters. One account credits Henry Heth with masterminding the little attack and Colonel John

Marshall Stone of the 2nd Mississippi of Joseph R. Davis's Brigade with leading the operation, spearheaded by 80 members of William MacRae's sharpshooters. Because this single source is not corroborated by other evidence, it has not been included in the text. See Chapman, *More Terrible Than Victory*, 281-282.

6. Dunlop, *Lee's Sharpshooters*, 253-254; Benson, "Reminiscences," in Berry G. Benson Papers, SHC, 619-621.

7. Charles Gilbert Gould to "Brother Aron," March 30, 1865 and to "Dear Mother," March 29, 1865, both in Captain Charles Gilbert Gould Collection, UVM.

8. Wiley, ed., *Norfolk Blues*, 212; Caldwell, *The History of a Brigade of South Carolinians*, 267.

9. Captain John Hardeman to "Dear Captain," March 28, 1865, in Gregory A. Coco Collection, Harrisburg Civil War Round Table Collection, USAMHI; Noah Collins, Memoir, in Isaac Spencer London Collection, North Carolina Department of Archives and History; Samuel Hoey Walkup, Diary, March 27, 1865, in Samuel Hoey Walker Papers, SHC; Octavius A. Wiggins, "Thirty-Seventh Regiment," in Clark, ed., *North Carolina in the Great War*, II, 670; J. Warren Keifer to "My Dear Wife," March 27, 1865, in Joseph Warren Keifer Papers, LC; Dunlop, *Lee's Sharpshooters*, 254-255; *OR* pt. 3, 202. Major Jackson Lafayette Bost of the 37th North Carolina stated that nearly all of his regiment supported Wooten's attack, the regiment suffering none killed "but some wounded, about five privates." See Bost to James H. Lane, July 31, 1867, in James Lane Papers, Auburn University. Scales was at home on sick leave during the spring campaign of 1865. Colonel Hyman was the ranking officer of the 13th North Carolina. See Taylor L. Rawley, "The Pender-Scales Brigade," in Clark, ed., *North Carolina in the Great War*, IV, 554.

10. Wiley, ed., *Norfolk Blues*, 213; Captain John Hardeman to "Dear Captain," March 28, 1865, in Gregory A. Coco Collection, Harrisburg Civil War Round Table Collection, USAMHI; J. Warren Keifer to "My Dear Wife," March 27, 1865, in Joseph Warren Keifer Papers, LC; Robert Pratt to "My Dear Brother Sid," March 27, 1865, in Robert Pratt Papers, VTHS. Captain Hardeman of the 45th Georgia wrote that Major Arthur McClellan delivered the flag of truce on behalf of General Wright. McClellan's brother was Major General George B. McClellan, former general-in-chief of all Union armies and the recently defeated Democratic candidate for president.

11. Dunlop, *Lee's Sharpshooters*, 255; Abraham T. Brewer, *History Sixty-first Regiment Pennsylvania Volunteers 1861-1865* (Pittsburgh, 1911), 136; George H. Mellish to "Dear Mother," March 27, 1865, in George H. Mellish Papers, HEH; Morse, "The 'Rebellion Record' of an Enlisted Man," in *National Tribune Scrapbook*, 98; George A. Cary, Diary, March 27, 1865, in Cary Family Papers, University of Maine; Benedict, *Vermont in the Civil War*, I, 579; J. Warren Keifer to "My Dear Wife," March 27, 1865, in Joseph Warren Keifer Papers, LC; Benson, "Reminiscences," in Berry G. Benson Papers, SHC; Wiggins, "Thirty-Seventh Regiment," in Clark, ed., *North Carolina in the Great War*, II, 670. Sergeant Brewer

of the 61st Pennsylvania was not a participant in the battle, but made his evaluation as the regiment's postwar historian.

12. Sheridan, *Personal Memoirs*, II, 124-125; Welcher, *The Union Army*, I, 1046-1049; Starr, *The Union Cavalry in the Civil War*, II, 421-423; *OR* pt. 3, 58, 67. Both Custer and Merritt had received brevets to major general.

13. Sheridan, *Personal Memoirs*, II, 126-129; Grant, *Personal Memoirs*, II, 436-438. These two first-hand accounts vary slightly in the details of the March 26 meeting, but agree on the conversation's essential content. Grant's written orders may be found in *OR* pt. 1, 50-51. It is curious that Grant would feel compelled to structure his orders so that in the event of an incomplete victory, public opinion in the North would not turn against the continued prosecution of the war. There is little indication that the political climate among the Northern people or in Washington favored a negotiated peace in the early spring of 1865. One thoughtful student of the campaign speculates that Grant simply acceded to Sheridan's arguments against the cavalry joining Sherman and concocted the story of the intentional deception to conceal this strategic concession. See Starr, *The Union Cavalry in the Civil War*, II, 425-426.

14. Sheridan, *Personal Memoirs*, II, 129-133. Sherman apparently originated the idea to visit Grant at City Point. He left Goldsboro, N.C. on March 25, arrived in Morehead City the next day, and there boarded a boat to City Point. He arrived on the afternoon of the 27th. Sherman mentioned nothing about meeting Sheridan or discussing his preferences for Sheridan's role in the imminent offensive. See William Tecumseh Sherman, *Memoirs of General W. T. Sherman*, 2 vols. (New York, 1875, reprint, New York, 1990), II, 810-811 and Simon, ed., *The Papers of Ulysses S. Grant*, XIV, 206, 236-237. Grant told Sherman as early as March 22 that he envisioned Sheridan destroying the South Side and Danville railroads and "from that point I shall probably leave it to his discretion either to return to this Army . . . or go and join you. . . ." See Simon, ed., *The Papers of Ulysses S. Grant*, XIV, 202-203.

The Eppes House, Appomattox Manor, is the centerpiece of the City Point Unit of Petersburg National Battlefield and is open to the public. The cabin Grant used as his headquarters and which served as the venue for the memorable council of war between Sherman, Sheridan, and Grant on the night of March 27 has been restored and returned to its original location by the National Park Service. Hancock Station was located just west of Jerusalem Plank Road, present-day (2000) Crater Road, about one mile south of Flank Road in the City of Petersburg. There is nothing on the ground to indicate its precise location.

15. Grant's March 28 order may be found in *OR* pt. 1, 52. Sheridan's account of his receipt of these orders is in Sheridan, *Personal Memoirs*, II, 134-135. See Starr, *The Union Cavalry in the Civil War*, II, 427 for an excellent analysis of these orders.

16. Orders for the Army of the Potomac emanated, of course, from that army's commander. Meade issued his original orders on March 27 and then modified them on March 28 in regard to the movements of Warren and Humphreys. See *OR*

pt. 3, 198-199, 224. Ord reported his movement across the James and Appomattox rivers in *OR* pt. 1, 1160. See also Edward G. Longacre, *Army of Amateurs*, 283-285. Longacre estimates that the four divisions that accompanied Ord numbered 20,000 men. Humphreys, *The Virginia Campaign*, 323, guessed that Ord's force included about half of the 32,000 infantry in the Army of the James and nearly all of the army's 1,700 cavalry. A Sixth Corps soldier thought that Ord's black troops alone numbered "10 or 12 thousand." He was impressed as well with their appearance and resolve: "They were tough looking felows and appeard to be anxious for the fight and sayed they had not forgot Fort Pilow yet[.] I should hate to be a Reb and fall in their hands poor felows. . . ." See William L. Phillips to "Father and Mother," March 31, 1865, in William L. Phillips Letters, SHSW. While the infantry divisions would find places in the Federal works, Mackenzie's troopers would guard the Army of the Potomac's wagon trains near Reams Station, then later supplement Sheridan near Dinwiddie Court House and Five Forks. See *OR* pt. 1, 1244.

The portion of Vaughan Road that provided the route first for Warren and then Humphreys on March 29, survives in 2000 as VA 605 in Dinwiddie County. Its intersection with Quaker Road exists as the junction of VA 605 and VA 660. It should be noted that the approximate route of the historic Vaughan Road from Petersburg to Dinwiddie Court House may be traveled by following VA 675 southwest from its intersection with VA 604. The track of Vaughan Road then follows VA 613, VA 670, and VA 605. Vaughan Road then becomes VA 660 as it heads southwest and finally turns west to follow VA 703 into Dinwiddie Court House. Some portions of this modern road network are not on historic alignments.

17. *OR* pt. 3, 198-199.

18. George H. Mellish to "Dear Mother," March 28, 1865, in George H. Mellish Papers, HEH; Oliver Edwards, Memoir, Illinois State Historical Library, 219-220. As will be seen, Sheridan strongly preferred the Sixth Corps over Warren's men. The bonds forged between Sheridan and the Sixth Corps in the Shenandoah Valley were powerful.

19. Charles W. Wall to "Dear Mother," March 16, 1865, in Wall Family Papers, Cornell University; Lothrup Lincoln Lewis, Diary, March 14, 21, 1865, in Lothrup Lincoln Lewis Collection, LC; John B. Southard to "My Dear Sister," March 16, 1865, in Southard Family Correspondence, New-York Historical Society; Olcott and Lear, *The Civil War Letters of Lewis Bissell*, 348-349.

20. Evidence regarding the effective strength of the opposing cavalry forces in late March yields uncertain conclusions. See Freeman, *R. E. Lee*, IV, 22-27; Freeman, *Lee's Lieutenants*, III, 656; *OR* pt.1, 390; Starr, *The Union Cavalry in the Civil War*, II, 430. Lee's cavalry divisions were commanded by major generals W. H. F. "Rooney" Lee and Thomas L. Rosser, and Colonel Thomas T. Munford, who led Major General Fitzhugh Lee's division while that officer assumed overall control of the cavalry. Rosser's Division, including Munford's Brigade, had returned to the Petersburg-Richmond front from the Shenandoah Valley with their small commands by March 28 in response to Sheridan's departure. Sheridan stated that he had 9,000 effective troopers in his three divisions. However, the returns for

March 31 showed 13,136 officers and men plus 290 gunners present for duty, not including Mackenzie's command. It is possible but unlikely that the horse shortage idled more than 4,000 cavalrymen. See *OR* pt. 1, 1101 and pt. 3, 391.

On March 27, Longstreet suggested adding Pickett's Division to the cavalry to counteract Sheridan's potential move to cut the railroads or join Sherman. See *OR* pt. 3, 1357. As will be seen in the text, the concentration at Five Forks evolved over the next 48 hours. Freeman stated that Lee learned on March 28 that "Federal infantry and artillery were continuing the march in great strength toward their left," and credited Lee's knowledge to the report of an eighteen-year-old girl living within the lines. Only Ord's troops were moving in any strength on March 28, and they were well short of the Confederate left that day. Moreover, their movement was not yet fully detected or appreciated at Confederate headquarters. Lee's concentration at Five Forks resulted from a sound analysis of likely Federal intentions rather than any evaluation of actual Union troop movements. Freeman provided a table that lists the complete deployment of the Army of Northern Virginia as of March 27. The average density of troops from north of the James to beyond Burgess's Mill was 1,140 men per mile.

21. *OR* pt. 3, 203, 231; Homer Curtis to "Dear Friends," March 29, 1865, in Homer Curtis Letters, YU; Memorandum Book of Daniel Schaffner, March 28, 1865, in Schaffner Family Collection, Civil War Papers, Pennsylvania Historical and Museum Commission; George H. Mellish to "Dear Mother," March 30, 1865, in George H. Mellish Papers, HEH; Rhodes, ed., *All for the Union*, 222-223. The burned house Wright referenced was the Jones mansion on Church Road.

22. Sheridan, *Personal Memoirs*, II, 135-141. Custer reined up at Malone's Bridge, the place where modern (2000) VA 703 crosses Rowanty Creek. Rowanty Creek is formed by the confluence of Hatcher's Run and Gravelly Run.

23. *OR* pt. 3, 253-255; William H. Powell, *The Fifth Army Corps (Army of the Potomac): A Record of Operations During the Civil War in the United States of America, 1861-1865* (New York, 1896, reprint, Dayton, Oh., 1984), 776. Warren's report that Dinwiddie Court House was undefended came second hand from "an old negro who has been hiding in the woods" and who had spoken to someone who had visited an unoccupied Dinwiddie Court House the previous day. A very helpful tactical overview of the campaign from March 29 through April 1 is provided in Ed Bearss and Chris Calkins, *The Battle of Five Forks* (Lynchburg, Va., 1985).

24. Francis A. Walker, *History of the Second Army Corps in the Army of the Potomac* (New York, 1887, reprint, Gaithersburg, Md., n.d.), 657; *OR* pt. 3, 249; Bearss and Calkins, *Battle of Five Forks*, 18-20. By necessity, the Second Corps established its line of battle through the countryside and not along any existing roadway. Thus, its deployment and movements required great exertion.

25. Freeman, *R. E. Lee*, IV, 27-29; Bearss and Calkins, *Battle of Five Forks*, 20-22.

26. Bearss and Calkins, *Battle of Five Forks*, 22. Wise's fourth regiment, the 34th Virginia, guarded Boydton Plank Road southward toward Dinwiddie Court House.

27. Bearss and Calkins, *Battle of Five Forks*, 22-28; Joshua Lawrence Chamberlain, *The Passing of the Armies: An Account of the Final Campaign of the Army of the Potomac, Based upon Personal Reminiscences of the Fifth Army Corps* (New York, 1915, reprint, Gettysburg, Pa., 1994), 42-53. Casualties at the Battle of Lewis's Farm, or as it is sometimes styled, the Battle of Quaker Road, totaled 53 killed, 306 wounded, and 22 missing for Warren, and an estimated 250 for the Confederates, although the actual figure may have been higher. The Lewis's Farm battlefield is privately owned and unmarked save for a single plaque along VA 660. The remains of an old home, alleged to contain materials from the original Lewis House, survive precariously in 2000 along a grassy farm lane. Except for a few modern homes, the battlefield retains a high degree of integrity.

28. Bearss and Calkins, *Battle of Five Forks*, 28-29; Humphreys, *The Virginia Campaign*, 326; Walker, *History of the Second Army Corps*, 657.

29. *OR* pt. 1, 53, pt. 3, 1363, 1365; Freeman, *R. E. Lee*, IV, 29; Peter S. Carmichael, *Lee's Young Artillerist: William R. J. Pegram* (Charlottesville, Va., 1995), 159.

30. Caldwell, *The History of a Brigade of South Carolinians*, 269; Benson, ed., *Berry Benson's Civil War Book*, 180; Dunlop, *Lee's Sharpshooters*, 258; Cadmus M. Wilcox, "Notes on the Richmond Campaign," in Cadmus M. Wilcox Papers, LC.

31. Benson, ed., *Berry Benson's Civil War Book*, 180; Caldwell, *The History of a Brigade of South Carolinians*, 270; Lane, "Glimpses of Army Life," in *SHSP*, XVIII, 421; Colonel William Joseph Martin and Captain Edward R. Outlaw, "Eleventh Regiment," in Clark, ed., *North Carolina in the Great War*, I, 602; John H. Robinson, "Fifty-Second Regiment," in Clark, ed., *North Carolina in the Great War*, III, 251; Hess, "Lee's Tarheels," 714; Freeman, *R. E. Lee*, IV, 30; Samuel H. Walkup to "My own best beloved Minnie," March 30, 1865, in Samuel Hoey Walkup Papers, SHC; Wiley, ed., *Norfolk Blues*, 213.

Humphreys, in *The Virginia Campaign*, 326, stated that "General Hill extended to his right in the course of the night of the 29th, and early in the morning of the 30th, McGowan's and McRae's [sic] brigades, moving into the intrenchments on the White Oak road on Johnson's left, Scales's and Cooke's brigades into the intrenchments in front of Burgess's mill and along the south side of Hatcher's Run . . . while Lane's, Davis's, McComb's, and Thomas's brigades held those maintained by Hill north of Hatcher's Run." Humphreys overlooked the separation of McGowan's pickets from this movement to the right. A soldier in the 2nd Maryland Battalion of McComb's Brigade reported that a part of his unit assumed responsibility for "the line formerly held by Gen. Davis' brigade," meaning that McComb's men spread out to the southwest as well as to the northeast on March 29. See Ammen, "Maryland Troops in the Confederate Army," I, 168, in Thomas Clemens Collection, USAMHI. Lane felt that Lee chose McGowan's Brigade to move to the right rather than his because the South Carolinians were "fresher." Lane probably referred to the fighting his Tarheels had experienced on the 25th and the 27th. At a density of 1,100 men per mile, Lee's front line was merely 1/10 as strong in manpower as his line of battle at Fredericksburg had been in December 1862. See Freeman, *Lee's Lieutenants*, II, 341, n. 17.

32. J. Warren Keifer to "My Dear Wife," March 29, 1865, in Joseph Warren Keifer Papers, LC; Rhodes, ed., *All for the Union*, 223; Haines, *Fifteenth New Jersey*, 298-299.

33. Charles Gilbert Gould to "Dear Mother," March 29, 1865, in Captain Charles Gilbert Gould Collection, UVM; Britton and Reed, eds., *To My Beloved Wife and Boy at Home*, 345; *OR* pt. 3, 259-261.

34. Horace Porter, "Five Forks and the Pursuit of Lee," in Robert Underwood Johnson and Clarence Clough Buel, eds., *Battles and Leaders of the Civil War*, 4 vols. (New York, 1887-1888), IV, 708. Porter identified Grant's camp on the night of March 29 as being "in an old corn-field just south of [Vaughan Road], close to Gravelly Run. See Porter, *Campaigning With Grant*, 426.

35. *OR* pt. 3, 266.

36. Porter, "Five Forks and the Pursuit of Lee," 709; Sheridan, *Personal Memoirs*, II, 142-143. The horse was named Breckinridge after the Confederate general on whose staff its former owner served. Sheridan had captured the animal at the Battle of Missionary Ridge in November 1863. Major General John C. Breckinridge had led an army in the Shenandoah Valley, served with Lee during the Overland Campaign, and become Confederate secretary of war since his service in Tennessee.

37. Sheridan, *Personal Memoirs*, II, 142-146. Grant's message to Sheridan may be found in *OR* pt. 3, 325. Sheridan's claim to have so persuasively influenced Grant's decision must be taken with a grain of salt. Grant's own version of this episode named Grant's chief of staff, Brigadier General John A. Rawlins, as being the advocate of cancellation, not Grant himself. The general-in-chief confirmed Sheridan's ebullient optimism but stopped short of crediting the cavalryman with changing his mind. See Grant, *Personal Memoirs*, II, 438-439. Horace Porter provided yet another version of this incident in *Campaigning With Grant*, 428-429. For more on Sheridan's reference to Burnside's Mud March, see A. Wilson Greene, "Morale, Maneuver, and Mud: The Army of the Potomac, December 16, 1862-January 26, 1863," in Gary W. Gallagher, ed., *The Fredericksburg Campaign: Decision on the Rappahannock* (Chapel Hill, N.C., 1995), 171-217.

38. Starr, *The Union Cavalry in the Civil War*, II, 434. Brigadier General Henry E. Davies's brigade of Crook's division accompanied Devin. Colonel J. Irvin Gregg's Pennsylvanians received the assignment to guard Stony Creek, and Colonel Charles H. Smith's brigade remained behind at the village. See *OR* pt. 1, 1102.

39. *OR* pt. 1, 1122. Sheridan reported at 2:45 p.m. that his cavalry had taken Five Forks, but this was in error. See *OR* pt. 3, 323. The John Boisseau House was located near what is the modern (2000) intersection of VA 661 and VA 627. The house no longer stands. These roads are now called Boisseau and Courthouse roads, respectively. This farmstead is usually marked on maps simply "J. Boisseau." John Boisseau, although related to Joseph G. Boisseau of Tudor Hall, was not his brother. Some of the roadways in 1860s Dinwiddie County carried multiple names

or were referenced in various ways by the visiting military. For purposes of clarity, the road leading northwest from John Boisseau's toward Five Forks will be called Courthouse Road. At John Boisseau's, Courthouse Road and Crump Road merged to form Adams Road, modern VA 627, which led south to Dinwiddie Court House.

40. Freeman, *R. E. Lee*, IV, 30-32; Freeman, *Lee's Lieutenants*, III, 657-660. In 2000, Claiborne Road survives close to its wartime track as VA 631 and White Oak Road follows its east-west course as VA 613.

41. Powell, *The Fifth Army Corps*, 778-780; William Swinton, *Campaigns of the Army of the Potomac: A Critical History of Operations in Virginia Maryland and Pennsylvania From the Commencement to the Close of the War, 1861-5* (New York, 1866, reprint, Secaucus, N.J., 1988), 586-587.

42. Humphreys, *The Virginia Campaign*, 327; Swinton, *Campaigns of the Army of the Potomac*, 587; Wilcox, "Notes on the Richmond Campaign," in Cadmus M. Wilcox Papers, LC; Caldwell, *The History of a Brigade of South Carolinians*, 270. Wilcox provided the lineup of brigades in his and Heth's divisions. To the left of Scales was Cooke's Brigade straddling Hatcher's Run, followed by Davis's Brigade, McComb's Brigade, Lane's Brigade, and Thomas's Brigade. Wilcox estimated that along this line of five miles the troops stood ten feet apart. No doubt, McComb's regiments shifted northeast to help Lane cover MacRae's portion of the line. As explained later in the text, two of MacRae's regiments would return to this front before the April 2 attack. The exact positions of these brigades are difficult to determine. Caldwell elevated the fight in which Colonel Ashford was wounded to a serious skirmish. "The volleys were at times almost as fierce as those of battle," he remembered. The Crow House sat southeast of Boydton Plank Road near Burgess's Mill. It is no longer extant and its site is not publicly accessible.

43. *OR* pt. 3, 311.

44. *OR* pt. 3, 303-305, 314, 318-321; Stevens, "The Storming of the Lines of Petersburg," in *PMHSM*, VI, 419; Lieutenant Robert Pratt, Journal, March 31, 1865, in VTHS; Homer Curtis to "Dear Friends," March 30, 1865, in Homer Curtis Letters, YU; Rhodes, ed., *All for the Union*, 223-224.

45. J. Warren Keifer to "My Dear Wife," March 30, 1865, in Joseph Warren Keifer Papers, LC.

46. *OR* pt. 3, 284-285, 317.

47. *OR* pt. 3, 285, 325; Starr, *The Union Cavalry in the Civil War*, II, 436-437.

48. *OR* pt. 3, 285, 312.

49. *OR* pt. 3, 313.

50. *OR* pt. 3, 305, 313.

51. *OR* pt. 3, 286-287, 321; Stevens, "The Storming of the Lines of Petersburg," in *PMHSM*, VI, 419; Philip R. Woodcock, Diary, March 30, 1865, in David Ward Collection, Lakeville, Connecticut; Britton and Reed, eds., *To My Beloved Wife and Boy at Home*, 345-346; William L. Phillips to "Father and Mother," April 1, 1865, in William L. Phillips Letters, SHSW; Rhodes, ed., *All for the Union*, 224.

The first attack order was withdrawn before the troops actually left camp for their jump-off points. They did move out after Wright received the go-ahead for the second time. Daniel Schaffner of the 87th Pennsylvania noted that a whiskey ration was drawn, tipping him off that rough work lay ahead. See Memorandum Book of Daniel Schaffner, March 31, 1865, in Schaffner Family Collection, Civil War Papers, Pennsylvania Historical and Museum Commission. Wright received Meade's orders canceling the offensive sometime after 2:10 a.m., for at that time Wright sent Meade a message requesting immediate instructions, lest the attack be aborted so late that he could not return his troops to their lines without being seen by the Confederates. See *OR* pt. 3, 371.

52. *OR* pt. 3, 334-335. Accounts disagree about the weather on the morning of March 31. Theodore Lyman wrote that "the rain held up about ten A.M. and the sun once more shone." Robert S. Westbrook in the history of the 49th Pennsylvania recorded, "Rain, rain, rain, this morning . . . it has cleared off at noon and is pleasant;" Horace Porter recalled, "The rain had continued during the night of March 30, and on the morning of the 31st the weather was cloudy and dismal." See Agassiz, ed., *Meade's Headquarters*, 330; Robert S. Westbrook, *History of the 49th Pennsylvania Volunteers* (Altoona, Pa., 1898), 237; Porter, *Campaigning With Grant*, 430. Freeman in *R. E. Lee*, IV, 34, wrote, "It had been raining since about 3 A.M., and was raining [well after dawn]."

53. Freeman, *R. E. Lee*, IV, 32. Freeman provides a summary of the density of the Confederate line at midnight March 30-31 on page 33. Hunton arrived on Anderson's line during the morning of March 30. See *OR* pt. 1, 1287. Grimes had been promoted to major general on February 15, the last such appointment made in Lee's army. Hill had been ill most of the winter and officially went on sick leave March 20. He convalesced at the home of his uncle, Colonel Henry Hill, in Chesterfield County. See Robertson, *General A.P. Hill*, 312-313.

54. Freeman, *R. E. Lee*, IV, 33-34; Caldwell, *The History of a Brigade of South Carolinians*, 270-271; Bearss and Calkins, *Battle of Five Forks*, 54. Moody was ill on March 31 and could not command his brigade. Caldwell stated that McGowan's Brigade received orders to get under arms "about eight or nine o'clock." It was about two miles between the South Carolinians' original position west of Burgess's Mill and their deployment area west of Claiborne Road. Allowing time for the regiments to form into column and, once underway, to digress occasionally from White Oak Road during their march, McGowan's journey consumed an estimated 90 minutes . This timetable is consistent with reports that described McGowan's deployment as occurring virtually simultaneously with the Union attack.

55. Bearss and Calkins, *Battle of Five Forks*, 54; Caldwell, *The History of a Brigade of South Carolinians*, 271; Freeman, *R. E. Lee*, IV, 33-34.

56. The best narrative of the Battle of White Oak Road may be found in Bearss and Calkins, *Battle of Five Forks*, 56-72. Warren's perspective is provided in *OR* pt. 1, 811-818. Bushrod Johnson's summary is in *OR* pt. 1, 1287-1288. Meade approved Warren's plan, but by the time that word reached Fifth Corps headquarters, the battle was already joined. See *OR* pt. 3, 362. Ayres's brigades involved in this attack

were commanded by colonels Frederick Winthrop and James Gwyn, both of whom had been brevetted brigadier general. Colonel Richard Coulter's brigade of Crawford's division provided the support. Coulter had also received a brevet promotion.

57. Caldwell, *The History of a Brigade of South Carolinians*, 272-273. Crawford's other two units were commanded by Colonel John A. Kellogg and Brigadier General Henry Baxter. Colonel Andrew W. Denison's Maryland Brigade of Ayres's division was posted on the division's left flank and was the target of McGowan's attack.

58. *OR* pt. 1, 677, 814-815; Bearss and Calkins, *Battle of Five Forks*, 61-64. The two brigades involved from Miles's division were commanded by colonels Henry J. Madill and John Ramsey.

59. Chamberlain, *The Passing of the Armies*, 72-74; *OR* pt. 3, 362.

60. Chamberlain, *The Passing of the Armies*, 74-76.

61. Chamberlain, *The Passing of the Armies*, 72. Casualties at the Battle of White Oak Road numbered 61 killed, 323 wounded, and 86 missing in Humphreys's corps; 126 killed, 811 wounded, and 470 missing in Warren's corps; and about 800 Confederates, of whom 71 belonged to McGowan's Brigade. See Bearss and Calkins, *Battle of Five Forks*, 127; *OR* pt. 1, 1288; Caldwell, *The History of a Brigade of South Carolinians*, 275. A portion of the White Oak Road Battlefield is preserved by the Civil War Preservation Trust (formerly the Association for the Preservation of Civil War Sites) in collaboration with Dinwiddie County. These organizations have provided a short walking trail and several interpretive signs along an impressive stretch of surviving Confederate fortifications running east from the Claiborne Road-White Oak Road intersection.

62. *OR* pt. 3, 380; Bearss and Calkins, *Battle of Five Forks*, 32. The exact timing of this correspondence between Sheridan and Grant is not provided. Sheridan implied that he asked for the Sixth Corps on the night of March 30-31 and stated that Grant's reply arrived on the morning of March 31. See Sheridan, *Personal Memoirs*, II, 146-147.

63. Freeman, *Lee's Lieutenants*, III, 660; Bearss and Calkins, *Battle of Five Forks*, 36.

64. Bearss and Calkins, *Battle of Five Forks*, 32-36. Sheridan's report of the action on March 31 may be found in *OR* pt. 1, 1102-1103. Those of Merritt, Devin, Gibbs, Custer, Crook, Davies, and Smith as well as those of lesser cavalry officers follow Sheridan's in the same volume. Brook Road followed the course of modern (2000) VA 605, now called Turkey Egg Road.

65. Bearss and Calkins, *Battle of Five Forks*, 37-44; Sheridan, *Personal Memoirs*, II, 150-151; Mark J. Crawford, "Dinwiddie Court House: Beginning of the End," in *America's Civil War*, XII, No. 1, (March 1999), 50-56.

66. Bearss and Calkins, *Battle of Five Forks*, 44-45; Starr, *The Union Cavalry in the Civil War*, II, 439-442; Sheridan, *Personal Memoirs*, II, 151-153. Colonel William Wells commanded the brigade Custer left behind with the wagons when Pennington and Capehart rode forward. Although the ground over which this

far-ranging battle was fought retains in 2000 a semblance of its wartime appearance, no part of the Dinwiddie Court House Battlefield is consciously preserved or interpreted.

67. Chris Calkins, "The Battle of Five Forks: Final Push for the Southside," in *Blue & Gray Magazine*, IX, No. 4 (April 1992), 17; Bearss and Calkins, *Battle of Five Forks*, 46; *OR* pt. 3, 381; Porter, "Five Forks and the Pursuit of Lee," 711. Mark J. Crawford estimates in a recent study that Pickett's losses numbered "between 800 and 1,000 men." See "Beginning of the End," in *America's Civil War*, XII, No. 1, 55. Sheridan's confidence may not have been as unshakable as Porter related. In a message sent to Grant reporting the outcome of the battle, Sheridan said of Pickett's command, "This force is too strong for us. I will hold on to Dinwiddie Court House until I am compelled to leave." In his memoirs, Sheridan implied that the arrival of Devin and Davies bolstered his courage. See *OR* pt. 3, 381; Sheridan, *Personal Memoirs*, II, 153-154.

68. Longacre, *Army of Amateurs*, 287-288; Westbrook, *49th Pennsylvania Volunteers*, 237; *OR* pt. 3, 374-375, 378-379.

69. Charles G. Morey to "Dear Mother," March 31, 1865, in Charles G. Morey Papers, Stuart Goldman Collection, USAMHI; J. Warren Keifer to "My Dear Wife," March 31, 1865, in Joseph Warren Keifer Papers, LC; Britton and Reed, eds., *To My Beloved Wife and Boy at Home*, 346.

70. *OR* pt. 3, 344-345, 372; "The Fall of Petersburg-The Share of the Sixth Corps in its Capture," in *Philadelphia Weekly Press*, June 1, 1937; Cadmus M. Wilcox, "Defense of Batteries Gregg and Whitworth, and the Evacuation of Petersburg," in *SHSP*, IV, 23-24; Wilcox, "Notes on the Richmond Campaign," and Wilcox, "Autobiography," 13-14 in Cadmus M. Wilcox Papers, LC; William MacRae, Appomattox Campaign Report, in Lee Headquarters Papers, VHS. Wilcox reported that his horse was shot twice by a Union sharpshooter that day. Lane implied that this mishap temporarily removed Wilcox from command, compelling Lane to assume divisional authority on March 31, a responsibility Lane clearly did not relish. See Lane, "Glimpses of Army Life," in *SHSP*, XVIII, 421. MacRae's two detached regiments would eventually take position on Lane's right, just west of Duncan Road, where they would be fully engaged during the April 2 Breakthrough.

71. Britton and Reed, eds., *To My Beloved Wife and Boy at Home*, 346; Porter, "Five Forks and the Pursuit of Lee," 710; Humphreys, *The Virginia Campaign*, 337; Porter, *Campaigning With Grant*, 432. Dabney's Mill was a portable sawmill and the structure itself was long gone by the time Grant arrived at the site on March 31. Its location was marked by a pile of sawdust. See Noah Andre Trudeau, *Out of the Storm: The End of the Civil War April-June 1865* (Boston, 1994), 16. The site of Grant's headquarters is located in 2000 along the south side of VA 613, Dabney Mill Road, east of that road's crossing of Interstate 85, at the elbow of a 90-degree turn in the roadway. There is nothing on the ground to indicate the site.

72. Sheridan, *Personal Memoirs*, II, 153-154; *OR* pt. 3, 340-342, 365; 381; Agassiz, ed., *Meade's Headquarters*, 331. A good analysis of the evolving Union

strategy on the night of March 31 may be found in Starr, *The Union Cavalry in the Civil War*, II, 442-446.

73. *OR* pt. 3, 381.

74. *OR* pt. 3, 366-367.

75. Sheridan, *Personal Memoirs*, II, 156-157; *OR* pt. 3, 419-420.

76. Roger Hannaford, "Reminiscences," quoted in Starr, *The Union Cavalry in the Civil War*, II, 445; Trudeau, *Out of the Storm*, 21.

77. Freeman, *Lee's Lieutenants*, III, 660; *OR* pt. 3, 363-365. Dr. James Boisseau should not be confused with Dr. Albert Boisseau (or John Boisseau or Joseph Boisseau, for that matter) whose home near Church Road in the Sixth Corps sector had been burned by Union skirmishers on October 4,1864, and whose brother, Joseph, owned Tudor Hall. The Dr. James Boisseau house is no longer standing.

78. Freeman, *R. E. Lee*, IV, 36; Calkins, "The Battle of Five Forks," 18.

79. Freeman, *Lee's Lieutenants*, III, 662-664. William Paul Roberts was the youngest Confederate general, being just 23 years old at Five Forks. Scant evidence remains of Pickett's fortifications, but the Five Forks battlefield itself is splendidly preserved as a unit of Petersburg National Battlefield.

80. Freeman, *Lee's Lieutenants*, III, 664-665; *OR* pt. 1, 1300. Anderson's battered command could afford to weaken its front no more than could Heth or Wilcox. At last, Confederate resources had been stretched to their limits, and—as the events of the next 24 hours would demonstrate—beyond.

81. The progress of the various Federal units on the morning of April 1 may be followed in Humphreys, *The Virginia Campaign*, 339-344. See also Bearss and Calkins, *Battle of Five Forks*, 76.

82. Humphreys, *The Virginia Campaign*, 344; Sheridan, *Personal Memoirs*, II, 160; Porter, "Five Forks and the Pursuit of Lee," 711-712. Colonel Orville Babcock of Grant's staff delivered the message authorizing Sheridan to relieve Warren at his pleasure. Grant wrote, "I was so much dissatisfied with Warren's dilatory movements in the Battle of White Oak Road and in his failure to reach Sheridan in time, that I was much afraid that at the last moment he would fail Sheridan." Warren's movements on the 31st can hardly be deemed dilatory, and the text speaks of the good reasons for his failure to reach Sheridan by midnight. Grant's motives for delegating to Sheridan the authority to do what neither Grant nor Meade had done more likely sprang from Warren's long history of contentious subordination than from specific acts of incompetence during the spring campaign. See Grant, *Personal Memoirs*, II, 445. An outstanding analysis of Warren's removal may be found in Stephen W. Sears, *Controversies and Commanders: Dispatches from the Army of the Potomac* (Boston, 1999), 253-287.

83. Humphreys, *The Virginia Campaign*, 346-347; Sheridan, *Personal Memoirs*, II, 161.

84. It is beyond the scope of this narrative to provide the tactical details of the Battle of Five Forks. Excellent accounts may be found in Bearss and Calkins, *Battle of Five Forks*, 92-109; Humphreys, *The Virginia Campaign*, 347-353; Calkins, "The Battle of Five Forks," 22, 41-52; and Trudeau, *Out of the Storm*, 28-45. Gravelly Run

Church Road is in 2000 called Tranquility Lane, VA 628. The road no longer extends across its namesake stream. The church itself has not survived.

85. Freeman, *Lee's Lieutenants*, III, 665-667. The scene of the shad bake is outside of the National Park boundaries, but may be roughly located by following a small road, aptly named Shad Bake Lane, running east from VA 627 a few hundred yards north of where that road crosses Hatcher's Run.

86. Trudeau, *Out of the Storm*, 45.

87. *OR* pt. 1, 836; Trudeau, *Out of the Storm*, 44-45. For a brief account of Warren's Court of Inquiry, see Humphreys, *The Virginia Campaign*, 357-361. Voluminous Federal and Confederate testimony survives from this inquiry, making Five Forks one of the best documented of all Civil War battlefields. The government published the evidence presented in the Warren inquiry in 1883 under the title *Proceedings, Findings, and Opinions of the Court of Inquiry Convened by Order of the President of the United States in the case of Gouverneur K. Warren*. Oliver Edwards in an unpublished memoir wrote that, "It was a painful duty to both Grant and Sheridan as they both appreciated Warren's great ability as an engineer officer." See Edwards, Memoir, Illinois State Historical Library, 222.

88. Freeman, *R. E. Lee*, IV, 41-43; Caldwell, *The History of a Brigade of South Carolinians*, 278-281. Freeman provides a table summarizing the Confederate deployment on the night of April 1 indicating that merely 133 men per mile guarded the Confederate line west of Burgess's Mill—a regiment of Scales's Brigade and the sharpshooters of MacRae's Brigade. Freeman, however, unaccountably neglects to include McGowan's Brigade in his calculations. Church Crossing is in 2000 the community of Church Road located where the byway leading north from Five Forks, VA 627, intersects the South Side Railroad.

89. Porter, *Campaigning With Grant*, 441; Sheridan, *Personal Memoirs*, II, 165.

90. Porter, *Campaigning With Grant*, 441-443. The same account may be found in Porter, "Five Forks and the Pursuit of Lee," 714-715; Agassiz, ed., *Meade's Headquarters*, 333. Grant had specifically assigned Porter to be his liaison with Sheridan on April 1, representing the general-in-chief's views and reporting regularly on the conduct of the day's events. See Porter, "Five Forks and the Pursuit of Lee," 711.

CHAPTER SIX

Final Preparations

Ambrose Powell Hill rose early on the morning of April 1 to conduct an exhaustive and exhausting personal inspection of his entire corps front south and west of Petersburg. Observers noticed that the general appeared frail and that he spoke little, to either the staff officers who accompanied him or the troops he examined behind the lines. "He seemed lost in contemplation of his immediate position," remembered one of Hill's aides.[1]

The enfeebled Virginian, prematurely returned from sick leave, saw little on his ride from Fort Gregg to Burgess's Mill to cheer him through his physical debilities. The engineers had unquestionably done their job. Their earthen and log fortifications rose mightily out of the Dinwiddie landscape. But General Lee's decisions to deploy portions of Hill's corps on the far western reaches of the Confederate perimeter, and the attrition of combat and desertion, had emaciated the ranks in Hill's sector. The works "would have been impregnable if defended by any adequate force," declared one North Carolinian, "but . . . in fact were occupied by a mere skirmish line." Moving from east to west, Hill saw Thomas's Georgia brigade and Lane's North Carolinians of Wilcox's Division, and McComb's Tennesseans (along with the 2nd Maryland Battalion), Joseph R. Davis's Mississippi regiments, and Cooke's Tarheels, all of Heth's Division. Around Burgess's Mill, MacRae's men and most of Scales's Carolinians hugged their fortifications. These seven brigades numbered something over 8,300 men, meaning that the average density on Hill's front amounted to about 1,380 troops per mile (or less than one soldier every yard). "Our line from the dam in front of Battery 45 to Burgess' Mill did not appear to me any stronger than a horsehair," commented one Virginia officer. After their fight with the Fifth Corps the previous day, McGowan's men rested near Claiborne Road beyond Hill's sphere of influence.[2]

"You need not send my clothes, nor flour, nor anything else to me, my dearest, we will either be killed or captured or the road will be destroyed before this letter reaches you."

The soldiers of the Third Corps recognized intuitively what Hill had witnessed during his inspection, fully realizing the precarious situation they faced. "All during the day of the 1st of April there was a feeling of unrest and apprehension, not only among the individuals, but even the animals," wrote one Confederate. "I have no recollection of having spent a more thoroughly disagreeable day. . . ." Hill's troops could hear the firing in the direction of Five Forks, and rumors circulated that disaster had befallen Confederate arms. Colonel Samuel H. Walkup of the 48th North Carolina, in Cooke's Brigade, presciently

reflected in a letter home the grim fatalism that infected many of Hill's officers and men on the evening of April 1:

> You need not send my clothes, nor flour, nor anything else to me, my dearest, we will either be killed or captured or the road will be destroyed before this letter reaches you. Lee will have evacuated Richmond or be captured before April closes and perhaps before ten days. Our officers and men are all well, but greatly discouraged. I have kept this letter back to see if the news would change, but it grows worse every day. . . . Be prepared for bad news from Lee's army.[3]

General Lee returned to his Turnbull House headquarters on April 1, more aware than anyone of the depth of the crisis at hand. His army's survival depended upon Longstreet arriving before the Federals could exploit the advantage gained at Five Forks. The probable consequences of a Union offensive haunted the minds of more humble Confederates that night as well. A Virginia artillerist stationed near Thomas's entrenchments noted the recent removal of McGowan's, MacRae's, and Scales's troops from his vicinity and the gossamer battle line described by the remaining infantry. "It is apparent to the most common observation that a very small effort on the part of the enemy would carry the portion of our lines," he confided to his diary, "and if this was done, our army would be cut in two beyond even the hope of reconstruction (in consideration of our small

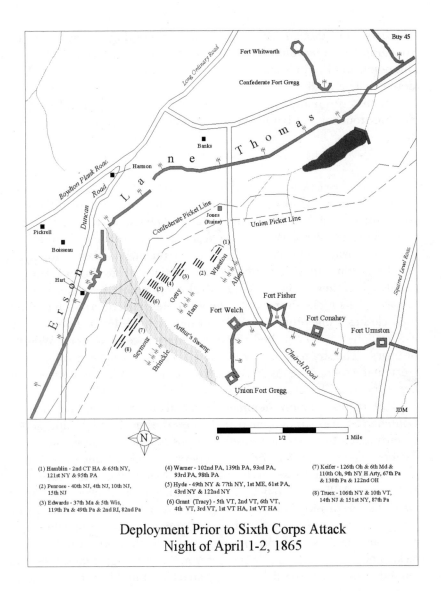

(1) Hamblin - 2nd CT HA & 65th NY,
    121st NY & 95th PA

(2) Penrose - 40th NJ, 4th NJ, 10th NJ,
    15th NJ

(3) Edwards - 37th Ma & 5th Wis,
    119th Pa & 49th Pa & 2nd RI, 82nd Pa

(4) Warner - 102nd PA, 139th PA, 93rd PA,
    93rd PA, 98th PA

(5) Hyde - 49th NY & 77th NY, 1st ME, 61st PA,
    43rd NY & 122nd NY

(6) Grant (Tracy) - 5th VT, 2nd VT, 6th VT,
    4th VT, 3rd VT, 1st VT HA, 1st VT HA

(7) Keifer - 126th Oh & 6th Md &
    110th Oh, 9th NY H Arty, 67th Pa
    & 138th Pa & 122nd OH

(8) Truex - 106th NY & 10th VT,
    14th NJ & 151st NY, 87th Pa

Deployment Prior to Sixth Corps Attack
Night of April 1-2, 1865

numbers), and though I have heard or seen nothing to lead me to the conclusion, yet I feel almost certain that if an assault is made, it will be at this point, and I cannot but think that the hour is not far distant when my doubts will be verified."

At that very moment, the Yankee high command was placing the finishing touches on a battle plan that would make a prophet of the young cannoneer.[4]

*   *   *

On the morning of April 1, Wright's Sixth Corps occupied the lines from just east of Fort Wadsworth on the Petersburg Railroad to Fort Sampson, near Peebles's Farm, a front of more than two miles. No midnight muster had disturbed their rest, so the men awakened refreshed and found time to honor the trifling traditions of the first of April by "fool[ing] all they could . . . & it mad[e] considerable merriment to[o]." Some soldiers took advantage of the welcome sunshine to wash and dry their clothes, while others lounged in camp or wrote letters home. Tense expectation, however, belied the calm appearance in General Wright's bivouacs. "The strain upon our nerves is great," one officer wrote, "and I feel that the sooner the suspense is ended the better. We get no news at all, but every officer looks anxious."[5]

Part of that anxiety stemmed from unconfirmed reports that the Confederates had strengthened their lines during the night and added infantry and artillery to their position opposite Wright's command. These rumors triggered the fear of a Confederate attack, a concern that had lingered since the close of hostilities on March 25. The tussle over McIlwaine's Hill on March 27 had only fueled Union worries. Wright instructed his division commanders to exercise additional vigilance along the picket lines and to ensure that no Confederate sortie be allowed to penetrate the blue cordon protecting the Sixth Corps camps. "The picket-line in front of each brigade is unusually strong," Frank Wheaton reminded his key subordinates. "Any attacking force less than a line of battle our pickets should destroy with ease." Reports continued to flow from the signal tower near Peebles's Farm describing the movement of Confederate wagons, placement of Southern artillery, and even the traffic on the South Side Railroad. In general, however, Wright could report to General Meade that "all [was] quiet on my front during the past twenty-four hours."[6]

The Sixth Corps leaders, while attentive to defensive measures, had by no means forsaken thoughts of attack. The plans for the dawn assault on

March 31, though issued and suspended twice the previous night, had not been abandoned. In fact, Wright had developed his strategy for puncturing the Confederate line several days earlier based on careful reconnaissance conducted by the Vermont Brigade commander, Lewis Grant.

"Aunt Liddy" Grant had made it his business to investigate the Confederate defenses throughout the winter and early spring. The capture of the Southern picket line on March 25 allowed him a much better perspective from which to conduct his inspections, and on the 26th he identified terrain he judged particularly vulnerable to an attack. A ravine, carrying one of the minor tributaries of Arthur's Swamp, split the Confederate fortifications opposite Fort Welch. This depression was only 50 or 60 feet wide where it crossed the Rebel works, but it broadened into a flat marsh as it approached the Union picket lines. At one time, the entire ravine had been choked with timber, but during the course of the winter the growth had all been cut, leaving behind a tangled carpet of stumps. Because of the swampy nature of this ground, the once-thick tree cover, and the emplacement of artillery on either side of the drainage, the Confederates had not deemed it necessary to extend their entrenchments across the miniature valley. Moreover, openings in the works and breaks in the abatis on either side of the stream bed allowed wood-gathering parties and sentries to traverse the area in front of the Confederate works. "It seemed quite certain to me that this was a weak point in the enemy's lines and that a column could be sent through them before any considerable force could be rallied to oppose it," thought Grant.[7]

The Vermonter reported these findings to his division commander, George Getty, and the two officers rode to the spot so Getty could assess the possibilities for himself. A day or two later, Getty notified his subordinate that both Wright and Meade had agreed to examine the ravine, and that he wanted his brigadier to join the distinguished party. In the company of various staff representatives, the four generals made their observations, with Grant serving as tour guide. Neither Meade nor Wright shared their opinions on the scene, but shortly after returning to his headquarters, Getty informed Lewis Grant that his ground had been approved for the attack. Moreover, Getty's division had been given the honor of leading it, and the division commander wished to place the Vermont Brigade in the front of the formation. "I understood this not only to be a recognition of the fine qualities of the Brigade but a recognition of the fact that I had first discovered & called attention to what seemed the weak point in the enemy's line," wrote Grant. When Wright informed Meade on the evening of March 30 that only one point along his line promised a successful attack,

Brigadier General Lewis Grant

Massachusetts MOLLUS Collection, Carlisle Barracks, Pennsylvania

he no doubt referred to the ravine both officers had studied a few days earlier.[8]

On the afternoon of April 1, while Sheridan and Warren attempted to destroy the Confederate right, U.S. Grant and Meade considered affairs elsewhere along the Union front. Meade acted on the assumption that Lee would strip the Confederate lines to meet the crisis on his western flank and, at 4:00 p.m., ordered Wright to resurrect the attack orders deferred on the night of the 30th:

> You will assault the enemy's works in your front at 4 a.m. to-morrow morning. Should this assault prove successful you will follow it up with all the force under your command, except the garrisons of the inclosed works and supports to the batteries you leave in the lines. After carrying the enemy's line you will push for the Boydton plank road and endeavor to establish communication with the assaulting columns on your right and left. Major-Generals Parke and Ord will assault at the same time. The point for attacking will be left to your judgment and knowledge of the enemy's works.[9]

The timing and intent of these orders raise several questions. There is no direct evidence that on the afternoon of April 1 Grant authorized an April 2 dawn attack. His own testimony agreed with those of the witnesses at his Dabney's Mill headquarters who stated that the attack orders emerged subsequent to receiving word of Sheridan's victory at Five Forks. Yet, Meade had no authority to assure Wright that Ord would move forward in concert with the Sixth Corps without Grant's explicit concurrence, because Ord reported directly to Grant. It is highly unlikely that Meade would have unilaterally assumed this authority, so Meade must have sent his directive to Wright with the knowledge and blessing of the lieutenant general. Evidently, Grant and Meade had agreed to reissue the March 30 attack orders prior to learning of Sheridan's fate at Five Forks as something of a contingency, in expectation of good news from Little Phil. Wright, Parke, and Ord would certainly appreciate a twelve-hour lead time to prepare an optimal assault, and if for any reason the anticipated attack became ill advised, it could easily be canceled as it had been two days earlier.

By about 8:30 p.m., Grant informed Meade of the results at Five Forks. The lieutenant general immediately began to worry that Lee would concentrate a mighty counter blow against Sheridan in the morning. "Some apprehensions filled my mind lest the enemy might desert his lines during the night, and by falling upon General Sheridan before assistance could reach him, drive him from his position and open the way for retreat," wrote Grant. He told Meade to employ Humphreys's corps to prevent this, and asked that Meade "inform Parke of this and tell him to be on the watch to go in."[10]

This message began a flurry of communication between Meade and Grant in which Meade struggled to understand the general-in-chief's true intentions. Meade immediately replied that his earlier orders to Wright and Parke "to attack to-morrow at 4 a.m. . . . were peremptory" and wondered if Grant wished those orders to be modified. Grant responded that the Ninth and Sixth Corps should "feel for a chance to get through the enemy's lines at once, and if they can get through should push on to-night. All our batteries might be opened at once without waiting for preparing assaulting columns." Grant wished only that the artillery begin a bombardment and that Parke and Wright advance a reconnaissance designed to ascertain if the Confederates continued to defend their lines in strength, or if Lee had indeed drastically weakened them to confront Sheridan in the morning. Only if Meade's army found Lee's defenses manifestly vulnerable, should it move forward without further preparation.[11]

Meade, however, partially misinterpreted Grant's instructions. At 9:00 p.m., he ordered Humphreys, Wright and Parke to "feel for a chance to get through the enemy's lines at once, and if you can get through push on to-night," a directive that accurately reflected Grant's conception. But Meade concluded his dispatch in a way that altered Grant's meaning: "Let your batteries be opened without waiting for the time to form assaulting columns; attack without delay."[12]

At 9:24 p.m., Meade received another message from Grant clarifying what he desired from Parke, Wright and Humphreys. This time, Meade understood. He immediately forwarded Grant's correspondence to his corps commanders well before any hasty attack could commence. He also reassured the general-in-chief that "I have modified my orders to conform with your dispatch. . . ." Before Grant received that comforting note he dashed another missive to Meade at 9:50 p.m., protesting that the army commander had misconstrued his purpose. Although not a word of this exchange could be considered harsh or critical, the frustration experienced by both men during this muddled hour is evident.[13]

The confusion between Grant and Meade on the evening of April 1 seems unnecessary considering that both officers occupied headquarters in close proximity near Dabney's Mill. The afternoon and evening of April 1 clearly represented a time when great strategic questions would be addressed, particularly after news of Sheridan's victory arrived. Under such circumstances, it is natural to expect that Grant and Meade would have shared a table in one or the other's tent to avoid delays in transmitting orders and, more to the point, to ensure that no question could arise about the plan of action. Meade suffered from a terrible cold on April 1 which may have contributed to his decision to remain at his own headquarters and communicate with Grant by dispatch. More likely, the explanation lies in force of custom and personality. The two men certainly maintained a proper and mutually respectful professional relationship throughout the campaign. Grant issued orders to Meade; Meade issued orders to his corps commanders. Each general had a role to play, and neither trampled upon the other's prerogatives. The separation, functional and physical, that allowed this arrangement to work, however, mitigated against a warmer rapport that would have avoided the exasperating, if ultimately harmless, correspondence on the night of April 1.[14]

No such confusion marred General Wright's preparations. At 10:05 p.m., Wright acknowledged receipt of Meade's orders and reported that arrangements were underway to begin the artillery bombardment and ready his skirmishers to advance at once. An hour later, the Sixth Corps commander informed Meade that, "Everything will be ready. The corps will go in solid, and I am sure will make the fur fly." He affirmed that his officers fully understood the morning attack plan and what was expected of them: "If the corps does half as well as I expect we will have broken through the rebel lines fifteen minutes from the word 'go.'" Meade passed along this buoyant message to Grant, who admitted that "I like the way Wright talks; it argues success." Shortly before midnight, Wright confirmed that he would launch his offensive at 4:00 a.m. "I may be able to attack at an earlier hour," wrote the corps commander, "but in order to almost insure success I think the attack better be made at 4 a. m., when my formation will be fully made." Meade replied at 12:25 a.m. that Wright should advance as soon as he felt that "there is a chance of success." Finally at 1:30 a.m., after receiving positive orders from Grant to initiate the offensive at 4:00 a.m., Meade instructed Wright that "you will attack the enemy's line at 4 a.m. to-day. All orders conflicting with this are suspended."[15]

Long before then, Wright's officers had prepared to execute an attack at whatever hour the high command deemed right. About 5:00 p.m., Wright issued detailed orders for an assault in accordance with Meade's original instructions, sent an hour earlier. The offensive would begin at 4:00 a.m. April 2, at the sound of a signal gun fired from Fort Fisher. The area between the left of the Sixth Corps, at the latitude of forts Cummings and Sampson, and the ruins of the Jones House along Church Road, a span of a little more than one mile, defined the breadth of the attack front. Getty's division would be the spearhead, supported on the right by

Wheaton and on the left by Truman Seymour, the latter two divisions recessed in echelon. Wright intended that each brigade maintain a front the length of a regiment, providing a relatively narrow but deep assault formation designed to generate and sustain maximum drive. The troops would advance to the Union picket line prior to the attack and there await the signal to charge.

Wright determined that only a token force would remain in the permanent fortifications from Fort Howard on the right to forts Gregg, Sampson, and Cummings on the left. Just ten percent of the usual complement of troops along the connecting rifle pits would man the earthworks, the balance of the corps, some 14,000 men, being committed to the assault. A battery of artillery would accompany each infantry division while two batteries poised in reserve, the rest of the Sixth Corps guns staying behind in the works. Captain George W. Adams of Battery G, First Rhode Island Light Artillery, organized a volunteer contingent of twenty cannoneers armed with rammers, lanyards, and friction primers for use with any enemy artillery captured during the assault. Wright arranged to remove the obstructions in front of the Union lines to facilitate rapid movement, and designated sharpshooters to "be so disposed as to be rendered most effective." The orders emphasized the importance of perfect silence prior to the assault, to maintain secrecy.[16]

If these instructions sounded familiar to Wright's division commanders, it was because they virtually mirrored the aborted attack orders issued 48 hours earlier. "The columns will move generally as directed in the attack proposed for the morning of the 31st ultimo," Wright affirmed, and "are to be considered strictly confidential."[17]

Despite this admonition, the man assigned responsibility for the key point of the Sixth Corps attack formation, Lewis A. Grant, took unusual measures to transmit his orders to his subordinates:

> I had not only called my commanding officers together & pointed out to them the ground & explained to them what was expected of us, but knowing the advance would be in the dark & that our path was beset with thick pine stumps from which the rebels had cut their wood, & that disorganization and some confusion would likely occur in the advance without the opportunity to reform, I had the men all called out in their company streets before we left camp & had the matter fully explained to them what we were expected to do.

Grant felt that such extensive dissemination of information was "unmilitary," but decided that the daunting task ahead warranted full disclosure to the troops expected to execute it. The brigade would be placed directly in rear of the skirmish line with its left near the ravine that Grant had earlier identified as the key terrain feature. Upon the firing of the signal gun, the attack would commence in silence so as to preserve the element of surprise until the last possible moment. The left flank of each regiment would hug the ravine for the entire distance to the enemy works with the troops to the right advancing accordingly. Once Grant felt satisfied that the company officers understood their roles, he ordered them back to their bivouacs to explain the attack plan to the rank and file.[18]

Getty's other brigade commanders, James Warner and Thomas Hyde, conducted briefings similar to the one hosted by Grant. In addition to essential information about the assault formations, officers received instructions to leave their horses behind and learned that men in the first ranks of each brigade were not to cap their rifles. This expedient would discourage the instinct to stop and return fire, the deadly tactical mistake in a frontal attack. Hyde briefed the six regimental commanders in his brigade atop the signal tower behind Fort Fisher. He outlined his intended unit formation and explained that the combat soldiers would be preceded by 40 axemen to dismantle the Rebel obstructions. The men would leave their canteens and knapsacks in camp to ensure the greatest facility of movement and reduce the potential for noise.[19]

Wheaton issued written orders at 10:00 p.m., apparently feeling that a meeting with his brigade commanders was unnecessary. His directive specified that Oliver Edwards's brigade would take the lead, followed by William H. Penrose's New Jersey Brigade and Joseph E. Hamblin's four regiments. Edwards was to conform to the movement of Getty's division on his left, while Penrose and Hamblin kept back 50 and 100 paces, respectively, to prevent crowding. Once Edwards had breached the Confederate line, Penrose would move up to Edwards's right and Hamblin to the right of the Jersey boys. Wheaton emphasized the need for silence and admonished his men to strike no matches and speak only when necessary and then in the lowest of tones. Only the men in the first lines of each brigade were to cap their loaded rifles.[20]

Edwards called a council of war to inform his regimental commanders of their roles. The brigade commander had studied the terrain and noted "that there was a zig zag opening through the enemy's four lines of obstructions, for the passing of reliefs to the skirmish line and I selected land marks to guide my brigade by, for a night attack."[21]

Similarly, Colonel Hubbard of the 2nd Connecticut Heavy Artillery summoned his company commanders to personally deliver the news of the attack. Hubbard made no effort to conceal his concern. Looking at once both very grave and sorrowful, Hubbard told his line officers, "Gentleman, I have sent for you to tell you that we have a serious duty to perform and that very soon." Hubbard went on to deliver a rather ominous description of the task faced by the regiment:

> Gentlemen, we are going to have a h——l of a fight at early daylight as General Grant has made up his mind to take Petersburg and Richmond to morrow morning and I want you fellows to simply tell your first sergeant[s] to have the men fall in ready to march as I have suggested, at 1 o'clock a.m. Now you can go to your quarters and if any of you have anything to say to your folks, wives or sweethearts make your story short and get what sleep you can for h——l will be tapped in the morning. Each company will have five or six axes to cut through the abatis or sharpened sticks in pole horses where we come to them and God only knows how many of us will ever come out of this d———d fight. Good night, gentlemen, hoping our forces may be successful.

Hubbard added that if any of his soldiers received wounds before the assault commenced, line officers were to muzzle their cries so that the enemy would not discern the presence of an attacking force so near to their picket line.[22]

There is no evidence of a meeting in the Third Division on the evening of April 1. Seymour sent word of the impending offensive via regular channels, the news arriving about the same time that Wheaton circulated his orders. "At 10:00 o'clock our lines were formed and our instructions given us," reported an officer in the 6th Maryland, "and then we laid down to try to get some sleep, if possible, to rest . . . for the fateful ordeal we knew we were to engage in. . . ."[23]

Rumors of the impending attack orders circulated through the Sixth Corps ranks even before official word reached the camps. One soldier, claiming to have come directly from Wright's headquarters, told his comrades in the 10th Vermont that, "boys, you are in for it and no mistake." His mates reacted with incredulity. "See here," blustered one Vermonter, "everybody knows that this is the first day of April, but we are feeling serious to-night, and if you try to spring any April-fool hoax on us we will drown you in the first pond that we come to." The "witness" protested that his tale was true and proceeded to outline plans for the pre-dawn assault. "Nonsense," replied a listener. "You don't believe that Grant is silly enough to try such a thing. They licked us out of our boots at Cold Harbor, with only half the chance they have here. That is just what 'Old Bob' has been waiting for all Winter, and the General who does what the other fellow wants him to, is a fool or a lunatic, and Grant isn't either."[24]

Soon enough, however, rumor became fact, and the soldiers responded to yet another notice to prepare for hazardous action. Few of the men viewed these latest orders as a false alarm. "All knew that bloody work was before us," admitted Lewis Grant, but according to brigade commander Warren Keifer, "the officers and men [were] in fine spirits." Aunt Liddy even detected a certain lightheartedness in the ranks as the troops went about their preparations for the assault. The soldiers filled cartridge boxes and canteens and examined their muskets. They put rations in their haversacks and made sure that their pipes and tobacco were as accessible as their ammunition.[25]

The careful observer might also have noted that many soldiers undertook tasks that indicated anything but a casual approach to the impending work. Some wrote what they feared would be their last letter home. Others gave messages to non combatants to pass along "in case of accidents." Playing cards and useless clothing, symbols of sin or excess, littered the ground. Some Northern boys scrawled their names and units on slips of paper, affixing them to their uniforms so, if necessary, their bodies could be identified. "We returned to our quarters, feeling that it was to be the most desperate fight of the war," remembered one New Englander. Hazard Stevens heard that "the remark was frequent among the men, 'Well, good-by, boys, that means death.'" Lewis Grant interpreted these reactions as merely the recognition among the troops that "the responsibility of going through rested upon them," but he detected no lack of determination among the men to discharge the duty assigned them.[26]

Wright fully recognized what a formidable obstacle the Confederate defenses presented. "The works in front of the chosen point of attack were known to be an extraordinarily strong line of rifle pits, with deep ditches and high relief, preceded by one or two lines of abatis," he wrote. "At every few hundred yards of this line were forts or batteries well supplied with artillery. These lines might well have been looked upon by the enemy as impregnable, and nothing but the most resolute bravery could have overcome them."[27]

The Sixth Corps commander could take comfort in the knowledge that the high command did not expect his men to reduce the Confederate position alone. Grant and Meade had arranged for all the forces arrayed against Lee's diminishing defenses to advance in unison on the morning of April 2. Parke received Meade's orders for the attack at 4:50 p.m. April 1 and promptly issued instructions to his division commanders. "Substantially the same arrangements for the assault were made as had been previously made for the assault ordered for the morning of the 31st," reported Parke. He directed that two of his divisions and a brigade from his third target the enemy's works opposite Fort Sedgwick, the attack to be coordinated with Wright's offensive farther west.[28]

To the left of the Sixth Corps, Ord's divisions of the Army of the James received Grant's directives to cooperate with Wright's assault. The lieutenant general recognized that the particularly swampy terrain confronting Ord posed a challenge and advised his subordinate to push his reserves to the right, where they would be able to support Seymour's division should that officer require help. "I do not wish you to fight your way over difficult barriers against defended lines," Grant told Ord. Instead, he advised that Ord determine if the Confederates had abandoned their lines and pursue them if they had fled.[29]

General Humphreys digested the same afternoon order from Meade that actuated Wright and Parke. The Second Corps would target the Confederate strongpoint near the Crow House, on the southwest bank of Hatcher's Run. During the evening, however, Humphreys's orders changed. Miles's division marched west to reinforce Sheridan, and Meade suspended Humphreys's attack, instructing him to hold the balance of the Second Corps in readiness to "take advantage of anything that might arise in the operations of the remainder of the army."[30]

Wright would garner support for his attack from one additional source. Between 8:30 p.m. and 9:00 p.m., Grant instructed Meade to order both the Sixth and Ninth corps artillery to open a bombardment. The lieutenant general hoped that a concentrated shelling would cause Lee to abandon his works and thus, presumably, alleviate the need for a potentially costly infantry assault. Meade passed along Grant's instructions to Wright and Parke, who relayed them to their artillery commanders, Captain Andrew Cowan of the 1st New York Light Battery, in the Sixth Corps, and Colonel John C. Tidball of the 4th New York Heavy Artillery, under Parke's command. Shortly before 10:00 p.m., Tidball called all his battery commanders together and explained the nature of their assignment. Cowan dashed through his subordinates' camps and transmitted the orders as well. About 10:00 p.m., some 150 guns opened on the Confederate works from the Appomattox River east of Petersburg as far west as forts Welch and Gregg.[31]

The iron barrage lasted some three hours. Cowan characterized the effort as "a moderate fire," but those infantrymen who experienced the shelling remembered it as an awesome spectacle. A soldier in the 126th Ohio thought that "never in the history of time was such firing heard on this side of the Atlantic. Those miles and miles of huge engines of war seemed fairly to leap into the air, the very earth beneath quaking and trembling at each discharge of those war monsters which sent shot and shell into the enemy's camp so rapidly that there was a constant flash as of lightning in intense darkness." A brigade commander in Humphreys's corps called the cannonade "the most noisy and terrific I have ever heard," while Lewis Grant thought the sight to be "magnificent and terrible." In the colorful words of a Pennsylvanian, "That long line of cannons that had been mute the previous days, as if hanging in rapt attention upon the momentous issues of this battle, from the Appomattox to Hatchers Run, now opened their brazen throats in one wild universal triumphant peal of thunder! The very earth shook for many miles around, and the sound reverberated, over mountain and through valley, for scores of miles away." Captain Michael Kelly of the 2nd Connecticut Heavy Artillery thought that the artillery display seemed as if "the devils in hell were fighting in the air."[32]

Cadmus Wilcox endured the bombardment which he termed "an almost incessant cannonade, solid shot and shell whizzing through the air and bursting in every direction, at times equal in brilliancy to a vivid meteoric display." The Confederates responded vigorously to the Union guns, compelling Elisha Hunt Rhodes to draw intimidating conclusions about what the infantry would face at dawn. "The noise was terrific, and the shriek of the shot and shell gave us an idea of what we might expect in the morning," wrote the Rhode Islander. "The whole night was hideous with screaming shells and bombs tracing networks of livid fire over the peaceful heavens," recalled a Pennsylvania soldier, rendering the experience "ever to be remembered by everyone who witnessed it."[33]

The cannonade eventually expended its venom about 1:00 a.m. By then, Ulysses S. Grant had completed his labors and "tucked himself into his campbed, and was soon sleeping as peacefully as if the next day were to be devoted to a picnic instead of a decisive battle," according to Colonel Porter. But no one in the Sixth Corps slept at that hour. While the big guns roared along the Union front, orders arrived for the troops to break camp and begin moving forward to assume positions for the upcoming contest. Wheaton's division, on the right, began shifting first, departing between 10:00 p.m. and 10:30 p.m. Special instructions arrived to secure any accoutrements that might make a noise. The soldiers placed their tin cups inside their haversacks, firmly strapped their canteens under their waist belts, and secured their bayonets in scabbards to prevent them from clanking. Once again, the officers enjoined silence on the columns that by midnight covered the two or more miles from Wheaton's bivouacs to Fort Fisher. The obstructions between that strongpoint and Fort Welch had been cleared to allow passage for the troops who padded catlike toward the advanced Union picket line. Here, at least one regimental commander ordered all his troops to remove the caps from their rifles to prevent the accidental shooting of the officers slated to lead the attack.[34]

Prior to Wheaton's arrival, Getty's division began to advance from its nearby encampments through the Federal entrenchments between forts Welch and Fisher. "Each regiment, as it crossed the works, was conducted by an officer familiar with the ground to its designated position, on reaching which it lay down," recalled one of Getty's staff officers. "A heavy mist made the moonless night more dark and gloomy," remembered Thomas Hyde, "and the raw air of midnight saw us quietly moving to our allotted places." Clouds of acrid artillery smoke hugged the ground, impeding the already difficult passage toward the jump-off points. Lieutenant Pratt of the 5th Vermont had been relieved from picket duty about 10:00 p.m. and returned to camp to prepare for the trek back to the front lines. "All I know thought of home and how many chances there were of getting killed," wrote Pratt.[35]

Seymour's division began its movement at midnight as well, taking position about 400 yards northwest of Fort Welch. With whispered orders guiding their way, the men of the 6th Maryland moved forward in the gloom, carrying 40 rounds of ammunition in their cartridge boxes and three days rations in their haversacks. "There were no light hearts in the corps that night, but there were few faint ones," thought Warren Keifer. "The soldiers of the corps knew the strength and character of the works to be assailed. . . . The night added to the solemnity of the preparation for the bloody work."[36]

Through the darkness and mist, a troop of some 50 horsemen could be seen observing the movement of the corps through the fortifications and toward the Union picket line. Two riders occupied the head of this formation. General Wright, the tall, stout figure of brusque manner, and Wright's assistant adjutant general, Major Charles H. Whittelsey, "slightly built, with a dash of comical hauteur in his deportment," watched as rank upon rank of ghostly blue figures emerged from the Federal abatis and into the open ground between the forts and the sentry posts. One of the orderlies carried the corps banner, "a blue swallow-tail, with white cross in the centre, on which was inscribed the figure six in red, thus giving the three national colors. . . ." Most of the rest of the Sixth Corps officers, in accordance with their orders, had left their mounts in the rear and marched on foot with their men toward their assigned places.[37]

Some of the troops had reached their designated positions, and others continued to make their way toward their jump-off points when a sharp musketry opened along the picket lines. Differing accounts explain the origin of this fire. Corporal Clinton Beckwith of the 121st New York believed that the Union pickets initiated the conflict "to cover the noise of our forming." Hazard Stevens agreed that "just as the head of the column [was] getting into position, the pickets opened fire. . . ." Thomas Hyde felt less charitable toward the blueclad sentry he blamed for precipitating the clash: "Our pickets had been strictly cautioned not to fire, but as we lay thickly packed on the rising ground behind them, some idiot fired his piece."[38]

The historian of the 61st Pennsylvania argued that the Confederates began the exchange, having become "aware that some unusual movement was being made on our side." Lieutenant Colonel Rhodes offered a more asinine explanation: "A mule belonging to the Brigade Pioneer Corps and loaded with picks and shovels broke loose and made for the front. The entrenching tools rattled at such a rate that the Rebels thought that something was up and opened a terrible fire." The 87th Pennsylvania's historian explained that the Confederates began shooting when they heard the chilled Federals banging their feet together to keep warm in the cold night air. Vermonters Lieutenant Charles H. Anson and Major Aldace F. Walker simply concluded that "some unknown cause" or "some unlucky chance" brought on the gunfire that contained unambiguously serious consequences for the waiting Federals.[39]

Union witnesses variously described the fire between the picket lines as "quite brisk," "lively," "severe and galling," and "the most severe fire I saw from a picket line." Such a volume of lead underscored the high state of readiness maintained by the Southern videttes. Wright had cautioned his commanders to retain perfect silence until the signal gun cued them to make their charge, but this necessity rendered the engagement along the picket line a one-sided affair. Corporal Oscar Waite of the 10th Vermont allowed that "we would have enjoyed the fracas but for the fact that . . . we couldn't give away our position by mixing in, so we lay there and took it, and when a fellow got hit he hardly dared grunt for fear the rebels would hear him." This inability to return the Confederate fire was "misery intensified" to the prone Federals, particularly when the thuds and stifled outcries indicated that a Rebel bullet had found its mark. "This was a tough place to stay," confessed a soldier in the 5th Wisconsin, "with nothing to do but lie there and take our medicine."[40]

The casualties began to mount behind the Union picket line. John Bragg of the 5th Wisconsin was killed and Jim Witter of the same regiment narrowly avoided injury when a Minie ball struck the stock of his rifle instead of his leg. At the other end of the line, Colonel Truex reported that "a number were killed and wounded" in his Third Division brigade. Southern projectiles found five or six men in the 10th Vermont, but the most severe loss occurred in Hyde's brigade of Getty's division. Lieutenant Colonel Erastus D. Holt, commanding the 49th New York, received a mortal wound, as did Lieutenant Colonel John W. Crosby of the 61st Pennsylvania. Holt survived long enough to be transferred to a hospital at City Point, but Crosby perished shortly after he was struck.[41]

The highest-ranking casualty of the picket fire was, ironically, the tactical architect of the offensive. Lewis Grant lay on the ground with his staff, enduring, like the rest of his Vermonters, the intense musketry, when a ball struck the left side of his head, cutting through his hat and scalp. Fortunately for Grant, the missile had not sustained sufficient velocity to penetrate his skull. Like most head wounds, Grant's bled profusely, and an aide assisted him to the rear. Command of the Vermont Brigade devolved upon Lieutenant Colonel Amasa S. Tracy of the 2nd Vermont.[42]

Grant's wound occurred shortly before the picket firing gradually diminished to an uneasy silence. Orders eventually reached the blueclad pickets to cease firing, and the Yankees yelled across the lines, "April Fool, Johnnies," in an attempt to provide a rationale for the unusually spirited exchange. The shaken Federals moved up closer to the now-quiet sentry posts and laid down again on the muddy earth. Hazard Stevens painted a graphic picture of the seemingly interminable time that remained until the first light of dawn would bring on the attack:

> This harassing picket firing at length died away. The night was pitchy dark. It was deadly chill and raw. The troops lay benumbed and shivering on the damp ground, anxiously awaiting the signal, the death-call to many a brave and beating heart. The artillery fire still rolled and thundered along our lines, especially on the Ninth Corps line, but the enemy had ceased to reply to it, and in front all was still. How long it seemed waiting in the darkness and cold![43]

Once the Confederate rifle fire faded away and the rumble of the Ninth Corps artillery echoed only faintly along the Sixth Corps front, Wright's officers made their final deployments for the attack. George Getty's Second Division remained the vanguard of a formation that many participants described as a wedge. Getty left a detachment of the 61st Pennsylvania of Hyde's brigade in Fort Urmston and the 62nd New York of Warner's brigade in forts Tracy and Keene, but placed the rest of his troops in the carefully planned positions outlined earlier in the evening. Each of his three brigades formed a compact column with a narrow front, the left of his formation resting on the ravine that Grant had identified as the key terrain feature of the assault. The troops took position immediately behind the picket line at a distance averaging roughly 600 yards from the Confederate works and about a third of that distance south of the Rebel picket line. The ground between the Federals and their targets had been cleared of all vegetation, but was littered with stumps and obstructed by several lines of abatis.[44]

Getty placed Grant's brigade, now under the command of Colonel Tracy, on the left of his division with its left resting on the lip of the ravine. Grant had designated his old regiment, the 5th Vermont under Lieutenant Colonel Ronald A. Kennedy, to occupy the position of honor at the head of the brigade. "It was battle-scarred and war-worn, and did not present a long line, but it was composed of veterans from many a well-fought field," wrote Grant with evident pride. Kennedy was to press through the ravine and remain as a rallying point for the rest of the Vermonters. Tracy's 2nd Vermont lay behind Kennedy with instructions to follow the 5th Vermont, bear right at the Confederate lines, and capture the artillery battery known to be just northeast of the ravine. Major William J. Sperry's 6th Vermont formed up next in line, ordered to move left of the ravine at the Confederate line and reduce the batteries in that direction. Captain George H. Amidon's 4th Vermont and Lieutenant Colonel Horace W. Floyd's 3rd Vermont would move left and right, respectively, from their positions as fourth and fifth units in column. The 1st Vermont Heavy Artillery fell to earth behind Floyd. This oversized unit split into two battalions as it had during the fighting on March 25. Major George D. Sowles and Captain Darius J. Safford commanded the battalions while Lieutenant Colonel Charles Hundson directed the regiment, which was to bring up the rear and act as supports for the brigade as needed. Grant considered the Vermonters "the apex or entering wedge of the Echelon," a distinction disputed by Thomas Hyde. There can be no doubt, however, that none of the Sixth Corps units deployed forward of the Vermonters, and Grant's brigade clearly possessed responsibility as "the directing column," using Getty's phraseology. Grant selected the position along the left bank of the ravine because the drainage itself "was full of stumps and because the opening in the enemy's abatis was at our right of the ravine."[45]

Hyde's brigade formed on Grant's right in four lines of battle, each line containing approximately equal numbers. "General Wright told me we would attack in a wedge-like formation, and that my brigade should be the point of the wedge," claimed Hyde. Although Hyde's six regiments indisputably comprised the center of Getty's formation, and his lead units occupied a position nearly as close to the Confederate works as did the 5th Vermont, Hyde's contention that his brigade bore responsibility for leading the charge conflicts with Getty's own statement that the Vermonters would set the pace for the assault.[46]

Hyde arranged his brigade with Major George H. Selkirk's 49th New York and Lieutenant Colonel David J. Caw's 77th New York regiments in the front ranks. The 1st Maine Veteran Volunteers under Lieutenant Colonel Stephen C. Fletcher occupied the second line and a portion of Colonel George F. Smith's 61st Pennsylvania the third. Hyde's remaining two regiments, the 43rd New York under Lieutenant Colonel Charles A. Milliken and the 122nd New York commanded by Lieutenant Colonel Horace W. Walpole, deployed in the fourth line of battle. Like the Vermonters, Hyde's front ranks formed "just in rear of the picket-line."[47]

Warner's First Brigade took position on the far right of Getty's division. Warner arrayed his troops in column of regiments five deep. The 102nd Pennsylvania under Lieutenant Colonel James Patchell drew the distinction of deploying in the front rank. Major James McGregor of the 139th Pennsylvania placed his unit in the second line, while Captain B. Frank Hean divided the large 93rd Pennsylvania in two battalions, arranging them in front of Fort Gregg in the third and fourth lines of Warner's formation. The 98th Pennsylvania led by Lieutenant Colonel Charles Reen occupied the fifth and final line.[48]

Wheaton's First Division took position to the right of Getty, each of his three brigades deployed in echelon. Wheaton selected Edwards's command to form some 25 paces to the right-rear of Warner's column of regiments. Edwards ordered 75 men of the 37th Massachusetts, commanded by Captain John C. Robinson and Second Lieutenant Harrie A. Cushman and armed with Spencer repeating rifles, to fan out and cover the entire brigade front as a skirmish line. He also assigned twenty men from the pioneer corps under Lieutenant David M. Donaldson to clear the Confederate obstructions once the attack signal had sounded. In the event these soldiers needed assistance, Edwards distributed a "sufficient quantity of axes along the first line, to be used in case the axmen had trouble."[49]

That first line consisted of Captain Archibald Hopkins's 37th Massachusetts on the right and Colonel Thomas S. Allen's 5th Wisconsin on the left, closest to the Pennsylvanians of Warner's brigade. Edwards deployed three regiments 300 paces behind the first line. Lieutenant Colonel Gideon Clark in command of the 119th Pennsylvania took position on the right of Edwards's second line, with Lieutenant Colonel Baynton J. Hickman's 49th Pennsylvania on Clark's left. Elisha Hunt Rhodes placed his 2nd Rhode Island on the far left of the second line, behind the 5th Wisconsin. Three hundred steps farther back, Colonel

Isaac C. Bassett positioned the 82nd Pennsylvania to form the third line of Edwards's brigade.[50]

Thirty paces in the rear of the right of Edwards's brigade, Wheaton posted the Garden Staters of Penrose's New Jersey Brigade. Penrose positioned Colonel Stephen R. Gilkyson's 40th New Jersey, some 500 strong, in the front of his column of regiments. Behind the 40th waited Lieutenant Colonel Baldwin Hufty and the 4th New Jersey, followed in order by Major James W. McNeely's 10th New Jersey and Major Ebenezer W. Davis's 15th New Jersey. The 40th New Jersey was a new regiment yet to experience a real baptism of fire. Moreover, enough of its members had deserted during the previous weeks to make the green unit notorious within the proud brigade. The tough-minded Penrose may have selected this shaky regiment for front line duty both to deter its members from skulking during the attack and to absorb its share of the expected casualties, thus sparing the veteran regiments some measure of danger.[51]

Hamblin's brigade deployed 30 paces in the rear of the right of the New Jersey Brigade in keeping with Wheaton's careful alignment. However, whereas Edwards had formed three lines of battle and Penrose four, Hamblin elected to post his four regiments in two lines of two units each. He placed Hubbard's 2nd Connecticut Heavy Artillery on the left of the front line, in close contact with Penrose's troops. To the Nutmeggers' right, Hamblin deployed his old unit, the 65th New York, now commanded by Lieutenant Colonel Henry C. Fisk. Behind Fisk, Hamblin positioned the 95th Pennsylvania under the direction of Lieutenant Colonel John Harper. The last of Hamblin's regiments, the 121st New York under Lieutenant Colonel Egbert Olcott, formed on Harper's left. Hamblin's brigade comprised the right flank of Wright's entire attack formation. As a means of protection therefore, Hamblin employed a select body of Spencer-equipped sharpshooters from the 49th Pennsylvania to serve both as a skirmish line and to watch the right of his brigade and the entire corps.[52]

Seymour's division anchored Wright's left flank. Colonel Keifer placed his seven regiments in three lines of battle, the right flank of each resting near the opposite side of the ravine from the Vermonters. After some difficulty negotiating the marshy terrain in the darkness of the early morning, and coping with the Confederate picket fire, Keifer managed to shuffle his units into position by 3:00 a.m. Like Grant and Hyde, Keifer's front line fell to earth just behind the advanced Union picket posts. Because Lieutenant Colonel Binkley of the 110th Ohio was acting as corps officer of the day and had charge of the picket line, Captain William D. Shellenberger led Binkley's Ohioans to their key position on the right of

Colonel J. Warren Keifer

Massachusetts MOLLUS Collection, Carlisle Barracks, Pennsylvania

Keifer's front line. From here, they would be able to move forward on the west side of the ravine once the Vermonters had commenced their assault along the east bank. Lieutenant Colonel Hill of the 6th Maryland filed in beside the Buckeyes, in the center of Keifer's front line. A contingent of about 100 men of the 126th Ohio under Colonel Benjamin F. Smith formed the left flank of the first line. The rest of that veteran regiment served as pickets and occupied the front-line rifle pits behind which their comrades deployed.[53]

The third of the three heavy artillery regiments serving as infantry in the Sixth Corps belonged to Keifer's brigade. Lieutenant Colonel James W. Snyder placed the outsize 9th New York Heavy Artillery in a second line. Behind the heavies, Keifer positioned the 122nd Ohio under Lieutenant Colonel Charles M. Cornyn on the right near the ravine, Colonel Matthew R. McClennan's 138th Pennsylvania in the center, and the 67th Pennsylvania under Major William G. Williams (of the 126th Ohio) on the left. Keifer's third line of battle rested merely ten paces behind the 9th New York Heavy Artillery.[54]

The second of Seymour's brigades belonged to William Truex, who commanded five regiments from New York, Pennsylvania, and Vermont. Truex managed to deploy somewhat earlier than Keifer. By 12:30 a.m., he had reached his designated ground on Keifer's immediate left some 400 yards in front of Fort Welch and just twenty paces behind the Union picket line. At this point, the Confederate pickets stood a mere 150 yards from the Union positions. Truex selected the 10th Vermont under Lieutenant Colonel George B. Damon to take the right of the first line, and the 106th New York led by Lieutenant Colonel Alvah W. Briggs to form on Damon's left. These two regiments remained quiet during the brunt of the picket firing, which claimed its share of victims from Truex's disciplined soldiers. "There had been a big rain not long before," remembered one Vermonter, "and the ground was partly flooded; our lines were straight, and when we came to lie down it was a lucky man that didn't find himself stretched out in a shallow puddle of almost freezing water." Enduring the deadly riflry and lying on the cold, wet ground "was not conducive to cheerfulness, warmth or comfort," agreed another observer.[55]

Truex placed the 151st New York under Lieutenant Colonel Charles Bogardus on the left of the second line and his old comrades of the 14th New Jersey, led by Lieutenant Colonel Jacob J. Janeway, on the right behind the 10th Vermont. These troops formed about 75 yards behind the leading regiments. The third line of Truex's brigade was manned by the 87th Pennsylvania, led on April 2 by Captain James Tearney. "This . . . regiment was composed almost entirely of raw troops, five companies having joined it within two weeks of this movement, and most of whom had never before been under fire," explained Truex. Like Wheaton, Seymour had arranged for pioneers to lead the attack and clear the Confederate abatis in advance of the charging infantry.[56]

Once the infantry had reached their jump-off points, the artillery duel had died down, and the picket fire finally abated, the last of the attack

Union fortifications outside Petersburg. *National Archives*

elements in Wright's battle plan began to adopt their final positions. All of Captain Cowan's guns had participated in the bombardment of the Confederate lines from their embrasures and platforms in the main Federal fortifications. But about 2:00 a.m., Cowan instructed the three battery commanders designated to accompany the infantry to move quietly out of the works and reassemble near Fort Fisher preparatory to reporting to their respective divisions.[57]

Captain William A. Harn, of the 3rd New York Independent Battery, left Fort Urmston and joined General Getty about 3:00 a.m. with his four light twelve-pounders. Captain Crawford Allen, Jr., commanding Battery H, 1st Rhode Island Light Artillery, reported to Wheaton's division with four Napoleons. At the same time, Lieutenant John R. Brinckle of Battery E, 5th U.S. Artillery, brought his four smoothbores to Seymour's division on the left of the corps. Lieutenant Orsamus R. Van Etten of the 1st New York Independent Battery, Captain Augustin N. Parsons of Battery A, 1st New Jersey Light Artillery, and Captain Adams of Battery G, 1st Rhode Island Light Artillery, all retained their three-inch ordnance rifles in the fortifications. Adams, however, personally reported with his twenty volunteers in preparation for manning the captured guns expected to fall into Federal hands.[58]

At last all was quiet, except for the muffled breathing of more than 14,000 men in blue poised for the cannon blast which, after nearly four years of unprecedented American mayhem, would trigger the attack that might determine the outcome of the war. The men waited amidst an atmosphere charged with unspoken determination and palpable fear, surrounded by comrades but alone with their thoughts. "Here we lay & rest for the greatest days work in the history of the war," remembered a Connecticut captain. Officers nervously glanced at their watches. The time had arrived for the long-awaited assault to begin. Ears strained for the sound of the signal gun from Fort Fisher. It was 4:00 a.m.[59]

*   *   *

For the soldiers in Wilcox's Division arrayed opposite the Sixth Corps, the hostilities on the night of April 1-2 merely confirmed their deep concern that they were perched upon the brink of momentous events. Corporal Joseph S. Kimbrough of the 14th Georgia performed picket duty that evening after enjoying his evening meal of cornbread and a slice or two of bacon. "Just as the shadows of night began to gather I returned to the picket line (which, by the way, was about as strong as the line of breastworks) in the face of a heavy cannonade from the enemy's lines, directed principally against our skirmish line," wrote Kimbrough. "At the picket line I found the men all in the rifle pits expecting a charge from the Yankee lines." Most of the picket firing occurred to the right of Kimbrough's position, so he did not engage in the skirmishing on the Sixth Corps front. "Sleep was weighing my eyelids down, and I retired about fifty yards from the rifle pit, rolled myself up in my blanket by a smoldering fire, and slept to the music of shrieking shot and shell from Yankee batteries."[60]

Whatever rest Kimbrough's comrades managed to gain that night must have been marred by worries about the approaching dawn. No more than 2,800 Confederate infantry occupied positions within rifle range of five times as many Federals silently poised to launch their attack. Lane's four North Carolina regiments stood precisely in the path of the Union wedge. The Tarheels spread their thin ranks over a distance of about one-and-a-quarter miles, their left resting on a small stream in front of the Banks House and their right terminating near the Hart House, a few hundred yards southeast of Tudor Hall. Lane placed the 33rd North Carolina, commanded by Colonel Robert V. Cowan, on his left. Thomas Wooten, the renowned sharpshooter, deployed his 18th North Carolina to Cowan's right, and the 37th North Carolina under Major Jackson Lafayette Bost formed on Wooten's right. Beyond the right flank of the 37th lay the ravine across which no entrenchments had been built. On the west side of that drainage, Captain T. James Linebarger positioned the last of Lane's regiments, the 28th North Carolina.[61]

Lane reported 1,162 officers and men present for duty on February 28, 1865, but those numbers probably decreased slightly during March due to desertions, sickness, and minor losses sustained during the fighting on March 25. Numerous sources described Lane's line as being extremely weak. Wilcox reported that the men stood "at places less than ten [paces apart], others at other points more than thirty." The historian of the 18th North Carolina stated that the Tarheels in his brigade "were some twenty feet apart in the trenches, beyond the Jones house," and another man in that regiment remembered the deployment as being one man for every twelve paces. These estimates appear exaggerated given the amount of front protected by Lane's men and the number of soldiers available to defend it. Assuming Lane's strength to be about 1,100 on the night of April 1-2, and calculating the distance between the Banks House drainage and the Hart House plateau as 6,500 feet, simple division yields a figure of one soldier approximately every six feet. In some places, such as the ravine between the 37th North Carolina and 28th North Carolina, no Confederate troops occupied the front, and in others, artillerists worked their guns. To admit, however, that Confederate accounts generally overstated the intervals between Lane's troops on the morning of April 2 does nothing to diminish the odds they faced. One Confederate cleverly characterized the Confederate line as a "cob-web force." Lane's men must have felt lonely indeed.[62]

The North Carolinians did enjoy a measure of protection on their flanks. To the northeast, Thomas's Brigade of Georgians covered a little more than a mile of the line connecting with Lane's left and extending to the site of the old dam across Rohoic Creek just below powerful Battery 45. Thomas led four regiments, although the precise order of their deployment is unknown. The 14th Georgia was commanded by Colonel Richard Lester and the 35th Georgia by Colonel Bolling H. Holt; Thomas Simmons's 45th Georgia and Major James B. Duggan's 49th Georgia had already tussled with the Sixth Corps during the Confederate counterattack on March 25. While the Georgians' precise strength cannot be determined, it likely did not exceed that of Lane.[63]

On Lane's immediate right rested Colonel William Joseph Martin's 11th North Carolina and Lieutenant Colonel Eric Erson's 52nd North Carolina, both of MacRae's Brigade. On the night of March 31 these two units, numbering some 280 men, had reported to General Cooke on the east side of Hatcher's Run. After dark on April 1, Cooke instructed them to move back toward the left "to relieve a portion of McComb's Brigade[,] occupying from the right of McGowan's Winter Quarters [Tudor Hall] [on] the left[,] to the Battery in front of McComb's Winter Quarters on the right." Colonel Erson had command of this movement, and his Tarheels arrived at their destinations about 1:00 a.m. Some members of the 26th North Carolina band had not made the short march west a few days before, and greeted their returning comrades. Shortly before daybreak, one of MacRae's pickets rushed back to the main line of works sporting a fresh wound. "Seeing us there [he] advised us to go to the rear," recalled musician Julius A. Lineback, "saying that there was every indication that a heavy force was being massed in our front, and that if a charge was made, this line could not possibly be held by the few men, they being strung out to a distance of 8-10 feet."[64]

The Confederate pickets who made life so miserable for the Sixth Corps on the night of April 1-2 and took the lives of men like colonels Holt and Crosby, belonged primarily to Sam McGowan's Brigade. While many of the South Carolina sharpshooters moved west with the bulk of their comrades on the night of March 29, about 150 of the brigade pickets stayed behind. Federal accounts testified to the intensity of their fire in the chilly darkness, but the number of videttes guarding the Confederate front lines that night must have been tiny, even when sentries from Lane's, Thomas's, and MacRae's brigades are counted. Despite the strength of the new picket posts, improved for about one week since the fighting on March 25, the soldiers behind the main fortifications could not expect more than token resistance by their skirmishers in the event of a concerted Federal attack.[65]

Lane, Thomas, and Erson could also depend on artillery fire to supplement their defense. Between Battery 45 on the left of Thomas's position and the right flank of Erson's detachment, no fewer than seven prepared artillery redans frowned out against would-be Union attackers. As late as March 29, the cannoneers assigned to this portion of the line labored diligently to construct even more works to protect their guns.

It is difficult to state with any certainty which batteries manned any of these positions on the night of April 1-2. Gunners from Lieutenant Colonel Charles Richardson's Battalion of Brigadier General R. Lindsay Walker's Third Corps artillery bore at least partial responsibility for this portion of Hill's line. Charles R. Grandy's Battery, the Norfolk Light Artillery Blues, had fired from positions near Tudor Hall on March 25 along with elements of the Crenshaw Battery, otherwise known as Captain Thomas Ellet's Virginia Light Artillery. On March 26, two of Grandy's smoothbores moved some 700 or 800 yards northeast of Tudor Hall to the vicinity of Lane's left flank to bolster the defense of Fort Gregg and Battery 45. Apparently, the other two batteries belonging to Richardson's Battalion—the Donaldsonville Artillery of Louisiana commanded by Captain R. Prosper Landry, and Captain Joseph D. Moore's Huger Battery of Virginia—moved from positions east of the Jerusalem Plank Road toward the west, at least part of the Huger Battery being posted near Burgess's Mill. Two rifled pieces belonging to the Norfolk Light Artillery Blues occupied one of the redans near the Boisseau House in the pre-dawn hours of April 2, where Captain Grandy peered out into the darkness toward the unseen Federals, wondering what the dawn had in store for his Virginia cannoneers.[66]

Less than three miles away, another Virginian, Robert E. Lee, lay partially undressed in his quarters at the Turnbull House. As the gray chieftain found uneasy rest, he could hear the boom of the Union artillery and, perhaps, the staccato sound of the musketry that blazed along his lines in the darkness. A short distance east on Cox Road at the outskirts of Petersburg, A. P. Hill also sought rejuvenation in the comfort of his temporary home, the Venable cottage, which he shared with his wife and daughters. Hill's personal inspection, and the information that reached Lee from various sources throughout the day and into the evening, convinced both men that the coming dawn would be as important as any new day since the armies' arrival at Petersburg nearly ten months earlier.

For one of these men, April 2 would mark the unhappy culmination of a bitter campaign to create a nation. For the other, that spring Sunday would provide his last worldly sunrise.[67]

NOTES

1. Robertson, *A. P. Hill*, 313; Freeman, *Lee's Lieutenants*, III, 676. Major General William Mahone's Division of Hill's corps occupied the defenses of the Howlett Line in Chesterfield County and did not receive a visit from its corps commander on April 1.

2. Martin and Outlaw, "Eleventh Regiment," in Clark, ed., *North Carolina in the Great War*, I, 602; William W. Chamberlaine, *Memoirs of the Civil War Between the Northern and Southern Sections of the United States of America 1861-1865* (Washington, 1912), 114-115. The strength and density of Hill's line between Thomas's left and Burgess's Mill is extrapolated from the tables provided by Freeman in *R. E. Lee*, IV, 33, 42-43. If Wilcox's line of two and one-quarter miles contained an average density of 1,100 men per mile, then Lane and Thomas (plus the portion of McGowan's sharpshooters who remained) must have numbered about 2,500 muskets. If Heth's front from Lane's right to Burgess's Mill, a distance of three and three-quarters miles, contained 1,565 men per mile, then these five brigades must have numbered about 5,868 men. Freeman estimates the total number of troops between Lieutenant Run and Claiborne Road as approximately 12,500, including Major General Bryan Grimes's division of John B. Gordon's corps on the left, and the skeleton force sent to replace Richard H. Anderson's departed brigades west of Burgess's Mill.

3. Percy G. Hawes, "Last Days of the Army of Northern Virginia," in *Confederate Veteran*, XXVII (1919), 341; Samuel H. Walkup to "My own best beloved Minnie," April 1, 1865, in Samuel Hoey Walkup Papers, SHC.

4. Freeman, *R. E. Lee*, IV, 42; Wiley, ed., *Norfolk Blues*, 215.

5. Stevens, "The Storming of the Lines of Petersburg," in *PMHSM*, VI, 419-20; Britton and Reed, eds., *To My Beloved Wife and Boy at Home*, 346; Memorandum Book of Daniel Schaffner, April 1, 1865, in Schaffner Family Collection, Civil War Papers, Pennsylvania Historical and Museum Commission; Homer Curtis to "Dear Fannie," April 1, 1865, in Homer Curtis Letters, YU; Rhodes, ed., *All for the Union*, 224. Fort Sampson was located southwest of Peebles's Farm and due south of Union Fort Gregg on the left end of the Union "fishhook." The fort is no longer extant.

6. *OR* pt. 1, 637, pt. 3, 401-403, 421, 426-27. Early on the morning of April 1, Meade moved his headquarters from Vaughan Road to near Grant's command post at Dabney's Mill. See Cleaves, *Meade of Gettysburg*, 313.

7. The evidence for crediting Lewis Grant with selecting the point of the Sixth Corps attack comes primarily from his correspondence with Getty and Hazard Stevens in the 1880s. Grant had read Humphreys's campaign monograph and knew of George G. Benedict's project to write the history of the Vermont troops in the war. Grant wanted to ensure that he and Getty received full recognition for determining the place where "the great closing battle of the war" would be fought. Stevens employed Grant's information in the preparation of his article published in the *Papers of the Military Historical Society of Massachusetts.* Grant wrote his own article, which appeared in 1887. Captain Merritt Barber, Grant's assistant adjutant general, confirmed his chief's version of events in a detailed letter written in 1892. None of the principals ever disputed the accounts published by Grant, Benedict, or Stevens, so there appears to be no reason to question their veracity. See L. A. Grant to "My Dear General," (George W. Getty), December 31, 1883 and January 5, 1884, and Lewis A. Grant to Hazard Stevens, February 13, 1884, all in the Hazard Stevens Papers, LC; Stevens, "The Storming of the Lines of Petersburg," in *PMHSM*, VI, 419; Grant, "The Old Vermont Brigade at Petersburg," in *Glimpses of the Nation's Struggle*, 396-397; Benedict, *Vermont in the Civil War*, I, 582-583, 601; Merritt Barber to General T.S. Peck, November 4, 1892, in VTHS.

Grant's ravine is a prominent feature along the Breakthrough Trail at Pamplin Historical Park. There are also remains of two military dams across the ravine, one near the Confederate works and the other several hundred yards downstream. Apparently the Confederates recognized the weakness of this position and attempted to correct it by damming the waters of the little tributary of Arthur's Swamp which drained the ravine. No documentary evidence has been found regarding these engineering features, but it is known that the Confederates created other inundations nearby. The absence of any mention of these dams suggests that the inundations were not present during Grant's reconnaissance or on April 2.

8. Stevens said that the reconnaissance involving Meade, Wright, Getty, and Lewis Grant occurred on March 27, but Grant hedged on identifying the exact day. None of the other principals mentioned the episode, and Barber merely timed it subsequent to the March 26 reconnaissance by Grant and Getty. Wright's dispatch to Meade on March 30 was cited in Chapter Five. It may be found in *OR* pt. 3, 312. Grant was not the only Sixth Corps general searching for weak points in the Confederate defenses. Wheaton examined the Rebel works in the company of Lieutenant Colonel Elisha Hunt Rhodes on March 28. "Together we crawled through the slashing until we nearly reached the enemy's pickets, with our glasses, we counted the cannon in their works, and tried to select positions for our troops to occupy in the coming assault," wrote Rhodes. See Rhodes, "The Second Rhode Island Volunteers at the Siege of Petersburg," 457-458.

9. *OR* pt. 1, 603, pt. 3, 422.

10. *OR* pt. 1, 54, pt. 3, 397.

11. *OR* pt. 3, 397.

12. *OR* pt. 3, 407.

13. *OR* pt. 3, 397-399, 422.

14. For evidence of Meade's illness see *OR* pt. 3, 423; Cleaves, *Meade of Gettysburg*, 317.

15. *OR* pt. 3, 399, 422-423, 452, 477.

16. *OR* pt. 1, 902, pt. 3, 423-424; Stevens, "The Storming of the Lines of Petersburg," in *PMHSM*, VI, 420-421. The Sixth Corps enjoyed some experience with successful frontal assaults employing tactics and formations like those envisioned for this attack. For example, on May 3, 1863, elements of the Sixth Corps successfully breached the famous stone wall and sunken road below Marye's Heights near Fredericksburg, and on May 10, 1864, portions of Wright's command penetrated the west face of the "Mule Shoe" salient at Spotsylvania.

17. *OR* pt. 3, 425.

18. Lewis A. Grant to Hazard Stevens, February 13, 1884, in Hazard Stevens Papers, LC; Grant, "The Old Vermont Brigade at Petersburg," in *Glimpses of the Nation's Struggle*, 397.

19. Penrose G. Mark, *Red: White: and Blue Badge. Pennsylvania Veteran Volunteers. A History of the 93rd Regiment, known as the "Lebanon Infantry" and "One of the 300 Fighting Regiments" from September 12th, 1861 to June 27th, 1865* (Harrisburg, Pa.: 1911), 321; Hyde, *Following the Greek Cross*, 250-251.

20. *OR* pt. 3, 427. It should be noted that Wheaton's orders relative to loaded but uncapped rifles were inconsistent with the directives for Getty's division. Because the first ranks needed to maintain their momentum to avoid stalling the entire formation in a deadly field of fire, it made more sense for those men to carry uncapped rifles into the attack. Perhaps Wheaton decided that the first ranks would fire a volley and subsequent attackers would close with the bayonet.

21. Augustus Woodberry, *The Second Rhode Island Regiment: A Narrative of Military Operations* (Providence, R.I., 1875), 341; Oliver Edwards, Memoir, Illinois State Historical Library, 223.

22. Soule, "Recollections of the Civil War," in *New Milford* (Conn.) *Gazette*, July 5, 12, 1912. Soule may have embellished his account a little. Captain Michael Kelly also attended this meeting with Hubbard and described the regimental commander as "excited but calm, determination in his eyes." As Hubbard explained the nature of the impending offensive, Kelly remembered him encouraging his subordinate commanders to perform well, and doing so "in great glee," leaving a somewhat different impression of Hubbard's mood than that described in the text. See Michael Kelly, Diary, April 1, 1865, CHS.

23. J. Warren Keifer to "My Dear Wife," April 1, 1865, in Joseph Warren Keifer Papers, LC; Eichelberger, Memoir, in Civil War Miscellaneous Collection, USAMHI.

24. Waite, "Three Years with the Tenth Vermont," 243-245. It should be noted that Waite cited the witness as having gathered his information at a grand meeting of all the corps commanders at Sixth Corps headquarters. Such a meeting never occurred, but because the rest of the tale rings true, it is included in the text as a repeated rumor.

25. Frank C. Morse to "Dear Nellie," April 1, 1865, in Frank C. Morse Papers, Massachusetts Historical Society; Grant, "The Old Vermont Brigade at Petersburg," in *Glimpses of the Nation's Struggle*, 399; J. Warren Keifer to "My Dear Wife," April 1, 1865, in Joseph Warren Keifer Papers, LC; Mark, *History of the 93rd Regiment*, 321.

26. Col. Robert L. Orr, "Before Petersburg: The Wedge-Shaped Assault and the Sixty-first Pennsylvania's Share in It," in *Philadelphia Weekly Press*, December 19, 1886; Woodberry, *The Second Rhode Island Regiment*, 341; Stevens, "The Storming of the Lines of Petersburg," in *PMHSM*, VI, 422; Lewis A. Grant to Hazard Stevens, February 13, 1884, in Hazard Stevens Papers, LC. Orr's account is repeated virtually verbatim in two regimental histories, Mark, *History of the 93rd Regiment*, 321, and Brewer, *History Sixty-first Regiment Pennsylvania Volunteers*, 137.

27. *OR* pt. 1, 903.

28. *OR* pt. 1, 1015-1016, pt. 3, 428-429.

29. *OR* pt. 1, 1160-1161, pt. 3, 431.

30. *OR* pt. 1, 678-679, pt. 3, 406-409. Grant's desire on the evening of April 1 to determine if the Confederates had abandoned their lines on either side of Hatcher's Run resulted in minor demonstrations by both Ord and Humphreys. These probes revealed that the Confederates still held their works in some strength and resulted in the modifications in the attack orders for the morning of April 2 described in the text. What remains of the Crow House defenses, so prominent in all accounts of the fighting on the Second Corps front, is located on private property that is very difficult to access. The residence itself no longer exists.

31. *OR* pt. 3, 397-399, pt. 1, 1009, 1072, 1084, 1088, 1090; Hance E. Morgan, Diary, April 1, 1865, in *Civil War Times Illustrated* Collection, USAMHI. At 4:30 p.m. on April 1, Meade telegraphed to Grant, "I desire to have Brvt. Maj. Andrew S. Cowan, 1st N.Yk. Indp. Battery—assigned to duty with his brevet rank to enable him to act as chief of artillery 6. A.C.—Can you so assign him pending the orders of the President." Captain William A. Harn of the 3rd New York Battery had been acting as artillery brigade commander since January when Colonel Charles H. Tompkins had gone on leave. It is not clear why Meade sought Cowan's elevation to artillery command on the eve of battle. Harn commanded his own battery on April 2. See Simon, ed., *The Papers of Ulysses S. Grant*, XIV, 242; *OR* pt. 2, 331,744, pt. 3, 1013. Cowan held the brevet rank of major and Tidball the brevet rank of brigadier general. Tidball reported 131 guns on the Ninth Corps front, including 40 mortars. Cowan had 24 guns in the six batteries that remained along the Sixth Corps lines. See *OR* pt. 1, 660-661, 1009-1015, 1070-1071.

32. *OR* pt. 1, 1009-1010; Rousculf, "Petersburg: The Part Taken in the Action of April 2, 1865 by the 126th Ohio," in *National Tribune*, June 18, 1891; Robertson, ed., *Civil War Letters of Robert McAllister*, 602; Grant, "The Old Vermont Brigade at Petersburg," in *Glimpses of the Nation's Struggle*, 399; Memoir of Thomas F. McCoy, Col. 107th Pennsylvania, in Frank R. McCoy Papers, LC; Michael Kelly, Diary, April 1, 1865, CHS.

33. Wilcox, "Defense of Batteries Gregg and Whitworth, and the Evacuation of Petersburg," in *SHSP*, IV, 25; *OR* pt. 1, 1072; Rhodes, ed., *All for the Union*, 225; Memoir of Thomas F. McCoy, Col. 107th Pa, in Frank R. McCoy Papers, LC; Roberts, "War Reminiscences," in *Connecticut Western News*, January 11, 1912.

34. Porter, "Five Forks and the Pursuit of Lee," 716; Rhodes, ed., *All for the Union*, 225; Rhodes, "The Second Rhode Island Volunteers," in *Rhode Island Soldiers and Sailors Historical Society*, X, 461; "The Fall of Petersburg-The Share of the Sixth Corps in its Capture," in *Philadelphia Weekly Press*, June 1, 1937; Roberts, "War Reminiscences," in *Connecticut Western News*, January 18, 1912; Soule, "Recollections of the Civil War," in *New Milford* (Conn.) *Gazette*, July 12, 1912; Michael Kelly, Diary, April 1, 1865, CHS; Best, *History of the 121st New York State Infantry*, 208; Haines, *15th New Jersey*, 301; Westbrook, *49th Pennsylvania Volunteers*, 237.

35. Grant, "The Old Vermont Brigade at Petersburg," in *Glimpses of the Nation's Struggle*, 400; Stevens, "The Storming of the Lines of Petersburg," in *PMHSM*, VI, 421; Hyde, *Following the Greek Cross*, 251; Mark, *History of the 93rd Regiment*, 321; Journal of Robert Pratt, April 1, 1865, VTHS; Bvt. Maj. Charles H. Anson, "Assault on the Lines of Petersburg, April 2, 1865," in *War Papers Being Papers Read Before the Commandery of the State of Wisconsin Military Order of the Loyal Legion of the United States* (Milwaukee: 1891, reprint, Wilmington, N.C., 1993), I, 89; Darius Safford to "Dear Sister," April 16, 1865, in Sherman/Safford Papers, VTHS.

36. Chaplain Edwin Mortimer Haynes, *A History of the Tenth Regiment, Vermont Volunteers with Biographical Sketches of the Officers who fell in Battle and A Complete Roster of all the Officers and Men Connected With It—Showing All Changes By Promotion, Death or Resignation, During the Military Existence of the Regiment* (Lewiston, Me, 1870), 143-144; Grayson M. Eichelberger, Memoir, in Civil War Miscellaneous Collection, USAMHI; Keifer, *Slavery and Four Years of War*, II, 192. It is not clear if Seymour's division utilized the same breaks and clearings in the Union lines between forts Fisher and Welch to gain their jump-off points as did Wheaton and Getty, but it is logical to assume that they did. Despite the proximate time of departure for all three divisions, no source mentioned any conflicts between units while filing out of the works.

37. "The Battle of Sunday: Highly Interesting Details of the Operations of the Sixth and Ninth Corps," in *Milwaukee Sentinel*, April 10, 1865. The Sixth Corps Headquarters flag carried on the morning of April 2 is, in 2000, displayed in the Battlefield Center at Pamplin Historical Park.

38. Best, *History of the 121st New York State Infantry*, 209; Hazard Stevens, Journal, in George W. Getty Papers, Gibson-Getty-McClure Family Papers, LC; Hyde, *Following the Greek Cross*, 251-252.

39. Brewer, *History Sixty-first Regiment Pennsylvania Volunteers*, 137-138; Rhodes, ed., *All for the Union*, 225; George R. Prowell, *History of the Eighty-Seventh Regiment, Pennsylvania Volunteers, Prepared from Official Records, Diaries, and Other Authentic Sources of Information* (York, Pa., 1901),

220; Anson, "Assault on the Lines of Petersburg," 90; Aldace F. Walker, "The Old Vermont Brigade," in *Military Essays and Recollections: Papers Read Before the Commandery of the State of Illinois, Military Order of the Loyal Legion of the United States*, II, 205; Benedict, *Vermont in the Civil War*, I, 584. According to one account, the offending quadruped mentioned by Rhodes "was found next day inside Lee's lines, having received no additional injury." See James L. Bowen, *History of the Thirty-Seventh Massachusetts Volunteers* (Holyoke, Mass, 1884), 410.

40. C.[lark] F. Barnes, "Petersburg. A Boy's Experience in the Terrible Charge of April 2, 1865," in *National Tribune*, July 27, 1883; *OR* pt. 1, 982; Haynes, *A History of the Tenth Regiment, Vermont Volunteers*, 144; Darius Safford to "Dear Sister," April 16, 1865, in Sherman/Safford Papers, VTHS; Waite,"Three Years With the Tenth Vermont," II, 246; Mark, *History of the 93rd Regiment*, 321-322; Hyde, *Following the Greek Cross*, 251-252.

41. Barnes, " A Boy's Experience in the Terrible Charge of April 2, 1865"; *OR* pt. 1, 982; Haynes, *A History of the Tenth Regiment, Vermont Volunteers*, 144; Brewer, *History Sixty-First Regiment Pennsylvania Volunteers*, 137; Stevens, "The Storming of the Lines of Petersburg," in *PMHSM*, VI, 422-423; Hazard Stevens, Journal, in George W. Getty Papers, Gibson-Getty-McClure Family Papers, LC; Frederick D. Bidwell, *History of the Forty-Ninth New York Volunteers* (Albany, 1916), 85-86. Crosby was an old resident of Philadelphia and was considered "gallant, high-spirited, generous to a fault, and more than brave." This was his fourth wound of the war. See Brewer, *History Sixty-First Regiment Pennsylvania Volunteers*, 137.

42. Benedict, *Vermont in the Civil War*, I, 584; Anson, "Assault on the Lines of Petersburg," 90; Grant, "The Old Vermont Brigade at Petersburg," in *Glimpses of the Nation's Struggle*, 403. Tracy had commanded the brigade during the Battle of Cedar Creek in October and would later earn the Medal of Honor for his actions there. See George W. Parsons, *Put the Vermonters Ahead* (Shippensburg, Pa., 1996), 135.

43. Benedict, *Vermont in the Civil War*, I, 584; Barnes, "A Boy's Experience in the Terrible Charge of April 2, 1865"; Best, *History of the 121st New York State Infantry*, 210; Stevens, "The Storming of the Lines of Petersburg," in *PMHSM*, VI, 423.

44. *OR* pt. 1, 953-954. Credit for suggesting the wedge-shaped attack formation, a standard attack in echelon, albeit on a grand scale, apparently belongs to Getty. Hazard Stevens of Getty's staff explicitly ascribed the tactical arrangement to that officer. See "The Storming of the Lines of Petersburg," in *PMHSM*, VI, 419. The immodest Lewis Grant made no claim for devising the tactics. Clearly, the specific arrangements for the attack appeared under Wright's name in his order of April 1. See *OR* pt. 1, 902 and pt. 3, 423-424. Fort Urmston is well preserved and a part of Petersburg National Battlefield. Forts Tracy and Keene were located along the main Union defense line between Vaughan and Squirrel Level roads and are no longer extant.

45. *OR* pt. 1, 954, 968; Grant, "The Old Vermont Brigade at Petersburg," in *Glimpses of the Nation's Struggle*, 400; Lewis A. Grant to George W. Getty, December 31, 1883, in Hazard Stevens Papers, LC; Benedict, *Vermont in the Civil War*, I, 602; Merritt Barber to General T.S. Peck, November 4, 1892, VTHS. Grant had begun his service as the major of the 5th Vermont, rising to lieutenant colonel and then colonel until he was promoted to brigade command in February 1863.

46. Hyde, *Following the Greek Cross*, 249; Brewer, *History Sixty-First Regiment Pennsylvania Volunteers*, 136-137.

47. *OR* pt. 1, 975. Hazard Stevens suggested a somewhat different alignment, but Hyde's contemporary report is the more reliable source. See Stevens, "The Storming of the Lines of Petersburg," in *PMHSM*, VI, 421.

48. *OR* pt. 1, 962-965. It will be remembered that the 62nd New York remained behind to garrison forts Tracy and Keene. Again, Hazard Stevens remembered a different alignment in "The Storming of the Lines of Petersburg," in *PMHSM*, VI, 421.

49. *OR* pt. 1, 910, 941, 945; Oliver Edwards, Memoir, Illinois State Historical Library, 222; Bowen, "Lee in the Toils," in *Philadelphia Weekly Times*, May 2, 1885.

50. *OR* pt. 1, 941, 945, 948-952.

51. *OR* pt. 1, 910, 927-928. See Bilby, *Three Rousing Cheers*, 239-240 for the suggestion that Penrose placed the 40th New Jersey in the front line as an object lesson. The strength of that regiment was taken from the Morning Report Book, April 1, 1865, Book Records of Volunteer Union Organizations, Civil War, Record Group 94, NA.

52. *OR* pt. 1, 910, 931, 936, 940.

53. *OR* pt. 1, 978, 992, 1000, 1003, 1005; John R. King, "Sixth Corps at Petersburg," in *National Tribune*, April 15, 1920. Keifer's official report stated that the alignment of his first line of battle was from right to left, 110th Ohio, 126th Ohio and 6th Maryland. However, all the other sources indicate the order provided in the text. Colonel Smith of the 126th Ohio mentioned that the final deployment was accomplished "after considerable maneuvering, changing position of regiments, & c.," so perhaps Keifer remembered an earlier alignment before the 126th Ohio and 6th Maryland switched positions prior to the attack.

54. *OR* pt. 1, 992, 1002, 1006-1008. McClennan stated that the 138th Pennsylvania brought 12 officers and about 300 men into line.

55. *OR* pt. 1, 981-982, 992; Haynes, *A History of the Tenth Regiment, Vermont Volunteers*, 143-144; Waite, "Three Years With the Tenth Vermont," II, 246; Abbott, *Personal Recollections*, 261-262.

56. *OR* pt. 1, 981, 986, 989; Sergeant J. Newton Terrill, *Campaign of the Fourteenth Regiment, New Jersey Volunteers* (New Brunswick, N.J., 1884), 118; Abbott, *Personal Recollections*, 263. Truex's decision to place the rookies of the 87th Pennsylvania in his brigade's least important position differed from Colonel Penrose's orders to position the 40th New Jersey directly in the line of fire, and suggests Penrose's motive in doing so.

57. *OR* pt. 1, 1009-1010.

58. *OR* pt. 1, 660, 1009-1015.

59. Michael Kelly, Diary, April 2, 1865, CHS.

60. J.[oseph] S.[ydney] Kimbrough, "From Petersburg to Hart's Island Prison," in *Confederate Veteran*, XXII (1914), 498.

61. *OR* pt. 1, 1285; Lane, "History of Lane's Brigade," in *SHSP*, X, 57. Virtually all of the earthworks defended by Lane in his final disposition are well preserved as a part of Pamplin Historical Park.

62. Inspection Reports and Related Records Received by the Inspection Branch in the Confederate Adjutant and Inspector General's Office, Inspection Report P, No. 64, Inclosure 11, February 28, 1865, Microcopy 935, Roll 16, for Lane's Brigade, Record Group 109, NA; Wilcox, "Autobiography," 14-15, in Cadmus M. Wilcox Papers, LC; McLaurin, Eighteenth Regiment," in Clark, ed., *North Carolina in the Great War*, II, 61; Augustus Evander Floyd, Memoir, 12, VHS; Jones, "Last Days of the Army of Northern Virginia," in *SHSP*, XXI, 76. Calculations made on the basis of Confederate strength are necessarily estimates. Not only are the numbers of soldiers not precisely known, but their deployment is also subject to question. For example, the undeterminable number of Lane's troops serving on picket duty at any given time would diminish the density of the main-line defense proportionately.

63. Wilcox, "Autobiography," 15, in Cadmus M. Wilcox Papers, LC; McRea, *Red Dirt and Isinglass*, 303; *OR* pt. 1, 1272.

64. Eric Erson, "Report of Operations of 2 Regts. of MacRae's Brigade," April 11, 1865, in Lee Headquarters Papers, VHS; Julius A. Lineback, Diary, April 1, 1865, in Julius A. Lineback Papers, SHC; Chapman, *More Terrible Than Victory*, 286; Hess, "Lee's Tarheels," 717.

65. Caldwell, *The History of a Brigade of South Carolinians*, 269-270. It is clear that not all of McGowan's sharpshooters remained behind near the Boisseau House. See Benson, ed., *Berry Benson's Civil War Book*, 180.

66. Sources on the Confederate artillery are difficult to find. Wiley, ed., *Norfolk Blues*, 210-216, provides good information taken from the diary of one of the battery's privates. The table of organization for Hill's artillery may be found in *OR* pt. 1, 1273-1274. Information on Grandy's, Ellet's, and Moore's batteries may be found in Lee A. Wallace, A *Guide to Virginia Military Organizations 1861-1865* (Lynchburg, Va., 1986), 19, 21-22, 27. None of the Third Corps artillerists left reports. The best map showing the Confederate gun emplacements is entitled "Petersburg and Five Forks, From Surveys under the direction of Bvt. Brig. Gen. N. Michler, Maj. of Engineers By Command of Bvt. Maj. Gen. A.A. Humphreys," 1867, LC, Geography and Map Division. Confederate artillery did not necessarily limit its deployment to the specific positions prepared to accommodate cannon. There is also no reason to believe that Southern ordnance occupied every established artillery position on the morning of April 2. Walker had received promotion to brigadier general on February 18, 1865.

67. Freeman, *R. E. Lee*, IV, 43; Robertson, *A. P. Hill*, 314.

The Breakthrough

T he men of the Sixth Corps lay on the cold, damp ground behind their entrenched picket line early on the morning of Sunday, April 2, consumed by an excruciating anticipation of the orders to advance. "The breathless anxiety of the moment gave way to angry maledictions on the supposed tardiness of the signal gun, muttered between teeth set for desperate deeds," recorded a Pennsylvanian. A member of the 121st New York admitted, "I would rather charge than lie here in this suspense and misery." The eerie quiet of the pre-dawn darkness was broken only by residual artillery fire ringing from the Ninth Corps front, several miles to the east.[1]

Shortly before 4:00 a.m., General Wright and members of his staff rode forward to the picket line. By flickering match light, the officers checked their watches. Wright decided that the unusual darkness of the morning required that he postpone the assault until visibility improved. He waited nearly an hour, until 4:40 a.m., when "it had become light enough for the men to see to step, though nothing was discernible beyond a few yards distance." Knowing that the dim illumination would aid his attackers in the upcoming struggle, protecting them from unobstructed Southern marksmanship, the Sixth Corps commander could defer the operation no longer. This was the assault, after more than nine grueling months of campaigning around Petersburg, that promised to drive a permanent wedge into the heart of Robert E. Lee's defenses around the Cockade City and its lifeline to Richmond. Such an outcome would leave both Petersburg and the Confederate capital untenable, and as a consequence flush the Army of Northern Virginia into the open, where superior Federal numbers and resources might bring about the very end of the war. The possibilities must be tested, and the time for the trial had arrived.[2]

Captain Romeo H. Start of the 3rd Vermont Battery, stationed in Fort Fisher, received the fateful directive. His signal gun would launch 14,000 troops toward the Rebel embankments a few hundred yards distant in the misty darkness—fortifications one Federal soldier called "the strongest line of works ever constructed in America." Moments later, a now-anonymous Vermonter pulled the lanyard on his gun, and a solitary boom echoed across the clammy gloom that cloaked the waiting armies. Some Yankees heard an answering blast from the direction of the Ninth Corps, indicating acknowledgment of the attack signal. Most of Wright's subordinates grasped the meaning of Start's artillery shot, although some officers in the Vermont Brigade did not immediately comprehend its significance. The sporadic cannonading that had disturbed absolute silence along the Union line robbed Start's signal gun of its uniqueness. Quickly, however, acting brigade commander Lieutenant Colonel Tracy discerned that the time had at last arrived for his Green Mountain men to forge ahead. "It was a great relief, a positive lifting of a load of misery to be at last 'let at them,'" wrote one Federal.[3]

> The troops slowly climbed to their feet, helped by "many a prod with boot or sword, and many a smothered oath and order."

Word circulated through the ranks to rise up and go forward. The troops slowly climbed to their feet, helped by "many a prod with boot or sword, and many a smothered oath and order." The men shook off the malaise of hours spent on the raw, wet earth and confronted their natural reluctance to undertake a frontal attack. Officers continued to enforce the silence that had characterized the operation since midnight, intent on preserving the element of surprise until the last possible moment. Almost noiselessly, the soldiers crossed their entrenched picket line. The Union sentries advanced with them to occupy the Confederate rifle pits after the initial rush. Hazard Stevens remembered that "at a hundred yards' distance nothing could be seen, nothing could be heard, to show that 14,000 troops in one solid wedge were swiftly moving to the assault of those formidable works determined to break them, save the sound of a deep distant rustling, like a strong breeze blowing through the swaying boughs and dense foliage of some great forest."[4]

The attackers covered about two-thirds of the distance between the picket lines, less than 200 yards, when, according to a Vermonter, "the enemy's pickets, conscious of some power advancing upon them like a mighty ocean wave, with unbroken crest, delivered their fire and ran to cover in disorder." This "weak and scattering volley" obviated the need for maintaining silence. "A cheer, that had been heard on nearly every battle-field in Virginia, went up from 10,000 brave hearts, and told the story to friend and foe that the Sixth Corps was on a charge and pushing for the main works of the enemy," wrote Captain Merritt Barber of the Vermont Brigade. Colonel Stevens described the Union battle cry as "one full, deep, mighty cheer," that expressed "defiance, force, fury, determination, and unbounded confidence. . . . It swept away all lingering fears and doubts from every manly breast like mists before the whirlwind."[5]

The six regiments of Tracy's Vermont Brigade, some 2,200 officers and men, set the initial pace for the entire assault. As the 5th Vermont at the head of the column burst through the overmatched Confederate picket line, scooping up a number of prisoners in the process, the 2nd Vermont trailed at a distance of about 100 yards. The regimental commanders attempted to regulate a disciplined interval between their units, but circumstances soon conspired against the realization of any tactical symmetry.[6]

Maintaining command and control in the nearly pitch darkness proved impossible. The field and staff officers in the Vermont Brigade, like most of their comrades in the rest of the corps, entered the battlefield on foot. This limited mobility, when combined with the dim, pre-dawn light, made it difficult to see beyond the limits of a single company.[7]

Although the resistance offered by the Confederate picket line did little to slow the Vermonters' rush, it did serve notice to General Lane's North Carolinians and their artillery supports near the ravine that an attack had commenced. Tracy's leading regiments had not yet reached the first line of abatis when a sharp small arms fire began to pour down upon them in the naked field. "It was as dark as a black cat," wrote Captain Walter Smith of the 4th Vermont, and according to General Getty, the Confederate riflery "was now spitting along the whole line." Almost instantly, the Rebel cannons added their iron to the metallic rain confronting the New Englanders. Most of the Southern shells initially exploded beyond the charging troops, but the Confederate gunners soon found the range. "A well-directed musketry fire from the front and artillery fire from the forts on either hand . . . completely enfiladed the line," reported staff officer Barber, and as a result, the brave Vermont Brigade began to falter.[8]

Lieutenant Charles H. Anson of the 1st Vermont Heavy Artillery recognized that a crisis point in the offensive had arrived:

> Thick and fast came the cannon shot, thicker and faster came the bullets, when for a moment, perhaps two, possibly ten, the charging column wavered, seemed to hesitate, the cannons' flashes lit up the terrible scene, revealing the struggling mass as it swayed to the right and left, recovering from the first great shock of battle. Were they, of whom so much was expected, to fail?

Captain Barber agreed that the next few minutes would determine the outcome of the fight:

> This was the most critical moment throughout the entire engagement. Day was just beginning to dawn and very soon the enemy would be able to discover our precise position and movements. They had become apprised of the point of attack and were apparently beginning to appreciate its importance, and were hastening to meet it with all the strength at their disposal.

Officers struggled manfully to overcome what General Getty charitably described as "considerable confusion" among the Vermonters. A member of the 4th Vermont wrote that "half of the men broke for the rear," and Hazard Stevens affirmed that many of the troops halted and "a large number did not advance much beyond the picket pits."[9]

Captain Darius J. Safford of the 1st Vermont Heavy Artillery took what was, for him, unprecedented action in an attempt to rally the demoralized members of his command:

> I never saw anything that culminated in such grand and overwhelming success that came as near being a failure as that charge[.] the men dreaded it from the fact that it was night and they could not see where they were going very distinctly and also because they thought the works were very much stronger than they proved to be and expected to find a good line of battle in them. . . . they were cold and chilled from over four hours lying in the cold on the wet ground and . . . many of them refused to advance further than the rebel picket line. I never had to strike men with my saber before to make them advance but that day I did[,] a great many of them and then in earnest too as hard as I could with the flat of my sword[.][10]

It is impossible to determine with any precision how long the Vermont Brigade hesitated in the field between the captured Confederate rifle pits and the multiple lines of abatis. Certainly with each passing moment the incoming fire became increasingly fierce. Common sense and the instinct for survival suggested that of all the options available, remaining stationary in the middle of the shelterless field was the worst. While some of Tracy's men fell back, most mustered their courage and plunged ahead, according to Barber, "with a determination that knew no such word as fail." The Vermonters reached the rows of obstructions, dealing with these obstacles in a much more ad hoc manner than Wright's battle plan envisioned. Barber claimed that the leading regiments "brushed away [the abatis] like cobwebs," but other witnesses reported differently. "With a cheer we went on getting through the abatis the best way we could," admitted Robert Pratt of the 5th Vermont. Lewis A. Grant, writing from the accounts of others, stated that the left of the attack formation "became somewhat entangled in the stumps" while the rightmost troops found the opening in the abatis associated with the ravine.[11]

While crossing the ground in front of the obstructions, the Vermont Brigade suffered a large percentage of its total casualties. Lieutenant George O. French of the 1st Vermont Heavy Artillery fell instantly killed while urging his troops forward. A shell fragment struck Captain Erastus G. Ballou of the 2nd Vermont, inflicting a dangerous wound. Lieutenant Gardner C. Hawkins of the 3rd Vermont entered the battle as acting adjutant of the 4th Vermont and found himself near the lines of abatis while the men under his command endured some of the most severe fire of the attack. Noticing the troops around him beginning to waver, Hawkins sprang forward and dramatically brandished his sword, urging his soldiers to maintain their momentum and continue the charge. "The effect upon the regiment if not upon other regiments of the brigade was very pointed and decisive," testified one Vermonter. Shortly after rallying his men, Hawkins received a hideous wound to the face, the ball entering the right side of his nose, passing into his head, out through his left eye, and finally carving a gouge down his left cheek and ear. Despite his injury, Hawkins refused to leave the battlefield until he was assured that his comrades had completed their advance.[12]

With the obstructions passed and forward motion again on their side, the Vermonters rushed ahead with Sergeant Thomas H. McCauley of the 2nd Vermont at the point of the column bearing the brigade flag. That formation enjoyed much less organization than it had displayed just minutes earlier. The passage of the picket posts and abatis shattered regimental alignments, and the attack became more a matter of inexorable momentum than of textbook tactics. After a brief struggle along the parapet, many of the defenders (probably from the 18th North Carolina and 37th North Carolina) surrendered, some even resignedly encouraging their captors, indicating a desire that the bloodshed be ended. Major Jackson L. Bost of the 37th North Carolina managed to lead a group of his men out of the maelstrom. "I was driven from the works, the line on the right and left of me in the regt. was broken and the enemy were filing down in the rear of our works towards Petersburg," remembered Bost. "I had to

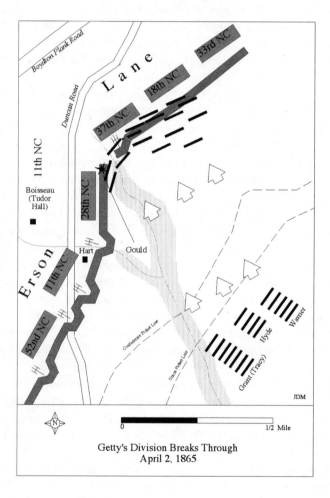

Getty's Division Breaks Through
April 2, 1865

fall back directly to the rear and formed a skirmish line as best I could to keep the enemy from advancing too fast in our rear, in order to give our wagons time to get out." The Federals found the situation very much to their liking. "[Our] men were perfectly beside themselves," remembered Stevens.[13]

The Vermonters claimed six Confederate guns as trophies of war. Four cannons positioned northeast of the ravine fell to the New Englanders along with two guns stationed southwest of the defile. It is difficult to gauge the resistance offered by the Rebel gunners on the attackers' right once the Vermonters had reached the redans. However, there can be no question that the cannoneers manning the artillery pieces southwest of the ravine and their infantry comrades refused to surrender quietly, as proven by the experience of Captain Charles G. Gould of Company H, 5th Vermont.[14]

Gould had grown up in Windham, Vermont, and from a very early age found himself drawn toward danger. When but two years old, Gould lost his balance while investigating the tempting aroma wafting from a pot of boiling applesauce fresh from the fire in his grandparents' home. The child tumbled into the searing liquid, suffering such horrific burns that he could not walk for four years. When the lad recovered, he developed a reputation around Windham as a daredevil, so it came as no surprise that at age 18 he enlisted in the army against his parents' wishes. Gould proved to be an excellent soldier and rose through the ranks to become a company commander in the 5th Vermont.[15]

On the morning of April 2, Gould and his command found themselves next to the leftmost company in the regimental alignment, the 5th Vermont, of course, occupying the very front rank of the attack formation. As the unit moved forward, Gould heard shouted orders from somewhere in the rear instructing the Vermonters to "bear to the left," prompting him to direct his company through the ravine to his left and up the opposite bank. The directive had, in fact, been aimed at the Vermont Brigade as a whole, which had generally obliqued to the right, away from the ravine, to avoid the severe fire being hurled at them from a strong point along the Confederate line. Gould's misapprehension of this intent, however, brought him and his men into a situation significantly more perilous than his grandparents' applesauce kettle.

Gould called a halt in the near darkness opposite a Confederate artillery position. The captain shouted for all the officers with him to identify themselves, and only Lieutenant Pratt responded. First sergeants Edward Brownlee and James Grace and some 50 other men had veered across the ravine with Gould. The 20-year-old New Englander realized that his small contingent stood between the Confederate line and the

Captain Charles G. Gould
5th Vermont

Courtesy of
Jack Mandaville

onrushing troops of Truman Seymour's division who, advancing in echelon on the Vermonters' left and rear, would soon be upon them. These bluecoats would, in the pre-dawn gloom, likely be unable to distinguish their allies from the Confederates whose fire made remaining motionless doubly impractical. Gould also believed that a body of the enemy now occupied the ground between his tiny vanguard and the rest of the brigade. This left him little option but to press ahead and try to subdue the guns that, at the moment, made life so tenuous for him and his men. Some veteran exclaimed "capture that battery," and in an instant the little knot of Vermonters dashed for the Confederate works.

Gould discovered a weak point in the abatis and, accompanied by Sergeant Brownlee and a few others, scrambled across the obstructions and toward the ditch and embankment of the Confederate fortifications. Most of Gould's party, however, opted to use a narrow opening in the abatis and thus fell behind their captain's pace. By now, Gould had lost direct contact with the rest of his men and focused entirely on covering the blazing real estate between himself and the enemy cannons. Maintaining the lead, with Sergeant Jackson Sargent of Company D following close behind carrying the regiment's state colors, Gould "jumped into the ditch and climbed the parapet" into the teeth of the Confederate battery.

As Gould appeared on the inside of the works, a leveled musket greeted him at point blank range. Fortunately for the Yankee captain, the gun misfired, but in the next moment a second Confederate guided his bayonet through Gould's mouth, the blade passing under his lip and emerging at the lower part of the jaw near his neck. Gould responded by thrusting his sabre through his attacker, killing the unfortunate Tarheel on the spot. Before his assailant fell, Gould felt the wrath of a third Southerner who slashed him with a sword, inflicting a nasty head wound. The close quarters fighting, too confused to allow the numerically superior Confederates to utilize their guns for fear of shooting their own men in the murky light, claimed Sergeant Brownlee and Corporal Charles A. Ford of the 5th Vermont, who had also managed to gain the ramparts.

Gould's own travails had not yet ended. Someone grabbed him by the overcoat and partially ripped off the garment, allowing another bayonet to plunge through his uniform coat and come to rest near a vertebrae in his upper back. "This was the most severe wound of the three," recalled Gould, "the bayonet entering the spine and penetrating it nearly to the spinal cord." The thrice-wounded captain now thought only of escape. He attempted to crawl over the parapet and into the relative protection of the moat. Too weak to accomplish his objective, Gould lay on the ground until Corporal Henry H. Recor of Company A appeared. Recor quickly recognized Gould's desperate situation and pulled the captain over the works and into the ditch, receiving a wound in the process of completing his life-saving rescue.

Amazingly, Gould maintained consciousness and sufficient strength to stagger rearward, where he encountered a line of Federal troops. He explained what had transpired and urged the reinforcements to charge the battery and recapture the flag that he assumed had been lost. He also, understandably, requested of a member of the brigade staff that someone be detailed to assist him to a safe place where he could receive medical attention.[16]

As it turned out, the fresh Union forces would have no Vermont flag to reclaim. Lieutenant Pratt, assuming Gould to be killed, had formed the remainder of their errant party in the moat and scrambled to and over the top of the works. Pratt's contingent captured the position and with it two guns and a number of prisoners, including a gray cannoneer whom Pratt slashed with his sabre a moment before the gunner could pull the lanyard on his loaded piece. By this time, Surgeon Samuel J. Allen of the 4th Vermont, medical director of Getty's division who had remained behind during the attack, could see from his vantage point at Fort Welch a widening dark line along the Confederate works representing the spreading Union domination of the enemy's position. The rest of the Vermont Brigade had scaled the works to the right of the ravine as intended, Colonel Tracy earning plaudits for his leadership. To the Vermonters' right, Hyde's brigade contributed to the expanding Federal victory by targeting the works in their front defended by the 18th North Carolina and 33rd North Carolina.[17]

Hyde shared with the Vermonters the brief confusion surrounding the firing of the signal gun. Soon enough, however, his 1,800 men in six regiments lurched ahead, responding to the brigade commander's muted orders of "Attention! Forward! Charge!" Hyde's four lines of battle managed to maintain intervals ranging from 100 to 250 yards during the advance. The leading units, the 49th New York and 77th New York, overran the Confederate picket posts in their front before the 43rd New York and 122nd New York in the rear line had even left their jump-off positions.[18]

"The charge was made in pitch darkness & is remarkable for that," thought Hyde as his regiments approached the edge of the formidable abatis. "The shot and shell from the enemy's forts were like so many rockets fired horizontally, and they were mostly a few feet over our head." Like the Vermonters, Hyde's units halted in the open field for a short time, attempting to reform in the inky chaos. The New Yorkers, Pennsylvanians, and Mainers became "bewildered in the darkness" and lost their formation, some drifting off toward the right, repeating the unintended movement that had occasioned Gould's shift across the ravine. As a result, comparatively few of Hyde's troops actually proceeded through the gaps in the abatis toward the Confederate line.[19]

Cowardice more than confusion robbed the 61st Pennsylvania of three-fifths of its strength during the attack. Of the 500 men aligned for the advance, some 300 were draftees, substitutes, or bounty men. "As we started the charge [these soldiers] disappeared and we never heard of them afterwards," remembered a bitter Thomas Hyde. "The 300 should all have been shot or hung." The balance of the 61st Pennsylvania, veterans all, acquitted themselves proudly in spite of the behavior of their reluctant comrades, and several performed acts of particular gallantry.[20]

Major Robert L. Orr had assumed field command of the regiment following the mortal wounding of Colonel John W. Crosby during the picket firing earlier in the morning. Orr coveted for his regiment the distinction of raising the first Union colors on the Confederate works and took steps to ensure that such an honor would be theirs. Both of Orr's color sergeants, John C. Mathews of Pittsburgh and Joseph Fisher of Philadelphia, understood their commander's ambition and prepared their banners for triumphant display by unfurling them from their covers prior to the charge. Orr instructed the color bearers to "dash forward at the word of command, plant the flags on the enemy's works in our front and 'keep them there.'"[21]

Once Hyde's attackers breached the abatis, with the aid of the two leading New York regiments who helped dismantle the woody obstructions, the 61st Pennsylvania along with the 1st Maine Veterans moved forward into the moat, resting for a moment to catch their breath before attempting the final lunge. Sergeant Fisher had preceded his regiment by some 50 yards during this advance, proudly waving his unit colors until a Confederate shot laid him low. Undaunted, the wounded Fisher attempted to crawl into the Confederate works to plant his flag but fainted before he could achieve his goal. Mathews seized the banner from Fisher's hands and, despite sustaining a bullet wound in the shoulder, raised the flag aloft and carried it into the Confederate line. Major Orr also grabbed one of the unit's colors and bore it forward. By this time, the members of Hyde's brigade who had continued the attack leapt "over the works like so many cats, [exchanging] bayonet thrusts" with their grayclad opponents. According to one account, the Confederates "were brushed away with an emphasis that precluded all ideas of an attempt to reform in any reasonable time to be made of use in barring our progress." Sergeant Augustus E. Floyd of the 18th North Carolina stated merely that "our line of battle was so thin the Yankees broke our lines." Some of the Tarheels surrendered while others fled to the rear. "After we got in[,] made them run in fine style," recorded a soldier in the 1st Maine Veterans.[22]

The third of Getty's brigades, James Warner's, began the attack on the right and slightly to the rear of Hyde's troops. In some respects, the experience of Warner's men mirrored that of their comrades in Tracy's and Hyde's brigades. Warner understood the signal to advance and, like the other brigade commanders, ordered his successive battle lines forward with 100 yard intervals separating the five waves. Warner's Pennsylvanians reached the Confederate rifle pits before they were discovered and easily overwhelmed the stunned Southern pickets. At this point, however, Warner's situation began to deteriorate. "The intervening space to their main works, owing to the darkness, the uneven and swampy character of the ground, and the artillery fire, was passed over in great confusion," Warner later admitted. The 102nd Pennsylvania in the vanguard of the brigade appeared disoriented, although they had not been physically repulsed by Southern fire. The 139th Pennsylvania, the unit following the 102nd Pennsylvania, quickly closed the gap between the two lines of battle. Major James McGregor feared that if his command waited until its sister regiment recovered its momentum, the entire column would be thrown into chaos while subjected to an unendurable torrent of lead and iron. By this time, artillery and infantry fire had already rendered the situation extremely perilous, so McGregor ordered his color sergeants forward, over the rifle pits, past the 102nd Pennsylvania, and up to the first line of abatis.[23]

McGregor's men happily discovered that the obstructions presented much less of a problem than they had anticipated. They drove through the tangle of sharpened timber, joined in the attack by members of the 102nd Pennsylvania and 93rd Pennsylvania. Sergeant Charles Marquette of the 93rd Pennsylvania, however, impaled himself on the point of one of the obstructions, causing a painful wound. Warner's leading regiments also suffered from Confederate bullets and shell, and from the darkness, which disoriented many attackers.

Major James A. Weston of the 33rd North Carolina, one of the Confederate outfits directly in Warner's path and the leftmost regiment in James Lane's formation, described his unit's position as "a mere skirmish line. . . . We fought desperately, but our thin line was pushed back by sheer force of numbers until it was broken in pieces. We then retreated behind our winter quarters and continued the contest, each man for himself." Major McGregor recalled the battle differently:

> Those of the regiment who had not been lost in the confusion, soon gained the enemy's main works, behind which were discovered many rebels, who appeared only too glad of the opportunity of going to our lines. I may here state that there was scarcely a shot fired by the enemy after the regiment had reached the abatis. A short halt was made on the enemy's works for the purpose of permitting the prisoners to pass over the works. . . .[24]

Colonel Warner entered the battle on horseback, one of the first mounted officers inside the fortifications. His brigade's relatively easy capture of their portion of the Confederate line may be ascribed in part to weakened Southern resistance caused by Tracy's and Hyde's slightly earlier conquests. In any event, Getty's division had swept aside half of Lane's Brigade as the first rays of light began to penetrate the Sunday morning gloom. To Getty's right, however, the warriors of Wheaton's First Division were writing their own version of the Breakthrough in blood.[25]

*   *   *

General Wheaton had specified that the advance of his three brigades would be conducted via the tactical maneuver of "guide left." Each of Wheaton's units would move toward the Confederate lines "as soon as the troops on [their] left had gained the prescribed distance of 100 paces between brigade lines." Although Wheaton reported that his division moved forward "upon a signal gun from Fort Fisher," other First Division witnesses contended that the attack did not commence until a second signal gun sounded, "for the first was not understood by our division commander." Oliver Edwards's Third Brigade, positioned on the division's left flank, no doubt became aware of Getty's advance to their immediate left, in addition to responding to the signal shots, and promptly "the word was passed along the line,'rise up!' and then 'forward!'"[26]

Edwards placed Colonel Tom Allen of the 5th Wisconsin in charge of his front line, which also included Edwards's old regiment, the 37th Massachusetts. "The rebs must have heard [the order to attack] for we were not yet over our own works when they commenced firing," wrote Private Clark F. Barnes of the 5th Wisconsin. "They seemed to be expecting company, and were all ready to receive us." The Badgers and Bay Staters had been preceded by what Edwards called his "forlorn hope," the contingent of Spencer-firing sharpshooters supporting a small group of axemen charged with dismantling the abatis protecting the Confederate works. Captain John Robinson, the commander of the marksmen, received a wound in the right arm near the shoulder while discharging this duty, but most of this Rebel fire was high. The barriers, however, proved to be even more troublesome than Wheaton expected. "All were astonished to find these obstructions such serious obstacles and so difficult to remove," admitted the Rhode Islander. The abatis at this particular location "was not only firmly secured by earth thrown over the trunks, but was strengthened by a double row of sharpened stakes firmly fixed in the ground." A soldier in the 5th Wisconsin remembered coming "near being impaled on those gut-punchers." But despite these problems, the advanced parties did their jobs. The ability of the Spencers to suppress enemy fire while the pioneers accomplished their mission especially impressed Colonel Edwards. "I consider a skirmish line armed with them fully equal to a line of battle armed with the Springfield," boasted the brigade commander.[27]

With some openings created in the obstructions, the time had come for Allen's line to forge ahead. "All along our front officers and men pushed through," recalled Wheaton. Not every participant, however, began the charge with confidence. Private Barnes confessed to experiencing more than a little trepidation when the orders reached him to advance:

> When I started on that charge I was not feeling very well; there was something the matter with my throat. I thought my heart would jump clear out of my mouth. The boys were yelling and charging all around me. I think I went more than half way across before I yelled and then I felt so much better that I was sorry I had not yelled when I started. I was much surprised at the great change in my feelings. After that whoop I think I could have tackled the whole so-called Southern Confederacy.

A red-headed member of Company E, 5th Wisconsin announced that the action promised to be too hot for him, and he calmly headed for the rear. Despite a menacing fire of canister and musketry, however, a hard core of Edwards's first line forced its way through the abatis and reached the ditch protecting a Confederate strongpoint.[28]

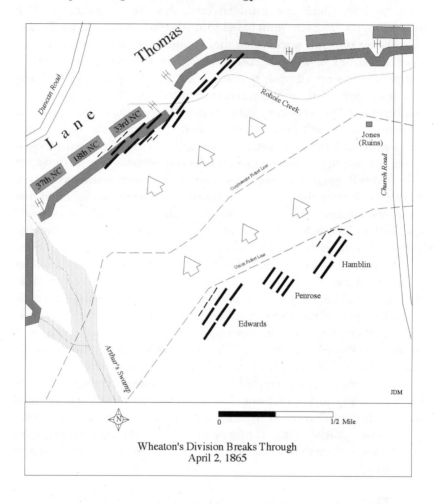

Wheaton's Division Breaks Through
April 2, 1865

The moat shielded a three-gun battery, and the depression soon filled with charging Federals faced with the daunting task of scaling the walls and subduing the artillerists and their infantry supports, men probably belonging to Lane's leftmost regiments, the 18th North Carolina and 33rd North Carolina. "I saw a comrade reach up and catch hold of a root," remembered Private Barnes. "I boosted him, and up he went. I then caught the same root, and some one helped me." Other members of the 5th Wisconsin tumbled into the Confederate lines as the Southern cannons roared defiantly in the brightening gloom.

To the Badgers' right, Company E, 37th Massachusetts led the scramble up the slope and onto the parapet. Corporal Richard E. Welch and Private Ansel R. Cook set the pace for their regiment, Welch accosting a Tarheel color bearer and seizing his flag. Lieutenant William A. Waterman of the 37th Massachusetts received a painful wound in the wrist during this brief hand-to-hand combat, while Private Michael Kelly and Corporal Luther M. Tanner were killed by the stubborn Confederates. Corporal Patrick Kelly, Michael's brother, bayoneted one of the North Carolina defenders as a wave of blue surged over the parapet and overwhelmed the outnumbered Southerners. In the 5th Wisconsin's sector, now virtually indistinguishable from the ground contested by the 37th Massachusetts, Sergeant Yates Lacy "did a little artistic bayonet work" of his own, and "the Johnny that he interviewed passed on to the sweet subsequently." After a fight that Captain Archibald Hopkins of the 37th Massachusetts termed "brief but sharp," Edwards's brigade found itself in command of three Confederate guns, about 40 prisoners, and Welch's banner. "It was a hard fought battle but it brought brilliant success, though with a terrible cost," wrote Private Edward P. Bridgman of the 37th Massachusetts.[29]

Edwards's second line of battle, consisting of the 2nd Rhode Island, 49th Pennsylvania, and 119th Pennsylvania, encountered less difficulty with the initial Confederate defenses than had Allen's contingent. Lieutenant Colonel Gideon Clark of the 119th Pennsylvania had overall command of the second line and easily guided his men over the Confederate picket posts. "The Rebels in the rifle pits threw down their guns and surrendered," remembered Elisha Hunt Rhodes. "They shouted 'Don't fire, Yanks!' and I ordered them to go to the rear, which they did on the run." Rhodes quickly reformed his regiment along the captured Confederate picket line, when an enthusiastic corporal shouted "Three cheers for Colonel Rhodes!" The men responded in full voice, but the noise attracted the attention of Confederate artillery: Rhodes counted four guns in a redoubt on his left and two more from a position to the right. The young colonel, like so many other sensible Union officers that morning, recognized that the open field was no place to linger. "Forward!" commanded Rhodes, and his men struck out for the ground between the artillery positions.[30]

Rhodes and his men reached the gaps in the abatis and made for the relative shelter of the moat. "The first I knew I fell into the ditch with a number of my men after me," Rhodes recalled. "The Rebels fired their cannon and muskets over our heads, and then we crawled up the slope and onto the parapet of their works, stepping right among their muskets as they were aimed over the work. It was done so quick that the Rebels had no chance to fire again but dropped their guns and ran." Rhodes had instructed his men to advance with uncapped muskets, so everything they had achieved thus far had transpired without discharging a shot. Now, the colonel shouted for his men to prime and fire, and instantly a Yankee volley rattled through the winter quarters abandoned days earlier by Samuel McGowan's men and temporarily occupied by Lane's North Carolinians.

Lieutenant Frank S. Halliday led a small party which seized two of the offending Rebel cannons and turned the guns around to supplement the rifle fire pouring into the fleeing Confederates. Some of the overwhelmed Southerners rallied in an attempt to reclaim their artillery. Corporal William Railton of the 2nd Rhode Island took control of one of the captured guns, which he had loaded to the muzzle with stones and scrap iron. Halliday suggested that the small party of Rhode Islanders abandon their prize in light of the determined Confederate counterattack closing upon them, but Railton replied, "If they come here I'll make them smell . . . brimstone." When the Confederates reached a distance of just 30 feet, Railton pulled the lanyard. The gun burst into fragments from the huge and irregular load, but the shot achieved its desired effect. "Such destruction of life I never saw, before or since," shuddered Halliday as the Rebel counterattack melted in a crimson burst.[31]

With his immediate objective achieved, Edwards sought to expand his grip on the compromised Confederate defenses: "I ordered Gen. Allen to change the front forward to the left with the first line and charge down the left inside the works, this line came out in front of Hyde's brigade 2nd Div., and met Col. Hyde as he came over the works." One of the Badgers more humbly described this movement as an order "to send a few shots to our left, just to help start the Johnnies down there, which we did." Not surprisingly, neither the outspoken Hyde nor Colonel Warner acknowledged that the First Division had helped them during the Breakthrough. Probably the arrival of the 5th Wisconsin and 37th

Colonel William H. Penrose

Massachusetts MOLLUS Collection, Carlisle Barracks, Pennsylvania

Massachusetts on the Second Division front fell well short of being tactically decisive.[32]

Edwards also instructed Colonel Clark to change his course to the right and sweep down the inside of the Confederate fortifications toward the northeast. In the process of executing this maneuver, Clark suffered a severe wound that would cost him his leg. Rhodes, who had begun a movement toward Boydton Plank Road, supported by the 82nd Pennsylvania, now reversed direction back toward the captured earthworks and then northeast, leading elements of his own regiment and Clark's command. The grayclad defenders in this sector contested the advance of Wheaton's First and Second brigades "vigorously," according to Clark's successor. Nevertheless, Rhodes's flank movement contributed to the fall of the works along the division's entire front, and when General Wheaton encountered Rhodes, he congratulated him "most heartily." In fact, a number of Edwards's men stopped to catch their breath and exchange handshakes, remembered Private Barnes, "for we knew that the end of the Confederacy was near."[33]

Edwards's support on the right came from the New Jersey Brigade. Colonel William Penrose was one of the few high-ranking Sixth Corps officers that morning to record difficulty in crossing the Confederate picket line, which in most places during the Breakthrough offered only token resistance. Penrose noted that his first two lines of battle, consisting of the shaky 40th New Jersey and the veteran 4th New Jersey, melded into one, "owing to the fact that the pickets which were to have advanced simultaneously with us did not, and the first line received the fire of the enemy's pickets, which was very severe." Eventually, the Southern sentries gave way, and Penrose's pioneers began chopping the strong abatis protecting the main Confederate line. By now all four New Jersey regiments had intermingled thanks to the delay in crossing the rifle pits and obstructions, and the darkness that shrouded Penrose's advance. In due course, openings in the abatis allowed the Garden Staters to renew their advance. The 40th New Jersey, true to its reputation, broke no fewer than three times, although according to one witness, "a portion did admirably." These stalwart men joined members from each of Penrose's other units in the ditch below the Confederate parapet.

Chaplain Alanson A. Haines of the 15th New Jersey credited the sharpshooters of the 37th Massachusetts with providing the vital covering fire that allowed Penrose's men to navigate the killing ground in front of the works. Nevertheless, the New Jersey Brigade drifted some 200 yards to the left of its intended targets and congregated below the works designated for capture by Edwards's brigade. As was the case in most places along the Breakthrough, Federal units overlapped and commingled so pervasively as to defy precise placement of regimental fronts.

Eventually, enough New Jerseyians accumulated in the moat to hazard the final assault. The men scrambled up the earthen slopes and into the Confederate lines. "The defenders of the fort showed the greatest obstinacy," admitted Haines, "some refusing to surrender, were shot down." Major Augustus Fay of the 40th New Jersey led this contingent into the midst of the defiant Carolinians, who greeted them with clubbed muskets and bayonets. Private William Cheatham of the 18th North Carolina represented the still-irrepressible spirit of Lane's men. Despite being overwhelmed as more and more New Jerseyians spilled into the

works, Cheatham refused to capitulate and paid for his determination with
a bayonet wound in his mid-section, delivered by a man from the 15th New
Jersey. The color-bearer of the 18th North Carolina zealously guarded his
banner, declining invitations to surrender his unit's emblem until Major
Fay wounded the hero and compelled him to drop the flag. Private Frank
Fesq of Company A, 40th New Jersey, captured the prize and would receive
the Medal of Honor for his efforts.

Captain Charles Paul of the 15th New Jersey, along with Captain James
Penrose of the brigade staff and a small body of men, advanced against two
rifled guns along the Confederate line. They managed to seize the cannons
and whirl them around, aiming at the now-retreating Confederates. The
officers loaded the pieces but could find no friction primers, so the
captured artillery remained mute. Two companies from the 37th
Massachusetts arrived and attempted to remove the guns as prizes of their
own, eliciting a bitter protest from the indignant New Jersey officers. When
Penrose's men eventually left their trophies to help sweep away
Confederate resistance to the northeast, the 37th Massachusetts succeeded
in taking the guns and, much to the irritation of Colonel Penrose, made
official claim of their capture. As the sun began to rise, the New Jersey
Brigade joined forces with elements of the 119th Pennsylvania and 2nd
Rhode Island to clear more of the works to their right, sending some 200
prisoners to the rear as tangible evidence of their success.[34]

Twenty paces to the right and rear of the New Jersey Brigade, Joseph
Hamblin awaited the signal gun from Fort Fisher that would launch the
four regiments of Wheaton's Second Brigade toward the Confederate
works. Hamblin's troops occupied the far right of the Sixth Corps
formation, opposite Thomas's Georgia Brigade. More ground separated
his Connecticut, New York, and Pennsylvania soldiers from the Southern
fortifications than anywhere else along Wright's front. Once the signal
sounded, the 2nd Connecticut Heavy Artillery and the 65th New York,
Hamblin's front line, dashed for the Rebel picket posts. The butternut
sentries "fired only one volley before we came onto them and took them
prisoners," reported a Connecticut lieutenant, "sending them back under
a very light escort as the idea was to keep all the men possible in that charge
on the morning of April 2."[35]

Captain James T. Stuart of the 49th Pennsylvania provided covering
fire with a line of his men armed with Spencers, much in the fashion of the
service rendered to Edwards's brigade by the 37th Massachusetts. With the
repeaters blazing away in support, Hamblin's front line of battle hastened
toward the particularly powerful obstructions that confronted the right
end of the Sixth Corps formation. The Yankees raced up a gentle slope,

attracting a mighty Georgia volley that "showed up in the partial darkness like a solid line of the most brilliant fireworks that I ever saw," remembered one New Englander. Fortunately for the Federals, darkness diminished the Southern marksmanship, most of the barrage passing over the attackers' heads.

The first line of barriers "was made of large round poles bored through with two inch holes and sticks drove through them and sharpened very sharp making one continuous bristling saw horse at least 4 1/2 feet high," recalled Lieutenant David Soule of the 2nd Connecticut Heavy Artillery. "These sections were chained together with short strong chains that had bolts at each end of the sections well fastened with nuts." The pioneers hacked away at these obstructions, a classic line of chevaux de frise, while the Federals maintained a steady fire in an attempt to lessen the deadly fusillade pouring down on them from the Confederate works. Eventually, the Yankees managed to split some of the sections in two, allowing the Connecticut and New York troops to tumble through. A second line of obstructions, this time an abatis, slowed the assault once again, allowing the Confederates to shoot more of their approaching enemies, including Lieutenant Colonel Jeffrey Skinner of the 2nd Connecticut Heavy Artillery, who fell wounded from a shell fragment that struck the right side of his chest.[36]

Hamblin admitted that once his leading troops reached the Confederate lines they became confused. The Nutmeggers and their New York comrades jumped into the moat, which here contained some standing water from the recent rains. Sergeant Edward S. Roberts of the 2nd Connecticut Heavy Artillery remembered seeing what he thought were hand grenades tossed down upon the gathering Yankee riflemen, who drove their bayonets into the fortifications to offer their comrades makeshift footholds. As the Federals clambered up the slippery slopes, they could not know if they "would get our heads blowed off or what, but as we came on top we could see the enemy running across the fields," recorded a New Englander. The atmosphere was filled with "sulphurus smoke" as the first rays of morning light illuminated the dramatic scene.

Hamblin's troops did not see such vicious hand-to-hand combat as the rest of Wheaton's division. Although officers such as Captain David S. Redding of the 45th Georgia attempted to rally small numbers of men to resist the Union onslaught, many of the Confederates opposite Hamblin's brigade received flank fire from behind the Confederate works courtesy of Edwards's and Penrose's successful attackers. Thus, they had already taken flight or been shot by the time Hamblin's men reached the parapet. "There were some dead behind the works and some wounded, all of them in their heads or shoulders for their works had protected their bodies," testified Lieutenant Soule. Lewis Bissell reported that a large number of Confederates surrendered to the 2nd Connecticut Heavy Artillery, including "a few slave soldiers." The rest of "rebeldom 'took to the woods' in great haste," exulted Sergeant Roberts. The triumphant Federals moved toward the abandoned winter quarters and began to search the vacated huts for cowering Confederates and potential plunder.

One Connecticut soldier opened the door to a cabin only to be greeted by a musket round that grazed his cheek. The stunned Federal responded with a shot of his own, killing his Rebel assailant. Other Yankees seized the hundreds of small arms left behind by Thomas's men and began smashing them against trees or on the ground. When one Union soldier grasped a captured rifle by the muzzle and swung it against a rock, the impact launched a bullet that passed through the man's leg and into the chin of one of his comrades. "This quieted the boy's ardor," according to a witness.[37]

Hamblin's second line, consisting of the 121st New York and the 95th Pennsylvania, endured the same steady artillery and musketry fire as the rest of the brigade while crossing toward the obstructions. "Our mighty charging column . . . rush[ed] with a continuous cheer, which together with the rattle of musketry and whiz and roar of the enemy's shells as they burst or richochetted [sic] through our ranks was something to be long remembered by those who had a part in the splendid achievement," wrote a member of the 95th Pennsylvania. The ranks of both regiments became separated by swampy ground in their front, and the units split right and left, entering the Confederate works at different places.[38]

Once inside the fortifications, some of Hamblin's men, including a detachment of the 2nd Connecticut Heavy Artillery, headed north toward the South Side Railroad. Some members of the 121st New York swarmed through the Rebel camps, steering for Boydton Plank Road. The bulk of Hamblin's men, however, turned to their right and moved up the line toward Petersburg, covering a considerable distance. They encountered canister fire from two Napoleons manned by the Norfolk Light Artillery Blues that had been repositioned to enfilade the interior of the rapidly disintegrating Confederate line. "As soon as this was done, we opened with one[-] second fuse case shot," remembered a Virginia artillerist. "Just as we fired the first shot inside our lines, a colonel shouted out that we were firing into our own men, a few of whom were flying from the rapidly advancing enemy who by this time were not more than fifty yards from our guns."

The Federals ignored the deadly blasts from Captain Grandy's smoothbores and overran the intrepid gray cannoneers. Confederate artillery and prisoners, including more than 200 captives claimed by the 121st New York alone, fell to the advancing Yankees. Private Francis Sprowl of Company F, 65th New York, loaded and fired two of the captured guns at their former owners as the Confederates unceremoniously abandoned their weapons. These shots and others like them found their marks, prompting one witness to observe that, "some of the boys in other regiments of the brigade said they never saw artillery used with such terrible effect. The ground was found strewn with their dead and wounded."[39]

> "The work accomplished by the division on this day was the most difficult I had ever seen troops called upon to perform."

Among the Confederate casualties that morning was Sergeant–Major Marion Hill Fitzpatrick of the 45th Georgia. Fitzpatrick and twelve of his comrades were all that remained of Company K, joined in the trenches by support personnel such as butchers, medical attendants, and army clerks. Battery H, 1st Rhode Island Light Artillery, accompanied Wheaton in his pre-dawn assault, and it may have been a shell fragment from the Rhode Islanders that found its way into Fitzpatrick's right thigh, inches below his hip. Unlike so many of the less fortunate Georgians that morning, selfless comrades removed Fitzpatrick from the battlefield before Federals overran the lines.[40]

Those victorious bluecoats "were perfectly wild with delight at their success in this grand assault," wrote division commander Wheaton. The ebullient Rhode Islander felt such pride in his unit's accomplishment that he would recommend all three of his brigade commanders and each of his regimental leaders for promotion, along with two officers in Battery H, 1st Rhode Island Light Artillery, 26 officers in Penrose's brigade, 24 officers in Hamblin's brigade, and 27 officers in Edwards's brigade. Wheaton also singled out more than 60 enlisted men for their distinguished service during the Breakthrough. "The work accomplished by the division on this day was the most difficult I had ever seen troops called upon to perform," thought Wheaton. "Massing and advancing in the dark they successfully assaulted strongly intrenched and elaborately obstructed lines with a determination and gallantry that could never be excelled."[41]

Never excelled? Perhaps not, but the troops of Truman Seymour's Third Division on the Sixth Corps left would earn the right that morning to lay their own claims to glory in the decisive penetration of Lee's lines southwest of Petersburg.

*   *   *

Warren Keifer bore responsibility for supporting Tracy's Vermonters on the left of the wedge, immediately across the landmark ravine on which Wright focused his assault. The Ohio brigade commander targeted one of the various gaps in the Confederate line as the key point of his tactical plan. "A narrow opening, just wide enough for a wagon to pass through, was known to exist in the enemy's line in front of my brigade," wrote Keifer, "though it was skilfully covered by a shoulder around it. . . . I determined to take advantage of it." Keifer directed the 6th Maryland, in the center of his front line, to move through the breach in the Southern works, holding its fire until it had gained the fortifications. Once behind the enemy defenses, the Marylanders would "open on the Confederates behind the works, taking them in flank, and, if possible, drive them out and thus leave for our other troops little resistance in gaining an entrance over the ramparts."[42]

With a "gray light in the east being barely discernible," Keifer's five regiments responded to the Fort Fisher signal gun without hesitation. "All suspense here ended," said Keifer. "Simultaneously the command, 'forward,' was given by all our officers, and the storming column moved promptly; the advanced line, with bayonets fixed, guns not loaded, the other line with guns loaded to be ready to fire, if necessary, to protect those in advance while passing the trenches." As was true with the other brigades in Wright's assault, few of Keifer's officers were mounted. [43]

The Confederate pickets delivered a sharp fire against Keifer's surging blue wave, assisted by incoming artillery toward the Federals' left. The Buckeyes and Marylanders in Keifer's front ranks, however, overwhelmed the Southern sharpshooters with momentum, drive, and superior numbers in lieu of their unloaded rifles, and made directly for the abatis fronting the main Confederate works. The Yankees forced their way through the obstructions, but not without encountering the usual problems. In some places, the attackers called on detachments of pioneers to chop apart and throw aside the fallen timber while absorbing a punishing fire at close range. "While we were doing this seven of our Pioneer comrades were killed in that one place," wrote Private Lorenzo Barnhart of the 110th Ohio. "It was dark but we were so close to there [sic] works that they could shoot us like rabbits."

Soon enough, the abatis yielded to Union axe blades, and with "enthusiastic cheers" Keifer's leading regiments dashed toward the

Confederate works, defended here by the 28th North Carolina. Captain William Shellenberger, temporarily directing the 110th Ohio on the right of Keifer's front line, fell with a wound in his left arm during this stage of the attack. Lane's accurate musketry and the relentless Southern artillery found dozens of other blue-jacketed marks, including Captain Elem Harter of the 110th Ohio who sustained a serious wound.[44]

The bluecoats utilized some of the material from the broken abatis to bridge the moat, again thrusting bayonets into the sides of the fortifications for steps. Other troops scrambled onto the shoulders of their comrades making human ladders of them to gain the parapet of Lane's bastion. In the meantime, Major Clifton Kennedy Prentiss, at the head of a contingent from the 6th Maryland, located the narrow opening identified by Keifer. Gaining the Confederate line, the Marylanders opened a flanking fire driving some of the surprised Tarheels to retreat. Other defenders greeted the Federals with clubbed muskets and riflery. "We had quite a lively time with the enemy when we entered [the works]," remembered a soldier in the 6th Maryland, "although I do not think it lasted more than five minutes."[45]

By then, Keifer's second and third-line units had also arrived to add their weight to the increasingly uneven contest. The 67th Pennsylvania struggled to get over reluctant members of the preceding regiments who had lain down behind the Confederate picket line to avoid incoming fire, but eventually the Pennsylvanians muscled their way toward the breastworks. The 9th New York Heavy Artillery obliqued to the left in front of Colonel Truex's brigade and captured four cannons, which they turned on the now-fleeing Confederates. Keifer captured the entire complement of Rebel artillery in his front, as many as six additional guns. Captain Grandy, in command of a section of rifled pieces from the Norfolk Light Artillery Blues, escaped Keifer's attackers, although the Yankees commandeered both of his guns and virtually all of his cannoneers.[46]

General Lane's assistant adjutant general, Major Edward Joseph Hale, remembered seeing some men mounting the works near where the right of Lane's Brigade connected with the two regiments from MacRae's Brigade to the southwest:

> I remarked to some one 'why there are the skirmishers, driven in,' & called out to know how near behind the enemy were. Just at the moment I observed a stand of colors in the work[s] & the person in command order his followers to fire. This was just before, or just at, dawn, and it was impossible to distinguish anything more than the color aforesaid (though not the color of the color) & the outlines of men against the sky.

Brigadier General
William MacRae

Miller,
Photographic History

Hale claimed that the astonished Tarheels "fought these people & all the hordes that passed over, step by step," but Keifer's penetration outflanked the 28th North Carolina on Lane's far right and forced it to fall back toward the Plank Road. Sergeant Hugh Torrence of Company B, 28th North Carolina, suffered a horrible wound about this time, a minie ball striking him in the right eye and exiting out the left eye. "I was officially reported killed," testified Torrence, but he survived his injury, being captured by the Sixth Corps as it swept beyond the Confederate works. Many of the members of Lane's Brigade who had not yet been shot or made prisoner withdrew to McGowan's abandoned winter quarters and fought among the huts. One of the North Carolinians emerged from a tent and killed Captain Henry H. Stevens of the 110th Ohio. Quickly recognizing his hopeless situation, the Confederate offered to surrender, but it is likely that Stevens's enraged comrades exacted instant vengeance on the unfortunate Rebel.[47]

As was true along the entire breadth of Wright's assault, the combat across the earthworks in Keifer's sector was brief but vicious, fought at close quarters with rifle, bayonet, and clubbed musket. Sergeant George F. Russer of Company B, 110th Ohio, lost his right arm as a result of hand-to-hand combat inside the Confederate works. Sergeant Richard Pierson of Company G of the same regiment led a small band into the fortifications and received a terrible wound in the process. Six officers and about twenty men of the 6th Maryland pierced Lane's defenses near the narrow opening, Color Sergeant David Laturn and Color Corporal William J. Brown planting the regimental banners on the parapet. Captain Thomas

Ocker and lieutenants Thomas Duff and Thomas H. Goldsborough all suffered serious injuries defending those flags.[48]

Major Prentiss strode at the head of that small contingent of Marylanders. As he crossed over the Confederate works and ascended the parapet "encouraging his command by his chivalric courage," a rifle ball "carried away a part of his breast bone immediately over his heart, exposing its action to view." Prentiss, a 29-year-old Baltimorian, had a younger brother, Private William Scollay Prentiss, who served in the 2nd Maryland Battalion (Confederate) in McComb's Brigade. William Prentiss also suffered an agonizing wound on the morning of April 2 that would require the amputation of his right leg.[49]

Numerous accounts describe with various degrees of poignancy the touching story of the Prentiss brothers during the Breakthrough. Sergeant John R. King of the 6th Maryland published a version long after the war guaranteed to tug at his readers' heart strings:

> After the enemy had been defeated[,] two of the 6th Md. men like many others were going over the field ministering to the wounded without regard to the uniform they wore [and] came upon a wounded Confederate, who after receiving some water, asked if the 6th Md. was any way near them.
>
> The reply was, 'We belong to that regiment. Why do you ask?' The Confederate replied that he had a brother in that regiment.
>
> 'Who is he?' he was asked.
>
> The Confederate said, 'Capt. Clifton K. Prentiss.'
>
> Our boys said, 'Yes, he is our Major now and is lying over yonder wounded.'
>
> The Confederate said: 'I would like to see him.' Word was at once carried to Maj. Prentiss. He declined to see him, saying, 'I want to see no man who fired at my country's flag.'
>
> Col.[Joseph C.] Hill, after giving directions to have the wounded Confederate brought over, knelt down beside the Major and pleaded with him to see his brother. When the wayward brother was laid beside him our Major for a moment glared at him. The Confederate brother smiled: that was the one touch of nature; out went both hands and with tears streaming down their cheeks these two brothers, who had met on many bloody fields on opposite sides for three years, were once more brought together.[50]

Every variation of the Prentiss saga agrees that the two brothers arrived at the same Sixth Corps field hospital. One witness, writing shortly after the war, described seeing Clifton and William brought into the hospital and placed in adjoining beds, not yet knowing of one another's fate or presence. Perhaps embellishing upon this account, the historian of the 14th New Jersey claimed that as the surgeons attended to the Prentiss brothers' wounds, the fraternal enemies met for the first time since the beginning of the war, "causing many to shed tears." Captain Erastus S. Norvell of the 6th Maryland claimed that he saw each of the brothers wounded within twenty yards of one another at virtually the same time, implying that the struggle that morning literally pitted brother against brother. Norvell's version is doubtful considering that McComb's troops were stationed considerably southwest of the Breakthrough and that the evidence is strong that Clifton suffered his wound during the early stages of the attack.

Another 6th Maryland veteran, Captain Grayson M. Eichelberger, added a final touch of Victorian sentimentality to the Prentiss story. In a memoir penned in 1912, Eichelberger stated that "Major Prentice [sic] had me read a letter from this brother only a few days before this battle. He had written to a sister in Baltimore and she forwarded the letter to the Major. In it he deplored the fate that compel[l]ed brother to fight against brother." It is easy to forgive the exaggerations in the recounting of the Prentiss boys' story—particularly since both wounds proved mortal; William died on June 23, 1865, and his older brother succumbed two months later.[51]

While Clifton Prentiss, the 6th Maryland, and the balance of Warren Keifer's brigade executed their attack against the right half of Lane's formation, Colonel Truex led the rest of Seymour's division toward the portion of the Confederate line defended by Lane's 28th North Carolina and Lieutenant Colonel Eric Erson's two regiments, the 11th North Carolina and 52nd North Carolina. With fewer than 300 men and in position for only a few hours, Erson inherited a nearly hopeless assignment to connect Lane's right with the left flank of McComb's Tennesseans and Marylanders. A six-gun artillery battery located on high ground a few hundred yards southwest of the Hart House, marked the key feature on this portion of the line. This battery would draw particular attention from the five regiments in Truex's brigade poised to respond to the signal from Fort Fisher.[52]

The First Brigade troops sprang forward at Truex's order, preceded by the axemen and sharpshooters who, while attempting to clear a path for the infantry, instantly encountered "a terrible fire of musketry and artillery," canister from the six-gun battery sweeping the field across which the Yankees now ventured. Lieutenant Colonel Jacob Janeway of the 14th New Jersey testified that due to the darkness and the fact that all five regiments began their advance simultaneously, "the men soon got mixed up in passing over the ground to the rebel works." The confusion proved so

Colonel William Truex

Massachusetts MOLLUS Collection,
Carlisle Barracks, Pennsylvania

pervasive that the 87th Pennsylvania, in Truex's third line, temporarily passed the first two lines of battle on their way toward the Rebel works.[53]

The charging Federals quickly overran the Confederate picket line and followed the fleeing gray sentries toward the main fortifications. The retreating graycoats inadvertently aided their opponents by shielding the Unionists from their comrades in the works, those Southerners withholding fire until the pickets cleared the range. Just as in Keifer's front, narrow openings in the line traversed by ramps beckoned Truex's men. The 10th Vermont, nearly 500 strong that morning, aimed for one of these gaps, while the 106th New York, moving on the Vermonters' left, encountered the "trip-up wire lines of abbatis," that slowed them down substantially. "The line was necessarily considerably broken in penetrating the abatis," reported Lieutenant Colonel Damon of the 10th Vermont, "and a portion of it became wholly disconnected from the command." With the flash of artillery from "the ugly-looking fort" illuminating this remarkable combat scene, Truex's men dashed into the moat or across the narrow causeways near the battery and engaged the overmatched defenders. "The greater portion of my command went into the fort near the unpainted barn outside of the enemy's works," reported Janeway, while Lieutenant Colonel Charles Bogardus of the 151st New York stated that "we . . . passed into a rebel fort, capturing two of the six pieces of artillery and two caissons in the fort."[54]

The stout-hearted Confederates faced an impossible situation. "On our left they came with a tremendous yell, while in our front they were advancing without noise," reported a private in the 11th North Carolina. "We directed our fire toward the noise, it not being light enough to see those in front." Erson's men stood five or six feet apart along the works, and Truex's charging masses quickly overwhelmed the thin butternut line.

"With fixed bayonets, and without firing a shot, we rushed across that driveway, which was so crowded that many were pushed off into the ditch," remembered a Vermonter. "As fast as we crossed we filed to the left, and kept on until the fort was almost surrounded. Then we halted, and every

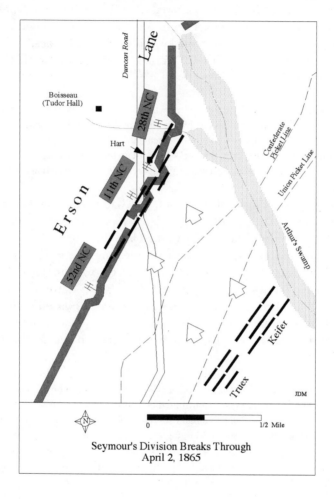

Seymour's Division Breaks Through
April 2, 1865

man yelled 'Surrender! Surrender!' All the reply we got was a volley from inside, so we shouted, 'Pile in. Don't let them reload,' and in we all went." Truex gave credit to the 10th Vermont for being first inside the works, but the 106th New York and 14th New Jersey quickly followed.[55]

The combat inside the fort followed a familiar script—brief, personal, and all in favor of the Yankees. That is not to say that the Federals gained their prize without cost. "It was plucky fighting on both sides," affirmed a New Englander. Private John C. Warlick of the 11th North Carolina remembered that:

> I was shooting at Yanks in front of me where they were thick as black birds. They had broke our line on our left & come on us on our left flank. I had seen them, but thought it was our own men until a Cap't who was in front of his men with sword drawn whacked me over the head twice. Before I realized my situation his men were right at his heels with fixed bayonets.[56]

One member of the 10th Vermont, who had been on rear-area guard duty for much of the previous campaign season, had long endured the teasing of his mates who mockingly warned him that during the final attack he could no longer avoid confronting the enemy. Desiring to prove his mettle, this soldier led the Vermonters' charge, was among the first to enter the enemy works, and dispatched three North Carolinians with his bayonet and clubbed musket before being wounded himself in the thigh. Corporal Oscar Waite of the same regiment recorded a lengthy, graphic tale regarding his experience with hand-to-hand battle in the six-gun battery:

> I had long considered 'bayonet exercise' my best hold, but on landing inside the fort found myself confronted by a lank six-foot rebel, who kept me so strictly on the defensive that I soon lost all conceit and backed off to where there was more room. My gun was loaded all this time, but I dared not lose my guard long enough to fire. While in the midst of this general mix-up I caught a glimpse of a clubbed musket almost whistling horizontally toward my head. The proper move would have allowed it to slide over, but that would give my first opponent the chance he was looking for. By partly parrying, though, the only result was a glancing kind of a shave that laid about half of my left eyebrow over on the other half. At the same instant, catching the first rebel off guard, I let go the small of my gun-stock with my right, and struck straight out with the butt of my gun, which reached the fellow's chest and 'floored' him. Then just as I turned to the clubbed-musket man, someone collared him from behind and pulled him over backwards. In about a minute the whole fracas was over, and the prisoners, said to be only 35 with whole skins, were marched to the rear.

Then I laid that loose flap of eyebrow in place, wound a handkerchief around it, and . . . as soon as the blood dried was able to remove the bandage. This was the first blood that the real graybacks had ever drawn, in my case, and I was really glad of something to show.[57]

Lieutenant Colonel Damon took command of the prisoners and, as Waite suggested, sent them to the rear without guards, Damon feeling the need for every one of his men on the front line. Some of the Carolinians who had not been captured or otherwise rendered hors de combat made their way through the winter quarters well behind the fortifications. Julius Lineback, a Tarheel musician, had sought shelter in the rear of the line before the Federal wave swept over the works. Once the Breakthrough occurred, "a long blue line, sparkling with flashes of musketry," began moving toward the Confederate camps. "Our men," remembered Lineback, "in pitifully small numbers [were] in full retreat. We needed no one to tell us what to do," admitted the musician:

"We got into the rear of the forts and mowed the Johnies down like grass."

Over fences, across fields, deep with soft ground from the rains, we made our way as best we could. To lighten our loads, some of us discarded what we thought we could best spare. I emptied my little sack of corn meal—the saving of weeks. One of the boys of a somewhat peculiar disposition had accumulated souvenirs & treasures of various kinds which he had in pouches strung around him. As he was floundering along, weighed down by his many possessions, he exclaimed, 'Oh Lord, what shall I do.' Another one, with more vehemence than reverence, volunteered the advice that he should 'throw away some them damned bags.'[58]

"We got into the rear of the forts and mowed the Johnies down like grass," boasted Private Simon B. Cummins of the 151st New York. "The Johns was panic strickened and run like sheep." A member of the 10th Vermont considered the battle "the most remarkable case of stampede and temporary disorganization . . . seen during the war." Among the witnesses to this victory was division commander Seymour who, in the company of Lieutenant John Brinckle, commander of Battery E, 5th U.S. Artillery, rode forward with the troops. "The bullets flew thick & fast & the shells burst everywhere, but on we went till the works were reached & our troops were soon over the parapet, though not without a short hand to hand fight," wrote Brinckle. "I made my horse go over the breast works & secured a trophy just as it was light enough to see the rebels scatter in every direction." Erson reported that "over two-thirds of my command were killed, wounded, and captured," though he admitted that he could not determine his exact losses. Truex claimed to have seized 300 prisoners during the initial Breakthrough while suffering relatively light casualties himself, partly because Keifer's brigade had compromised Erson's position and that of their supports, the 28th North Carolina, on their left.[59]

Credit for Wright's Breakthrough belonged entirely to the Sixth Corps infantry, although the long arm of the corps played a meaningful supporting role. Lieutenant Walter M. Knight led a section of Battery H, First Rhode Island Light Artillery forward with Wheaton's men and "opened fire on the enemy, doing good service." General Wheaton credited the Rhode Island cannoneers with "very handsomely compell[ing] a section of the enemy's artillery to retire," adding that had those Confederate guns been allowed to remain, "they might have materially retarded our advance." The Third New York Independent Battery and a section of Battery G, First Rhode Island Light Artillery under Lieutenant Reuben H. Rich advanced in support of Seymour's attack and unleashed counterbattery fire until the infantry closed with the Confederate defenders. Captain George Adams and his intrepid band of twenty detached cannoneers of Battery G, First Rhode Island Light Artillery "accompanied the assaulting columns [and] was of great service in the operations subsequent to the assault in turning the captured guns upon the enemy's columns and works, thereby adding much to the demoralization of the rebel forces," reported General Wright. Seven of the twenty volunteers from this battery won Medals of Honor for their accomplishments during the Breakthrough.[60]

Barely thirty minutes after the signal gun had launched the attack, Horatio Wright reported to Meade that "the corps has carried the works in front and to the left of the Jones house. Prisoners now coming in." At 5:30 a.m., Meade conveyed his congratulations to the Sixth Corps commander and also reported the good news to the general-in-chief, who passed it on to President Lincoln at City Point. Lincoln promptly wired his wife that "all now looks highly favorable," although no one suggested that the day's fighting had ended.[61]

But for hundreds of men in blue and gray, the struggle had indeed run its course—for that day and forever. Chief Engineer John G. Barnard estimated that Federal casualties during the Breakthrough numbered "some eleven hundred in killed and wounded, all of which occurred in the space of about fifteen minutes." A newspaper correspondent claimed that "in places the ditches were heaped with living and dying combatants, tumbled together promiscuously," while a Pennsylvania officer recalled that "it was a busy time for the stretcher bearer, and the ambulance man & the surgeon as well as for those who handled the artillery & the musket & the sword, and directed the movements. Ah! there was the festive scene of death—Death in the trenches—death in the air. . . ." Confederate losses during the Breakthrough may never be known, although it is clear that many more Southerners became prisoners than were killed or wounded.[62]

Another imponderable aspect of the Breakthrough attracted considerable attention from the Federal participants—both in the immediate aftermath of the victory and for years thereafter. Historian James M. McPherson has noted that, "Perhaps the only achievement that could eclipse the honor of taking enemy colors or retaking one's own was to plant the national flag on a captured enemy position." Certainly the distinction of being the first over the works and, collaterally, the first to carry the Northern colors into the Confederate line on April 2, generated multiple claimants.[63]

Almost half of the Sixth Corps regiments that participated in the Breakthrough—20 out of 42—stipulated in one form or another that they were the first to penetrate the works or raise a flag over the enemy line that morning. The aspirants for these accolades represented each of the eight brigades in the corps. Two regiments in particular, however, appear to own the strongest case for first breaching the Confederate fortifications.[64]

Lewis Grant argued vociferously after the war that the Vermont Brigade deserved recognition for being the first of Wright's units across Lee's lines:

> It is not strange, perhaps, that several different commands have claimed that they, or men of their command were first on the rebel works. In one sense their respective claims may be right—they were probably the first in their immediate front. But before they could reach or mount the works, the Vermont Brigade had scaled the works in their front & were driving out the rebels on the right & left as the other forces came up on the right & left. In the very nature of things (of the formation), the head of my column must have been 80 to 100 yards in advance of the head of any other column. Then came the other Brigades of our Division on my rear & right respectively, and the colors of the other Brigades still to the rear— so that the head of my column must have been nearly or quite 200 yards in advance of the head of either other Division.[65]

If Grant's boast on behalf of the Vermont Brigade may be believed, then Captain Charles G. Gould deserves recognition as the first man over the Confederate works. No fewer than four accounts, including Gould's own, affirm that the young line officer of the 5th Vermont led the New Englanders at the point of the wedge. "Capt. C. G. Gould, Company H, when the line advanced on the first fort of the enemy, scaled the works and entered considerably in advance of any of the rest of the command and commenced a hand-to-hand encounter, which came near costing him his life," reported Lieutenant Colonel Ronald Kennedy, the regimental commander. Captain Merritt Barber, who prepared the Vermont Brigade's after-action report, agreed: "It is confidently believed that Capt. Charles G. Gould, of the Fifth Vermont, was the first man of the Sixth Corps who mounted the enemy's works. His regiment was in the first line of the brigade and in the charge he was far in advance of his command." Lewis Grant testified that, "I have taken much pains to consider the evidence and it seems to me conclusive that Captain Gould was the first upon the works." Gould's own version of events concurred with those of his superiors: "It was officially reported and so far as I am aware has never been questioned, that I was the first one to enter the enemy's works. Although it can justly be attributed to chance more than any other cause, I have always believed the report to be true, and from all the circumstances connected with the engagement feel warranted in my belief."[66]

Sergeant John E. Buffington and the 6th Maryland of Keifer's brigade pose the most serious challenge to Captain Gould and the 5th Vermont's claim of notoriety. "It is not disputed here that my brigade was the first to enter the Rebel works and gain a position," Keifer told his wife the day following the Breakthrough. Truman Seymour reported that "for some moments after the entrance of this division the firing continued on our right, upon the other divisions of the corps," suggesting that if Keifer's was not the first brigade into the Confederate line, it subdued its opponents earlier than did Getty's and Wheaton's men. Six weeks after the Breakthrough, Keifer wrote his division commander that, "In compliance with your request I have the honor to state that I have made a full investigation as to who was in fact the first man from this brigade to enter the works of the enemy in front of Petersburg on the 2nd ult and am fully satisfied that Sergeant John E. Buffington, Co C 6th Maryland Volunteers was the first man to pass over the works." Buffington, a Carroll County, Maryland farmer, was one of six Federals who initially stormed the ramparts in the company of Major Prentiss. "It is admitted by the men that the Sergeant [Buffington] did not halt upon the works but sprang within them, the other five made a temporary halt on top of the works," testified Keifer.[67]

According to a postwar newspaper article, a donor made $400 available to General Grant as a reward for the first man who should raise the flag of the Union over Richmond. Because Richmond did not fall by assault, Grant allegedly decided to divide the reward three ways, including a portion to the Sixth Corps soldier "most conspicuous for gallantry in carrying the lines at Petersburg." The general-in-chief delegated responsibility for making this decision to General Wright who, if the article is to be believed, tellingly passed the decision on to General Seymour. The Third Division commander determined that Sergeant Buffington was "the first enlisted man of the Third Division who mounted the parapet of the enemy's lines at Petersburg, April 2, 1865." Buffington supposedly received his share of the $400 prize money, but not until 1908 would the government finally bestow upon him a Medal of Honor for his heroism during the Breakthrough.[68]

It is important to note that Seymour specified only that Buffington was the first man over the works from his division. This qualification thus dilutes Keifer's claim that his troops led the entire corps that Sunday morning. However, the testimony of Confederate general James Lane further confuses the matter. "My line was pierced by the enemy in strong force at the ravine in front of the right of the Thirty-seventh, near General McGowan's headquarters," wrote Lane. It is not possible to pinpoint the exact junction of the 37th North Carolina with the 28th North Carolina, but Lane's report implied that the two regiments connected on the line in front of Tudor Hall, that is, on Keifer's axis of attack. Was the ravine mentioned by Lane the one that divided the Vermonters from Keifer, or another drainage to the southwest, entirely in Seymour's sphere of influence? Of course, Gould's path of approach brought him and his small group of followers to the left of the Arthur's Swamp ravine as well, in approximately the same location as Prentiss's and Buffington's narrow opening. It is difficult, then, not to conclude that the initial Union penetration occurred near one of two surviving openings in the Confederate works located 200 and 400 yards southwest of the ravine. Which small band of Federals first reached the Confederate line here— that led by Gould or the one involving Prentiss and Buffington—defies absolute determination.[69]

Some participants in this discussion admitted that the chaotic circumstances of that portentous Sunday prevented the drawing of firm conclusions. Thomas Hyde acknowledged that, "several regiments of the brigade claim their colors as first on the works, but the darkness must leave that honor forever undecided." Merritt Barber, though certain that Gould climbed the Confederate parapet before any other man, felt less confident in deciding the sensitive issue of which unit in his Vermont Brigade first raised its colors on Lane's log-and-earthen fortifications: "The commander of the Fifth, Sixth, and Eleventh Vermont, each claims that the colors of his command were the first planted on the works, but owing to the darkness prevailing at the time the lines were reached, and the distance between the points at which these colors were placed on the works, it is impossible to decide the delicate question."

One now-anonymous observer probably best captured the truth of this issue when he wrote:

> That line was too extensive to be under one man's eyes from right to left at that moment, and it scarcely yet dawn. No man could then tell—no man can now tell—whose colors were the first to have been planted on the works, or whose men were the first to have entered those works, except in in his own immediate brigade front. Those honors belong to all who were on the front line, not to Vermont, not to New Jersey, not to New York, not to Ohio, not to Massachusetts, nor Wisconsin, nor Pennsylvania, as each have claimed, but to all in the Sixth Corps who were in the front line.[70]

At 5:30 a.m. on April 2, 1865, the controversy over whose flags first topped the Rebel line or which unit's worthies first scrambled their way over the Confederate parapet and into immortality lay in the future. The Sixth Corps assault and Breakthrough, as large in scale as the most famous frontal attacks in Civil War history, and characterized by one writer as "one of the most brilliant operations of modern warfare," had unquestionably succeeded in knocking the heart out of Robert E. Lee's Petersburg defenses.[71]

But the sun's glow in the eastern sky reminded the weary foes that the entire day still lay before them. The early success of the Sixth Corps suggested that the end to the long ordeal at Petersburg might be imminent. Would the Sixth Corps Breakthrough bring an end to the war itself?

NOTES

1. Brewer, *History Sixty-first Regiment Pennsylvania Volunteers*, 138; Best, *History of the 121st New York State Infantry*, 210; *OR* pt. 1, 968.

2. Terrill, *Fourteenth Regiment, New Jersey Volunteers*, 118; *OR* pt. 1, 902-903. Terrill stated that Wright's party appeared at 3:45 a.m. and that striking the match elicited a scattered fire from the Confederate pickets.

3. Benedict, *Vermont in the Civil War*, II, 727, I, 585; Walker, "The Old Vermont Brigade," 206; "The Fall of Petersburg," in *Philadelphia Weekly Press*, June 1, 1937; Terrill, *Fourteenth Regiment, New Jersey Volunteers*, 118; *OR* pt.1, 954, 962, 968; Anson, "Assault on the Lines of Petersburg," 90; Stevens, "The Storming of the Lines of Petersburg," in *PMHSM*, VI, 423; Brewer, *History Sixty-first Regiment Pennsylvania Volunteers*, 138; Hyde, *Following the Greek Cross*, 252. The 3rd Vermont Battery was assigned to the Reserve Artillery.

The sources disagree considerably regarding when the signal gun was fired. Estimates range from 3:30 a.m. to 5:00 a.m. Wright's testimony has been followed in the text as the most reliable. Likewise, some inconsistency surrounds the temporary confusion experienced in Getty's division subsequent to the discharge of the signal gun. Both Captain Merritt Barber, the staff officer who prepared the after-action report for the Vermont Brigade, and General Getty acknowledged a delay, and ascribed it to the cannonading on the Ninth Corps line. Colonel Hyde offered a rather implausible affirmation of the misunderstanding by blaming the masking of the signal gun on the racket from an artillery salute fired in honor of the victory at Five Forks. Hyde claimed to have clarified the situation personally by consulting with General Getty and then conveying to Colonel Tracy Getty's authorization to advance. Colonel Hazard Stevens wrote that an officer from Wright's headquarters, not brigade commander Hyde, visited Getty's division and inquired why the attack had not begun some ten minutes after the signal gun had been fired. Barber's report merely said that "soon . . . it was learned that the signal had been given. . . ." Wright reported that "the columns moved promptly at the signal, at 4:40 a.m. . . ." No other officers complained about the attack being deferred, suggesting that the lag between the firing of the signal gun and the commencement of the attack was practically indiscernible.

4. Stevens, "The Storming of the Lines of Petersburg," in *PMHSM*, VI, 423; "The Fall of Petersburg," in *Philadelphia Weekly Press*, June 1, 1937; Anson, "Assault on the Lines of Petersburg," 91; *OR* pt. 1, 962.

5. Stevens, "The Storming of the Lines of Petersburg," in *PMHSM*, VI, 423-424; Walker, "The Old Vermont Brigade," 205; Anson, "Assault on the Lines of Petersburg," 91; *OR* pt. 1, 968, 954, 962. Lieutenant Colonel Charles A. Milliken of the 43rd New York had command of the division's picket line on April 2. Milliken claimed that between 400 and 500 enemy soldiers came under his control after the Confederate picket line succumbed.

6. Benedict, *Vermont in the Civil War*, I, 581-582; *OR* pt. 1, 963, 954, 974.

7. Anson, "Assault on the Lines of Petersburg," 91.

8. Walter Wallace Smith to "Dear Parents," April 3, 1865, in Walter Wallace Smith Papers, Duke; Hazard Stevens, Journal, in George W. Getty Papers, Gibson-Getty-McClure Family Papers, LC; *OR* pt. 1, 968.

9. Anson, "Assault on the Lines of Petersburg," 92; *OR* pt. 1, 968-969, 954; Walter Wallace Smith to "Dear Parents," April 3, 1865, in Walter Wallace Smith Papers, Duke; Hazard Stevens, Journal, in George W. Getty Papers, Gibson-Getty-McClure Family Papers, LC.

10. Darius Safford to "Dear Sister," April 16, 1865, in Sherman/Safford Papers, VTHS.

11. *OR* pt. 1, 969; Journal of Lieutenant Robert Pratt, April 2, 1865, VTHS; Grant, "The Old Vermont Brigade at Petersburg," in *Glimpses of the Nation's Struggle*, 401; Anson, "Assault on the Lines of Petersburg," 92.

12. Letters Received, Sixth Army Corps, 1862-1865, Record Group 393, NA; *OR* pt. 1, 969. Hawkins was awarded the Medal of Honor for his actions on April 2 but did not survive his wounds.

13. Anson, "Assault on the Lines of Petersburg," 93; *OR* pt. 1, 954, 973; Walter Wallace Smith to "Dear Parents," April 3, 1865, in Walter Wallace Smith Papers, Duke; Jackson L. Bost to "Dear General" [James H. Lane], July 31, 1867, in James Lane Papers, Auburn University; Hazard Stevens, Journal, in George W. Getty Papers, Gibson-Getty-McClure Family Papers, LC; Walker, "The Old Vermont Brigade," 206. Lewis Grant misidentified Sergeant McCauley as Thomas I. McColley and called him a "mounted orderly at brigade headquarters."

14. Grant, "The Old Vermont Brigade at Petersburg," 401; Stevens, "The Storming of the Lines of Petersburg," in *PMHSM*, VI, 425. Available evidence does not permit identification of the guns captured by the Vermonters. A two-gun artillery redan still exists a few hundred feet northeast of the ravine along the Breakthrough Trail at Pamplin Historical Park and, no doubt, some of the ordnance seized by Tracy's men had been positioned there.

15. Howard Coffin, *Full Duty: Vermonters in the Civil War* (Woodstock, Vt., 1993), 336. Gould first enlisted as a private in the 11th Vermont, which became the First Vermont Heavy Artillery, on August 13, 1862. He received promotions to corporal, sergeant-major and second lieutenant in his regiment and on November 10, 1864 accepted promotion to captain in the 5th Vermont. See Jacob G. Ullery, *Men of Vermont* (Brattleboro, Vt., 1894), part III, 70.

16. Charles Gilbert Gould's adventure is mentioned in practically every published account of the Breakthrough. See for example, Parsons, *Put the Vermonters Ahead*, 145; Benedict, *Vermont in the Civil War*, I, 586-587; Anson, "Assault on the Lines of Petersburg," 92-93; Stevens, "The Storming of the Lines of Petersburg, " in *PMHSM*, VI, 425; and *OR* pt. 1, 969, 973, 975. Lewis Grant provided a somewhat garbled version of the Gould episode in his Memorandum of July 15, 1890 in Gould's pension file, Entry 501, Correspondence of the Records & Pension Office, File 240190, Record Group 94, NA, as well as in a letter to Hazard Stevens on February 13, 1884, in the Hazard Stevens Papers, LC. The narrative provided in the text is based on Gould's own testimony, printed in Benedict, *Vermont in the Civil War*, I, 593-596 and Gould to "My dear Bob" (Lieutenant Robert Pratt), July 7, 1882, made available to the author through the courtesy of Jack Mandaville of Maple Grove, Minnesota.

Gould not only survived his ordeal but recovered remarkably quickly. In just a few days, he was able to write his parents that, "My wounds are doing finely and will be well in a week or so." He also wrote his brother that, "Have got wounds enough to make a great deal of noise but they are all very light. Am up and out of doors all the time." See Gould to "Dear Parents," April 8, 1865, and Gould to "Brother Aron," April 4,1865, both in the Captain Charles Gilbert Gould Collection, UVM. Gould would be awarded the Medal of Honor in 1890, and a year later, Sergeant Sargent would receive the same recognition. Gould also received a brevet promotion to major for his deeds that morning. Gould settled in Washington, DC after the war, working for the Pension Office, War Department, and Patent Office.

The precise location of Gould's heroics is difficult to determine. There is no prepared Confederate artillery position that corresponds with a location close to the southwest bank of the ravine. There is, however, a narrow opening in the works and the remains of a traverse that might have been a part of an artillery position, visible along the Breakthrough Trail at Pamplin Historical Park. Gould's travails most likely occurred near this spot.

17. Walker, "The Old Vermont Brigade," 206-207; Pratt, Journal, April 2, 1865, VTHS; Robert Pratt to "Dear Brother Sid," April 9, 1865, courtesy of Jack Mandaville; *OR* pt. 1, 971. Two identical sources from the 61st Pennsylvania identify Hyde's opponents in the Breakthrough as "Heth's Tennesseans," but William McComb's brigade of Tennessee and Maryland troops occupied a position substantially to the southwest of where Hyde's brigade initially struck the Confederate line. See Brewer, *History Sixty-first Regiment Pennsylvania Volunteers*, 138, and Orr, "Before Petersburg," in *Philadelphia Weekly Press*, December 19, 1886.

18. *OR* pt. 1, 976; Hyde, *Following the Greek Cross*, 252; Thomas Hyde to "Dear Stevens," February 6, 1884, in Hazard Stevens Papers, LC.

19. Thomas Hyde to "Dear Stevens," February 6, 1884, in Hazard Stevens Papers, LC; Hyde, *Following the Greek Cross*, 253; *OR* pt. 1, 976.

20. Hyde, *Following the Greek Cross*, 254. The regimental history of the 61st Pennsylvania describes the performance of the unit's new recruits differently, claiming that they "seemed glad of the opportunity offered them to take part in battle, to be members of an organization whose deeds and works were part of the history of their country..." Although Hyde is not always the most reliable witness, in this case his blunt testimony seems more credible than the laudatory rhetoric normally decorating regimental histories. See Brewer, *History Sixty-first Regiment Pennsylvania Volunteers*, 138-139. Neither Hyde's official report nor his letter to Stevens mentions the 61st Pennsylvania, and the regimental commander filed no after-action report.

21. Orr, "Before Petersburg," in *Philadelphia Weekly Press*, December 19, 1886. Colonel George F. Smith commanded the 61st Pennsylvania on April 2, but his whereabouts are not recorded. Orr, who had been awarded a brevet promotion to lieutenant colonel, wrote his account from the perspective of the regimental field commander. See also, Brewer, *History Sixty-first Regiment Pennsylvania Volunteers*, 137-139.

22. Brewer, *History Sixty-first Regiment Pennsylvania Volunteers*, 138-139; Orr, "Before Petersburg," in *Philadelphia Weekly Press*, December 19, 1886; Hyde,

Following the Greek Cross, 253; Correspondence of the Records & Pension Office, File 378148, 263102, O-1748 (VS), Record Group 94, NA; Augustus Evander Floyd, Memoir, VHS; Lothrup Lincoln Lewis, Diary, April 2, 1865, in Lothrup Lincoln Lewis Collection, LC. Fisher, Mathews, and Orr all won the Medal of Honor for their actions during the attack.

23. *OR* pt. 1, 963-966.

24. *OR* pt. 1, 966; Clark, ed., *North Carolina in the Great War*, II, 576; Mark, *History of the 93rd Regiment*, 322. Marquette would earn the Medal of Honor for being, despite his injury, one of the first to plant a regimental flag on the Confederate works.

25. Benedict, *Vermont in the Civil War*, II, 388. Hyde also procured his horse and arrived on the Confederate lines atop his mount.

26. *OR* pt. 1, 910; Edwards, Memoir, 223, Illinois State Historical Library; Bowen, *History of the Thirty-Seventh Massachusetts*, 410; "The Fall of Petersburg," in *Philadelphia Weekly Press*, June 1, 1937.

27. Edwards, Memoir, 223, Illinois State Historical Libary; Barnes, "A Boy's Experience in the Terrible Charge of April 2, 1865," in *National Tribune*, July 27, 1883; Bowen, *History of the Thirty-Seventh Massachusetts*, 410 and "Lee in the Toils," in *Philadelphia Weekly Times*, May 2, 1885; Captain John C. Robinson to "Dear Father," April 4, 1865, courtesy of Fred D. Robinson, Chesterfield, Va.; *OR* pt. 1, 910; Oliver Edwards to Brig. Gen. R. A. Pierce, June 30, 1865, in Spencer Repeating Rifle Catalog, n.p., n.d, 24. Thomas Scott Allen was a 39-year-old native of New York who had relocated to Oshkosh, Wisconsin before the war. He was a miner, surveyor, and real estate agent and after the war served four years as Wisconsin's secretary of state.

28. *OR* pt. 1, 910; Barnes, "A Boy's Experience in the Terrible Charge of April 2, 1865," in *National Tribune*, July 27, 1883; Cyrus Spore, in *National Tribune*, December 11, 1884; Bowen, *History of the Thirty-Seventh Massachusetts*, 411.

29. Barnes, "A Boy's Experience in the Terrible Charge of April 2, 1865," in *National Tribune*, July 27, 1883; Bowen, *History of the Thirty-Seventh Massachusetts*, 411 and "Lee in the Toils," in *Philadelphia Weekly Times*, May 2, 1885; *OR* pt. 1, 945; Edwards, Memoir, 224, Illinois State Historical Library; unidentified article, c. July 1865, in *Gazette & Courier*, Northampton, Massachusetts, in Edward Payson Bridgeman Papers, SHSW. Corporal Welch captured the flag of the 37th North Carolina. This flag, in 2000, is on display in the Battlefield Center at Pamplin Historical Park.

30. Rhodes, ed., *All for the Union*, 225-226; Woodbury, *The Second Rhode Island Regiment*, 342-344.

31. Rhodes, ed., *All for the Union*, 226; Woodbury, *The Second Rhode Island Regiment*, 345-346.

32. Edwards, Memoir, 225, Illinois State Historical Library; Bowen, *History of the Thirty-Seventh Massachusetts*, 411; Barnes, "A Boy's Experience in the Terrible Charge of April 2, 1865," in *National Tribune*, July 27, 1883; *OR* pt. 1, 941, 952. Colonel Allen received a brevet promotion to brigadier general as of March 13,

1865, for "gallant and meritorious service." See Hunt & Brown, *Brevet Brigadier Generals in Blue*, 12.

33. Edwards, Memoir, 225, Illinois State Historical Library; Bowen, *History of the Thirty-Seventh Massachusetts*, 411; *OR* pt. 1, 941, 950-952; Barnes, "A Boy's Experience in the Terrible Charge of April 2, 1865," in *National Tribune*, July 27, 1883; Rhodes, ed., *All for the Union*, 226; Woodbury, *The Second Rhode Island Regiment*, 343.

34. The story of Penrose's role in the Breakthrough is provided in *OR* pt. 1, 927-929; Haines, *Fifteenth New Jersey*, 301-302; and Bilby, *Three Rousing Cheers*, 240.

35. Olcott and Lear, *The Civil War Letters of Lewis Bissell*, 360; Soule, "Recollections of the Civil War," in *New Milford* (Conn.) *Gazette*, July 12, 1912.

36. *OR* pt. 1, 940; Soule, "Recollections of the Civil War," in *New Milford* (Conn.) *Gazette*, July 12, 1912; Olcott and Lear, *The Civil War Letters of Lewis Bissell*, 360; Roberts, "War Reminiscences," in *Connecticut Western News*, January 18, 1912.

37. Soule, "Recollections of the Civil War," in *New Milford* (Conn.) *Gazette*, July 12, 1912; Olcott and Lear, *The Civil War Letters of Lewis Bissell*, 360; Roberts, "War Reminiscences," in *Connecticut Western News*, January 18, 1912; Thomas Jefferson Simmons to "My dear Captain and Old Comrade" [David S. Redding], April 22, 1905, in Civil War Miscellany-Personal Papers, Georgia Department of Archives and History. Bissell's reference to the capture of black Confederate soldiers, while not unique, was not literally true. No organized Confederate black units fought along Hill's line or anywhere else at Petersburg on April 2. Bissell must have encountered black teamsters, cooks, servants, or other non-combatants during the Breakthrough, some of whom were doubtless armed and fighting, and mistook these men for regular Confederate soldiers.

38. *OR* pt. 1, 936; Best, *History of the 121st New York State Infantry*, 209-210; "The Fall of Petersburg," in *Philadelphia Weekly Press*, June 1, 1937.

39. *OR* pt. 1, 931-932, 935-936, 938; Olcott and Lear, *The Civil War Letters of Lewis Bissell*, 361; Wiley, ed., *Norfolk Blues*, 216. The placement of this particular Confederate artillery opposite Hamblin's brigade is based on circumstantial evidence only. See note 46 below.

40. McCrea, *Red Dirt and Isinglass*, 305-306; *OR* pt. 1, 911-912. Fitzpatrick rode a train to Richmond where he received medical treatment, but the surgeons could do little with a wound so close to the hip. He died on April 6.

41. *OR* pt. 1, 910-911, 918-926.

42. Keifer, *Slavery and Four Years of War*, II, 193. A member of the 6th Maryland writing many years after the war confirmed Keifer's account, identifying the narrow opening as a "salla [sic] port for passing thru, perhaps 12 to 20 feet wide, blinded in front by a similar piece of fortification to hide the opening and it leaving a pass around each end." Grayson M. Eichelberger, Memoir, Civil War Miscellaneous Collection, USAMHI. An opening in the preserved Confederate works along the Breakthrough Trail in Pamplin Historical Park is most likely the

feature described by Keifer and Eichelberger. A traverse behind the main line, not in front of it as Eichelberger described, exists to one side of the gap, representing perhaps a portion of the parallel work built to protect the opening.

43. Keifer, *Slavery and Four Years of War*, II, 193-194. In his after-action report, Keifer claimed that the signal gun discharged precisely at 4:00 a.m. Truman Seymour made the same statement. Colonel Benjamin Smith of the 126th Ohio, Lieutenant Colonel James W. Snyder of the 9th New York Heavy Artillery, and Colonel Matthew R. McClennan of the 138th Pennsylvania all echoed Keifer's assertion that the gun sounded at 4:00 a.m., while Lieutenant Colonel Joseph C. Hill of the 6th Maryland and Major William G. Williams commanding the 67th Pennsylvania both reported that their orders to go forward arrived about 5:00 a.m. Despite these variations, descriptions of Seymour's actual attack relative to the assaults of the other divisions indicate that the signal gun that actuated Getty's division about 4:40 a.m. provided the cue for Seymour's troops as well. See *OR* pt. 1, 992, 978, 1005, 1003, 1002, 1008, 1000, and 1006.

44. *OR* pt. 1, 978, 1003; Rousculf, "Petersburg: The Part Taken in the Action of April 2, 1865 by the 126th Ohio," in *National Tribune*, June 18, 1891; Lorenzo Barnhardt, "Reminiscences of the Rebellion," ts. in the collection of Pamplin Historical Park. Shellenberger led the 110th Ohio because the unit's regular commander, Colonel Otho Binckley, was acting as corps officer of the day in charge of the picket line. Keifer boasted in his after-action report that, "not even a temporary check transpired in passing through and over the double line of abatis, ditch, and strong earth-works," but other evidence, such as that cited above, indicates that the Confederate defense was more stout than Keifer's report acknowledged. See *OR* pt. 1, 993.

45. Keifer, *Slavery and Four Years of War*, II, 194; Erastus S. Norvell, "Petersburg," in *National Tribune*, June 11, 1891. Keifer identified the location of his attack as being "just to the left (the enemy's right) of a salient angle in the enemy's line of works." There are three clues that help suggest this point on the ground. First, Keifer's brigade advanced to the left, or southwest, of the ravine that divided Seymour's division from Getty's division. Second, Keifer's attack targeted a narrow opening in the Confederate works. Third, a subtle salient existed in the Confederate works between the two branches of Arthur's Swamp and northeast of Duncan Road as depicted on maps of the Confederate line. Keifer's brigade front, then, probably extended from the southwest edge of the ravine, southwest to the western branch of Arthur's Swamp. The narrow opening utilized by the 6th Maryland is most likely the one that survives along the Breakthrough Trail at Pamplin Historical Park, but in the absence of more explicit evidence this must be considered merely informed speculation. Another gap in the Confederate line exists several hundred yards southwest of the narrow opening interpreted along the Breakthrough Trail. Although the current configuration of this opening clearly resulted from 20th-century logging operations, it may have existed in the original works in a different form and might have been the gap targeted by Keifer. See *OR*

pt. 1, 993 for Keifer's testimony, and Nathaniel Michler's map, "Petersburg and Five Forks," LC.

46. *OR* pt. 1, 1006,1002, 993; J. Warren Keifer to "My Dear Wife," April 3, 1865, in Joseph Warren Keifer Papers, LC; Keifer, *Slavery and Four Years of War*, II, 194; Wiley, ed., *Norfolk Blues*, 216. Keifer's letter to his wife claimed the capture of eight guns in the initial attack, including, presumably, the four corralled by the 9th New York Heavy Artillery. In his memoirs, he inflated the total to ten.

The whereabouts of the four guns of Grandy's Battery on the morning of April 2 is in some dispute. Private John H. Walters recorded that on March 25, the two rifles and two Napoleons of the battery "reached the right of McGowan's Brigade on the Boisseaux Farm . . . in a bottom." On March 26, Walters wrote that, "after dark, our two Napoleons were moved some seven or eight hundred yards farther to the left [northeast] to be prepared to lend a helping hand to Battery Gregg or [Battery] 45. . . ." Three days later, Walters testified that "our Napoleon sections were ordered to take position some seven or eight hundred yards further to the left," placing them something less than one mile northeast of Tudor Hall, while the rifled section under Captain Grandy's direct command remained near the Boisseau House. Westwood A. Todd of the 12th Virginia stated that on April 2, "a detachment [of the Norfolk Light Artillery Blues] with two Napoleons under Lt. James W. Gilmer were near the Boisseau House . . . and the remaining detachment with two rifled guns, under Captain Grandy . . . were posted several hundred yards to the right of Lt. Gilmer." Walters, as a member of the battery, is the more reliable witness. See Wiley, ed., *Norfolk Blues*, 210, 212, 214, 218.

47. Edward Joseph Hale to James H. Lane, May 20, 1867, in Lane Papers, Auburn University; Clark, ed., *North Carolina in the Great War*, II, 482; Hugh Torrence, Memoir, in Military Collection, Box 72, Folder 19, North Carolina Department of Archives and History; Keifer, *Slavery and Four Years of War*, II, 194.

48. Headquarters Letter Book, 1863-1865, April 10, 1865, in J. Warren Keifer Papers, LC; *OR* pt. 1, 1000.

49. The indisputable facts surrounding the Prentiss brothers' wounds on April 2 may be found in J. Warren Keifer to "My Dear Wife," April 3, 1865, in Joseph Warren Keifer Papers, LC (although Keifer misidentified William as a major); *OR* pt.1, 978, 1000; Keifer, *Slavery and Four Years of War*, II, 196; Compiled Service Records of Confederate General and Staff Officers and Non regimental Enlisted Men, Microcopy 321, Roll 16, Record Group 94, NA; Compiled Service Records of Federal Officers, Microcopy 384, Roll 155, Record Group 94, NA. Clifton K. Prentiss enlisted as a second lieutenant in Baltimore on July 31, 1862. He served on Seymour's staff during the summer and fall of 1864 and received his majority on December 2, 1864. William S. Prentiss transferred from the 1st Maryland Infantry to the 2nd Maryland Battalion in August 1862 when the 1st Maryland was disbanded. He was 26 years old in 1865.

50. King, "Sixth Corps at Petersburg," in *National Tribune*, April 15, 1920.

51. William Howell Reed, *Hospital Life in the Army of the Potomac* (Boston, 1866, Special Edition, 1881) 190-192; Terrill, *Fourteenth Regiment, New Jersey*

Volunteers, 120; E. S. Norvell, "Petersburg," in *National Tribune*, June 11, 1891; Eichelberger, Memoir, in Civil War Miscellaneous Collection, USAMHI; "The Battle of Sunday: Highly Interesting Details of the Operations of the Sixth and Ninth Corps," in *Milwaukee Sentinel*, April 10, 1865. Reed's account added the intriguing detail that two other Prentiss brothers arrived at the hospital to care for their wounded kinsmen, while Keifer in his memoirs claimed that a Prentiss brother, serving as a Union chaplain, helped nurse both Clifton and William. John H. Prentiss and Thomas Melville Prentiss were Clifton's and William's only surviving brothers in 1865. John was a doctor and Thomas was active in the Presbyterian Church, but corroborating evidence has not surfaced to prove that they were near Petersburg on April 2. Clifton died on August 20, 1865, in New York. For details on the Prentiss family see C. J. F. Binney, *The History and Genealogy of the Prentice Families of New England* (1883, new 4th edition, 1997).

52. Erson, "Report of 2 Regts. of MacRae's Brigade," in Lee Headquarters Papers, VHS. Predictably, it is difficult to pinpoint exact troop dispositions along the Confederate line. Erson stated in his report that the 11th North Carolina and the 52nd North Carolina, under his command, received orders from General Cooke to relieve a portion of McComb's Brigade "occuppying from the right of McGowan's Winter Quarters to the left [,] to the Battery in front of McComb's Winter Quarters on the right." Lane stated that "the right of the Twenty-eighth rest[ed] near the brown house in front of General McRae's [sic] winter quarters" [the Hart House]. This would place the junction of the 28th North Carolina and the 11th North Carolina somewhere near the Hart House, perhaps just northeast of current (2000) VA 670, Duncan Road. The six-gun battery occupied a prominent knoll over which Duncan Road currently passes. Because the Confederate works survive in 2000 a few hundred yards northeast and southwest of the Hart House, it is possible to trace the course of the now-missing line with reasonable accuracy, including the artillery position. See Lane, "History of Lane's North Carolina Brigade," in *SHSP*, X, 57.

53. *OR* pt. 1, 982, 986; Haynes, *A History of the Tenth Regiment, Vermont Volunteers*, 336-337; Abbott, *Personal Recollections*, 265.

54. Waite, "Three Years with the 10th Vermont," II, 246; Haynes, *A History of the Tenth Regiment, Vermont Volunteers*, 355; *OR* pt. 1, 990, 986, 989; Abbott, "Personal Recollections," 268. Waite wrote after the war that, "We, i.e. center, might have struck the fort on the left but our part of Reg. went through the road and gap on the right. . ." See Waite to George G. Benedict, December 29, 1886, in Benedict Papers, UVM. Janeway's intriguing reference to the unpainted barn outside of the enemy's works suggests an outbuilding associated with the Hart House, although no other references to this structure have been found.

55. Jacob S. Bartlett, "The War Record of J. S. Bartlett," in J.S. Bartlett Papers, SHC; William J. Martin, "The Eleventh North Carolina Regiment," in *SHSP*, XXIII, 55-56; Waite, "Three Years with the 10th Vermont," II, 246.

56. Abbott, *Personal Recollections*, 267; John C. Warlick to Edward Outlaw, December 1, 1901, quoted in *More Terrible Than Victory*, 291-292.

57. Waite, "Three Years with the 10th Vermont," II, 246-247. Sergeant Charles H. Whittamore of the 10th Vermont was the object of the teasing.

58. *OR* pt. 1, 990-991; Julius Lineback, Diary, April 1 [April 2], 1865, in Julius A. Lineback Papers, SHC.

59. Melvin Jones, ed., *Give God the Glory: Memoirs of a Civil War Soldier* (n.p., 1979), n.p. [letter of Simon B. Cummins to "Dear Father and Mother," April 3, 1865]; Abbott, "Personal Recollections," 270; Erson, "Report of 2 Regts. of MacRae's Brigade," in Lee Headquarters Papers, VHS; John R. Brinckle to "My Dear Brother," April 14, 1865, and to "My Dear Sister," April 10, 1865, both in John Rumsey Brinckle Papers, LC; *OR* pt. 1, 982. Captain Lemuel Abbott of the 10th Vermont characterized his brigade's assault as "comparatively speaking . . . a bloodless affair," noting "how little resistance there really was in front of the First Brigade excepting that of the one fort which so stubbornly held out." See Abbott, *Personal Recollections*, 269. Corporal Oscar Waite ascribed his regiment's minimal losses to Confederate fear of hitting their retiring pickets, thus limiting the Southern fire. See Waite, "Three Years with the 10th Vermont," II, 246. Private Simon B. Cummins of the 151st New York stated that "we did not loose [sic] many." See Jones, ed., *Give God the Glory*.

60. *OR* pt. 1, 902, 911-912, 1010. The distinguished cannoneers included Corporal James A. Barber, Private John Corcoran, Private Charles D. Ennis, Sergeant John H. Havron, Corporal Samuel E. Lewis, Sergeant Archibald Molbone, and Private George W. Potter. See Letters Received Enlisted Branch, Entry 409, File B-6920 (EB) for Corcoran and Entry 409, File C-7026 for Potter, and Correspondence of the Records & Pension Office, Entry 501, File 515708 for Barber, Havron, Lewis, and Molbone and File 334821 for Ennis, all in Record Group 94, NA.

61. *OR* pt.3, 478, 453; Roy P. Basler, ed, *The Collected Works of Abraham Lincoln*, 8 vols. (New Brunswick, N.J., 1953-1955), VIII, 381.

62. Barnard, *Report on the Defenses of Washington*, 151; "The Battle of Five Forks," in *Cincinnati Daily Gazette*, April 7, 1865; Memoir of Thomas F. McCoy, Col. 107th Pennsylvania, in Frank R. McCoy Papers, LC.

63. McPherson, *For Cause and Comrades*, 85.

64. The units that, one way or another, take credit for leading the Breakthrough include, from Getty's division, the 5th Vermont, 1st Vermont Heavy Artillery, 6th Vermont, 61st Pennsylvania, 122nd New York, 139th Pennsylvania, and 93rd Pennsylvania; from Wheaton's division, the 95th Pennsylvania, 2nd Connecticut Heavy Artillery, 5th Wisconsin, 37th Massachusetts, 15th New Jersey, and 4th New Jersey; from Seymour's division, the 6th Maryland, 110th Ohio, 126th Ohio, 9th New York Heavy Artillery, 10th Vermont, 106th New York, and 87th Pennsylvania.

65. Lewis A. Grant to Hazard Stevens, February 13, 1884, and December 31, 1883, both in Hazard Stevens Papers, LC. It should be recalled that Grant had been wounded during the picket firing earlier in the morning and did not personally participate in the Breakthrough.

66. *OR* pt. 1, 975, 978, 969; Benedict, *Vermont in the Civil War*, I, 596-597; Memorandum by L.A. Grant, July 15, 1890, in Correspondence of the Records & Pension Office, File 240190, Record Group 94, NA.

67. J. Warren Keifer to "My Dear Wife," April 3, 1865, in Joseph Warren Keifer Papers, LC; King, "Sixth Corps at Petersburg," in *National Tribune*, April 15, 1920; J. Warren Keifer to Truman Seymour, May 19, 1865, Headquarters Letter Book 1863-1865, in Joseph Warren Keifer Papers, LC.

68. "Medal of Honor For Marylander," in *Westminster* (Md) *Sentinel*, March 28, 1908.

69. *OR* pt. 1, 1285. Major General Cadmus M. Wilcox, Lane's superior officer, at least partially corroborated Lane's identification of the Breakthrough by stating that, "The Confederate lines, were broken at several points between Petersburg & Hatcher's Run, one near Boisseau's house, near where Lane & McCombs [sic] brigades joined. . . ." Wilcox confused Erson's two regiments of MacRae's Brigade with McComb's troops who were next in line to the southwest. Erson's troops had reported, perhaps without Wilcox's complete knowledge, to the right of Lane's men after midnight on April 2. See Wilcox, "Notes on the Richmond Campaign," in Cadmus M. Wilcox Papers, LC. It is worth noting that no account has been located that either states or implies that Keifer's and Grant's brigades overlapped during their attacks, although it seems clear that at least Gould's and Prentiss's tiny bands hit the Confederate line near the same place and at about the same time.

70. *OR* pt. 1, 976, 971-972; Unidentified clipping in the files of Petersburg National Battlefield.

71. "The Battle of Sunday," in *Milwaukee Sentinel*, April 10, 1865.

CHAPTER EIGHT

Consequences
of the Breakthrough

Gened Wright and his subordinate Sixth Corps commanders faced two important challenges after capturing the Confederate works in their front. First, they had to restore command and control over their troops, whose organization had deteriorated in the chaos of victory. Secondly, the officers needed to develop and implement a clearly defined plan for exploiting their spectacular success. Some of the same elements that had contributed to Wright's achievement now inhibited his ability to capitalize on the Breakthrough. The sheer volume of the assault over an extensive area, conducted in limited light with an emphasis on drive rather than maintenance of distinct zones of authority, left the triumphant Union units in disarray. Brigade and division lines overlapped. Regimental commanders lost visual and audible contact with their companies. Any given colonel might find his troops scattered between the former Confederate picket line and the abandoned Southern camps. It would take time to sort everyone out and reestablish combat-ready formations.[1]

Once Wright and his officers found the means to realign their men, what would be their next objective? Wright's general directive for the assault issued the previous day had stated that, "Should we succeed in breaking the enemy's line and gaining the Boydton plank road the subsequent movements of the corps will be in conformity with the orders of

Major-General Meade already promulgated." Those orders, communicated by Meade on April 1, specified that, "After carrying the enemy's line you will push for the Boydton plank road and endeavor to establish communication with the assaulting columns on your right and left." [2]

Meade's plan to predicate Wright's post-Breakthrough objectives on the undefinable fates of John G. Parke's and Edward O. C. Ord's attacks left room for various interpretations of the Sixth Corps goals. A staff officer in Getty's division understood the corps mission to involve a sweep down the enemy's works toward Hatcher's Run, clearing the front for the Twenty-fourth and Second corps, thus allowing the combined forces to reverse direction and assail the interior Petersburg defenses. Brigade commander Hyde told his regimental subordinates that they were to "keep right on and cut [the] Southside R.R." after piercing the Confederate works. The historian of the Vermont Brigade stated that the Green Mountain boys received orders to "halt, re-form and await further orders" after their attack. [3]

"In the ardor of the movement it was quite impossible to check the advance of the troops."

Turn left? Go forward? Stop? Army commander Meade did little to alleviate the confusion. "I have not sent [Wright] any orders," the Pennsylvanian admitted to General Grant, "relying on his judgment and the fact of his knowing the operations on his right and left." Nothing indicates, however, that immediately after the Breakthrough Wright understood that Parke's assault several miles to the east had bogged down amidst the warrens of the Confederate entrenchments south of Petersburg, or that Ord would not order his units to advance until well after the Sixth Corps had completed its attacks. Wright would have to improvise his tactics, but first he needed to regain control of his divisions. [4]

Doing this would prove no easy task. "In the ardor of the movement it was quite impossible to check the advance of the troops," Wright confessed. Each of the Sixth Corps divisions pressed forward all vaguely aiming for Boydton Plank Road in pursuit of fleeing Confederates and unknowable opportunities. Getty's brigades in the center of Wright's formation set the example for the entire corps. Although some Second Division regiments attempted to halt along the captured earthworks to collect prisoners and organize for the next advance, most of Getty's soldiers rushed forward "without halting or re-forming, regardless of order

. . . firing on the fugitives, all cheering, until it seemed as if all bonds of discipline were broken."[5]

About one-half mile beyond the captured Confederate lines, swarms of bluecoats reached Boydton Plank Road. As additional Southerners fell prisoner along the highway, the Federals snipped the telegraph lines that paralleled the road. A member of the Signal Corps came equipped with a portable battery that he attached to the severed wires, allowing him to eavesdrop on Confederate transmissions. Meanwhile, elements of Hyde's and Tracy's brigades forged ahead to the South Side Railroad— arriving, according to one account, at 5:10 a.m. Fifteen skirmishers from the 61st Pennsylvania were among the first Federals to reach the tracks. Private Jacob S. Baker of Company B scaled a pole and cut more telegraph wire while troops from the 1st Maine Veterans, 122nd New York, and 4th Vermont captured and burned a small wagon train, sending the teams to the rear. A few of the men even attempted to dislodge some rails before officers herded the gleeful marauders back toward the captured Confederate line.[6]

Some of Getty's lieutenants established a picket line some 400 yards north of Boydton Plank Road. These sentries bore responsibility for maintaining a vigil against possible Confederate counter-offensives, but their main task was to prevent the haphazard advance of Federal regiments. Their efforts failed, however, as troops from Wheaton's division whisked past these videttes toward the South Side Railroad. Discipline and organization enjoyed no greater sway in the First Division than in Getty's command, with the possible exception of a portion of Edwards's brigade. Colonel Isaac C. Bassett of the 82nd Pennsylvania led Edwards's third line of battle "directly to the front, to the south side railroad, and cut the telegraph line to Richmond," according to Edwards. It may have been these Pennsylvanians who breached Getty's makeshift skirmish line. Bassett's men were joined by portions of the 5th Wisconsin and 37th Massachusetts, who also reached the railroad and fired into a train of cars. The 2nd Rhode Island and 49th Pennsylvania remained near the Plank Road and, like the 139th Pennsylvania of Warner's brigade, eventually established a reasonably well-ordered core of troops ready to react to any new instructions.[7]

The bulk of both the 121st New York and the 2nd Connecticut Heavy Artillery of Hamblin's brigade forged straight ahead after the Breakthrough, while most of the 65th New York and 95th Pennsylvania turned to the right and moved northeast along the Confederate works. An officer in the 121st New York testified that "a lot of us fellows charged over the field to the road, and fired into the running Rebs, and also into some wagons which were passing. We also twisted off the telegraph wires with our bayonets, continuing our firing at everything in sight." Lieutenant Soule of the 2nd Connecticut Heavy Artillery affirmed that some of his men tore up a section of the South Side Railroad, "for no one knew w[h]ere Gen Lee's army was, whether up at Petersburg, on the retreat, or skedaddled. . . ." Getty and Wheaton experienced only limited resistance from the residue of the vanquished Confederate battle line, "owing to the dimness of the twilight [making it] difficult at first to distinguish friend from foe," remembered a retreating North Carolinian.[8]

On the left flank of Wright's corps, Seymour's Third Division suffered the same disabling lack of cohesion that plagued Getty and Wheaton. An officer in the 10th Vermont of Truex's brigade led a few men through the abandoned Confederate camps just behind the captured works, hesitant to plunge ahead in the lingering darkness without any discernible organized force around which to rally. The small party approached a hut and, peering through the open door, saw two Confederates, one lying on the floor and the other sitting on the edge of his bunk, apparently debating whether to dress. The Vermonter crept up to the cabin and craned his neck around the corner, demanding the surrender of its occupants. Neither Rebel responded and to the officer's surprise, he discovered that both Confederates were dead. "The sitting man's body had been so perfectly balanced when instantly killed it had remained in its lifelike sitting position," recalled the Vermonter. "The discovery that he was dead was startling in the dim morning light which, on leaning forward after a step inside the cabin, revealed the pallor of his face and look of death."

Soon enough, however, live Confederates began to scramble from various hiding places in the camp, "half-clad, some without hats, pants, shoes, guns, etc., showing how completely they had been surprised, offering to surrender, but . . . afraid when directed to go to the rear of our lines to go alone through them for fear of being misunderstood and shot." The Vermonter described his captives as "comical-looking long haired, shriveled, half-clad and starved cadaverous-looking specimens of humanity." Despite his arrogance, the officer remained reluctant to advance without a much larger supporting cast than that which accompanied him at the time.[9]

Keifer's brigade, on Seymour's right, dashed ahead despite the opinion of the commander of the 138th Pennsylvania that "after crossing the works the organization of the brigade appeared to dissolve." Captain Eichelberger of the 6th Maryland was among the first of Keifer's men to venture beyond the Confederate ramparts, and he soon found himself at the Pickrell House, General Heth's hastily abandoned headquarters. "In

[Heth's] bedroom I found his Div. flag," recalled Eichelberger. "I set it down in the hall and ran upstairs thinking to find someone as prisoners. All were gone—When I came back to the hall my captured flag was gone—and another got the credit, and perhaps a medal, for picking up my captured flag."

Keifer reported that the 138th Pennsylvania and the 122nd Ohio of his command pressed across the Plank Road, captured more Confederates in a remote encampment, and eventually destroyed the telegraph lines and "tore up two rails on the South Side road." Captain Norvell of the 6th Maryland and Major Arthur McClellan of Wright's staff accompanied this group, which Norvell estimated at about 500 strong. The enthusiastic soldiers engaged in various acts of destruction or otherwise milled about searching for targets of opportunity.

The two Yankee officers soon recognized that their small party enjoyed neither unity of command nor any visible support. McClellan departed to locate the rest of the division and seek guidance from higher authority. After a period of time in which Norvell heard nothing from his companion, the captain decided to return to the captured breastworks himself. There he found Seymour, who inquired with some vigor, "Captain, where the devil have you been?" Norvell described the situation near the railroad, whereupon Seymour instructed him to "bring them in at once." Assisted by other officers, Norvell helped shepherd the ranging Third Division men back toward the Plank Road while, along the rest of Wright's front, organization gradually replaced victorious chaos. Among the stray bluecoats from Seymour's division were a twenty-five-year-old corporal from Centerville, Pennsylvania, named John Mauk and his friend and comrade from Company F, 138th Pennsylvania, Private Daniel Wolford. These two ordinary Union soldiers were about to participate in one of the Breakthrough's most extraordinary and significant consequences.[10]

*   *   *

The artillery pyrotechnics that had preceded Wright's attack could be plainly heard on the western outskirts of Petersburg, where Ambrose Powell Hill sought fitful rest at the Venable cottage in the company of his wife and two daughters. Across the road at the Widow Knight's house, "Indiana," Colonel William H. Palmer also found his sleep disturbed by the nighttime cannonading. The Third Corps chief of staff arose and wakened Major William Norborne Starke, a colleague on Hill's staff, requesting Starke to determine the origin and effect of the artillery fire. Starke departed on his fact-finding mission around 3:00 a.m. and returned before daylight, reporting "that the enemy had part of our line near the Rives' salient, and that matters looked critical on the lines in front of the city." Starke then took this ominous information to General Hill at his Venable cottage quarters.[11]

Shortly thereafter, Hill, dressed in a white linen shirt recently made by his wife, appeared at Indiana and inquired of Palmer whether any word had been received from his division commanders, Henry Heth or Cadmus Wilcox. Palmer replied in the negative, having no information beyond that provided by Major Starke. Hill returned to his headquarters tent and requested that his horse be saddled and made ready for use. As a black servant led Hill's dapple-gray mount, Champ, toward the general, Colonel Palmer dashed up, seeking permission to accompany his chief. Hill denied the request but ordered Palmer to awaken the rest of the staff and see to the hitching of the headquarters wagons. Hill intended to ride to General Lee's headquarters to confer with his commander, and then return to Indiana with instructions for the morning's activities.[12]

The general rode first to his couriers' quarters, where he found Sergeant George W. Tucker grooming his horse in the near darkness of the early dawn. Hill ordered Tucker to assign two orderlies to join him on the short trip to Lee's headquarters and for the sergeant to follow as soon as he could ready his own mount. Hill knew that Tucker made it his custom to have two horses saddled at all times for instant employment during periods of crisis. Tucker assigned Private William H. Jenkins and another man named Kirkpatrick to gallop behind the rapidly departing Hill. Tucker quickly completed his own equestrian preparations and swung into the saddle only minutes after the departure of Hill, Jenkins, and Kirkpatrick.

"Edge Hill," Lee's headquarters overlooking the intersection of Cox and Long Ordinary roads, lay one and one-half miles west of Indiana, so Hill and his trailing aides needed little time to reach their destination. Immediately upon their arrival, however, Hill ordered Kirkpatrick to reverse field and report portentous news to Third Corps headquarters. Hill had apparently spotted the fugitives from Wilcox's Division streaming back from their broken fortifications and surmised that serious problems must have befallen his sector of the line. He told Kirkpatrick to inform Colonel Palmer of the emergency and to summon Palmer and the rest of the staff to ride west and prepare to rally the troops. This was the first intimation at corps headquarters that Hill's defenses had collapsed. Hill and Jenkins dismounted in front of Edge Hill, the Turnbull House, as Tucker reigned up.[13]

Lieutenant General Ambrose Powell Hill

Library of Congress

Hill entered the Turnbull House and found Lee in his room, half-dressed and showing evidence of a poor night's rest. General Longstreet, who had arrived a little earlier from north of the Appomattox River, rested in another chamber. As Hill and Lee compared notes on the rapidly unfolding crisis, Colonel Charles S. Venable of Lee's staff burst into the house with graphic verification of what Hill had discerned during his ride to Edge Hill. Venable had spotted "wagons and teamsters dashing rather wildly down the River Road (Cox's) in the direction of Petersburg." The staff officer had also conferred with a wounded Confederate, who told him that Yankee skirmishers were at that very moment prowling about Brigadier General Nathaniel H. Harris's abandoned winter quarters, which lay about one-half mile south of army headquarters![14]

Lee immediately instructed Venable to ascertain the circumstances that had allowed Union soldiers to penetrate so deeply behind Hill's lines. Hill leapt to his feet and strode out of the room with Venable, unwilling to delegate such a critical assignment solely to a staff officer. The two men mounted their horses and, joined by Tucker and Jenkins, rode south. After traveling but a short distance, Hill stopped to gaze through his field glasses toward the unknown dangers ahead of them. The four riders carefully proceeded a few moments longer until they reached Cattail Run, a small tributary of Rohoic Creek, where they stopped to water their horses and gather their thoughts. Scattered shots suddenly broke the uneasy silence, and the specter of armed men arose in the dim light before them. Out of the murky landscape appeared two fully-equipped Yankees. Tucker and Jenkins reacted instantly and rode down upon the intruders, demanding and securing their uncontested surrender. The Federals, no doubt, had been as surprised to encounter a party of mounted Confederates as Hill's little entourage had been to see them. "Jenkins, take them to General Lee," intoned Hill, while Tucker, Venable, and the general continued their ride, marginally protected by a half-dozen stray Confederates informally marshaled by Venable as a screen.[15]

The shallow valley created by Cattail Run shielded Hill's tiny escort from Harris's deserted huts, where Venable had spotted the Union troops. A young courier from Colonel Thomas H. Carter's Second Corps artillery, Percy G. Hawes, had joined Hill's party after being rousted from his encampment near Mayfield, the Whitworth House, by some Sixth Corps adventurers. Hawes confirmed Venable's report and warned Hill that numerous Yankees lurked over the rise around Harris's huts, an admonition that the capture of the two Union prisoners seemed to verify. Venable added his voice of caution to that of Hawes, citing General Lee himself as the source of concern for Hill's safety. Hill courteously acknowledged Lee's consideration, but assured Venable that he had no object in mind other than to gain communication with his right. It seemed that everyone shared the same solicitude for Hill's well being.

As the group ascended the slope toward Harris's winter quarters, Tucker joined Venable and Hawes in raising a protest. "Please excuse me,

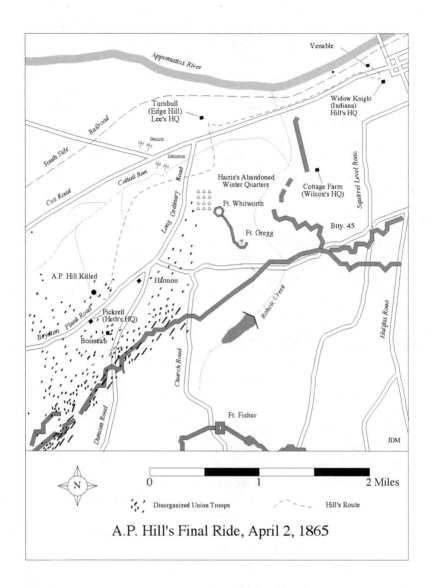

A.P. Hill's Final Ride, April 2, 1865

General, but where are you going?" he asked. "Sergeant, I must go to the right as quickly as possible," Hill replied, but acceding to warnings now thrice repeated, the general agreed to alter his route: "We will go up this side of the branch to the woods, which will cover us until reaching the field in rear of General Heth's quarters[;] I hope to find the road clear at General Heth's."[16]

The party's course now followed the stream bed of Cattail Run in a generally southwesterly direction. After riding a short distance, Hill spotted artillery on Cox Road some 300 or 400 yards to the north. The general inquired about the identity of the guns, and Venable replied that they belonged to Lieutenant Colonel William T. Poague's Battalion of Third Corps artillery, recently arrived from Dutch Gap, along Major General William Mahone's line north of the Appomattox River. Hill ordered Venable to deploy Poague's gunners (probably only Captain Charles F. Johnston's Albemarle Artillery and Captain Nathan Penick's Pittsylvania Battery) to protect Lee's headquarters and the interior Petersburg defenses from the looming threat now gathering to the south and west. Venable complied, requesting that young Hawes join him. This left only Tucker and Hill to continue the increasingly dangerous journey toward the Pickrell House.[17]

Sergeant Tucker recognized full well the peril that now faced his corps commander. "From that time on I kept slightly ahead of the General," wrote Tucker. "I had kept a Colt's army pistol drawn since the affair of the Federal stragglers." The two riders crossed Long Ordinary Road and passed through some woods along Cattail Run advancing almost two miles until they emerged into a field north of Boydton Plank Road opposite the Harmon House and Duncan Road, less than one-half mile northeast of Heth's headquarters. During this entire span, neither Hill nor Tucker saw another soul and few words passed between them. At one point, the pensive general told Tucker, "Sergeant, should anything happen to me you must go back to General Lee and report it."[18]

Hill and Tucker halted in the clearing and scanned their expanded field of vision. The sergeant could see that the Plank Road was full of troops. Hill used his binoculars to render a positive identification. "They are there," stated the general, Tucker correctly understanding that the men were Federals.

"Which way now, General?" Tucker inquired.

Hill pointed down the hill toward a strip of woods that ran parallel to the Plank Road. "We must keep on to the right."

Tucker spurred ahead and covered about two-thirds of the distance to the sheltering forest, defined by a perimeter of several large trees. The intrepid aide noticed a half-a-dozen or more Federals in the timber, two of whom dashed behind one of the oaks and leveled their guns, one atop the other, at Tucker and Hill. The two Union soldiers were Corporal Mauk and Private Wolford.[19]

The pair of Pennsylvanians had been wending their way back toward the captured Confederate works after experiencing the high adventure of tearing up track on the South Side Railroad and firing on a wagon train along Cox Road. They had seen a covey of their comrades in blue making coffee and eating breakfast on the other side of the Plank Road and had thought to join them in a little repast before renewing their search for the rest of their unit. As Wolford and Mauk entered some swampy woods they noticed "two men on horseback coming from the direction of Petersburg, who had the appearance of officers." These riders, of course, were Hill and Tucker.

The four antagonists had now assumed their positions. Mauk and Wolford enjoyed the advantage of cover and superior weapons. Hill and Tucker controlled the pace of the confrontation and possessed the initiative.

"We must take them," ordered Hill, drawing from his holster a Colt Navy pistol.

"Stay there, I'll take them," replied the loyal Tucker, closing on the Pennsylvanians to a distance not exceeding twenty yards. "If you fire, you'll be swept to hell!" shouted the Confederate sergeant. "Our men are here—surrender!"

By now the range had diminished to ten yards with Hill riding to the right of Tucker. The affair had assumed some of the character of an Old West showdown at high noon. Would either side fire? Who would pull the trigger first? Wolford's courage began to fail and he lowered the rifle from his shoulder. Mauk, with only an instant to reach a decision, told his partner, "I cannot see it. Let us shoot them." Wolford aimed his rifle again and both weapons erupted with streaks of orange flame at virtually point blank range. Tucker reached out to his right toward Champ and grabbed the horse's bridle. Somehow, the nervous Wolford had missed his mark. Quickly wheeling to the left, Tucker looked around him and saw Hill sprawled on the ground motionless, his limbs extended in an attitude of death. Mauk's round had severed Hill's left thumb and passed directly through the general's heart, exiting through his back. The corps commander was probably dead before he hit the ground.[20]

While none of the accounts of Hill's death mention the time that the episode occurred, it is possible to estimate the hour based on the sequence of events leading to Mauk's mortal shot. Hill's ride to the Turnbull House occurred after he received Starke's information about the Union penetration at Rives Salient. Because that attack began at 4:30 a.m., Starke could not possibly have returned to Indiana with such news until 5:00 a.m., and possibly later. Because Hill had seen the results of Wright's Breakthrough on the way to Edge Hill, the Virginian's ride to Lee's headquarters probably took place between 5:00 a.m. and 5:30 a.m. Allowing for the passage of a quarter of an hour between the time of Hill's arrival at the Turnbull House and the time that he, Venable, Tucker, and Jenkins left on their reconnaissance, Hill probably began his final ride about 5:45 a.m. Such a schedule would account for the presence of Union troops so far behind the fractured Confederate line. The general's route between Edge Hill and Mauk's fateful oak tree covered some two miles, a trip made cautiously with several documented stops. Thus, Hill and Tucker most likely encountered Mauk and Wolford between 6:30 a.m. and 6:45 a.m.

Sergeant Tucker maintained control of Champ and quickly reversed course, throwing himself across the neck of his mount to present as small a target as possible. Once inside the shelter of the woods, Tucker changed horses and directed the swifter Champ back toward Lee's headquarters "as fast as the nature of the ground would permit." Tucker dodged stray parties of Federals but felt that the imperative nature of his mission demanded that he risk moving through open ground on the most expeditious route to Edge Hill. He guided Champ through Harris's forsaken winter camp, passing surprised Federals along the way, and gained the cover of Cattail Run. Soon he spotted a party of mounted Confederates who proved to be Longstreet and his staff. Shortly thereafter, Palmer and other members of Hill's military family appeared, having responded to Kirkpatrick's earlier message, and Tucker briefed everyone on the sad state of affairs. Palmer accompanied Tucker the remaining distance to Edge Hill, where they found Lee, dressed in an unsoiled suit of gray cloth, wearing a new sword and belt, standing south of Cox Road across from the Turnbull House.[21]

Tucker was well known throughout the army, and the sight of him, not Hill, astride Champ must have provided Lee with some intimation of the bad news Tucker now delivered. "I reported to [Lee] General Hill's last order to me," remembered the sergeant. "General Lee then asked for details. . . ." Tucker provided a full account of the circumstances surrounding Hill's death. Tears filled the general's eyes as a sorrowful expression overwhelmed his careworn countenance. "He is at rest now, and we who are left are the ones to suffer," said Lee. Ever mindful of the personal considerations of war even at such a critical time, Lee instructed Palmer and Tucker to repair to the Venable cottage and inform Mrs. Hill of her loss. "Colonel, break the news to her as gently as possible," he admonished Palmer.[22]

Once Tucker had galloped away from the fatal clearing, Mauk and Wolford departed as well. "We knowing not what was on our flank, and not being able to see in that direction, backed out and went farther down the swamp, and crossed to the men on the hill," recalled Mauk. However, curiosity overcame the Pennsylvanian's initial fear, and the corporal decided to return to the field and learn what he could about the brave officer he had shot. In a matter of moments, Mauk spied what he thought to be a skirmish line advancing in his direction. He withdrew and, gathering a dozen or so of his coffee-boiling comrades, devised a makeshift formation of his own. Mauk, acting more like a colonel than a corporal, waited until the approaching figures reached hailing distance and then ordered them to halt, which they did. "Throw up your arms, advance, and give an account of yourselves," instructed Mauk.

The party consisted of six or eight men wearing Union uniforms and carrying weapons and about an equal number of unarmed Confederates. Mauk's questioning revealed that his captives were a party of Federals leading their small group of Rebel prisoners to the rear. Mauk accepted the apparent truth of the situation and released them. Before departing, one of the guards asked the corporal if there had been a man killed in the vicinity. Mauk replied that he had slain an officer in the nearby swampy woods. The party then headed off in the direction Mauk indicated.

This group of soldiers may, in truth, have been a portion of the 5th Alabama Battalion, Hill's headquarters unit, searching for their general's remains. Tucker credited these men with the rescue of Hill's body while it was still warm, and Venable said that the recovery occurred "in less than half an hour after General Hill was killed." The stratagem of pretending to be a Federal detachment escorting captured Confederates seems a plausible way to penetrate a country swarming with the enemy. The question, however, as to how the Alabamians may have obtained Union uniforms must remain an open one.[23]

Only later did Mauk find these circumstances suspicious. He and Wolford eventually returned to their unit, where they reported their adventure to their colonel, Matthew R. McClennan. As rumors of Hill's death circulated throughout the Army of the Potomac later in the day, the inquisitive McClennan sent Mauk and Wolford to Keifer's headquarters. Eventually, the two men reported to General Wright himself. The Sixth Corps commander listened to their story and then asked the imminently notorious corporal if he knew who he had shot. "I told him I did not," replied Mauk, who by now must have been totally mystified about why his morning's escapade had attracted such high level attention. "You have killed General A. P. Hill of the Confederate army," said Wright, Mauk and Wolford not guessing until that moment the identity of their victim in the clearing.[24]

Hill's corpse arrived at the Venable cottage a few minutes after Colonel Palmer had appeared to break the news to the pregnant widow, Dolly Hill. Palmer heard Mrs. Hill singing inside the building as he rapped on the door. When she answered Palmer's knock, Mrs. Hill threw up her hands and shouted, "The General is dead. You would not be here if he had not been killed." Palmer made arrangements to transport the distraught family to safety under the escort of several members of Hill's staff, including the general's nephew, Captain Frank Hill, and the courier, Private Jenkins. As admiring hands lifted General Hill's body onto a dilapidated wagon, the Virginian's face was covered with his military cape.[25]

First Thomas "Stonewall" Jackson, then "Jeb" Stuart, and now A. P. Hill; events had conspired to deprive General Lee of some of his most valued subordinates. Now, however, the fate of his army itself rested in the balance as the Federals began to exploit the advantage created by Wright's Breakthrough.

*   *   *

Although the collapse of Erson's, Lane's and Thomas's commands created a huge breech in Lee's defensive perimeter, it did not destroy all the resistance along the Third Corps front. Henry Heth could still count three intact brigades positioned from Hatcher's Run northeastward to the ragged southwest margin of the Breakthrough. John R. Cooke's North Carolinians, some 600 strong, defended the works on either bank of Hatcher's Run, including an installation known as the Free Nigger Fort northeast of the stream. To Cooke's left, the five regiments of Joseph R. Davis's Brigade occupied the line. These troops, predominantly Mississippians, were led that morning by Colonel Andrew M. Nelson of the 42nd Mississippi. Brigadier General William McComb's Tennessee brigade, including the 2nd Maryland Battalion, defended what had now become Heth's left, southwest of and adjacent to the Breakthrough. McComb had 500 or 600 rifles in place that morning, endowing the Confederates with roughly 1,600 remaining men astride and northeast of Hatcher's Run. Heth assigned Cooke overall responsibility for this portion of the line, the division commander himself directing the mixed forces west of Hatcher's Run. Just as along Thomas's, Lane's, and Erson's fronts, powerful artillery bolstered the thin Southern ranks in at least half-a-dozen fixed gun emplacements between McComb's entrenchments and Hatcher's Run.[26]

Gradually, the Sixth Corps officers restored order in their commands and began to assemble a new attack formation designed to overrun Cooke's defenses. Seymour's division aligned perpendicular to the captured Confederate works with its left on the inside of the entrenchments. The Vermont Brigade, now under the de facto command of Lieutenant Colonel Charles Mundee of Getty's staff, dressed on Seymour's right in descending numerical order, the 1st Vermont Heavy Artillery (11th Vermont) on the left and the 2nd Vermont on the right. Hyde's brigade formed to the right of the Vermonters and Warner's regiments to the right of Hyde. Wheaton had been preparing to steer his division toward Petersburg when Wright sent him orders to dispatch the two brigades nearest the rest of the corps to assist Seymour and Getty. Wheaton whisked William H. Penrose's and Oliver Edwards's commands to the left, where they filed in on Warner's right. Hamblin's brigade remained along the captured Confederate line to protect the position against a potential counterattack. This new Union deployment stretched across Boydton Plank Road, but by no means did it resemble the well-ordered formation that had facilitated the Breakthrough. The blueclad officers did their best to perfect their combat alignments, but the seven brigades that now faced southwest toward McComb, Nelson, and Cooke would depend more on firepower and high morale than parade-ground tactics to achieve their next objective.[27]

Their initial target lay some 300 yards to the southwest. Here, a battery mounting four guns, known informally as Fort Alexander and occupied by the Purcell Artillery of Richmond commanded by Captain George M. Cayce, seemed ripe for the picking. In the distance, the Federals could see butternut infantry forming at right angles to their works, preparing to support the guns. Seymour's men, among them the 10th Vermont of Truex's brigade and the 6th Maryland and 9th New York Heavy Artillery from Keifer's command, overran the battery "without serious opposition" and quickly turned the captured ordnance upon the Confederates farther down the line. Lieutenant Samuel W. Angel of the 6th Maryland secured the colors of the Purcell Artillery as a trophy of war. Using this brief halt to catch their breath and reorganize their ranks, the Federals lurched forward again, this time heading for Fort Davis, an emplacement some 400 yards to the southwest on the opposite side of the marshy terrain formed by a small but treacherous watercourse named Rocky Branch.[28]

This two-gun battery lay within McComb's original zone of control. The Tennesseans and Marylanders scrambled to establish a line of battle,

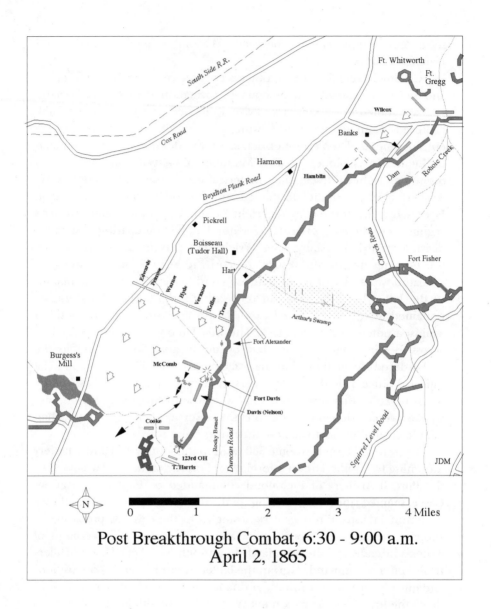

Post Breakthrough Combat, 6:30 - 9:00 a.m.
April 2, 1865

the 250 men of the 2nd Maryland Battalion being the first to present an organized front against the swarming bluecoats who waded through the breast-deep swamp. "Form your men first," McComb ordered the commander of the 2nd Maryland, "and I'll form the rest of the brigade on your Marylanders."[29]

While McComb's Maryland infantry poured "a severe musketry fire" upon the charging Yankees, and the guns in Fort Davis roared in support, a hodgepodge of Third Division units swept up to the fort's embankment, their uniforms soaked with the waters of Rocky Branch. Color bearers from the 14th New Jersey hoisted their banners on the works, and after brief fighting along the parapet, the Confederates withdrew a few hundred yards into a surviving patch of woods. From there, they maintained such a strong blanket of fire that the victorious Federals could not sustain their momentum. Among the Union casualties lay Adjutant James M. Read of the 10th Vermont, who suffered a wound to the foot that would require amputation, and four days later prove mortal. The advance over the rough ground did further violence to the Sixth Corps organization as well, creating an opportunity that McComb's Brigade did not squander.[30]

Twenty minutes had passed since Fort Davis had fallen. Somehow, General Heth learned of its capture and sent a courier, J. C. Bingham, with orders for McComb to retake the position. General McComb needed no such encouragement, however, for he and a staff officer, Captain John Allen, had worked mightily to rally the brigade for a countercharge. "Gen. McComb was using his most persuasive manner, telling the men of their many glorious deeds and that he was then prepared to sacrifice his own life if necessary," remembered Bingham. "Capt. John Allen . . . not so choice in his language, was making the air blue as he dashed among those in the rear, urging them to the front."

Just then a small but perfectly ordered line of men appeared, and McComb recognized the detachment as some of the brigade sharpshooters led by Lieutenant Fergus S. Harris. The lieutenant approached McComb and Allen as the staff officer explained the desperate situation facing the brigade: "Harris, the men are badly demoralized. I don't believe we can retake the battery. Can you lead them?"

Harris replied with a firm resolve: "These men will fight, Captain. Let me lead them with my sharpshooters."

Harris's marksmen had been isolated in the picket posts in front of the main line and had been delayed in making their way back to the works, fearful of being mistaken for attacking Federals. By the time Harris reported, however, McComb had managed to rally the 2nd Maryland Battalion and the 1st, 7th, and 14th Tennessee regiments to assist the sharpshooters. The general crafted a line of battle on both sides of the works and at right angles to them, then gave the command to advance. With McComb and Allen encouraging the men above the roar of musketry, "Harris jerked off his hat, waved it in the air, and struck a brisk trot toward the enemy, hurrahing at the top of his voice." McComb watched proudly as his veteran troops executed their counterattack. "I never saw our boys make a more gallant charge," beamed the brigadier. "We drove the enemy over the branch into Genl. Wilcox['s] line."[31]

"Before we were prepared the enemy was upon us in a counter charge, and the fort, with its guns, was lost, and some of our men were taken," recalled Colonel Keifer. Sergeant Henry W. Manson of the 7th Tennessee was among the sharpshooters who shrieked the Rebel Yell and plowed into the stunned Unionists in what he termed "a regular devils' picnic." Manson found himself moving through the brigade's winter quarters when he spied a "tall, angular Federal, standing on the works more exposed to the fire than anyone." The bluecoat pointed his rifle at Manson and let go a round that ricocheted off the corner of a soldiers' hut, spraying bark in Manson's face. "With a prayer for the soul of the bravest Yankee I ever saw[,] my trusty Sharpe's rifle was aimed at the tall man's breast, and at the crack of the gun he fell from the earthworks," remembered Manson.[32]

Those Federals not captured scrambled back through the swamp toward the safety of Fort Alexander to the northeast. Lieutenant Angel of the 6th Maryland sustained a mortal wound while rallying his company during this withdrawal. The fighting at Fort Davis had lasted less than ten minutes, demonstrating for the first—but not the only time that morning—that A. P. Hill's men retained sufficient morale and firepower to execute a tactical offensive.[33]

Some members of the 2nd Maryland Battalion began working the artillery pieces at Fort Davis, but almost immediately the victorious Rebels began to contend with counterbattery fire emanating from the occupied emplacement to the northeast. Major William Wood of the 9th New York Heavy Artillery had command of some of the captured Confederate ordnance and executed good practice on the two guns in Fort Davis. Other artillery came under the control of less experienced cannoneers. An unidentified officer shouted to a group of soldiers from the 10th Vermont to serve one of the captured guns. "I didn't fancy that kind of a job," admitted Corporal Oscar E. Waite, "but having been recognized, and not caring to ignore so special an invitation," Waite reported just as another impressed crew launched a shell that exploded high in the tops of some pines hundreds of yards beyond McComb's position. "My artillery experience had been confined to Fourth of July celebrations, but having watched the battery men at drill, and having, while supporting batteries, seen them in actual practice. . . . I started without hesitation."

Waite swabbed the gun and saw to the loading of the piece, someone offering the good advice to be sure that the projectile did not explode over their own men. Taking aim at a Rebel officer mounted near the fort, Waite pulled the lanyard. "That shell seemed to pass almost under that horse's nose, and exploded near the ground in front of the rebel line; and its course over the heads of our men was filled with dark whirling objects . . . . 'Were all those hats?'" Waite inquired with some anxiety. "That was all right," replied an officer who had watched the round through his field glasses. "Just right, nothing but hats. Give them another just like it, only a little <u>higher</u>."[34]

Time was the ally of the Federals. Major Wood's marksmanship (undoubtedly more than the contributions of the amateur cannoneers of the 10th Vermont) helped silence the second of McComb's artillery pieces while various units from Seymour's division poised to renew their offensive. Lieutenant Colonel Bogardus of the 151st New York estimated that the Federals advanced again across the swamp about 7:00 a.m. A polyglot of regiments from Truex's and Seymour's brigades once again splashed through Rocky Branch and up to the parapet of the fort.[35]

Major Wyllys Lyman of the 10th Vermont, caught up in the spirit of the moment, exhorted his men to "Follow me, and we'll bag those fellows. Come on every one of you. . . . Rally on your colors!" A German soldier, a member of another regiment, came under the steely glare of the excited major. "Vot you means," protested the immigrant. "Dose iss not my colors." The German began to leave when Lyman, known to the Vermonters as something of a fop, "jump[ed] like a cat for a mouse [and] grabbed the fellow's collar" giving him "a quick wheel in the right direction." The major had developed a reasonably efficient line of battle and soon had it making tracks for Fort Davis. Corporal Waite told the rest of the story:

Coming to a soggy, nearly flooded valley, where the invisible stepping places were indicated by little tufts of rushes, we hesitated. Our Dandy Major, slick as though just out of a band-box, sprang to the front, and we started on the jump. Just then, the rebels, being attacked from the other side, began to pour out of the fort like wheat from a bag. The Major swung his sabre, and yelling for us to hurry, jumped from one of those tussocks. Just then our big impressed Dutchman jumped for the same one, and bumping the open-mouthed Major, who had landed first, sent him sprawling like a big frog, into that murky-bottomed water. Like a jack from a box, the half-crumpled Major sprang to his feet, and between coughing fits managed to shout, 'Go on, men! Left half-wheel! I'll be there.'

Witnesses to this little episode could not help but halt and enjoy a belly laugh at the expense of these two characters. But soon everyone regained their composure and, along with the rest of Seymour's men, reached the fort and helped round up prisoners.[36]

Waite's comment that the Confederates sustained an attack from another direction referenced the participation of the Vermont Brigade in this assault. The New Englanders had formed on Seymour's right at the outset of the movement down the Confederate line, but they had encountered several obstacles in addition to their grayclad enemies. The first was the terrain. "The whole command pushed forward vigorously through thickets, swamps, and pine woods, soon losing all organization again in the eagerness of the men to surpass each other in the pursuit of the enemy," reported a Vermont officer. The second impediment to the brigade's effectiveness arrived in the person of Charles Mundee.

Because the brigade's regular commander, Lewis A. Grant, had fallen wounded during the picket firing before the Breakthrough, Colonel Tracy of the 2nd Vermont had led the brigade through the Confederate works. Getty dispatched Mundee, his assistant adjutant general, with orders to help guide Tracy's command in its post-Breakthrough maneuvers. Unbeknownst to Getty, Mundee was drunk. Perhaps the alcohol, combined with the stimulation of the moment, prompted the staff officer to overstep the authority Getty had assigned him. Instead of reporting merely as a guide, Mundee relieved Tracy of command and personally assumed tactical control of the Vermonters. Colonel Tracy must have been surprised at his unwarranted and unexplained removal, but recognized that in the immediate presence of the enemy it would be worse than irresponsible to debate the issue. The inexperienced and inebriated Mundee certainly added nothing to the efficiency of the Vermonters as they struggled forward toward McComb's flank.[37]

By this time, however, Heth realized that his left had been irretrievably compromised. "As soon as I found that the enemy had possession of the Boydton Plank Road and that he was moving down this road my position being no longer tenable I gave orders to withdraw to Sutherland's Station on the S.S. Rail Road," reported Heth. Cooke, who had joined the beleaguered Tennesseans and Marylanders at Fort Davis, passed along the withdrawal orders to McComb. "Genl. Cook[e] told me the enemy were pushing out the road in our rear and they would cut us off," wrote McComb. "We had more prisoners than we had men in our command & Genl. Cook[e] said we would have to give them a verbal parole as we could'nt take them out." McComb remembered "not the least confusion" during the retreat, but more probably, the situation bordered on the chaotic. Captain Walter Smith of the 4th Vermont described charging down the Confederate works, "gob[b]ling up Johnies[,] artillery and every thing." Sergeant Lester G. Hack of the 5th Vermont jerked the colors of the 23rd Tennessee from a stubborn Rebel who attempted to rally a small group of McComb's soldiers. Among those men was Sergeant Manson of the 7th Tennessee, who received a gunshot wound to the leg while trying to protect the unit from Mundee's flank attack. "By this time the line was broken and the enemy had it all their own way," Manson recalled.[38]

Once McComb's Brigade began its withdrawal, the Mississippians of Nelson's [Davis's] Brigade stood directly in the path of the now unstoppable Union juggernaut. "I . . . sent orders to Colonel Nelson commanding Davis' Brigade to withdraw at once and also to [the] officer commanding my Brigade to retire up [the] right bank of the creek," reported Cooke. "Colonel Nelson was very slow in obeying the order and in consequence I think, very unnecessarily surrendered his command." In fairness to Nelson, he did not so much capitulate to the advancing Yankees as he abdicated responsibility for attempting to orchestrate an orderly withdrawal. Lieutenant Colonel George W. Shannon of the 11th Mississippi, for example, merely moved his regiment to Hatcher's Run where he disbanded it, every man for himself. Some fugitives negotiated the stream by swimming while others floated across on logs. Judging his situation hopeless, the color bearer of the 11th Mississippi "tore the flag of the regiment into shreds, tied them to the flag-staff and threw them into Hatcher's Run," moments before most of the 11th found itself surrounded and prisoners of war. Nelson, along with approximately 70 officers and men of the 42nd Mississippi, surrendered to Captain George G. Tilden, Lieutenant Julius S. Dorman, and about 50 men from the 1st Vermont Heavy Artillery, who also seized two cannons in the process. Davis later reported that only twenty members of his brigade escaped.[39]

McComb reached Hatcher's Run only to discover that "the enemy had possession of the bridge at Burgess Mill. My Brigade at this time was very much scattered & General Cooke said the only chance for escape was to swim." Some of the Tennesseans navigated safely across, but just 30 of the 2nd Maryland Battalion emerged intact from the fighting on April 2. Captain Augustus Merrill of the 1st Maine Veterans noticed the fugitives on the far bank of Hatcher's Run. With a party of fifteen soldiers representing half-a-dozen-regiments, Merrill utilized an old mill dam to gain the left bank of the stream. Once across, his little band liberated Captain John Tifft of the 9th New York Heavy Artillery, who had been moving under guard toward the west. The intrepid Yankees bluffed 64 Confederates into surrendering before withdrawing back across Hatcher's Run, snagging five more graycoats along the way. Many years later, Thomas Hyde recommended Merrill for a Medal of Honor in recognition of his brave leadership during this episode.[40]

By 7:45 a.m., all organized resistance northeast of Hatcher's Run had evaporated. Only Cooke's Brigade survived in any semblance of order from the three hours of fighting that had proven so devastating to the Third Corps of the Army of Northern Virginia. Four brigades, Thomas's, Lane's, McComb's, and Davis's, had been all but removed from the strategic equation, along with the half of MacRae's North Carolinians who had participated in the morning's combat. While Heth hurried northwest toward Sutherland Station with the remaining elements of his division, the Sixth Corps began to tally the fruits of its stunning achievement.

One Federal claimed that 6,000 or 7,000 Confederates surrendered to the Sixth Corps on the morning of April 2, clearly an absurd exaggeration. But many officers reported either careful estimates or studied accounting of the trophies yielded by Hill's men. "This brigade captured 10 pieces of artillery immediately after entering the works . . . also a large number of prisoners, 3 battle-flags, and Major General Heth's division headquarters flag," boasted Keifer. He later expanded his total number of captured cannons to fourteen. Seymour credited his division with the seizure of "some twenty-odd guns and many hundred prisoners, with four flags." General Wright first reported that his command had taken "1,000 prisoners and a great many guns," but shortly thereafter raised his estimate to "many guns and flags, and I think from 2,000 to 3,000 prisoners." Grant later guessed that the Sixth Corps had corralled 3,000 Confederates that morning. This estimate is probably close to the mark. Heth and Wilcox had some 4,500 men on their line at dawn, counting cannoneers. Deducting the significant percentage of Cooke's soldiers who escaped, and a reasonable allowance for the uncertain number of Southerners killed during the attacks, anecdotal evidence supports the notion that the vast majority of the remaining Confederates became prisoners. The Breakthrough and its subsequent action, then, resulted in one of the most serious reverses ever suffered by a corps of the Army of Northern Virginia. No wonder Sergeant Albert C. Harrison of the 14th New Jersey wrote home on April 2 that, "The Confederacy is gone up."[41]

*   *   *

While the Sixth Corps prepared for, and then executed, its momentous assault, General Ord's detachments from the Army of the James played a meaningful if decidedly supporting role in the morning's success. By the evening of March 29, three divisions of Ord's infantry had taken their positions beyond the left flank of Wright's Sixth Corps. Brigadier General Robert S. Foster's three brigades of the Twenty-fourth Corps occupied General Humphreys's old entrenchments between the Sixth Corps and Hatcher's Run. Foster had tendered his resignation a few days earlier "for private reasons," but at his corps commander's, Major General John Gibbon's, request Foster had agreed to remain in the field until the current campaign had been decided. Brigadier General John W. Turner's Independent Division linked Foster's left with the right flank of the Second Corps farther west. Brigadier General William Birney's Twenty-fifth Corps division of United States Colored Troops remained in reserve. Between March 30 and April 1, Ord's soldiers jousted with the Confederates, displaying much "patience, endurance, and pluck," sustaining and inflicting casualties, but effecting no material change in the strategic situation along their front.[42]

Grant intended that Ord's troops participate in the mass assault ordered for the morning of April 2. Ord explained on the eve of the attack, however, that the landscape between his divisions and the enemy consisted of a "bay-gall, or morass" and expressed some hesitation about the practicality of a large-scale frontal movement across such inhospitable terrain. The lieutenant general appreciated Ord's situation and told the army commander on the night of April 1 that, "I think as you have such difficult ground to go over your reserves had better be pushed well over to the right, so that they can help [General Wright] or go in with you, as may be required." Grant modified these orders before midnight:

> If it is impracticable for you to get through in your front I do not want you to try it, but you can in that case draw out of your lines more men as a reserve, and hold them to throw in where some one else may penetrate. . . . Understand, I do not wish you to fight your way over difficult barriers against defended lines. I want you to see, though, if the enemy is leaving, and if so follow him up.

Grant, truly exercising his authority as general-in-chief of all armies, kept Ord informed of Wright's attack plans while Gibbon passed along to his division commanders the orders to suspend their proposed assaults. Thus, at the first hint of light, while the Sixth Corps challenged Thomas, Lane, and Erson, Ord's men remained in their fortifications, alert to circumstances both on their flanks and in their front that might prompt them to move.[43]

Those circumstances evolved before 6:00 a.m. Wright reported his great success to Grant but expressed in unusually strong terms his perceived need for immediate assistance to preserve his victory: "I must be re-enforced or I shall lose all that I have gained. My rear also should be looked after, as I only left a brigade where I broke through." Grant informed Ord of Wright's achievement. "Now is the time to push your men to the right," he ordered, "leaving your line very thin, and go to [Wright's] assistance." Ord responded by sending five brigades to the northeast, Foster's three under colonels Thomas O. Osborn, George B. Dandy, and Harrison S. Fairchild, and most of Lieutenant Colonel Andrew Potter's and Colonel William Curtis's brigades of Turner's division. Gibbon retained Brigadier General Thomas M. Harris's West Virginia brigade of Turner's command, which advanced along the corps picket line, and the three sable brigades of Birney's division.[44]

General Turner had instructed Harris to advance a strong skirmish line toward the Confederate position shortly before daybreak. The division commander suspected that the graycoats in his front may have abandoned their lines during the night or might, even then, be in the act of withdrawing. The 123rd Ohio of Potter's brigade moved forward to reinforce Harris's men, who crept ahead in the dim light. When the attack orders arrived, the Buckeyes joined Harris's three Mountaineer regiments in charging the portion of Cooke's line northeast of Hatcher's Run. The Federals struck the works "at the point where [the Confederate] lines begin to refuse on the north[east] bank of Hatcher's Run," explained Harris, "striking them at the fort which defends the angle and from that to the run, a distance of about 300 yards. . . ." Harris's thrust captured two guns, three battle flags, two line officers, and 28 men. Evidently the Confederates offered but feeble resistance, because Harris reported that he accomplished his success "without loss on my part . . . the greater portion of the defending force making good their retreat whilst my men were struggling through a very dense difficult slashing in front of these works." The 123rd Ohio received credit for most of the captures. Harris enjoyed his bloodless victory because Cooke's men northeast of Hatcher's Run had already begun the withdrawal necessitated by Seymour's and Getty's sweep down the line.[45]

Harris's troops had no sooner subdued their opponents than a Sixth Corps staff officer arrived on the scene with news of Wright's achievements across Hatcher's Run. "Soon a line of glittering bayonets were seen advancing towards us," wrote a member of Seymour's 14th New Jersey, "and Major-General Gibbons [sic] informed Gen. Wright that the advancing column belonged to the 24th Corps." Gibbon remembered meeting both Wright and Getty as he entered the captured Confederate ramparts, and Ord proudly informed Grant that "Harris' brigade has taken the works on the north [east] side of Hatcher's Run." The two corps commanders, along with General Getty, assessed the happy tactical situation. Gibbon suggested that because Confederate resistance had evaporated on their front, perhaps their combined troops should reverse field and push rapidly toward Petersburg. Gibbon's idea contained the unspoken hope that Lee's army might collapse if aggressively tested, and consequently the end not only of the campaign, but of the war itself, became possible for those commanders willing to undertake bold initiatives.[46]

Just then, however, Joseph Hamblin entertained no such thoughts. The Sixth Corps brigade commander had his hands full with a body of Rebels apparently determined to regain everything that had been lost during the morning's actions.

*   *   *

The four regiments of Hamblin's brigade had remained behind along the captured Confederate works when the rest of Wright's corps pivoted southwest toward Hatcher's Run. With the dispersion of Lane's and Thomas's troops, the next Confederate units in line to the northeast belonged to Brigadier General William R. Cox's Brigade of Major General Bryan Grimes's Division of the Second Corps. Cox's North Carolinians defended a mile of works in shockingly sparse array, one man per ten paces. Cox did enjoy the benefit of an intact picket line and ample artillery support, and when Lieutenant Colonel Henry E. Peyton of Lee's staff found Cox, he implored the Tarheel brigadier to contain the Breakthrough on his front "at all ventures." Cox recognized that his now-exposed right invited disaster, particularly because a long unoccupied traverse running diagonally to the right of his brigade would provide an ideal shelter for any Yankees inclined to turn his flank. "At this moment, I discovered an engineer corps composed of 350 negroes, under the command of a Colonel, who were used for strengthening our works," remembered Cox. "I requested Colonel Peyton to place this corps under my command, which he did. Using them as dummies, I extended them on this unoccupied line, and as only their heads were exposed, the enemy naturally supposed they were there to meet any assault that might be made." Hamblin's men, whether they actually saw Cox's ersatz black battalion or not, never attacked the Carolinian's makeshift line. Instead, the isolated Northerners found themselves contending with a Confederate counterattack that came not from the east, but from the north.[47]

General Wilcox had been resting at Cottage Farm, his division's headquarters along Cox Road between the Venable and Turnbull houses, when about daylight the sound of unusually strong firing prompted him to ride toward the front. It is curious that Hill had not shared with Wilcox his concern for the brewing trouble along the Third Corps line during the predawn hours while the corps commander rode past Cottage Farm on his way to Edge Hill. Perhaps Hill assumed that Wilcox was already at the front, or in his anxiety, simply overlooked the obvious and failed to instruct one of his aides to check with Wilcox's headquarters. In either event, the Confederate high command certainly employed flawed communications on this critical morning.

General Lane had already dispatched Lieutenant George H. Snow of the 33rd North Carolina to Cottage Farm with news of the Breakthrough when the division commander encountered some of Lane's fugitives, perhaps Snow among them, near Fort Gregg, an outwork west of Lee's interior lines overlooking Boydton Plank Road. Wilcox quickly absorbed the essentials of the morning's combat, and when Lane arrived, the two officers reviewed their tactical options. Lane argued against making a stand at Fort Gregg and its complementary strongpoint to the north, Fort Whitworth, "because I knew, from personal observation, that the works, where my line had been broken, were held by an overwhelming force." Wilcox, however, believed that by reclaiming the initiative, the Confederates might restore their lost lines or, at least, blunt additional Federal advances until reinforcements could arrive from north of the Appomattox River.

Wilcox and Lane thus went about the task of organizing a strike force from the flotsam and jetsam washed up around Fort Gregg by the Sixth Corps tidal wave. Using the ramparts of the little bastion as a rallying point, Lane, Thomas, and Wilcox managed to align some 600 troops in battle formation, Lane's Carolinians on the right and Thomas's Georgians on the left. This diminutive demi-division moved forward and, in Lane's words, "drove the enemy beyond the branch, near the house occupied by Mrs. Banks."[48]

The attack landed upon about 80 men representing all four regiments of Hamblin's brigade, along with some First Division sharpshooters, all under the command of Lieutenant Colonel Henry C. Fisk of the 65th New York and Lieutenant Colonel John Harper of the 95th Pennsylvania. While some of Hamblin's forces had pushed forward to the Plank Road after the Breakthrough, the little party accompanying Fisk and Harper moved to the right, expanding the breach to the northeast. Whatever actual fighting was associated with Wilcox's mini-offensive must have been brief and comparatively bloodless. The victorious Confederates reoccupied a portion of their lost fortifications and opened on the withdrawing Federals with two recaptured guns. Lane's men established a new line facing west along Church Road, perpendicular to the original Confederate works.[49]

Wilcox's counteroffensive did little more than define the northeastern limits of the Sixth Corps Breakthrough and accomplished nothing to diminish the enormity of the catastrophe suffered by Hill's corps. More than four miles of the Confederate line remained in Union hands, stretching northeast from Hatcher's Run nearly to Church Road. Five Confederate brigades and a portion of a sixth had been driven from their works, Lane's and Thomas's still sufficiently potent to muster a limited counterattack, but McComb's, Davis's, Cooke's, and Erson's either routed from the field or virtually eliminated from the order of battle.

General Lee had seen evidence of the Breakthrough from the Turnbull House, had been informed of Hill's death, and by mid-morning had learned more about General Pickett's defeat at Five Forks the previous day. The Confederate commander clearly grasped the magnitude of the emergency that now confronted him. The Breakthrough had separated the survivors of the Five Forks calamity and the other troops west of Hatcher's Run from the units still defending the Petersburg perimeter. The brigades east of Hatcher's Run had suffered a devastating attack and likely faced renewed assaults from Grant's victorious legions. Lee realized that the most he could hope to accomplish was to hold Petersburg and Richmond until nightfall could shield a retreat and permit him to reconcentrate his divided army somewhere to the west along the Richmond and Danville Railroad. About 10:00 a.m., Lee dictated a fateful message to Secretary of War John C. Breckinridge. Lee's aide, Lieutenant Colonel Walter H. Taylor, repeated Lee's words to a telegrapher, who relayed them to the capital. Breckinridge read the portentous communication at 10:40 a.m.:

> I see no prospect of doing more than holding our position here till night. I am not certain that I can do that. If I can I shall withdraw to-night north of the Appomattox, and, if possible, it will be better to withdraw the whole line to-night from James River. The brigades on Hatcher's Run are cut off from us; enemy have broken through our lines and intercepted between us and them. . . . Our only chance . . . of concentrating our forces, is to do so near Danville railroad, which I shall endeavor to do at once. I advise that all preparation be made for leaving Richmond to-night.[50]

As Lee's message arrived at the War Department, Postmaster General John H. Reagan, Secretary of State Judah P. Benjamin, and other

Colonel Joseph E. Hamblin

Massachusetts MOLLUS Collection, Carlisle Barracks, Pennsylvania

Confederate officials completed an anxious vigil along with the secretary of war, who had spent a restless night at his office awaiting news from the Petersburg front. Breckinridge accepted Lee's grim analysis with the studied calm of a former field commander and dispatched a messenger to share the report with President Davis, who at that moment was a block away at worship in St. Paul's Church.

April 2 was communion Sunday and the genteel congregation of St. Paul's knelt to receive the sacrament. As Reverend Charles F. E. Minnigerode intoned the service, the church sexton, William Irving, strode down the aisle, tapped Davis on the shoulder, and handed the president a note. A gray pallor darkened Davis's countenance as he read the dispatch. The ever-dignified chief executive rose "with singular gravity and determination," remembered one observer, and quietly left the sanctuary. The president hastened to his office in the Customs House, where he telegraphed Lee, acknowledging receipt of the bad news and lamenting that " the loss of many valuables . . . for the want of time to pack and of transportation" would be the cost of such short notice of the need to leave the capital. When Lee received this ungenerous rebuke, he tore the offending telegram into pieces, revealing

> "I think it is absolutely necessary that we should abandon our position to-night. I have given all the necessary orders on the subject to the troops, and the operation, though difficult, I hope will be performed successfully."

a temper only rarely displayed. The general-in-chief had been providing the administration with warnings of the potential evacuation of Richmond for nearly two months, and momentarily the gray chieftain indulged his frustration at the injustice of Davis's remarks. Nevertheless, Lee replied deferentially to the president's message. "I think it is absolutely necessary that we should abandon our position to-night," he advised. "I have given all the necessary orders on the subject to the troops, and the operation, though difficult, I hope will be performed successfully."[51]

After defending Petersburg for more than nine arduous months, Lee could now measure the duration of the campaign in hours. Yet the question remained, how many hours? For while the Davis administration bundled papers, emptied warehouses, and readied trains to escape the doomed capital, and Lee focused on the necessary arrangements to extricate his gallant army from the protective mantle of the Cockade City's defenses, thousands of soldiers in blue moved relentlessly toward the remaining lines of Confederate resistance. It was not yet noon. The sheltering cloak of darkness would not appear for another eight hours.

Before the Army of Northern Virginia could undertake a new campaign to reach General Joseph E. Johnston in North Carolina, it would have to find the will and the means to survive a more immediate trial—a test that in the late morning of April 2 came swinging northeast along Boydton Plank Road, aiming straight at Petersburg.

NOTES

1. Stevens, "The Storming of the Lines of Petersburg," in *PMHSM*, VI, 424; Stevens, Journal, in George W. Getty Papers, Gibson-Getty-McClure Family Papers, LC.

2. *OR* pt. 3, 424, 422.

3. Stevens, "The Storming of the Lines of Petersburg," in *PMHSM*, VI, 420; Hyde, *Following the Greek Cross*, 251; Benedict, *Vermont in the Civil War*, I, 583-584. Stevens's account described essentially what transpired and cited no evidence that such a plan had been developed prior to the Breakthrough. Therefore, it is quite possible that Stevens wrote from hindsight rather than from the perspective of what was intended at the time of the Breakthrough.

4. *OR* pt. 3, 455. Meade sent this correspondence to Grant at 8:00 a.m., well after Wright had begun his movement to the southwest.

5. *OR* pt. 1, 903, 966; Stevens, "The Storming of the Lines of Petersburg," in *PMHSM*, VI, 424.

6. Mark, *History of the 93rd Regiment*, 322; Letters Received, Sixth Army Corps, 1862-1865, Part II, Entry 4414 [Captain Caspar Kaufman, 61st Pennsylvania], April 21, 1865, Record Group 393, NA; Lothrup Lincoln Lewis, Diary, April 2, 1865, in Lothrup Lincoln Lewis Collection, LC; Stevens, "The Storming of the Lines of Petersburg," in *PMHSM*, VI, 424; Stevens, Journal, in George W. Getty Papers, Gibson-Getty-McClure Family Papers, LC. Stevens said that about 100 men of the 122nd New York and 4th Vermont were engaged in the wagon burning.

7. *OR* pt. 1, 966, 910; Edwards, Memoir, 223-225, Illinois State Historical Library; Rhodes, ed., *All for the Union*, 226-227.

8. *OR* pt. 1, 931-932; Best, *History of the 121st New York State Infantry*, 210-211; Soule, "Recollections of the Civil War," in *New Milford* (Conn.) *Gazette*,

July 19, 1912; J.[ackson] L. Bost to James Lane, July 31, 1867, in Lane Papers, Auburn University. Major Bost was a member of the 37th North Carolina.

9. Abbott, *Personal Recollections*, 270-274.

10. *OR* pt. 1, 1008, 993; Keifer, *Slavery and Four Years of War*, II, 195; Eichelberger, Memoir, Civil War Miscellaneous Collection, USAMHI; Norvell, "Petersburg," in *National Tribune*, June 11, 1891. Private George Loyd, Company A, 122nd Ohio, did get the credit for capturing Heth's flag. See *OR* pt. 1, 994. A biographical sketch of Mauk and Wolford may be found in Matthews, "How General A. P. Hill Met His Fate," in *SHSP*, XXVII, 35-36. Both men hailed from Bedford County, Pennsylvania and were laborers before enlisting in the Union army on August 29, 1862.

11. George W. Tucker, "Death of General A.P. Hill," in *SHSP*, XI, (1883), 565-566. Tucker's account also appeared in "Annals of the War: Death of Gen. A.P. Hill," in *Philadelphia Weekly Times*, November 24, 1883. A variety of sources, primary and secondary, are useful in describing the events surrounding A.P. Hill's death, Tucker's account being the single most valuable. Two recent syntheses of the story appear in Robertson, *A.P. Hill*, 314-318, and Trudeau, *The Last Citadel*, 369-370 and 373-375. Both of these narratives describe Hill's inability to sleep on the night of April 1-2 due to a combination of worry and the physical ailments that plagued the general, and have Hill arising at 3:00 a.m. to seek information at his military headquarters. This is an assertion not directly supported by Tucker's account. Clearly, Starke's report related to Parke's attacks against Major General John B. Gordon south of Petersburg along the Jerusalem Plank Road, attacks that did not begin until about 4:30 a.m., making it illogical for Hill and Palmer to be discussing any Federal penetrations at 3:00 a.m. Tucker said that Palmer awoke Starke between 2:00 a.m. and 3:00 a.m., so Starke's departure from Indiana probably occurred around 3:00 a.m. It is difficult to understand, however, why a Third Corps staff officer (Starke carried the title of acting assistant adjutant general) would explore the situation on the Second Corps front and not have traveled to Wilcox's and Heth's sectors as well.

The Venable House belonged to James M. Venable, a member of the Virginia Senate. The home no longer exists, its site obliterated by railroad tracks and warehouses. The Widow Knight was Isabella E. Knight, whose husband, John, died in October 1863. No longer extant, the Knight House stood at what in 2000 is the intersection of Wythe and Atlantic streets in Petersburg.

12. Tucker, "Death of Hill," in *SHSP*, XI, 566. The detail about the linen shirt comes from Robertson, *A. P. Hill*, 314. Hill's horse is described as "dapple-gray" by William Woods Hassler in *A. P. Hill: Lee's Forgotten General* (Richmond, 1962), 240. Robertson calls Champ "iron-gray" in *A. P. Hill*, 291.

13. Tucker, "Death of Hill," in *SHSP*, XI, 566. Efforts to identify courier Kirkpatrick more completely have been unsuccessful.

14. Charles S. Venable to G. Percy Hawes, December 25, 1883, in "Further Details of the Death of General A. P. Hill," in *SHSP*, XII, 185-186. Considerable uncertainty and contradiction exists concerning this aspect of A. P. Hill's final

hours. Venable claimed that Hill reached the Turnbull House "before light," but given the circumstances he described, Hill's arrival must have been sometime after 5:00 a.m., almost certainly before sunrise but not literally "before light." Venable also placed Longstreet at Lee's headquarters at 1:00 a.m., but Longstreet stated in *From Manassas to Appomattox*, 604, that he reached Edge Hill "before the first rays of morning," probably before Hill but not nearly as early as 1:00 a.m. Freeman in *R. E. Lee*, IV, 44, says Longstreet arrived about 4:00 a.m. Freeman in *Lee's Lieutenants*, III, 677, has Venable interrupting a conversation between Lee and Hill, however, in his *R. E. Lee*, IV, 44, he places Lee and Longstreet together upon Venable's arrival. Venable's testimony placed Hill in the room with Lee while Longstreet napped in an adjacent space. Tucker mentioned nothing about Hill even entering the Turnbull House! Robertson in *A.P. Hill*, 315, states and Trudeau in *The Last Citadel*, 370, implies that the three generals were in conference when Venable appeared with news of the Yankees' proximity. The fact that the Federals were present in the immediate neighborhood may indeed have been news to Hill and Lee, but as stated in the text, Hill had dispatched Kirkpatrick before entering Edge Hill with the report that his line was in crisis, so Venable's breathless account must be discounted at least so far as the implication that his reconnaissance was the first to discover that the Confederate works on Hill's front had been penetrated.

15. Venable to Hawes in, "Further Details of the Death of General *A.P. Hill*," in *SHSP*, XII, 186; Tucker, "Death of *A.P. Hill*," in *SHSP*, XI, 567. Although it is not possible to identify the Confederates who temporarily boosted Hill's firepower, they probably belonged to Lane's Brigade. Major Jackson L. Bost of the 37th North Carolina recalled falling "back obliquely towards Petersburg to a publick road (name not known) on which Gen. Lee's Hd Qrs were and South of the latter place when I found some artillery and Col. Cowan of 33rd Regt., with a small number of his men." See Bost to "Dear General," [James H. Lane], July 31, 1867, in James Lane Papers, Auburn University. Venable and Tucker provided differing details regarding this portion of Hill's last ride. The text is a blend of their two accounts, reconciled in the most logical fashion.

Adjutant Edward J. Hale of Lane's Brigade added an interesting footnote to this portion of Hill's story. Hale claimed to have seen Hill and his party riding along Cattail Run from a vantage point west of Fort Whitworth. Hale said he also spotted the Union skirmishers who threatened to surprise Hill, and dispatched three men to provide a warning. Just moments earlier, Hale claimed to have encountered General Longstreet "who came leisurely riding up... with one leg over the pommel of his saddle. He replied, very indifferently, that there wasn't anything to do—or there was no use to do anything." See Hale to "My dear General [James H. Lane]," June 13, 1884, in James Lane Papers, Auburn University. Of course, by 1884 the campaign among some former Confederates to discredit Longstreet's wartime performance was already in progress. Hale's letter, in addition to positioning the massive Longstreet in a most unlikely riding posture, may be more a product of this manifestation of the "Lost Cause" mythology than a strict accounting of the facts.

16. Hawes, "Last Days of the Army," in *Confederate Veteran*, XXVII, 341; Percy G. Hawes to Rev. J. William Jones, March 21, 1884, in "Further Details of the Death of General A. P. Hill," in *SHSP*, XII, 184-185; Tucker, "Death of A. P. Hill, in *SHSP*, XI, 567. It is impossible to reconcile Hawes's account completely with those of Tucker and Venable. Hawes's conversation with Hill may have taken place prior to the capture of the Union prisoners, but because Hawes mentioned nothing about this incident, it is difficult to prove the sequence of events. These three primary sources provide different and not always corroborating details of Hill's final ride either because they were not always in each other's or Hill's immediate presence during the ride to Cattail Run or because the memories of the witnesses, clouded by anywhere from eighteen to 54 years of intervening time, had become unreliable.

17. Hawes, "Last Days of the Army," in *Confederate Veteran*, XXVII, 341; Venable to Hawes in, "Further Details of the Death of General A. P. Hill," in *SHSP*, XII, 186; Monroe F. Cockrell, ed., *Gunner With Stonewall: Reminiscences of William Thomas Poague* (Jackson, Tenn., 1957, reprint, Wilmington, N.C., 1987), 110; W. Cullen Sherwood and Richard L. Nicholas, *Amherst Artillery Albemarle Artillery and Sturdivant's Battery* (Lynchburg, Va., 1996), 152. Poague stated in his memoirs that on April 1 he had sent Penick's and Johnston's batteries to report to Colonel Hilary P. Jones at Petersburg. Not until 9:00 a.m. on April 2 did Poague appear at the Turnbull House with the rest of his battalion, long after Hill had been shot. When Poague arrived, Penick was still deployed along Cox Road while Johnston had been sent "to a fort in rear of Fort Gregg." It is possible that only Penick's Battery was on Cox Road when Hill spotted the unidentified guns, but it is more likely that Johnston adopted his position behind Fort Gregg later, but certainly before 9:00 a.m.

18. Tucker, "Death of A. P. Hill," in *SHSP*, XI, 567-568. Tucker mistook Long Ordinary Road for Boydton Plank Road when describing this stage of Hill's final ride. Long Ordinary Road was a byway that connected Cox Road with the Plank Road. U.S. 1, inconveniently styled Boydton Plank Road in 2000, approximates the course of Long Ordinary Road between VA 142 (historic Boydton Plank Road) and VA 226 (Cox Road) in Dinwiddie County. Tucker likewise underestimated the distance to the field near Heth's headquarters but very accurately stated the distance from the field to the Harmon House.

William Frierson Fulton of the 5th Alabama Battalion published a challenge to this portion of Tucker's narrative. Fulton claimed that "I was in charge of a skirmish line, and Gen. Hill on his horse, followed by probably two couriers, was making for a skirt of woods already occupied by the enemy scouts. Observing my line of skirmishers he sent his courier to order me to advance my line to those woods and hold the enemy in check. Just a few moments after I saw him brought out of the woods by his courier, on his horse, dead!" Fulton's account is suspect. Not only is it uncorroborated by supporting evidence, but it clearly contradicts other accounts of the recovery of Hill's body. Still, Fulton does provide some rationale for the proximity of the 5th Alabama Battalion to the site of Hill's death.

See William Frierson Fulton, II, *Family Record and War Reminiscences*, n.p., n.d., 136-137.

19. Tucker, "Death of A. P. Hill," in *SHSP*, XI, 568. Mauk's rifle was the upper one, suggesting that he may have been standing behind the tree while Wolford kneeled below his comrade.

20. Tucker, "Death of A. P. Hill," in *SHSP*, XI, 568; John W. Mauk, "The Man Who Killed General A. P. Hill," in *SHSP*, XX (1892), 350-351. These two accounts of Hill's death, unlike the sources for Hill's ride, agree in most details. Hawes, "Last Days of the Army," in *Confederate Veteran*, XXVII, 341-342 stated that a bullet grazed Tucker's shoulder and cut his jacket, but Tucker never mentioned receiving such a wound. For the details of Hill's injuries see G. Powell Hill, "First Burial of General Hill's Remains," in *SHSP*, XIX (1891), 185. Tucker misstated that the ball "struck the General's pistol hand." See "Death of A. P. Hill," in *SHSP*, XI, 569. General James A. Walker in his oration at the dedication of the Hill statue in Richmond on May 30, 1892 stated that after Hill was shot he turned to Tucker and said,"Take care of yourself." Because Tucker did not mention Hill speaking to him and, given the devastating nature of Hill's wound, Walker probably fabricated this assertion. See "Unveiling of the Statue of General Ambrose Powell Hill," in *SHSP*, XX, 383.

Speculation has occasionally arisen suggesting that Hill intentionally exposed himself to Mauk's deadly fire—in essence, that Hill committed suicide. This psycho-analysis derives from a statement Hill allegedly made on March 29 while visiting Richmond that he "did not wish to survive the fall of Richmond." The actual events surrounding Hill's death do not reveal any behavior inconsistent with the general's long-standing reputation for personal bravery bordering on rashness. Venable attributed Hill's "reckless" disregard of his life that morning to an "anxious devotion to duty and love for his troops." Moreover, Richmond had not fallen when Hill took his last ride, and although Hill realized that the military situation at Petersburg was desperate, nothing indicates that he considered it hopeless. See Hill, "First Burial of General Hill's Remains," in *SHSP*, XIX, 185, "Further Details of the Death of General A.P. Hill," in *SHSP*, XII, 185, and Robertson, *A.P. Hill*, 312.

The approximate location of Hill's death is marked by a small granite monument situated on private property behind the Sentry Woods subdivision off A. P. Hill Drive in Dinwiddie County. Access to this poignant, if humble marker in 2000 is via an unmarked trail beginning at the far end of the circular A. P. Hill Drive. A map of the site is available at Pamplin Historical Park.

21. Tucker, "Death of A.P. Hill," in *SHSP*, XI, 568-569; Longstreet, *From Manassas to Appomattox*, 605; Mauk, "The Man Who Killed General A.P. Hill," in *SHSP*, XX, 351; Hawes, "Last Days of the Army," in *Confederate Veteran*, XXVII, 341.

22. Tucker, "Death of A. P. Hill," in *SHSP*, XI, 569; Hawes to Jones, March 21, 1884, in "Further Details of the Death of General A. P. Hill," in *SHSP*, XII, 184; Hawes, "Last Days of the Army," in *Confederate Veteran*, XXVII, 342; Freeman, *R. E. Lee*, IV, 45-47. Robertson in *A. P. Hill*, 318, states that Palmer began reciting the

details of Hill's death to Lee, "but broke down in tears and motioned to Tucker to finish the account." Trudeau, in *The Last Citadel*, 375, repeats this detail. The accounts cited by Robertson do not reveal the source of this version of the story.

23. Mauk, "The Man Who Killed General A. P. Hill," in *SHSP*, XX, 351; Venable to Hawes, December 25, 1883, in "Further Details of the Death of General A. P. Hill," in *SHSP*, XII, 187; Tucker, "Death of A. P. Hill," in *SHSP*, XI, 569. It is possible, of course, that the 5th Alabama Battalion obtained their blue uniforms from prisoners or the dead encountered on their way toward Hill's death site, or that they maintained a small supply of such uniforms for use in extraordinary situations.

24. Mauk, "The Man Who Killed General A. P. Hill," in *SHSP*, XX, 351; *OR* pt. 1, 1008. These sources do not indicate the time of Mauk's interview with Wright, but it probably occurred sometime in the afternoon. McClennan's report crediting Mauk and Wolford with Hill's death is dated April 2, demonstrating that the Federals had pieced together the incident the same day that it occurred. Given the fact that word of Hill's death took time to circulate through the Confederate army, and that prisoners from that army must have been the bearers of the news to the Federals, some time had to elapse between Mauk's and Wolford's return to their unit and their interview with Wright. Moreover, it is improbable that Wright and Keifer would be interviewing a corporal and a private about the death of even a high-ranking Confederate officer while combat responsibilities demanded their attention. It should be noted that as late as 7:55 a.m. April 3, Wright found it necessary to confirm Hill's death, indicating either that some doubt had remained regarding the episode even twenty-four hours after it occurred, or that Wright felt that he had not adequately reported what he knew to be true. See *OR* pt. 3, 521 for the text of a dispatch from Wright to Meade citing the discovery of a letter in Petersburg informing Hill's mother of her son's death. "We have much other evidence to show that he was killed in the attack of this corps yesterday," Wright averred. Colonel Theodore Lyman of Meade's staff also indicated that it was not until the morning of April 3 that he, and presumably Meade, "learned [of] the death of Lieutenant-General A. P. Hill, who was killed by one of our stragglers whom he tried to capture." See Agassiz, ed., *Meade's Headquarters*, 341.

25. Robertson, *A. P. Hill*, 319-320. Hill was buried in the Winston family cemetery in the Coalfield area of Chesterfield County on the estate of a kinsman at 2:00 p.m. April 4. In 1867 his remains were removed to Hollywood Cemetery and in 1891 they were reinterred one more time at the intersection of Laburnum Avenue and Hermitage Road in Richmond, where they rest under a statue of the general. For the details of Hill's various burials, see Robertson, *A. P. Hill*, 320-324.

26. Ammen, "Maryland Troops in the Confederate Army," 175, in Thomas Clemens Collection, USAMHI; John R. Cooke and Henry Heth, in Lee Headquarters Papers, VHS; Trudeau, *The Last Citadel*, 369. William McComb wrote that "I had about as many men on the Skirmish line as I had in the main line." McComb had ridden beyond the left flank of his brigade during the Breakthrough and had to use a ruse to escape from the Federals swarming behind the captured

Confederate works. See William McComb, "Recollections of 1864-1865," Museum of the Confederacy. An article in the May 30, 1899 edition of the *Lebanon* (Tenn.) *Democrat* entitled "Archer's Brigade, Capt. Fergus S. Harris Relates Some Interesting Incidents of Its Members," challenged Ammen's identification of the location of the Free Nigger Fort. "Back of the Claypole house was the line of forts called free Negro Batteries," wrote Harris. The Claypole House was nearly two miles northeast of Hatcher's Run in front of the Confederate line. The Nathaniel Michler map shows six fixed gun emplacements between the six-gun battery and the refused line on the east bank of Hatcher's Run. See Michler, "Petersburg and Five Forks," LC. Much of the Confederate line, including artillery positions, survives intact on private property in 2000. The works along Cooke's front nearest Hatcher's Run are particularly stunning.

27. Haynes, *A History of the Tenth Regiment Vermont Volunteers*, 145; Stevens, "The Storming of the Lines of Petersburg," in *PMHSM*, VI, 427; *OR* pt. 1, 910-911, 969.

28. John R. Cooke, in Lee Headquarters Papers, VHS; Haynes, *A History of the Tenth Regiment, Vermont Volunteers*, 145; *OR* pt. 1, 1000; Alfred Seelye Roe, *The Ninth New York Heavy Artillery* (Worcester, Mass., 1899), 225. Lieutenant Colonel George B. Damon of the 10th Vermont, who is quoted in the account printed in Haynes, said that only two guns occupied this work. Lieutenant Colonel Joseph C. Hill of the 6th Maryland and the account published in Roe said four. Brigadier General McComb indicated that the left flank of his brigade "was resting to the right of the Purcell Battery." Samuel Z. Ammen of the 2nd Maryland Battalion identified this position as Fort Alexander. See McComb to "Major," April 11, 1865, in Lee Headquarters Papers, VHS, and Ammen, "Maryland Troops in the Confederate Army," I, 175, in Thomas Clemens Collection, USAMHI. This installation should not be confused with another Confederate fort sometimes called Fort Alexander. See Chapter Nine, Note 12. For the identification of the gun emplacement as Fort Davis, named after Joseph Davis, whose brigade had occupied the area earlier in the campaign, see Randolph McKim, "The Second Maryland Infantry—An Oration Delivered in the State House at Annapolis, May 7, 1909," in *Confederate Veteran*, XVII (1909), 458. Of course, this installation should not be confused with Union Fort Davis, located on the Federal siege line along Jerusalem Plank Road.

29. Haynes, *A History of the Tenth Regiment, Vermont Volunteers*, 145; *OR* pt. 1, 1002; Roe, *The Ninth New York Heavy Artillery*, 226; Ammen, "Maryland Troops in the Confederate Army," I, 176, in Thomas Clemens Collection, USAMHI. Private William S. Prentiss very probably received the wound that resulted in the meeting with his brother, Clifton, during this portion of the battle. See Chapter Seven.

30. Haynes, *A History of the Tenth Regiment, Vermont Volunteers*, 145; *OR* pt. 1, 986, 1000, 1002; Roe, *The Ninth New York Heavy Artillery*, 226; Grant, "The Old Vermont Brigade at Petersburg," in *Glimpses of the Nation's Struggle*, 402.

31. "Last Charge of Lee's Army," in *Confederate Veteran*, V (1897), 565; William McComb to Lamar Hollyday, December 16, 1876, in "Maryland Troops in the Confederate Service," in *SHSP*, III (1877), 136; McComb, "Recollections." McComb promoted Harris to captain as reward for his brave charge. See "Trio of Comrades at Memphis Reunion," in *Confederate Veteran*, X (1902), 320.

32. Haynes, *A History of the Tenth Regiment, Vermont Volunteers*, 145; Keifer, *Slavery and Four Years of War*, II, 196; Dr. Henry W. Manson, "Story From the Ranks," in *Confederate Veteran*, I (1893), 68.

33. Keifer, *Slavery and Four Years of War*, II, 196; *OR* pt.1, 1000; McComb to Hollyday, in "Maryland Troops in the Confederate Service," in *SHSP*, III, 136.

34. McComb, "Recollections"; Haynes, *A History of the Tenth Regiment, Vermont Volunteers*, 146; *OR* pt. 1, 1000, 1002; Waite, "Three Years With the Tenth Vermont," II, 247-248.

35. *OR* pt. 1, 989,1000, 1002.

36. Waite, "Three Years With the Tenth Vermont," II, 248-249. Waite did not mention Lyman by name, but that officer held the majority in the 10th Vermont on April 2.

37. *OR* pt. 1, 969-971; Benedict, *Vermont in the Civil War*, I, 597-598; Lieutenant Robert Pratt, Journal, April 2, 1865, in VTHS. Captain Merritt Barber concealed Mundee's condition in his official report, which lauded the staff officer as leading the attack "with conspicuous gallantry throughout all the subsequent movements. . . . With a perfect disregard of all danger, and by his example, as well as by the skill with which he handled the command, contributed in a very great degree to the glorious achievements that day performed by the Vermont brigade." Of course, just because Mundee was unqualified for line command and physically impaired does not mean that he lacked personal courage.

38. Henry Heth, in Lee Headquarters Papers, VHS; McComb to Hollyday, in "Maryland Troops in the Confederate Service," in *SHSP*, III, 136; McComb, "Recollections"; Walter Wallace Smith to "Dear Parents," April 3, 1865, in Walter Wallace Smith Papers, Duke; Walter F. Beyer and Oscar F. Keydel, eds., *Deeds of Valor: How America's Heroes Won the Medal of Honor* (Detroit, 1905); Benedict, *Vermont in the Civil War*, I, 203; *OR* pt. 1, 970; Manson, "Story From the Ranks," in *Confederate Veteran*, I, 68. Manson became a prisoner and on April 4 saw the Federal he had shot during the counterattack at Fort Davis. The men exchanged stories about the episode and passed a pleasant time together, "the one that walked waited on the one that couldn't walk, and the two who had shot at each other would have risked their lives each in the other's defense."

39. John R. Cooke, in Lee Headquarters Papers, VHS; Love, *The Prairie Guards*, 18; Benedict, *Vermont in the Civil War*, II, 387; Joseph R. Davis to Jefferson Davis, April 4, 1865, in Edwin M. Stanton Papers, LC. Benedict indicated that Nelson was wounded and "expressed regret that he had not discovered the small number of his captors sooner." Nelson, a judge in civilian life, remained a prisoner until June 18, 1865.

40. William McComb and John R. Cooke, in Lee Headquarters Papers, VHS; William McComb to Lamar Hollyday, in "Maryland Troops in the Confederate Service," in *SHSP*, III, 136; Ammen, "Maryland Troops in the Confederate Army," I, 176, in Thomas Clemens Collection, USAMHI; *OR* pt. 1, 977-78; Thomas W. Hyde to Redfield Proctor, September 26, 1891, in Letters Received, Volunteer Service Branch, Entry 496, File 4396 (VS) 1879, Record Group 94, NA. Merrill identified his prisoners as being Virginia sharpshooters, but he must have been mistaken. Heth's division contained no Virginia units. Merrill received the Medal of Honor. See "A Profitable Reconnoissance (sic)" in Beyer and Keydel, eds., *Deeds of Valor*, 519-520 for Merrill's version of the story.

41. Chapman, *More Terrible Than Victory*, 293-296; J. Warren Keifer's report of artillery captured on April 2, 1865 in Headquarters Letter Book, 1863-1865, in Joseph Warren Keifer Papers, LC; Henry Heth in Lee Headquarters Papers, VHS; Norvell, "Petersburg," in *National Tribune*, June 11, 1891; *OR* pt. 1, 979, 993, pt. 3, 479; Grant, *Personal Memoirs*, II, 448; Albert C. Harrison to "Dearest Parents," April 2,1865, in Olsen, ed., *Upon the Tented Field*, 307.

42. Longacre, *Army of Amateurs*, 287-288; Trudeau, *The Last Citadel*, 379; *OR* pt. 1, 1160; Gibbon, *Personal Recollections*, 293. Gibbon speculated that given the outcome of the campaign, "I don't think [Foster] ever regretted making the change."

43. *OR* pt. 3, 430-431, 492; John Gibbon to John W. Turner, April 2, 1865, in John Wesley Turner Papers, USAMHI.

44. *OR* pt. 3, 479, 492; pt. 1, 1161, 1174, 1203. Wright's plea for help is untimed and may actually have been sent after the corps began its sweep southwest toward Hatcher's Run. In either case, it is clear that Grant directed Ord to move to Wright's assistance shortly after he learned of the Breakthrough, whether Wright solicited the help then or a little while later.

45. *OR* pt. 1, 1174, 1214, 1221.

46. *OR* pt. 1, 1221; Terrill, *Fourteenth Regiment, New Jersey Volunteers*, 119; Gibbon, *Personal Recollections*, 299-300.

47. William R. Cox, "The Anderson-Ramseur-Cox Brigade," in Clark, ed., *North Carolina in the Great War*, IV, 453. Cox volunteered that "I presume it may be safely said it is the only time during the war when negroes were employed in aiding us to fight our battles." No Federal source mentioned encountering a line of battle such as that described by Cox.

48. Wilcox, "Defence of Batteries Gregg and Whitworth and the Evacuation of Petersburg," in *SHSP*, IV, 25-26; James H. Lane, "The Defence of Battery Gregg—General Lane's Reply to General Harris," in *SHSP*, IX (1881), 104-105. Wilcox wrote that his counterattack "recaptured the lines to the vicinity of Boisseau's house," but this is highly unlikely. Nothing in the Federal accounts of this action suggests that the Confederate attack swept over the more than one mile of the original Confederate line between the Banks House and Tudor Hall, as Wilcox boasted. Moreover, the division commander's testimony is in conflict with Lane's. Lane stated in his published report that he "cleared the works as far as the

branch on which the left of the Thirty-third rested the night previous," which is merely a different way of describing the ground than as provided in the text. Wilcox's tardy appearance during one of his division's most critical hours does not speak well for his generalship on April 2, although his eagerness to restore his line cannot be faulted.

49. *OR* pt. 1, 911, 932, 1285; Lieutenant Dallas M. Rigler to James H. Lane, June 17, 1867, in "The Defence of Fort Gregg," in *SHSP*, III, 26. Wheaton mentioned only the 95th Pennsylvania and 65th New York in describing this action, but Hamblin specifically stated that portions of the 121st New York and 2nd Connecticut Heavy Artillery were also present, a contention sustained by accounts from soldiers in those units. No doubt, more than 80 men had originally moved to the right after the Breakthrough, but that is the number that Wheaton claimed met Wilcox's 600 attackers. Hamblin is wrong, however, both in claiming that his brigade moved a mile to the right after their breakthrough and that they held this point until nearly noon. Wilcox's attack occurred well before then, probably between 8:00 a.m. and 9:00 a.m.

50. Freeman, *R. E. Lee*, IV, 49; *OR* pt. 3, 1378; Dowdey and Manarin, eds., *The Wartime Papers of R. E. Lee*, 924-925.

51. Accounts of the exchange of messages between Lee, Breckinridge, and Davis may be found in Freeman, *R. E. Lee*, IV, 49-55; Furgurson, *Ashes of Glory*, 319-321; Davis, *Jefferson Davis*, 603-604; and William C. Davis, *Breckinridge: Statesman Soldier Symbol* (Baton Rouge, 1974), 502. The text of the correspondence is in *OR* pt. 3, 1378, and Dowdey and Manarin, eds., *The Wartime Papers of R. E. Lee*, 924-926. William C. Davis believes that President Davis had learned of the contents of Lee's first message to Breckinridge from Postmaster General Reagan while the president was on his way to St. Paul's. If this is true, then whatever shock witnesses discerned in Davis's reaction to receiving the notice in church may have been more perceived than real, or manufactured in the literature for dramatic retelling.

CHAPTER NINE

The Defense and Capture of Fort Gregg

Colonel Thomas O. Osborn's brigade of Ohio, Pennsylvania, and Illinois troops led the Federal advance from Hatcher's Run toward Petersburg and the redefined limits of the Sixth Corps Breakthrough. Osborn, a thirty-two-year-old Chicago lawyer, had helped recruit the 39th Illinois at the outset of the war, one of the four regiments now moving northeast behind the conquered Confederate earthworks. Until this day, Osborn's only prominent action during nearly four years of service had been his participation in Benjamin Butler's attack on Drewry's Bluff in May 1864, during which a wound had cost the colonel the use of his right arm. The events of April 2 would soon replace Drewry's Bluff as the most important combat of Osborn's military career.[1]

Osborn's offensive sprang from General Ord's 6:50 a.m. directive that Twenty-fourth Corps commander John Gibbon send all available manpower to assist the Sixth Corps. Osborn's troops found themselves at the head of Robert S. Foster's division, the brigades of colonels George B. Dandy and Harrison S. Fairchild falling into column behind Osborn. The Chicagoan's route took him along the captured Confederate works to the vicinity of the Pickrell House where, at approximately 8:30 a.m., his regiments gained Boydton Plank Road, about the same time that brigadier generals Lane and Thomas were driving against Joseph Hamblin's brigade near the Banks House. Colonel William B. Curtis's and Lieutenant Colonel Andrew Potter's brigades of John W. Turner's Twenty-fourth Corps division used a different path to support Hamblin, traveling behind the original Sixth Corps lines toward the Union signal tower near Fort Fisher.[2]

Osborn learned of the Confederate counterattack while en route to the scene of the Breakthrough. The brigade commander promptly ordered his troops to adopt the "double-quick" and deployed the 62nd Ohio as skirmishers. Osborn then established a line of battle, forming the 199th Pennsylvania on the right with their right flank resting on the former Confederate fortifications, the 67th Ohio in the center, and his own 39th Illinois on the left. Dandy and Fairchild would form on Osborn's left once they arrived.[3]

"We found everything in confusion. Our lines had been ruptured everywhere."

Cadmus M. Wilcox, from his vantage point near Fort Gregg, could see Osborn's developing formation and recognized that a new crisis confronted his overmatched Confederate forces. As Wilcox pondered how his scattered and outnumbered troops might deal with this impending Federal threat, Colonel Charles S. Venable of General Lee's staff galloped up with welcome news. Brigadier General Nathaniel H. Harris's Mississippi brigade of William Mahone's Third Corps division had crossed the Appomattox River and would arrive near Fort Gregg in a matter of minutes. Venable no sooner completed his report than Harris's small contingent appeared. Wilcox ordered the Mississippians to move westward along Boydton Plank Road and present a line of battle to the approaching bluecoats, with skirmishers in advance. "It was [my] purpose to delay the forward movement of the enemy as much as possible," explained Wilcox, "in order that troops from the north side of the James river might arrive and fill the gap between the right of our main Petersburg lines and the Appomattox."[4]

Harris guardedly advanced his undersized brigade, guiding on Boydton Plank Road. "We found everything in confusion," testified one of the Mississippians. "Our lines had been ruptured everywhere, and the Union troops were in possession." Harris's forces proceeded about 400 yards before deploying at right angles to the highway. "The ground being undulating, I threw back both flanks, behind the crest on which I formed, and exposed my centre in order that I might induce the enemy to believe that there was a continuous line of battle behind the ridge," wrote Harris. "The enemy were evidently misled by this device, as they made the most careful dispositions, and forming two lines of battle, advanced with the utmost caution."

Major General Cadmus Marcellus Wilcox

Library of Congress

From his vantage point on the little rise, Harris gained his first clear view of Osborn's brigade supported by the rest of Foster's division. "It was a grand but awful sight," thought one of the Confederates, "the Federals moving with the same precision as though on parade . . . the glint and glimmer of their guns shone like a wave of silver." Supported by a couple of artillery pieces posted in their rear, Harris's men opened a "brisk fire" on the approaching Yankees. General Harris paced behind his thin line of riflemen, encouraging them to "stand like iron, my brave boys, stand like iron." Incoming Federal fire claimed a few Mississippi victims.[5]

This light Confederate cannonade and the appearance of Harris's Brigade had a less daunting effect on the Federals than the Confederate general first assumed. Osborn quickly ordered his men to charge, causing both Harris's skirmish line and Lane's and Thomas's troops along Church Road to pull back without offering serious resistance. Harris remembered that Wilcox had instructed him "not to suffer myself to be cut off, but to hold the enemy in check as long as possible, and then fall back slowly toward Batteries Gregg and Whitworth." The Federals recaptured two twelve-pounder Napoleons that had been seized during Wilcox's recent counterattack and scooped up some two dozen prisoners who either failed or declined to make a withdrawal. An officer in the 37th North Carolina of Lane's Brigade stated that his detachment's occupation of the Church Road line lasted all of fifteen minutes. Colonel James C. Briscoe of the 199th Pennsylvania confirmed that Osborn's advance occurred about 9:00 a.m., indicating that the Federals had repaired the temporary setback experienced by Hamblin's brigade in less than an hour and with literally no loss of life.[6]

Had Osborn been able to see the commander of the opposing Mississippi troops, he would have recognized much of himself in his Confederate counterpart. Nathaniel Harrison Harris, like Osborn, was a young lawyer in command of a brigade that included his own former regiment. Harris, a native of Natchez, Mississippi, had studied law in New Orleans before the war and relocated to Vicksburg to practice his profession. In the spring of 1861, at the age of 26, Harris raised a company of infantry that became a part of the 19th Mississippi. The youthful attorney rose through his unit's ranks to become its colonel in April 1863. Lee promoted him to brigadier general the following winter, and Harris's command was one of the two Confederate brigades to defend the Bloody Angle at Spotsylvania. The Overland Campaign and subsequent action at Petersburg had reduced Harris's four regiments to about 600 effectives by April 2.[7]

At midnight April 1-2, Mahone had ordered Harris to place his command "in readiness to move at a moment's warning." That notice arrived just one hour later. Harris had quickly removed his brigade from its position on the south end of his division's formation north of Swift Creek in Chesterfield County, leaving about one-third of his troops to maintain the picket line. The remainder of the brigade had begun moving toward the Richmond-Petersburg Turnpike, taking with them only their rifles, canteens, and cartridge boxes to ensure the most rapid possible progress.

Harris remembered that his troops displayed "fine spirits . . . marching with a quick, lively step." As the column headed south toward the Cockade City, Harris could hear the "deep, heavy and incessant roar of artillery, and the sharp rattle of musketry" that indicated to him that "a more than ordinary conflict on the lines around that devoted city" was in progress. The racket about Petersburg stood in sharp contrast to the situation along Mahone's front on Bermuda Hundred that night. "Not having heard of the disaster at Five Forks the day previous, we could not imagine the cause of the alarm, as everything was perfectly quiet on our front," recalled Private Thomas T. Roche of the 16th Mississippi.[8]

By sunrise, Harris's four Mississippi regiments, the 12th, 16th, 19th and 48th, had arrived near Petersburg. They made their way up the left bank of the Appomattox River toward and across the pontoon bridge near the village of Matoaca, the hard marching column stretching out for nearly half a mile. "I met Gen. Lee a short distance from the bridge, mounted and accompanied by several members of his staff," remembered Harris. "I at once reported to him for orders." The general-in-chief asked one of his aides if Major General John B. Gordon's line south and east of Petersburg had managed to remain intact. Learning that it had, Lee directed Harris's welcome, if modest, reinforcements toward Boydton Plank Road with instructions to report to General Wilcox "near the Newman House." This had been Harris's camping ground during the winter, so the young brigadier knew the area intimately. Harris reported to Wilcox within two hours of arriving on the south side of the Appomattox. The division commander, having already sent Lane and Thomas forward to dislodge Hamblin, appeared to Harris as being "without an organized command." Another Mississippian thought the dismounted Wilcox to be "inclined to be a little profane that morning," because the general observed enthusiastically that each of the Mississippians was "equal to one hundred of those d—d cowardly fellows." Harris advanced his brigade as Wilcox indicated, but upon the approach of Osborn's bluecoats, the Mississippi brigadier realized "the futility of attempting to check the advancing lines of the enemy with my small force (about four hundred men) in such an exposed position, [so] I fell back to the vicinity of the Newman House, where I again met Wilcox."[9]

General Wilcox went about the business of forging a new defense with the minimal resources available to him. He positioned fragments of Lane's and Thomas's men in the sunken reaches of Boydton Plank Road facing south and extending east to Rohoic Creek, where they connected with the thinly deployed Tarheels of Brigadier General William R. Cox's Brigade. Wilcox placed still other Georgians and North Carolinians south of the

Brigadier General James H. Lane

Plank Road near the creek itself, while about 125 of Lane's and Thomas's much-traveled veterans reported to Fort Gregg. Here they joined a handful of former artillerists who had been converted to infantrymen and sent to Fort Gregg a few days earlier.[10]

This Confederate bastion and its sister strong point, Fort Whitworth, squatted about one mile west of the Dimmock Line on the north side of Boydton Plank Road. Lee had ordered these outworks constructed in the fall of 1864, when he extended his main defense line from Battery 45 southwest to Hatcher's Run. The engineers had positioned the small forts so they could arrest the advance of enemy forces toward Petersburg or the

Appomattox River should the primary works be breached. A lesser emplacement, styled Fort Owen in honor of Lieutenant Colonel William Miller Owen, a Louisiana artillery officer who was in command of the forts, lay just south of Fort Gregg a quarter mile beyond Boydton Plank Road.[11]

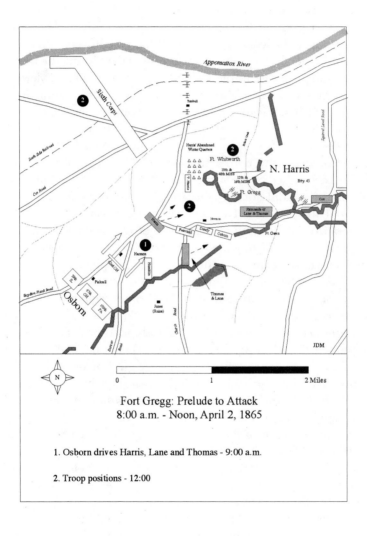

Fort Gregg: Prelude to Attack
8:00 a.m. - Noon, April 2, 1865

1. Osborn drives Harris, Lane and Thomas - 9:00 a.m.

2. Troop positions - 12:00

One historian described Fort Gregg as "a plump semicircle of packed earth lying on the muddy plain, protected by a trench fourteen feet wide and six feet deep, its earthen walls eight feet thick, topped with a palisade of logs. There were embrasures for six guns, and inside, a firing step so that riflemen could man loopholes." A wall of loopholed pine trunks eighteen or twenty inches in diameter enclosed the rear or northern side of the fort. The tiny garrison had stockpiled a considerable amount of artillery ammunition in pyramid formations inside of Fort Gregg. Six hundred yards to the north, the less imposing Fort Whitworth linked itself to Gregg by means of an incomplete trench, an indication that during the long, idle months of winter no one in the Confederate high command viewed the two little citadels as possessing much strategic worth. Coincidentally, Harris's Brigade had encamped in this neighborhood during the winter, and remnants of their temporary quarters dotted the open fields west of the forts. The Mississippians had thought so little of Fort Whitworth that they had "converted the timber supports into firewood, thus rendering [the fort] easily washed by the Winter rains," according to a member of the 16th Mississippi. "It did not have the strength of an ordinary rifle pit."[12]

When Thomas's and Lane's men arrived back at Fort Gregg, cannoneers from the Washington Artillery of Louisiana commanded by Lieutenant Francis McElroy joined them with two three-inch rifles. Former teamsters previously converted into artillerists supplemented McElroy's gunners, who rolled their twin pieces into the embrasures facing southwest. Soon, the 12th and 16th Mississippi regiments of Harris's Brigade filed into Fort Gregg with perhaps 200 men led by Lieutenant Colonel James H. Duncan of the 19th Mississippi. After Osborn's advance had prompted the Mississippians to retire, Wilcox met with Harris and instructed the brigadier to split his understrength brigade in half, Harris personally deploying the 19th and 48th Mississippi in Fort Whitworth, supporting the four guns in position there. Wilcox thought that Fort Gregg now contained "as many men as could fire conveniently." Thus, at about 11:00 a.m., the garrison of Fort Gregg mustered perhaps 350 men at its peak, with Fort Whitworth's defenders numbering something over 200.[13]

Wilcox knew that Major General Charles W. Field's Division of Longstreet's corps was en route to the south side of the Appomattox. Clearly, Wilcox's mission would be to hold what remained of the western defenses of Petersburg until Field could provide fresh manpower. Harris received word from Lee's headquarters to "supply my command with plenty of ammunition, as he expected me to hold the two works until Longstreet [Field] arrived." Wilcox rode up to the defenders at Fort Gregg and addressed them in a loud voice: "Men, the salvation of Lee's army is in your keeping; you must realize the responsibility, and your duty; don't surrender this fort; if you will hold the enemy in check for two hours Longstreet, who is making a forced march, will be here, and the danger to the army in the trenches will be averted." Perhaps a total of 1,000 Confederates remained west of Rohoic Creek arrayed in forts Whitworth, Gregg, and Owen, and along Boydton Plank Road facing south and west. On the horizon, a blue host many times that number began to gather, flushed with victory and seeking to land the knockout blow to the Confederacy. Federal artillery fire cut short Wilcox's inspirational speech. The men in Fort Gregg strained their voices to be heard over the incoming shells: "Tell General Lee that Fort Gregg will never be surrendered."[14]

* * *

While Osborn's brigade deserved sole credit for driving Lane, Thomas, and Harris from their advanced positions into the ramparts of forts Gregg and Whitworth, the Prairie Stater's four regiments were not the only Unionists assembling in the fields west of the Confederate strong points. By 9:00 a.m., General Wright had learned from officers on Grant's staff that the situation west and north of Hatcher's Run did not require Sixth Corps attention. The Second and Fifth corps, plus Philip Sheridan's cavalry, bore responsibility for subduing the remaining Confederates in that precinct, so Wright ordered his seven brigades to reverse field and follow Foster and Turner toward Petersburg. These troops moved out shortly before 10:00 a.m., marching in parallel columns on the inside of the captured Confederate line. "As the exultant veterans advanced along the works, passing the Red House, near where they had broken through in the early morning, their enthusiasm knew no bounds," according to one Vermont soldier.[15]

Getty's Second Division assumed the lead and arrived without incident opposite the Confederate forts in support of Gibbon's divisions. The Vermont Brigade placed its right flank on Boydton Plank Road with James Warner's brigade to their left and Thomas Hyde's brigade on the division's left, their left flank refused. Getty's men suffered marginally from Confederate artillery fire after their deployment. Some guns belonging to Lieutenant Colonel William T. Poague's Confederate battalion positioned on Getty's left along Cox Road proved particularly annoying. These pieces frequently changed position and managed to enfilade Getty's line. "The shelling from front and right was also severe," reported the division commander. The Federals unlimbered their own artillery in reply, while the infantry hugged the reverse slope of a gentle ridge, seeking shelter from the bothersome Confederate shells.[16]

Colonel Penrose's New Jersey Brigade and Oliver Edwards's six regiments, both of Wheaton's division, followed Getty's men toward Petersburg. Edwards formed on Hyde's left, while Penrose's Jerseymen formed in echelon on the far left of the entire Sixth Corps formation, touching the tracks of the South Side Railroad. These First Division reinforcements also complained of Confederate artillery fire during their approach toward the Petersburg lines.[17]

The two brigades of Truman Seymour's Third Division also countermarched from Hatcher's Run, but they were not destined to confront the Confederates between the Appomattox River and Boydton Plank Road. Moving to the right of the path followed by Gibbon's corps, Seymour's men recrossed the captured Confederate line and occupied the abandoned Rebel picket posts opposite Fort Fisher. Hamblin's brigade, the slightly bruised victims of Lane's and Thomas's counterattack earlier in the morning, obeyed Wheaton's directive to shift entirely out of the Sixth Corps sector, reporting to General Parke on the Ninth Corps front south of Petersburg.[18]

Although Hamblin's strength would thus be unavailable to the Federal forces arrayed opposite the Confederate forts, Brigadier General Thomas M. Harris's troops soon arrived to compensate for Hamblin's departure. Harris's men, aided by the 123rd Ohio of Potter's brigade, had been the only troops from the Twenty-fourth Corps that morning to fight along Hatcher's Run. Harris learned, as had Wright, that responsibility for dealing with whatever Confederate resistance remained west and north of that stream rested with others. "My command was reformed within twenty minutes," reported Harris and "we advanced . . . meeting with no opposition until within about a mile of the outer chain of forts on the south[west] side . . . of Petersburg, where the enemy had disposed his forces to resist our farther progress." Harris responded to Gibbon's order to deploy, along with the arriving brigades of Curtis and Potter, in support of Foster's division opposite forts Gregg and Whitworth. Thus, eleven Federal brigades from the Sixth and Twenty-fourth corps, perhaps 15,000 men, spanned the ground in a long arc between the South Side Railroad to and beyond Boydton Plank Road. "We evidently now had the enemy by the throat but he still held tenaciously to his line," observed Gibbon.[19]

General Grant had been following the morning's exciting events from his headquarters on Dabney's Mill Road, near the area of February's Battle of Hatcher's Run. As word of first Wright's and then Gibbon's successes reached him, Grant telegraphed the good news to the troops in Bermuda

Hundred and north of the James River. The most important recipient of Grant's dispatches waited anxiously at City Point. President Abraham Lincoln eagerly devoured the reports from his commanding general, passing Grant's descriptions of the rapidly unfolding events almost verbatim to Secretary of War Edwin M. Stanton in Washington.[20]

Grant learned from Ord at about 8:30 a.m. of Thomas Harris's breaching of the Confederate line at Hatcher's Run and the dispatch of the rest of Gibbon's corps to assist Wright. The lieutenant general now felt duty bound to ride to the front in order to coordinate the movements of the two corps (from different armies) involved in the follow-up to the Breakthrough. Accompanied by his headquarters entourage, Grant reached the captured Confederate works, urging his horse up and over the parapet. He arrived just as a large body of Rebel prisoners, prizes from Wright's Breakthrough, made its way to the rear shepherded by Federal escorts. "Some of the guards told the prisoners who the general was, and they manifested great curiosity to get a good look at him," remembered a member of the general's staff. One witness etched a vivid, if possibly embellished, portrait of Grant's chance encounter with the tangible human evidence of Lee's collapsing defense:

> I returned to the works with my numerous prisoners, others surrendering en route, just in season to see General Grant . . . and his retinue of about one hundred pass inside the enemy's works by the fort we had taken, going toward Petersburg. He was mounted on a proud-stepping dark charger, dressed with unusual care and never appeared to better advantage. The occasion inspiring it, he was a perfect picture of a conquering hero, but seemed all unconscious of it. The artist who could put Grant and his suite on canvas as he appeared then would win renown. As Grant's eye caught the motley group of prisoners with me, who were regarding him with silent, open-mouthed wonder, he slightly smiled, drew in his horse a little as though to speak or in doubt of his safety, seeing the rebs had guns, but finally dashed on, an impressive picture not only in the midst of war, but surrounded by grand fortifications and the victorious and defeated living, wounded, dying and dead, real heroes of both the blue and the gray; never to be forgotten by those who were fortunate enough to see it.[21]

As Grant rode forward he encountered "a division of Wright's corps, flushed with success, and rushing forward with a dash that was inspiriting beyond description," according to Colonel Horace Porter of the commander's party. The troops that spotted Grant belonged, in fact, to both Seymour's and Wheaton's divisions. If their appearance inspired Grant, his presence stirred them with equal ardor. "As soon as the soldiers saw the Lieutenant-General, they shouted, 'Boys, here's General Grant, three cheers for him,' and all along the line as he rode on his black horse, Jeff. Davis, the men cheered him with the wildest enthusiasm," remembered a member of the 14th New Jersey. "He rode with head uncovered, and bowed his thanks for the soldiers' hearty greeting." Lieutenant David Soule of the 2nd Connecticut Heavy Artillery expressed amazement that the most powerful soldier in the world "sat on his horse, in a plain blouse suit, if I had not have known him by sight I would have said he and his staff were just an ordinary bunch of cavalrymen in their fatigue suits."[22]

Grant and Meade found one another amidst this welter of mutual admiration, and the two commanders exchanged words of congratulation. Generals Wright, Seymour, Getty, and Wheaton also located the lieutenant general, who had the opportunity to express to these Sixth Corps officers his especial appreciation for what they had accomplished that morning. By 10:45 a.m., Grant had established headquarters in the Banks House, a two-story frame dwelling located south of the Plank Road barely one mile southwest of Fort Gregg. "Everything has been carried from the left of the Ninth Corps," he informed City Point. "The Sixth Corps alone captured more than 3,000 prisoners. The Second and Twenty-fourth Corps both captured forts, guns, and prisoners from the enemy, but I cannot yet tell the number. . . . All looks remarkably well." As Grant dictated this buoyant news to the president, he thought to mention one additional tactical detail: "We are now closing around the works of the city immediately enveloping Petersburg."

Forward of that line stood the two tiny forts upon which Wilcox relied to buy the time needed to save Petersburg and perhaps the Confederacy. A few hundred Mississippians, North Carolinians, Georgians, Louisianians and Marylanders readied ammunition, double-checked rifles and cannons, and pulled their hats just a little tighter around their heads. The storm of battle, one of the most dramatic combat episodes of the entire war, was about to break upon them.[23]

*   *   *

Not every Confederate officer agreed with Cadmus Wilcox that forts Gregg and Whitworth should be defended at all costs. Brigadier General Reuben Lindsay Walker, Third Corps chief of artillery, dispatched Captain Richard Walke, his assistant inspector general, to order the withdrawal of all the guns in both emplacements in order to save them from almost certain capture once the Federals commenced their assault. At Fort Whitworth, General Harris earnestly but unsuccessfully protested the removal of the four rifled pieces positioned there. McElroy's two rifles in Fort Gregg remained in position only because the Unionists had already approached too closely for them to be extricated safely.[24]

James Lane also considered the twin forts a death trap, even before Wilcox had orchestrated the counterthrust that dislodged Hamblin's troops. Now, on the brink of the inevitable attack, Lane reiterated this opinion to his division commander, feeling satisfied "that every man in the Fort would be killed or captured, & I wanted to save as many as I could." Wilcox granted Lane permission to redeploy to the left near Rohoic Creek, where a number of his North Carolinians had previously taken position. Lane promptly sent aides into Fort Gregg to retrieve as many of his Tarheels as he could before the hammer blow fell upon the overmatched defenders. In the confusion of the moment, not many of Lane's men responded to their general's messengers. Those who did leave departed with the disdain of the steadfast Mississippians ringing in their ears.[25]

These eleventh-hour reductions unfolded as John Gibbon prepared to unleash his corps against the two Confederate bastions. The Twenty-fourth Corps commander retained tactical control of the field, assuring that the operation—and the glory that would accrue from it—would belong to his two divisions. With Getty and Wheaton extending the line to his left, Seymour in position behind Foster, and Turner's brigades arriving in immediate support, Gibbon set in motion the plan he had devised to reduce the forts and, perhaps, capture Petersburg, whose spires could be seen looming beyond the Southern defenses.[26]

None of the Twenty-fourth Corps artillery along Hatcher's Run had accompanied Gibbon's infantry on its march toward Petersburg. Gibbon recognized that assistance from the long arm would not only aid his impending attack, but might prevent grayclad reinforcements from bolstering the forts. He assigned Lieutenant Colonel Peter S. Michie, chief engineer of the Army of the James, responsibility for locating available batteries to augment his offensive. Michie hustled to Fort Fisher, where Captain Romeo H. Start of the 3rd Vermont Battery answered his breathless request for guns. As the cannoneers from the Green Mountain State rumbled forward with four pieces, a section of the 1st New York Battery under Lieutenant William Sears also joined Michie's makeshift battalion. These guns advanced opposite Fort Owen south of Fort Gregg, in position to bombard both Gregg and Whitworth as a precursor to Gibbon's infantry assault.[27]

The Twenty-fourth Corps troops began to deploy for the offensive on a low ridge some 800 yards south of Fort Gregg. Osborn's brigade, advanced beyond its comrades as a result of its morning foray, established position first. Colonel Osborn shook out the 62nd Ohio as brigade skirmishers, the Buckeyes approaching to within 150 yards of Fort Gregg, where they halted in a small ravine. The rest of the brigade remained on the higher ground as the balance of Foster's division formed for the assault.[28]

Dandy's brigade filed in on Osborn's immediate left. Colonel Dandy placed the 11th Maine on the left of the brigade formation on Boydton Plank Road southwest of Fort Gregg. The 100th New York and 10th Connecticut formed successively to the right of the Pine State men, making connection with Osborn's troops. Two companies from the 11th Maine, supplemented by troops from other regiments in the brigade, advanced as skirmishers, Dandy's men deploying about 12:15 p.m. Prior to the assault, Dandy sent word to Lieutenant Colonel Jonathan A. Hill, commanding the 11th Maine, to shift farther right in order to improve his connection with the 100th New York. For reasons that eluded the brigade commander, Hill instead took his regiment out of formation to the left and halted among the abandoned Confederate winter camps opposite Fort Whitworth. Foster's main battle line thus consisted of the four regiments of Osborn's brigade and the 100th New York and 10th Connecticut of Dandy's command.[29]

Colonel Fairchild's brigade of Foster's division and two brigades of Turner's division supported Osborn and Dandy. Fairchild's troops occupied the ground to the left and slightly to the rear of Dandy's regiments. Behind them the veterans of Andrew Potter's and William B. Curtis's brigades moved northward from the main Union line. The third of Turner's brigades, the West Virginians of Thomas Harris's command, reported to Foster for orders. The Hoosier general directed Harris to take position on the far left of the corps, opposite Fort Whitworth. By 1:00 p.m., all six brigades of Gibbon's corps were on the field, glaring across a few hundred yards of open, intermittently swampy ground at the twin mounds of earth and logs that stood between them and Petersburg.[30]

The troops in forts Gregg and Whitworth, outnumbered by the assembled Federals in their immediate front by a margin of eight or nine to one, had not been idle while Gibbon prepared his assault. Nathaniel Harris had sent incendiaries to torch the cabins west of Fort Whitworth, built by his own troops as winter quarters but now promising shelter to the potential attackers. While these structures burned and smoldered, the Mississippians and their comrades busily collected and loaded the extra rifles that had been either abandoned during the morning's actions or warehoused in the forts. Many of these Confederates had defended the Bloody Angle at Spotsylvania the previous spring and recalled how critical spare weapons had been. The garrison positioned extra boxes of rifle ammunition along the parapet as well. Defenders might have been in short supply; firearms and bullets were not.[31]

With the removal of the artillery from Fort Whitworth, only the two rifles in Fort Gregg, supplemented ineffectively by ordnance in Battery 45 on the inner Confederate line, aided the outnumbered foot soldiers. In fact, Harris believed that the act of removing the artillery from Fort Whitworth precipitated Gibbon's decision to launch his assault.[32]

Although such an explanation appears nowhere in the Union commander's accounts, there can be no question that the appearance of Foster's division, with Turner's in close proximity, etched an indelible picture in the minds of many Southern soldiers. "Ah, what a contrast, what a soul-sickening spectacle to behold," thought one member of the 16th Mississippi. "25,000 men, flushed with recent victory, to be hurled against 250 . . . half-starved heroes, whose hearts of steel qualled not even at such fearful odds." While this witness's estimate of the blueclad force exceeded a reality sufficiently daunting to require no exaggeration, a less emotional participant recalled that "Gibbon's columns approached in fine order, and by its numbers alone, seemed about to envelop the works." Harris once again exhorted the men in Fort Whitworth to "stand like iron, my brave boys, stand like iron," while Captain R. R. Applewhite of the 12th Mississippi used much the same language to encourage the defenders in Fort Gregg. Colonel Duncan provided more specific instructions to his expectant troops, ordering them not to fire until told to do so. "All around the walls of Fort Gregg was the cry of the officers, 'Keep down men, keep down' . . . with their suspension drawn to a tension indescribable," remembered one Mississippian.[33]

About 1:00 p.m., Gibbon issued General Foster the attack orders, which channeled that tension into what army commander Ord would call "a desperate courage worthy of a better cause." Foster immediately committed Osborn's and Dandy's brigades to the assault against Fort Gregg, and Osborn's regiments moved forward in quick time at right shoulder shift arms. Once the Chicagoan's formation had crossed the marshy streamlet a couple of hundred yards south of Fort Gregg, Osborn "gave the command charge, when the brigade, with cheers, swept up the ascent at the double-quick under a terrible fire of grape, canister, and minie-balls tearing through the ranks."[34]

Colonel Briscoe of the 199th Pennsylvania, on Osborn's right, recalled that the last 300 yards in front of the fort "form[ed] a perfect natural glacis" and that crossing this ground cost his unit its most severe losses. Briscoe received a leg wound 75 yards from the fort's moat, but along with many of his men, the colonel pushed into the ditch. There he discovered that the recent rains had filled the moat to a significant depth, particularly on the right or southeast side of the fort. Wounded men fell face down in the muddy water, where they risked drowning unless rescued by friendly hands. The Pennsylvanians struggled to jam their bayonets into the slippery sides of the earthwork in order to rise above the muck.[35]

The 39th Illinois advanced to the immediate left of the 199th Pennsylvania. Private Michael Wetzel, a member of Company I, remembered that Fort Gregg "was as full of men as ever a dog was of fleas." As the Suckers approached the moat, Rebel fire became especially fierce. "Grape was being planted, not as farmers plant corn, two to four in a hill, but by the bucket full, perhaps barrel, for two of the men of my company who were killed each had three grapeshot through them," recalled Wetzel. Wetzel sustained a serious arm wound just as he reached the moat and tumbled in. Half buried in the mud at the bottom of the ditch and showered by the loose dirt kicked up by comrades clinging to the fort's slope, he desperately grasped at the pants leg of a friend. The man recognized him, and "with a pocketknife cut my equipments from my body and coat-sleeve from my arm, and tied my handkerchief around the arm, the knot being placed over the artery, which had been severed, and my life was thus saved."[36]

Sergeant George W. Burton of Company E was not nearly so lucky. A few feet from the moat a burst of Confederate fire riddled him with bullets, causing him to stagger into the ditch, the national colors he carried tumbling to the ground in the process. Lieutenant Oliver Sproul of the 199th Pennsylvania saw what had happened and grabbed the Stars and Stripes, planting the banner in the side of the fort, perhaps the first of the many Union flags destined to fly from the ramparts of Fort Gregg that afternoon.[37]

In the meantime, the 67th Ohio on the left of Osborn's original formation reached the fort near its southwest angle. The Buckeyes worked their way toward the back of the works using the ditch as a sheltered avenue of approach. The farther they advanced, however, the deeper the water became until they were completely thwarted in their attempt to reach Gregg's palisaded rear entrance, "the water in that part of the ditch being so deep that the men could not wade through it," reported regimental commander, Colonel Alvin C. Voris. The 62nd Ohio had also charged into the ditch, having sustained horrific losses while crossing the open ground south of the fort. "When we moved forward the enemy opened on the solid column, first with one piece of artillery, then with another, cutting a wide swath the full length of the column, and eight or ten feet wide," remembered Lieutenant Robert Davison. Like the rest of Osborn's

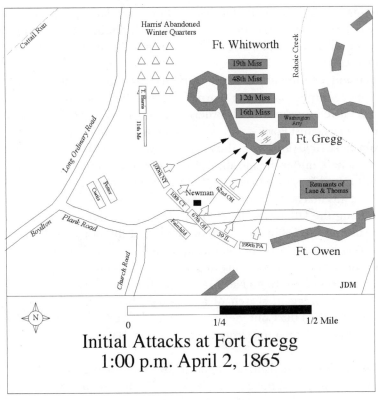

Initial Attacks at Fort Gregg
1:00 p.m. April 2, 1865

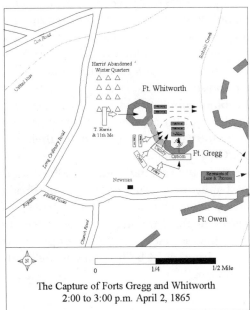

The Capture of Forts Gregg and Whitworth
2:00 to 3:00 p.m. April 2, 1865

swarming brigade, the men of the 62nd Ohio struggled to climb to the top of the parapet, retain their footing in the muddy ditch, or avoid trampling upon the wounded and dying who sought safety against the face of the fortress walls.[38]

Division commander Foster instructed George Dandy to join the attack once either Osborn or Turner had initiated the offensive. When Osborn moved forward, Dandy ordered his two available regiments to join in the effort against Fort Gregg. "The assault was commenced at a distance of from 200 to 300 yards from the works, and was made at the double-quick, without a halt, under the most terrific fire of musketry and artillery I have ever witnessed," reported Dandy. "Many of our brave men went down, but the work was reached without faltering."[39]

Among the fallen was the colonel's brother, Major James H. Dandy, commanding the 100th New York on the left of the brigade's formation. Major Dandy, "who by his heroic example had succeeded in animating the men with a more than ordinary degree of fearlessness," thought Captain Edwin Nichols of the 100th New York, was killed while trying to pass to the rear of Fort Gregg in search of a way into the stubborn fortification. Nichols described the Confederate resistance as "a terrible fire of musketry and canister," echoing the experience of Osborn's troops immediately on their right.[40]

The 10th Connecticut, commanded by Lieutenant Colonel Ellsworth D. S. Goodyear, filled the gap between the 100th New York and the 67th Ohio of Osborn's brigade. "To reach [Fort Gregg] we had to charge across an open plain not only in the face of a well-directed fire from the fort, but also subject to a cross-fire upon both flanks," wrote Corporal Joseph E. Parmelee of Company A. The 10th Connecticut suffered horrendous losses as they dashed across the open ground, Colonel Goodyear sustaining wounds to his face and shoulder. Confederate fire also claimed one of the color-bearers, the blue Connecticut state flag plunging to the ground beside him. Parmelee and Private George W. Philips grasped the fallen banner and made for the parapet, determined that theirs would be the first standard on Fort Gregg. Philips and Parmelee reached the bastion's earthen walls near the southwest angle and scrambled wildly up the slope with the distinctive banner of the Nutmeg State visible to other members of the regiment. "Every brave man this way," shouted Private Winfield F. Works, "our flag is on the fort!" It is impossible to judge whether the 10th Connecticut or 39th Illinois deserve the honor of placing the first flag on Fort Gregg, although veterans of both regiments debated the issue with some fervor after the war.[41]

Six Union regiments now packed the sodden ditch below Fort Gregg on its southern, eastern and western sides, or lined the ground immediately in front of the moat. "The garrison," admitted Colonel Dandy, "although surrounded, refused to surrender and continued to fire upon our men, while from Fort Baldwin [Whitworth] a destructive fire was also poured in upon the backs of our troops exposed in that direction."[42]

The Confederates in Fort Gregg had watched Foster deploy and withheld their fire until the blue ranks had approached within effective rifle range. "We pelted them right merrily," remembered one exultant Mississippian who shared the perspective of his comrades that multiple Union attacks had been thrown back. While Federal accounts universally reported that Foster's two brigades reached the moat of Fort Gregg without hesitation, albeit while sustaining heavy losses, Nathaniel Harris's version of the battle reflected that of every other Confederate participant:

> Gregg repulsed assault after assault—the two remnants of regiments, which had won glorious honor on so many fields, fighting this, their last battle, with most terrible enthusiasm, as if feeling this to be the last act of the Drama for them. And the officers and men of the Washington Artillery fighting their guns to the last, preserved untarnished the brilliancy of reputation acquired by their corps. Gregg raged like the crater of a volcano, emitting flashes of deadly battle-fires, enveloped in flame and cloud, wreathing our flag, as well in honor, as in the smoke of death.

The Confederates counted two, three, or even four attacks before Gibbon's men succeeded in reaching the ditch. "Again and again came rapid firing, and Gibbon's men recoiled," stated a member of the 48th Mississippi. "A second and third attempt were likewise beat off with tremendous loss to the Federals." From his vantage point near Rohoic Creek, Cadmus Wilcox averred that "three or four times were they seen to give way and then renew the attack." A cannoneer from the Washington Artillery agreed that the Federals "were thrice driven back by our messengers of destruction and death. Again and again they charged, until upon this little spot, it was like unto the fire of hell . . . amid the crashing rain of leaden missiles, severing soul from body."[43]

These seemingly irreconcilable versions of the same event might be explained by the uneven and slightly staggered advances made by Osborn and Dandy, which may have appeared to the beleaguered Confederates as separate orchestrated assaults. There is no question that once these two brigades had bogged down around the fort, Colonel Dandy sent Captain Frank Hawkins to General Foster with a request for additional troops. Foster ordered Colonel Fairchild to reinforce his sytmied comrades.

Fairchild immediately summoned Major Frank W. Tremain, ranking officer of the 89th New York, and Major Hyron Kalt, in temporary command of the 158th New York: "Majors, there is a fort which has withstood the attack of a brigade of 'new troops.' Now I want you to take your two 'old regiments' and take it." The officers enthusiastically assented and hustled off to ready their men.[44]

The 89th New York, a unit that had fought under Fairchild as early as the spring of 1862, led the reinforcements toward the left or western side of Fort Gregg. Tremain was killed after covering less than 100 yards, but his men gained the moat, mingling indiscriminately with Dandy's troops to their right. The 158th New York piled in soon thereafter, losing Lieutenant Edward Riley, the regimental adjutant, in the process. With the rest of Fairchild's brigade waiting in reserve, the bulk of Foster's entire division—eight regiments—encircled Fort Gregg with numbers that exceeded the remaining strength of the garrison by at least ten to one.[45]

Nevertheless, the defenders of Fort Gregg maintained their determination to retain their position, or at least to sell their lives dearly for the time needed to prevent Petersburg's demise. "It would be impossible to describe the scene in Fort Gregg at this time," wrote one Confederate. "Our enthusiastic spirits found vent in such rebel yelling as was never heard before. . . . We all yelled and cheered like madmen, and fought like demons." One of Lane's men remembered that as the ammunition began to expire (or the frantic soldiers could not locate the reserve cartridges) "our men threw bats and rocks at them in the ditch."[46]

With Foster's division almost entirely committed and Fort Gregg defiantly resisting all efforts to reduce it, Gibbon summoned the remainder of his available forces to the fray. The corps commander ordered General Turner to engage his three brigades, Thomas Harris's against Fort Whitworth, and Potter's and Curtis's in support of Foster's stalled division at the base of Fort Gregg.[47]

Potter and Curtis had moved up to within striking distance of the fort once Osborn and Dandy had executed their attack. These two veteran brigades now arose and advanced virtually simultaneously, Potter's three regiments on the right and Curtis's three units on the left. "Like reapers [we] went to the harvest of death," remembered a member of the 12th West Virginia, "over ground already thickly strewn with the dead of the brigade which preceded [us], through a storm of grape and canister that caused the heart of every observer to stand in fear for the fate of the brave men who undauntedly dashed onward." Colonel Curtis, a 43-year-old merchant from (of all places) Sharpsburg, Maryland, galloped back and forth encouraging his troops to maintain their momentum despite the fort's brutal blanket of fire.[48]

Curtis's troops absorbed terrible punishment not only from Fort Gregg but from Fort Whitworth as well. "We would go ahead a little, then fall to the ground to dodge the canister, then at it again," said a West Virginian. Sergeant Albert G. Leach of the 12th West Virginia lamented the order, issued by "some fool," to halt within 50 yards of the fort. "We lost several of our best men there," Leach reported. Leach's comrades, along with troops from the 54th Pennsylvania and 23rd Illinois, lurched forward and at last reached the moat below Fort Gregg, where they joined the survivors of Foster's assaults. Foster's men "were in the ditch—packed there like sardines in a box—making no effort to get into the fort," recalled Private William Bennett of the 54th Pennsylvania. "The only way we could get to the fort was to go over the top of the men in the ditch. They were in a perilous position, and could not help themselves. They were unable to take the fort nor could they get away from it."[49]

Andrew Potter directed his Ohio and Massachusetts troops to the right and then executed a half-wheel movement to the left, which brought the 116th Ohio directly in front of Fort Gregg facing north. The Buckeyes found their progress thwarted not only by Confederate fire but by the prone bodies of Foster's men hugging the ground below the fort. "It was sure death to remain here many minutes longer," observed one of Potter's men. "The order was given, 'Forward'—and now each one vies with his comrade for the ditch. It was a race for life." With the 116th Ohio connecting with Curtis's 12th West Virginia on its left, and the 34th Massachusetts advancing to the right of the Buckeyes, most of Turner's six regiments plunged into the moat, where they fused in one muddled mass with Foster's motionless hordes. Now, the greater part of 14 Union regiments, perhaps 4,000 soldiers, had reached the walls of Fort Gregg. Would this milling multitude reprise the gruesome experience of the Crater and await their fate at the bottom of a muddy hole? Momentum, morale, and mass suggested otherwise.[50]

The tactical key to Fort Gregg lay at the northwestern corner of the fort, where the unfinished trench ran toward Fort Whitworth. "There was a weak point on the side of Gregg, where the ditch was incomplete," reported one of the Confederates, and eventually the Federals exploited this vulnerable spot to gain the little bastion's interior. In truth, however, the final attack had little to do with innovative tactics or perspicacious orders of Union officers targeting discernible weaknesses in the emplacement's defenses. Rather, the decisive combat at Fort Gregg provided an example all too often repeated in the Civil War, in which masses of maddened men collided at point-blank range in a fury of indescribable mayhem.[51]

The addition of Turner's two brigades to the stalled remnants of Foster's eight regiments swept the entire Federal force into renewed action through sheer volume of humanity. There was simply not enough real estate in front of and below Fort Gregg to shelter so many men simultaneously. The Federals comprehended through raw instinct that they must either move forward or fall back behind adequate cover in order to avoid being slaughtered by the fort's unyielding garrison. Moving forward essentially meant moving up—scaling the slippery walls of the earthwork or rushing around the moat to the unfinished trench or against the palisaded sallyport in the rear. The Yankees, acting as individuals or in small groups subject to the shouted instructions of line officers, simultaneously attempted all three maneuvers.

Down in the moat, the Federals began to dig steps into the sides of the fort and prepared to boost one another up the slope and onto the parapet. The Confederates could hear Union officers screaming direction and encouragement as the men gouged frantically into the packed clay in order to claw their way to the top. A Georgian inside Fort Gregg described the scene from the garrison's perspective:

> Upon the tiptoe of expectancy, with guns in hand and pointed across our breastworks every living member of our little garrison... was watching for the heads of the enemy to appear. First we saw the flags, next the bayonets bobbed in sight and then the heads of the Federals rising up out of the ditch. We poured volley after volley into them. Some escaped our murderous fire; many were killed upon the breastworks; some few were shot and fell inside the fort. So the first effort to scale our fort met with a signal defeat.[52]

The Yankees, although jammed together cheek by jowl in the muddy hell of the moat, managed to shove and hoist one another up to the ramparts. "Our men in ascending could not use their guns, and in some instances threw pebbles and sand into the faces of the enemy to blind them," wrote a member of the 12th West Virginia. The color-bearer of that regiment, a man named Adams, had fallen seriously wounded when Private Joseph R. Logsdon picked up the flag and scaled the works, only to be cut down as he planted the flag on the parapet. The regimental symbol tumbled into the fort, where it motivated the Northerners to follow it into the jaws of Fort Gregg's combat-crazed defenders. "The noise outside [of Fort Gregg] was fearful, frightful and indescribable" recalled a Mississippian, "the curses and groaning of frenzied men could be heard over and above the din of musketry. Savage men, ravenous beasts!"[53]

The 12th West Virginia's flag was not the only Union banner to reach the crest of Fort Gregg during this stage of the battle. The colors of the 39th Illinois, initially raised on the slope of the fort, now ascended toward the ramparts where the Confederates attempted to capture it. "As fast as they showed themselves on top of the parapet we shot them down," boasted a member of the 39th Illinois. "They became so excited that one of them took his bayonet and threw it with all his might at the flag, but fortunately missing the standard [bearer] and tearing a large hole in the center of the flag." Seeing this, Colonel Osborn began grabbing the men of his command, physically lifting them up to protect the banner of his old regiment and to "take this fort before the enemy receives reinforcement." The brigade commander hoisted one of his men onto the ramparts near the left end of the ditch about ten or twelve feet from the northwest corner of the fort. This soldier raised his rifle to shoot at a Confederate who stood only a musket-length away. A second Southerner quickly appeared and unloosed a minie ball that raked the side of the Yankee's neck, knocking him senseless. When this Federal regained consciousness, a dead man was laying across his back. He rolled the corpse away, picked up his rifle, and returned to the fray.[54]

The garrison also suffered from this intense combat, and its small numbers diminished by the minute. Colonel Duncan distributed his men along the firing steps as best he could, detailing a mere 25 troops to guard the palisaded gate in the fort's rear. The Confederates now seized artillery projectiles and used them as makeshift grenades against the desperate attackers clambering up the walls. "Our men hurled them on the heads of the enemy in the ditch," testified a Mississippian. "The fuses of the bomb shells were fired and rolled on them. This work did not stop until all or nearly all of the solid cannon balls and shells were gone." The Southerners also bombarded their attackers with bricks salvaged from the chimneys of the winter quarters.[55]

Such desperation signaled that the outcome of the struggle had been all but determined. The Federals began to rush into the fort via the trench line running toward Fort Whitworth. Others burst through the crumbling sallyport while still more appeared along the fort's blood-drenched southern parapet. "They were yelling, cursing, and shooting with all the frenzy and rage of a ho[r]de of merciless barbarians," according to a North Carolinian. The Unionists spent little time on the parapet. "Down boys, down," yelled their officers. "Charge down it is," remembered Private William Stark of the 34th Massachusetts of Potter's brigade. "Plunge, slide or jump down among the bright polished steel. Foot to foot. No loading and firing now. Bayonet every man."[56]

"There were so many Federals coming over the parapet in the last charge we could not shoot them all," testified the garrison medical officer, surgeon George Richards. That did not mean, however, that the intrepid Confederates succumbed to the overwhelming odds. The combat raged for another 25 minutes as Yankee and Rebel exchanged hand-to-hand blows of the most horrific nature. "The whole wall was covered with bluecoats," remembered an officer in the 33rd North Carolina, while from his vantage point in the rear, Wilcox counted half a dozen Federal flags flying from the ramparts. "We broke our guns and used the barrels for clubs," said Sergeant Joseph B. Thompson of the 16th Mississippi. "It was not my fortune to witness, much less participate in, a more desperate hand-to-hand conflict during the war," shuddered a soldier in the 39th Illinois. "The men used the butts of their guns and bayonets, while our officers were equally as busy with their swords. Inch by inch the Johnnies were forced to yield their ground, but it was not until more than half the fort was in our possession before they would surrender." One Federal remembered hearing a Confederate officer exhorting his men to "Die, boys, die but never surrender." This Northerner observed that "steel . . . has a wonderful power to change opinions, especially when pointed at the breast. . . . They fought like demons."[57]

Private Lawrence Berry of the Washington Artillery refused to face the inevitable. This cannoneer had just participated in loading his piece with a double round of canister as the Federals rushed toward the muzzle of the cannon screaming, "Don't fire that gun; drop the lanyard, or we'll shoot!" The fearless Berry defied them with an outburst of bravado. "Shoot and be damned!" he replied as the charge from his muzzle mowed a path of bloody destruction across the packed earth of Fort Gregg, killing and wounding perhaps two dozen attackers. The enraged Unionists riddled Berry with minie balls and dispatched other members of the gun crew as well.[58]

The Federals who entered Fort Gregg were appalled at the vision that greeted them. "The interior of the fort was a pool of blood, a sight which can never be shut from memory," testified a New Yorker. "The rebels had recklessly fought to the last." Amidst the unspeakable horror of this sickening spectacle, the surviving Confederates dropped their rifles, raised their arms, and finally acknowledged defeat. "When we rushed over the top the sight was truly terrific," remembered a Union officer. "Dead men and the dying lay strewn all about, and it was with the greatest difficulty that we could prevent our infuriated soldiers from shooting down and braining all who survived of the stubborn foe." A Confederate participant agreed that some infuriated Yankees continued their detail of death even after the garrison had capitulated:

> Many of our captors were under the influence of whisky, and all were exasperated that we should have made such a stubborn fight, entailing on them a bloody massacre, when resistance was useless and vain. So the cry was kill, and but for their officers, who with cocked pistols made the men desist, all of us would have been murdered, and then too the jam of men in the fort gave us some protection, for it was impossible almost to shoot a Confederate without hitting a Federal. We lost about forty men killed in the fort after its capture, and fully that many Federals were killed by their own men.[59]

Colonel Curtis reported that Captain William A. Smiley of the 12th West Virginia accepted the formal surrender of Fort Gregg, tendered by Colonel Duncan. Smiley asked Duncan why the garrison had continued to fight once the outcome of the uneven contest had been determined. The Mississippi officer explained that the noise inside Fort Gregg had been so intense and that his men were so excited that he could not make his wishes to surrender the fort heard until the Federals had physically subdued his troops. Another member of the 12th West Virginia offered a different if implausible explanation for the Confederates' incredible fortitude: "They had been drinking whisky and gunpowder."[60]

* * *

The 19th Mississippi and 48th Mississippi in Fort Whitworth certainly had not been imbibing exotic cocktails, but they had been rapt observers of the drama unfolding a few hundred yards south of them at Fort Gregg. "We could hear them cheering every time we repulsed the Yankees," remembered a soldier in the 12th Mississippi. Nathaniel Harris and his two regiments aided the defense of Fort Gregg even more materially by pouring an effective flanking fire against the left and rear of Gibbon's men as they clustered along the western fringes of the fort. [61]

Harris could concentrate on assisting the defenders of Fort Gregg because the Federals ventured no simultaneous effort to capture Fort Whitworth. That is not to say, however, that the ground west of Fort Whitworth contained no Union soldiers. The 11th Maine of Dandy's brigade had drifted to that neighborhood prior to the initial assault on Fort Gregg as had Thomas Harris's three West Virginia regiments of Turner's division. Foster had suggested that Harris move to his left when the Mountaineers arrived following their successful combat at Hatcher's

Run. Harris, a 47-year-old physician, maneuvered his brigade opposite the abandoned Confederate winter camps and charged into the ruins of that military village, deploying within 150 yards of Fort Whitworth. Here the bluecoats hunkered down, seeking shelter not only from Fort Whitworth's musketry, but from enfilade fire at Fort Gregg. Harris's left was exposed as well, because the Sixth Corps troops arrayed toward the Appomattox River had not established a tight connection with the West Virginians.[62]

While Osborn, Dandy, Fairchild, Potter, and Curtis attacked Fort Gregg, Thomas Harris contented himself with "pouring a perfect storm of balls" into Fort Whitworth. The decisive push onto the ramparts of Fort Gregg, and the advance of Wright's troops on his left, signaled Harris that the time had come for his brigade to attack Fort Whitworth, a conclusion understood equally as clearly by the two small Mississippi regiments inside the little bastion. "As soon as Gregg fell, we of Whitworth saw that 'our turn came next' and girded our loins for the fray," remembered Captain Frank H. Foote of the 48th Mississippi. Foote and his comrades took inspiration from their regimental banner that flew proudly in the afternoon breeze as Thomas Harris's Unionists readied themselves for the assault:

> The flag of the 48th Miss. floated above us, and many balls pierced its folds that day, and twice was it shot from its staff. The third time it was attached to a rifle, and defiantly flaunted in the faces of our assailants. Gen. [Nathaniel] Harris mounted the parapet and waved the flag over our heads, and shouted 'Give 'em hell, boys.'[63]

The West Virginians now arose and began to rush toward Fort Whitworth. Just then, an officer from Lee's staff arrived in the fort, carrying orders for Nathaniel Harris to withdraw the garrison because fresh Confederate troops had at last arrived to man the interior lines of the Petersburg defenses. "The order to evacuate Battery Whitworth was given to the commanders of the 19th and 48th regiments, but as the enemy was close upon us and we were nearly enveloped and under a cross fire, our withdrawal was made without much regard to order," admitted General Harris. Captain Foote described the retreat a little more colorfully:

> Seeing that our 'blue-belly' friends had a hankering after that particular spot, and having urgent business at Petersburg to answer roll-call we left them in possession as soon as our Gen. Harris gave the word,'every man for himself. . . .' Our rapid movement of change of base was fraught with much fun, and I noticed how Col. Phelps, [sic] of the 19th Miss, gathered his cumbersome limbs together for the mighty effort. As he cleared the gorge he shied to the left, and a bullet came crashing beside him. The

uncertainties of life came before him, and with a 2:40-gait he lit out. Another ball spent of its mission and fury struck him in the back, and oh, my, you should have seen that 180-pound six-foot man 'git.' I laughed until I was weak. . . .

Our General (N. H. Harris) was a portly man devoid of fear, and aggressive. He did not relish the 'homestretch,' and soon became tired. The run exhausted him, and while catching his breath he said to me,'I'll be d—d if I run any more.' Just then his brother and Aid-de-Camp, Capt. Will Harris, threw up his hat, in defiance of repeated summons to surrender, expecting it to fall in front of him, and he would pick it up as he passed, but it fell behind him and he stopped to pick it up just as the Federals fired a hasty volley at us. The volley stimulated Gen. Harris, his brother, and myself to renewed exertions, so much so that I believe that we led the boys into the last ditch of Petersburg, spitting into spray the placid waters of Old Town Creek.[64]

Thomas Harris reached Fort Whitworth just as the Mississippians were leaving. The Federals scooped up four officers and 65 enlisted men and found two dead and two wounded Confederates in the fort as well. Harris's West Virginians pursued a short distance—the chase that so motivated Foote and the Harris brothers—and "secured a few more prisoners, and a few were picked up by my skirmishers, raising the number to about eighty-five in all," reported Thomas Harris. The 11th Maine, errant comrades of Dandy's men now in possession of Fort Gregg, also moved into Fort Whitworth.[65]

The capture of Fort Whitworth may have been relatively bloodless, but the struggle for Fort Gregg left a legacy of carnage long remembered by the men in blue and gray who fought there on April 2. "I never saw so many dead in so small a place lying just where they had fallen," testified a Northern officer. A Confederate witness agreed: "The ground was nearly covered with dead and wounded Yankees for a considerable distance in front. The ditch was full of dead, dying, wounded, and living but scared Yankees." Another Southerner recalled that, "the dead of the enemy lay literally in heaps, much thicker than they were in front of the stone fence at Fredericksburg, or in the angle at Spotsylvania Courthouse," while a soldier from the 16th Mississippi wrote that "for one hundred yards

"For one hundred yards in front of the work the ground was completely covered with one trembling mass of human beings."

in front of the work the ground was completely covered with one trembling mass of human beings."

Nathaniel Harris estimated that the engagement lasted from about 1:00 p.m. until 3:00 p.m. During that time, eighteen Union regiments participated in the attacks against the twin forts, all but Thomas Harris's brigade and the 11th Maine focusing upon Fort Gregg. Corps commander Gibbon, calling the assault against Fort Gregg "one of the most desperate of the war," tallied 122 Union officers and men killed and 592 wounded during the two-hour struggle, a number that greatly exceeded the combined garrisons of Whitworth and Gregg.[66]

Osborn's brigade suffered a disproportionate share of the Federal losses. His four regiments counted 43 killed and 183 wounded during the battle. Dandy's butcher's bill amounted to 28 killed and 145 wounded, the 10th Connecticut experiencing the most severe regimental losses in Gibbon's corps with 89 of its men left on the field. Andrew Potter's three regiments lost 80 men killed and wounded while the 12th West Virginia of Curtis's brigade suffered 20 casualties.[67]

Confederate losses are, as always, more difficult to determine. Harris's killed and wounded in Fort Whitworth were minimal, but the story in Fort Gregg was much different and unspeakably grimmer. One of the earliest casualty estimates appeared in a campaign history published in 1866, in which former war correspondent William Swinton asserted that Fort Gregg's "two hundred and fifty defenders had been reduced to thirty." It is difficult to understand how Swinton arrived at that figure. The Union officers conducting the attack reported some 56 dead Confederates within Fort Gregg and gathered about 250 prisoners, in addition to the 70 Mississippians seized in Fort Whitworth. One Confederate account estimated the number of losses inside the fort as "about 50 or 60 men," while another asserted that the number of prisoners captured by the Federals totaled only 170.[68]

Nathaniel Harris admitted that "the two regiments defending Battery Gregg suffered severely, but the loss was not as great as Swinton states." Harris was correct, assuming Swinton believed that less than three dozen Confederates survived the battle. Clearly, however, few of Fort Gregg's defenders escaped unscathed from the little emplacement. Those who did not fall in the fort's defense found themselves prisoners of war, marched to the observation tower near Fort Fisher, and then forwarded to City Point en route to Point Lookout, Maryland. The bulk of Fort Whitworth's garrison managed to gain the safety of the inner Confederate line along with the fragments of Lane's, Thomas's and Cox's commands, whose positions had faced south along Boydton Plank Road east of Fort Gregg.

Here they found a welcome reception from fresh Confederate troops whose appearance had rendered the sacrifices at forts Whitworth and Gregg tactically worthwhile.[69]

The new units belonged to Brigadier General Henry "Rock" Benning's Georgia Brigade and Brigadier General John Bratton's South Carolinians, both of Field's First Corps division. On the evening of April 1, following receipt of the news of Pickett's disaster at Five Forks, Lee had ordered Longstreet to transfer Field's 4,600 men from north of the James River to the Petersburg front. Receiving instructions from Lee to accompany his troops in person, "Old Pete" made arrangements to remove Field's five brigades from their front-line positions and then hurried to meet with the army commander. Longstreet arrived ahead of his men and thus was present when A. P. Hill appeared at the Turnbull House in the early hours of April 2.[70]

Benning's and Bratton's commands defended the right of Field's line so were best situated to reach the depot of the Richmond & Petersburg Railroad. Longstreet arranged to send these two brigades to Petersburg by rail, expecting the remainder of Field's men, Brigadier General William F. Perry's Alabamians, Brigadier General George T. Anderson's Georgians, and the Texas-Arkansas brigade, to march overland. "Prepare transportation to Petersburg for two brigades of Field's division over railroad at once," barked an order from Longstreet's staff. "The troops will start from camp as soon as they can get ready." As the First Corps officers better understood the magnitude of the emergency along Lee's Petersburg lines, Longstreet's staff scrambled to find rail transportation for all of Field's units. "The other brigades will have to go by railroad," they concluded. "They cannot march and reach Petersburg in time or in good condition." It would take at least five hours to return the cars from the Cockade City and pick up two additional brigades, however, so the immediate responsibility would rest alone with Benning and Bratton. The Confederates made arrangements to mask Field's departure with Major General Joseph B. Kershaw's infantry division, Brigadier General Martin W. Gary's cavalry brigade, and various reserve, militia, and local defense troops.[71]

The Army of Northern Virginia's creaking transportation infrastructure performed just well enough during this crisis. Benning's Georgians, the vanguard of Field's reinforcements, marched out from Petersburg along Cox Road just as Gibbon prepared to attack forts Whitworth and Gregg. Longstreet deployed Benning to the right and rear of the forts, closer to the river, filling a dangerous void in the Confederate defenses. As Bratton and other elements of Field's division appeared,

Longstreet placed them on the high ground of the old Dimmock Line, extending from Battery 45 at Boydton Plank Road northward to the Appomattox River. With Cox's relatively intact brigade anchoring the left of this formation, aided by the fugitives from Lane's, Thomas's, and Harris's units, the Confederates had found "the last ditch" of their Petersburg defenses.

The threat posed by Gibbon's offensive had been defused by the heroics at Fort Gregg, but elsewhere along the blazing battle lines other emergencies demanded the attention of Robert E. Lee.[72]

NOTES

1. For a biographical sketch of Thomas Ogden Osborn, see Ezra J. Warner, *Generals in Blue* (Baton Rouge, 1964), 351-352. Details regarding Osborn's wound may be found in Herbert M. Schiller, M.D., *The Bermuda Hundred Campaign* (Dayton, Ohio, 1988), 200, n. 11.

2. *OR* pt. 1, 904, 1174, 1179, 1215; Wilcox, "Defence of Batteries Gregg and Whitworth, and the Evacuation of Petersburg," in *SHSP*, IV, 27. Exact timing of these actions is difficult to establish. Foster stated that, "At about 8 a.m. on the 2d . . . . I moved to the right through the enemy's works . . . relieving General Hamblin's brigade. . . ." Gibbon timed the commencement of the movement to the right at 6:50 a.m., although Osborn said he began at 6:00 a.m. A regimental commander in Osborn's brigade asserted that the shift started at 5:00 a.m., which is clearly too early. Dandy reported that his brigade began to move at 9:00 a.m., which is clearly too late! Ord wrote Grant at 8:10 a.m. that "All my white troops, except Harris' brigade, have gone to help Wright." See *OR* pt. 3, 493. The distance from Hatcher's Run to the Pickrell House is a little less than four miles, and even without any opposition, such a march through a recent battlefield along the captured Confederate line could not have been accomplished in barely an hour. Osborn's arrival on Boydton Plank Road about 8:30 a.m. seems a reasonable estimate and conforms with Lane's attack against Hamblin, which occurred no earlier than 8:00 a.m. and no later than 9:00 a.m.

3. *OR* pt. 1, 1185, 1179.

4. Wilcox, "Defence of Batteries Gregg and Whitworth, and the Evacuation of Petersburg," in *SHSP*, IV, 26.

5. Trudeau, *The Last Citadel*, 381; Archie K. Jones, "The Battle of Fort Gregg," in *New Orleans Times-Picayune*, December 13, 1903; John Y. Riley, "Fort Gregg. Thermopylae of the South," in an unidentified newspaper clipping in the collection of Pamplin Historical Park; Nathaniel Harris to William Mahone, August

2, 1866, in Personal Papers Collection, William Mahone Papers, 1866-1895, Library of Virginia; Buxton R. Conerly, "How Fort Gregg Was Defended April 2, 1865," in *Pike County Mississippi 1798-1876. Pioneer Families and Confederate Soldiers Reconstruction and Redemption* (Nashville, 1909), 231-233. Harris did not identify the guns that supported him, but Thomas T. Roche of the 16th Mississippi said they belonged to the Washington Artillery. See Thomas T. Roche, "Fighting for Petersburg," in *Philadelphia Weekly Times*, May 5, 1883.

6. *OR* pt. 1, 1185, 1190; Nathaniel Harris to William Mahone, August 2, 1866, in Personal Papers Collection, William Mahone Papers, 1866-1895, Library of Virginia; Lieutenant Dallas M. Rigler to General James H. Lane, June 17, 1867, in "Defence of Fort Gregg," in *SHSP*, III, 26. Two interesting accounts seemingly credited black troops instead of Osborn's brigade with this successful attack. Lieutenant David Soule of the 2nd Connecticut Heavy Artillery described an assault "done by a small colored brigade officered by white men as we learned by orderlies passing by" that roughly comports with the events surrounding Osborn's approach. Isaac O. Best, the regimental historian of the 121st New York, also reported an attack by a "colored brigade" but included details of a bayonet charge and hand to hand combat. The only black troops in the area belonged to Brigadier General William Birney's division of the Twenty-fifth Corps, and their reports clearly indicated that they did not participate in the fighting on the morning of the 2nd. Moreover, none of the other accounts, Union or Confederate, mentioned any serious fighting associated with this maneuver. According to a recent study of black troops in the Union army, "Throughout the morning and well into the afternoon, the black division [Birney's] was given no specific assignment but instead was relied upon to act as a general reserve." Therefore, it is difficult to understand to what action Soule and Best referred. See Soule, "Recollections of the Civil War," in *New Milford* (Conn.) *Gazette*, July 19, 1912, Isaac O. Best, "The Siege and Capture of Petersburg," in Isaac O. Best Papers, Schoff Civil War Collection, University of Michigan, and Noah Andre Trudeau, *Like Men of War* (Boston, 1998), 427.

7. Biographical information on Harris may be found in several compendiums including Patricia L. Faust, ed., *Historical Times Illustrated Encyclopedia of the Civil War* (New York, 1986), 344-345 and Richard N. Current, ed., *Encyclopedia of the Confederacy*, 4 vols. (New York, 1993), II, 746. The other brigade defending the Bloody Angle was Brigadier General Samuel McGowan's South Carolinians.

8. Roche, "Fighting for Petersburg," in *Philadelphia Weekly Times*, May 5, 1883; Conerly, "How Fort Gregg Was Defended, April 2, 1865," 230-231; Nathaniel H. Harris to William Mahone, August 2, 1866, in Personal Papers Collection, William Mahone Papers, 1866-1895, Library of Virginia. Private Robert B. Thetford of the 12th Mississippi said that Harris left "about one-half of the brigade behind" on their march to Fort Gregg, but no other source documented such a compromised response to Mahone's summons. See Robert B. Thetford, "Commands Holding Fort Gregg," in *Confederate Veteran*, XXIX, (1921), 335.

9. Nathaniel Harris to James Longstreet, February 12, 1894, in "Nineteenth Mississippi Regiment," in *Confederate Veteran*, VI (1898), 70; Frank H. Foote,

"Front of Petersburg. The Confederate Defense of Fort Gregg, Va. April 2, 1865," in *National Tribune*, May 1, 1890; Roche, "Fighting for Petersburg," in *Philadelphia Weekly Times*, May 5, 1883; Jones, "The Battle of Fort Gregg," in *New Orleans Times-Picayune*, December 13, 1903. Douglas Southall Freeman says nothing about Harris's brief meeting with Lee that morning and mistakenly wrote that Harris's Brigade had not accompanied the rest of Mahone's Division to Bermuda Hundred. See *Lee's Lieutenants*, III, 682, n. 30. The upper pontoon bridge was also known as the Battersea or Battersea Cotton Factory Bridge and was located beyond the western outskirts of Petersburg near the little industrial village of Matoaca. The Newman House was located a few hundred yards west of Fort Gregg on the north side of Boydton Plank Road on the grounds of modern (2000) Central State Hospital. It is no longer extant.

10. Lieutenant Dallas M. Rigler to General James H. Lane, June 17, 1867, in "The Defence of Fort Gregg," in *SHSP*, III, 26; Wilcox, "Defence of Batteries Gregg and Whitworth, and the Evacuation of Petersburg," in *SHSP*, IV, 27; George Skoch, "The Last Ditch," in *Civil War Times Illustrated*, XXVII, No. 9 (January 1989), 15; Chamberlaine, *Memoirs of the Civil War*, 115-116. Major Edward J. Hale of Lane's staff tallied 27 men and five officers from the brigade in Fort Gregg, but believed that Lane's own estimate of 30 or 40 with nine or ten officers was probably correct. Counting the artillerists and some of Thomas's men, Hale estimated that 100 to 150 men occupied the fort prior to Harris's arrival. See Edward J. Hale, Jr., to "My dear General," [James H. Lane], May 20, 1867, in Lane Papers, Auburn University. Rigler of the 37th North Carolina estimated that 75 members of Lane's Brigade occupied the fort. Rohoic Creek is often called Old Town Creek in the contemporary literature.

11. Napier Bartlett, "The Defence of Fort Gregg," in *SHSP*, III, 82-83; William Miller Owen, *In Camp and Battle with the Washington Artillery of New Orleans* (Boston, 1885), 368. Fort Owen was constructed on the night of March 25-26 to compensate for the destruction of the dam impounding Rohoic Creek, which, according to Owen, had washed away. Work on Fort Owen continued at least through March 28. See also R.A. Brock to Secretary Southern Historical Society, August 20, 1891, in "The Artillery Defenders of Fort Gregg, in *SHSP*, XIX, 66-67. It will be recalled that knowledge of this inundation contributed to Wright's decision to focus his attack on April 2 against a portion of the line not potentially affected by the flooding.

12. Skoch, "The Last Ditch," 15; Burke Davis, *To Appomattox: Nine April Days, 1865* (New York, 1959), 73-74; Conerly, "How Fort Gregg Was Defended April 2, 1865," 231; Foote, "Front of Petersburg," in *National Tribune*, May 1, 1890. An excellent description of the fort is contained in George W. Kennedy, "Defending Fort Gregg, A Johnny Reb's Story of the Surrender on April 2, 1865," in *National Tribune*, May 15, 1902. Fort Gregg remains in an outstanding state of preservation in 2000 and is owned and interpreted by Petersburg National Battlefield. Fort Whitworth also survives on the grounds of Central State Hospital, but has been converted for use as a picnic and recreation area and is somewhat deteriorated.

Fort Whitworth is sometimes called Fort Alexander or Fort Baldwin in contemporary accounts. Brigadier General Edward Porter Alexander, James Longstreet's chief of artillery, claimed that "Fort Alexander" was named after him. See Gallagher, ed., *Fighting for the Confederacy*, 515. A Mississippi soldier explained that the Fort Baldwin designation sprang, ironically, from a member of the 19th Mississippi, Private William R. Baldwin of Company F, who, as punishment for some minor infraction, had to march along the ramparts of Fort Whitworth shouldering a log. Calling the emplacement Fort Baldwin was thus a sarcastic gesture that found its way into some of the subsequent accounts of the battle. See Foote, "Front of Petersburg," in *National Tribune*, May 1, 1890.

13. Nathaniel Harris to James Longstreet, February 12, 1894, in "Nineteenth Mississippi Regiment," in *Confederate Veteran*, VI, 70; Skoch, "The Last Ditch," 15; Wilcox, "Defence of Batteries Gregg and Whitworth, and the Evacuation of Petersburg," in *SHSP*, III, 28; Giles Cooke, Diary, April 2, 1865, VHS; Riley, "Fort Gregg. Thermopylae of the South"; "The Battle of Fort Gregg," in *New Orleans Times-Picayune*, April 1, 1900; A.E. Strother, "Heroic Defense of Ft. Gregg by a Handful of Confederates," in *Atlanta Journal*, October 26, 1901. The former teamsters had been converted to service in the 4th Maryland Battery commanded by Captain Walter S. Chew.

The composition and strength of the garrison at Fort Gregg was earnestly and sometimes bitterly debated by Confederate veterans, particularly the North Carolinians who claimed that they received inadequate credit for participating in the battle. See numerous examples in the James Lane Papers, Auburn University and in Lane, "The Defence of Battery Gregg," in *SHSP*, IX, 104-105 and *SHSP*, III, 19-26. General Lane went so far as to claim that Harris's Brigade contributed only token reinforcements to his Tarheels in Fort Gregg. Wilcox confirmed that troops from Lane's, Harris's and Thomas's brigades manned the fort, but asserted that there were fewer of Thomas's men than North Carolinians or Mississippians, and that "the most of Harris' brigade was ordered to Fort Whitworth." See Wilcox, "Defence of Batteries Gregg and Whitworth, and the Evacuation of Petersburg," in *SHSP*, III, 28, and Wilcox, "Notes on the Richmond Campaign," in Cadmus M. Wilcox Papers, LC. Napier Bartlett somehow determined that the number of troops in Fort Gregg was precisely 214. See "The Defence of Fort Gregg," in *SHSP*, III, 82.

This postwar debate notwithstanding, the historical record clearly indicates that prior to Gibbon's attack, the garrison consisted of Duncan's two Mississippi regiments, smaller numbers of Lane's and Thomas's men, and the Louisiana and Maryland cannoneers. Some of the converted teamsters had been serving as artillerists since the previous October. McElroy belonged to the Third Company of Washington Artillery and his unit remained south of Petersburg in Gordon's Second Corps sector. McElroy's command at Fort Gregg was a provisional one only.

14. Nathaniel Harris to James Longstreet, February 12, 1894, in "Nineteenth Mississippi Regiment," in *Confederate Veteran*, VI, 70; Skoch, "The Last Ditch," 15;

Trudeau, *The Last Citadel*, 382; Jones, "The Battle of Fort Gregg," in *New Orleans Times-Picayune*, December 13, 1903.

15. *OR* pt. 1, 904, 911, 955; Anson, "Assault on the Lines of Petersburg," 96. Sources do not agree regarding the precise time the Sixth Corps units started their return march toward Petersburg. Getty stated that the movement began at 9:00 a.m.; Wheaton put the time at 9:45 a.m.; Anson said "about 10:00 o'clock." Wright's substantial correspondence with Meade was not explicit about when he learned that he was not needed beyond Hatcher's Run. The timing of various dispatches implies, however, that this occurred about 9:00 a.m., well after Foster and Turner began their march toward Petersburg and about the same time that Osborn's appearance prompted the Confederates to retire toward the forts. The Red House mentioned by Anson was the Harmon House, located near the intersection of Duncan and Boydton Plank roads, the site of which is owned by Pamplin Historical Park.

16. *OR* pt. 1, 955; Anson, "Assault on the Lines of Petersburg," 96. Captain Crawford Allen's Battery H, First Rhode Island Light Artillery and Captain William A. Harn's 3rd Battery, New York Light Artillery provided Getty's ordnance support.

17. *OR* pt. 1, 904, 911. Private William L. Phillips of the 5th Wisconsin was wounded in the arm during the march toward Petersburg and later died of this wound. See S. Brimhall to "Mr. Phillips," May 15, 1865, in William L. Phillips Letters, SHSW.

18. *OR* pt. 1, 904, 983, 1005-1006; Haynes, *A History of the Tenth Regiment, Vermont Volunteers*, 146. For Hamblin's subsequent role in the fighting on April 2, see Chapter Ten.

19. *OR* pt. 1, 1215, 1217, 1221; Gibbon, *Personal Recollections*, 300. The Federal brigades included those of Penrose, Edwards, Warner, Grant, Hyde, Osborn, Dandy, Fairchild, Potter, Curtis, and Harris. Gibbon reported that his two divisions numbered 7,916 men on their way across the James and Appomattox rivers. His six brigades in front of forts Gregg and Whitworth must have numbered between 7,000 and 7,500 men on the morning of April 2. See Gibbon, *Personal Recollections*, 294. Getty's division plus Penrose and Edwards represented roughly five-eighths of the 14,000 men involved in the Breakthrough. Accounting for casualties sustained during the attack, and some straggling, Wright's five brigades in question may have numbered between 7,500 and 8,000 men. Of course, Truex's and Keifer's brigades of Seymour's division were in supporting distance, as were Birney's black troops who moved up in the rear of the front lines between Boydton Plank Road and Cox Road. See *OR* pt. 1, 1236-1243.

20. Grant, *Personal Memoirs*, II, 449; *OR* pt. 3, 448; Basler, ed., *The Collected Works of Abraham Lincoln*, VIII, 382.

21. *OR* pt. 3, 493; Grant, *Personal Memoirs*, II, 449; Porter, *Campaigning with Grant*, 446; Abbott, *Personal Recollections*, 273-274. It is impossible to determine with any precision where Grant reached the Confederate line. His encounter with the Confederate prisoners (whom he estimated at 3,000 in number) and the action that had just occurred between Osborn and Wilcox suggests he might have struck

the line at the far southwestern edge of Wright's Breakthrough, far enough from the Fort Gregg area to ensure his safety but still within the zone of where most of the Confederate prisoners surrendered. Abbott's reference to "the fort we had taken" could refer to the six-gun battery along Duncan Road, seized during the Breakthrough by Abbott's own unit, Truex's brigade of Seymour's division.

22. Terrill, *Fourteenth Regiment, New Jersey Volunteers*, 119; Soule, "Recollections of the Civil War," in *New Milford* (Conn.) *Gazette*, July 19, 1912. Abbott and Soule presented contrasting descriptions of Grant's appearance. Given the lieutenant general's preference for unadorned military attire, Soule's recollection is probably the more accurate. There is some evidence to suggest that troops other than Seymour's and Hamblin's, both located on the south side of the captured Confederate works, also saw Grant. See Hyde, *Following the Greek Cross*, 256-257, and Charles R. Paul, Diary, April 2, 1865, in Murray G. Smith Collection, USAMHI. Captain Paul of the 15th New Jersey served on Penrose's staff and was mentioned explicitly by Wheaton for "conspicuous gallantry in the assault on the enemy's works near Petersburg, Va., April 2, 1865." See *OR* pt. 1, 919.

23. Grant, *Personal Memoirs*, II, 449; Porter, "Five Forks and the Pursuit of Lee," 717; Trudeau, *The Last Citadel*, 377; *OR* pt. 3, 449. The Banks House survives as a detached portion of Pamplin Historical Park, although its rural setting is threatened in 2000 by nearby industrial development.

24. Harris to Mahone, August 2, 1866, in Personal Papers Collection, William Mahone Papers, 1866-1895, Library of Virginia; Bartlett, "The Defence of Fort Gregg," in *SHSP*, III, 84-85. Captain William W. Chamberlaine claimed that he was the officer sent by Walker to order the guns removed from Fort Gregg: "I . . . found Lieut. Col. Eschelman at the stream [Rohoic Creek] near the limbers, and delivered the message. . . . But there was not time enough to send the limbers with the horses to the Fort and withdraw the guns before the first assault." Chamberlaine, *Memoirs of the Civil War*, 117. Harris misidentified the staff officer sent by Walker as "Captain Walker, A.A.G. of Gen Walker," and Lieutenant Colonel William Miller Owen referred to him as "Lieutenant Walke."

The identity of the artillery withdrawn from Fort Whitworth is difficult to determine. Harris failed to mention the name of the captain in charge of the guns. Wise identified the cannons as belonging to the Washington Artillery under command of Lieutenant Henry A. Battles. However, Owen stated that Battles and his guns occupied Fort Owen on the morning of April 2 and that Battles was captured there. Most of the rest of the Washington Artillery was located south of Petersburg near Fort Mahone. See Wise, *The Long Arm of Lee*, II, 931, Owen, *In Camp and Battle with the Washington Artillery*, 368-371, and Napier Bartlett, *Military Record of Louisiana* (Baton Rouge, 1964), 213-214. Frank H. Foote of the 48th Mississippi stated in a postwar article that, "a Georgia Battery of Parrott guns was placed in [Fort Whitworth], but they might just as well have been in Jericho as there, for their fire of rifled shell and shot was perfectly useless." See Foote, "Front of Petersburg," in *National Tribune*, May 1, 1890. No other direct evidence corroborates this identification, although there were four Parrott Rifles in Colonel

Allen S. Cutts's Battalion of Georgia artillery under Walker's command, two in Battery A and two in Battery C, which also had two three-inch rifles. See Wise, *The Long Arm of Lee*, II, 914-915. Lieutenant Colonel William T. Poague made a reference to "some other guns—of what command I never knew" in his account of the fighting near the Turnbull House on the morning of April 2. It is possible that these unidentified pieces wound up at Fort Whitworth. See Cockrell, ed., *Gunner With Stonewall*, 111, and endnote 8, Chapter Ten. Trudeau in his fine account of the fighting at Fort Gregg states that cannon fire from Fort Whitworth punished the attackers at Gregg, but this assertion is in direct contradiction to Harris's testimony cited above. See *The Last Citadel*, 385.

25. Lane, "The Defence of Battery Gregg," in *SHSP*, IX, 104; Edward J. Hale to "My dear General" [Lane], June 13, 1884, in Lane Papers, Auburn University; Trudeau, *The Last Citadel*, 383. The foregoing does not suggest that Lane or the North Carolinians were cowardly, but rather that the general felt that a better defensive deployment could be made either along the dam at Rohoic Creek or in the inner defenses themselves.

26. *OR* pt. 1, 1174, 1194, 1215.

27. *OR* pt. 1, 1165-1166, 1010, 1224-1225; Benedict, *Vermont in the Civil War*, II, 728-729; Charles A. Story, "The 3d Vt. Battery at Fort Gregg," in *National Tribune*, July 9, 1891.

28. *OR* pt. 1, 1186; W.[illiam] F. Outland, "Fort Gregg a Picnic," in *National Tribune*, April 7, 1904. Outland served in the 67th Ohio.

29. *OR* pt. 1, 1194-1195, 1199; Charles A. Rolfe, "Fort Gregg Again," in *National Tribune*, March 2, 1893. Dandy's brigade included the 24th Massachusetts and the 206th Pennsylvania, but neither of these units were present in any strength on April 2. The 206th Pennsylvania had been left behind in the trenches north of the James and the bulk of the 24th Massachusetts was performing provost duty on Bermuda Hundred. One company, at least, of the 24th Massachusetts did participate in the action in front of Fort Gregg, as Rolfe mentioned them specifically in his account of the battle. Osborn's brigade included a detachment of the 85th Pennsylvania, about 125 men assigned as provost guard for division headquarters, commanded by Lieutenant Absalom S. Dial. See William E. Chick, "Fort Gregg Again," in *National Tribune*, January 8, 1891, and *OR* pt. 1, 577. Osborn and Dandy thus brought perhaps 2,500 men to bear against Fort Gregg in the initial attack.

30. *OR* pt. 1, 1194, 1203, 1217, 1221.

31. Wilcox, "Defence of Batteries Gregg and Whitworth, and the Evacuation of Petersburg," in *SHSP*, IV, 28; Conerly, "How Fort Gregg Was Defended on April 2, 1865," 233.

32. Jones, "The Battle of Fort Gregg," in *New Orleans Times-Picayune*, December 13, 1903; Davis, *To Appomattox*, 75; Bartlett, "The Defence of Fort Gregg," in *SHSP*, III, 85; Nathaniel Harris to William Mahone, August 2, 1866, in Personal Papers Collection, William Mahone Papers, 1866-1895, Library of Virginia. Jones stated that "our two pieces did not fire more than two shots before both guns were dismounted, and the gunners took shelter in the bomb-proof."

Most of the Federal accounts, however, made graphic mention of canister and shell fire, which could only have come from Fort Gregg. Jones's assertion must be in error. William Poague's artillery took position behind Rohoic Creek after falling back from the Turnbull House, but Poague made no claim that his guns played a meaningful role in the defense of Fort Gregg. See Cockrell, ed., *Gunner With Stonewall*, 112.

33. Riley, "Fort Gregg,"; Conerly, "How Fort Gregg Was Defended," 232, 234; Thetford, "Commands Holding Fort Gregg," in *Confederate Veteran*, XXIX, 335; Strother, "Heroic Defense of Ft. Gregg," in *Atlanta Journal*, October 26, 1901.

34. *OR* pt. 1, 1161, 1174, 1186; Gibbon, *Personal Recollections*, 300.

35. *OR* pt. 1, 1190; Samuel R.W. Snyder, "The Assault on Fort Gregg," in *National Tribune*, February 5, 1903; W.[illiam] J. Britton, "Fort Gregg—First Colors Up," in *National Tribune*, April 21, 1904.

36. Michael Wetzel, "Fort Gregg: A One-Armed Comrade's Descriptions of its Capture," in *National Tribune*, August 21, 1890. Wetzel, like many Civil War soldiers, probably misused the term "grapeshot" in referring to canister. Grapeshot was a naval artillery round, only rarely used on land. His rescuer was Sergeant Ernest W. Tateburg of Company I. The Civil War-era nickname for people from Illinois was Suckers. I am indebted to my friend, the distinguished historian and professional Hoosier, Alan T. Nolan, who many years ago called my skeptical attention to this unglamorous moniker for residents of my native state, for which I still owe him a Chicago steak dinner.

37. "Fort Gregg Again," in *National Tribune*, February 19, 1891; William E. Chick, "Fort Gregg Again," in *National Tribune*, January 8, 1891 and "Capture of Fort Gregg," in *National Tribune*, June 12, 1902. Burton survived his wounds.

38. *OR* pt. 1, 1189; Robert Davison, "How Fort Gregg Was Taken," in *National Tribune*, March 10, 1904.

39. *OR* pt. 1, 1195.

40. *OR* pt. 1, 1202.

41. Joseph B. Parmelee, "That Little Mix-Up at Fort Gregg," in *National Tribune*, June 19, 1902; Joseph B. Parmelee, "First Flag on Fort Gregg," in *National Tribune*, September 15, 1904; James M. Rogers, "Who Led the Assault on Fort Gregg," in *National Tribune*, January 29, 1891; William L. Norton, "Fort Gregg Again," in *National Tribune*, October 29, 1891.

42. *OR* pt. 1, 1195.

43. Jones, "The Battle of Fort Gregg," in *New Orleans Times-Picayune*, December 13, 1903; Harris to Mahone, August 2, 1866, in Personal Papers Collection, William Mahone Papers, 1866-1895, Library of Virginia; Nathaniel Harris to James Longstreet, February 12, 1894, in "Nineteenth Mississippi Regiment," in *Confederate Veteran*, VI, 70; Owen, *In Camp and Battle with the Washington Artillery*, 372; Foote, "Front of Petersburg," in *National Tribune*, May 1, 1890; Conerly, "How Fort Gregg Was Defended," 234; Wilcox, "Autobiography," 16-17, and Wilcox, "Notes on the Richmond Campaign," both in Cadmus M. Wilcox Papers, LC; Benjamin F. Eschelman, "The Washington Artillery: Address of

Colonel B.F. Eschelman at Their Reunion," in *SHSP*, XI, 252; Gordon W. McCabe, "Defence of Petersburg," in *SHSP*, II, 301. William Chamberlaine is the authority for placing Wilcox's command post "just in rear of Fort Gregg, by the little stream." See *Memoirs of the Civil War*, 118.

44. *OR* pt. 1, 1195, 1203; James E. Northrup to "My Dear Sir" (Captain R. R. Duncan), March 24, 1891, "After Many Years," in *Culpeper* (Va.) *Exponent*, May 3, 1901.

45. *OR* pt. 1, 1203; Rev. J. Dunley Ferguson, "At Fort Gregg," in *National Tribune*, February 11, 1892.

46. Strother, "Heroic Defense of Ft. Gregg," in *Atlanta Journal*, October 26, 1901; Rigler, "The Defence of Fort Gregg," in *SHSP*, III, 27.

47. *OR* pt. 1, 1174, 1215.

48. Frederick H. Patton to "Dear Friends," April 16, 1865, in "Fort Gregg Again," in *National Tribune*, March 3, 1892.

49. Thomas W. Hibbs, "Just How Fort Gregg Was Captured," in *National Tribune*, June 30, 1904; Albert G. Leach, "Fort Gregg," in *National Tribune*, January 15, 1891; William Bennett, "Fort Gregg," in *National Tribune*, May 12, 1904.

50. *OR* pt. 1, 1217; Captain Ransom Griffin, "The 116th Ohio at Fort Gregg," in *National Tribune*, August 22, 1912; George K. Campbell, "Capture of Fort Gregg," in *National Tribune*, March 6, 1902; William B. Stark, "Petersburg to Appomattox," in *Atlantic Monthly*, CLXII, 250.

51. Bartlett, "The Defence of Fort Gregg," in *SHSP*, III, 84; "Fort Gregg Again!" in *National Tribune*, February 19, 1891.

52. Strother, "The Defense of Ft. Gregg," in *Atlanta Journal*, October 26, 1901.

53. Jones, "The Battle of Fort Gregg," in *New Orleans Times-Picayune*, December 13, 1903; Frederick H. Patton to "Dear Friends," April 16, 1865, in "Fort Gregg Again," in *National Tribune*, March 3, 1892; *OR* pt. 1, 1219; Daniel Maxwell, "Also at Fort Gregg," in *National Tribune*, November 14, 1912. The only two men in the 12th West Virginia with the surname Adams were privates Emanuel Adams of Company D and Eli Adams of Company K.

54. "Fort Gregg Again!" in *National Tribune*, February 19, 1891.

55. Conerly, "How Fort Gregg Was Defended on April 2, 1865," 234-235; George W. Kennedy, "Defending Fort Gregg, A Johnny Reb's Story of the Surrender on April 2, 1865," in *National Tribune*, May 15, 1902; Lieutenant Alvis B. Howard to "General Lane," June 3, 1867, in "The Defence of Fort Gregg," in *SHSP*, III, 25-26.

56. F.[rederick] H. Patton to "Dear Friends," April 16, 1865, in "Fort Gregg Again," in *National Tribune*, March 3, 1892; Conerly, "How Fort Gregg Was Defended on April 2, 1865," 235; Howard to "General Lane," June 3, 1867, in "The Defence of Fort Gregg," in *SHSP*, III, 26; Stark, "Petersburg to Appomattox," in *Atlantic Monthly*, CLXII, 250.

57. Richards quoted in Skoch, "The Last Ditch," 18; Lieutenant Frank B. Craige to General James H. Lane, June 4, 1867, in "The Defence of Fort Gregg," in *SHSP*, III, 25; Wilcox, "Autobiography," 16, and Wilcox, "Notes on the Richmond

Campaign," both in Cadmus M. Wilcox Papers, LC; Wilcox, "Defence of Batteries Gregg and Whitworth, and the Evacuation of Petersburg," in *SHSP*, IV, 29; J.E. Gaskell, "Last Engagement of Lee's Army," in *Confederate Veteran*, XXIX (1921), 261; "Fort Gregg Again!" in *National Tribune*, February 19, 1891; Stark, "Petersburg to Appomattox," in *Atlantic Monthly*, CLXII, 250.

58. William Miller Owen, "The Artillery Defenders of Fort Gregg," in *SHSP*, XIX, 70; "The Battle at Fort Gregg," in *SHSP*, XXVIII, 266. Another version of this story identifying the defiant Confederate as a Georgian named Giles may be found in Strother, "The Defense of Fort Gregg," in *Atlanta Journal*, October 26, 1901.

59. Trudeau, *The Last Citadel*, 388; Jones, "The Battle of Fort Gregg," in *New Orleans Times-Picayune*, December 13, 1903. "We felt very indignant when we saw the Federal troops fire down on its brave defenders after they had crowned the ramparts," wrote William W. Chamberlaine in *Memoirs of the Civil War*, 118.

60. *OR* pt. 1, 1220; Maxwell, "Also at Fort Gregg," in *National Tribune*, November 14, 1912; Hibbs, "Just How Fort Gregg Was Captured," in *National Tribune*, June 30, 1904.

61. Thetford, "Commands Holding Fort Gregg," in *Confederate Veteran*, XXIX, 336; Nathaniel Harris to James Longstreet, February 12, 1894, in "Nineteenth Mississippi Regiment," in *Confederate Veteran*, VI, 71.

62. *OR* pt. 1, 1182, 1221-1222.

63. *OR* pt. 1, 1222; Foote, "Front of Petersburg," in *National Tribune*, May 1, 1890.

64. Nathaniel Harris to James Longstreet, February 12, 1894, in "Nineteenth Mississippi Regiment," in *Confederate Veteran*, VI, 71; Nathaniel Harris to William Mahone, August 2, 1866, in Personal Papers Collection, William Mahone Papers, 1866-1895, Library of Virginia; Foote, "Front of Petersburg," in *National Tribune*, May 1, 1890. No field officer named Phelps served in the 19th Mississippi. Foote probably referred to Colonel Richard W. Phipps of that regiment. Wilcox claimed he issued the order to Harris to evacuate Fort Whitworth. See Wilcox, "Defence of Batteries Gregg and Whitworth, and the Evacuation of Petersburg," *SHSP*, IV, 19.

65. *OR* pt. 1, 1182, 1222.

66. John G. Barnard, letter of April 2, 1865, in John G. Barnard Papers, Duke; Thetford, "Commands Holding Fort Gregg," in *Confederate Veteran*, XXIX, 336; Jones, "The Battle of Fort Gregg," in *New Orleans Times-Picayune*, December 13, 1903; Roche, "Fighting for Petersburg," in *Philadelphia Weekly Times*, May 5, 1883; Nathaniel Harris to James Longstreet, February 12, 1894, in "Nineteenth Mississippi Regiment," in *Confederate Veteran*, VI, 71; *OR* pt. 1, 1174. Major Giles Cooke, an officer on Lee's staff, agreed that "about 3 pm the firing slackened. . . .", Giles Cooke, Diary, April 2, 1865, VHS.

67. *OR* pt. 1, 1186, 1195, 1217; Frederick H. Patton to "Dear Friends," April 16, 1865, in "Fort Gregg Again," in *National Tribune*, March 3, 1892. The summary of casualties listed in *OR* pt. 1, 594-595 includes losses suffered between March 29 and April 9, 1865, so it is not possible to extract precisely the numbers lost on April 2.

68. Swinton, *Campaigns of the Army of the Potomac*, 603; *OR* pt. 1, 1174, 1179, 1217, 1219; "The Battle at Fort Gregg," in *New Orleans Times-Picayune*, April 1, 1900; Kennedy, "Fort Gregg. An Account of the Capture by One of its Defenders," in *National Tribune*, July 17, 1902. William Swinton served as a war correspondent covering the Army of the Potomac for the *New York Times*. Swinton earned the enmity of a number of Union generals for his tendency to criticize the army's performance. See J. Cutler Andrews, *The North Reports the Civil War* (Pittsburgh, 1985), 65, and Emmet Crozier, *Yankee Reporters 1861-65* (New York, 1956), 22 for information about Swinton. Gibbon reported 55 Confederate dead inside Fort Gregg, Foster said 57, and Curtis and Potter, 56. Swinton's assertion has been adopted by other writers telling the story of Fort Gregg. See for example "McCabe, "Defence of Petersburg," in *SHSP*, II, 301; Eschelman, "The Washington Artillery," in *SHSP*, II, 252; Todd, "Reminiscences of the War Between The States," 288, in Westwood A. Todd Papers, SHC; and Newman, "The Old Forty-Ninth Georgia," in *Confederate Veteran*, XXXI, 181.

69. Nathaniel Harris to James Longstreet, February 12, 1894, in "Nineteenth Mississippi Regiment," in *Confederate Veteran*, VI, 71; "The Battle at Fort Gregg," in *New Orleans Times-Picayune*, April 1, 1900; Wilcox, "Defence of Batteries Gregg and Whitworth, and the Evacuation of Petersburg," in *SHSP*, IV, 29.

70. Freeman, *Lee's Lieutenants*, III, 675; Longstreet, *From Manassas to Appomattox*, 602; *OR* pt. 1, 1372-1374. For the meeting between Lee, Longstreet, and Hill, see Chapter Eight.

71. *OR* pt. 1, 1372-1375.

72. Longstreet, *From Manassas to Appomattox*, 606-607; Freeman, *R. E. Lee*, IV, 52; Wilcox, "Defence of Batteries Gregg and Whitworth, and the Evacuation of Petersburg," in *SHSP*, IV, 29; Wilcox, "Autobiography," 17, in Cadmus M. Wilcox Papers, LC; Jackson L. Bost to "Dear General" [James Lane], July 31, 1867, in Lane Papers, Auburn University; Nathaniel Harris to James Longstreet, February 12, 1894, in "Nineteenth Mississippi Regiment," in *Confederate Veteran*, VI, 71. The exact timing of Benning's arrival is difficult to determine. Major Giles Cooke of Lee's staff said that, "Benning's brigade of Longstreet's Corps came to our position about 12 M." Harris stated that, "As we were retiring and crossing [Old] Town Run, Benning's Brigade made its advance near the Cox road." Longstreet also timed Benning's appearance as occurring prior to the Federal attacks against Fort Gregg, an assertion repeated by Douglas S. Freeman. Longstreet stated that "the other brigades of Field's division came up" while Gibbon's attack was underway. It seems safe to conclude that Benning's vanguard arrived sometime proximate to Gibbon's first efforts to capture Fort Gregg, and that by the time Lee ordered Harris to evacuate Fort Whitworth, the bulk of Field's Division had appeared along the inner defense line. Obviously, the officers responsible for finding rail transportation from Richmond to Petersburg had done their jobs well.

CHAPTER TEN

Hold On Until Nightfall

G eneral Robert E. Lee appeared "self-contained and serene" at his Edge Hill command post along Cox Road west of Petersburg. The man on whom the fate of the Army of Northern Virginia had depended for so many months reached deep into his much-tested reservoir of fortitude, courage, and military acumen to marshal every resource to meet the current exigency. Lee knew full well that defending Petersburg had become a forlorn hope, as he clearly indicated to the secretary of war, the president, and Smith S. Nottingham, a neighboring civilian who chose the crisis-laden morning of April 2 to pay a social call on the Confederacy's ranking soldier.

"General, do you think the reinforcements will be here from Richmond in time to restore the lines?" inquired Nottingham.

When Lee calmly replied in the negative, the visitor posed an even tougher question: "Then you will have to give us up?"

"Yes sir," answered Lee politely, terminating the interview with a courteous request to be remembered to the Nottingham family.[1]

Lee had spoken frankly to the nervous countryman. The Sixth Corps Breakthrough ended any expectation that Confederate forces might maintain an enduring grip on the Cockade City. Nevertheless, Lee drew a sharp distinction between abandoning Petersburg and forsaking his army and with it, the Confederate cause. His immediate objective was to hold Petersburg's inner defenses until darkness would allow him to extricate his divisions in relative safety. He would then strike southwest, in hopes of joining Joseph Johnston's army in North Carolina. Although Lee's decision to send Nathaniel Harris's Mississippians to bolster the defense of forts Gregg and Whitworth would blunt John Gibbon's pending threat, when other bluecoats began to appear in force along Cox Road opposite Edge Hill, Lee would be unable to muster infantry reserves to block their path. Instead, Marse Robert relied on a collection of cannoneers who, with their artillery alone, would attempt to buy the time necessary for Charles W. Field's Division to file into the empty trenches of the Dimmock Line, west of the city.[2]

"Everybody seemed busy packing up and removing headquarters belongings."

That artillery belonged exclusively to the Third Corps battalion of William T. Poague. On the morning of April 1, Lee's chief of artillery, Brigadier General William N. Pendleton, had taken the initiative to order two of Poague's five batteries from their reserve positions near the Howlett House in Chesterfield County to the western outskirts of Petersburg. Those seven guns of Captain Nathan Penick's Pittsylvania (Virginia) Battery and Captain Charles F. Johnston's Albemarle (Virginia) Artillery had arrived near the Turnbull House by the morning of April 2, the same guns that General Hill had directed Charles S. Venable to deploy during Hill's fatal reconnaissance earlier that morning. Penick commanded two ten-pounder Parrott rifles and two three-inch rifles, while Johnston's battery consisted of one Napoleon smoothbore and two ten-pounder Parrotts. About 9:00 a.m., Poague himself arrived in Petersburg with the remaining guns of his battalion. After reporting to General Pendleton, who had summoned the balance of Poague's ordnance at Lee's request the previous night, the officers and artillerists rumbled west on Washington Street, which became Cox Road as it left the limits of town. Soon the cannoneers reported to the Turnbull House, where according to Poague, "everybody seemed busy packing up and removing headquarters belongings."[3]

The frenzy at Edge Hill resulted from the appearance of Sixth Corps soldiers returning from Hatcher's Run. Getty's division and two brigades of Wheaton's command, the New Jersey Brigade and Edwards's six regiments, had arrived late in the morning in support of Gibbon's troops. These men initially deployed in a long line extending from Boydton Plank Road on the right to the South Side Railroad on the left, a distance of more than a mile and a half. As Gibbon readied the Twenty-fourth Corps for its assault against Fort Gregg, Getty concentrated his supporting troops to the north, where they came under an annoying fire from Penick's and Johnston's artillery, which by this time had been augmented by the other batteries of

Poague's Battalion. Two Napoleons under Major Thomas A. Brander fired with a "marked effect on the flank of the enemy" from a vantage point on Cox Road about three-quarters of a mile west of the Turnbull House. Captain Addison W. Utterback's Warrenton (Virginia) Battery took position some five hundred yards southwest of Edge Hill, while Poague assigned Lieutenant John W. Yeargain's Madison (Mississippi) Battery and Graham's (North Carolina) Battery under Captain Arthur B. Williams to defend the Turnbull House itself from positions to its north.[4]

Captain William A. Harn's 3rd New York Light Artillery and Captain Crawford Allen's Battery H, 1st Rhode Island Light Artillery unlimbered their guns and replied to the bothersome fire emanating from Poague's cannoneers. One of these Federal shells crashed through the Turnbull House itself, perhaps the immediate source of the consternation Poague observed when he arrived with Brander's section and Utterback's, Yeargain's and Williams's batteries. More likely, the obvious preparations for an infantry attack against Poague's position alerted the headquarters personnel at Edge Hill that they faced imminent danger. Veteran officers understood all too well that without infantry support, Poague's artillery could not withstand a determined assault by Union foot soldiers.[5]

Getty and Wheaton repositioned their five brigades to establish a line from just south of Cox Road northward to the Appomattox River. This northward shift created a gap between Getty's right and Gibbon's left opposite Fort Whitworth, but the Unionists did secure their northern flank on the river. Getty's division formed most of the Sixth Corps front opposite the Turnbull House, with the Vermont Brigade deployed on the right, Warner's men in the center, and Hyde's troops occupying the left. Although a few shallow swales offered limited shelter, and the counter battery fire contributed by Harn and Allen provided some relief from Poague's relentless barrage, General Getty realized that remaining stationary made little sense. Moreover, once Gibbon launched his initial attack against Fort Gregg, unity of action dictated that the Sixth Corps confront the Confederates arrayed opposite them as well.[6]

The redeployment of the Sixth Corps had compelled Brander's section to fall back and Utterback's and Johnston's batteries to withdraw to a point about 500 yards east of the Turnbull House. Poague placed his Mississippi battery under Lieutenant Yeargain north of the Turnbull House near the river, with Williams's Tarheel artillerists in support on the Mississippians' left, and Penick's Virginia gunners to their left on Cox Road. These thirteen pieces and their experienced crews, assisted perhaps by a handful of Lee's headquarters personnel, faced the five Union brigades now poised to begin another charge.[7]

Getty sent Lieutenant Charles H. Anson, formerly of the 1st Vermont Heavy Artillery but then serving on Getty's staff, to notify the brigade commanders of his intention to attack. "To ride along the line amid that terrible storm of shot and shell seemed an impossibility, and live," thought Anson. Mounted on his "faithful, fearless, sure-footed horse . . . with a tight grasp on the rein," the staff officer delivered his message to Lieutenant Colonel Charles Mundee of the Vermont Brigade, then to Warner and Hyde. The Vermonters had formed in a single line with the 1st Vermont Heavy Artillery on the right and the 2nd, 3rd, 5th, 6th, and 4th Vermont regiments extending in that order to the left. Captain Darius J. Safford of the 1st Vermont Heavy Artillery shook out a skirmish line, and the whole brigade, joined by the rest of the division, started forward at once, the Vermonters' right flank hugging Cox Road for alignment. "The enemy poured in a very heavy fire of shot and shell from a battery on our right which completely enfiladed our lines," reported Captain Merritt Barber of the Vermont Brigade, "and a perfect hail-storm of canister from a battery of four guns planted in the garden of the Turnbull House . . . directly in front." Major James McGregor of the 139th Pennsylvania, to the Vermonters' left, gauged the incoming fire from Poague's guns as "about as heavy . . . as ever the regiment was under from artillery." Our "three brigades attempted to charge the hill," echoed Colonel Hyde, "but the canister fire was so hot and the division now so small and wearied, the . . . attack was a failure." Poague, who never identified the "guns from other commands" which assisted his battalion with enfilading fire from south of Cox Road, confirmed that "the first assault on this part of our lines was broken and the enemy driven back into the woods along the road."[8]

Poague remembered "a considerable delay" following the repulse of Getty's first attack. The Confederate cannoneer must have watched with no little satisfaction and relief as the leading regiments of brigadier generals Henry L. Benning's and John Bratton's brigades filed into view behind him, heading from their river crossings toward positions behind the sheltering ramparts of the Dimmock Line. But Getty and Wheaton also used this pause to improve their tactical situation. Getty sent Anson to direct Colonel Edwards to renew the offensive by advancing against the right flank of Poague's Battalion. Edwards reacted skeptically at first to such orders from an unknown officer. "Who in h—l are you?" barked the brigade commander, who, once convinced of the authenticity of the instructions, promptly took steps to cooperate.[9]

Hyde's brigade, on Edwards's right, also received orders to move to the left and front to help subdue the deadly artillery. "At this time my three left regiments were wholly extended as skirmishers to the left and rear to

Colonel Thomas W. Hyde

Massachusetts MOLLUS Collection, Carlisle Barracks, Pennsylvania

protect that flank, and were along the South Side Railroad and the bank of the Appomattox," reported Hyde. While arranging his three remaining regiments for the attack, Hyde dispatched a lieutenant and 50 men from the 1st Maine Veterans with orders "to shoot the battery horses, as we knew we could get on their flank, and they were probably standing hitched to the

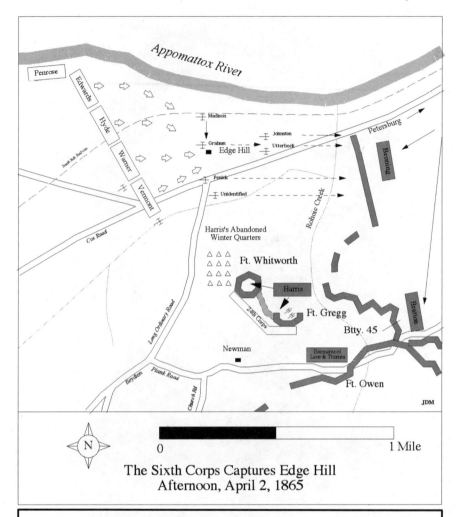

The Sixth Corps Captures Edge Hill
Afternoon, April 2, 1865

Five of the eight Sixth Corps brigades had by midday on April 2 deployed opposite General Lee's headquarters at the Turnbull House, Edge Hill. Lee had no infantry available for the defense of Edge Hill and relied entirely on artillery from Lieutenant Colonel William T. Poague's Battalion. The Gray cannoneers repulsed one Union attack, but a second Federal assault drove Lee's gunners to new positions across Rohoic Creek.

caissons and would be a fine mark from that side." One-half mile to the south, Lieutenant Colonel Horace W. Floyd of the 3rd Vermont embraced precisely the same tactic. Floyd unleashed "a few men as skirmishers, with orders to advance on the double-quick and shoot the horses of the battery

Colonel James M. Warner

Massachusetts MOLLUS Collection. Carlisle Barracks, Pennsylvania

to prevent its being removed," a "daring feat" that "was accomplished with perfect success."[10]

Poague prepared to contest any renewal of the Federal offensive from his positions around the Turnbull House, but the flanking movement against his far right initiated by Edwards, Hyde, and Warner rendered his situation untenable. "We were in imminent danger of being bagged," confessed the Virginia artillerist, who ordered his cannoneers to limber their pieces and make for the rear. By this time, Getty's second assault was underway. Hyde led his demi-brigade through some wetlands under persistent fire from Poague's still-servicable guns. Hyde's casualties included two color bearers from the 1st Maine Veterans. "The first five hundred men across [the swamp] made a run for the battery... as we went up the hill amid the roar of guns and whir of canister, amid Yankee cheers and rebel yells," recalled Hyde. "The din was terrible! Brass Napoleons were never better served, but they were doomed."[11]

As Hyde's men rushed in from the northwest, the Vermonters pushed forward into the yard of the Turnbull House, which by now was defended only by Yeargain's immobile smoothbores. The rest of Poague's guns escaped about the same time that General Lee also quit his long-defended Petersburg command post. Joined in his departure by the headquarters telegrapher and Lieutenant Colonel Walter H. Taylor of his staff, Lee took the time to order that a borrowed chair be removed for eventual return to its owner, then reluctantly turned his mount to the rear. "This is a bad business" he observed to Taylor as the proximity of the Yankees caused him to spur Traveller into a gallop amid a shower of hot fire that claimed a nearby horse. Poague also effected a dramatic getaway:

> I made my escape by jumping an ordinary plank fence, fortunately being
> mounted on my brother Jim's horse, Josh, who was a great jumper. I had
> gotten but a short distance when a bullet whizzed near my head, fired by an
> officer who was stopped by the fence. I turned in my saddle and sent a shot
> in return and then waving him an adieu, galloped to the road and joined our
> retiring artillery which was safely withdrawn to the east bank of a creek
> along which Longstreet's line was being formed.[12]

Federal soldiers from multiple commands swarmed about the Turnbull House as Lieutenant Yeargain raised a white flag in token of surrender. Colonel Floyd ordered his victorious men to cease fire, and moved forward to accept the prize of the Mississippi ordnance. Captain Robinson Templeton also approached with a squad of the 1st Vermont Heavy Artillery precipitating an intramural debate with Floyd about who would claim the captures. "Just at this moment the skirmish line of the First Brigade of this division coming up on the left and not observing the white flag, opened fire on the battery, when the men turned and fled," reported a Vermont officer. The offending Federals may have actually been from Warner's 37th Massachusetts of Wheaton's division, two companies of which had moved forward under cover near Edge Hill. A squad of the 93rd Pennsylvania led by Sergeant Hiram Layland also helped silence the

Confederate cannon. Poague testified that the Mississippi cannoneers took advantage of this opportunity and "escaped by putting the buildings between them and their assailants, who halted as soon as they reached the abandoned pieces."[13]

Deprived of their human trophies, the Vermonters sorted out custody of the four Napoleons and then took stock of their own losses. Most poignant among them was Captain Charles C. Morey of Company E, 2nd Vermont, who fell mortally wounded during the final attack. Morey had enlisted in April 1861 and had worked his way through the ranks from private to captain. The young New Englander had participated in 27 battles during his four years in uniform and earned a reputation, according to one of his comrades, as "faithful and fearless [being] considered one the most reliable officers in the regiment. It seems a hard fate to perish in the last struggle, after having passed safely through so many."[14]

Captain Morey, lieutenants William H. Humphrey and William F. Tilson, both of the 4th Vermont, and an unknown number of their Sixth Corps colleagues became casualties during the last substantial combat they would engage in on this momentous day. That is not to say that Wright's troops merely collapsed at Edge Hill. Lieutenant Colonel Hazard Stevens of Getty's staff, seeing Charles Field's men filing in behind Petersburg's inner defenses and believing that "a thousand fresh men could have broken through," rode frantically in search of Getty to urge him to renew the assault. En route, Stevens encountered Colonel Penrose commanding the New Jersey Brigade, which had been only lightly engaged in the struggle against Poague's cannoneers. Penrose expressed reluctance to attack without explicit orders, but after some reflection, he moved ahead, joined by Colonel Hyde and some of Hyde's brigade. As these officers and their troops crested the ridge at Edge Hill and advanced east toward Rohoic Creek, fire from Confederate sharpshooters began to rain into them. One of the bullets struck Lieutenant Alvin A. Messer of the 1st Maine Veterans, killing him as he rode next to Colonel Hyde. Another projectile rattled off Colonel Penrose's belt plate. The accoutrement saved the brigade commander's life but nonetheless knocked him out of the saddle and onto the ground, where he convulsed with pain.[15]

In addition to the fire directed from the Dimmock Line, the Sixth Corps contended with artillery shelling from across the Appomattox River. Major Brander had led Penick's Battery across the bridge near Matoaca, and, according to Poague, "secured a position opposite the enemy's left from which he stirred up great commotion. . . ." According to a soldier in the 61st Pennsylvania, "the aim of these guns was splendid and their shots told on us with much effect." Once again, the four Napoleons of Crawford

Allen's Rhode Island artillery offered counter battery fire. Allen split his attention between Brander on the north side of the river, and other Confederate guns in the Dimmock Line, no doubt Poague's refugees from Edge Hill. This two-front artillery duel cost Allen a number of his cannoneers, but ultimately succeeded in providing some cover for the beleaguered Federal infantry.[16]

That infantry included the Vermont Brigade, which advanced from Edge Hill to the banks of Rohoic Creek, absorbing "an enfilading fire from batteries on either hand, and a desultory fire of sharpshooters posted in the inner defenses." Members of the 4th Vermont, on the far left of the brigade, penetrated the Confederate lines deeper than any Sixth Corps unit. Using a fallen tree to tiptoe across Rohoic Creek, these men crept up the eastern slope of that stream's diminutive valley and brought some Confederate artillery under fire. But that was as far as any Unionist advanced. "The men being now worn out by want of sleep, having eaten nothing since the night previous, and completely exhausted by the labors of this long day, were withdrawn to a ravine to the right side of the [Cox] road," wrote Captain Barber.[17]

Exhaustion was the universal theme of accounts from the five Sixth Corps brigades west of Petersburg on the late afternoon of April 2. "The regiment was . . . permitted to enjoy that rest which they so much needed," reported Major McGregor of the 139th Pennsylvania. "The line was advanced . . . to within a mile of the city, when the weary, hungry troops sought the rest so much needed, having been under arms for twenty, and engaged in battle sixteen hours," agreed Charles Anson. Lieutenant Robert Pratt of the 5th Vermont simply wrote in his journal, "We were completely tired out." General Grant, perhaps recognizing the depleted condition of the soldiers knocking on Petersburg's western portal, rejected the recommendations of "prominent officers" to order a resumption of the offensive. One of those officers might well have been Sixth Corps commander Horatio Wright. Colonel Edwards reported that Wright had asked him if he felt that he could "put my brigade into Petersburgh and I told him yes." Wright replied, with implied disappointment, "I have orders to halt." After the war, Colonel Horace Porter explained Grant's reasoning:

> He was firm in his resolve not to sacrifice the lives necessary to accomplish [the forced capture of Petersburg]. He said the city would undoubtedly be evacuated during the night, and he would dispose the troops for a parallel march westward, and try to head off the escaping army. And thus ended the eventful Sunday.

Grant did order an artillery bombardment to commence at 5:00 a.m. on April 3, to be followed by an assault an hour later, indicating that he entertained at least some doubt that Lee would forsake Petersburg before dawn. But for the time being, the Union general-in-chief was content. "All seems well with us," he wired City Point, "and everything quiet just now. I think the President might come out to pay us a visit to-morrow."[18]

The Sixth Corps withdrew to high ground just east of the Turnbull House, completed a line of entrenchments, and went into camp for the night. The Vermont Brigade established its headquarters at Edge Hill, the officers amusing themselves by rummaging through the detritus of Lee's recent occupancy. At that moment, the Confederate commander must have been content to have traded his command post for the survival of his army, because the resources he had brought to bear along the western perimeter of Petersburg were meager indeed. Charles Field, whose division opposed Wright's brigades along Cox Road, observed that "the enemy, finding us not inclined to give way for him, contented himself with forming line in front of us, but out of range." From the Confederate standpoint, Union satisfaction with the status quo late on the afternoon of April 2 provided a reprieve from the prospect of immediate defeat and, perhaps, the opportunity to escape to the west and build new hope for victory in combination with Johnston's forces.[19]

Would Grant have been successful had he hazarded another assault late that day? General Cadmus Wilcox reported that the infantry in Lee's last line deployed in "not less than five foot intervals between the men [and] the right of the line did not rest on the Appomattox . . . there [being] an interval of about one mile between it and the river." This would suggest that an opportunity existed either to punch through Field's thin defenses or to orchestrate an envelopment around the exposed right of the makeshift line. However, the firepower and resiliency of Poague's heroic gunners should not be discounted. They could effect a crossfire from both sides of the Appomattox and visit severe punishment on massed troops passing across the open ground between the Turnbull House and Rohoic Creek. Field's actual strength once south of the river is impossible to calculate with any precision, but he started his journey with some 4,600 men. Three of Horatio Wright's eight brigades were elsewhere on the afternoon of April 2, and those present "were too tired to congratulate ourselves on the victory, and did not care if Petersburg was in sight and near," according to the usually optimistic Thomas Hyde. Lee's relative ability to defend his last line resembled his vulnerable condition that morning, but the offensive capabilities of the Sixth Corps had been clearly diminished during the intervening twelve hours. In order to have captured

Petersburg from the west on the afternoon of April 2, Wright would have needed help—help potentially available from the Second Corps.[20]

* * *

Andrew A. Humphreys's three divisions had played an active if secondary role in the Union operations since March 29. Grant had assigned the Second Corps a position on the left of the Federal line, providing both support for E.O.C. Ord's forces to their right and a floating connection with Gouveneur K. Warren's troops on their left. From their entrenchments south of Boydton Plank Road near Burgess's Mill, Humphreys's ten brigades sparred for three days with Confederate troops, primarily units from Harry Heth's and Cadmus Wilcox's divisions of A. P. Hill's corps. Nelson A. Miles's participation on Warren's right during the Battle of White Oak Road on March 31 marked the most significant combat contribution rendered by the Second Corps during this period. At 6:30 p.m. on April 1, General Meade had ordered Humphreys to launch a dawn assault against a Confederate strongpoint southwest of Hatcher's Run known as the Crow House Redoubt. Grant and Meade intended this attack to be the western-most element of their grand offensive that would include Ord, Wright, and Parke's Ninth Corps. Later that evening, however, Grant modified his plan. Fearful that Lee might detach soldiers from the western end of his lines to threaten Sheridan at Five Forks, the lieutenant general, through Meade, instructed Humphreys to probe the enemy earthworks that night, searching for signs of such a shift. Miles's division, on Humphreys's left, would strike immediately if it detected Southern infantry moving toward Sheridan. In the absence of Confederate troop movements, Miles was to march west on White Oak Road to reinforce Sheridan.[21]

Humphreys began jabbing at the Confederates along Hatcher's Run about 9:30 p.m., but he discovered no reduction in Rebel strength or resolve. "The enemy were found to be vigilant, and opened with their artillery," reported Humphreys. Similarly, General Miles discerned no movement afoot to march against Sheridan. Consequently, about 11:00 p.m., Miles's division began its trek toward Five Forks. Miles's departure prompted Grant and Meade to rethink the wisdom of compelling Humphreys to attack the Crow House Redoubt the next morning. "As one division of the Second Corps is now ordered away," wrote Grant to Meade at 1:25 a.m. April 2, "General Humphreys need not attack the Crow House, but be in readiness to take advantage of any weakening of the enemy in his front." Thus, when the rest of the army advanced that morning,

Humphreys confined his remaining two divisions, under brigadier generals William Hays and Gershom Mott, to forays against the Confederate picket line.[22]

With the rising sun came word at Second Corps headquarters of Wright's success to the northeast. "I directed General Hays to try and carry the Crow house redoubt and General Mott to strain every effort in his front," reported Humphreys. By 7:30 a.m., the Confederate picket line was in Federal hands. Thirty minutes later, Hays carried the Crow House works and the fortifications adjacent to them.[23]

The victims of these attacks belonged to elements of four brigades: Samuel McGowan's and Joseph Hyman's (commanded that day by Colonel Thomas S. Gallaway) of Wilcox's Division, and parts of John R. Cooke's and William MacRae's of Heth's command. Cooke's troops straddled Hatcher's Run, occupying the Crow House fortifications and their adjacent trenches. McGowan's, Hyman's, and MacRae's men defended the works extending westerly from Burgess's Mill along White Oak Road. "We could hear the keen cracking of muskets away over in the direction of Petersburg," recalled a member of the 13th North Carolina of Hyman's brigade. "Nearer and nearer it came—a storm of thunder and lightning by shells and a hail-storm of rifle bullets. Finally the blue clouds of Union soldiers burst through the woods, shooting and charging." A soldier in the 27th North Carolina of Cooke's command also remembered gauging the course of the approaching battle by the prevalence of Rebel yells or Yankee cheers: "After a while the 'huzza' seemed to prevail, and soon a courier . . . came rushing into our fort. Very shortly afterwards we were ordered out of our works and in a few minutes were on the retreat from Petersburg."[24]

While Cooke and MacRae executed a hasty but relatively orderly withdrawal under the competent eye of Henry Heth, McGowan's five regiments and the 13th North Carolina of Hyman's brigade bought time. McGowan's South Carolinians maintained their position in the works, firing on the attacking Federals "with a unanimity and an accuracy that beat them clear off the field, and secured us from molestation for at least a little while," according to a staff officer. The Palmetto Staters took advantage of this respite to scurry northwest, while some of the brigade's sharpshooters smashed rifles against trees to prevent them from falling into enemy hands. Their Tarheel comrades guarded the little bridge at Burgess's Mill spanning Hatcher's Run "not quitting it till the enemy were close upon [their] rear, left flank, and . . . front," wrote General Wilcox. Between 8:00 a.m. and 9:00 a.m., all the graycoats had evacuated their entrenchments and were streaming toward Sutherland Station on the South Side Railroad.[25]

Humphreys ordered all three of his divisions to give chase, albeit from opposite directions. Mott's brigades, followed by Hays's command, were directed to move west on White Oak Road, and then turn north on Claiborne Road, through what had been the heart of the March 31 battlefield. Miles's division, having found no emergency on Sheridan's front requiring its presence, had rested a couple of hours near Little Phil's camps then reversed course. About 7:30 a.m., it began marching east on White Oak Road also heading for the Claiborne Road intersection, where it prepared to encounter the Confederates. Colonel Robert Nugent, commanding Miles's Second Brigade, and Colonel Henry J. Madill, the Third Brigade commander, formed line of battle and advanced through some woods toward the old Confederate line. To the Federals' delight, they discovered that the works had remained abandoned. The Yankees quickly redeployed inside the empty Southern fortifications, then resumed their advance northward along Claiborne Road.[26]

Miles, however, would pursue the Confederates alone. Before either Mott or Hays could commence their march down White Oak Road, General Meade arrived in their midst along the captured Confederate works near Burgess's Mill. The army commander instructed Humphreys to send those two divisions northeastward on Boydton Plank Road to support Wright's corps, not west to join Miles. Meade further ordered his subordinate to meet personally with Miles and direct his division to "move toward Petersburg by the first right-hand fork road after crossing Hatcher's Run and connect with the other divisions." Implicit in this strategy was the belief that Sheridan's cavalry and Brigadier General Charles Griffin's Fifth Corps infantry could handle whatever Confederate resistance remained to the northwest.[27]

Humphreys quickly rode west on White Oak Road, then north on Claiborne Road to locate Miles and communicate Meade's directive. He overtook his First Division commander about a mile north of Hatcher's Run, where he also encountered the indomitable Philip Sheridan. The bandy-legged Irishman still considered Miles under his direct command and intended that Miles's division (supported by the Fifth Corps, which was marching in its rear) destroy the Confederate forces lurking in the neighborhood. Humphreys informed Sheridan of Meade's desire for Miles to move east toward Petersburg.

The two distinguished generals offered conflicting accounts of what transpired next. Humphreys claimed that "upon learning from [Sheridan] that he had not intended to return General Miles' division to my command, I declined to assume further command of it, and left it to carry out General Sheridan's instructions, whatever they might be." Humphreys then rode off to rejoin Hays and Mott. Sheridan remembered the conversation differently: "I relinquished command of the division. . . . I have always since regretted that I did so, for the message Humphreys conveyed was without authority from General Grant, by whom Miles had been sent to me, but thinking good feeling a desideratum just then, and wishing to avoid wrangles, I faced the Fifth Corps about and marched it down to Five Forks. . . ." Because Miles is silent on the issue, it is unclear under whose authority the First Division commander now acted, both Humphreys and Sheridan having departed, and both claiming to have deferred control of Miles's brigades to the other. In any event, Miles proceeded north on Claiborne Road without the guidance of either Sheridan or Humphreys and without the support of Hays, Mott, or any of the Fifth Corps.[28]

This turn of events boded ill for the Federals. Heth's men had recovered from their morning reversal. McGowan's sharpshooters continually annoyed Miles's pursuers, "making a stand at any favorable point," reported one of the South Carolinians. Cooke's Brigade deployed "first one regiment and then another as skirmishers to retard the enemy," allowing the bulk of Heth's motley command to deploy along Cox Road south of the railroad near Sutherland Station. Lieutenant James Fitz James Caldwell of McGowan's staff described the Confederate position:

> This line ran, for nearly half its length, just on the edge of a highway, and for its whole length, was almost parallel with the South Side Railroad. The right of the Confederate line rested by a large house on the west of the road by which we came; our left against a country church. . . . The railroad was a hundred yards in rear of the left of the line, and passed through a deep cut here. We were on the summit of a perfectly smooth open ridge, which commanded the slope towards our enemy for six or eight hundred yards. At about that distance ran a small stream and a ravine. Beyond the ravine rose a ridge, similar to the one we occupied, but covered partly with large oaks, partly with pines.[29]

Heth had selected a place, anchored between Sutherland Tavern on his right and Ocran Methodist Church on his left, from where he could defend the railroad and take maximum advantage of favorable terrain and a good field of fire. His entire front measured about one-half mile in length. McGowan's Brigade occupied the left with MacRae's, Hyman's, and Cooke's troops to their right in that order. Orr's Rifles of McGowan's command refused the left flank of the line and the South Carolina sharpshooters deployed several hundred yards in advance to serve as skirmishers. The soldiers prepared hasty barricades of fence rails and "other stuff we could find near at hand, adding such dirt as we could dig up with our bayonets, tin cups, plates, etc." recalled a North Carolinian. They bolstered their position with one cannon at the church, two in the center of the line, and four near Sutherland Tavern. By about 11:00 a.m., the Confederates were ready. Lieutenant Caldwell estimated that McGowan's brigade numbered about 1,000 men and that the entire force at Sutherland Station could not have exceeded 4,000 troops. Before all his preparations had been completed, a courier from Lee approached Heth with word of A.P. Hill's death and orders that the division commander "must take command of the corps and report in person to [Lee] as soon as possible." Heth passed command of the field to General Cooke and hastened toward Petersburg.[30]

While the Confederates readied their position for defense, Miles's four brigades continued their northward march along Claiborne Road. The division numbered some 8,000 troops, at least twice as strong as Cooke's waiting defenders. Madill's all-New York brigade led Miles's column. Madill, a Pennsylvania attorney by profession, had celebrated his 36th birthday three days earlier and carried with him the distinction of two brevets for gallant and meritorious service. Nugent's Irish Brigade moved up in close support of Madill. Nugent's army experience before the war and service at the head of the 69th New York prior to his elevation to brigade command marked him also as an accomplished officer. When the hasty Rebel entrenchments rose into view, Miles's Federals deployed in line of battle, Madill's brigade on the left and Nugent's in support to their right.[31]

Miles's men were exhausted. They had marched most of the night and all of the morning, and their attack preparations revealed their ragged condition. "Our line resembled a line broken by the fire of the enemy, rather than a line about to charge against their works," observed a chaplain in Madill's brigade. Nevertheless, about noon Madill received Miles's order to advance and the bluecoats moved forward, angling toward the right end of Cooke's compact formation.[32]

The Federal assault lacked polish and finesse, but compensated for its uneven alignment with fierce determination and enthusiasm. "Although at least a half a mile from us, they did not advance at even a moderate pace, nor even halt to dress their lines," wrote Lieutenant Caldwell. "But, with yells of mingled confidence and ferocity, they rushed forward rapidly, disordering their line and breaking through all control." McGowan's sharpshooters, acting as skirmishers, directed a spirited fire against the blue wave, and then fell back to take position on Cooke's flanks. On came the New Yorkers until they had closed to within several hundred yards of

Major General Henry Heth

Library of Congress

their Rebel antagonists, where "they raised the shout with greater vigor than ever, and stormed toward the works." The Union cheers elicited a response in kind from Cooke's veterans, who unloosed "a cool, well-directed and destructive fire" upon the two Federal brigades. The Confederate volleys "rolled a perfect sheet of lead across the open interval,

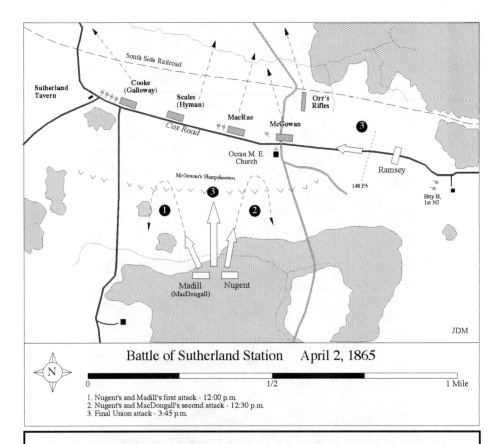

Battle of Sutherland Station   April 2, 1865

1. Nugent's and Madill's first attack - 12:00 p.m.
2. Nugent's and MacDougall's second attack - 12:30 p.m.
3. Final Union attack - 3:45 p.m.

Brigadier General Nelson A. Miles's Second Corps division counter-marched from Five Forks on the morning of April 2 in pursuit of four Confederate brigades. These troops, under the overall command of Major General Henry Heth, had been driven from their entrenchments near Burgess's Mill and along White Oak Road early that morning. Heth's soldiers executed a fighting retreat then halted along a modest ridge line near Sutherland Station on the South Side Railroad. A lack of coordination between Union commanders Phil Sheridan and Andrew A. Humphreys left Miles alone to deal with Heth. Two Union attacks failed between noon and 1:00 p.m.. Several hours later, Miles launched a third attack that routed the Confederate defenders and resulted in the capture of the South Side Railroad.

striking down scores of the enemy, opening great gaps in their line, and destroying all concert and all order," reported Caldwell. Colonel Madill fell with a disabling if not fatal wound, so Miles tapped a 25-year-old Scotsman, Colonel Clinton Dugald MacDougall of the 111th New York, to extricate the brigade. Once the Federals began their retreat McGowan's sharpshooters closed upon each flank of the broken line, "driving home with fearful accuracy every discharge of their deadly rifles." The ground was littered with blue-jacketed bodies in the wake of Miles's impetuous attack, the 4th New York Heavy Artillery alone counting 97 casualties. Delirious with their success on what had been an otherwise-disastrous day for Southern arms, Cooke's brigades "gave vent to a wild and derisive yell" in celebration of their victory.[33]

In short order, the Federals gave evidence that they intended to silence the Confederate jubilation. After informing Humphreys of his unsuccessful assault, Miles directed MacDougall to ready his brigade for another attack, supported this time by artillery as well as Nugent's bloodied regiments. At 12:30 p.m., the Yankees set off again, veering toward their right this time, against McGowan's end of the line. Their spirits remained high, as demonstrated by their "cheering vociferously," as they swept against the South Carolina skirmishers. One of the sharpshooters thought that the Unionists "fought with the desperation of veterans with minds made up to succeed," but, just as with the first effort, high morale and competent leadership could not overcome the lead and iron pouring from the Confederate works. "We opened upon them at three or four hundred yards," wrote Caldwell, "tore fearful rents in their line, covered the ground with dead and dying, and sent forth, above the roar of artillery and musketry, ringing peals of cheers, which proclaimed the last soldiers of the Confederacy still unsubdued." MacDougall's right arm fell limp with a painful flesh wound, and the Federals withdrew to the shelter of their wooded ridge, chased by the sharpshooters, who reestablished their forward positions after suffering minimal losses. "I never saw finer fighting anywhere than was done by the . . . little brigades at Southerland [sic] Station," thought another South Carolinian. "I stood upon a stump on the hill to the eastward of the Federal column where the left wing of sharpshooters were contending with the Federal right, and great tears of overwhelming admiration flowed down my cheeks in streams, as I contemplated the grand courage of that glorious little band of unfaltering heroes, fighting to the very death for a cause already lost. I could hardly stand it."[34]

Courage permeated the field. On the far Confederate right, a tiny band of about 70 men from the 22nd North Carolina under the leadership of Captain C. Frank Siler occupied a patch of woods toward which a full Union regiment, the 39th New York, advanced. Siler lifted his hat in one hand and his sword in the other and dashed along his tiny line encouraging the troops, eliciting an admiring comment from General Cooke, and holding fast against odds of more than four to one. An unnamed Federal soldier displayed fortitude of a different kind. Following the repulse of the second Union attack, this man found himself lying between the lines suffering from a broken thigh. When approached by Confederate skirmishers, he begged his captors to shoot him, both to put an end to his misery and to fulfill his vow never to become a prisoner. When the Southerners quite naturally declined to murder the poor fellow, the wounded Yankee removed a pocketknife from its hiding place and cut his own throat, accomplishing his purpose and leaving a gruesome impression the witnesses would never forget.[35]

Relative quiet now enveloped the battlefield south of Sutherland Station, a silence broken only by desultory artillery firing. Several hours passed during which both sides prepared for a renewal of the contest. Cooke saw no opportunity or rationale for assuming the offensive. His four small brigades were isolated, cut off from Confederate forces to the east, and out of touch with whatever remained of George Pickett's and Richard H. Anderson's commands to the west. McGowan shifted the bulk of his sharpshooter battalion from its skirmish position in front of the brigade to the far left to strengthen that exposed flank, but there was precious little else the Confederate generals could do but "lay still and await the awful finale."[36]

Miles, on the other hand, entertained no thought of abandoning his opportunity to capture the South Side Railroad and redeem the reputation of his division. "I now determined to carry the position by an attack on the enemy's [left] flank," Miles reported. He called upon the Fourth Brigade, led by 26-year-old Colonel John Ramsey, to deploy one regiment to the left, and another to the right. This latter unit, the 148th Pennsylvania, would screen the movement of the rest of Ramsey's brigade, which received orders from Miles to "assault the enemy's position." Miles assigned a staff officer, Captain Silas J. Marlin, to conduct Ramsey's five remaining Pennsylvania and New York regiments in rear of the 148th Pennsylvania's skirmishers where they formed a line of battle under the crest of a hill, out of sight of McGowan's advanced troops. "The whole preparations were made in a most incredible short time," thought Ramsey, "the officers working energetically and the men obeying orders with alacrity."[37]

Miles logged the commencement of his third attack at 2:45 p.m., although the actual time may have been as much as an hour later. Captain A. Judson Clark's Battery B, First New Jersey Light Artillery opened an effective fire from a position near Cox Road about 1,200 yards southeast of the Confederate line, while Ramsey poured across the combat-littered landscape toward McGowan's vulnerable left flank. With MacDougall's and Nugent's brigades pressing the Confederates on their fronts, Miles had at last marshaled a force sufficiently strong and well disposed to earn the victory that had thus far eluded him. "In overwhelming force the blue columns of the enemy were discovered advancing from all directions," remembered a South Carolinian. "The Federal line on the flank pressed against the Rifle regiment with steadiness and resolution," agreed Lieutenant Caldwell, "and the line in our front moved more closely to us." McGowan's Brigade gamely fought against a foe that enclosed them on two sides. "Our lines opened fire in full chorus at long range," reported Captain William S. Dunlop, "and as the enemy closed upon us the vigor of our defense increased, until the entire line was enveloped in one living cloud of blue coats, whose muskets spurted fire and smoke and death." In short order, the Union columns converged, raining a frontal and enfilading fire along the South Carolinians' ranks. "The whole line now pushed forward with resistless fury, determined for victory," reported Colonel Ramsey.[38]

Ramsey placed the 53rd Pennsylvania on the far right of his formation, with orders to seize the railroad tracks. Once the Pennsylvanians accomplished this task the enemy resistance, which had remained fierce, began to crumble. "With one last, desperate, fruitless effort, the Confederates dashed the contents of their faithful rifles into the very teeth of their overpowering assailants, broke and fled the field, leaving our dead and wounded, with a number of prisoners, in their hands," admitted Dunlop. Discipline in McGowan's Brigade evaporated, and every man decided for himself whether to fight, run, or surrender on the spot. "So there was a Babel of tongues," remembered Caldwell, "a hurrying, thronging, watching, and planning—until, at last, there came a rupture, some staying behind in despair, some disputing the progress of the enemy, retiring, some fleeing for life."[39]

A private in the 148th Pennsylvania picked up one of McGowan's regimental flags, then discarded it in the excitement of the moment, allowing a soldier in the 4th New York Heavy Artillery to claim the prize. As Cooke's brigades collapsed in short order from east to west, Miles's troops collected some 600 prisoners and two of Cooke's artillery pieces in a scene described by one Confederate as "perfect bedlam." Ramsey considered the outcome an "eminently . . . happy [and] glorious one," achieving, at last the literal goal of Grant's offensive: the capture of the South Side Railroad.[40]

Cooke's Brigade, farthest removed from the Confederate left, escaped the battlefield in a comparatively disciplined fashion. Such was not the case with McGowan's, Hyman's, and MacRae's survivors. The preferable retreat route lay to the northwest, but many of the discomfited Confederates headed due north, where they soon encountered the unfordable waters of the swollen Appomattox River. Caldwell considered this retreat "the most disorderly movement I ever saw among Confederate troops." Panic, despair, and confusion animated the fugitives' actions. "I several times attempted to reform the line, but without success," lamented General MacRae. "A weary, mortified, angry stream of men poured through the fields and roads," according to Caldwell, all striving to put distance between themselves and their Federal pursuers. Some of the South Carolinians found a small skiff that could accommodate no more than four men at a time, and used this humble craft to ferry token numbers to the north bank. Most of the Confederates turned upstream in search of a ford, bridge, or sheltering terrain, at last finding relief in the setting sun. "So we wandered—strung along the river bank for miles, straggling through brush and brier, floundering in the beds of small streams or in mud-holes filled by the recent heavy rains, and pressing forward to some points undetermined in our own minds," remembered Lieutenant Caldwell.[41]

The decisive outcome at Sutherland Station might have proved even more devastating for the Confederates had Miles organized an earnest pursuit of his vanquished foes. Not unlike the Sixth Corps following the capture of the Turnbull House position, Miles's men had approached their limit of combat endurance. They had enjoyed practically no sleep since the night of March 31, and the bitter fighting at Sutherland Station had claimed 366 casualties in the division. Moreover, Miles understood that his mission, as defined earlier by Sheridan, was to "drive the enemy toward Petersburg," so instead of turning west or north, Miles followed the railroad and the parallel River Road eastward for about two miles, until he encountered General Humphreys.[42]

Humphreys had received a message from Meade about 2:30 p.m. that Miles was in trouble. "You will give him aid, sending a division if you can spare it," instructed the army commander. By that time, Mott's and Hays's divisions had completed their northeastward march on Boydton Plank Road and were in position to reinforce either Wright or Gibbon, who were involved in their respective struggles against Poague's artillery to the north and forts Whitworth and Gregg, near the Plank Road. Mott had reported as early as 11:25 a.m. that "I am now going into position on the left of General Wright." While Colonel Robert McAllister's primarily New Jersey brigade remained in support, by early afternoon Mott had deployed his other two brigades "in line of battle with the Sixth and Twenty-fourth Corps." Brigadier General Regis De Trobriand placed his First Brigade between Wright and Gibbon, filling the gap that had existed since late morning, when Getty and Wheaton had shifted northward toward Cox Road.

Brigadier General Byron R. Pierce took his Second Brigade to the left of the Sixth Corps about 1:15 p.m. and arrayed it parallel to the Appomattox River. From this point, Pierce reported using his sharpshooters to dislodge a Confederate battery, probably Brander's guns, which had been annoying the Sixth Corps from the north side of the river. By late afternoon, Pierce had shifted to his right, across Cox Road, and deployed facing Petersburg from the vicinity of Fort Whitworth. Both De Trobriand and Pierce sustained light casualties in pursuance of their duty as reserves.[43]

Hays's division had followed Mott up Boydton Plank Road in the morning. It had advanced to a point on Cox Road about a mile west of the Turnbull House when Humphreys turned it around and aimed it westward, toward Sutherland Station. "I moved [as] rapidly as possible by the Cox Road," reported Humphreys, "expecting, if the enemy were still in front of Miles, to take them in flank." Of course, by the time Humphreys appeared with his Second Division, Miles had already won the battle and commenced his march toward Petersburg. Miles returned to the depot at Sutherland, where he disposed his troops to protect the railroad, and then made camp. Hays also bivouacked in the area, while Mott's division bedded down along the battle line west of Rohoic Creek.[44]

The story of the Second Corps on April 2 had been one of missed opportunities. General Humphreys wrote after the war that "probably the whole force [Cooke's four brigades] would have been captured in the morning had the Second Corps continued its march toward Sutherland Station." Assuming any degree of competent leadership, Humphreys's judgment was sound. Had the Federals maneuvered all three of their Second Corps divisions against Cooke's bedraggled contingent, wholesale capture or annihilation awaited the understrength Carolinians.[45]

Eventually, of course, Miles alone drove the Confederates from their lines at Sutherland Station, but it required three attacks and nearly five precious hours to do so. Had Miles exercised more care in the preparation of his initial assault, he might have shortened the time needed to dislodge Cooke, and thus increased his chance of overwhelming the entire crowd. As it was, Miles's understanding of his objective after the Battle of Sutherland Station allowed most of Cooke's survivors to escape. Instead of vigorously pursuing the graycoated fugitives with the fresh troops of Colonel George W. Scott's First Brigade, Miles turned east where the only soldiers he encountered belonged to Hays's redundant reinforcements.

For their part, neither Hays nor Mott accomplished much in proportion to their numbers. No one can gainsay their morning success along Hatcher's Run, but these two divisions had virtually no influence on the fighting anywhere else. Humphreys, Meade, Sheridan, and Grant all bear responsibility for squandering the potential impact of some 13,000 men.

The Second Corps commander became more of a pawn than a protagonist on April 2, exercising practically no independent leadership. Squeezed between the territorial arrogance of Phil Sheridan and the reactive orders of George Meade, Humphreys presided over a divided corps that bounced between Five Forks, Petersburg's western suburbs, and Sutherland Station. Meade miscalculated when he instructed Humphreys to countermarch Hays from Cox Road west of Petersburg to Miles's relief. As a result, Hays influenced neither battlefront that afternoon. Would Hays's presence west of Rohoic Creek have emboldened Meade and Grant to renew the assaults that had driven Lee into his last ditch? The record is silent on the question, but neither of the ranking Federal generals hinted that they considered Humphreys's troops as anything more than reserves. Mott's division, after all, had been available since before noon for offensive employment on either Wright's or Gibbon's fronts, but received no orders to do so.

If Grant and Meade thus appeared satisfied with affairs on the western side of their April 2 operation, how did they view Union fortunes south of the city?

* * *

The man responsible for those fortunes, Ninth Corps commander John G. Parke, harbored grave reservations about his unit's assignment on the morning of April 2. The same orders that would launch Wright's divisions on their Breakthrough applied to the Ninth Corps as well, but during the pre-dawn hours of that momentous Sunday Parke revealed a marked pessimism about the prospects for his impending assault. "The enemy reply to our artillery with all their batteries, and the skirmishers develop an infantry force still in our front," he wired Meade's headquarters at 1:15 a.m. "I fear that unless we find a weak place the attack ordered at 4 will not be attended with success." In fifteen minutes, the anxious Parke sent an almost identical message to his superior, followed a quarter of an hour later by a pointed request to cancel the offensive: "Our only hope of success in the assault ordered at 4 o'clock was in a surprise. That is now entirely lost. Does the major-general commanding intend that under these circumstances the assault shall be made?" After an hour of anxious waiting, Parke received his response: "Your dispatches of 1:15, 1:30, and 1:45 were received and referred to the lieutenant-general who ordered this attack. No answer."[46]

Parke's caution stemmed largely from the nature of the works he was expected to conquer. His axis of assault would be northward along Jerusalem Plank Road, the major southbound highway out of Petersburg. The Confederates defended a cluster of six forts there, enhanced from their origins in the Dimmock Line with long traverses, and still numbered, from east to west, batteries 25 through 30. These strongpoints contained artillery that, in the words of one Federal, "swept the approaches in every direction." The most prominent position along this line, Battery 29, squatted several hundred yards west of the Plank Road and somewhat in advance of the rest of the emplacements. The soldiers called it Fort Mahone, but it became better known as "Fort Damnation," the Rebel counterpart of Union Fort Sedgwick—"Fort Hell" in the soldiers' parlance—which sat a few hundred yards south of the Confederate line. In advance of the entrenchments, Southern troops had laced the open ground with the usual maze of obstructions. An inner line of works behind the main fortifications provided a reserve position, eminently defensible should the Federals breach the trenches in front.[47]

The inevitable scarcity of infantry marked the only weakness in the Confederate defense. Major General Bryan Grimes's Division of the Second Corps bore responsibility for the line from the Crater west to Battery 45. Grimes counted merely 2,200 men in his four veteran brigades to defend some three-and-a-half miles of entrenchments, supplemented only by two battalions of Virginia reserves. Grimes positioned Battle's Alabama Brigade, commanded by twenty-nine-year-old Colonel Edwin L. Hobson, at the forts straddling the Plank Road, with Grimes's old North Carolina brigade, led by Colonel David G. Cowand, in support on their right. Brigadier General William R. Cox's Tarheels extended Grimes's line to the west. Colonel Edwin A. Nash, in command of Cook's Georgia Brigade, defended the entrenchments east of the highway, connecting there with the divisions of brigadier generals Clement Evans and James A. Walker. "Along the line of works we occupied we had but one man to five or six feet, an ordinary skirmish line," remembered one Confederate. Grimes rotated one-third of his men to the picket line and kept another third of them alert in the trenches at all times, so concerned was he about the security of his position. The artillery bombardment that commenced about 10:00 p.m. on April 1 only heightened Grimes's anxiety.[48]

General Meade's 9:00 p.m. orders reached Parke a few minutes before the Union guns opened. Like Wright farther west, the Ninth Corps commander misinterpreted Meade's directive as instructions to initiate an immediate attack. The misunderstanding resulted in Parke advancing a strong skirmish line along his entire front. "The enemy was found

Confederate dead in Fort Mahone's muddy trenches. April 1865. *National Archives*

prepared and in full force" reported Parke, except for the Confederates opposite Brigadier General Simon G. Griffin's brigade of Brigadier General Robert B. Potter's Second Division, one-half mile west of Fort Sedgwick. Griffin surprised the Confederates here and captured eight officers and 241 men. Once it became clear, however, that the offensive would not begin until early the next morning, Griffin withdrew his brigade and marched toward Jerusalem Plank Road, where Parke began to deploy his forces for the dawn attack he so dreaded.[49]

Parke had seven brigades in his corps and he intended to employ parts of five of them in his offensive. He assigned Potter's division to the sector west of Jerusalem Plank Road, with Griffin's troops in front and elements of Colonel John I. Curtin's brigade in support. On their right, east of the highway, Brigadier General John F. Hartranft aligned his two brigades of Pennsylvanians in a single column four regiments deep, their left flanks resting on the road, with two regiments in reserve. At 2:00 a.m., five of the six regiments belonging to Colonel Samuel Harriman's brigade of Brigadier General Orlando B. Willcox's First Division reported to Hartranft from the Union lines east of Petersburg. Harriman ordered the 38th Wisconsin, 109th New York, and 8th Michigan to form on the right of Hartranft's division, while retaining his other two units in support. Pioneers armed with axes to dismantle the obstructions would precede the assault formation. All told, Parke designated eighteen regiments to charge against the three under strength Confederate brigades in his immediate front, with four additional regiments available for instant support.[50]

Parke established his command post at Fort Rice, about midway between the Norfolk & Petersburg Railroad and Jerusalem Plank Road, and waited for the appointed hour when his corps would spring into action. That hour arrived at 4:00 a.m., when the first element of Parke's plan unfolded. The two remaining brigades of Willcox's division conducted a demonstration along a front running from the Crater north to the Appomattox River designed to draw attention from the true targets south of the city. "Some of the enemy's picket-pits were captured near the old Crater," reported Willcox. "The pickets of the Third and Second Brigades, strongly re-enforced, advanced handsomely, the artillery opened vigorously, and large portions [of Confederate troops] were drawn down to oppose what they considered a real attack in force." Willcox managed to snag a handful of Rebel prisoners and actually controlled a small section of the main Confederate line for a brief period until the graycoats drove the intruders back. By then, however, Parke had initiated his primary offensive.[51]

A signal gun fired at 4:30 a.m. loosed the Federal legions, which advanced in concert on both sides of Jerusalem Plank Road. On General Potter's front west of the highway, Griffin designated three companies of the 31st Maine as a storming party to lead the assault directly up the road toward Battery 28. Pioneer troops accompanied these New Englanders, assigned the task of clearing away the abatis flanking both sides of the thoroughfare. Griffin then stacked six regiments in a column, led by the 179th New York, to blast through the gaps. "Just at daybreak, at a preconcerted signal, the column moved forward in connection with General Hartranft's division, which joined us on our right," reported Griffin. "Nothing could exceed the coolness and intrepidity with which both officers and men, under a terrific fire, advanced to the attack." The Yankees reached the Confederate works and encountered a water-filled ditch, much like the moat that surrounded Fort Gregg. "Some of the men fell in as they rushed ahead to climb the high, slanting ascent and were unable to get out and were drowned," remembered a soldier in the 31st Maine. The momentum and depth of the Federal attack formation, however, soon mastered this obstacle, and Griffin's brigade "capture[d] their complete line of works, with many pieces of artillery . . . sending hundreds of prisoners to the rear."[52]

Once Griffin succeeded in capturing Battery 28 and the works to its immediate west, Colonel Curtin ordered his four regiments to advance against Fort Mahone. The 39th New Jersey led Curtin's brigade, supported in line by the 48th Pennsylvania, 45th Pennsylvania, and 58th Massachusetts. The Garden Staters tore away the abatis fronting Fort Damnation and clawed their way to and over its muddy ramparts "under very heavy fire of grape and musketry." Three cannon and a few prisoners fell into the Jerseymen's hands as the rest of Curtin's attacking force approached the walls of the fort. Soon, the 39th New Jersey rejoined them, driven back to the outside of the works by a ripping fire from the reserve Confederate positions to the north and on both flanks of Fort Mahone. A piece of shrapnel claimed the life of Colonel George W. Gowan, commander of the 48th Pennsylvania, during this stage of the battle. His regiment, however, and their comrades from Pennsylvania and Massachusetts, managed to cross into Fort Mahone and advance as far as some supporting trenches before they, too, encountered an unendurable leaden hurricane from the front and flanks. By this time Potter had also suffered a severe wound, and command of the division devolved upon General Griffin. Finding further progress impossible, Griffin ordered the disorganized-if-triumphant survivors of his two brigades to hold their ground and await the outcome of events east of the road.[53]

Hartranft's division, which was to conform to the movements of Griffin's brigade, employed much the same tactics that proved so successful west of the highway. The Third Division's pioneers cut the wires connecting sections of chevaux-de-frise and swung them apart, in Hartranft's words, "in the manner of opening a gate." The Confederate

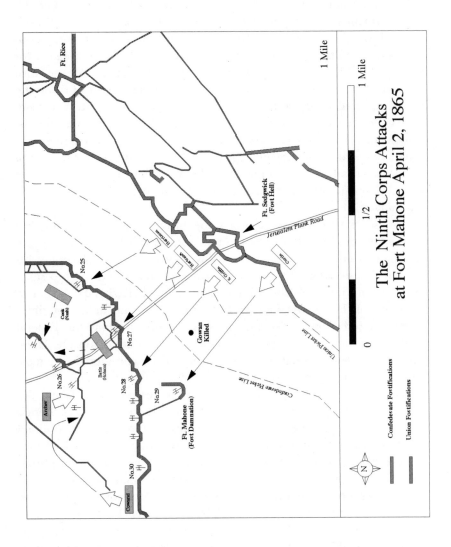

The Ninth Corps Attacks
at Fort Mahone April 2, 1865

defenders poured rifle and canister fire into the dimly seen ranks of blue. "I could hear the thud as [canister rounds] hit men, their cries of agony, curses and cheers, and by the flash of bursting mortar shells could see men falling all about in the rear," wrote one Pennsylvanian. But soon, Hartranft's determined troops clambered over the walls of Battery 27, controlling some 400 yards of the Confederate line east of the Plank Road and proudly claiming three battle flags as evidence of their achievement.[54]

Harriman's three regiments formed the final component of Parke's assault formation. Led by the 38th Wisconsin, the First Division troops disposed of multiple rows of chevaux-de-frise and abatis and headed for Battery 25. The attackers "mounted the embankment of the fort, bayoneting and shooting the men at the cannon in the act of firing the same," reported Lieutenant Colonel Colwert K. Pier of the 38th Wisconsin. "The national flag carried by the color-guard of this regiment was the first planted on the captured work." Harriman's infantry turned their five commandeered cannons against the Confederates in the reserve lines until a detachment of the 1st Connecticut Heavy Artillery arrived to man the guns. Harriman's troops secured some 68 Confederate prisoners during this initial rush.[55]

Hobson's Alabamians absorbed the brunt of Parke's assault, but Cook's Georgia Brigade east of the road also recoiled in the face of the onslaught. General Grimes acted swiftly amidst the crisis sweeping his division. He summoned Cowand's North Carolinians and the two small battalions of Virginians under Lieutenant Colonel Fletcher H. Archer to the point of danger. As soon as these reinforcements arrived, Grimes ordered a series of counterattacks designed first to limit the Federal advance and then to regain as much of the lost real estate as possible. These efforts would lead to what one Confederate soldier considered "the most desperate [struggle] of all the war."[56]

Grimes placed four artillery pieces in the reserve works facing the captured entrenchments, a stratagem that proved critical to Confederate success. These guns belched forth blankets of canister that confined Parke's troops to the territory they had gained during their initial assaults, in some places even forcing the Federals to the outside of the captured works. Late in the morning, Grimes organized an offensive with Cowand and Archer on his right, and Hobson and Cook on his left. The Confederates lurched forward into a labyrinth of trenches, redoubts, and traverses occupied haphazardly by the game-but-disorganized survivors of Parke's dawn initiative. "The fight was from traverse to traverse as we slowly drove them back," recalled a Confederate. "The Yankees would get on top of them and shoot down on our men, and as we would re-take them our men did the same thing." Adding to the terror of this small-unit combat, huge mortar shells rained down upon the Confederates, exploding in spectacular and often deadly fashion.[57]

Grimes organized another assault about 1:00 p.m., underscoring Parke's urgent request for fresh troops. A few minutes before this second counterattack, the Ninth Corps commander wired Meade, expressing his fear that "the enemy [will] get between Wright and me. I should have reinforcements at once." The two brigades responding to this call belonged to Joseph Hamblin of the Sixth Corps and Colonel Charles H.T. Collis, commanding the Independent Brigade deployed at Meade Station along the United States Military Railroad behind Willcox's line. Hamblin began his march about 1:00 p.m. and arrived at Fort Sedgwick by 2:20 p.m. Collis's four regiments preceded Hamblin by a few minutes and advanced to Griffin's front west of the Plank Road. The appearance of these fresh levies heartened Parke. "I feel greatly tempted to make another push," he informed General Meade.[58]

The North Carolinian opposing him, however, beat him to the punch. About 3:00 p.m., Grimes focused the third of his counterblows against Fort Mahone and the trenches surrounding it. The onrushing Confederates took shelter in the warren of fortifications and opened a vicious, often masked leaden hail from behind logs and through gaps in the barricades. "The fire from guns of every calibre was furiously savage," recalled a Pennsylvania artillerist. "I saw the men of my regiment load their guns behind the traverses, climb to the top, fire down into the ranks of the enemy, roll off and reload and repeat the same," wrote one North Carolinian. Sometimes the fighting was hand-to-hand, and the tactics defied any discernible regimental organization. Curtin's troops gradually withdrew from their advanced positions in the face of this grim pressure. Griffin's brigade fared somewhat better, the 56th Massachusetts conspicuous for its tenacity in resisting

"I saw the men of my regiment load their guns behind the traverses, climb to the top, fire down into the ranks of the enemy, roll off and reload and repeat the same."

Grimes's attack. Nevertheless, the Confederates managed to regain a portion of Fort Mahone, scooping up "a large number of prisoners," according to General Grimes. At this juncture, Collis's brigade dashed

onto the scene and succeeded "under a fierce artillery and musketry fire in driving back the enemy and reoccupying the line" east of Fort Mahone.[59]

By 3:45 p.m., Parke was able to report that "the enemy has again been repulsed. Our line wavered a little, but we still hold our ground. Collis is in and Hamblin will support center of right. Our men are very weary, but with this support we hope to hold without fail." Collis and Griffin proposed to renew their attacks against Fort Mahone, an idea that intrigued the Ninth Corps commander for a moment. "But the exhausted condition of my troops forced me to reluctantly abandon the idea," rethought Parke. The butcher's bill, at least, justified his conclusion. Hartranft lost 594 men in his two brigades, and Harriman contributed 184 to the casualty list sustained east of Jerusalem Plank Road. Potter's division suffered 722 losses on April 2, making the entire tally of killed, wounded, and captured in the Ninth Corps exactly 1,500 men.[60] Bryan Grimes's casualties are unknown, but his outnumbered forces undoubtedly suffered in proportion to Parke's. The Confederates had also fought themselves to a frazzle, one powder-begrimed Tarheel testifying that he had fired more than 200 rounds during the day.[61]

A stalemate now descended upon the battlefield south of Petersburg. The armies held irregular and alternating sections of the Confederate works, particularly west of Jerusalem Plank Road. John B. Gordon, Grimes's superior officer, had fared better than any other Confederate corps commander that day. A. P. Hill was dead and his replacement, Harry Heth, had been isolated from the remnants of his command. Richard Anderson and his troops were fugitives far to the west of Petersburg and irrelevant to the city's defense, while James Longstreet commanded a fraction of his First Corps south of the Appomattox gamely clinging to the western portion of the Dimmock Line, Lee's innermost bastion. Gordon's Second Corps, on the other hand, had repulsed Willcox's demonstration east of Petersburg and, thanks to Grimes's grit, had at least partially redeemed all but about a 200-yard section of the lines in his front. Gordon recalled that he "was in the act of concentrating for a supreme effort to restore this last breach, when Colonel Charles Marshall of General Lee's staff reached me with a message from the commander-in-chief." Marshall related the sad tidings of the day's disasters elsewhere and the absolutely desperate condition of the Army of Northern Virginia. "In the face of this almost complete crushing of every command defending the entire length of our lines on my right, the restoration of the remaining breach in my front could contribute nothing toward the rescue of Lee's army," wrote Gordon. Lee instructed the young Georgian instead to "maintain my compact line around this last breach, prevent, if possible, Grant's effort to send through it his forces into the city, and at any sacrifice hold my position until night, and until all other commands could be withdrawn."[62]

The dreadful contest for Petersburg had almost run its course.

NOTES

1. Quoted from the *Richmond Dispatch*, August 8, 1897, in Freeman, *R. E. Lee*, IV, 50 and Trudeau, *Out of the Storm*, 61. The Smith S. Nottingham home was just east of Edge Hill, separated by only a fence and a few hundred yards. Nottingham owned 70 acres which he bought in either 1861 or 1862. This building is no longer extant.

2. For the details regarding Harris's arrival and Field's appearance along the Confederate line, see Chapter Nine.

3. William Nelson Pendleton, "The Artillery of the Army of Northern Virginia in the Last Campaign and at the Surrender," in *SHSP*, IX, 419; *OR*, pt. 1, 1280; Cockrell, ed., *Gunner With Stonewall*, 110; Wise, *The Long Arm of Lee*, II, 914. Pendleton's manuscript report, which differs slightly from his published ones, may be found in the Lee Headquarters Papers, VHS. For Hill's deployment of Poague's guns, see Chapter Eight.

4. Cockrell, ed., *Gunner With Stonewall*, 110-111; Pendleton, "The Artillery in the Last Campaign," in *SHSP*, IX, 419; Wise, *The Long Arm of Lee*, II, 914. The identity of the the guns commanded by Major Brander is unclear. Neither Poague nor Pendleton shed light on the question. Captain Thomas A. Richards, the commander of the Madison Battery, was absent on April 2. For information on the initial deployment of the Sixth Corps opposite Fort Gregg and the Turnbull House, see Chapter Nine.

5. Stevens, "The Storming of the Lines of Petersburg," in *PMHSM*, VI, 430. Also see Chapter Nine, note 16 for Harn's and Allen's deployment.

6. Trudeau, *The Last Citadel*, 376; *OR*, pt. 1, 963; Hyde, *Following the Greek Cross*, 256; Anson, "Assault on the Lines of Petersburg," 96.

7. Cockrell, ed., *Gunner With Stonewall*, 111; Pendleton, "The Artillery in the Last Campaign," in *SHSP*, IX, 419. Yeargain had four Napoleons and Williams had two Napoleons and a three-inch rifle to complement Penick's four rifled pieces. Brander's two guns are not further identified. See Wise, *The Long Arm of Lee*, II, 914.

8. Anson, "Assault on the Lines of Petersburg," 96; *OR*, pt. 1, 970, 966; Hyde, *Following the Greek Cross*, 257; Cockrell, ed., *Gunner With Stonewall*, 111. The guns that enfiladed the Vermont Brigade could have belonged to Captain Edward Graham's Petersburg (Virginia) Battery of Lieutenant Colonel Preston Chew's Battalion, and Captain John J. Shoemaker's Lynchburg (Virginia) Battery of Major James Breathed's Battalion, both of the Horse Artillery. Pendleton mentioned four

pieces of horse artillery, but placed them north of Cox Road. It is entirely possible that these guns had shifted to the southeast and pummeled the Vermonters as they began their charge against the Turnbull House. Clearly, the canister fire mentioned in Barber's report came from Penick's Battery. See *OR*, pt. 1, 1280.

9. Cockrell, ed., *Gunner With Stonewall*, 111; Anson, "Assault on the Lines of Petersburg," 97. Anson did not name the officer who questioned his identity, but did identify him as the commanding officer of a brigade of the First Division. Because Edwards's brigade was closest to Getty's left flank, it is presumed that Edwards, not New Jersey Brigade commander William H. Penrose, was the man to whom Anson spoke.

10. *OR*, pt. 1, 976, 970; Hyde, *Following the Greek Cross*, 257. Hyde's 1st Maine Veterans and 61st Pennsylvania comprised two of the three regiments that participated in the final charge. Hyde identified the officer in charge of the horse assassination party as "Lieutenant Nichols."

11. Cockrell, ed., *Gunner With Stonewall*, 112; Hyde, *Following the Greek Cross*, 257-258. A small stream drains the ground across which Hyde advanced west of the Turnbull House, but nothing like the "swamp where many sank to the waist," as Hyde described, exists there in 2000. This area has been a residential subdivision for years. Every battery in Poague's Battalion included Napoleons except Penick's, so it cannot be stated with certainty to which batteries Hyde referred, but he probably saw the Madison Battery, which had not abandoned its position.

12. *OR*, pt. 1, 970; Cockrell, ed., *Gunner With Stonewall*, 112; Freeman, *R. E. Lee*, IV, 50-51. The stream mentioned by Poague is Rohoic Creek.

13. *OR*, pt. 1, 970, 964; Bowen, *History of the Thirty-Seventh Massachusetts*, 412; Mark, *History of the 93rd Regiment*, 323; Cockrell, ed., *Gunner With Stonewall*, 112. Colonel Robert L. Orr of the 61st Pennsylvania claimed, without convincing foundation, that his regiment actually captured the guns at the Turnbull House. See Orr, "Before Petersburg," in *Philadelphia Weekly Press*, December 19, 1886. Several accounts misidentified the captured guns as belonging to Williams's North Carolina Battery. See Trudeau, *The Last Citadel*, 376; Hyde, *Following the Greek Cross*, 258; Benedict, *Vermont in the Civil War*, I, 590. Captain Williams wrote after the war of his battery's experience on the afternoon of April 2: "We succeeded in holding the enemy in check a short time, but were compelled to fall back to our inner line around Petersburg." See Clark, ed., *North Carolina in the Great War*, I, 549. Bowen's account misidentified Yeargain's guns as belonging to Captain John C. Carpenter's Second Corps battery.

14. Parsons, *Put the Vermonters Ahead*, 147-148; *OR*, pt. 1, 970; Wilbur Fisk to "Editor Freeman," April 9, 1865, in Wilbur Fisk Letters, LC; Captain Ephraim W. Harrington to "Friend Morey," April 3, 1865, in Stuart Goldman Collection, Charles Morey Papers, USAMHI. Harrington wrote Morey's father to apprise him of his son's death:

"He was killed in action near Petersburg yesterday after noon. I was by his side when he fell. he was killed by a Grape Shot. Striking him in the right shoulder and breaking it badly. he lived about twenty minutes after he was hit. I stayed with him untill he breathed his last. He never spoke after he was hit but he knew me about one minute. I closed his eyes and saw him carryed off the Field by some of the men of his own company and they burryed him with as much respect as possable. There was a Chaplin with the men when he was burryed and he made a Prayer at his grave. He is burryed where he can easyly be found by any one if it is your wish to get his Body. his name written on a board and nailed on a Tree by his Head. . . ."

15. *OR*, pt. 1, 970; Stevens, "The Storming of the Lines of Petersburg," in *PMHSM*, VI, 432; Hyde, *Following the Greek Cross*, 259-260. The Sixth Corps casualty reports for April 2 do not discriminate in regard to location or timing. The vast majority of those losses occurred during the Breakthrough, but the assault against Edge Hill did account for some of the killed and wounded that day.

16. Cockrell, ed., *Gunner With Stonewall*, 112; Brewer, *History Sixty-first Regiment Pennsylvania Volunteers*, 140. This source stated that Allen lost eighteen gunners during this action, which is at odds with other evidence. See Chapter Eleven, note 15. Pendleton credited Brander with three guns on the north side of the river, but does not identify them. See Pendleton, "The Artillery in the Last Campaign," in *SHSP*, IX, 419.

17. *OR*, pt. 1, 971; Benedict, *Vermont in the Civil War*, I, 592.

18. *OR*, pt. 1, 966, 976; pt. 3, 449; Anson, "Assault on the Lines of Petersburg," 97; Journal of Robert Pratt, April 2, 1865, VTHS; Edwards, Memoir, Illinois State Historical Library, 225-226; Porter, "Five Forks and the Pursuit of Lee," 718; Grant, *Personal Memoirs*, II, 453. Other than Edwards's reference to General Wright, little is known about the corps commander's whereabouts during the afternoon fighting or his influence on the battle. If, indeed, Wright was one of the advocates of the offensive, he displayed yet again his odd tendency to alternate between boldness and over caution.

19. *OR*, pt. 1, 971; Stevens, "The Storming of the Lines of Petersburg," in *PMHSM*, VI, 432; Benedict, *Vermont in the Civil War*, I, 604; Otis F.R. Waite, *Vermont in the Great Rebellion Containing Historical and Biographical Sketches, Etc.* (Claremont, N.H., 1869), 194; Hazard Stevens, Journal, in George W. Getty Papers, Gibson-Getty-McClure Family Papers, LC; Field quoted in Trudeau, *The Last Citadel*, 389.

The question of Edge Hill's fate that afternoon is an interesting one. Walter Taylor stated that shortly after he and General Lee evacuated Edge Hill, the house "was soon enveloped in flames." Douglas Southall Freeman repeats this assertion in his biography of Lee, referring to the Vermont Brigade headquarters of the evening as the Turnbull House "site." Private John W. Haley of the 17th Maine, a member of Brigadier General Byron R. Pierce's Second Corps brigade, confirmed Taylor's assessment: "We soon came to the ruins of the Turnbull house, lately the headquarters of General Robert E. Lee, now a pile of smoking cinders with official documents flying around." See Taylor, *Four Years With General Lee*, 150, Freeman, *R. E. Lee*, IV, 51, n.40, and Ruth L. Silliker, ed., *The Rebel Yell and the*

Yankee Hurrah: The Civil War Journal of a Maine Volunteer, Private John W. Haley, 17th Maine Regiment (Camden, Me., 1985), 257.

However, persuasive evidence suggests that Edge Hill was at least sufficiently habitable on the night of April 2 to accommodate the substantial number of Federal witnesses who said they were in it. For example, one Union soldier wrote, "some of the officers of the Sixth Corps, had the pleasure of sleeping in the house where Gen. Lee had had his headquarters during the entire winter, and which he had left only a few hours before the arrival of the Sixth Corps." See Mark, *History of the 93rd Regiment*, 324. Mary E. Nottingham, a young neighbor girl of the Turnbulls, wrote that on April 3 she and her family returned to their home "and were just in sight of our house when the flames burst from the Turnbull house." See "Recollections of General Lee," in *Richmond Dispatch*, August 8, 1897. See also *OR*, pt. 1, 638 documenting the establishment of a Union station of observation at the Turnbull House on the night of April 2. Perhaps the fire that Taylor saw and Haley confirmed either consumed an outbuilding and not the main dwelling, or it was not so devastating a blaze as they implied.

20. Wilcox, "Notes on the Richmond Campaign," in Cadmus Wilcox Papers, LC; Hyde, *Following the Greek Cross*, 260. Field surrendered 4,953 men at Appomattox Court House a week later.

21. *OR*, pt. 1, 675-678; pt. 3, 406, 409; Trudeau, *The Last Citadel*, 390-391. What the Federals called the Crow House Redoubt was actually two small enclosed forts connected by infantry trenches. Confederate accounts sometimes referred to the Crow House works as Fort Euliss or Fort Eustiss. The property belonged to 75-year-old William Crow, who owned 360 acres on the southwest side of Hatcher's Run.

22. *OR*, pt. 1, 678-679; pt. 3, 452. Colonel Henry J. Madill estimated that his brigade departed toward Five Forks at 2:00 a.m., April 2. See Henry Madill, Diary, April 2, 1865, in Gregory A. Coco Collection, Harrisburg Civil War Round Table Collection, USAMHI.

23. *OR*, pt. 1, 679.

24. Wilcox, "Defence of Batteries Gregg and Whitworth, and the Evacuation of Petersburg," in *SHSP*, IV, 30; James A. Graham, "Thirteenth Regiment,"II, 684; Adjutant Graham Daves, "Twenty-Second Regiment," II, 176; and Capt. R.S. Williams, "Twenty-Seventh Regiment," I, 455, all in Clark, ed., *North Carolina in the Great War*. Hyman's command was known officially as Scales's Brigade. The portion of Cooke's command positioned northeast of Hatcher's Run had participated in the fighting against the Sixth Corps during the Federal movement to the southwest following the Breakthrough, while two regiments of MacRae's Brigade had been overrun by Truman Seymour's division during the Breakthrough itself. See Chapters Eight and Seven, respectively, for these actions.

25. Trudeau, *The Last Citadel*, 391-392; William MacRae, Appomattox Campaign Report, in Lee Headquarters Papers, VHS; Wilcox, "Defence of Batteries Gregg and Whitworth, and the Evacuation of Petersburg," in *SHSP*, IV, 30; Benson, ed., *Berry Benson's Civil War Book*, 188-189; Caldwell, *The History of a Brigade of*

South Carolinians, 281. The 13th North Carolina's defense of the bridge over Hatcher's Run near Burgess's Mill collapsed under the pressure from the Sixth Corps as well as Hays's division. Although the Union sources do not explicitly credit troops from other corps, it is clear that Hays's attack, Harris's attack, and the Sixth Corps pursuit to Hatcher's Run all shared the same geography prior to Heth's retreat.

26. *OR* pt. 1, 679, 711, 715, 724-725, 729, 733-734, 737-738, 740, 746, 1288; Madill, Diary, April 2, 1865, in Gregory A. Coco Collection, Harrisburg Civil War Round Table Collection, USAMHI. Union accounts of Miles's march on the morning of April 2 agree in most details. However, Colonel Clinton MacDougall of the 111th New York reported "a severe skirmish, in which the enemy used artillery very freely" along the Confederate lines behind White Oak Road. More typical was the commentary of Colonel John Ramsey, commander of the Fourth Brigade: "entered the enemy's works at the point where the White Oak road runs through them, the works being occupied without any loss. The march was continued through the enemy's late camp, without any incident of note. . . ." Miles's men had been posted south of White Oak Road on April 1 prior to marching west to join Sheridan, so they realized that the Confederates occupied this portion of their line as far west as Claiborne Road, at least until sunset. Bushrod Johnson had evacuated the Claiborne Road–White Oak roads intersection beginning about 6:30 p.m., allowing Miles to use White Oak Road to join Sheridan. However, on the morning of April 2, Miles's officers had every right to worry that Johnson's troops might have returned or that the Confederates driven from Hatcher's Run might make a stand in the old fortifications at the White Oak Road–Claiborne roads intersection.

27. *OR* pt. 1, 679; Humphreys, *The Virginia Campaign*, 367. Griffin had replaced Warren in command of the Fifth Corps the previous evening. The 2000 incarnation of the road Meade wished Miles to follow is VA 632, Olgers Road.

28. *OR* pt. 1, 679; Sheridan, *Personal Memoirs*, II, 172-173. It is quite possible, of course, that Miles moved north on his own accord after both Humphreys and Sheridan declined to issue him orders. Humphreys obscured this issue in his campaign history, writing that when he caught up with Miles, the division commander was on the brink of combat with the Confederates at Sutherland Station. See Humphreys, *The Virginia Campaign*, 367. Miles stated in his report that Sheridan ordered him to "drive the enemy toward Petersburg", but the context of these instructions, if given in the morning, is unclear. See note 42 below.

29. Benson, ed., *Berry Benson's Civil War Book*, 189; Graham, "Twenty-Seventh Regiment," in Clark, ed., *North Carolina in the Great War*, II, 455; Caldwell, *The History of a Brigade of South Carolinians*, 281-282.

30. Caldwell, *The History of a Brigade of South Carolinians*, 282; Graham, "Twenty-Seventh Regiment," II, 455, and Robinson, "Fifty-Second Regiment," III, 251, both in Clark, ed., *North Carolina in the Great War*; Chris M. Calkins, *The Appomattox Campaign, March 29-April 9, 1865* (Conshohocken, Pa., 1997), 48; Trudeau, *The Last Citadel*, 393. Federal forces blocked Heth's route to Edge Hill as well as his path back to Sutherland Station. The acting corps commander thus

crossed the Appomattox River to escape, but from there could exercise no command over the remnants of the Third Corps. Ocran Methodist Church and Sutherland Tavern exist in 2000 in the Sutherland community along U.S. 460. The present church sits on the original location and is reported to have elements of the 1865 building under its modern brick facade. Sutherland Tavern has been partially restored and is open to the public as a museum called Fork Inn. An interesting display there highlights the Battle of Sutherland Station and the history of the structure.

31. *OR*, pt. 1, 62, 734. The Second Corps counted 21,167 men present for duty on March 31. Four of its ten brigades belonged to Miles. For information on Madill and Nugent, see Hunt & Brown, *Brevet Brigadier Generals in Blue*, 375, 451.

32. *OR*, pt. 1, 738; Chaplain Ezra Simmons of the 125th New York quoted in Trudeau, *The Last Citadel*, 394.

33. Caldwell, *The History of a Brigade of South Carolinians*, 282-283; Dunlop, *Lee's Sharpshooters*, 274-275; Graham, "Twenty-Seventh Regiment," in Clark, ed., *North Carolina in the Great War*, II, 455; Wilcox, "Defence of Batteries Gregg and Whitworth, and the Evacuation of Petersburg," in *SHSP*, IV, 31; *OR*, pt. 1, 733-734. Madill was wounded in the right side above the hip joint. See Madill, Diary, April 2, 1865, in Gregory A. Coco Collection, Harrisburg Civil War Round Table Collection, USAMHI.

34. *OR*, pt. 1, 711, 734; pt. 3, 467; Wilcox, "Defence of Batteries Gregg and Whitworth, and the Evacuation of Petersburg," in *SHSP*, IV, 31; Caldwell, *The History of a Brigade of South Carolinians*, 283-284; Dunlop, *Lee's Sharpshooters*, 275-276.

35. "Captain C. Frank Siler, Hero of Heroes," in *Confederate Veteran*, XV (1907), 90; *OR*, pt. 1, 738; Daves, "Twenty-Second Regiment," in Clark,ed., *North Carolina in the Great War*, II, 176; Caldwell, *The History of a Brigade of South Carolinians*, 284.

36. Wilcox, "Defence of Batteries Gregg and Whitworth, and the Evacuation of Petersburg," in *SHSP*, IV, 31; Caldwell, *The History of a Brigade of South Carolinians*, 284-285; Dunlop, *Lee's Sharpshooters*, 276. Pickett's Division and Anderson's troops under Bushrod Johnson had assembled the previous night at Church Road Crossing along the South Side Railroad about two and a half miles north of Five Forks. On April 2 they moved toward the Appomattox River, hoping to escape across that stream. Finding the river swollen beyond fording, the Confederates established a defensive position at an intersection called Scott's Cross Roads. Here they tangled with Sheridan's cavalry late in the day. See Calkins, *The Appomattox Campaign*, 53-55 and Freeman, *Lee's Lieutenants*, III, 681-682.

37. *OR*, pt. 1, 711, 746.

38. *OR*, pt. 1, 711, 746, 792; Dunlop, *Lee's Sharpshooters*, 276-277; Caldwell, *The History of a Brigade of South Carolinians*, 285-286. It is difficult to pinpoint Clark's precise location during the final attack. William MacRae said that the final Union attack began about 5:00 p.m. Major Seward F. Gould of the 4th New York Heavy Artillery timed the assault at 3:45 p.m. Trudeau estimates that Ramsey began

his attack a little before 4:00 p.m. See William MacRae, Appomattox Campaign Report, in Lee Headquarters Papers, VHS; *OR*, pt. 1, 733; Trudeau, *The Last Citadel*, 396.

39. *OR*, pt. 1, 746; Dunlop, *Lee's Sharpshooters*, 277; Caldwell, *The History of a Brigade of South Carolinians*, 286.

40. *OR*, pt.1, 712, 726, 733, 746; Dunlop, *Lee's Sharpshooters*, 277; Trudeau, *The Last Citadel*, 397. Private Josiah Phillips of the 148th Pennsylvania was the original captor of the unidentified South Carolina flag. Private Frank Denio of Company M, 4th New York Heavy Artillery, was the soldier who later picked it up and claimed the credit. Of course, unorganized elements of the Sixth Corps had reached the South Side Railroad immediately following the Breakthrough, but they had not remained astride the tracks. Wheaton's and Getty's divisions had also blocked the tracks as they deployed opposite Edge Hill prior to Miles's successful action.

41. William MacRae, Appomattox Campaign Report, in Lee Headquarters Papers, VHS; Dunlop, *Lee's Sharpshooters*, 277-278; Wilcox, "Autobiography," 14-15, in Cadmus M. Wilcox Papers, LC; Caldwell, *The History of a Brigade of South Carolinians*, 286-288; Benson, ed., *Berry Benson's Civil War Book*, 190-191; Wilcox, "Defence of Batteries Gregg and Whitworth, and the Evacuation of Petersburg," in *SHSP*, IV, 31-32; Trudeau, *The Last Citadel*, 397.

42. *OR*, pt. 1, 679-680, 686, 712. Miles's division had suffered 331 casualties on March 31 during the fighting along White Oak Road, so the unit had been substantially bled and marched during that 48-hour period. Exactly when Sheridan conveyed such orders to Miles is a mystery. There is no record of Sheridan and Miles communicating during or immediately after the Battle of Sutherland Station, and during the morning's command confusion between Sheridan and Humphreys a directive to "drive the enemy toward Petersburg" would have been an odd one, given the situation at the time. Perhaps Miles's memory failed him in regard to this detail of his report. River Road, VA 601, follows the course of the wartime River Road east from the Sutherland area in 2000.

43. *OR*, pt. 1, 679, 777, 782, 785-786; pt. 3, 467, 474. Mott mentioned placing his right near the Sully House, a dwelling that does not appear on the wartime maps.

44. *OR*, pt. 1, 679-680, 760, 762, 782, 786. Colonel William A. Olmstead, commanding Hays's First Brigade, reported that his unit had advanced "to and near Mr. Cogswell's house, on Cox's road." A wartime map indicates the "Cogville" house south of Cox Road about one mile west of the Turnbull House. See Nathaniel Michler, *Sketch of the Entrenched Lines in the Immediate Front of Petersburg*, Map 609, LC.

45. Humphreys, *The Virginia Campaign*, 369.

46. *OR*, pt. 3, 482-483. Parke was not alone in his trepidation about attacking the Confederate fortifications in his front. Lieutenant Alonzo R. Case of the 207th Pennsylvania wrote in his diary on March 31, "The Men all dread the charging of these works as they do <u>Death itself!</u> And they all seam to think that it cant be did,

and I hope that it wont have to be." Alonzo Rufus Case, Diary, Gregory A. Coco Collection, Bendersville, Pennsylvania.

47. Trudeau, *The Last Citadel*, 357. Battery "A", Sumter (Georgia) Artillery, four Napoleons and two ten-pounder Parrotts commanded by Captain Hugh M. Ross, defended Fort Mahone. Battery "B", Sumter (Georgia) Artillery, six Napoleons, commanded by Captain George M. Patterson, was in Battery 27. All of the fortifications mentioned in the text disappeared long ago. An impressive monument to Pennsylvania troops in the Ninth Corps occupies part of the site of Fort Mahone in 2000.

48. Gallagher, ed., *Extracts of Letters of Major-General Bryan Grimes*, 104-105; Cyrus B. Watson, "Forty-Fifth Regiment," in Clark, ed., *North Carolina in the Great War*, III, 56-57; Allen, *Lee's Last Major General*, 243-244. Cox's Tarheels played a peripheral role in defending against the Breakthrough and Parke's attack. See Chapter Eight. The density of troops on the line in Gordon's corps was 870 per mile. See Freeman, *R. E. Lee*, IV, 42.

49. *OR*, pt. 1, 1016, 1054. For information about Meade's orders that night, see Chapter Six and *OR*, pt. 3, 407.

50. *OR*, pt. 1, 1016, 1043, 1054, 1061. Hartranft left the 209th Pennsylvania and the 200th Pennsylvania, both of Lieutenant Colonel William H. H. McCall's brigade, in reserve. Harriman placed the 37th Wisconsin and 27th Michigan in reserve. Potter left the 7th Rhode Island, 35th Massachusetts, 36th Massachusetts, 51st New York, 9th New Hampshire, and 11th New Hampshire to garrison the forts on his division's line.

51. *OR*, pt. 1, 1016-1017, 1039-1040. Nothing remains of Union Fort Rice. The 51st Pennsylvania of Harriman's brigade also participated in Willcox's operation.

52. *OR*, pt. 1, 1054, 1059; Maine soldier quoted in Trudeau, *The Last Citadel*, 361.

53. *OR*, pt. 1, 1054, 1057; Trudeau, *The Last Citadel*, 361-362. Although Potter survived until 1887, his April 2 wound bothered him for the remainder of his life and was cited as a contributory cause of his death. A handsome monument to Colonel Gowan stands in 2000 near where that officer suffered his fatal wound. It is maintained by the National Park Service on a small plot of land surrounded on all sides by commercial development. Gowan's name is sometimes spelled Gowen.

54. *OR*, pt. 1, 1062; Pennsylvanian Miles C. Huyette quoted in Trudeau, *The Last Citadel*, 361.

55. *OR*, pt. 1, 1043, 1045-1046. The reports of Harriman and his officers misidentified the Confederate work they captured east of Jerusalem Plank Road, Battery 25, as Fort Mahone.

56. Gallagher, ed., *Extracts of the Letters of Major-General Bryan Grimes*, 105-106; Watson, "Forty-Fifth Regiment," in Clark, ed., *North Carolina in the Great War*, III, 57. Archer's units were the 3rd Battalion Virginia Reserves and the 44th Virginia Battalion, both of which were composed of men from Petersburg and surrounding counties. Fletcher Archer was an attorney before the war and a veteran of the Mexican War.

57. Gallagher, ed., *Extracts of the Letters of Major-General Bryan Grimes*, 106-107; Watson, "Forty-Fifth Regiment," in Clark, ed., *North Carolina in the Great War*, III, 57; Quote in Trudeau, *The Last Citadel*, 362-363.

58. Gallagher, ed., *Extracts of the Letters of Major-General Bryan Grimes*, 107; *OR*, pt. 1, 1062, 1091-1092, 932; pt. 3, 485-486; Trudeau, *The Last Citadel*, 363. John J. Ingraham of the 121st New York of Hamblin's brigade referred to Fort Mahone as "Fort Heaven," apparently in contrast to Fort Sedgwick's moniker of Fort Hell. See Ingraham to "Dear Parents," April 16, 1865, in John J. Ingraham Papers, Cornell University. The site of Meade Station is interpreted in Petersburg National Battlefield.

59. *OR*, pt. 1, 1055, 1058, 1092; William McClelland, "A Brave Battery," in *Philadelphia Weekly Times*, June 18, 1887; Gallagher, ed., *Extracts of the Letters of Major-General Bryan Grimes*, 107; Watson, "Forty-Fifth Regiment," III, 57-58, and Col. Thomas S. Kenan, "Forty-Third Regiment," III, 16-17, both in in Clark, ed., *North Carolina in the Great War*; Trudeau, *The Last Citadel*, 363-365.

60. *OR*, pt. 3, 486, pt. 1, 1056, 1065. Hartranft's Second Brigade and Griffin's brigade of Potter's division sustained the greatest casualties on April 2. No single regiment lost more than the 207th Pennsylvania, which reported 185 losses between March 29 and April 9, the vast majority suffered on April 2. Collis reported 85 casualties from March 29-April 9, most of them likewise absorbed on April 2. See *OR*, pt. 1, 590.

61. Gallagher, ed., *Extracts of the Letters of Major-General Bryan Grimes*, 107; Watson, "Forty-Fifth Regiment," in Clark, ed., *North Carolina in the Great War*, III, 58.

62. Gordon, *Reminiscences of the Civil War*, 420-421; Trudeau, *The Last Citadel*, 365-366. Gordon's wife had given birth to a son in Petersburg on April 1, adding a touch of personal poignancy to his evacuation orders.

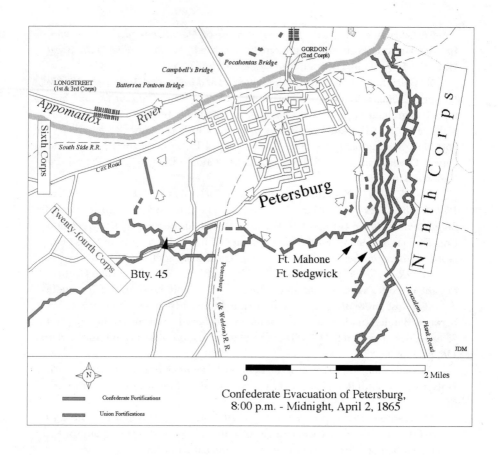

Confederate Evacuation of Petersburg,
8:00 p.m. - Midnight, April 2, 1865

0   1   2 Miles

Confederate Fortifications

Union Fortifications

CHAPTER ELEVEN

The Fall of Petersburg

While the armies grappled south and west of Petersburg on April 2, the townspeople endured a day fraught with the almost-unbearable certainty of calamity. "The greatest excitement prevails every where and with everybody this morning," wrote one Petersburg woman. "Every kind of rumor in circulation; people are flying in every direction; we all try and keep composed." Civilians, of course, had no access to the cheerless battlefield intelligence that hour by hour defined the magnitude of the crisis confronting the Army of Northern Virginia. But the steady stream of incoming ambulances, the intensity of the shelling and other sounds of combat, and the unhappy reports of grayclad soldiers as they arrived wounded or demoralized in the streets of town, gave credence to the most frightening predictions.[1]

Any lingering doubts about Petersburg's fate evaporated in the afternoon when officials began burning tobacco warehouses, a desperate expedient to deny their valuable contents to the Federal army. Quartermaster and commissary officers opened the doors to their repositories, offering food and equipment to anyone wishing to claim it. The estimated 3,000 sick and wounded in Petersburg's remaining military hospitals were told to evacuate the doomed city, "the moans mingling with the cries of women, the shrieking and bursting of shell, and the hoarse orders of men in authority."[2]

In contrast to these increasingly disordered conditions in Petersburg, the situation at army headquarters remained remarkably calm. General Lee had relocated his command post from the Turnbull House to Captain Robert D. McIlwaine's home, known as Cottage Farm, between Edge Hill and the city's western limits. There, Lee faced a logistical task of enormous complexity. His army was scattered, parts of it isolated far to the west, some of it in Chesterfield County or north of the James, and the remnants of Petersburg's defenders holding their lines just west, south, and east of town. Lee still sought, as he had for more than a month, to join Joseph Johnston's forces in North Carolina. Along the way, he would have to reunite his divided command and subsist it during a long, difficult trek to the southwest.

"Lee . . . drafted the orders that would leave Petersburg entirely defenseless for the first time in nearly four years."

Lee determined to effect his escape via the Richmond & Danville Railroad, the only avenue available to the Confederates now that the Yankees controlled the South Side Railroad. The army would rendezvous forty miles west of Petersburg at Amelia Court House, the closest point on the Richmond & Danville Railroad convenient to all elements of his fractured command. From there, the Army of Northern Virginia would work its way southwest to Danville and into the Tarheel State where—together with Johnston—Confederate arms might remain viable. Amelia lay on the south side of the Appomattox River, so the troops defending Petersburg would have to negotiate two crossings of that watercourse to reach their destination. The Confederates north of the James would be required to cross that river as well as the Appomattox. Only those units separated from the rest of the army beyond Five Forks and Sutherland Station could avoid a river crossing, but they faced their own crisis amid these desperate circumstances.

By 3:00 p.m., Lee had completed his planning and, in the presence of generals Longstreet, Heth, and Wilcox, drafted the orders that would leave Petersburg entirely defenseless for the first time in nearly four years:

> General Longstreet's and Hill's corps will cross the pontoon bridge at Battersea Factory, and take the River road, north side of Appomattox, to Bevill's Bridge to-night. General Gordon's corps will cross at Pocahontas and railroad bridges, his troops taking Hickory road, following General Longstreet to Bevill's Bridge, and his wagons taking the Woodpecker road to Old Colville, endeavoring not to interfere with Mahone's troops from Chesterfield Court-House, who will take the same road. General Mahone's division will take the road to Chesterfield Court-House, thence by Old Colville to Goode's Bridge. Mahone's wagons will precede him on the

same road or take some road to his right. General [Richard S.] Ewell's command will cross the James River at and below Richmond, taking the road to Branch Church, via Gregory's, to Genito road, via Genito Bridge to Amelia Court-House. The wagons from Richmond will take the Manchester pike and Buckingham road, via Meadville, to Amelia Court-House. The movement of all troops will commence at 8 o'clock, the artillery moving out quietly first, infantry following, except the pickets, who will be withdrawn at 3 o'clock. The artillery not required with the troops will be moved by the roads prescribed for the wagons, or such other as may be most convenient. Every officer is expected to give his unremitting attention to cause the movement to be made successfully.

The last troops to leave the city, Lee instructed, would destroy the bridges connecting Petersburg with Chesterfield County to prevent the Federals from launching an immediate pursuit after dawn.[3]

Once he had circulated the orders for Petersburg's evacuation, Lee notified Secretary of War John C. Breckinridge of the certainty of his withdrawal. "It is absolutely necessary that we should abandon our position to-night, or run the risk of being cut off in the morning," he explained to the Kentuckian. "I have given all the orders to officers on both sides of the river, and have taken every precaution that I can to make the movement successful. It will be a difficult operation, but I hope not impracticable." By the time this joyless dispatch reached Richmond around 7:00 p.m., the dismantling of the capital was already well under way.[4]

In Petersburg, the city's habitually optimistic authorities had no choice but to admit the unthinkable. The destruction of military supplies in the city signaled Lee's all-but-certain intention to remove his army. Members of the city council convened an emergency meeting at which they named a committee to call on the general-in-chief to ascertain his specific plans. Moreover, if the soldiers did indeed abandon Petersburg's defense, the councilmen made plans to meet their blueclad conquerors to seek protection for the citizens and their property.

Mayor William W. Townes and councilmen James Boisseau and Charles F. Collier comprised the committee charged with consulting General Lee. They proceeded to Cottage Farm, only to find the general absent. In a short while, however, Lee returned and met with the local dignitaries. "The General was apparently calm and collected, but very reticent," remembered Councilman Collier, "only replying to the committee that he would communicate with us at the residence of Mr. [D'Arcy W.] Paul, in the city of Petersburg, that . . . night at 10 o'clock." The delegates returned dejectedly to their doomed city, knowing that their nine-month ordeal was about to end in disaster.[5]

At the appointed hour Major Giles A. Cooke of Lee's staff arrived at the Paul house on Union Street, where the entire city council awaited his report. As the solons expected, Cooke confirmed that the army would abandon Petersburg by midnight, transferring control of the city to its civilian authorities. Absorbing the import of Cooke's information, the councilmen decided to reconvene at Reverend Paul's at 4:00 a.m., then divide into pairs or small groups assigned to monitor each of the highways entering Petersburg. Wherever the Federals were encountered, these appointed representatives would offer the city's surrender, thereby, they hoped, forestalling wholesale destruction at the hands of vengeful occupation troops.[6]

Councilman Collier and Mayor Townes spent the hours after Cooke's departure wandering the streets, observing the unforgettable scenes that signaled an end to their authority and their way of life. "As we walked," wrote Collier, "Lee's soldiers, in large bodies, in squads, and singly, passed along through the streets towards the bridges over the Appomattox leading into Chesterfield County." By then, most of the Confederate field artillery had been safely removed and the infantry withdrawn from their front-line positions. Field's Division and what remained of A. P. Hill's corps west of Petersburg used the Battersea Bridge to reach the north bank. Gordon's survivors filed through town toward the Campbell, Pocahontas, and railroad bridges.[7]

General Lee's intentions became clear to the men in the ranks after sunset. "Darkness had gathered over the gory field when I noticed that the artillery was being quietly removed from the works, while staff officers and field officers were unusually conspicuous," wrote a Georgian in Thomas's Brigade. "I knew this meant a retreat or change of base." A Tarheel soldier marching through Petersburg that long night realized the army's situation only when he saw the "noble women . . . weeping as in the agony of despair," at the passing of the troops. The local populace thronged the streets, joining Collier, Townes, and their neighbors, drawn by the need to witness for themselves that their faithful protectors would no longer shield them from the unspeakable. "There was no sleeping in Petersburg that night," remembered a brigade commander, "no night except for the darkness."[8]

Although conditions in Petersburg after midnight compared favorably with the hellish scene that consumed the Richmond business district during those chaotic first hours of April 3, enough was ablaze in the Cockade City to catch the attention of many observers. "Great fires were raging in the city, for the authorities were burning the big warehouses filled with all kinds of army stores," wrote one Confederate. "The flames

Campbell's Bridge over the Appomattox River looking northwest
from Petersburg toward Ettrick.

National Archives

were leaping skyward, illuminating the city and surrounding country."
Individual troops broke ranks to gather loot that filled unguarded
buildings or spilled into the streets. Inevitably, liquor found its way down
soldiers' throats, adding another level of instability to the fragile
equilibrium. Despite these complications, Lee's forces reached the bridges
with remarkable efficiency.   A Virginian remembered crossing the
Pocahontas Bridge in the heart of Petersburg about 10:00 p.m., expecting
the Yankees to open fire at any moment. He also made note of the stacked
fuel placed around the span, set to ignite when the last Confederate had
crossed the river.[9]

Some civilians joined the exodus, including a number of escaping
slaves who crossed the Appomattox amid the confusion. Most residents,
however, chose to remain in Petersburg, deciding that protecting their
homes was the preferable of two distasteful options. Among them were
former general and Mrs. Roger A. Pryor, who had arrived from Cottage
Farm, most recently Lee's temporary headquarters, and taken up lodging
in a rented house. Mrs. Pryor had locked her husband, a recent parolee
from a Union prison camp, in an upstairs room to prevent the ailing but
ardent patriot from yielding to his passions and departing with the army.

When the doorbell rang late in the night, Mrs. Pryor found Mayor Townes, who had come to inquire if Pryor would like to join him and Councilman Collier on their mission to surrender Petersburg. "Oh, he cannot—he cannot," protested Mrs. Pryor, citing the general's weakened physical condition and the mental agony that surrendering his own home would cause him. The mayor compassionately declined to press the matter.[10]

In the meantime, Lee's army continued to cross the Appomattox River, organized units gradually yielding to small bands of stragglers, then to individuals completely separated from their comrades and commands. The officers charged with destroying the spans faced a difficult decision regarding when to set the bridges ablaze. While they understood that not every soldier or loyal citizen wishing to flee Petersburg had done so, dawn was approaching and with it, inevitably, the Union army. They knew that their imperative duty was to ensure that the roiling waters of the swollen Appomattox separated Lee's army from its would-be pursuers. "Just before the last troops crossed . . . the torch was applied to the bridges," remembered a Virginia soldier. "How many of our men were cut off I cannot say," recalled another Confederate, "but I am certain there were some who had to swim that night or surrender the next morning." A loud explosion preceded the destruction of the spans in town, "the timbers of [one] bridge rising skyward and changing ends like arrows." The evacuation of Petersburg utterly devastated many of Lee's men. "O, how sad I felt to think so noble a little city should soon be in Yankee hands," wrote North Carolina artillerist James W. Albright. Another Confederate expressed absolute despair at the events of the evening. "I am almost demoralized," wrote Sergeant James E. Whitehorne of the 12th Virginia. "I can't see what will become of us. . . . I'll never see the calm moon again without remembering this sad night."[11]

*   *   *

Of course, the events of April 2 had ensured that many men wearing both blue and gray would never see a moon of any variety again. The combat on the final day of the Petersburg Campaign resulted in one of the larger combined losses of any twelve-hour period during the entire war.

Attrition in the Sixth Corps occurred during the Breakthrough, as a result of the fighting toward Hatcher's Run, and in the afternoon sparring near the Turnbull House. Getty's division suffered at least 395 and perhaps as many as 414 casualties on April 2, most of this loss occurring in the morning assault. The Vermont Brigade absorbed more than its share of the division's attrition. "The casualties of the day were 2 commissioned officers and 24 enlisted men killed; 10 officers and 151 men wounded, and 7 enlisted men missing; in all, 196," reported Lewis A. Grant, himself numbered among the wounded. The oversized 1st Vermont Heavy Artillery endured greater losses than any of its sister regiments. Warner's brigade lost 103 men on April 2, and Hyde's Third Brigade reported 96 killed, wounded, or missing.[12]

Frank Wheaton's First Division reported 321 losses on April 2, the majority suffered by Edwards's Third Brigade. Edwards's six regiments, who, like the Vermonters, had formed on the left and in advance in their divisional formation during the predawn offensive, counted 194 casualties, some 60% of the entire divisional loss. The 5th Wisconsin accounted for nearly half the brigade casualties, suffering twelve killed and 70 wounded, while the 37th Massachusetts lost 36 men that day. Penrose's New Jersey Brigade lost 75 men. Hamblin's Second Brigade sustained only 52 casualties, reflecting in part its assignment to remain behind during the struggle to reach Hatcher's Run.[13]

Truman Seymour reported 327 losses in his Third Division, a number almost identical to Wheaton's, but distributed throughout only two brigades. Warren Keifer's Second Brigade absorbed the majority of the division's losses. Of the 166 officers and men killed, wounded, or captured on April 2 in the brigade, nearly 40% fell in the 9th New York Heavy Artillery, the large unit's losses being more than twice the total of any two other regiments' combined casualties. William S. Truex's First Brigade reported 161 killed or wounded on April 2.[14]

Artillerists of the Sixth Corps added their names to Wright's casualty list. Of the nineteen cannoneers reported hurt on April 2, eleven belonged to Captain Crawford Allen's Battery H, 1st Rhode Island Light Artillery. Wright's total corps loss of 1,081 included 123 killed, 899 wounded, and 59 missing. The permanent Sixth Corps hospitals treated 804 of these wounded men and then transferred them via the United States Military Railroad to the Depot Hospital at City Point. "By daylight the wounded began to come in, and from this time until four P.M. the surgeons were occupied in dressing wounds, extracting bullets and amputating limbs," according to a Union soldier visiting the corps hospitals. "There were the usual sad and terrible scenes of suffering and death."[15]

Second Corps losses on April 2 totaled 422, the vast majority sustained in the fighting at Sutherland Station. General Parke reported a total of 1,719 casualties in the Ninth Corps, most of them inflicted during the fighting along Jerusalem Plank Road. John Gibbon's Twenty-fourth Corps suffered 714 killed or wounded on April 2, almost exclusively during the attacks at Fort Gregg. Discounting minor losses experienced by the Fifth

Corps, Twenty-fifth Corps, and Sheridan's cavalry, Federal troops south of the Appomattox River counted 3,936 casualties in the fighting around Petersburg on April 2.[16]

To put that number into perspective, more Northern soldiers fell at Petersburg on April 2, 1865 than at First Manassas or Malvern Hill in Virginia, at Franklin or Fort Donelson in Tennessee, at Champion Hill or Brice's Cross Roads in Mississippi, at Resaca or Kennesaw Mountain in Georgia, or at any number of other more celebrated engagements. Breaking the backbone of the rebellion came at a heavy price for the Union army on April 2, 1865.[17]

Information regarding Confederate casualties on April 2 is sketchy. One student has calculated that the Sixth Corps captured some 3,980 Confederates during the course of the day, including 2,100 by Getty's division, 990 by Seymour's brigades, and 890 by Wheaton's troops. The ten regiments that faced the Sixth Corps during the Breakthrough suffered an estimated loss of 19 killed, 27 wounded, and 1,022 captured. Added to these educated guesses are the approximately 380 dead and captured at Forts Gregg and Whitworth, the 600 prisoners and uncounted killed and wounded at Sutherland Station, and the unknown but substantial losses around Fort Mahone and along the line to Hatcher's Run. At least 5,000 and perhaps as many as 5,500 Confederate soldiers became casualties on April 2, the vast majority of them prisoners of war. There were so many captured graycoats that Grant first estimated them to number 10,000 or 12,000—an exaggeration by at least a factor of two. Nevertheless, Lee's losses on April 2 amounted to about 10% of his entire command, a tragic day for the Army of Northern Virginia and one rarely equaled during the course of the war.[18]

*   *   *

As darkness enveloped the quiet battle lines west of Petersburg, a member of the 15th New Jersey speculated about conditions beyond Rohoic Creek, inside the Confederate fortifications. "We could only conjecture what was taking place within the city," he admitted. Of course, those grayclads who had avoided capture, or death, were at that very moment in the process of abandoning the unhappy town. Meanwhile, the Rebel captives provided unintended entertainment for their Yankee guardians that night, as recorded by a Vermonter:

> Large squads of the prisoners were taken by here, and of course every
> fellow that could leave his bed, had to go out to the road to pay his respects

to the Johnnies. I thought they looked remarkably well, considering what had been said of their condition. Their faces looked grim and dusty, of course, but I couldn't see any sign at all of their having suffered from starvation. And their clothes and general appearance were as good as ours generally are, after we have been marching and fighting for some length of time.

The Federals enjoyed biting (if not outright malicious) banter with the captives, inquiring sarcastically about conditions in Richmond and Petersburg and wishing them well in their trips to Northern prison camps. "Most of them were good natured about it," commented an admiring Yankee. "Damn it, you needn't laugh," replied one Confederate to the jibes of his blue-jacketed captors, "you ought to have done this before."[19]

Timely or overdue, the Federal general-in-chief considered the day's results to be "one of the greatest victories of the war." Lesser lights agreed. "We have had glorious success," wrote the chaplain of the 37th Massachusetts. "Unbounded enthusiasm prevails. Vociferous cheering rends the very air. . . ." At 4:40 p.m., from his headquarters at the Banks House near Boydton Plank Road, and exactly twelve hours from the commencement of Wright's attack, Grant wrote to Lincoln inviting the president to meet with him the following day. The chief executive responded with enthusiasm. "Allow me to tender to you and all with you the nation's grateful thanks for this additional and magnificent success," he beamed. "At your kind suggestion I think I will meet you to-morrow."[20]

While Grant arranged for his rendezvous with the president, the Sixth Corps completed preparations for the bombardment and attack scheduled to commence at 5:00 a.m. April 3. "The troops will be under arms at 4 a.m. to-morrow," instructed Wright. "The command will be held in readiness to assault the enemy's works in case he should be found to be evacuating or show signs of weakness."[21]

In the predawn hours of April 3, however, evidence mounted suggesting that the Cockade City would fall without a fight. Rapt bluecoated observers east, south, and west of Petersburg watched as flames from the city's buildings illuminated the night sky. These Federals drew the obvious conclusion from the conflagrations. The city "had been burning during the day," wrote a Northern reporter, "but its appearance now was heightened by its vivid contrast with the darkness of night, and was sublime beyond expression." Confederate deserters confirmed suspicions that Lee was evacuating his lines and that few troops remained to contest a Federal occupation. At least one intrepid Union volunteer made his way into Petersburg to verify these assertions, and returned with eye-witness affirmation of the Confederate withdrawal.[22]

East of the city, in the lines held by Brigadier General Orlando B. Willcox's Ninth Corps division, Lieutenant Colonel Ralph Ely, in command of Willcox's Second Brigade, issued orders at 1:30 a.m. for two of his regiments, the 1st Michigan Sharpshooters and the 2nd Michigan, "to hold themselves in readiness to make a demonstration on the right of my front at 4 a.m. and perhaps sooner." An hour later, Ely received orders to commence his probe immediately, based on the testimony of a deserter "that the rebels had all left except the picket-line." Ely instructed a staff officer to awaken the two Wolverine regiments and order them to "throw out scouts and a heavy skirmish line and occupy the main rebel works if possible." Should this mission prove a success, the rest of the brigade was to follow the two lead regiments, who themselves were to "advance . . . rapidly, but cautiously, forward and plant a color upon some public building in the city."[23]

South of Petersburg, John F. Hartranft, commanding Parke's Third Division, ordered skirmishers from his brigades "to advance . . . and feel for the enemy," while notifying the rest of his division to remain on alert for a possible movement toward the city. Hartranft circulated these instructions at 3:00 a.m., just minutes before Ely unleashed his two Michigan regiments toward Petersburg via the City Point Road. At 3:20 a.m., west of town, Oliver Edwards received orders from General Wright, through his division commander Frank Wheaton, to "press the enemy." Edwards moved at once to execute his instructions. Thus, Federal forces from three fronts moved simultaneously toward what they suspected to be abandoned or weakly-held Confederate lines, each with the expectation of being the first Union troops to enter Petersburg.[24]

The 1st Michigan Sharpshooters and the 2nd Michigan began their advance at 3:10 a.m., occupying the main Confederate earthworks without opposition. The Westerners gave voice to their joy and relief through "three hearty cheers," and pressed carefully ahead into Petersburg itself. Slowed both by the terrain and a reasonable caution in the dark, predawn shadows, the Michiganders entered the city about an hour after they had left their own lines. At 4:25 a.m., the Federals reached the short street that led to the Petersburg courthouse, the Cockade City's handsome signature building and symbol of municipal authority. Major Clement A. Lounsberry, Ely's assistant adjutant general, who had accompanied the troops, encountered one of the city's deputations charged with surrendering Petersburg to the Union military. "Major Lounsberry was met in front of the court-house by three citizens bearing a flag of truce and a communication from the mayor and common council tendering the surrender of the town, and requesting that persons and private property be respected," reported Ely. "But the gallant major could listen to no proposition until the 'old flag' was floating from the highest point of the court-house steeple. . . ."

Ely recorded that at precisely 4:28 a.m., the 1st Michigan Sharpshooters hoisted their regimental banner above the Petersburg courthouse, while moments later the 2nd Michigan raised its flag above the Customs House at the nearby corner of Union and Tabb streets. Color Sergeant William T. Wixcey belonged to the group that entered the courthouse and lofted the first Union colors to preside over the city since the spring of 1861. "It was yet dark when we made our way into the court-house and up the winding stairs into the clock tower," he recalled. "For want of a better place to display our colors we opened the door of the clock face and thrust them out through it, and there, for the first time in years, floated the dear old flag. . . . Our hearts were too full for utterance, so we clasped hands and shed tears of joy, for we knew that the beginning of the end had come." Eventually, Lounsberry accepted the surrender document from the local officials, the text of which appeared in Ely's report:

> Lieut. Gen. U.S. Grant, commanding the Armies of the U.S. or The Major-General Commanding U.S. Forces in front of Petersburg: General: The city of Petersburg having been evacuated by the Confederate troops, we, a committee authorized by the common council , do hereby surrender the city to the U.S. forces, with a request for the protection of the persons and property of its inhabitants.[25]

While this dramatic scene unfolded, Colonel Alfred B. McCalmont, commanding Hartranft's First Brigade, arrived at the courthouse and encountered Lieutenant Colonel Ely. McCalmont could not deny that the Michiganders had beaten his Pennsylvanians to the building, but he did assert that "I am satisfied . . . that this brigade was the first which entered the limits of the city in a body." McCalmont quietly withdrew to the outskirts of town, content with his claim that to his troops belonged the honor of first occupying Petersburg. The confluence of these Ninth Corps units in the heart of the city sounded to one Confederate officer, engaged in superintending the final destruction of the bridges, like the "shouting and shrieking [of] so many Serbs—my heart ached in contemplations of what might be done by them. . . ."[26]

The third arm of the converging Union pincers, Edwards's brigade of Wheaton's division, moved out of its trenches toward the western Confederate defenses about 4:00 a.m. The division pickets led the advance under the command of Captain Miles L. Butterfield, Wheaton's acting

Petersburg Courthouse

Massachusetts MOLLUS Collection, Carlisle Barracks, Pennsylvania

engineer officer. What exactly transpired next remains a matter of debate. According to Butterfield, shortly after his skirmishers left the forward Union lines, "I discovered in the morning light, what I supposed to be a carriage, and a flag of truce on the works occupied by the rebels the night before." Approaching the vehicle in the company of another officer,

Butterfield claimed to have heard one of its occupants say, "We wish to surrender the City." Butterfield reported that the party included Mayor Townes, D.W. Paul, and two members of "the Common Council, [who] handed me a letter addressed to General Grant, or any General commanding the Union forces before Petersburg." The captain allegedly dashed immediately to Sixth Corps headquarters and showed the letter to General Wright. The corps commander reportedly instructed Butterfield to rejoin the civilian authorities and tell them that the Union forces "will take possession [of Petersburg] at once." Butterfield supposedly returned to the mayor and accompanied him and his party into the city, "thereby being the first Union officer to enter Petersburg after the surrender."[27]

Councilman Charles Collier offered a different version of these events. Collier recorded that he and Mayor Townes had reached the Model Farm west of Petersburg on foot, about dawn, carrying a white handkerchief tied to a walking stick as a flag of truce. Not having seen a Union soldier, the two dignitaries were startled when they heard the report of a signal gun in the neighborhood of Fort Gregg, "and instantaneously, there sprang forth, as from the bowels of the earth . . . a mighty host of Federal soldiers, and then followed such a shout of victory as seemed to shake the very ground on which we stood." According to Collier, this wave of bluecoats swept past the astonished officials, who tried in vain to arrest the attention of some high-ranking commander in order to tender the surrender of Petersburg. "The officers would not take time to stop to hear what we had to say, the men rushing ahead to enter the city, but bade us come along with them, they (the officers) promising to protect us and to protect our people." Collier claimed that he and Mayor Townes reached the courthouse only to find "the whole building, steeple and all, festooned with small Federal flags." They felt their mission had been accomplished, however, even though they had not been afforded the formal opportunity to capitulate to the Union authorities.[28]

Colonel Edwards authored yet a third scenario. According to the brigade commander, "I ordered my skirmish line to advance, when we moved forward into the City. Just outside we met a hack with a white flag, and Mayor Towne (sic), Alderman Paul and two other Aldermen surrendered the city to me." Edwards further claimed that no other Union troops were present for at least 30 minutes following the surrender, except the handful of Ninth Corps men who raised the flag over the courthouse. "As soon as I received the surrender I halted the 6th Corps skirmish line, and sent the 37th Mass into the City as Provost Guard," testified Edwards, counting on the Bay-Staters' Spencer rifles to preserve order. The historian of the 15th New Jersey introduced an additional wrinkle into Edwards's story, suggesting that Mayor Townes and company first encountered Major Augustus Fay of the 40th New Jersey, the officer commanding the picket line (not Butterfield), who referred Townes to Colonel Edwards.[29]

It is difficult to reconcile these divergent accounts, all of which appeared well after the war. However, Butterfield's and Edwards's versions suffer from the appearance of self-promotion. Collier certainly had no ego invested in his recital of events, and the specter of eager Union soldiers rushing forward in the enthusiasm of the moment contains the ring of truth. It is hard to imagine that Butterfield would have had the time to make a round trip between the Model Farm and Wright's headquarters, wherever they might have been that fluid morning, before line authorities like Edwards would have seized control of troop movements. Perhaps the actual events along Cox Road that morning may never be known in all their detail. There can be no question, however, that Union troops entered Petersburg from the east, south, and west at roughly the same moment, and that by raising a flag above the courthouse, the Michiganders from Ely's brigade committed the overt act which resulted in the de facto surrender of the Cockade City.

Thousands of Northern soldiers now poured into the streets of town, although the vast majority of Grant's forces remained in their fortifications and did not partake in the memorable scenes that awaited the occupying troops. Hamblin's brigade of Wheaton's division approached the city from the south, having spent the previous afternoon in support of the Ninth Corps. When it reached Petersburg's business district, some of the men made their way toward the Pocahontas Bridge which, though ablaze, had not yet collapsed into the Appomattox River. Enlisting the help of fellow troops and local blacks, the ersatz firefighters succeeded in dousing the flames and saving the bridge. Other Yankees spotted Confederate stragglers and gobbled them up before they could effect their escape in small craft.[30]

Among the captives was Corporal Joseph S. Kimbrough of the 14th Georgia. The exhausted Kimbrough had fallen asleep and spent the night in Petersburg with a number of his worn-out comrades. About an hour after daylight, the "hoarse huzzas" of the Federals awoke the slumbering stragglers who snatched up their rifles and made for the bridges over the Appomattox. Seeing the railroad span in ruins and the Pocahontas Bridge in flames filled Kimbrough with dread: "No language can describe my feelings as I gazed across that muddy, swollen stream and realized that there was no chance to cross nor time to escape." Kimbrough bent his rifle across a rock and tossed his faithful weapon into the swirling waters of the Appomattox before the Federals arrived and demanded his surrender.[31]

The 121st New York received the assignment of placing United States flags on the public buildings throughout Petersburg, explaining Councilman Collier's observation that the courthouse had been "festooned" with Union banners. Other members of Hamblin's brigade indulged in less patriotic activities. "We secured a lot of Confederate currency and postage stamps, and routed out a lot of stragglers and sneaks, hid about the city," wrote one New Yorker. "At the Commissary we secured some nice hams and some apple jack that was quite smooth, and under its softening influence we forgave a good many of our foes." Black house servants took delight in telling the Yankees about Confederate soldiers hiding in private homes, and when the Unionists entered these dwellings to collect their prisoners, the women, remembered one Federal, "gave us a startling exhibition of their ability to blackguard us." Other Petersburg women displayed more restraint as they implored the Northern troops to share the captured foodstuffs. "Ladies begging me to give them something to eat," wrote Lieutenant Philip R. Woodcock of the 121st New York. "Had an entertaining time with them. Ladies fainted away which required my help."[32]

Petersburg's black population far exceeded the hungry women in their enthusiastic reception of the Union troops. "By the time we were fairly in the city streets, the colored brother (and sister) had caught on that something was up," wrote Captain James Deane of the 2nd Connecticut Heavy Artillery. "And what praise they did bestow on us—even my big awkward horse came in for a share of admiration." Another Connecticut soldier recalled that "as we entered the street there was a line of shanties inhabited by darkies who were on top of their houses and fences waving their hats shouting,'The Lord bless the Yankees, the Lord bless the Yankees.'" New Englander Michael Kelly remembered that "in Petersburg the colored portion of the people were wild with singing, praysing [sic] God for sending the Yankee hosts to free them, clap[p]ing hands, backs to the posts, houses rocking right & left singing hymns, shaking hands, pushing one another with joy. . . . We were overjoyed."[33]

As thrilled as were the blacks to see Hamblin's regiments, they reserved their warmest welcome for the United States Colored Troops of Brigadier General William Birney's Twenty-fifth Corps division. Elements of all three of Birney's brigades marched into the city as early as 6:00 a.m. "We were among the first troops to enter Petersburg," wrote Sergeant–Major William McCoslin of the 29th USCT, "and the orderly, well-behaved disposition of our command elicited the praise of our officers, and the universal commendations of the people, sobriety and decorum being the order of the day." The chaplain of the 127th USCT remembered that the black population thronged the streets and sang spirituals, celebrating their liberation with Biblical analogy.[34]

Colonel James Hubbard of the 2nd Connecticut Heavy Artillery temporarily assumed the duties of provost marshal in Petersburg and immediately took steps to secure the streets. One Confederate prisoner thought that "everything was in terrible commotion. Irish women, negro women, men, and boys were running hither and thither, some of them with slabs of bacon on their heads and others with sacks and bundles of various sorts and sizes." Councilman Collier credited Hamblin with establishing a reasonable degree of order in what could easily have devolved into anarchy. "Every effort was made by the Federal officers and troops to protect the persons and property of our citizens," explained the Councilman. "Safeguards were sent to every house for which they were asked . . . . Everything was at once systemized by the military, and comparative order and quiet reigned under martial law." "A little pillaging was done," confessed one Connecticut soldier, but soon enough, guards protected the stores and extinguished smoldering fires, a legacy of the night's destruction.[35]

Hamblin's regiments and Birney's black troops were not the only Federals to occupy Petersburg on the morning of April 3. Edwards assigned the 37th Massachusetts with their repeating weapons as guards while other soldiers from west of Petersburg drifted into the city, fulfilling a less formal role. Lieutenant Robert Pratt of the 5th Vermont accompanied Getty's divisional skirmishers and noted that the town's businesses were all deserted. "There was nothing strange about the appearance of this city," noted a member of the 10th Vermont, "except its remarkable silence. Stores, shops, and all public buildings were closed; nearly all the male inhabitants had fled with the army, save old men and negroes." Before long, however, some enterprising Northern merchants who had supplied the Union army behind the lines appeared to fill the void left by Petersburg's devastated commercial community.[36]

About 10:00 a.m., Hamblin received orders to return to his old camps south of town preparatory to rejoining the Sixth Corps, which had already departed toward the west. General Parke assumed responsibility for garrisoning Petersburg with one of his Ninth Corps divisions. He selected Willcox's troops for this task. Assisted by some borrowed cavalry, Willcox established firm control of the city's precincts, conducted a reconnaissance across the river to ascertain the route of Lee's retreat, and in the course of the next 48 hours snared more than 1,000 prisoners, 830 small arms, and seven battle flags. "In two hours," boasted Willcox, "Petersburg . . . was as quiet, and property and persons as safe as in Washington, an instance of discipline and good conduct on the part of the troops unsurpassed in military history."[37]

Roger A. Pryor proved to be the biggest catch netted during the Union occupation. As early as 7:30 a.m. April 3, Wright reported that Colonel Hamblin had interviewed Pryor, who confirmed the Confederate evacuation and testified that General Lee was "very bitter and disposed to fight it out to the last." Captain James Deane of the 2nd Connecticut Heavy Artillery claimed to have picked Pryor up and brought him to Hamblin, both for interrogation and as an informed source for offering "suggestions as to the placing of guards to prevent destruction of public property." Captain Butterfield reported having seen Pryor at Councilman William R. Mallory's home that morning, Pryor expressing relief that the war was almost over. Mrs. Pryor confirmed that three "German-looking soldiers" had barged into their home and marched her husband off for destinations unknown.[38]

Federal officers ranged across the entire city, motivated more by curiosity than by the expectation of unearthing a prominent prisoner. "Marks of bombardment were plentiful on all sides," recalled a New Yorker, "chimneys down, holes through brick walls and little drifts of debris, mortar and brick, in yard and street." Despite this damage, Captain Michael Kelly of the 2nd Connecticut Heavy Artillery liked what he saw of the conquered town. "This is a beautiful city, splendid and beautiful buildings composed of banks, halls, churches, court house, [and] many factories," wrote Kelly. "It contains about 20,000 inhabitants." Colonel Theodore Lyman of Meade's staff was less impressed. "The main part of the town resembles Salem [Massachusetts], very much, plus the southern shiftlessness and minus the Yankee thrift," he judged. Lyman, however, did admit that the houses on Market Street were "all very well kept and with nice trees." The New Englander next ventured to Blandford Cemetery and then to the Crater. He grew reflective about the empty fortifications whose former inhabitants had once visited mayhem and death upon the Union army, the scarred earth now mutely symbolic of the end of a long, sad chapter in a long, sad war. "Upon these parapets, whence the rifle-men have shot at each other, for nine long months, in heat and cold, by day and by night, you might now stand with impunity and overlook miles of deserted breastworks and covered ways!" wrote Lyman. "It was a sight only to be appreciated by those who have known the depression of waiting through summer, autumn and winter for so goodly an event!"[39]

Lyman and Meade completed their tour and returned to the heart of town, arriving at 21 South Market Street, the handsome, Italianate brick residence of Thomas Wallace, president of the Petersburg branch of the

Exchange Bank of Virginia. Here they encountered Grant and his staff, attracting a crowd of blacks attempting to sell the Union officers Confederate money! By this time, Grant had ordered most of his forces west from the Petersburg entrenchments as the first step of his campaign to prevent Lee from reaching Danville and Johnston's army in North Carolina. As early as 6:00 a.m., Wright had received instructions to travel west with his whole command, moving in the wake of the Second Corps. By 7:30 a.m., Wright had executed those orders, lacking only Hamblin's brigade, which was still prowling about Petersburg. Once orders arrived for Hamblin's regiments to join their Sixth Corps comrades, only Willcox's men remained in town, excluded from the campaign's final installment.[40]

General Meade left the Wallace House before President Lincoln arrived. The chief executive had departed City Point by rail about 9:00 a.m. accompanied by Admiral David Dixon Porter, naval Captain John S. Barnes, bodyguard William Crook, and Lincoln's son, Tad. The train chugged into Hancock Station, just west of Jerusalem Plank Road, about 10:00 a.m. Captain Robert Lincoln, the president's other surviving son, greeted his father on behalf of General Grant, on whose staff the young Lincoln now served. Grant had provided a small cavalry escort for the distinguished party as well as his own horse, Cincinnati, for Lincoln to ride. Once mounted, the entourage moved north along Jerusalem Plank Road, encountering Hamblin's men marching out of town to gather their knapsacks and rejoin their division. "We met President Lincoln, and Admiral Porter . . . and we cheered them," recorded Sergeant Edward S. Roberts of the 2nd Connecticut Heavy Artillery. Lincoln enjoyed the admiration of his troops much more than the quick tour he received of the Fort Mahone area, still littered as it was with unburied corpses from the previous day's combat. Crook, the President's bodyguard, noticed that Lincoln's face again "settled into its old lines of sadness" while viewing the carnage, and one of the cavalry escort thought he saw tears in the president's eyes.[41]

Lincoln arrived at the Wallace House sometime between 10:30 a.m. and 11:00 a.m. Grant and members of his staff had been seated on the front porch of the house, but upon the president's approach, Grant rose and descended the steps. Lincoln "dismounted in the street, and came in through the front gate with long and rapid strides, his face beaming with delight," remembered Colonel Horace Porter of Grant's staff. "He seized General Grant's hand as the general stepped forward to greet him, and stood shaking it for some time, and pouring out his thanks and congratulations with all the fervor of a heart which seemed overflowing with the fullness of joy. I doubt whether Mr. Lincoln ever experienced a happier moment in his life." The general responded warmly but with his usual reserve. "He didn't appear exultant, and he was as quiet as he had ever been," recalled Crook.[42]

Lincoln repeated his congratulations to Grant on his great victory of the previous day and said, one might imagine with a twinkle in the presidential eye, "Do you know, general, I have had a sort of sneaking idea for some days that you intended to do something like this." "Old Abe" then mentioned that he had guessed that William T. Sherman's army, now in North Carolina, would have played a role in the conquest of Petersburg. Grant replied that he had been anxious to arrange events so that the Army of the Potomac would earn the sole honor of defeating Lee: "I said to him that if the Western armies should be even upon the field, operating against Richmond and Lee, the credit would be given to them for the capture, by politicians and non-combatants from the section of country which those troops hailed from." Grant feared that intersectional bickering would result if the eastern army did not win its own major campaign. Lincoln allowed that he had never considered the question in that light, being so fully occupied with the notion of victory that he had not cared where that victory originated or with whom.

Lincoln spent the next half an hour discussing his views on reconstruction and his commitment to a lenient policy toward the vanquished South. While Colonel George H. Sharpe, the army's chief of military information, tamed a restless and hungry Tad with sandwiches, the two dignitaries remained in conversation, hoping to receive word that Richmond had fallen. During this historic meeting, Mr. Wallace emerged onto the porch and invited Grant and Lincoln to sit inside his home. Wallace had known Lincoln in earlier years when both were Whig politicians. Grant declined the gesture on the basis that he was smoking one of his ubiquitous cigars, so the famous pair conducted their entire meeting out of doors. After the passage of some 90 minutes, the two most important men of the Union cause concluded their discussions. "When our conversation was at an end Mr. Lincoln mounted his horse and started on his return to City Point, while I and my staff started to join the army, now a good many miles in advance," wrote Grant.[43]

Ironically, it was not long after Lincoln's departure that a dispatch arrived informing Grant that Union troops had entered Richmond. The general-in-chief took leave of Petersburg and, like his victorious army, moved west, shadowing the Army of Northern Virginia from the south side of the Appomattox River. Grant halted for the night at Sutherland Station, where he established his headquarters. There, he wrote Sherman a long dispatch, informing his friend that Petersburg and Richmond had fallen

Lieutenant Colonel Elisha Hunt Rhodes

Massachusetts MOLLUS Collection, Carlisle Barracks, Pennsylvania

and that the Confederates were moving west toward the Richmond &
Danville Railroad. "If Lee goes beyond Danville you will have to take care of
him with the force you have for a while," advised the general-in-chief. But
Grant hoped that he would reach the junction of the South Side and

Danville railroads at Burkeville ahead of his opponents, thus blocking the Confederates' direct path into North Carolina. In such an instance, Grant wrote, "there will be no special use in you going any farther into the interior of North Carolina. There is no contingency that I can see except my failure to secure Burkeville that will make it necessary for you to move on to the Roanoke [River] as proposed when you were here." Strategic considerations addressed, Grant allowed himself two concluding sentences reflecting his assessment of the achievement consummated on April 2: "This army has now won a most decisive victory and followed the enemy. This is all that it ever wanted to make it as good an army as ever fought a battle."[44]

> "We heard today that Richmond had been evacuated and is in flames. Well, let it burn, we do not want it. We are after Lee, and we are going to have him."

While Ulysses S. Grant wrote William T. Sherman, young Lieutenant Colonel Elisha Hunt Rhodes scribbled a few lines in his diary somewhere on Cox Road west of Petersburg. It was Rhodes who, as a captain, exactly four months earlier, had expressed regret at leaving the Shenandoah Valley for an uncertain future in the trenches at Petersburg. It had been Rhodes's hope then that his change of venue would hasten the end of the war, though in those cold, wet quarters south of Petersburg it was difficult to understand how. On the night of April 3, 1865, however, the picture had become clear. "We heard today that Richmond had been evacuated and is in flames," wrote the Rhode Islander. "Well, let it burn, we do not want it. We are after Lee, and we are going to have him." Rhodes was right. In six days, the incomparable Robert E. Lee would surrender his storied divisions at Appomattox Court House, and the collapse of other Southern armies and the Confederacy itself would quickly follow.[45]

* * *

The rifles and cannons at last fell silent. Over time, the meaning, rather than the conduct, of the Civil War would absorb the nation's attention, and the sacrifices of the men in blue and gray who fought the final battles at Petersburg—the engagements that brought an end to America's four-year nightmare—assumed a new significance. With every passing year, these farm boys from the Carolinas, store clerks from New

York, and their thousands of comrades, witnessed the continual transferal of their personal experiences to the repository of national memory, with the growing realization that their trials, triumphs, and tragedies marked an unprecedented milestone in the destiny of their common country.

Today the uniforms they wore, the equipment they used, the letters they wrote to loved ones, and the landscapes their lifeblood made sacred, comprise a unique inheritance to be treasured by modern Americans. It was their generation's story. It is our enduring, inescapable legacy.

NOTES

1. Wilcox, "Defence of Batteries Gregg and Whitworth, and the Evacuation of Petersburg," in *SHSP*, IV, 25; Wiley, ed., *Norfolk Blues*, 217.

2. Wiley, ed., *Norfolk Blues*, 217; John Herbert Claiborne, "Last Days of Lee and His Paladins," in George S. Bernard, ed., *War Talks of Confederate Veterans* (Petersburg, Va., 1892, reprint, Dayton, Oh., 1981), 240; Sara Agnes (Mrs. Roger A.) Pryor, *Reminiscences of Peace and War* (New York, 1904), 348. Tobacco valued at more than $1,000,000 went up in flames in Petersburg. See Henderson, *Petersburg in the Civil War*, 136.

3. Lee's orders in *OR*, pt. 3, 1379. The elements of Longstreet's, Hill's, and Gordon's troops mentioned in Lee's orders were south of the Appomattox, defending the Petersburg fortifications. Most of Major General William Mahone's Division of Hill's corps was in the Howlett Line in Chesterfield County. Lieutenant General Richard S. Ewell's command was north of the James River. For a detailed analysis of Lee's strategic problem, see Freeman, *R. E. Lee*, IV, 53-57. The Army of Northern Virginia's withdrawal from Petersburg and its entire campaign to Appomattox Court House is covered in maps and text by Christopher M. Calkins in *From Petersburg to Appomattox* (Farmville, Va., 1983, reprint, 1993).

4. *OR*, pt. 3, 1379. Lee had notified Breckinridge of the need to abandon Richmond on the morning of April 2. See Chapter Eight. For a graphic description of the evacuation of Richmond on the night of April 2, see Fergurson, *Ashes of Glory*, 322-336.

5. Charles F. Collier, "War Recollections. Story of the Evacuation of Petersburg, by an Eye-Witness, in *SHSP*, XXII, 70-71. Charles Fenton Collier had been elected several times to the Virginia House of Delegates and replaced Roger Pryor in the Confederate Congress in 1862. He served as Petersburg's mayor on two occasions after the war. D'Arcy W. Paul had been the president of the Petersburg Savings and Insurance Company and was a prominent citizen. He was also a leading Methodist clergyman. See Current, ed., *Encyclopedia of the Confederacy*, I,

367-368 on Collier, and Henderson, *Petersburg in the Civil War,* 17, 165, n. 12 on Paul.

6. Collier, "War Recollections," in *SHSP*, XXII, 71.

7. Collier, "War Recollections," in *SHSP*, XXII, 71; Freeman, *Lee's Lieutenants,* III, 684. Colonel Henry L. Abbot, commanding the siege train of Grant's forces, reported that the Federals captured 30 guns at Petersburg as well as 22 pieces "from their Appomattox water batteries; also 4 from their line in front of Bermuda Hundred." See *OR*, pt. 1, 663. The Campbell Bridge was located where in 2000 VA 36 carries traffic across the Appomattox River between Petersburg and Ettrick. The Pocohantas Bridge comports roughly to the location of the 2000 span linking Petersburg with Colonial Heights on U.S. 1 and 301. The Railroad Bridge, of course, served the Richmond & Petersburg Railroad.

8. Kimbrough, "From Petersburg to Hart's Island Prison," in *Confederate Veteran,* XXII, 499; Trudeau, *The Last Citadel,* 401; Henry Kyd Douglas, *I Rode With Stonewall* (Chapel Hill, N.C., 1940), 330.

9. I.[saac] G.[ordon] Bradwell, "Last Days of the Confederacy," in *Confederate Veteran,* XXIX, 57; James W. Albright, Diary, April 2, 1865, in James W. Albright Papers, SHC.

10. Henderson, *Petersburg in the Civil War,* 135; Pryor, *Reminiscences of Peace and War,* 350. Pryor had resigned his commission in the spring of 1863 and served as a special courier with the cavalry until his capture on November 27, 1864, near Petersburg. The house occupied by the Pryors probably stood at the southeast corner of Davis and Hinton streets. The dwelling is no longer extant, but an ornate iron fence likely associated with the structure is visible on the lot in 2000.

11. Bradwell, "Last Days of the Confederacy," in *Confederate Veteran,* XXIX, 57; James W. Albright, Diary, April 2, 1865, in James W. Albright Papers, SHC; J.[ames] E. Whitehorne, Diary, April 2, 1865, in J.E. Whitehorne Papers, SHC.

12. *OR*, pt. 1, 908, 957, 967; Stevens, "The Storming of the Lines of Petersburg," in *PMHSM*, VI, 434; Hazard Stevens Papers, LC. For detailed discussions of individual casualties in the Vermont Brigade, see Benedict, *Vermont in the Civil War,* I, 121-122, 151, 175, 202-203, 230, 604-605; II, 388.

13. *OR*, pt. 1, 912; unidentified newspaper clipping in the files of Petersburg National Battlefield; undated article c. July 1865, *Northampton* (Mass.) *Gazette & Courier,* in the Edward Payson Bridgeman Papers, SHSW.

14. *OR*, pt. 1, 908, 995.

15. Earl Fenner, *The History of Battery H First Regiment of Rhode Island Light Artillery in the War to Preserve the Union 1861-1865* (Providence, 1894), 66-67; *OR*, pt.1, 629, 908; Haines, *Fifteenth New Jersey,* 302-303. Seven officers commanding either brigades or regiments in the Sixth Corps became casualties during the fighting on April 2. They included Brigadier General Lewis A. Grant commanding Second Brigade, Second Division, and regimental commanders Lieutenant Colonel Gideon Clark of the 119th Pennsylvania, Lieutenant Colonel Charles Reen of the 98th Pennsylvania, Lieutenant Colonel Erastus D. Holt of the 49th New York, Lieutenant Colonel John W. Crosby of the 61st Pennsylvania, Major

Clifton K. Prentiss of the 6th Maryland, and Captain William D. Shellenberger of the 110th Ohio.

16. *OR*, pt. 1, 680, 1020, 1174.

17. Casualty figures for other battles were taken from *Civil War Sites Advisory Commission Report on the Nation's Civil War Battlefields, Technical Volume II: Battle Summaries* (Washington, 1998).

18. Bryce A. Suderow, "Confederate Strengths & Losses from March 25-April 9, 1865," typescript in the files of Pamplin Historical Park; Stevens, "Storming the Lines of Petersburg," in *PMHSM*, VI, 434; Trudeau, *The Last Citadel*, 377; Simon, ed., *The Papers of Ulysses S. Grant*, XIV, 323, 330. Grant told Sherman on April 3 that "We have about 12,000 prisoners. . . . From all causes I do not estimate his loss at less than 25,000." See *OR*, pt. 3, 510. The losses in Lane's, Thomas's, and MacRae's brigades during the Breakthrough were calculated by Dr. Arthur W. Bergeron, Jr., historian at Pamplin Historical Park, from the rosters of those units. Earl J. Hess in his study of MacRae's Brigade counted 669 losses in that unit on April 2, 657 of them prisoners, representing as much as 60% of the brigade's total strength. Of course, this number includes those lost during the Breakthrough, at Hatcher's Run, and at Sutherland Station. See "Lee's Tarheels," 728. Few days saw Lee's strength diminished by 10% or more. Sharpsburg in September 1862, May 3, 1863 at Chancellorsville, the final two days at Gettysburg, and May 12, 1864 at Spotsylvania come to mind in this necessarily imprecise exercise in casualty and strength calculation. During the retreat to Appomattox, of course, the Army of Northern Virginia hemorrhaged at an unprecedented rate.

19. Haines, *Fifteenth New Jersey*, 302; Wilbur Fisk to "Editor Freeman," April 9, 1865, in The Papers of Wilbur Fisk, LC.

20. Grant to Julia Dent Grant, April 2, 1865, and Grant to Col. T.[heodore] S. Bowers, City Point, April 2, 1865, in Simon, ed., *The Papers of Ulysses S. Grant*, XIV, 330, 327; Frank C. Morse to "My dear Nellie," April 4, 1865, in Frank C. Morse Papers, Massachusetts Historical Society; *OR*, pt. 3, 449.

21. *OR*, pt. 3, 450, 481-482.

22. *New York Times* reporter J. R. Hamilton, as quoted in Trudeau, *The Last Citadel*, 402.

23. *OR*, pt. 1, 1047.

24. *OR*, pt. 1, 1063, 1047; Oliver Edwards to G.N. Galloway, August 20, 1879, in unidentified newspaper clipping in the files of Petersburg National Battlefield.

25. *OR*, pt. 1, 1047-1048; William T. Wixcey, "First Flag in Petersburg," in *National Tribune*, July 4, 1907. As the editor of the *Bismarck Tribune* after the war, Lounsberry would scoop the world by sending to the *New York Herald* the first news of the battle at Little Big Horn. My thanks to Dr. Richard J. Sommers for this interesting aside. The Petersburg courthouse still stands in 2000 and retains its wartime appearance and elegance. Its silhouette serves as part of Petersburg's municipal logo.

26. *OR*, pt. 1, 1063, 1067; Giles A. Cooke, Diary, April 12, 1865, VHS. A recent account identifies the 200th Pennsylvania as leading McCalmont's brigade into the

city, but the colonel stated that "a line of skirmishers, under the command of Lieutenant-Colonel [Mish T.] Heintzelman, Two hundred and eighth Pennsylvania Volunteers, and Lieut. Col. L.[evi] A. Dodd, Two hundred and eleventh Pennsylvania Volunteers, preceded the column a few rods." See Calkins, *The Appomattox Campaign*, 65 and *OR*, pt. 1, 1067.

27. M.[iles] L. Butterfield, "Personal Reminiscences with the Sixth Corps, 1864-5," in *War Papers Being Papers Read Before the Commandery of the State of Wisconsin Military Order of the Loyal Legion of the United States*, IV, 88-89; *OR*, pt. 1, 913. Butterfield had been a member of the 5th Wisconsin.

28. Collier, "War Recollections," in *SHSP*, XXII, 71-72. According to Henderson, *Petersburg in the Civil War*, 43, "The Model Farm, about a mile west of the city limits, had been built before the war as an agricultural experiment station. There was a large barn, stables, and a double row of cottages framing an open space of approximately an acre."

29. Edwards, Memoir, Illinois State Historical Library; Edwards to G.N. Galloway, August 20, 1879, in unidentified newspaper clipping, Petersburg National Battlefield; Haines, *Fifteenth New Jersey*, 303; Bilby, *Three Rousing Cheers*, 241-242; Bowen, *History of the Thirty-Seventh Massachusetts*, 412.

30. Britton and Reed, eds., *To My Beloved Wife and Boy at Home*, 347; Trudeau, *The Last Citadel*, 406-407. The railroad bridge had been destroyed before the Federals arrived.

31. Kimbrough, "From Petersburg to Hart's Island Prison," in *Confederate Veteran*, XXII, 499-500.

32. Record Book, GAR Post 391, courtesy of David Ward, Lakeville, Connecticut; Best, *History of the 121st New York State Infantry*, 212-213; Philip R. Woodcock, Diary, April 3, 1865, David Ward Collection, Lakeville, Connecticut.

33. James Deane, "Following the Flag: The Three Years Story of a Veteran," ts., CHS; Roberts, "War Reminiscences," in *Connecticut Western News*, February 1, 1912; Michael Kelly, Diary, April 3, 1865, CHS.

34. Trudeau, *Like Men of War*, 428-429.

35. Roberts, "War Reminiscences," in *Connecticut Western News*, February 1, 1912; Kimbrough, "From Petersburg to Hart's Island Prison," in *Confederate Veteran*, XXII, 500; Collier, "War Recollections," in *SHSP*, XXII, 72.

36. Bowen, *History of the Thirty-Seventh Massachusetts*, 412; Journal of Lieutenant Robert Pratt, April 3, 1865, VTHS; Haynes, *A History of the Tenth Regiment, Vermont Volunteers*, 147.

37. *OR*, pt. 1, 932, 1019, 1040.

38. *OR*, pt. 3, 521; Deane, "Following the Flag: The Three Years Story of a Veteran," ts., CHS; Butterfield, "Personal Reminiscences With the Sixth Corps," 89; "The Sixth Corps," in *New York Herald*, April 7, 1865.

39. George L. Kilmer, "Petersburg: Historic Incidents of the Closing Days Before the City. Taking Possession." in *Philadelphia Weekly Times*, November 28, 1885; Michael Kelly, Diary, April 3, 1865, CHS; Agassiz, ed., *Meade's Headquarters*, 340-341.

40. Agassiz, ed., *Meade's Headquarters*, 341; Henderson, *Petersburg in the Civil War*, 137; Grant, *Personal Memoirs*, II, 459; *OR*, pt. 3, 520-521, 524. The Wallace House still stands as a private residence in 2000. Its modern address is 204 South Market Street.

41. Edward S. Roberts, Diary, April 3, 1865, CHS. An excellent account of Lincoln's visit to Petersburg may be found in Trudeau, *The Last Citadel*, 410-412.

42. Porter, *Campaigning With Grant*, 450; Crook quoted in Trudeau, *The Last Citadel*, 411; Henderson, *Petersburg in the Civil War*, 137.

43. Trudeau, *The Last Citadel*, 411-412; Porter, *Campaigning With Grant*, 450-452; Grant, *Personal Memoirs*, II, 459-461. One unsubstantiated version of this story has Lincoln requesting permission from Wallace's son to enter the house. "You are not going to let that man come into the house!" cried the youngster. "I think it would not do to try to stop a man from coming in who has fifty thousand men at his back," replied the elder Wallace, who then joined the two dignitaries on the porch. See William S. McFeely, *Grant, A Biography* (New York, 1981), 213-214. Sharpe's official title was deputy provost marshal general. See Edwin C. Fishel, *The Secret War for the Union* (Boston, 1996), 287, 647,n.57.

44. *OR*, pt. 3, 510.

45. Rhodes, ed., *All for the Union*, 227.

The Breakthrough in Perspective

T he charge of Major-Gen. Wright's veterans under cover of the darkness and mist, preceding the break of day, will forever live in history as one of the grandest and most sublime actions of the war," predicted Sergeant J. Newton Terrill of the 14th New Jersey. "When it is remembered how much depended on them, and what would have been the consequences if they failed, the country will treasure as household words the names of Wright, Getty, Seymour, Wheaton, and other generals who led the oft-tried but never defeated men of the 6th corps to victory, on the morning of Sunday, April 2d."[1]

Sergeant Terrill's forecast has hardly stood the test of time. The Sixth Corps Breakthrough of April 2, 1865 usually goes unmentioned in accounts of the Civil War, and the officers responsible for leading the attack are familiar only to serious students of the conflict. Although the battlefield itself retained much of its historical integrity over the decades, until the recent establishment of a private historical park (see Appendix), the woods and fields where the Sixth Corps achieved its great triumph remained unknown to all but a handful of relic hunters. In point of fact, neither the participants, the press, nor the rival armies even bestowed a traditional name upon the engagement. One will search in vain for a reference to the Battle of Boisseau Farm or the Battle of Duncan Road, and thus this author settled for promoting the battle's common reference as "the breakthrough" into a proper noun.

The surrender of Petersburg and the occupation of Richmond, of course, left the citizenry of the North elated, even if they possessed a less-than-perfect understanding of the military events that elicited such seminal consequences. "Your dispatch announcing the fall of Richmond and Petersburg and the rout of Lee's army has electrified our people," wrote Governor Richard J. Oglesby of Illinois in an April 3 telegram to the secretary of war. "We are firing salutes over the restoration of the Union, and the hearts of our people are throbbing in unison with the reverberation of Grant's artillery. God bless Abraham Lincoln, E. M.Stanton, U. S. Grant, W. T. Sherman, Phil Sheridan, and the soldiers of the Union!"[2]

One Maine soldier wrote that "the jubilee of this day, [April 3] or night, was one that a man sees only once in a lifetime." In Philadelphia, an observer called April 3 "the brightest day in the history of the war." The news of the collapse of Lee's Petersburg lines precipitated unfettered celebration in the City of Brotherly Love, according to this man: "We have all been intoxicated with excitement. . . . I never saw anything like the scene here. . . . Men, women, & children all . . . frantic with joy." The *Milwaukee Sentinel* described the victory on April 2 as "the most complete and triumphant achievement of the kind this war has witnessed," while President Lincoln's more measured evaluation simply referred to the Breakthrough and its immediate consequences as a "magnificent success."[3]

The soldiers and officers of the Army of the Potomac shared an appreciation for the magnitude of their victory on April 2. But in addition to recognizing the dimensions of their battlefield triumph, the troops also understood the tactical achievement that compelled the evacuation of Virginia's two most important cities.

As early as April 2 itself, General Grant referred to the fighting of that momentous day as "one of the greatest victories of the war." Army commander Meade would cite the "gallant" Sixth Corps Breakthrough as "the decisive movement of this campaign which resulted in the capture of the Army of Northern Virginia." Captain Charles G. Gould of the 5th Vermont, whose heroics earned him the probable distinction of being the first Yankee over the works that morning, simply said, "We have whipped the Rebels big." Brigadier General Lewis A. Grant, whose Vermonters led the Sixth Corps attack, characterized the capture of the Petersburg lines as "the breaking of the back bone of the rebellion."[4]

As is true for all bibliographical facets of the last days at Petersburg, the Confederate viewpoint is more elusive. A correspondent from the 6th Vermont wrote on April 3 that one Southern officer to whom he had been talking recognized that the fighting of the previous day "would do more towards ending the war than anything else." James Eldred Phillips of the

12th Virginia left a brief but poignant account of the day's activities in his diary: "The Army of Northern Va. got whip[p]ed badly. The killed & wounded was large. An awful sad day in the Army & I reckon all over the country."[5] Most Confederate participants, however, tended to include the Sixth Corps Breakthrough and its consequent fighting on April 2 as part of the tragic continuum that concluded one week later at Appomattox Court House.

Similarly, historians have viewed the final battles at Petersburg, from March 25 to April 2, through the lens of an inevitability that has robbed this bitter combat of much of its drama and significance. Naturally, the more pre-knowledge one brings to the end of the Petersburg Campaign, the less contingency remains. Hindsight informs us that by the spring of 1865, the outcome of the Civil War had been determined. All that remained was to "play out the string." This ahistorical approach ignores the perspective of the soldiers whose lives were at stake during the final weeks of the war. The men of the Sixth Corps, who executed the Breakthrough, did not consider themselves robotic pawns in the achievement of a foregone conclusion. The Breakthrough left an impression on the minds of these volunteers that would remain for the rest of their lives. Colonel J. Warren Keifer told his wife on the night of April 2 that he had seen "the most daring deeds of gallantry performed today that ever was performed by soldiers." Captain Charles E. Perkins of the 2nd Rhode Island felt that surviving "the storming of the works" to be able to see the surrender of Lee's army "cansels all of the hardships that I have seen and gorn (sic) through." For a soldier in the 2nd Vermont, the victory of April 2 relieved him from feeling inferior to the Union armies from the West: "We can . . . shake hands with our Western comrades without feeling reproached, as if our ill luck had left the burden of the work for them to do. We . . . have shown them that we can do something besides retreat, fight and die; we . . . have shown them that we can win victories as well."[6]

Perhaps a soldier from the 126th Ohio best characterized the "ever-memorable morning of April 2, 1865," not just for his comrades, but for all students of this campaign, including readers of this modest attempt to recount the events and context of the Breakthrough: "Never, to my dying day, shall I forget that sublime, fearful, magnificent spectacle, which no brush could paint or pen describe."[7]

Notes

1. Terrill, *Fourteenth Regiment, New Jersey Volunteers*, 120.

2. *OR*, pt. 3, 544.

3. Major John Mead Gould, *History of the First-Tenth-Twenty-ninth Maine Regiment* (Portland, Me., 1871), 571-572; Albert Harper to "My Dear Parents," April 3, 1865, in John Harper Papers, HSWP; "The Battle of Sunday: Highly Interesting Details of the Operations of the Sixth and Ninth Corps," in *Milwaukee Sentinel*, April 10, 1865; Basler, ed., *The Collected Works of Abraham Lincoln*, VIII, 383.

4. Simon, ed., *The Papers of Ulysses S. Grant*, XIV, 330; Anson, "Assault on the Lines of Petersburg," 97-98; Mark, *History of the 93rd Regiment*, 324; Benedict, *Vermont in the Civil War*, I, 600; Walker, "The Old Vermont Brigade," 207; Captain Charles G. Gould to "Dear Parents," April 4, 1865, in Captain Charles Gilbert Gould Collection, UVM; Lewis A. Grant to Hazard Stevens, December 31, 1883 and February 13, 1884, both in Hazard Stevens Papers, LC; Stevens, "The Storming of the Lines of Petersburg," in *PMHSM*, VI, 435.

5. George H. Mellish to "Dear Mother," April 3, 1865, in George H. Mellish Papers, HEH; James Eldred Phillips, Diary, April 2, 1865, VHS.

6. J. Warren Keifer to "My dear Wife," April 2, 1865, in Joseph Warren Keifer Papers, LC; Captain Charles E. Perkins to "Dear Sister," April 10, 1865, in *Civil War Times Illustrated* Collection, USAMHI; Wilbur Fisk to "Editor Freeman," April 9, 1865, in The Papers of Wilbur Fisk, LC. One Federal artillerist detected as early as April 18 that the Sixth Corps was not receiving due recognition for its achievements on April 2, and blamed the slight on a lack of competent correspondents reporting on the activities of the corps. See John R. Brinckle to "My Dear Sister," April 18, 1865, in John Rumsey Brinckle Papers, LC.

7. Rousculf, "Petersburg: The Part Taken in the Action of April 2, 1865 by the 126th Ohio," in *National Tribune*, June 18, 1891.

The Battlefields Today

Major Thomas J. Wooten, former commander of the Sharpshooter Battalion of James H. Lane's Brigade, addressed a group of Confederate veterans in Lumberton, North Carolina sometime after the war. Wooten waxed eloquent about the sacrifices of Lee's troops at Petersburg and then predicted, "when the future historian shall publish to the world the true story of the siege of Petersburg, men and women from every clime will make annual pilgrimage to those battle fields. . . ."[1]

Wooten's prophecy has been only partially realized. The Petersburg battlefields draw tens of thousands of visitors each year, but compared to the historic landscapes at Fredericksburg, Manassas, Antietam, or especially Gettysburg, attendance at Petersburg-area sites lags considerably behind. The reasons for this relative lack of interest in the Petersburg Campaign are many and varied. The literature on this critical chapter of Civil War military history is much less substantial than that for operations conducted earlier in the Eastern Theater. A handful of narratives treat various aspects of the nine-and-a-half months of action at Petersburg, but only one recent monograph attempts to cover the entire campaign. The definitive tactical history of operations at Petersburg—a monumental task, to be sure— remains to be written.[2]

Moreover, the roster of army leaders at Petersburg includes a number of comparatively obscure personalities whose late-war rise to power deprives them of a large reputation or a modern following. Unquestionably, Robert E. Lee and Ulysses S. Grant dominate the

Petersburg saga, but especially by 1865, many of the best-known subordinate commanders had either departed the military stage or had been reduced to a secondary role. On the Federal side, Winfield Scott Hancock, John Sedgwick, and (for better or worse) Ambrose E. Burnside had all been replaced by the relatively unknown Andrew Λ. Humphreys, Horatio G. Wright, and John G. Parke. Colorful or admired figures like Daniel E. Sickles, Philip Kearny, and John F. Reynolds had been disabled or killed.

Lee's army operated at Petersburg without some of the icons of the Confederacy. Thomas J. "Stonewall" Jackson had been dead more than a year when the campaign commenced. James Ewell Brown Stuart perished almost exactly a year after Jackson. James Longstreet missed the first four months of the Petersburg operations due to a wound sustained in May, and even upon his return, his diminished capacity reduced him to commanding the most static section of Lee's lines. Richard S. Ewell experienced what amounted to a nervous breakdown in May, and his subsequent role at Petersburg was even less visible than Longstreet's. Only Ambrose Powell Hill remained in command at the corps level throughout the entire last year of the war, but his poor health periodically compelled him to relinquish the field as well. This command attrition compromised the entire Army of Northern Virginia, so that by 1865 its table of organization contained numerous personalities whose popular images resonate but faintly to modern students of the war.

Interest in Petersburg's story also suffers from a misguided perception that events around the Cockade City possessed little influence on the outcome of the war. Moreover, some observers consider Lee's position around Petersburg and Richmond a fatal trap from which there was no practical escape, and believe that the gray chieftain conducted his campaign in a vacuum devoid of possible victory. The ill-conceived corollary to this notion is that the military action that did occur was tactically uninteresting—the sort of digging, sniping, and line extension that defines true siege warfare and stultifies most readers.[3]

Finally, Petersburg's southerly latitude effects its visibility and popularity as a tourist destination. Many battlefields and other historic sites lie between Southside Virginia and the population centers of the mid-Atlantic or northeastern states from where most of Virginia's out-of-state tourism originates. Travelers from New Jersey, Pennsylvania, and New York often run out of time or interest in touring Civil War battlefields long before their mini-vans reach the Appomattox River.

Happily for those who care about America's Civil War heritage, this limited attention to the Petersburg Campaign has little to do with the quality of the historic resources that remain to be explored. Petersburg is the Alaska of Civil War sites in the East. Nowhere is there a greater concentration of pristine but undeveloped battlefields than in Dinwiddie County, although how long that will remain true is difficult to foretell. Added to the well-preserved private sites around Petersburg is an excellent and growing infrastructure of publicly accessible landscapes that allow the history-seeker an opportunity to learn the Petersburg story on the very ground on which it was written.[4]

The flagship of the region's park lands is the Petersburg National Battlefield. This sprawling unit of the National Park system includes several distinct destinations ranging in size from hundreds of acres to small plots containing but a single monument. The main unit of the National Battlefield, located between Petersburg and Fort Lee on Virginia 36, features a visitor center with a comprehensive museum and an aging but emotionally effective audio-visual presentation covering the entire campaign. Adjacent to the visitor center, a short walk leads to Battery Five, scene of the dramatic fighting on June 15, 1864 which marked the beginning of the campaign. A four-and-one-half mile driving tour parallels the Union siege lines past Fort Stedman, ending at the Crater. A complete tour of this portion of the National Battlefield could take four hours or more, including sampling the handful of short, interesting walks available at many of the tour stops.

A few miles northeast of the Crater in Hopewell, the National Battlefield's City Point Unit preserves Union logistical headquarters at the breathtaking confluence of the James and Appomattox rivers. This small but fascinating reserve features the restored cabin used by Grant during the winter of 1864-1865 as well as exhibits in Appomattox Manor, a refurbished plantation home presiding over one of Virginia's most scenic settings.

The Union and Confederate earthworks that once comprised an unbroken ring around Petersburg still survive in surprising abundance. In addition to vestiges of fortifications passively preserved in the yards of Petersburg dwellings and deep within Dinwiddie woodlots, the City of Petersburg has inherited responsibility from the National Park Service for long stretches of breastworks south and west of town. A drive along Defense Road traces several miles of Lee's works west of Jerusalem Plank Road, today's Crater Road. Farther south, a similar experience may be enjoyed by touring Flank Road, a modern thoroughfare that follows the Ninth and Sixth Corps lines southwest of the historic city. Fort Wadsworth, a Union installation constructed to protect the Petersburg Railroad, remains under National Park Service jurisdiction in a splendid state of preservation.

The 1865 battlefields described in this book offer a fascinating day of touring, for those properly equipped with maps and a sense of adventure. Although most of the expansive Hatcher's Run battlefield is indiscernible amidst a featureless expanse of private land, a small section of the battlefield is preserved by the Civil War Preservation Trust, formerly the Association for the Preservation of Civil War Sites. Visitors to Hatcher's Run may read a state highway marker along Dabney Mill Road and then take a short walk to find a monument commemorating the death of Major General John Pegram, who perished near that spot on February 6.

The wide-ranging combat on March 25 resulting in the capture of miles of the Confederate picket line offers little to the modern tourist. None of the battlefield land is publicly accessible, and the eastern portion of the field has been obliterated by the recent construction of a steel recycling plant. Likewise, the scene of the March 27 Confederate attack at McIlwaine's Hill is inaccessible and devoid of historic ambience. Tourists may visit the Union forts from which the Sixth Corps attacks on March 25 originated along the western-most portion of Flank Road. These original emplacements are still owned by the National Park Service, although the National Battlefield offers sparse interpretation, and access into the overgrown forts is fraught with the usual reptilian, entomological, and botanical hazards typical of Virginia woodlands.

The Lewis Farm battlefield along Quaker Road retains a remarkable degree of visual integrity, despite being entirely privately owned. A lone highway marker along Quaker Road interprets the action. The story is better told at White Oak Road, where a joint project of the Civil War Preservation Trust and Dinwiddie County has resulted in an admirable, if diminutive battlefield park. A self-guided trail leads along a well-preserved portion of the Confederate line, and wayside markers describe the see-saw action that occurred there on March 31. Although there is nothing to attract a visitor to the Dinwiddie Court House battlefield, Five Forks is a different matter. Here, the National Park Service has acquired virtually the entire battlefield and is in the slow process of restoring it to its 1865 appearance. A modest visitor center at the crossroads is staffed during the busy travel season, and wayside exhibits allow a reasonably satisfying self-guided tour. Five Forks is a true gem in the rough and, if adequately funded for visitor development, could become one of the best military history sites in the country.

A new institution has protected the site of the Sixth Corps Breakthrough and developed it into an impressive visitor experience. Pamplin Historical Park & The National Museum of the Civil War Soldier is a privately owned preserve funded by the philanthropic descendants of the property's wartime owners. The action on April 2 is interpreted in a state-of-the-art museum styled the Battlefield Center, that places the Breakthrough in its historic context and features fiber-optics battle maps, interactive computers, an audio-visual program, and an impressive array of artifacts. Beginning just outside the building, a nearly two-mile system of walking trails leads visitors along incredibly well-preserved fortifications, interpreted with signs and recorded messages. About half of the original Confederate line breached by the Sixth Corps on the morning of April 2 is included within Pamplin Historical Park's 422 acres. The park also features Brigadier General Samuel McGowan's Tudor Hall headquarters and The National Museum of the Civil War Soldier. This outstanding new facility tells the story of the common soldier of the Civil War, including the tens of thousands of men in blue and gray who fought at Petersburg.

Little remains of the Sutherland Station battlefield, but visitors interested in this aspect of the campaign should visit Fork Inn, the old Sutherland home. The private owners of the house have converted it into an eclectic museum including exhibits about the April 2 battlefield. Farther east, near Pamplin Historical Park, a small marker in a patch of woods indicates the place where A. P. Hill fell while trying to reach the Century House, Henry Heth's headquarters, which still stands in private ownership off U.S. 1, Boydton Plank Road. The poignant setting for the afternoon action at Forts Gregg and Whitworth remains in a reasonably evocative condition, although their mutual relationship is now severed by the four lanes of Interstate 85. Fort Gregg is owned by the National Park Service, which has provided minimal visitor access to and interpretation of this Confederate bastion of bravery and fortitude. Fort Whitworth has been converted for recreational use by the administration at Central State Hospital which owns the fort, but both emplacements retain more than a little of their structural integrity.

The city of Petersburg is rife with reminders of the campaign. Visitor destinations include the Siege Museum on Bank Street, which tells the story of life in the Cockade City while the armies fought around it, and Old Blandford Church, now a unique Confederate Memorial featuring stained glass windows by Louis Comfort Tiffany. Inquiries at the city's Visitor Center in Old Town guide tourists to other historic structures which played a key role in the Petersburg story. General Lee's High Street headquarters still stand, as does the Wallace House, where Lincoln and Grant met on the morning of April 3. The beautiful courthouse downtown remains the city's most prized building, as it was in 1865 when Michiganders displayed the Union flag from its clock tower signaling the end of the long ordeal for soldiers and citizens alike.[5]

A complete tour of these Petersburg Campaign sites could easily absorb three days or more—as long as the most hardy battlefield tramper needs to cover Gettysburg or the Fredericksburg-area battlefields in detail. Moreover, with several potential exceptions, the odds are that at each of these places the visitor will find himself virtually or literally alone, distracted little by the presence of fellow tourists. But visitors to Petersburg's battlefields are never really alone. Stand at Fort Fisher at dawn, at Five Forks at sunset, or at the head of the ravine along the Breakthrough Trail at Pamplin Historical Park on a crisp winter day. Close your eyes. Listen. The men who wrote this story will be all around you.

NOTES

1. Charles Leonard Van Noppen, "Biographical Sketch of Thomas Jones Wooten," in Charles Leonard Van Noppen Papers, Duke.

2. Trudeau's *The Last Citadel* is the best single source on the entire campaign. A number of monographs deal with specific chapters of the campaign, by far the most impressive being Richard J. Sommers's *Richmond Redeemed*, which covers Grant's Fifth Offensive in September-October 1864. See the Bibliography for more secondary sources addressing the Petersburg Campaign. Petersburg has not been the subject of a popular film or television program, two key stimulators of visitation to historic sites.

3. Lee's ability to keep Grant at bay might have soured the Northern voters during the 1864 elections on the Lincoln administration and continued prosecution of the war. Union victories in Atlanta, the Shenandoah Valley, and at Mobile Bay offset Lee's apparent invincibility. Sherman's destruction of Lee's supply system in Georgia and the Carolinas and Sheridan's desolation of the Valley and the James River and Kanawha Canal sealed Lee's doom at Petersburg and Richmond.

4. Check the endnotes throughout the main text for information about the present condition and modern location of historic sites associated with the Petersburg Campaign.

5. For more information regarding visiting the historic sites in and around Petersburg, contact the following organizations: Petersburg National Battlefield, 1539 Hickory Hill Road, Petersburg, VA 23803; Pamplin Historical Park & The National Museum of the Civil War Soldier, 6125 Boydton Plank Road, Petersburg, VA 23803; City of Petersburg Visitor Center, 425 Cockade Alley, Petersburg, VA 23803 and City of Hopewell Visitor Center, 4100 Oaklawn Blvd., Hopewell, VA 23860.

Order of Battle

April 2, 1865

FEDERAL FORCES

Lt. Gen. Ulysses S. Grant

Army of the Potomac
Maj. Gen. George G. Meade

Second Army Corps
Maj. Gen. Andrew A. Humphreys

First Division
Brig. Gen. Nelson A. Miles

First Brigade
Col. George W. Scott
26th Michigan
5th New Hampshire
2nd New York Heavy Artillery
61st New York
81st Pennsylvania
140th Pennsylvania

Second Brigade
Col. Robert Nugent
28th Massachusetts (five companies)
63rd New York
69th New York
88th New York (five companies)
4th New York Heavy Artillery

Third Brigade
Colonel Henry J. Madill (w);
Col. Clinton D. MacDougall
7th New York
39th New York
52nd New York
111th New York
125th New York
126th New York (battalion)

Fourth Brigade
Col. John Ramsey
64th New York (battalion)
66th New York
53rd Pennsylvania
116th Pennsylvania
145th Pennsylvania
148th Pennsylvania
183rd Pennsylvania

Second Division
Brig. Gen. William Hays

First Brigade
Col. William Olmsted
19th Maine
19th Massachusetts
20th Massachusetts
7th Michigan
1st Minnesota (two companies)
59th New York
152nd New York
184th Pennsylvania
36th Wisconsin

Second Brigade
Col. James P. McIvor
8th New York Heavy Artillery
155th New York
164th New York
170th New York
182nd New York

Third Brigade
Brig. Gen. Thomas A. Smyth
14th Connecticut
1st Delaware
12th New Jersey
10th New York (battalion)
108th New York
4th Ohio (four companies)
69th Pennsylvania
106th Pennsylvania (three
companies)
7th West Virginia (four companies)

Unattached
2nd Company Minnesota
Sharpshooters

Third Division
Brig. Gen. Gershom Mott

First Brigade
Brig. Gen. Regis de Trobriand
20th Indiana
1st Maine Heavy Artillery
40th New York
73rd New York
86th New York
124th New York
99th Pennsylvania
110th Pennsylvania

Second Brigade
Brig. Gen. Byron R. Pierce
17th Maine
1st Massachusetts Heavy Artillery
5th Michigan
93rd New York
57th Pennsylvania
105th Pennsylvania
141st Pennsylvania

Third Brigade
Col. Robert McAllister
11th Massachusetts
7th New Jersey
8th New Jersey

11th New Jersey
120th New York

Artillery Brigade
Maj. John G. Hazard

Fifth Army Corps
Brig. Gen. Charles Griffin

First Division
Brig. Gen. Joseph J. Bartlett

First Brigade
Brig. Gen. Joshua L. Chamberlain
185th New York
198th Pennsylvania

Second Brigade
Col. Edgar M. Gregory
187th New York
188th New York
189th New York

Third Brigade
Col. Alfred L. Pearson
1st Maine Sharpshooters
20th Maine
32nd Massachusetts
1st Michigan
16th Michigan
83rd Pennsylvania
91st Pennsylvania
118th Pennsylvania
155th Pennsylvania

Second Division
Brig. Gen. Romeyn B. Ayres

First Brigade
Col. James G. Grindlay
5th New York (veteran)
15th New York Heavy Artillery
140th New York
146th New York

Second Brigade
Col. David L. Stanton
1st Maryland
4th Maryland
7th Maryland
8th Maryland

Third Brigade
Col. James Gwyn
3rd Delaware
4th Delaware
8th Delaware (three companies)
157th Pennsylvania (four companies)
190th Pennsylvania
191st Pennsylvania
210th Pennsylvania

Third Division
Brig. Gen. Samuel W. Crawford

First Brigade
Col. John A. Kellogg
91st New York
6th Wisconsin
7th Wisconsin

Second Brigade
Brig. Gen. Henry Baxter
16th Maine
39th Massachusetts
97th New York
11th Pennsylvania
107th Pennsylvania

Third Brigade
Col. Richard Coulter
94th New York
95th New York
147th New York
56th Pennsylvania
88th Pennsylvania
121st Pennsylvania
142nd Pennsylvania

Unattached
1st Battalion New York Sharpshooters

Artillery Brigade
Col. Charles S. Wainwright

Sixth Army Corps
Maj. Gen. Horatio G. Wright

First Division
Brig. Gen. Frank Wheaton

First Brigade
Col. William H. Penrose
1st & 4th New Jersey (battalion)
2nd New Jersey (two companies)
3rd New Jersey
10th New Jersey
15th New Jersey
40th New Jersey

Second Brigade
Col. Joseph E. Hamblin
2nd Connecticut Heavy Artillery
65th New York
121st New York
95th Pennsylvania

Third Brigade
Col. Oliver Edwards
37th Massachusetts
49th Pennsylvania
82nd Pennsylvania
119th Pennsylvania
2nd Rhode Island
5th Wisconsin

Second Division
Brig. Gen. George W. Getty

First Brigade
Col. James M. Warner
62nd New York
93rd Pennsylvania
98th Pennsylvania
102nd Pennsylvania
139th Pennsylvania

Second Brigade
Brig. Gen. Lewis A. Grant (w);
Lt. Col. Amasa S. Tracy;
Lt. Col. Charles Mundee
2nd Vermont
3rd Vermont
4th Vermont
5th Vermont
6th Vermont
1st Vermont Heavy Artillery

Third Brigade
Col. Thomas W. Hyde
1st Maine (veteran)
43rd New York (five companies)
49th New York (five companies)
77th New York (five companies)
122nd New York
61st Pennsylvania

Third Division
Brig. Gen. Truman Seymour

First Brigade
Col. William S. Truex
14th New Jersey
106th New York
151st New York (five companies)
87th Pennsylvania
10th Vermont

Second Brigade
Col. J. Warren Keifer
6th Maryland
9th New York Heavy Artillery
110th Ohio
122nd Ohio
126th Ohio
67th Pennsylvania
138th Pennsylvania

Artillery Brigade
Capt. Andrew Cowan

Ninth Army Corps
Maj. Gen. John G. Parke

First Division
Brig. Gen. Orlando B. Willcox

First Brigade
Col. Samuel Harriman
8th Michigan
27th Michigan
109th New York
51st Pennsylvania
37th Wisconsin
38th Wisconsin

Second Brigade
Lt. Col. Ralph Ely
1st Michigan Sharpshooters
2nd Michigan
20th Michigan
46th New York
60th Ohio
50th Pennsylvania

Third Brigade
Lt. Col. Gilbert P. Robinson;
Col. James Bintliff
3rd Maryland (four companies)
29th Massachusetts
57th Massachusetts
59th Massachusetts
18th New Hampshire
14th New York Heavy Artillery
100th Pennsylvania

Acting Engineers
17th Michigan

Second Division
Brig. Gen. Robert B. Potter (w);
Brig. Gen. Simon G. Griffin

First Brigade
Col. John I. Curtin
35th Massachusetts
36th Massachusetts

58th Massachusetts
39th New Jersey
51st New York
45th Pennsylvania
48th Pennsylvania
7th Rhode Island

Second Brigade
Brig. Gen. Simon G. Griffin;
Col. Walter Harriman
31st Maine
2nd Maryland
56th Massachusetts
6th New Hampshire
9th New Hampshire
11th New Hampshire
179th New York
186th New York
17th Vermont

Third Division
Brig. Gen. John F. Hartranft

First Brigade
Lt. Col. William H. H. McCall
200th Pennsylvania
208th Pennsylvania
209th Pennsylvania

Second Brigade
Col. Joseph A. Mathews
205th Pennsylvania
207th Pennsylvania
211th Pennsylvania

Artillery Brigade
Col. John C. Tidball

Independent Brigade
Col. Charles H. T. Collis
1st Massachusetts Cavalry (eight
companies)
61st Massachusetts
80th New York
68th Pennsylvania
114th Pennsylvania

Cavalry
Maj. Gen. Philip H. Sheridan

Army of the Shenandoah
Brig. Gen. Wesley Merritt

First Division
Brig. Gen. Thomas C. Devin

First Brigade
Col. Peter Stagg
1st Michigan
5th Michigan
6th Michigan
7th Michigan

Second Brigade
Col. Charles L. Fitzhugh
6th New York
9th New York
19th New York
17th Pennsylvania
20th Pennsylvania

Third (Reserve) Brigade
Brig. Gen. Alfred Gibbs
2nd Massachusetts
6th Pennsylvania (six companies)
1st United States
5th United States
6th United States

Third Division
Brig. Gen. George A. Custer

First Brigade
Col. Alexander C. M. Pennington
1st Connecticut
3rd New Jersey
2nd New York
2nd Ohio

Second Brigade
Col. William Wells
8th New York
15th New York
1st Vermont

Third Brigade
Col. Henry Capehart
1st New York (Lincoln)
1st West Virginia
2nd West Virginia
3rd West Virginia

**Second Division
(Army of the Potomac)**
Maj. Gen. George Crook

First Brigade
Brig. Gen. Henry E. Davies, Jr.
1st New Jersey
10th New York
24th New York
1st Pennsylvania (five companies)
2nd United States Artillery, Battery A

Second Brigade
Col. J. Irvin Gregg
4th Pennsylvania
8th Pennsylvania (eight companies)
16th Pennsylvania
21st Pennsylvania
1st US Artillery Batteries H and I

Third Brigade
Col. Charles H. Smith
1st Maine
2nd New York Mounted Rifles
6th Ohio
13th Ohio

Army of the James
Maj. Gen. Edward O. C. Ord

Defenses of Bermuda Hundred
Maj. Gen. George L. Hartsuff

Infantry Division
Maj. Gen. Edward Ferrero

First Brigade
Col. Gilbert H. McKibbin
41st New York
103rd New York
2nd Pennsylvania Heavy Artillery
104th Pennsylvania

Second Brigade
Col. George C. Kibbe
6th New York Heavy Artillery
10th New York Heavy Artillery

Artillery
Col. Henry L. Abbot

Separate Brigade
Brig. Gen. Joseph B. Carr
38th New Jersey
20th New York Cavalry, Cos. D and F
16th New York Heavy
Artillery, Cos. E and H
184th New York
1st U.S. Colored Cavalry, Cos. E and I
3rd Pennsylvania Heavy Artillery
(detachment)

Twenty-Fourth Army Corps
Maj. Gen. John Gibbon

First Division
Brig. Gen. Robert S. Foster

First Brigade
Col. Thomas O. Osborn
39th Illinois
62nd Ohio
67th Ohio
85th Pennsylvania
199th Pennsylvania

Third Brigade
Col. George B. Dandy
10th Connecticut

11th Maine
24th Massachusetts
100th New York
206th Pennsylvania

Fourth Brigade
Col. Harrison S. Fairchild
8th Maine
89th New York
148th New York
158th New York
55th Pennsylvania

Third Division
Brig. Gen. Charles Devens

First Brigade
Col. Edward H. Ripley
11th Connecticut
13th New Hampshire
81st New York
98th New York
139th New York
19th Wisconsin

Second Brigade
Col. Michael T. Donohoe
8th Connecticut
5th Maryland
10th New Hampshire
12th New Hampshire
96th New York
118th New York
9th Vermont

Third Brigade
Col. Samuel H. Roberts
21st Connecticut
40th Massachusetts
2nd New Hampshire
58th Pennsylvania
188th Pennsylvania

Independent Division
Brig. Gen. John W. Turner

First Brigade
Lt. Col. Andrew Potter
34th Massachusetts
116th Ohio
123rd Ohio

Second Brigade
Col. William B. Curtis
23rd Illinois
54th Pennsylvania
12th West Virginia

Third Brigade
Brig. Gen. Thomas M. Harris
10th West Virginia
11th West Virginia
15th West Virginia

Artillery
Maj. Charles C. Abell

Twenty-Fifth Army Corps
Maj. Gen. Godfrey Weitzel

First Division
Brig. Gen. August V. Kautz

First Brigade
Col. Alonzo G. Draper
22nd USCT
36th USCT
38th USCT
118th USCT

Second Brigade
Brig. Gen. Edward A. Wild
29th Connecticut
9th USCT
115th USCT
117th USCT

Third Brigade
Brig. Gen. Henry G. Thomas
19th USCT
23rd USCT

43rd USCT
114th USCT

Attached Brigade
Col. Charles S. Russell
10th USCT
28th USCT

Second Division
Brig. Gen. William Birney

First Brigade
Col. James Shaw, Jr.
7th USCT
109th USCT
116th USCT

Second Brigade
Col. Ulysses Doubleday
8th USCT
41st USCT
45th USCT
127th USCT

Third Brigade
Col. William W. Woodward
29th USCT
31st USCT

Artillery Brigade
Capt. Loomis L. Langdon

Cavalry Division
Brig. Gen. Ranald S. Mackenzie

First Brigade
Col. Robert M. West

Second Brigade
Col. Andrew W. Evans

*   *   *

CONFEDERATE FORCES

Gen. Robert E. Lee

Army of Northern Virginia
Gen. Robert E. Lee

First Army Corps
Lt. Gen. James Longstreet

Pickett's Division
Maj. Gen. George E. Pickett

Steuart's Brigade
Brig. Gen. George H. Steuart
9th Virginia
14th Virginia
38th Virginia
53rd Virginia
57th Virginia

Corse's Brigade
Brig. Gen. Montgomery D. Corse
15th Virginia
17th Virginia
29th Virginia
30th Virginia
32nd Virginia

Hunton's Brigade
Brig. Gen. Eppa Hunton
8th Virginia
18th Virginia
19th Virginia
28th Virginia
56th Virginia

Terry's Brigade
Maj. William W. Bentley
1st Virginia
3rd Virginia
7th Virginia
11th Virginia
24th Virginia

Field's Division
Maj. Gen. Charles W. Field

Perry's Brigade
Brig. Gen. William F. Perry
4th Alabama
15th Alabama
44th Alabama
47th Alabama
48th Alabama

Anderson's Brigade
Brig. Gen. George T. Anderson
7th Georgia
8th Georgia
9th Georgia
11th Georgia
59th Georgia

Benning's Brigade
Brig. Gen. Henry L. Benning
2nd Georgia
15th Georgia
17th Georgia
20th Georgia

Gregg's Brigade
Col. Robert M. Powell
3rd Arkansas
1st Texas
4th Texas
5th Texas

Bratton's Brigade
Brig. Gen. John Bratton
1st South Carolina
5th South Carolina
6th South Carolina
2nd South Carolina (Rifles)
Palmetto State Sharpshooters

Kershaw's Division
Maj. Gen. Joseph B. Kershaw

Du Bose's Brigade
Brig. Gen. Dudley M. Du Bose

16th Georgia
18th Georgia
24th Georgia
3rd Georgia Battalion Sharpshooters
Cobb's Legion
Phillips Legion

Humphreys's Brigade
Col. William H. Fitz Gerald
13th Mississippi
17th Mississippi
18th Mississippi
21st Mississippi

Simms's Brigade
Brig. Gen. James P. Simms
10th Georgia
50th Georgia
51st Georgia
53rd Georgia

Artillery
Brig. Gen. Edward P. Alexander

Haskell's Battalion
Lt. Col. John C. Haskell

Huger's Battalion
Maj. Tyler C. Jordan

Second Army Corps
Maj. Gen. John B. Gordon

Grimes's Division
Maj. Gen. Bryan Grimes

Battle's Brigade
Col. Edwin L. Hobson
3rd Alabama
5th Alabama
6th Alabama
12th Alabama
61st Alabama

Grimes's Brigade
Col. David G. Cowand
32nd North Carolina
43rd North Carolina
53rd North Carolina
2nd North Carolina Battalion

Cox's Brigade
Brig. Gen. William R. Cox
1st North Carolina
2nd North Carolina
3rd North Carolina
4th North Carolina
14th North Carolina
30th North Carolina

Cook's Brigade
Col. Edwin A. Nash
4th Georgia
12th Georgia
21st Georgia
44th Georgia

Archer's Battalion
Lt. Col. Fletcher Archer
3rd Battalion Virginia Reserves
44th Virginia Battalion

Early's Division
Brig. Gen. James A. Walker

Johnston's Brigade
Col. John W. Lea
5th North Carolina
12th North Carolina
20th North Carolina
23rd North Carolina
1st North Carolina Battalion,
Sharpshooters

Lewis's Brigade
Capt. John Beard
6th North Carolina
21st North Carolina
54th North Carolina
57th North Carolina

Walker's Brigade
Maj. Henry Kyd Douglas
13th Virginia
31st Virginia
49th Virginia
52nd Virginia
58th Virginia

Gordon's Division
Brig. Gen. Clement A. Evans

Evans's Brigade
Col. John H. Lowe
13th Georgia
26th Georgia
31st Georgia
38th Georgia
60th Georgia
61st Georgia
9th Georgia Battalion Artillery
12th Georgia Battalion Artillery
18th Georgia Battalion Infantry

Terry's Brigade
Col. Titus V. Williams
2nd Virginia
4th Virginia
5th Virginia
10th Virginia
21st Virginia
23rd Virginia
25th Virginia
27th Virginia
33rd Virginia
37th Virginia
42nd Virginia
44th Virginia
48th Virginia

York's Brigade
Col. Eugene Waggaman
1st Louisiana
2nd Louisiana
5th Louisiana
6th Louisiana
7th Louisiana

8th Louisiana
9th Louisiana
10th Louisiana
14th Louisiana
15th Louisiana

Artillery
Brig. Gen. Armistead L. Long
Braxton's Battalion
Cutshaw's Battalion
Johnson's Battalion
Lightfoot's Battalion
Hardaway's Battalion
Stark's Battalion

Third Army Corps
Lt. Gen. Ambrose Powell Hill (k);
Maj. Gen. Henry Heth

Heth's Division
Maj. Gen. Henry Heth;
Brig. Gen. John R. Cooke

Davis's Brigade
Col. Andrew M. Nelson
1st Confederate Battalion
2nd Mississippi
11th Mississippi
26th Mississippi
42nd Mississippi

Cooke's Brigade
Brig. Gen. John R. Cooke
15th North Carolina
27th North Carolina
46th North Carolina
48th North Carolina
55th North Carolina

MacRae's Brigade
Brig. Gen. William MacRae
11th North Carolina
26th North Carolina
44th North Carolina
47th North Carolina
52nd North Carolina

McComb's Brigade
Brig. Gen. William McComb
2nd Maryland Battalion
1st Tennessee (Provisional Army)
7th Tennessee
14th Tennessee
17th Tennessee
23rd Tennessee
25th Tennessee
44th Tennessee
63rd Tennessee

Wilcox's Division
Maj. Gen. Cadmus M. Wilcox

Thomas's Brigade
Brig. Gen. Edward L. Thomas
14th Georgia
35th Georgia
45th Georgia
49th Georgia

Lane's Brigade
Brig. Gen. James H. Lane
18th North Carolina
28th North Carolina
33rd North Carolina
37th North Carolina

McGowan's Brigade
Brig. Gen. Samuel McGowan
1st South Carolina (Provisional Army)
12th South Carolina
13th South Carolina
14th South Carolina
Orr's Rifles

Scales's Brigade
Col. Joseph H. Hyman
13th North Carolina
16th North Carolina
22nd North Carolina
34th North Carolina
38th North Carolina

Mahone's Division
Maj. Gen. William Mahone

Forney's Brigade
Brig. Gen. William H. Forney
8th Alabama
9th Alabama
10th Alabama
11th Alabama
13th Alabama
14th Alabama

Weisiger's Brigade
Brig. Gen. David A. Weisiger
6th Virginia
12th Virginia
16th Virginia
41st Virginia
61st Virginia

Harris's Brigade
Brig. Gen. Nathaniel H. Harris
12th Mississippi
16th Mississippi
19th Mississippi
48th Mississippi

Sorrel's Brigade
Col. George E. Taylor
3rd Georgia
22nd Georgia
48th Georgia
64th Georgia
2nd Georgia Battalion
10th Georgia Battalion

Finegan's Brigade
Col. David Lang
2nd Florida
5th Florida
8th Florida
9th Florida
10th Florida
11th Florida

Artillery
Brig. Gen. Lindsay Walker
McIntosh's Battalion
Poague's Battalion
Thirteenth Virginia Battalion
Richardson's Battalion
Pegram's Battalion

Anderson's Corps
Lt. Gen. Richard H. Anderson

Johnson's Division
Maj. Gen. Bushrod R. Johnson

Wise's Brigade
Brig. Gen. Henry A. Wise
26th Virginia
34th Virginia
46th Virginia
59th Virginia

Wallace's Brigade
Brig. Gen. William H. Wallace
17th South Carolina
18th South Carolina
22nd South Carolina
23rd South Carolina
26th South Carolina
Holcombe Legion

Moody's Brigade
Brig. Gen. Young M. Moody
41st Alabama
43rd Alabama
59th Alabama
60th Alabama
23rd Alabama Battalion

Ransom's Brigade
Brig. Gen. Matthew W. Ransom
24th North Carolina
25th North Carolina
35th North Carolina
49th North Carolina
56th North Carolina

Artillery
Col. Hilary P. Jones
Blount's Battalion
Stribling's Battalion
Coit's Battalion
Smith's Battalion

Cavalry Corps
Maj. Gen. Fitzhugh Lee

Fitzhugh Lee's Division
Brig. Gen. Thomas T. Munford

Payne's Brigade
Col. Reuben B. Boston
5th Virginia
6th Virginia
8th Virginia
36th Virginia Battalion

Munford's Brigade
Brig. Gen. Thomas T. Munford
1st Virginia
2nd Virginia
3rd Virginia
4th Virginia

Gary's Brigade
Brig. Gen. Martin W. Gary
7th Georgia
7th South Carolina
Hampton Legion
24th Virginia

W. H. F. Lee's Division
Maj. Gen. William H. Fitzhugh Lee

Barringer's Brigade
Brig. Gen. Rufus Barringer
1st North Carolina
2nd North Carolina
3rd North Carolina
4th North Carolina

Beale's Brigade
Capt. Samuel H. Burt
9th Virginia
10th Virginia
13th Virginia
14th Virginia

Roberts's Brigade
Brig. Gen. William P. Roberts
4th North Carolina
16th North Carolina Battalion

Rosser's Division
Maj. Gen. Thomas L. Rosser

Dearing's Brigade
Brig. Gen. James Dearing
7th Virginia
11th Virginia
12th Virginia
35th Virginia Battalion

McCausland's Brigade
16th Virginia
17th Virginia
21st Virginia
22nd Virginia

Artillery
Lt. Col. Preston Chew
Breathed's Battalion
Chew's Battalion

Bibliography

MANUSCRIPTS

Auburn University Libraries, Special Collections, Auburn, Alabama
James Lane Collection
Benjamin Mason Confederate Letters

Carroll County Historical Society, Westminster, Maryland
Lewis Rosenburger Diary

Gregory A. Coco Collection, Bendersville, Pennsylvania
Alonzo Rufus Case Diary

Connecticut Historical Society, Hartford
James Deane, "Following the Flag: The Three Years' Story of a Veteran 1862-1865."
Michael Kelly Diary
Edward S. Roberts Diary

Cornell University, Rare and Manuscript Collections, University Library, Ithaca, New York
John J. Ingraham Papers
Wall Family Papers

Duke University, William R. Perkins Library, Durham, North Carolina
John G. Barnard Papers
John Franklin Heitman Papers
Patterson-Cavin Family Papers
Charles Leonard Van Noppen Papers
Walter Wallace Smith Papers
John C. Warlick Letters

Georgia Department of Archives and History, Atlanta
Civil War Miscellany-Personal Papers
David S. Redding Papers

Historical Society of Western Pennsylvania, Pittsburgh
John Harper Papers

Henry E. Huntington Library, San Marino, California
George H. Mellish Papers

Illinois State Historical Library, Springfield
Oliver Edwards Memoir

Library of Congress, Manuscripts Division, Washington
John Rumsey Brinckle Papers
Wilbur Fisk Papers
Lemuel Thomas Foote Papers
Gibson-Getty-McClure Families Papers
George W. Getty Papers
Hazard Stevens Journal
Joseph Warren Keifer Papers
Lothrup Lincoln Lewis Collection
Frank R. McCoy Papers
Montgomery Cunningham Meigs Papers
Winthrop Henry Phelps Papers
Edwin M. Stanton Papers
Hazard Stevens Family Papers
Cadmus Marcellus Wilcox Papers

Library of Virginia, Richmond
William Mahone Papers-Personal Papers Collection
Nathaniel Harris Letter, August 2, 1866

Maine Historical Society, Portland
William Bryant Adams Papers

Jack Mandaville Collection, Maple Grove, Minnesota
Charles G. Gould to Robert Pratt, July 7, 1882, ts.

Massachusetts Historical Society, Boston
Frank C. Morse Papers

Minnesota Historical Society, St. Paul
John H. Macomber Papers

Museum of the Confederacy, Eleanor S. Brockenbrough Library, Richmond, Virginia
William McComb, "Recollections of 1864-1865."
Joseph Mullen, Jr. Diary
Papers Presented by M.[ark] Newman to The Committee of Ladies in Savannah Georgia, January 28, 1896
William Nelson Pendleton, Order Book, June 5, 1862-April 1, 1865

National Archives, Washington
Book Records of Volunteer Union Organizations, Record Group 94
Descriptive List and Letter Book, 15th New Jersey Infantry
Descriptive List and Order Book, 5th Wisconsin Infantry
Morning Report Book, 40th New Jersey Volunteers
Compiled Service Records of Confederate General and Staff Officers, and Nonregimental Enlisted Men, Record Group 94
Microcopy No. 331, Roll 121
Microcopy 321, Roll 16

Compiled Service Records of Federal Officers, Record Group 94
Military Record of Clifton K. Prentiss, Microcopy 384, Roll 155
Correspondence of the Records and Pension Office

Inspection Reports and Related Records Received by the Inspection Branch in the Confederate Adjutant and Inspector General's Office, Inspection Report P, Record Group 109
No. 37, Inclosure 46, Microcopy 935, Roll 12, 14, Inspection Reports for Wilcox's Division, November 30, 1864, December 31,1864
No. 64, Inclosure 3, Microcopy 935, Roll 16, Inspection Report for MacRae's Brigade, February 27, 1865
No. 64, Inclosure 9, Microcopy 935, Rolls 14-16, Inspection Reports for McGowan's Brigade, December 27, 1864, January 27, 1865, February 28, 1865
No. 64, Inclosure 11, Microcopy 935, Roll 16, Inspection Report for Lane's Brigade, February 28, 1865

Inspection Reports and Related Records, Record Group 94
Inspection Report of Maj. Stevens, 2d Div., 6th Corps, February 7, 1865, 3rd Brigade

Bushrod Rust Johnson Papers
Letters Received Enlisted Branch, Sixth Army Corps, 1862-1865, Record Group 94
Letters Received, Volunteer Service Branch, Record Group 94
Letters Received, Sixth Army Corps, 1862-1865, Record Group 393
Letters Sent Book, Sixth Army Corps, 1864-1865, Record Group 393

Regimental Order Books, Record Group 393
37th Massachusetts Infantry, 1862-1865
122nd New York Infantry, 1862-1865
Circular, Headquarters 3rd B[riga]de., 1st Div[ision], 6th A.[rmy] C.[orps], January 9., 1865

New Jersey Historical Society, Newark
Franklin Jones Papers

New-York Historical Society, New York
Southard Family Correspondence

Norfolk Public Library, Norfolk, Virginia
John Walters Diary

North Carolina Department of Archives and History, Raleigh
Isaac Spencer London Collection
Noah Collins Memoir

Military Collections
Hugh Torrence Memoir

Ohio Historical Society, Archives/Library Division, Columbus
William McVey Papers

Pamplin Historical Park, Dinwiddie County, Virginia

Ts. letters of Edward A. [last name unknown] of the 37th Massachusetts
Lorenzo Barnhart,"Reminiscences of the Rebellion."
Bearss, Edwin C. "The Sixth Corps Scores A Breakthrough." Unpublished report prepared for the National Park Service
Resolutions Adopted By McGowan's Brigade, South Carolina Volunteers
Riley, John Y. "Fort Gregg. Thermopylae of the South." unidentified newspaper clipping
Spencer Repeating Rifle Catalog, n.p., n.d.
Suderow, Bryce A. "Confederate Strengths and Losses from March 25-April 9, 1865." t.s., May 1987, revised Sept. 29, 1991.

Pennsylvania Historical and Museum Commission, Harrisburg

Schaffner Family Collection
Civil War Papers

Petersburg National Battlefield, Petersburg, Virginia

Oliver Edwards to G.N. Galloway, August 20, 1879, unidentified newspaper clipping

Fred C. Robinson Collection, Midlothian, Virginia

Captain John C. Robinson Papers

Ed Root Collection, Coopersburg, Pennsylvania

Peter Cullen to The Honorable Mr. [Newton D.] Baker, Secretary of War,   October 24, 1916.

Rutgers University Library, New Brunswick, New Jersey

James Denton Letters

State Historical Society of Wisconsin, Madison

Edward Payson Bridgman Papers
George W. Buffum Letters, 1864-1865
William L. Phillips Letters

United States Army Military History Institute, Carlisle Barracks, Pennsylvania

Civil War Miscellaneous Collection
Corporal John Preston Campbell Papers
Grayson M. Eichelberger Memoir
Dayton E. Flint Papers

Civil War Times Illustrated Collection
Hance Morgan Diary

Thomas Clemens Collection
Samuel Z. Ammen, "Maryland Troops in the Confederate Army."

Stuart Goldman Collection
Charles C. Morey Papers

Harrisburg Civil War Round Table Collection,
Gregory A. Coco Collection

Capt. John Hardeman, Letter
Henry J. Madill, Diary
Siebert Family Papers
Sgt. Aldus Jewell Papers

Northwest Corner Civil War Round Table Collection
Philip R. Woodcock Diary
Theodore F. Vaill Papers

Murray G. Smith Collection
Charles R. Paul Papers
The John Wesley Turner Papers

University of Maine, Raymond H. Fogler Library, Orono
Cary Family Papers

University of Michigan, William L. Clements Library, Ann Arbor
   James S. Schoff Collection
Anonymous Union Spy Intelligence Journal, November 2, 1864-March 30, 1865
George Henry Bates Letters
Isaac O. Best, "The Siege and Capture of Petersburg."

University of North Carolina,Southern Historical Collection, Chapel Hill
James W. Albright Papers

   J.[acob] S. Bartlett Papers
"The War Record of J.S. Bartlett. A Private in Company E-First Regiment of North Carolina
Volunteers From Yorktown to the Appomatox"

Berry G. Benson Papers
Willis G. Briggs Papers
Meeta Rhodes Armistead Capehart Papers
William H. Forney Papers
Fries and Schaffner Papers
James A. Graham Papers
William A. Graham Papers
Lenoir Family Papers
Julius A. Lineback Papers and Diary

Breckinridge Long Papers
William S. Long Memoir

William Nelson Pendleton Papers
Leonidas La Fayette Polk Papers
Proffit Family Papers

Westwood A. Todd Papers
"Reminiscences of the War Between the States April 1861-July 1865."

Samuel Hoey Walkup Papers
J.[ames]E. Whitehorn Papers

University of South Carolina, South Caroliniana Library, Columbia
Samuel Lewers Dorroh Papers
Hammond, Bryan, and Cummings Family Papers
Samuel McGowan Papers
Templeton Family Papers
Andrew Bowie Wardlaw Papers

University of Southern Mississippi, McCain Library and Archives, Hattiesburg
Andrew and Mary Burwell Letters

University of Vermont, Bailey-Howe Library, Burlington
George G.[renville] Benedict Papers
Captain Charles Gilbert Gould Collection
Joseph Case Rutherford Papers

University of Virginia, Alderman Library, Charlottesville
Heth-Selden Papers
Henry Heth Memoir

University of Wisconsin, The Golda Meir Library, Milwaukee
Warren Williams Papers

Vermont Historical Society, Montpelier
Merritt Barber to General T.S. Peck, November 4, 1892
George J. Howard Letters
Lieutenant Robert Pratt Papers
Sherman/Safford Family Papers

   Oscar E. Waite Papers
"Three Years With the Tenth Vermont."

Virginia Historical Society, Richmond
Giles Buckner Cooke Diary
Elizabeth Lewis Selden Dimmock Papers
Augustus Evander Floyd Memoir
Robert Edward Lee Papers

   Lee Headquarters Papers
Erson, Lt. Col. Eric. "Report of Operations of 2 Regts. of MacRae's Brigade." April 11, 1865.

St. Paul's Church Vestry Book

David Ward Collection, Lakeville, Connecticut
GAR Record Book, CJ Powers Post 391
Philip R. Woodcock, Diary

Winthrop University, Dacus Library, Rock Hill, South Carolina
William J. Miller Memoir

Yale University Library, New Haven, Connecticut
  Bernhard Knollenberg Collection
    Homer Curtis Letters

NEWSPAPERS

Cincinnati Daily Gazette
Connecticut Western News (Canaan)
Lebanon (Tenn.) *Democrat*
The Medium (Abbeville, S.C.)
Milwaukee Sentinel
New Orleans Times-Picayune
New York Herald
Philadelphia Weekly Press
Philadelphia Weekly Times
Portsmouth (N.H.) *Daily Morning Chronicle*
Richmond Dispatch
Westminster (Md.) *Sentinel*
The Winsted (Conn.) *Herald*

OFFICIAL PUBLICATIONS

Barnard, Brevet Major General J.[ohn] G. *A Report on the Defenses of Washington to the Chief of Engineers, U.S. Army.* Washington: U.S. Government Printing Office, 1871.
Civil War Sites Advisory Commission Report on the Nation's Civil War Battlefields Technical Volume II: Battle Summaries. Washington: The Secretary of the Interior, 1998.
Lykes, Richard Wayne. *Campaign for Petersburg.* Washington: U.S. Government Printing Office, 1970.
The War of the Rebellion: A Compilation of the Official Records of the Union and Confederate Armies. 130 vols. Washington: U.S. Government Printing Office, 1880-1901.

ADDRESSES, ARTICLES, AND ESSAYS

Adams, Ida Bright, ed. "The Civil War Letters of James Rush Holmes." *The Western Pennsylvania Historical Magazine*, 44, no. 2 (June 1961): 105-127.
Anson, Bvt. Major Charles H. "Assault on the Lines of Petersburg, April 2, 1865." In *War Papers Being Papers Read Before the Commandery of the State of Wisconsin Military Order of the Loyal Legion of the United States.* 4 vols. Milwaukee: Burdick, Armitage & Allen, 1891-1914, 1: 85-98. Reprint, Wilmington, N.C.: Broadfoot Publishing Company, 1993.
Barnes, C.[lark] F. "Petersburg. A Boy's Experience in the Terrible Charge of April 2, 1865." *National Tribune*, July 27, 1883.
Bartlett, Napier. "The Defence of Ft. Gregg." *Southern Historical Society Papers*, 3 (1875): 82-86.
"Battle at Fort Gregg." *Southern Historical Society Papers*, 28 (1900): 265-267.
Bennett, William. "Fort Gregg." *National Tribune*, May 12, 1904.
Bowen, James L. "Lee in the Toils." *Philadelphia Weekly Times*, May 2, 1885.
Bradwell, I.[saac] G.[ordon], "Holding the Lines at Petersburg." *Confederate Veteran*, 28 (1920): 457-459.

— "Last Days of the Confederacy." *Confederate Veteran* 29 (1921): 56-58.
Britton, W.J. "Fort Gregg—First Colors Up." *National Tribune,* April 21, 1904.
Butterfield, M.[iles] L. "Personal Reminiscences With the Sixth Corps." In *War Papers Being Papers Read Before the Commandery of the State of Wisconsin Military Order of the Loyal Legion of the United States.* 4 vols. Milwaukee: Burdick, Armitage & Allen, 1891-1914, 4: 85-93. Reprint, Wilmington, N.C.: Broadfoot Publishing Company, 1993.
Caldwell, J.[ames] F.[itz] J.[ames] "Reminiscences of the War of Secession." In Snowden, Yates, ed. *History of South Carolina.* 5 vols. Chicago: The Lewis Publishing Co., 1920, 2: 822-831.
Calkins, Chris. "The Battle of Five Forks: Final Push for the South Side." *Blue & Gray Magazine,* 9, no. 4 (April 1992): 8-22, 41-52.
Campbell, G.[eorge] K. "Capture of Fort Gregg." *National Tribune,* March 6, 1902.
Chamberlain, Brevet Major-General Joshua L. "The Military Operations on the White Oak Road, Virginia, March 31, 1865." In *War Papers Read Before the Commandery of the State of Maine, Military Order of the Loyal Legion of the United States.* 4 vols. Portland, Me.: The Thurston Print; Lefavor-Tower Company, 1898-1915, 1: 207-253. Reprint, Wilmington, N.C.: Broadfoot Publishing Company, 1992.
Chick, William E. "Fort Gregg Again." *National Tribune,* January 8, 1891.
— "Capture of Fort Gregg." *National Tribune,* June 12, 1902.
Claiborne, John Herbert, M.A., M.D. "Personal Reminiscences of the 'Last Days of Lee and His Paladins.'" *Southern Historical Society Papers,* 28 (1900): 18-58.
Collier, Charles F. "War Recollections: Story of the Evacuation of Petersburg, by an Eye-Witness." *Southern Historical Society Papers,* 22 (1894): 69-73.
Conerly, Buxton R. "How Fort Gregg was Defended April 2, 1865." In Conerly, Luke Ward. *Pike County Mississippi 1798-1876. Pioneer Families and Confederate Soldiers Reconstruction and Redemption.* Nashville: Brandon Printing Company, 1909.
"A Confederate Airship. The Artis Avis Which was to Destroy Grant's Army." *Southern Historical Society Papers,* 28 (1900): 303-305.
Cooke, Maj. Giles B. "When With General Lee." *Confederate Veteran,* 37 (1929): 182-183.
Crawford, Mark J. "Dinwiddie Court House: Beginning of the End." *America's Civil War,* 12, No. 1 (March 1999): 50-56.
Davison, Robert. "How Fort Gregg Was Taken." *National Tribune,* March 10, 1904.
"Defence of Fort Gregg." *Southern Historical Society Papers,* 3 (1875): 19-28.
Eichelberger, G.[rayson] M. "Who Took My Flag?" *National Tribune,* December 22, 1910.
Eschelman, Colonel B.[enjamin] F. "The Washington Artillery: Address of Colonel B. F. Eschelman at Their Reunion." *Southern Historical Society Papers,* 11 (1883): 247-254.
Ferguson, Rev. J. Dunley. "At Fort Gregg." *National Tribune,* February 11, 1892.
Flagg, George. "Marching to Appomattox." *National Tribune,* May 30, 1918.
Foote, Frank H. "Front of Petersburg, The Confederate Defense of Fort Gregg, Va., April 2, 1865." *National Tribune,* May 1, 1890.
"Fort Gregg Again!" *National Tribune,* February 19, 1891.
"Further Details of the Death of General A.P. Hill." *Southern Historical Society Papers,* 12 (1884): 183-187.
Gaskell, J.E. "Last Engagement of Lee's Army." *Confederate Veteran,* 29 (1921): 261-262.
Glatthaar, Joseph T. "Black Glory: The African-American Role in Union Victory." In Boritt, Gabor ed. *Why The Confederacy Lost.* New York: Oxford University Press, 1992, 133-162.
Goolsby, Pvt. J.C. "The Crenshaw Battery, Pegram's Battalion, Confederate States Artillery." *Southern Historical Society Papers ,* 28 (1900): 336-377.
Grant, Brigadier-General Lewis A. "The Old Vermont Brigade at Petersburg." In *Glimpses of the Nation's Struggle. A Series of Papers Read Before the Minnesota Commandery of the Loyal Legion of the United States.* St. Paul: St. Paul Book and Stationery Company, 1887, 381-403. Reprint, Wilmington, N.C.: Broadfoot Publishing Company, 1992.

Greene, A. Wilson. "Morale, Maneuver, and Mud: The Army of the Potomac, December 16, 1862-January 26, 1863." In Gallagher, Gary W., ed., *The Fredericksburg Campaign: Decision on the Rappahannock.* Chapel Hill: The University of North Carolina Press, 1995, 171-227.

Griffin, Ransom. "The 116th Ohio at Fort Gregg." *National Tribune,* August 22, 1912.

Hall, Austin. "The Sixth Corps: The Part it Took in the Action of April 2, 1865." *National Tribune,* January 8, 1891.

Harris, Nathaniel H. "Nineteenth Mississippi Regiment." *Confederate Veteran,* 6 (1898): 70-71.

Hawes, Percy G. "Last Days of the Army of Northern Virginia." *Confederate Veteran,* 27 (1919): 341-344.

Hibbs, T.[homas] W. "Just How Fort Gregg Was Captured." *National Tribune,* June 30, 1904.

Hill, G. Powell. "First Burial of General Hill's Remains." *Southern Historical Society Papers,* 19 (1891): 183-186.

Hollyday, Lamar. "Maryland Troops in the Confederate Service." *Southern Historical Society Papers,* 3 (1875): 130-139.

Houghton, Henry. "The Ordeal of Civil War: A Recollection." *Vermont History,* 41 (Winter, 1973): 31-49.

Jones, Captain A.[rchie] K. "The Battle of Fort Gregg." *New Orleans Times-Picayune,* December 13, 1903.

Jones, Thomas G. "Last Days of the Army of Northern Virginia." *Southern Historical Society Papers,* 21 (1893): 57-103.

Kennedy, George W. "Defending Fort Gregg. A Johnny Reb's Story of the Surrender on April 2, 1865." *National Tribune,* May 15, 1902.

— "Fort Gregg. An Account of the Capture by One of its Defenders." *National Tribune,* July 17, 1902.

Kilmer, George L. "Petersburg: Historic Incidents of the Closing Days Before the City. Taking Possession." *Philadelphia Weekly Times,* November 28, 1885.

Kimbrough, J.[oseph] S.[ydney] "From Petersburg to Hart's Island Prison." *Confederate Veteran,* 22 (1914): 498-500.

King, John R. "Sixth Corps at Petersburg." *National Tribune,* April 15, 1920.

Lane, James H. "The Defence of Battery Gregg." *Southern Historical Society Papers,* 9 (1881): 102-107.

—"Glimpses of Army Life in 1864." *Southern Historical Society Papers,* 18 (1890): 406-422.

—"History of Lane's North Carolina Brigade." *Southern Historical Society Papers,* 9 (1881): 353-361.

—"History of Lane's North Carolina Brigade." *Southern Historical Society Papers,* 10 (1882): 206-213.

"Last Charge of Lee's Army." *Confederate Veteran,* 5 (1897): 565.

Leach, Albert G. "Fort Gregg." *National Tribune,* January 15, 1891.

McCabe, Capt. W. Gordon. "Defence of Petersburg." *Southern Historical Society Papers,* 2 (1876): 257-306.

McClelland, William. "A Brave Battery." *Philadelphia Weekly Times,* June 18, 1887.

"McComb and Staff." *Southern Historical Society Papers,* 16 (1888): 107.

McElroy, John. "The Appomattox Campaign." *National Tribune,* April 18, 1912.

McKim, Randolph. "The Second Maryland Infantry—An Oration Delivered in the State House at Annapolis, May 7, 1909." *Confederate Veteran,* 17 (1909): 458.

Martin, W.[illiam] J.[oseph] "The Eleventh North Carolina Regiment." *Southern Historical Society Papers,* 23 (1895): 42-56.

Matthews, James P. "How General A.P. Hill Met His Fate." *Southern Historical Society Papers,* 27 (1899): 26-38.

Maxwell, Daniel. "Also at Fort Gregg." *National Tribune,* November 14, 1912.

Merritt, Maj.-Gen. Wesley. "The Appomattox Campaign." *In War Papers and Personal Reminiscences 1861-1865 Read Before the Commandery of the State of Missouri, Military Order of the Loyal Legion of the United States.* St. Louis: Becktold & Co., 1892, 108-131. Reprint, Wilmington, N.C.: Broadfoot Publishing Company, 1992.

Morse, W.[illiam] E. H. "The 'Rebellion Record' of an Enlisted Man." In *National Tribune Scrapbook.* Washington: The National Tribune, 1909, 83-101.

Newman, Mark, compiler. "The Old Forty-Ninth Georgia." *Confederate Veteran,* 31 (1923): 181.

Northrup, James E. Letter to Captain R.R. Duncan, March 24, 1891. In "After Many Years." *Culpeper* (Va.) *Exponent,* May 3, 1901.

Norton, William L. "Fort Gregg Again." *National Tribune,* October 29, 1891.

Norvell, E.[rastus] S. "Petersburg." *National Tribune,* June 11, 1891.

Orr, Robert L. "Before Petersburg: The Wedge-Shaped Assault and the Sixty-first Pennsylvania's Share in It." *Philadelphia Weekly Press,* December 19, 1886.

Outland, W.F. "Fort Gregg a Picnic." *National Tribune,* April 7, 1904.

Owen, William Miller. "The Artillery Defenders of Fort Gregg." *Southern Historical Society Papers,* 19 (1891): 65-71.

Patton, F.[rederick] H. Letter to "Dear Friends," April 16, 1865. In "Fort Gregg Again." *National Tribune,* March 3, 1892.

Parmelee, Joseph E. "First Flag on Fort Gregg." *National Tribune,* September 15, 1904.

— "That Little Mix-Up at Fort Gregg." *National Tribune,* June 19, 1902.

Pendleton, William Nelson. "The Artillery of the Army of Northern Virginia in the Last Campaign and at the Surrender." *Southern Historical Society Papers,* 9 (1881): 418-424.

Perry, William M. "At Petersburg. Comrade Perry Fires the Last Shot in Defense of the Sixth Corps." *National Tribune,* August 20, 1891.

Porter, Horace. "Five Forks and the Pursuit of Lee." In Johnson, Robert Underwood and Buel, Clarence Clough, eds. *Battles and Leaders of the Civil War.* 4 vols. New York: The Century Company, 1887-1888, 4: 708-722.

Rhodes, Elisha H. "The Second Rhode Island Volunteers at the Siege of Petersburg, Va." In *Personal Narratives of the Events in the War of the Rebellion, Being Papers Read Before the Rhode Island Soldiers and Sailors Historical Society, Military Order of the Loyal Legion of the United States.* 10 vols. Providence: Sidney S. Rider; N. Bangs Williams & Co.; Published by the Society, 1878-1915, 10: 430-465. Reprint, Wilmington, N.C.: Broadfoot Publishing Company, 1992.

Rigler, Lt. D.[allas] M. to James H. Lane, June 17, 1867. In "The Defence of Fort Gregg." *Southern Historical Society Papers,* 3 (1877): 19-28.

Roberts, Edward S. "War Reminiscences." *Connecticut Western News,* January 4, 1912.

Robertson, James I., Jr., ed. "The Boy Artillerist: Letters of Colonel William Pegram, C.S.A." *Virginia Magazine of History and Biography,* 98 (April 1990): 221-260.

Roche, Thomas T. "Fighting for Petersburg." *Philadelphia Weekly Times,* May 5, 1883.

Rogers, James M. "Who Led the Assault at Fort Gregg?" *National Tribune,* January 29, 1891.

Rousculf, Solomon. "Petersburg: The Part Taken in the Action of April 2, 1865 by the 126th Ohio." *National Tribune,* June 18, 1891.

Siler, Captain C. Frank. "Hero of Heroes." *Confederate Veteran,* 15 (1907): 90.

Skoch, George. "The Last Ditch." *Civil War Times Illustrated,* 27, No.9 (January 1989): 12-18.

Snyder, Samuel R. W. "The Assault on Fort Gregg." *National Tribune,* February 5, 1903.

Soule, David E. "Recollections of the Civil War." *New Milford* (Conn.) *Gazette,* June 28, 1912.

Stark, William B. "Petersburg to Appomattox." *Atlantic Monthly,* 162 No.2 (August 1938): 248-254.

Stevens, Brevet Brigadier-General Hazard. "The Storming of the Lines of Petersburg By the Sixth Corps, April 2, 1865." In Ropes, John Codman and Dwight, Theodore F., eds. *Papers of the Military Historical Society of Massachusetts.* 15 vols. Boston: The Military Historical Society of

Massachusetts, 1895-1918, 6: 409-435. Reprint, Wilmington, N.C.: Broadfoot Publishing Company, 1989.

Story, C.A. "The 3d Vt. Battery at Fort Gregg," *National Tribune*, July 9, 1891.

Strother, A. E. "Heroic Defense of Ft. Gregg by a Handful of Confederates." *Atlanta Journal*, October 26, 1901.

Thetford, R.[obert] B. "Commands Holding Fort Gregg." *Confederate Veteran*, 29 (1921): 335-336.

"Trio of Comrades at Memphis Reunion." *Confederate Veteran* 10 (1902): 320.

Tucker, G.[eorge] W. "Death of General A. P. Hill." *Southern Historical Society Papers*, 11 (1883): 564-569.

— "Death of General A.P. Hill." *Philadelphia Weekly Times*, November 24,   1883.

"Unveiling of the Statue of General Ambrose Powell Hill." *Southern Historical Society Papers*, 20 (1892): 352-395.

Vandiver, Frank. "The Food Supply in the Confederate Armies, 1865." *Tyler's Quarterly Historical and Genealogical Magazine*, 26 (October 1944): 209-210.

Walker, Aldace F. "The Old Vermont Brigade." In *Military Essays and Recollections Papers Read Before the Commandery of the State of Illinois, Military Order of the Loyal Legion of the United States.* 8 vols. Chicago: A.C. McClurg and Company, 1891-1923, 2: 189-209. Reprint, Wilmington, N.C.: Broadfoot Publishing Company, 1992-1993.

Wetzel, M. "Fort Gregg: A One-Armed Comrade's Description of its Capture." *National Tribune*, August 21, 1890.

"Who Killed General A.P. Hill?" *Southern Historical Society Papers*, 20 (1892): 349-351.

Wilcox, Maj. Gen. C.[admus] M. "Defence of Batteries Gregg and Whitworth, and the Evacuation of Petersburg." *Southern Historical Society Papers*, 4 (1877): 18-33.

Winter, George J. "A Battalion of Sharpshooters." *Transactions of the Huguenot Society of South Carolina*, 79 (1974): 89-101.

Wixcey, William T. "First Flag in Petersburg." *National Tribune*, July 4, 1907.

PRINTED PRIMARY SOURCES

Abbott, Major Lemuel Abijah. *Personal Recollections and Civil War Diary 1864.* Burlington, Vt.: Free Press Printing Co., 1908.

Agassiz, George R., ed. *Meade's Headquarters 1863-1865. Letters of Colonel Theodore Lyman from The Wilderness to Appomattox.* Boston: The Atlantic Monthly Press, 1922.

Alexander, E.[dward] Porter. *Military Memoirs of a Confederate.* New York: Charles Scribner's Sons, 1907. Reprint, Dayton, Oh.: Press of Morningside Bookshop, 1977.

Basler, Roy P., ed. *The Collected Works of Abraham Lincoln.* 8 vols. New Brunswick, N.J.: Rutgers University Press, 1953-1955.

Benson, Susan Williams, ed. *Berry Benson's Civil War Book.* Athens: University of Georgia Press, 1992.

Bernard, George S., ed. *War Talks of Confederate Veterans.* Petersburg, Va.: Fenn & Owen, 1892. Reprint, Dayton, Oh.: Press of Morningside Bookshop, 1981.

Billings, John D. *Hardtack and Coffee or The Unwritten Story of Army Life.* Boston: George M. Smith & Co., 1889. Reprint, Gettysburg, Pa.: Civil War Times Illustrated, 1974.

Britton, Ann Hartwell and Reed, Thomas J., eds. *To My Beloved Wife and Boy at Home: The Letters and Diaries of Orderly Sergeant John F.L. Hartwell.* Madison, N.J.: Fairleigh Dickinson University Press, 1997.

Chamberlain, Joshua Lawrence. *The Passing of the Armies: An Account of the Final Campaign of the Army of the Potomac, Based upon Personal Reminiscences of the Fifth Army Corps.*

New York: G.P. Putnam's Sons, 1915. Reprint, Gettysburg, Pa.: Stan Clark Military Books, 1994.

Chamberlaine, William W. *Memoirs of the Civil War Between the Northern and Southern Sections of the United States of America 1861-1865.* Washington: Press of Byron S. Adams, 1912.

Cockrell, Monroe F., ed. *Gunner With Stonewall: Reminiscences of William Thomas Poague.* Jackson, Tenn.: McCowat-Mercer Press, 1957. Reprint, Wilmington, N.C.: Broadfoot Publishing Company, 1987.

Dana, Charles A. *Recollections of the Civil War With the Leaders at Washington and in the Field in the Sixties.* New York: D. Appleton and Company, 1898.

Douglas, Henry Kyd. *I Rode With Stonewall.* Chapel Hill: The University of North Carolina Press, 1940.

Dowdey, Clifford and Manarin, Louis H., eds. *The Wartime Papers of R.E. Lee.* New York, Bramhall House, 1961.

Dunlop, William S. *Lee's Sharpshooters; or The Forefront of Battle.* Little Rock: Tunnah & Pittard, Printers, 1899. Reprint, Dayton, Oh.: Morningside Bookshop, 1982.

Early, Jubal Anderson. *Autobiographical Sketch and Narrative of the War Between The States.* Philadelphia: J.B. Lippincott Company. Reprint, Wilmington, N.C.: Broadfoot Publishing Company, 1989.

Floyd, Dale E., ed. *"Dear Friends at Home. . ." The Letters and Diary of Thomas James Owen, Fiftieth New York Volunteer Engineer Regiment, during the Civil War.* Washington: Office of the Chief of Engineers, 1985.

Fulton, William Frierson, II. *Family Record and War Reminiscences.* n.p. n.d.

Gallagher, Gary W., ed. *Fighting for the Confederacy: The Personal Recollections of General Edward Porter Alexander.* Chapel Hill: The University of North Carolina Press, 1989.

Gibbon, John. *Personal Recollections of the Civil War.* New York: G.P. Putnam's Sons, 1928. Reprint, Dayton, Oh.: Press of Morningside Bookshop, 1988.

Gordon, General John B. *Reminiscences of the Civil War.* New York: Charles Scribner's Sons, 1903. Reprint, Baton Rouge: Louisiana State University Press, 1993.

Grant, Ulysses S. *Personal Memoirs of U.S. Grant.* 2 vols. New York: Charles L. Webster & Company, 1885. Reprint, New York: Bonanza Books, 1974.

Grimes, Bryan. *Extracts of Letters of Major-General Bryan Grimes to his wife, written while in active service in the Army of Northern Virginia Together With Some Personal Recollections of the War, Written by Him After its Close, Etc.* Raleigh, N.C.: Alfred Williams & Co., 1884. Reprint with an introduction by Gary W. Gallagher, Wilmington, N.C.: Broadfoot Publishing Company, 1986.

Hammock, Mansel, ed. *Letters to Amanda.* Culloden, Ga.: n.p., 1976.

Hyde, Thomas W. *Following the Greek Cross or, Memories of the Sixth Army Corps.* Boston and New York: Houghton, Mifflin and Company, 1894. Reprint, Gaithersburg, Md.: Olde Soldier Books, Inc., 1988.

Johnston, Joseph E. *Narrative of Military Operations.* New York: D. Appleton and Company, 1874.

Jones, Melvin, ed. *Give God the Glory: Memoirs of a Civil War Soldier.* n.p., 1979.

Keifer, Joseph Warren. *Slavery and Four Years of War; A Political History of Slavery in the United States Together With a Narrative of the Campaigns and Battles of the Civil War in Which the Author Took Part: 1861-1865.* 2 vols. New York: G.P. Putnam's Sons, 1900.

Longstreet, James. *From Manassas to Appomattox.* Philadelphia: J.B. Lipponcott Company, 1896. Reprint, Secaucus, N.J.: The Blue and Grey Press, 1985.

Lowe, Jeffrey C. and Hodges, Sam, eds. *Letters to Amanda: The Civil War Letters of Marion Hill Fitzpatrick, Army of Northern Virginia.* Macon, Ga.: Mercer University Press, 1998.

McFadden, Janice Bartlett Reeder, ed. *Aunt and the Soldier Boys.* Santa Cruz, Cal.: Moore's Graphic Arts, 1970.

Marshall, Jeffrey D., ed. *A War of the People: Vermont Civil War Letters.* Hanover, N.H.: University Press of New England, 1999.

Morrison, James L., Jr., ed. *The Memoirs of Henry Heth.* Westport., Conn.: Greenwood Press, 1974.

Nevins, Allan, ed. *A Diary of Battle: The Personal Journals of Colonel Charles S. Wainwright 1861-1865.* New York: Harcourt, Brace & World, Inc., 1962.

Olcott, Mark with David Lear, ed. *The Civil War Letters of Lewis Bissell. A Curriculum.* Washington: The Field School Educational Foundation Press, 1981.

Porter, Horace. *Campaigning With Grant.* New York: The Century Co., 1897. Reprint, Alexandria, Va.: Time-Life Books, 1981.

Priest, John Michael, ed. *Turn Them Out to Die Like a Mule: The Civil War Letters of Hospital Steward John N. Henry, 49th New York, 1861-1865.* Leesburg, Va.: Gauley Mount Press, 1995.

Pryor, Sara Agnes (Mrs. Roger A.). *Reminiscences of Peace and War.* New York: The Macmillan Company, 1904.

Reed, William Howell. *Hospital Life in the Army of the Potomac.* Boston: William V. Spencer, 1866.

Rhodes, Robert Hunt, ed. *All for the Union: The Civil War Diary and Letters of Elisha Hunt Rhodes.* New York: Orion Books, 1985.

Roberston, James I., Jr., ed. *The Civil War Letters of General Robert McAllister.* New Brunswick, N.J.: Rutgers University Press, 1965.

Rosenblatt, Emit & Ruth, eds. *Hard Marching Every Day: The Civil War Letters of Private Wilbur Fisk, 1861-1865.* Lawrence, Kans., University Press of Kansas, 1992.

Sheridan, Philip H. *Personal Memoirs of P.H. Sheridan.* 2 vols. New York: Charles L. Webster & Company, 1888.

Sherman, William Tecumseh. *Memoirs of General W.T. Sherman.* 2 vols. New York: D. Appleton & Company, 1875.

Silliker, Ruth L., ed. *The Rebel Yell and the Yankee Hurrah: The Civil War Journal of a Maine Volunteer, Private John W. Haley, 17th Maine Regiment.* Camden, Me.: n.p., 1985.

Simon, John Y., ed. *The Papers of Ulysses S. Grant.* 22 vols. to date. Carbondale, Ill.: Southern Illinois University Press, 1967-

Southwick, Thomas P. *A Duryee Zouave.* Brookneal, Va.: Patrick A. Schroeder Publications, 1995.

Sparks, David, ed. *Inside Lincoln's Army. The Diary of Marsena Rudolph Patrick, Provost Marshal General, Army of the Potomac.* New York: Thomas Yoseloff, 1964.

Stevens, George T. *Three Years in the Sixth Corps.* Albany, N.Y.: S.R. Gray, Publisher, 1866. Reprint, Alexandria, Va.: Time-Life Books, 1984.

Stiles, Robert. *Four Years Under Marse Robert.* New York: Neale Publishing Company, 1903. Reprint, Dayton, Oh.: Morningside House, 1988.

Taylor, James E. *The James E. Taylor Sketchbook: With Sheridan Up the Shenandoah Valley in 1864: Leaves from a Special Artist's Sketchbook and Diary.* Dayton, Oh.: Morningside House, Inc., 1989.

Taylor, Walter H. *Four Years With General Lee: Being a Summary of the More Important Events Touching the Career of General Robert E. Lee, in the War Between the States: Together with an Authoritative Statement of the Strength of the Army Which He Commanded in the Field.* New York: D. Appleton and Co., 1877. Reprint, Robertson, James I., Jr., ed. New York: Bonanza Books, 1962.

Tisdale, Jean, ed. *Dear Companion.* Spindale, N.C.: Kaleidoscope Publishers, 1997.

Townsend, George Alfred. *Campaigns of a Non-Combatant.* New York: Blelock & Company, 1866. Reprint, Alexandria, Va.: Time-Life Books, 1982.

Tyler, Mason Whiting. *Recollections of the Civil War With Many Original Diary Entries and Letters Written from the Seat of War, and with Annotated References.* New York: G.P. Putnam's Sons, 1912.

Underhill, Charles Sterling, arranger. *"Your Soldier Boy Samuel": Civil War Letters of Lieut. Samuel Edmund Nichols, Amherst '65 of the 37th Regiment Massachusetts Volunteers.* Buffalo, N.Y.: Privately Printed, 1929.

Wiley, Kenneth. *Norfolk Blues: The Civil War Diary of the Norfolk Light Artillery Blues.* Shippensburg, Pa: Burd Street Press, 1997.

Wiley, Bell Irvin, ed. *Recollections of a Confederate Staff Officer.* Jackson, Tenn.: McCowat-Mercer Press, 1958. Reprint, Wilmington, N.C.: Broadfoot Publishing Company, 1987.

Wright, Stuart T., ed. *The Confederate Letters of Benjamin H. Freeman.* Hicksville, N.Y.: Exposition Press, 1974.

UNIT HISTORIES

Armstrong, James. *Carolina Light Infantry's Record in the Great War. The Story of a Gallant Company.* Charleston: Walker, Evans & Cogswell Co., 1912.

Baquet, Camille. *History of the First Brigade, New Jersey Volunteers.* Trenton: MacCrellish & Quigley, 1910.

Beaudry, Paul Stephen. *The Forgotten Regiment: History of the 151st New York Volunteer Infantry Regiment.* Cleveland: InChem Publishing, 1995.

Best, Isaac O. *History of the 121st New York State Infantry.* Chicago: Lieut. Jas. H. Smith, 1921. Reprint, Baltimore: Butternut and Blue, 1996.

Bidwell, Frederick David. *History of the Forty-Ninth Volunteers.* Albany, N.Y.: J. B. Lyon Co., Printers, 1916.

Bilby, Joseph G. *Three Rousing Cheers: A History of the Fifteenth New Jersey from Flemington to Appomattox.* Hightstown, N.J.: Longstreet House, 1993.

Bowen, James Lorenzo. *History of the Thirty-Seventh Regiment Mass. Volunteers, in the Civil War of 1861-1865, With a Comprehensive Sketch of the Doings of Massachusetts as a State, and of the Principal Campaigns of the War.* Holyoke, Mass.: Clark W. Bryan & Company, Publishers, 1884.

Brewer, Abraham T. *History of the Sixty-first Regiment Pennsylvania Volunteers 1861-1865.* Pittsburgh: Art Engraving and Printing Co., 1911.

Caldwell, J.[ames] F.[itz] J.[ames] *The History of a Brigade of South Carolinians Known First as "Gregg's," and Subsequently as "McGowan's Brigade."* Philadelphia: King & Baird, Printers, 1866. Reprint, Dayton, Oh.: Morningside Press, 1984.

Chapman, Craig S. *More Terrible Than Victory: North Carolina's Bloody Bethel Regiment.* Washington: Brassey's, 1998.

Clark, Walter, ed. *Histories of the Several Regiments and Battalions from North Carolina in the Great War 1861-'65. Written by Members of the Respective Commands.* 5 vols. Goldsboro, N.C.: Nash Brothers, 1901. Reprint, Wendell, N.C.: Broadfoot's Bookmark, 1982.

Crew, Roger T. and Trask, Benjamin H. *Grimes' Battery, Grandy's Battery and Huger's Battery Virginia Artillery.* Lynchburg, Va.: H.E. Howard Inc., 1995.

Crowell, Kathy, compiler. *"The Onondagas: A History of the 122d Regiment, New York Volunteers."* Fayetteville, N.Y.: n.p., 1998.

Davenport, Alfred. *Camp and Field Life of the Fifth New York Volunteer Infantry (Duryee Zouaves).* New York: Dick and Fitzgerald, 1879. Reprint, Gaithersburg, Md., Butternut Press, 1984.

Fenner, Earl. *The History of Battery H First Regiment of Rhode Island Light Artillery in the War to Preserve the Union 1861-1865.* Providence: Snow & Farnham, Printers, 1894.

Gould, Maj. John Mead. *History of the First-Tenth-Twenty-ninth Maine Regiment.* Portland, Me: Stephen Berry, 1871.

Haines, Alanson A. *History of the Fifteenth Regiment New Jersey Volunteers.* New York: Jenkins & Thomas, Printers, 1883. Reprint, Gaithersburg, Md.: Olde Soldier Books, n.d.

Haynes, Chaplain Edwin Mortimer. *A History of the Tenth Regiment, Vermont Volunteers with Biographical Sketches of the Officers who fell in Battle and A Complete Roster of all the Officers and Men Connected With It—Showing All Changes By Promotion, Death or Resignation, During the Military Existence of the Regiment.* Lewiston, Me.: Journal Steam Press, 1870.

Hess, Earl J. "Lee's Tarheels: Pettigrew's North Carolina Brigade in the Civil War." Unpublished manuscript provided to the author courtesy of Hess, November 2, 1999.

Lewis, Osceola. *History of the One Hundred and Thirty-Eighth Regiment, Pennsylvania Volunteer Infantry.* Norristown, Pa.: Wills, Iredell & Jenkins, 1866.

Love, D.[avid] C. *The Prairie Guards. A History of Their Organization, Their Heroism, Their Battles and Their Triumphs.* Columbus, Ga.: n.p., 1890.

McDaid, William K.. "Four Years of Arduous Service: The History of the Branch-Lane Brigade in the Civil War." Ph.D dissertation, Michigan State University, 1987.

Mark, Penrose G. *Red: White: and Blue Badge. Pennsylvania Veteran Volunteers. A History of the 93rd Regiment, known as the "Lebanon Infantry" and "One of the 300 Fighting Regiments" from September 12th, 1861 to June 27th, 1865.* Harrisburg, Pa.: Aughinbaugh Press, 1911.

Mills, George H. *History of the 16th North Carolina Regiment in the Civil War.* Rutherfordton, N.C.: The Western Vindicator Press, 1897. Reprint, Hamilton, N.Y.: Edmonston Publishing Co., Inc., 1992.

Olsen, Bernard A., ed. *Upon the Tented Field.* Red Bank, N.J.: Historic Projects, Inc., 1993.

Owen, William Miller. *In Camp and Battle With the Washington Artillery of New Orleans.* Boston: Ticknor and Company, 1885.

Parsons, George W. *Put the Vermonters Ahead: The First Vermont Brigade in the Civil War.* Shippensburg, Pa.: White Mane Publishing Company, Inc., 1996.

Powell, William H. *The Fifth Army Corps (Army of the Potomac): A Record of Operations During the Civil War in the United States of America, 1861-1865.* New York: G.P. Putnam's Sons, 1896. Reprint, Dayton, Oh.: Press of Morningside Bookshop, 1984.

Prowell, George R. *History of the Eighty-Seventh Regiment, Pennsylvania Volunteers, Prepared from Official Records, Diaries, and Other Authentic Sources of Information.* York, Pa.: Press of the York Daily, 1901.

Roe, Alfred Seelye. *The Ninth New York Heavy Artillery. A History of Its Organization, Services in the Defenses of Washington, Marches, Camps, Battles, and Muster-Out, With Accounts of Life in a Rebel Prison, Personal Experiences, Names and Addresses of Surviving Members, Personal Sketches, and a Complete Roster of the Regiment.* Worcester, Mass: Published by the Author, 1899.

Sherwood, W. Cullen and Nicholas, Richard L. *Amherst Artillery, Albemarle Artillery, and Sturdivant's Battery.* Lynchburg, Va.: H.E. Howard, Inc., 1996.

Terrill, Sergeant J. Newton. *Campaign of the Fourteenth Regiment, New Jersey Volunteers.* New Brunswick, N.J.: Daily Home News Press, 1884.

Tompkins, D.[aniel] A.[ugustus] *Company K, Fourteenth South Carolina Volunteers.* Charlotte, N.C.: Observer Printing and Publishing House, 1897.

Underwood, George C. *History of the Twenty-Sixth Regiment of the North Carolina Troops in the Great War 1861-'65.* Goldsboro, N.C.: Nash Brothers Book and Job Printers, 1901. Reprint, Wendell, N.C.: Broadfoot's Bookmark, 1978.

Walker, Francis A. *History of the Second Army Corps in the Army of the Potomac.* New York: Charles Scribner's Sons, 1887. Reprint, Gaithersburg, Md.: Olde Soldier Books, n.d.

Westbrook, Robert S. *History of the 49th Pennsylvania Volunteers.* Altoona, Pa.: *Altoona Times* Printers, 1898.

Woodbury, Augustus. *The Second Rhode Island Regiment: A Narrative of Military Operations in Which the Regiment was engaged from the Beginning to the End of the War for the Union.* Providence: Valpey, Angell and Company, 1875.

SECONDARY PUBLISHED SOURCES

Allen, T. Harrell. *Lee's Last Major General: Bryan Grimes of North Carolina.* Mason City, Ia.: Savas Publishing Company, 1999.

Andrews, J. Cutler. *The North Reports the Civil War.* Pittsburgh: The University of Pittsburgh Press, 1985.

Bache, Richard Meade. *Life of General George Gordon Meade.* Philadelphia: Henry T. Coates & Co., 1897.

Baltz, Louis J. *The Battle of Cold Harbor, May 27-June 13, 1864.* Lynchburg, Va.: H. E. Howard, Inc., 1994.

Barefoot, Daniel B. *General Robert F. Hoke: Lee's Modest Warrior.* Winston-Salem, N.C.: John F. Blair, Publisher, 1996.

Barrett, John G. *The Civil War in North Carolina.* Chapel Hill: The University of North Carolina Press, 1963.

Bartlett, Napier. *Military Record of Louisiana, Including Biographical and Historical Papers Relating to the Military Organizations of the State: A Soldier's Story of the Late War, Muster Rolls, Lists of Casualties in the Various Regiments (So Far as Now Known), Cemeteries Where Buried, Company Journals, Personal Narratives of Prominent Actors, etc.* New Orleans: L. Graham and Co. Printers, 1875.

Bearss, Ed and Calkins, Chris. *The Battle of Five Forks.* Lynchburg, Va.: H.E. Howard, Inc., 1985.

Benedict, G.[eorge] G.[renville] *Vermont in the Civil War. A History of the part taken by the Vermont Soldiers and Sailors in the War for the Union 1861-5.* 2 vols. Burlington, Vt.: The Free Press Association, 1886-1888.

Bennett, William W. D.D. *A Narrative of The Great Revival which prevailed In the Southern Armies.* Philadelphia: Claxton, Remson & Haffelfinger, 1877. Reprint, Harrisonburg, Va.: Sprinkle Publications, 1989.

Bergeron, Arthur W., Jr. *Tudor Hall: The Boisseau Family Farm.* Richmond, Va.: Dietz Press, 1998.

Beyer, W.[alter] F. and Keydel, O.[scar] F., eds. *Deeds of Valor: from records in the archives of the United States: How America's Heroes Won the Medal of Honor.* Detroit: The Perrien-Keydel Company, 1907.

Binney, C.J.F. *The History and Genealogy of the Prentice Families of New England.* n.p., 1883.

Blake, Nelson M. *William Mahone of Virginia: Soldier and Political Insurgent.* Richmond, Va.: Garrett & Massie, 1935.

Bowman, Col. S.[amuel] M.[illard] and Irwin, Lt.-Col. R.[icard] B.[ache] *Sherman and His Campaigns; A Military Biography.* New York: Charles B. Richardson, 1865.

Bradley, Mark L. *Last Stand in the Carolinas: The Battle of Bentonville.* Campbell, Cal.: Savas Publishing Company, 1996.

Brown, J. Willard. *The Signal Corps, U.S.A., in the War of the Rebellion.* Boston: U.S.Veteran Signal Corps Association, 1896. Reprint, Baltimore: Butternut and Blue, 1996.

Bushong, Millard K. *Old Jube: A Biography of General Jubal A. Early.* Boyce, Va.: Carr Publishing Company, 1955.

Calkins, Christopher M. *The Appomattox Campaign: March 29-April 9, 1865.* Conshohocken, Pa.: Combined Books, 1997.

— *From Petersburg to Appomattox*. Farmville, Va.: *The Farmville Herald*, 1983.

Carmichael, Peter S. *Lee's Young Artillerist : William R.J. Pegram*. Charlottesville, Va.: University Press of Virginia, 1995.

Cavanaugh, Michael A. and Marvel, William. *The Petersburg Campaign: The Battle of the Crater, "The Horrid Pit" June 25-August 6, 1864*. Lynchburg, Va.: H.E. Howard, Inc., 1989.

Cleaves, Freeman. *Meade of Gettysburg*. Norman: University of Oklahoma Press, 1960.

Coffin, Howard. *Full Duty: Vermonters in the Civil War*. Woodstock. Vt.: The Countryman Press, Inc., 1993.

Cooling, Benjamin Franklin. *Jubal Early's Raid on Washington 1864*. Baltimore: The Nautical & Aviation Publishing Company of America, 1989.

Cornish, Dudley Taylor. *The Sable Arm: Black Troops in the Union Army, 1861-1865*. New York: Longmans, Green, 1956. Reprint, Lawrence, Kans.: University Press of Kansas, 1987.

Crofts, Daniel W. *Reluctant Confederates: Upper South Unionists in the Secession Crisis*. Chapel Hill: The University of North Carolina Press, 1989.

Crozier, Emmet. *Yankee Reporters: 1861-65*. New York: Oxford University Press, 1956.

Cummings, Charles M. *Yankee Quaker Confederate General: The Curious Career of Bushrod Rust Johnson*. Rutherford, N.J.: Fairleigh Dickinson University Press, 1971. Reprint, Columbus, Oh.: The General's Books, 1993.

Davis, Burke. *To Appomattox: Nine April Days, 1865*. New York: Rhinehart, 1959.

Davis, William C. *Breckinridge: Statesman Soldier Symbol*. Baton Rouge: Louisiana State University Press, 1974.

— *Death in the Trenches: Grant at Petersburg*. Alexandria, Va.: Time-Life Books, 1986.

— *Jefferson Davis: The Man and His Hour*. New York: Harper Collins Publishers, 1991.

Donald, David Herbert. *Lincoln*. New York: Simon & Schuster, 1995.

Eckert, Ralph Lowell. *John Brown Gordon: Soldier Southerner American*. Baton Rouge: Louisiana State University Press, 1989.

Elliott, Joseph Cantey. *Lieutenant Richard Heron Anderson: Lee's Noble Soldier*. Dayton, Oh.: Morningside House, 1985.

Fishel, Edwin C. *The Secret War for the Union*. Boston: Houghton Miflin Company, 1996.

Fonvielle, Chris E., Jr. *The Wilmington Campaign: Last Days of Departing Hope*. Campbell, Cal.: Savas Publishing Company, 1997.

Freeman, Douglas Southall. *R. E. Lee: A Biography*. 4 vols. New York: Charles Scribner's Sons, 1934-1935.

— *Lee's Lieutenants: A Study In Command*. 3 vols. New York: Charles Scribner's Sons, 1942-1944.

Furgurson, Ernest B. *Ashes of Glory: Richmond at War*. New York: Alfred Knopf, 1996.

Gallagher, Gary W., ed. *Lee The Soldier*. Lincoln, Neb.: University of Nebraska Press, 1996.

— *Struggle for the Shenandoah: Essays on the 1864 Valley Campaign*. Kent, Oh.: Kent State University Press, 1991.

Gordon, Lesley J. *General George E. Pickett in Life & Legend*. Chapel Hill: The University of North Carolina Press, 1999.

Hamlin, Percy Gatling. *Old Bald Head" (General R.S. Ewell):The Portrait of a Soldier*. Strasburg, Va.: Shenandoah Publishing House, Inc., 1940.

Hassler, William Woods. *A.P. Hill: Lee's Forgotten General*. Richmond,Va.: Garrett & Massie, 1962.

Henderson, William D. *Petersburg in the Civil War: War at the Door*. Lynchburg, Va.: H.E. Howard, Inc., 1998.

Horn, John. *The Petersburg Campaign: The Destruction of the Weldon Railroad, Deep Bottom, Globe Tavern, and Reams Station, August 14-25, 1864*. Lynchburg, Va.: H.E. Howard, Inc., 1991.

Howe, Thomas J. *The Petersburg Campaign: Wasted Valor June 15-18, 1864.* Lynchburg, Va.: H.E. Howard, Inc., 1988.

Humphreys, Andrew A. *The Virginia Campaign of '64 and '65. The Army of the Potomac and The Army of the James.* New York: Charles Scribner's Sons, 1883. Reprint, Wilmington, N.C.: Broadfoot Publishing Company, 1989.

Humphreys, Henry H. *Andrew Atkinson Humphreys: A Biography.* Philadelphia: The John C. Winston Company, 1924. Reprint, Gaithersburg, Md.: Ron R. Van Sickle Military Books, 1988.

Jordan, David M. *Winfield Scott Hancock: A Soldier's Life.* Bloomington, Ind.: Indiana University Press, 1988.

Lewis, Thomas A. *The Guns of Cedar Creek.* New York: Harper & Row, 1988.

Longacre, Edward G. *Army of Amateurs: General Benjamin F. Butler and the Army of the James, 1863-1865.* Mechanicsburg, Pa.: Stackpole Books, 1997.

Lowry, Thomas P., M.D. *The Story the Soldiers Wouldn't Tell: Sex in the Civil War.* Mechanicsburg, Pa.: Stackpole Books, 1994.

McCrea, Henry Vaughan. *Red Dirt and Isinglass: A Wartime Biography of a Confederate Soldier.* Marianna, Fla.: Chipola Press, 1992.

McFeely, William S. *Grant: A Biography.* New York: W.W. Norton, 1981.

McPherson, James M. *Battle Cry of Freedom.* New York: Oxford University Press, 1988.

— *For Cause and Comrades.* New York: Oxford University Press, 1997.

Marvel, William. *Burnside.* Chapel Hill: The University of North Carolina Press, 1991.

Matter, William D. *If It Takes All Summer: The Battle of Spotsylvania Court House.* Chapel Hill: The University of North Carolina Press, 1988.

Miller, J. Michael. *The North Anna Campaign: "Even to Hell Itself."* Lynchburg, Va.: H.E. Howard, Inc., 1989.

Murdock, Eugene Converse. *Patriotism Limited 1862-1865. The Civil War Draft and the Bounty System.* Kent, Oh.: Kent State University Press, 1967.

Naisawald, L. Van Loan. *Grape and Canister: The Story of the Field Artillery of the Army of the Potomac, 1861-1865.* New York: Oxford University Press, 1960. Reprint, Washington: Zenger Publishing Company, 1983.

Nash, Howard P., Jr. *Stormy Petrel: The Life and Times of General Benjamin F. Butler 1818-1893.* Rutherford, N.J.: Fairleigh Dickinson University Press, 1969.

Nolan, Alan T. *Lee Considered: General Robert E. Lee and Civil War History.* Chapel Hill: The University of North Carolina Press, 1991.

Oberseider, N. L. and Savery, Suzanne. *Four Self-Guided Walking Tours: Petersburg Virginia.* Petersburg: City of Petersburg Museums, 1995.

O'Connor, Richard. *Sheridan the Inevitable.* Indianapolis: The Bobbs-Merrill Company, Inc., 1953.

Pfanz, Donald C. *Richard S. Ewell: Portrait of a Soldier.* Chapel Hill: The University of North Carolina Press, 1998.

Power, J. Tracy. *Lee's Miserables: Life in the Army of Northern Virginia from the Wilderness to Appomattox.* Chapel Hill: The University of North Carolina Press, 1998.

Priest, John M. *Antietam: The Soldiers' Battle.* Shippensburg, Pa.: White Mane Publishing Company, 1989.

Rable, George C. *The Confederate Republic: A Revolution Against Politics.* Chapel Hill: The University of North Carolina Press, 1994.

Rhea, Gordon C. *The Battle of the Wilderness, May 5-6, 1864.* Baton Rouge: Louisiana State University Press, 1994.

— *The Battles for Spotsylvania Court House and the Road to Yellow Tavern May 7-12, 1864.* Baton Rouge: Louisiana State University Press, 1997.

Robertson, James I., Jr. *General A.P. Hill: The Story of a Confederate Warrior.* New York: Random House, 1987.

— *Soldiers Blue and Gray*. Columbia, S.C.: University of South Carolina Press, 1988.

Robertson, William Glenn. *The Battle of Old Men and Young Boys, June 9, 1864*. Lynchburg, Va.: H.E. Howard, Inc., 1989.

Rollins, Richard, ed. *Black Southerners in Gray: Essays on Afro-Americans in the Confederate Armies*. Murfreesboro, Tenn.: Southern Heritage Press, 1994.

Schiller, Herbert M., M.D. *The Bermuda Hundred Campaign*. Dayton, Oh.: Morningside House, Inc., 1988.

Sears, Stephen W. *Controversies and Commanders: Dispatches from the Army of the Potomac*. Boston: Houghton Mifflin Company, 1999.

Sommers, Richard J. *Richmond Redeemed: The Siege at Petersburg*. Garden City, N.Y.: Doubleday & Company, Inc., 1981.

Starr, Stephen Z. *The Union Cavalry in the Civil War*. 3 vols. Baton Rouge: Louisiana State University Press, 1979-1985.

Stedman, Charles M. *Memorial Address Delivered May 10th, 1890, at Wilmington, N.C. by Hon. Charles M. Stedman. A Sketch of the Life and Character of General William MacRae, with an Account of the Battle of Reams Station*. Wilmington, N.C.: Wm. L. DeRossett, Jr., Photo-Engraver and Printer, 1890.

Swinton, William. *Campaigns of the Army of the Potomac, A Critical History of Operations in Virginia Maryland and Pennsylvania from the Commencement to the Close of the War 1861-5*. New York: Charles B. Richardson, 1866. Reprint, Secaucus, N.J.: The Blue & Grey Press, 1988.

Symonds, Craig L. *Joseph E. Johnston: A Civil War Biography*. New York: W.W. Norton & Company, 1992.

Taylor, Emerson Gifford. *Gouverneur Kemble Warren: The Life and Letters of an American Soldier 1830-1882*. Boston: Houghton Mifflin Company, 1932. Reprint, Gaithersburg, Md.: Ron R. Van Sickle Military Books, 1988.

Thomas, Emory M. *The Confederate Nation: 1861-1865*. New York: Harper & Row Publishers, 1979.

— *Robert E. Lee, A Biography*. New York: W.W. Norton & Company, 1995.

Trudeau, Noah Andre. *Bloody Roads South: The Wilderness to Cold Harbor, May-June 1864*. Boston: Little, Brown and Company, 1989.

— *The Last Citadel: Petersburg, Virginia June 1864-April 1865*. Boston: Little, Brown and Company, 1991.

— *Like Men of War: Black Troops in the Civil War 1862-1865*. Boston: Little, Brown and Company, 1998.

— *Out of the Storm: The End of the Civil War April-June 1865*. Boston: Little, Brown and Company, 1994.

Ullery, Jacob G. *Men of Vermont*. Brattleboro, Vt.: Transcript Publishing Co., 1894.

Waite, Otis F. R. *Vermont in the Great Rebellion containing Historical and Biographical Sketches, Etc.* Claremont, N.H.: Tracy, Chase and Co., 1869.

Walker, Aldace F. *The Vermont Brigade in the Shenandoah Valley 1864*. Burlington, Vt.: The Free Press Association, 1869

Wellman, Manly Wade. *Giant in Gray: A Biography of Wade Hampton of South Carolina*. New York: Charles Scribner's Sons, 1949. Reprint, Dayton, Oh.: Morningside Bookshop, 1988.

Wert, Jeffry D. *From Winchester to Cedar Creek: The Shenandoah Campaign of 1864*. Carlisle, Pa.: South Mountain Press, Inc., 1987.

— *General James Longstreet: The Confederacy's Most Controversial Soldier—A Biography*. New York: Simon & Schuster, 1993.

Wiley, Bell Irvin. *The Life of Billy Yank: The Common Soldier of the Union*. Indianapolis: Bobbs-Merrill Co., 1952.

— *The Life of Johnny Reb: The Common Soldier of the Confederacy.* Indianapolis: Bobbs-Merrill Co., 1943.

Williams, T. Harry. *P.G.T. Beauregard: Napoleon in Gray.* Baton Rouge: Louisiana State University Press, 1955.

Winslow, Richard Elliott III. *General John Sedgwick: The Story of a Union Corps Commander.* Novato, Cal.: Presidio Press, 1982.

Wise, Jennings Cropper. *The Long Arm of Lee or The History of the Artillery of the Army of Northern Virginia.* 2 vols. Lynchburg, Va.: J.P. Bell Co., 1915. Reprint, Richmond, Va.: Owens Publishing Co., 1988.

Wise, Stephen R. *Lifeline of the Confederacy: Blockade Running During the Civil War.* Columbia, S.C.: University of South Carolina Press, 1988.

Yearns, Wilfred Buck. *The Confederate Congress.* Athens: The University of Georgia Press, 1960.

REFERENCE WORKS

Boatner, Mark Mayo III. *The Civil War Dictionary.* New York: David McKay Company, Inc., 1959.

City Point Unit, Petersburg National Battlefield, Site Bulletin, n.d.

Current, Richard N., ed. *Encyclopedia of the Confederacy.* 4 vols. New York: Simon & Schuster, 1993.

Faust, Patricia L., ed. *Historical Times Illustrated Encyclopedia of the Civil War.* New York: Harper & Row, 1986.

Hewett, Janet B., ed. *The Roster of Confederate Soldiers 1861-1865.* 16 vols. Wilmington, N.C.: Broadfoot Publishing Company, 1995-1996.

—, ed. *The Roster of Union Soldiers 1861-1865.* 26 vols. to date. Wilmington, N.C.: Broadfoot Publishing Company, 1997-.

Hunt, Roger D. & Brown, Jack R. *Brevet Brigadier Generals in Blue.* Gaithersburg, Md.: Olde Soldier Books, Inc., 1990.

Krick, Robert K. *Lee's Colonels: A Biographical Register of the Field Officers of the Army of Northern Virginia.* Dayton, Oh.: Press of Morningside Bookshop, 1979.

John Milner Associates, Inc. *Historic Structure Report for Tudor Hall Dinwiddie County, Virginia.* 2 vols. West Chester, Pa.: John Milner Associates, Inc., 1995.

Report of the Adjutant General of the State of Illinois. 9 vols. Springfield: Phillips Bros., 1900-1902.

Sifakis, Stewart. *Who Was Who in the Civil War.* New York: Facts on File, 1988

Wallace, Lee A., Jr. *A Guide to Virginia Military Organizations 1861-1865.* Lynchburg, Va.: H.E. Howard, Inc., 1986.

Warner, Ezra J. *Generals in Blue: Lives of the Union Commanders.* Baton Rouge: Louisiana State University Press, 1964.

— *Generals in Gray: Lives of the Confederate Commanders.* Baton Rouge: Louisiana State University Press, 1959.

Welcher, Frank J. *The Union Army 1861-1865: Organization and Operations.* 2 vols. Bloomington, Ind.: Indiana University Press, 1989-1993.

Yearns, Buck W. and Barrett, John G., eds. *North Carolina Civil War Documentary.* Chapel Hill: The University of North Carolina Press, 1980.

MAPS

Bergeron, Arthur W., Jr. Manuscript map of Sixth Corps Attack Formation, Pamplin Historical Park

Calkins, Christopher M. "General A.P. Hill's Last Ride-April 2, 1865, Near Petersburg, Virginia". Petersburg National Battlefield with accompanying text

Davis, George B., Perry, Leslie J., Kirkley, Joseph W. *Atlas to Accompany the Official Records of the Union and Confederate Armies.* Washington: Government Printing Office, 1891-1895. Reprint, New York: Arno Press, 1978.

Library of Congress, Geographical and Map Division, Washington

Bechler, Gustavus R. Military map referring to the campaign of the Army of the Potomac in Virginia, Maryland and Pennsylvania

Campbell, Albert H. Map of the vicinity of Petersburg 1864

   Lindenkohl, Adolph.

Military Map of Southeastern Virginia

Southern Virginia and northern North Carolina

   Michler, Nathaniel.

Map of the Battlefield of Five Forks

Petersburg and Five Forks

Petersburg Novb. 2nd 1864

Sketch of the entrenched lines in the immediate front of Petersburg

Nicholson, W. L. Map of Eastern Virginia

Perham, A.S. Map showing portions of the Federal and Confederate forces at the Battle of Five Forks fought April 1, 1865

Preston, Noble D. Map of Central Virginia From Dinwiddie C.H. to Appomattox C.H.

Russell, Robert E.L. The retreat from Petersburg, April 2-9, 1865

Sholl, Charles Military topographical map of eastern Virginia

Stevens, Walter H., Sketch of the Confederate and Federal Lines around Petersburg

   U.S. Army, Army of the Potomac, Engineer Department

Map of the lines of march of the Army of the Potomac from Culpeper to Petersburg, Virginia

Map showing the operations of the Army of the Potomac under command of Mag.[sic] Gen. George G. Meade, from March 29th to April 9th, 1865

Map of the Environs of Petersburg from the Appomattox River to the Jerusalem Plank Road

   U.S. Army, Corps of Engineers

South Central Virginia showing lines of transportation

Map showing the Federal and Confederate works during the siege of Petersburg, between the Appomattox River and Hatcher's Run, June 16, 1864 to April 3, 1865 Military Maps illustrating the operations of the armies of the Potomac & James

   U. S. Army, Corps of Topographical Engineers Central Virginia

Walker, L.E., Map of part of the Union lines during the siege of Petersburg, Virginia

   Weyss, John E.

Map of the Siege of Petersburg, 1864-5

Map of the Siege of Petersburg, 1864-5 (with overlay)
Grant's and Sheridan's Campaigns, 1864-1865
Map of the Seat of War in Virginia, 1865

Duke University, Perkins Library, Durham, North Carolina
US Army Maps of Petersburg

United States Department of the Interior, Geological Survey
Carson Quadrangle, 1969, Photo revised 1987
Dinwiddie Quadrangle, 1963, Photo revised 1971, Photo inspected, 1979
Petersburg Quadrangle, 1969, Photo revised, 1987
Sutherland Quadrangle, 1963, Photo revised 1971 and 1974

INDEX